THE
BEGINNINGS OF
MODERN AMERICAN
PSYCHIATRY
The Ideas of Harry Stack Sullivan

Originally published under the title
Psychoanalysis and Interpersonal Psychiatry

D1301897

THE
BEGINNINGS OF
MODERN AMERICAN
PSYCHIATRY

THE IDEAS OF
HARRY STACK SULLIVAN

Patrick Mullahy

SENTRY EDITION

Originally published under the title *Psychoanalysis and Interpersonal Psychiatry*

HOUGHTON MIFFLIN COMPANY BOSTON 1973

FIRST SENTRY PRINTING   C

Published by special arrangement with Science House, Inc.
The original hardcover edition, issued in 1970 under
the title *Psychoanalysis and Interpersonal Psychiatry:
The Contributions of Harry Stack Sullivan*, contained as an
Appendix Patrick Mullahy's essay "Experience and Conduct:
The Ethical Philosophy of John Dewey," which has
been omitted from this Sentry edition.
Otherwise the text is identical.

ISBN: 0-395-17228-4

Printed in the United States of America

to the memory of my grandmother
Bridget Hennelly

Preface

For almost an entire generation American psychiatry was largely dominated by Freudian psychoanalysis. Though it originally encountered a good deal of hostility, as was the case in Europe a generation earlier, when it was introduced to this country on a major scale by Brill and a few others it rapidly gained ascendancy. The influx of German and Austrian psychoanalysts in the 1930's was largely responsible for its dominance. In most of the large cities of the United States, psychoanalytic institutes were founded, to which young physicians were attracted and at which they were "trained." But almost from the beginning, classical psychoanalysis suffered an almost fatal flaw: dogmatism. How much this was a reaction due to the hostility that Freud originally met with in Europe, I do not know. As it turned out, psychoanalysis gradually became not only a technique of therapy and a method of psychological inquiry, but a "system" of ideas and assumptions about the nature of man. While much of this "system" was admittedly speculative when first it was created and made known by Freud, it gradually became accepted as established fact. Freud made many changes and modifications as he elaborated his system. But he not only quite explicitly stated that psychoanalysis was his creation, which was true, but he also adhered to the view that only he could make any appropriate and important additions and modifications, along with his devoted disciples, provided that he approved and accepted their work. Not only was an apprenticeship, if possible, under Freud himself, but otherwise under one of his followers, required in order to become a psychoanalyst, it was also necessary to adhere strictly to Freudian theory and technique. Hence there was little room left for original and independent minds. In Europe, Adler around 1912 was forced to withdraw. Jung, whom Freud once characterized as "my beloved son, in whom I am well pleased," also in 1913 left the psychoanalytic "movement" to create his own school. But in Europe, there never was a wholesale uncritical acceptance of Freud by the psychiatrists of various European countries.

It is not at all clear why psychoanalysis became so quickly dominant in this country. With one outstanding exception, by the mid-1930's America's greatest psychiatrists, such as White and Meyer, were dead. Then the psychoanalysts took over, with their (to many Americans) glamorous European backgrounds. Of course, during the 1920's, if one who wanted to be a psychoanalyst had the bad luck to be born in the United States, he might be able to go to Europe and study in Vienna or Berlin or Budapest. One could also have fun. In my younger days I listened for many hours to stories by American and emigré psychoanalysts of the romance and gaiety of continental European capitals. And then it all ended with the rise of Hitler, and the outbreak of World War II.

There is no question of the enormous contribution of Freudian psychoanalysis, despite its shortcomings, to American psychiatry. Freud helped to teach American psychiatry how to walk upright and talk. But did American psychiatry have to walk and talk in the Viennese style? According to the psychoanalysts, the answer was yes, unless one preferred to remain "superficial." And so Freudian psychoanalysis suffered the same fate in the United States that it suffered in Europe. Minor additions were permitted—and no more. As long as Freud was alive, only he could make major revisions, and some of them, such as the death instinct, were, to say the least, questionable. And so classical psychoanalysis eventually became inflexible and sterile.

Meanwhile Sullivan had begun his epochal work with patients suffering schizophrenic and related disorders. At first he tried to adhere to the classical Freudian model, but he soon found it was gravely defective. Working in the setting of a mental hospital, he absorbed and tested in his work with patients whatever he found valuable and discarded the rest. At Saint Elizabeth's hospital in Washington, D. C., where he was a liaison officer for the Veterans Administration, he came under the influence of William Alanson White, who had applied Freud's psychoanalytic principles in a nondogmatic, flexible fashion to the diagnosis and treatment of hospital patients. Since he also attended staff conferences at Johns Hopkins University's Phipps Clinic, he became familiar with and was influenced by Adolf Meyer's psychiatry, especially perhaps his approach to schizophrenia. But when Sullivan became director of clinical research at Sheppard and Enoch Pratt Hospital in Baltimore in 1925, he was already a full-fledged psychiatrist with revolutionary ideas, as the papers he published from 1924 onwards will demonstrate. Interpersonal relations came to be regarded as paramount in the etiology of mental illness. Intrapsychic processes were not, and could not be, separated from the social history and actual, current living of the individual. To claim otherwise, Sullivan thought, is as erroneous—and therapeutically disastrous—as to claim that one can walk without a ground to walk upon. Of course Freud never did—and never could—completely ignore interpersonal relations. But his focus of study always centered on intrapsychic occurrences as if they had a life of their own—but that is a long, complex story. Nowadays, I think it fair to say that most psychoanalysts pay much more attention to the individual's "object relations," which is, in effect, a watered-down version of interpersonal psychiatry.

It seems clear that for at least the first decade of his professional life Sullivan wanted to work within the psychoanalytic "movement" and purify it of Freud's more speculative ideas. But he met with little or no success, at least until the house that Freud built came under attack from a great number of independent psychiatrists and psychologists so that it has become shaken to its very foundations. At all events, Sullivan reached a point at which he decided to let Freudian psychoanalysis continue on its merry way. I scarcely need to add this is no adverse reflection on the genuine and lasting achievements of Freud, to whom Sullivan owed a great deal. (Certain of his professional and/or personal enemies have been in the habit of telling their students that "Sullivan hated Freud." There is no truth to that assertion.)

Immodesty compels me to remind the reader that more than twenty years ago I published *Oedipus—Myth and Complex: A Review of Psychoanalytic Theory*. In that book I succeeded, I think, in acquainting the general literate public with a respectable grasp of the fundamentals of psychoanalytic theory, Freudian and Neo-Freudian, as it then stood. Since that time my opinion of Freud has remained essentially unchanged but my appraisal of Sullivan has become greatly augmented. Infinitely more important is the fact that his work is gradually becoming understood and appreciated throughout a large part of the world.

Although psychoanalysis for a time became "the rage" in this country, as it never did in Europe, some American psychiatrists always regarded it with reserve. There were those who rejected it *in toto*. At the present time there are few "orthodox" psychoanalytic institutes left. But in places like New York and Boston they are still potent. Psychotherapy is no longer the more or less exclusive domain of psychoanalysis or of any one "school." (See, for example, R. Bruce Sloane, "The Converging Paths of Behavior Therapy and Psychotherapy," *International Journal of Psychiatry*, 8:493-501, 1969.) Despite the traditional hostility of the medical profession, psychologists have created "schools" and "centers" that adhere to one or another of various forms of psychotherapy. Psychiatry seems to be more eclectic than it was a generation ago. Neurologically and/or biochemically oriented psychiatrists are searching for the "causes" of mental illness in the nervous system or in the workings of the body as a whole. Of course, psychiatry is a long way from achieving a unitary theory of the "causes" of mental illness. Some workers in the field are skeptical of the possibility of any such overarching theory.

In any case, it seems wise to take a "long view," however difficult that may be for some. A hundred years from now the rivalry of the contemporary schools is likely to be as silent and stilled as the voices of the Medieval Schoolmen. In fact, this rivalry is already muted. The ever-accelerating pace of social change will have brought about conditions we cannot know. It is impossible to imagine what psychiatry will then be like, but one would have to be very naïve to believe that its task will be lessened, though some may dream of magic pills or even brain transplants. In the words of one psychoanalyst, Rudolf Ekstein, American mass society "is in danger of losing the personal element —the roots of true individualism—and developing instead a kind of ruthless individualism that can become impersonal, irresponsible, overcompetitive and violent" *(Psychiatry and Social Science Review,* August, 1969, p. 6). As knowledge grows the world becomes ever more complex, more "technological," more overpopulated, more and more endangered of ultimate and final disaster. So the fate of man is unknown and threatened by forces about which the individual has usually very little understanding and over which he seems to have little or no control. My essay in the Appendix deals at some length with a few of these matters. Meanwhile, psychiatry will be able to help the relatively fortunate few. And that is surely a worthwhile and satisfying job. A man can always enjoy tilling his own garden though he cannot clear and cultivate a wilderness.

This preface marks the completion of a job I started more than five years ago. My task was made all the more difficult because of almost constant interruptions due to the necessities of earning a living. There were times when I wished someone else had done it, but no one, to my knowledge, has attempted a fairly comprehensive exposition of Sullivan's ideas. A psychiatrist, one of his former students, I reflected, would be the ideal man. However, there does not seem to be anyone available who is willing to sacrifice thousands of hours for such a task. Since the value of Sullivan's work, the fertility of his ideas, the power of his therapeutic techniques, are now almost universally recognized to be great, in so far as they are understood, I believed the job had to be done. And it has been done; perhaps not as well as I should like, but well enough, I think, to make the task much easier for anyone else who may some day want to rework what I have attempted.

The most important reason for writing this book is that a large amount of Sullivan's early work is not easily available to the general reader or to the psychiatrist who spends six days a week treating patients, and the seventh, talking shop with his colleagues. A number of Sullivan's early papers have not been published in book form. They are still buried, so to speak, in journals that are stacked in university libraries. The only book that Sullivan ever wrote—and what a book! —was only recently made available in mimeographed form by the William Alanson White Psychiatry Foundation, Washington, D. C. to interested psychiatrists. It is unlikely that many have read it. In this book I have attempted to provide a panoramic review of all of Sullivan's important ideas. This exposition shall, I hope, fill many gaps that still exist in the knowledge of perhaps most psychiatrists and clinical psychologists regarding interpersonal psychiatry.

But I have tried to present something more than a mere explication. Whenever it seemed necessary I have attempted to explain ideas that have seemed to be, or might be, obscure. No doubt I have not succeeded perfectly. Although I yield to no one in my admiration of Sullivan's achievements I am not one of those who think that his work cannot be interpreted without the aid of divine revelation. If one is willing to engage in the long and laborious endeavor of studying his writings and lectures from the time they first appeared in print, I believe most of the obscurities will disappear. Not all of them, perhaps. There were some matters that Sullivan seems never to have thought through, and perhaps will always remain obscure. But I doubt that occasional obscure passages in his work amount to very much. The general drift of his thought is clear.

P.M.

Acknowledgments

W. W. Norton and Co., Inc., deserve my thanks, which I gladly give, for permission to quote extensively from all six of the volumes containing papers and lectures by Sullivan, all of which are mentioned in the body of the text as well as in the footnotes. Dr. Otto Allen Will, Jr., and the Editor-in-Chief of *Contemporary Psychoanalysis,* Dr. Arthur H. Feiner, have very generously permitted me to quote the long excerpt from Dr. Will's paper "Schizophrenia and the Therapeutic Field." To them and the publisher, The William Alanson White Psychoanalytic Society, and the William Alanson White Institute of Psychiatry, Psychoanalysis and Psychology, I wish to express my thanks.

I take pleasure in publicly expressing my appreciation to Brother Gregory Nugent, F. S. C., President, Manhattan College, for the 1969 Summer Grant he awarded me in order to assist me in the completion of this book.

Several talks I held with Dr. Maurice R. Green saved me from ignoring some of Sullivan's ideas on tension and anxiety. I am also indebted to him for reading Chapters 2 and 11.

Contents

Preface — vii

Acknowledgments — xiii

1 The Early Development of Sullivan's Theories — 1

2 The Development of Symbol Systems — 37

3 The Evolution of Sullivan's Theory — 75

4 The Evolution of Personality
in Interpersonal Relations — 119

5 The Modified Psychoanalytic Method, and Types
of Personalities and Typical Situations — 191

6 Dynamisms of Difficulty — 240

7 Personality and Interpersonal Relations — 284

8 The Development of Personality — 334

9 Clinical Entities — 424

10 Sullivan's Theory of Schizophrenia — 483

11 The Psychiatric Interview — 523

12 Some Recent Developments — 613

Bibliography — 675

Index — 689

THE
BEGINNINGS OF
MODERN AMERICAN
PSYCHIATRY

The Ideas of Harry Stack Sullivan

Originally published under the title
Psychoanalysis and Interpersonal Psychiatry

1/ *The Early Development of Sullivan's Theories*

Harry Stack Sullivan was born in Norwich, New York, on February 21, 1892.[1] His grandparents had immigrated to the United States from Ireland. When Sullivan was three years of age, his family moved from the county seat to a farm situated near the village of Smyrna. There he is said to have been surrounded by books and opportunities to appease his curiosity about nature. Not many associations with other children were possible, especially since the Sullivans, a Roman Catholic family, were the only people of the Roman Catholic faith in a Yankee Protestant community. Since Sullivan was the only surviving child—two other children having died in infancy—he knew isolation from very early in life. A close friend, the late Clara Thompson, in a memorial address, has described him as a lonely person from his earliest childhood.[2]

In addition, Sullivan was exposed to an unhealthy family situation from the very start. Thompson relates how his mother, who thought she had married beneath her, was a complaining semi-invalid with chronic resentment at the, to her, humble family situation. Sullivan apparently got little warmth from her. In the after years, he used to say that his mother was not interested in knowing the boy who was her son, that she used him as a "dummy" on which to hang her illusions. But through those trying years Sullivan clung to the belief that if he could only reach his father, he would experience understanding. According to Thompson this finally occurred after he had reached adult life. In my own recollection, Sullivan, who, on a few occasions, confided a little of his early life experience to me, was able to establish some rapport with the "old man" only after his mother had died. In any event, during Sullivan's childhood, he was more or less estranged from his father, also, who may have seemed to him, as Thompson describes Timothy Sullivan in her memorial address, shy and withdrawn but who, in fact, according to certain informants, was a quite capable person in every way, though perhaps puzzled or baffled by the behavior of a boy who preferred reading books to working on the farm. Like many another youngster living on a farm who has been cut off from close human relationships, the close "friends" of Harry's childhood were the livestock on the farm with whom he felt comfortable and less lonely. Anyone who has ever experienced a more or less similar background can testify that this is no mere attachment to "pets." In any case, according to Thompson's account, Sullivan had no companions and when he finally went to school he felt out of place, not knowing how to be "a part of the group." Apparently he underwent a traumatic adolescence. This was largely the early background of the master theorist of interpersonal relations, whom Redlich and Freedman have characterized as "America's most original modern psychiatrist."[3]

Not long after graduating from high school, he determind to study medicine and psychiatry. He worked his way through the Chicago College of Medicine and Surgery, where he received the M.D. degree in 1917. During World War I he served as a first lieutenant "immovably detailed as a junior member of the Board of Examiners for the Medical Corps of what is now the 6th Service Command Area."[4] After being discharged from military service, he "resolutely entered the field of his choosing," psychiatry. But almost immediately he was called to become (1919) assistant medical officer in the 8th District Headquarters of the Rehabilitation Division of the Federal Board for Vocational Education. Subsequently he went to Washington to become (1920-1921) executive medical officer of the Division. He did not leave the Government service, the writer in *Current Biography* says, until he had drafted policy and procedure for handling the many soldiers disabled by neuropsychiatric conditions, though nothing was then done about his recommendations.

Having returned to Chicago, he was recalled to Washington, D. C., to become (1922-1923) United States Veterans Bureau liaison officer at St. Elizabeth's Hospital.[5] "At last his career as a psychiatrist was launched."[6] There he made the acquaintance of the eminent psychiatrist, the late William Alanson White, a man who made a permanent impression on Sullivan's thought. In 1923, he went to Sheppard and Enoch Pratt Hospital, Baltimore, Maryland with the title of assistant physician. The superintendent of this institution was another eminent physician, the late Ross McClure Chapman, who is said to have been of every assistance to Sullivan. In 1925, Sullivan was made Director of Clinical Research, having been given "unlimited opportunities" for intensive study of patients suffering from schizophrenic disorders, a position he held for approximately five years. But he also continued to lecture there until 1933. While he was Director of Clinical Research he was given a unique opportunity to test some of his ideas in a quasi-experimental setup.

Mrs. Helen S. Perry, a former managing editor of *Psychiatry,* who has investigated Sullivan's setting up of the special ward, relates that some time near the end of the period during which he was formally connected with Sheppard and Enoch Pratt Hospital, probably for the last twelve months he worked there, he established a special receiving service.[7] Furthermore, as she says, the social structure of the ward was drawn to Sullivan's specifications, though it was based on certain changes he had already partially incorporated on other wards at Sheppard. This special ward, which he has described briefly in a published paper, "Socio-Psychiatric Research," consisted of six beds and was housed in a relatively new building that was separated from the other buildings.[8] There were three beds in each of two rooms in this special ward, the two rooms being separated from each other by intercommunicating sitting rooms and a corridor. Mrs. Perry says there were several wards in this building—75 beds in all—and Sullivan's influence on the other wards, she thinks, was probably also considerable. But Sullivan ran the special ward in such a way that it was uniquely cut off from the various hierarchical structures that exist in any hospital. The freedom with which Sullivan was allowed to run this ward is said to have been quite remarkable. For one thing, the special ward was wholly removed from the supervision of the Nursing Service—and that was no small innovation. No woman was allowed on this ward. It is said there were six attendants (plus various relief personnel) who worked in two 12-hour shifts. According to Mrs. Perry's account, the day shift was composed of four attendants and the night shift of two. Sullivan handpicked these attendants from the hospital at large, and he may have directly hired some of them. Despite the fact that they were low in the hierarchy, as all attendants were and are to this day in mental hospitals, these attendants were trained in an intensive way by Sullivan to become full-fledged assistants. Under Sullivan's tutelage and inspiration they apparently developed a remarkable esprit de corps, and possessed unusual integrity and devotion to the patients. This is partly indicated by the fact that for considerable periods of time patients were entrusted to the care of the assistants without direct intervention by Sullivan (whose dedication to his patients was unlimited) unless and until it was necessary, though no doubt he was kept thoroughly informed of the patients' behavior. Thus the ward became a testing ground of carefully supervised interpersonal relations.

The special ward was created, in part, for the purpose of sealing off the patients from the hierarchical values of any mental hospital—values that largely reflect the social world outside. As Perry so well says, to expect an individual who had suffered humiliation in his family and the world at large to find a cure in an institution riddled with outworn codes of hierarchical values seemed nonsensical to Sullivan. Since his patients were male schizophrenics, female nurses were excluded primarily because "the registered female nurse may become the prototype of the high-status female in an inferior male society" of patients. Also, the profession of nursing has certain inherent superordinate-subordinate standards that may obstruct the establishment of a sympathetic personal environment for the patient—a vital necessity in Sullivan's view. Still again, he considered that the medical education existing in the 1920's, and subsequently, was woefully inadequate, as he pointed out in "Training of the General Medical Student in Psychiatry."[9] In this paper he offered several extensive measures for improvement of medical education.

Sullivan claimed that it was during the course of his work at Sheppard and Enoch Pratt Hospital that he became convinced of the great importance of social factors in explaining mental illness, or its absence. From this period came the evolution of his interpersonal orientation though his becoming acquainted with social scientists undoubtedly enhanced and enriched it. From this time onward he began to look to the social sciences for help in understanding interpersonal relations. As a result of his efforts, a standing committee on the relations of psychiatry and the social sciences was established in the American Psychiatric Association. Ultimately he arrived at the conviction that interpersonal theory tends to merge with social psychology. Furthermore, he believed that psychiatric prognosis is largely a specialized technique of social psychology, though supplemented by a knowledge of human biology.

Despite Sullivan's intensive preoccupation with mental disorders and their treatment, he found time for teaching. From 1924 to 1930 he was an instructor in psychiatry at the University of Maryland's Medical School, where he quickly rose to the rank of associate professor.

From 1924 onward he published several papers. Many of them appeared in the *American Journal of Psychiatry* until *Psychiatry* was founded in 1937. In 1930, a series of Farewell Lectures that Sullivan delivered at Sheppard and Enoch Pratt was privately circulated. These lectures were incorporated in *Personal Psychopathology,* several versions of which were written by 1932 and also privately circulated among some of his psychiatric and social science colleagues. It seems a pity that Sullivan never published this work. Recently (1965) a mimeographed edition has been copyrighted by the William Alanson White Psychiatric Foundation. Though in the light of present knowledge it is uneven, I believe many of the ideas in it are still valuable, and I shall summarize them in this book.

Sullivan moved to New York in 1931 and entered private practice. From this time forward he had more opportunity to study patients suffering from obsessional neuroses. Obsessional states had long intrigued him because of a possible relationship to schizophrenic disorders.

In 1938, having become preoccupied with a "practical psychiatry" for the not very distant national emergency that he, like others, had anticipated, he left New York and returned to Washington. He became a consultant in psychiatry for the Selective Service System in 1940, serving in that capacity for more than a year.

In the 1930's and 1940's Sullivan was a psychiatric supervisor or consultant for numerous psychiatrists and clinical psychologists in the New York and Washington-Baltimore areas, many of whom have become distinguished members of their profession.

In the meantime, the William Alanson White Psychiatric Foundation was established in Washington in 1933 by several former associates of Dr. White. Sullivan was one of the three original signers of the Certificate of Incorporation. (The other two were Dr. Lucille Dooley and Dr. Ernest E. Hadley.) The Washington School of Psychiatry, one of the enterprises of the Foundation, was incorporated in 1936. But soon after Sullivan's death the School ceased to be a Training Institute in Sullivan's "variant" of traditional psychoanalysis, which he had called interpersonal psychiatry. Many of his former students and colleagues returned to the more or less orthodox psychoanalytic fold. The William Alanson White Institute of Psychiatry, Psychoanalysis and Psychology in New York City was originally a branch of the Washington School. In these institutions, when Sullivan was alive, candidates for training in psychiatry were given an opportunity to learn directly his theories and therapeutic "methods." Another enterprise of the Foundation is the publication of *Psychiatry,* which was started in 1937. For a time Sullivan was co-editor and then, until 1949, editor.

He was influential in the founding of the World Federation for Mental Health and was a lively participant in the UNESCO project studying tensions affecting international understanding and war.[10] These interests are reflected in the papers "Remobilization for Enduring Peace and Social Progress" and "Tensions Interpersonal and International: A Psychiatrist's View," now published in *The Fusion of Psychiatry and Social Science.*

On January 14, 1949, he died in Paris.

Aside from *Personal Psychopathology,* Sullivan never wrote a book. Fortunately, several series of lectures were recorded. Several of the lecture series have been published in book form. The books containing the lecture series are *Conceptions of Modern Psychiatry* (originally published in the journal *Psychiatry* in 1940),[11] *The Interpersonal Theory of Psychiatry,*[12] *The Psychiatric Interview,*[13] and *Clinical Studies in Psychiatry.*[14] Two additional volumes, *Schizophrenia as a Human Process*[15] and *The Fusion of Psychiatry and Social Science,*[16] which contain many papers previously published in scholarly journals, are also available. These two volumes contain valuable biographical information about Sullivan and excellent interpretive commentaries on his intellectual background and the development of his ideas by Mrs. Perry.

Many questions have been raised as to whom Sullivan owes what. This can be an interesting and valuable (when it is not a hostile) enterprise. Mrs. Perry has answered several of such questions in her commentaries. But I shall refrain from a wholesale investigation of that sort. It is, however, important to mention the following men because they influenced either his theories or therapeutic "methods" quite early in his career: Sigmund Freud, Carl G. Jung, William Alanson White, Adolf Meyer, Charles Horton Cooley, and George Herbert Mead.

Freud undoubtedly ranks first in Sullivan's indebtedness. For a brief period, Sullivan tried to formulate his ideas within the classical psychoanalytical framework, as one can see from the first two papers he published: "Schizophrenia: Its Conservative and Malignant Features," and the "Oral Complex." He found much in Freud's psychoanalysis that he could employ in a productive fashion, though, as time went on, with more and more modifications and additions, until, by the middle or late thirties, he had worked out his own theories of interpersonal relations and their distortions. And, since he died when he perhaps barely reached the peak of his creative endeavors, it is interesting to speculate on what he might have accomplished had he lived as long as Freud.

In treating mental patients, he did not employ the classical psychoanalytic "method" but a "variant" of it, which he explains in "The Modified Psychoanalytic Treatment of Schizophrenia."[17] Freud himself did not think that schizophrenic patients could be treated by his own "method." In dealing with schizophrenics, Sullivan rejected free association, at least until they had reached some insight into their situation or a significant degree of improvement. Often, when circumstances permitted, he then referred them to colleagues for regular psychoanalytic treatment.

During the early part of his professional life, that is, until he went into private practice in 1931, Sullivan dealt largely with schizophrenics and patients suffering other sorts of psychotic disturbances. Since the psychiatry of schizophrenia in those days when he worked at Sheppard and Enoch Pratt Hospital was rather crude, Sullivan devoted his time and energy not only to developing more adequate techniques of therapy but to creating a more adequate theoretical framework for the understanding and treatment of schizophrenia. These tasks in turn coupled with Sullivan's increasing experience led to the construction of a technique of psychotherapy suited to the neuroses, and to a theory which, however imperfect, would help clarify the problems and origins of the milder mental disorders. A study of all these matters is not easy and will take up considerable space in this book.

In the rest of this chapter and the next two chapters I will attempt the following: (1) expound and briefly summarize the gradual development of Sullivan's ideas on schizophrenia; (2) outline the fragmentary development of interpersonal theory that appeared in connection with his early researches; (3) explicate the techniques of therapy and methods of research he employed; (4) tell his overall philosophy of psychiatric inquiry and therapy; and (5) give a brief summary of some of his ideas on the logic and methodology of psychiatric research.

But before I begin to outline Sullivan's ideas on schizophrenia, I want to sketch very briefly his summarization of the life history of a young man who underwent "the grave psychosis." It is my hope that in this way my subsequent discussion will seem less recondite and more meaningful to students of psychology. One should also bear in mind that Sullivan believed schizophrenic experiences are not different in kind from the nightmares that normal people sometimes have.

Schizophrenia is notoriously difficult to understand—even by psychiatrists. Hence I think it desirable to make some introductory general statements about mental disorders that may help the general reader who lacks the time or the interest to familiarize himself with the theories and findings of psychiatrists and clinical psychologists regarding the etiology and symptoms of various disorders that come under the heading of mental illness or abnormal behavior.[18] Mental illness is usually broken down into several classifications, although they often vary somewhat with different writers. These classifications include the psychoneuroses (hysteria, obsessive-compulsive neurosis, for example); psychophysiologic disorders (migraine headaches, stomach ulcers, etc.); functional psychoses (schizophrenia, manic-depressive psychosis, etc.); character disorders (psychopathic personality, certain "types" of juvenile delinquency, etc.); alcoholism and drug addiction; acute and chronic brain disorders; and still other forms of abnormal behavior that I need not mention.

For the purposes of this book, I shall confine my introduction to a small number of statements about the psychoneuroses (or neuroses) and functional psychoses. Of necessity these statements are selective and not always accepted perhaps by all psychiatrists and clinical psychologists. The term "functional" means, roughly, that there is no discoverable organic basis for a particular form of mental illness. In the brief descriptions I am about to give, one should realize that ultimately they stem mainly from Freud and Sullivan though supplemented by a host of other lesser contributors. The general reader may, on reading about the behavior of the mentally ill, ask, "How do people get that way?" Coleman has characterized the "essential sequence" in the development of the neuroses as typically: "(a) faulty personality development—immaturities, distortions—resulting in specific weaknesses in personality structure; (b) evaluation of certain common life stresses as terribly dangerous and threatening; (c) arousal of severe anxiety [often linked up with intense conflict]; (d) development of neurotic [that is, more or less ineffectual and often self-defeating] defense patterns to cope with the threats and anxiety; and (e) finally vicious circles with lowered efficiency and a myriad of secondary symptoms such as chronic fatigue and dissatisfaction."[19]

There is no need for me to attempt to catalogue the symptoms more or less typical of the various forms of neuroses. A few illustrations will suffice. For example, in hysteria various physical illnesses are unconsciously simulated. The obsessive-compulsive person is bedeviled with thoughts and impulses that he knows are irrational but that still persist. In the so-called anxiety neurosis one suffers a diffuse ("free-floating") but often severe anxiety that cannot be referred to any particular threat or situation. The hypochondriac is preoccupied with actual or imagined bodily diseases, upsets, complaints, and the like. In neurasthenia the person experiences chronic fatigue, mild depression, irritability, and anxiety.

Sullivan and others have claimed that the difference between psychosis and neurosis is one of degree only. While all psychiatrists do not agree, I think it would be fruitless to pursue this controversy, which may be, in part, "semantic." In any event, the difference is usually considered to be important—sometimes vitally important. As a rule, the psychoses are much more severe and disabling than are the neuroses. According to Coleman's formulation, the latter "blend imperceptibly into the psychoses" with increasing degrees of personality disorganization. Still an obsessive-compulsive neurosis can be pretty disabling and enormously difficult to "treat." Nevertheless there are certain symptom groups characteristic of the psychoses that are much less evident or practically absent in the neuroses.

What was said about the "essential sequence" in the development of the psychoneuroses applies to a large extent in the development of the functional psychoses. But there are important differences, too. For example, in schizophrenia it appears that the person is subjected very early in life to anxiety-provoking experiences that help prepare the way, so to speak, for subsequent disastrous occurrences. It appears that neurotic persons are not subjected to unfortunate experience quite so early in life or at least not to the same degree. Still, any type of functional mental illness is the outcome of so many variables that it is difficult to be precise about its origins. Furthermore, so little is known about many of these variables that almost any statement about them must be regarded as tentative.

A reader may ask, Why does one person become neurotic while another becomes psychotic? There is no certain answer to that question, as yet, though Sullivan has some suggestive ideas and hypotheses. One may, if one wishes, fall back upon genetics, for example, claiming that this or that type of mental illness is nurtured by an hereditary predisposition. But this is, to say the least, controversial. Sullivan, in general, rejected the notion of such a predisposing factor, especially in the later phase of his career.

Before I take up his early formulations of schizophrenia, there is one more topic to be discussed briefly: psychotic symptoms. Like the neuroses, each type of psychosis is characterized by numerous symptoms. But there are two kinds of symptoms that are outstanding and common in the major functional psychoses: delusions and hallucinations. Again I shall avail myself of Coleman's clear and precise formulations. He defines delusions as false beliefs that the individual vigorously defends despite logical absurdity or proof to the contrary and despite their serious interference with his social adjustment. He mentions *delusions of sin and guilt* wherein the individual believes he has committed unforgivable sins that have brought calamity to others. A second sort of delusion—*hypochondriacal delusions*—has to do with beliefs relating to various horrible disease conditions, wherein one emits bad odors, is "rotting away," or is being "eaten away." There are *nihilistic delusions,* such that one believes nothing, including oneself, exists. The patient may have died several years ago, for example, though a vaporous form of his spirit may remain. *Delusions of persecution* are common. People are plotting against one, or threatening one or discriminating against one, and the like. Often allied with these, as I shall point out in a subsequent chapter, are *delusions of grandeur.* One believes he is a great person, or a great historical figure, or a great genius or—even God. *Delusions of reference* (according to Sullivan) among people who are *not* psychotic or considered to be such are not rare. One believes that others are talking about him, in the absence of any evidence, of course, referring to him in some way, or portraying his life in cartoons, and so on. Still again there are *delusions of influence,* wherein one believes that people are influencing him in various ways. For example, they employ complicated electrical gadgets that send out waves interfering with his thoughts or filling his mind with filth.

Hallucinations are experiences of perception without any apparent, appropriate objective stimulation to arouse them. They have been described as distortions or misinterpretations of perception. Auditory, visual, olfactory, gustatory, and tactile hallucinations occur. The patient "may hear voices telling him what to do" or commenting upon or criticizing all of his actions. Occasionally messages are received from God or from some organization telling the patient of great powers that have been conferred upon him or of his mission to save mankind.

"In some instances the voices are ascribed to specific persons such as God, some relative or friend, or 'enemies.' In other cases the patient insists that he has not the vaguest idea as to the identity of the person or persons talking. Similarly the voices may be well localized —they may come from the light fixture, or the window, or an imaginary telephone receiver which the patient holds to his ear—or they may seem to come from all directions."[20]

In Sullivan's view, delusions and hallucinations are disguised symbolic expressions of unconscious or dissociated impulses and emotional patterns. These impulses and emotional patterns may be "carry-overs" from some earlier period in the person's life. Thus, in this introductory explication, one may conceive of personality as comprising the ego or self and the unconscious and/or dissociated aspects of the "mind" as well.

Thus, in therapy the patient may often relate to the psychiatrist or, in Sullivan's language, integrate a situation with him, by means of, or in terms of, unconscious motives, impulses, emotional patterns. Needless to say, the psychiatrist has to learn to understand these occurrences, and his role in them.

E. W., at the time of the report in "Regression: A Consideration of Reversive Mental Processes" was twenty-five years of age, the third of three children, the other two being girls.[21] His father was a quiet, intelligent but "decidedly subordinated man." E. W.'s mother is said to have been of much intelligence but of exaggerated ideals of goodness and clever at showing her children pain at any infraction of her moral code. This code, according to Sullivan, was "so high" that, of the girls, neither succeeded in adaptation. One daughter had developed a speech disorder by the age of ten. The other, who was the second child, failing to "attach" her husband's affections, was unhappily married and sought much support from her mother. The son, E. W., who was the "baby" of the family, grew to puberty a "paragon." His feeling of social inadequacy became so great that, by the time he reached the third year of high school, it overpowered his "compensatory athletic satisfactions and even his obvious popularity." Using the pretext of having to go to work, or at least of wanting to go to work, he quit school.

Apparently this ruse enabled him to become comfortable especially since he "combined with it" his removal to a nearby town. He thus "got on" until the war. Then, preparing to "vindicate" himself by enlisting he again became caught "in the toils of his mother's tender dominion," for she insisted that he abandon his plans to enlist and return home. Sullivan asserts E. W. was thus emasculated, and was caught up in the draft.

Despite the disadvantageous compulsory service, he "made good." Aside from being unable to emulate the heterosexual virility demonstrated by his fellows, he was quite happy in his new surroundings, where he was well liked. When he returned home and lived under the parental eyes he immediately developed "nervousness." In the parental milieu, E. W.'s urge toward sex adjustment is said to have become much exaggerated. But he could not make a "frank attempt," so he resorted to the device of going to the theater and putting his elbow in juxtaposition with the breast of a woman. On doing this he would shortly experience orgasm. Even though this habit that he had developed was anything but satisfactory as a compromise at sex adjustment, he was driven to repeat the procedure again and again.

E. W.'s "economic adaptation" also suffered. His peace of mind is said to have become so impaired that his fellow workers (who presumably noticed something of his disturbed state) would tease him about masturbation. His situation took on the aspects of a vicious circle. Nightmares disturbed his sleep. There followed "frank insomnia." E.

W. became seriously disturbed. Having decided to "fight it out" with someone, he was dissuaded, Sullivan says, by the "elected victim," who was his sister's negligent husband. "He experienced a schizophrenic outbreak—hallucinatory remarks anent the honoring of women, ideas of reference, disordered behavior regarding his elder (unmarried) sister, dream-like prepotent thoughts, feelings of panic."

After he was received into the hospital, he accomplished a very fair adjustment, Sullivan says, until confronted by misadventure with a competitive situation involving him with a male hypomanic and two silly girls, whereupon he again "collapsed." Sullivan goes on to say that E. W. became tense, developed the idea that he must come into physical contact with the breasts of a motherly nurse, thereafter was disturbed, actively hallucinated again, and impulsively overactive.

Analytic investigation—that is, Sullivan's "variant" of Freud's psychoanalysis—progressed until it became evident to E. W. that his interest in men was strong; "he then 'left it to God,' and became inaccessible." Soon anguish over a persistent thought (fortified by occasional hallucinations), to the effect that his mother was a prostitute, drove him to cooperation again. Suddenly he became suicidal as he drew near to an appreciation of, or insight into, the dominant role of his "mother-fixation." It is said that he then became very disturbed, negativistic, actively combative, with feelings of influence, frank homosexual hallucinatory accusations, frank homosexual desires, mutism, sex pressure, and a succeeding vigorous ritual of asceticism to suppress the sex urge, and along with all this a vigilant wakefulness, refusal to sleep except on the floor, very prolonged standing, vigorous refusal of food, and the like. Having succeeded, after a time, in suppressing any consciousness of sexual impulses, he became "classically catatonic."

After months of apparently fruitless effort on Sullivan's part—months of "apparent oblivion" on the part of the patient—the latter one day wrote: "Dear Mother, I want you always to remain in my heart." Still later E. W. interrupted his long silence in order to ask permission to visit home. Months after that he gave no response to Sullivan though he entered into fairly normal conversation with his mother, telling her he was undecided as to whether he or his physician was "right."

Sullivan wrote that, on occasions when E. W. visited his home for dinner, the hospital attendant who accompanied him noted certain peculiarities of mood and behavior. "When these were discussed with his elder sister," Sullivan asserted, "she remarked on the striking resemblance of these to moods and conducts of his boyhood. He is jealous of his mother's attentions to the others, reacting with pouting and refusal to eat at the table with the family. . . . The regression of motives, even if not seen in a full scale of gradations, is seen in orderly outline."[22]

Before I begin a more or less systematic explication of Sullivan's ideas about, and interpretations of, schizophrenia, I must warn any Freudian-oriented reader that, in Sullivan's view, the "case" I have summarized is *not* to be rigidly interpreted in terms of the classical oedipal conflict. In a paper titled "Erogenous Maturation," Sullivan wrote that the Oedipus complex "must be recognized as a distortion, not as a biological development normal to the male [or female] child. It is a fraudulent symbol situation, the result of multiple vicious features of our domestic culture."[23] Whether or not one approves of Sullivan's free-swinging attack on the "domestic culture," one can easily see that he did not think the Oedipus complex is universal and biologically ordained, as Freud believed.

In any event, failure to resolve the Oedipus complex is not the nucleus of every neurosis or a central explanatory concept for understanding schizophrenia. The etiology of mental disorders is much more "complicated" than this. Several "variables" (some of which Freud recognized) have to be taken into account, as I shall attempt to explain.

Sullivan claimed, in "Psychiatric Training as a Prerequisite to Psychoanalytic Practice," that schizophrenics differ from other types of patients in that their motivation is peculiarly integrated so that they undergo with extraordinary ease reactivations of emotional configurations or "sets" that are seldom observed in other types of people.[24] The reactivations of such emotional patterns are so unpleasant that schizophrenics come to protect themselves by "distance," "indifference," and "apathy." Sullivan added that if one is dealing with an hysteric, one anticipates in the course of a successful psychoanalysis the reappearance of some very early emotional configurations, but the therapist begins at the level of one's fellow man in ordinary life. He discusses first more or less adult relationships as they are manifested, and from this level the therapist works gradually back to the earlier configurations in a manner that is fairly smooth, and fairly easy to follow. This technique is outlined in *Personal Psychopathology* and the *Psychiatric Interview*. Sullivan asserts that, in contrast to such a situation, when one has at last, by the skill of one's preliminary work, actually entered into relationships of intimacy with a schizophrenic, one passes suddenly from the realm of ordinary people, from the types of relationship that one recognizes among one's fellows from school years onward, into a type of interpersonal situation that can actually be referred only to the relationships that characterize the first three years of life. "Abruptly, often without warning, one finds oneself integrated by powerful motives of the type of hatred and primitive love for which our language is lacking terms."[25]

Earlier he wrote:

> Schizophrenics are individuals who have undergone a severe mental disorder which is characterized variously but is significant, for our purposes, because of a dissociation of the mental aspects of the life processes in such a fashion that the victim no longer amalgamates readily in ordinary social activities but instead finds himself surrounded by extraordinary caricatures of other people, engaging in bizarre activities more or less definitely injurious to him, the whole of his interpersonal relations resembling the phantasmagoria of the nightmare.[26]

Sullivan goes on to say that the schizophrenic's motivation is correspondingly, perhaps fundamentally, altered in a fashion leading him to what is popularly called insane activities, and he becomes a menace to himself and/or to others.

He describes the people who are later to become schizophrenic as usually relatively inconspicuous in the social fabric up to and into adolescence, but in the course of adolescence they become conspicuous indeed because of their bizarre behavior, and are thereupon conveyed hastily to a mental hospital—if they have not committed suicide. They tend to follow or adopt one of a few fairly definite courses of behavior in the mental hospital. According to Sullivan's account, they are, respectively, extraordinarily shy and uncommunicative or bitterly hostile because of the fancied enmity of everyone, or shy, silly, and childishly employed. As things stood in 1929, they tended markedly to remain thenceforth and forever in the mental hospital until at the end of a rather long and terrible life they died. In harmony with the usual psychiatric orientation prevailing until recently, they were expected to deteriorate in all or various of the human abilities to some curious vegetative state termed deterioration.

On the surface, the schizophrenic's life is said to be an excessively simple one. To the superficial observer he is often completely divorced from social influences. No longer does he respond in any ordinary fashion to the social forces that are impressed on him. Many of the cultural values of people in his society no longer interest him, be they ethical, artistic, or whatever. He is not even interested in taking food or avoiding contact with feces, urine, or whatnot.

His thinking is awry—not that he has really lost the capacity to think. But partly owing to certain poignantly traumatic experiences, or to a series of very unfortunate experiences extending over a period of years, he is decidedly uncertain about life. It seems that if one is sufficiently uncertain about life, one loses the cognitive assets that enable people to distinguish the products of autistic or purely subjective reverie processes from the products (thoughts, perceptions, behavior patterns) of experience with external reality. Once a person loses this ability to separate subjective fancy from external reality, he begins to sink into mental processes significantly like those one experiences when one is asleep or (Sullivan for a while believed) in the intrauterine state before birth. In "Peculiarity of Thought in Schizophrenia," Sullivan discusses the mental processes of the schizophrenic at length, a topic which I shall discuss subsequently in this chapter and in later chapters.[27] Once a partition of experience occurs in which a person during a considerable period of waking life is without the ability to distinguish what has true, and consensually (socially) acceptable external references and what is purely fantasy, he is definitely schizophrenic. It is these peculiarities, Sullivan wrote, relating to the abnormal partition of experience, that constitute the essence of schizophrenic behavior.

In the first paper Sullivan published, called "Schizophrenia: Its Conservative and Malignant Features,"[28] he sought, among other things, to combat the pessimism of many psychiatrists regarding schizophrenia. He was attempting to insure a new measure of interest in schizophrenic patients so that they "will cease to be regarded by so many as *a priori* inexplicable and hopeless." At the same time he warned against dilettantish or thoughtless or insensitive behavior on the part of a physician or nurse or attendant. Far more than any single action, Sullivan claimed, it is the general attitude of the physician toward the patient that determines his value. The schizophrenic patient is said to appreciate "all too definitely" the physician's attitude regarding the life situation presented by the patient. In this connection, certain philosophical and speculative anthropological notions (such as solipsism and Jung's "collective unconscious") or an allegedly scientific outlook that eliminates purpose from human life and "reduces the individual to organismic cravings in pitched battle," when embodied in the attitude of the physician, have much the same destructive influences on the patient as those to which he was previously subjected in the world, in various guises. Too much of the physician's own thinking is constituted of primitive processes of thought (autistic thought processes) for him to settle easily into the interpretation of the more primitive processes of the patient—at least until he shall have developed a certain measure of insight into certain unreflective attitudes embodied in his own intellectual and moral heritage.

Sullivan reiterated W. A. White's dictum to the effect that the psychiatrist must understand what the patient is trying to do. Therefore the element of motivation seems logically fundamental in attacking the problem of understanding and treating schizophrenia.

Sullivan maintained in the first paper he published that a schizophrenic psychosis may serve in at least some instances, a positive, constructive function. For example, he mentions a group of patients whom he had studied who had recovered with definite favorable change of personality, compared with their prepsychotic condition. Staff conferences of various hospitals had diagnosed the majority of them as suffering from *dementia praecox*, a primary disease entity. A large number of them had manifested markedly "psychopathic" traits in childhood. Their histories revealed such things as ungovernable temper tantrums, destructiveness, malicious behavior, emotional instabilities of high degree, excessive sensitiveness, extreme self-consciousness, severe neuroses. The postpsychotic personality in these cases is said to have showed the disappearance or mitigation of (personality) "defect," a greater adaptability or a greater self-satisfaction (self-esteem) such that the stress or tensions incident to ordinary life was much nearer the usual, that is, the average. Sullivan claims that an improvement from a seclusive, self-contained, or pent-up attitude with lack of the ability to use available outlets for the expression of distressing mental content to one in which the patient was relatively open and able to discuss his life problems was generally observed. Emotional or intellectual deterioration occurred in *none* of these cases such that the personality was reduced below the average of people similarly situated in the community. In fact, the psychosis, according to Sullivan, made subsequent social life possible, thus preserving an individual who previously had not been equal to the demands of everyday social intercourse. This group, where therapeutic endeavor was consistently encouraging, comes under the traditional clinical label of catatonic *dementia praecox*. Sullivan believed almost all initial schizophrenic psychosis should be considered of this category.

Sullivan also claims that, even in the group who came out of their psychosis with a decidedly paranoid adjustment to reality, there had been a change from an obviously ineffectual adaptation to one in which the social contacts of the individual caused him much less profound discomfort and in which emotional introversion and brooding gave way to the less individually destructive projection of discomfort and hate.

It must be obvious to any one, Sullivan said, that *the social milieu to which the patient had to return had a great deal to do with his future.* He thought that if the conservative reorganization or reconstruction of complexes and sentiments (later lumped together as "dynamisms") that appears to underlie a goodly share of the early schizophrenic phenomenology or symptomatology leads the patient undergoing treatment to the foreconscious belief that he can circumvent or rise above environmental handicaps, and this belief is the "presenting" or outstanding, notable, communicable feature of a comprehensive mental integration, or orientation, then his recovery will proceed; and if such reconstruction is not accomplished, the patient fails to recover. This failure is apparently due to the hopeless features of the social situation awaiting him.

Sullivan was not successful in his efforts to identify exactly the factors that cause milder maladjustive efforts to "pass over" into schizophrenia. Although in "Peculiarity of Thought in Schizophrenia" he stated that throughout his experience the complex etiology of schizophrenia culminated in a situation in which the sexual adequacy of the individual, according to the ideals he had acquired, was acutely unsatisfactory, Sullivan did not think, as he stated in "The Onset of Schizophrenia," that the "sex factor" was of exclusive importance.[29] He believed that "cultural distortions" provided by the home were of prime significance. Parents or their surrogates had provided the schizophrenic patient, when he was a child, with various kinds of experience from which he developed "erroneous attitudes" leading to maladjustment. All sorts of maladjustments were found in the history of patients who suffered the "grave psychosis." These maladjustments make one more vulnerable to the stresses of adolescence in Western society, and, even, sometimes, to apparently minor accidental events. Also, the pathogenic experiences and "erroneous attitudes" that have been acquired by schizophrenic patients, first in the home, are largely assimilated into the self, though some may remain or become dissociated.

A great number of Sullivan's patients manifested clear signs of coming trouble before the "break" or onset of schizophrenia. A number of them are said to have been brought to notice by the outcropping of behavior of a simple psychoneurotic sort. In some cases, according to Sullivan, unwitting attempts at hysterical incapacitations not only precede many psychoses but actually constitute much of the psychotic picture. Frank schizophrenic phenomena, in a small number of cases, for years were preceded by obsessive substitutive reactions. In these instances, also, the maladjustive phenomena were continued in the psychosis. Another complaint of considerable duration was neurasthenia. "The gradations from neurasthenic picture into schizophrenia would be easy to observe," Sullivan claims in "The Onset of Schizophrenia," "did we but attend more clearly to the mental state of quasi-normal adolescents." And he adds that anxiety conditions that deepen into schizophrenic panic occur in numbers. In another decade Sullivan was to conceive of anxiety as a central explanatory conception for the understanding of mental illness.

Thus, in potential patients, there was a significant grouping of irrational factors that interlock. One may find that a potential patient had developed many misapprehensions regarding his real potentialities of achievement. Such a youth's personality has evolved in such a fashion that he exaggerates, misunderstands, and conceals from himself various requirements for his satisfactions (and emotional security), and comes to believe that he needs certain "end-situations" that are superfluous and that he can dispense with certain others that are a part of the common biological heritage. He unwittingly elaborates a fabric of personal ideals "which have but a complex order of relationship to possibility," that is, ideals that are unrealistic and of doubtful attainment. Likewise, he will have fabricated notions concerning the estimation or appraisal that other people make of him that are "simply fantastic." Since all these factors interlock, it comes about that his energies are dissipated in pseudoproblems and defensive processes.

More generally, numerous maladjustive processes are found to have existed that were obstacles to the having of "useful experience." The irrational, unconscious protection of the self was a "central theme." In the further course of his studies, Sullivan began to realize that it was self-system functions, designed to protect self-esteem, that made the lives of troubled youth enormously complicated and destructive of personal efficiency, that is, personal adequacy.

Sullivan claimed in "The Onset of Schizophrenia" that it is never easy to say just when the schizophrenic patient has crossed the line into actual psychosis. In several cases, he said, he had found that there had occurred a brief phase of a marked psychotic condition some considerable time before the final break. He mentions a patient who when 17 years of age underwent an operation firmly convinced that he would not survive the anaesthetic. This patient came out of the anaesthetic minus his normal, that is, usual grasp on reality. For days things seemed to be quite unreal. In the patient's own words, he lived in a dream. In this alleged dreamlike state all sorts of trifling and wholly unrelated occurrences seemed fraught with great personal import, relating in some signal but uncomprehensible way to him: "The operation had been the occasion for some strange mutilation: he was changed in some curious fashion." Then, one morning, according to the patient, he awoke his old self. This patient, according to Sullivan, went on to the age of 25 years before the stress of "heterosexual adaptation" precipitated an exceptionally "paranoid" incipient schizophrenia.

Another patient, whom Sullivan also mentions, on receiving cocaine anaesthesia for a nasal operation, when he was 22 years of age, developed an extraordinary excitement like that seen in catatonia. This condition subsided after 30 hours, and nothing bizarre was manifested for the next three months. Then, as the date of his marriage drew near, he lapsed quickly into a severe catatonic schizophrenia.

Still another patient, "having accidentally discharged a gun in the direction of a beloved uncle, developed blocking and phenomena of stupor which lasted a few days." Then eight months later under circumstances in which both his heterosexual efforts and his strivings for prestige among his fellows failed disconcertingly he underwent a catatonic dissociation, which in every instance entails a regression to modes of experience characteristic of infancy and early childhood. (The latter is one of the things that made schizophrenia seem "mysterious" and incomprehensible to many psychiatrists and gravely hindered communication with schizophrenic patients.) Sullivan wrote that each one of this group of patients had come to a psychopathic type of adjustment quite early in life. The psychopath is, among other things, unable to profit from certain types of experience.

The onset of schizophrenia may be abrupt or insidious, a fact that is significant for its outcome. At any rate, in "The Onset of Schizophrenia," Sullivan said that his search for the phenomena actually constituting the onset had brought to light the following. A great deal of the early phenomenology, that is, the patient's experiences while still in a prepsychotic state, is an accentuation of the phenomena of almost any mild disorder. One will find that in psychopathological states generally there is a clear to vague impression that other people show an unfriendly interest in one. A great proportion of all maladjusted individuals are said to believe that they suffer invidious discussion. Belittling others in an unwitting effort to reduce them to a lower level than that adjudged to oneself may be evidenced in behavior and thinking. This also occurs indirectly by projection of "persecutory trends," in which one unconsciously attributes to other people one's own tendency to disparage them. The tendency to detract from the worth of others, either directly, or indirectly by unwittingly attributing to them belittling attitudes, may on slight excuse progress into notions that one is being slighted, annoyed, or definitely wronged. Many maladjusted people attach fantastic or illusory meanings to the behavior of others or to their own actions or even to inanimate events. Beliefs akin to delusions of mind reading and of more or less mysterious control by others are held by a remarkable number of people who are not regarded as psychotic. Hypochondriacal notions, somewhat grandiose self-appraisals, depressive depreciations of self and self-criticism can be found in a great many maladjusted people. Still again, among one large group of maladjusted persons, obsessions and preoccupations are typical.

The "prodromal," incipient period of schizophrenia (a condition in which the individual alternates between a state in which he lives the sort of life to which he is accustomed, that is, one in which his behavior is under the control of his "ego," and a state, of varying length, that is under the domination of dissociated tendencies) often includes characteristic features that Sullivan thought should receive special attention. Many patients are depressed for a long time before the outcropping of frank psychosis. According to Sullivan, their behavior and utterances reflect much unhappiness but is to be distinguished from the psychosis of depression (which he has described in *Conceptions of Modern Psychiatry*). He says they do not slow up physically and mentally nor suffer preoccupation with certain grief-provoking notions to the exclusion of more practical thinking. "Expressed loosely, they feel not that all is lost as a consequence of personal sins and errors, but that all is wrong for some more or less inscrutable reason, which may or may not pertain closely to some weakness or inadequacy or peculiarity of the individual—often alleged results of masturbation."[30] The situation is said to be always a maladjustment to assumed personal inadequacy, though this may elude the patient's consciousness entirely. "While the true depressive is preoccupied with thoughts of the enormity of the disaster, of punishment, hopelessness, and the like, the incipient schizophrenic is not the host of any simple content, but is burdened with pressing distresses and becomes more and more wrapped up in fantastic explanation and efforts at remedy."[31]

Pure depression is said to be a standstill of adjustment: the sufferer does not, or cannot, even attempt to resolve his problems. The depression of schizophrenia is "a most unhappy struggle." Schizophrenics try to escape from their situation by "mystic and more or less extraordinary efforts" while justifying themselves by "heroic measures." Several "case histories" in *Schizophrenia as a Human Process* help clarify these matters, but a discussion of such measures has no great significance for the purposes of this book and will not be dealt with here.

Another important group of phenomena of the incipient schizophrenic state is perplexity. In this state, extraconscious material is said to influence perceptions of reality toward the end that the patient becomes more and more entangled in contradictions, alternative notions, and illusions. Sullivan asserted that autochthonous thoughts appear and interfere unpleasantly with rational efforts. Insignificant occurrences persistently hold the individual's attention, giving rise to disturbing analogies.

Still again "fear states" (which in his subsequent career Sullivan reinterpreted as anxiety states, and conditions stemming from them) are factors important in many incipient schizophrenic conditions.

"Schizophrenic depression" as described above, perplexity, and "fear states" unite to constitute three "phenomenon-groups" that combine in the evolution of most schizophrenic psychoses.

It is a "fear state"—acute panic—that typically precipitates the *sudden,* abrupt onset of schizophrenia. The foreshadowed loss of respect in the eyes of others owing to certain uncontrollable cravings—loosely, homosexual cravings—as a rule brings about this panic. For example, one of Sullivan's patients, "hating his father with a great hate, and already lonely and unhappy," rapidly developed very severe panic after he had submitted to fellatio for the first time.[32]

Another patient, at age 19, who had never resolved a powerful but ambivalent attachment to his mother, was received into the hospital after a panic in which he walked the streets, believing that he was pursued by all the automobiles of a city, that every third house was alight, that he was going to be crucified or otherwise killed. In "Peculiarity of Thought in Schizophrenia," Sullivan has outlined the history of this "case," called E. K. Owing to considerations of space, I shall omit Sullivan's summary of the social difficulties of E. K.'s childhood and early chronological adolescence. At the age of 18, E. K. is said to have been definitely seclusive and decidedly overscrupulous, and at times showed compulsive behavior. To some extent he overcame these problems. Having taken a job with two bootleggers, he attended a mixed party on Halloween, "at which he had much trouble with his thinking" and reportedly would laugh frequently without cause. A few days later the psychosis is said to have been obvious.

When he was received into the hospital, he was tense, "scattered," rambling in conversation, troubled by constant thoughts pertaining to a desire to do fellatio, believing that, as he said, things had a blurred look, as if the world was coming to an end. He is said to have misinterpreted occurrences about him, to have believed that everyone thought him to be an oral pervert, to have had many delusions of reference and projections involving nearly everyone.

Not only had this patient never resolved a powerful but markedly ambivalent attachment to his mother, he had persistent strong emotional attitudes toward his father and at times, Sullivan says, a very disquieting desire to submit to sexual advances that he imagined his father making to him. Sullivan relates that at the age of eight E. K. was submitted to pederasty by his older brother, toward whom he maintained a strong conscious affection. E. K. maintained a perverse adaptation with active and passive pederasty, thereafter, with companions of approximately his own age. After one of his companions refused to reciprocate as the passive agent, telling some others of his use of the patient, his social difficulties became marked. Frequently he masturbated, to the accompaniment of homosexual phantasies. *"On an occasion when about 17,* he, having inserted a candle into the rectum," as he said, to increase satisfaction, on the approach of orgasm "withdrew the candle and thrust it into his mouth."[33] He remembered vividly that the orgasm was very powerful—a recollection that E. K. at first strongly resisted. Sullivan relates that he never repeated the procedure. He found out not long after this that several of his mates in the pederasty episodes were making what appeared to him successful heterosexual adjustments. But he was reduced to going to decidedly low houses of prostitution, where he achieved no satisfaction. . . . On a certain occasion after misinterpreting a statement he heard his roommate make, he "stumbled through some revealing recriminations to the astonishment and contempt of the other, and by night was in panic."

In "The Onset of Schizophrenia," Sullivan wrote that he had come to regard all initial manifestations of schizophrenic illnesses as strikingly uniform. "From the standpoint of content, there appear those processes and symbol elaborations customary in dreaming." The schizophrenic's cognitive operations, including his perceptions of reality, are distorted for the purpose of "representing" his personal situation and for efforts at solving it. Sullivan claims that it is at this stage that the patient believes he is watched and followed. The "observers" are sometimes symbolic representations of the ideals that, in a manner of speaking, cannot control his desires of "lower cultural value" by ordinary acts. In other instances the observers are personifications of the (to him) evil desires that "pursue him" to assault or "rob" or degrade him. In the first state of affairs exteriorization is said to take the form of the voice of God, and in the second situation, the hallucination of threats or foul epithets. This sort of content is said to connect with a more or less terrible affective situation of a primitive sort, namely a so-called insane mood that has existed prior to the clear-cut cognitive phenomena—the symbol elaborations customary in dreaming. (These matters are considerably elaborated in *Conceptions of Modern Psychiatry*.) Sullivan wrote that the motivation operating is in a general way conflicting groups of elaborated and more or less successfully repressed personal tendencies opposed by tendencies of the character of ideals, that is, "cultural controls" or mores. "The disturbance in reality-appraisal," Sullivan adds, "which has been slow in the prodromal stages, is now very swift, progressing to a state in which everything is involved in the cognitive efforts. This stage in which nothing is without an incomprehensible meaning, and the ordinary exchange of intelligence is palsied, may continue in relatively simple elaboration. This is the catatonic type of schizophrenia."[34]

In catatonic schizophrenia, the conflicts mentioned previously may remain unresolved, so that the struggle for personal security expands into cosmic dramas, and the psychic processes regress perhaps to the most primitive phase of personality development. However, Sullivan asserts that at any time this situation may pass into one of the following: (1) a massive resynthesis "amounting to recovery with profit" from the experience; (2) "a fragile reorganization prone to relapse under fresh difficulties"; (3) a "readjustment by paranoid processes," which, if successful, entails a *persistent paranoid state,* with "more or less of schizophrenic residues" or remnants, and which, if unsuccessful, entails an "unhappy jumble" of schizophrenic projections—of evil omen, since they are linked up with an attitude of destructive hatred; and (4) the practically irremediable hebephrenic type. In hebephrenia, destruction of the conflicts is achieved by disintegration of the acquired socially adopted tendencies (that is, roughly, "ego" motives), and along with this a dilapidation or disintegration of the developed structures (that is, roughly, toilet habits, eating habits, sexual behavior patterns, etc.) that influence manifestations of "simple native tendencies," such as physiological drives. There is, in other words, a disintegration of the entire personality makeup. Then the motivation of hebephrenics becomes juvenile, childish, or even infantile.

In Chapter 3 I will briefly discuss situations in which the *onset* of schizophrenia is more gradual and often insidious rather than abrupt though the end result is the same—or worse. However, for the sake of clarity, I wish to mention the following. There is no sudden, dramatic separation from ordinary living—or from "reality," as some writers would say. Instead, the sufferer is said to become gradually more and more peculiar until finally, because of some more or less spectacular occurrence, his mental illness is recognized. Therefore, it seems that in every occurrence of schizophrenia there is no single precipitating factor that more or less abruptly drives the individual into panic.[35]

Sullivan suggested a technique in "Schizophrenia: Its Conservative and Malignant Features" for treating acute and subacute states of schizophrenia, which, as I have already said, differs from orthodox psychoanalytic "method," though he claimed that some incipient and early states of schizophrenia can be and were analyzed directly, as August Hoch had demonstrated. Sullivan held that, in acute and subacute states, the application of the discoveries of psychoanalysis must be divorced from the method of free association in its usual form. The careful use of questions, in some instances, addressed to the patient, and to a trained assistant in the hearing of the patient, is said to have been found effective in stimulating perception, analysis, and resynthesis of psychotic content. Sullivan wrote also that in other cases recourse is to be had to primitive forms of thought exchange (unspecified), and utlilization of symbols, allegories, and even rituals for the induction in the disorganized individual of therapeutic experience assimilable at the levels of regression to which he has reverted. In later years he abandoned this notion.

When, toward the end of his career as Director of Clinical Research at Sheppard and Enoch Pratt Hospital, he was able to establish a special ward there, he impressed upon his assistants the importance of the first 24 hours of any patient on a ward. The data from the first 24 hours were carefully noted because the patient's initial encounter with the daily round in an institution might turn out to be crucial throughout his entire stay. Sullivan encouraged his assistants to spend a great deal of time with the new patient in a close and reassuring way and to be alert observers of whatever seemed to occur. The life of the patient on the ward was regarded as in many ways more crucial to his progress than the single hour a day usually spent with the doctor, partly because the patient's daily living provided more complex and varied data and in many ways more rewarding data as well.[36]

In "The Modified Psychoanalytic Treatment of Schizophrenia," Sullivan summarizes his procedures as follows:

The procedure of treatment begins with removing the patient from the situation in which he is developing difficulty, to a situation in which he is encouraged to renew efforts at adjustment with others. . . . The subprofessional personnel with whom the patient is in contact must be aware of the principal difficulty—*viz.*, the extreme sensitivity underlying whatever camouflage the patient may use. They must be activated by a well-integrated purpose of helping in the redevelopment or development *de novo* of self-esteem as an individual *attractive* to others. They must possess sufficient insight into their own personality organization to be able to avoid masked or unconscious sadism, jealousies, and morbid expectations of results. They must be free from the more commonplace ethical delusions and superstitions. . . .

Given the therapeutic environment, the first stage of therapy by the physician takes the form of providing an orienting experience. After the initial, fairly searching, interview, the patient is introduced to the new situation in a matter-of-fact fashion, with emphasis on the personal elements. In other words, he is made to feel that he is now one of a group, composed partly of sick persons—the other patients—and partly of well folk—the physician and all the others concerned. Emphasis is laid on the fact that something is the matter with the patient, and—once this is at least clearly understood to be the physician's view—that regardless of the patient's occasional or habitual surmise to the contrary, everyone who is well enough to be a help will from thenceforth be occupied in giving him a chance to get well. From the start he is treated as a *person among persons.*[37]

Sullivan adds that there is never to be an acceptance of his disordered thought and behavior as *outré* or crazy, or of a "never mind" technique that ignores the obvious. Everyone in this milieu is to regard the patient's outpouring of thought or the doing of acts as at least *valid* for the patient, and to be considered seriously as something that at least he should understand. The "individualism" of the patient's performances, Sullivan says, is neither to be discouraged nor encouraged, but when they seem clearly morbid, they are to be noted and perhaps questioned, instead. The questioning must arise from a desire to center the patient's attention on the discovery of the factors concerned. Violence, if it occurs, is to be discouraged *unemotionally,* and in the clearly expressed interest of *"the general or special good."*

Violence on the part of a patient often arises from panic, and such a state of affairs must be dealt with by the physician. On the other hand, if the patient seems obviously to increase in comfort (emotional security) without professional attention after the patient's introduction to care, the physician can profitably await developments. Sullivan claimed that a considerable proportion of these patients proceed in this "really human environment" to the degree of social recovery that permits analysis, without much contact with the supervising physician. Furthermore, patients who experienced this (as far as I know unprecedented) form of therapy became aware of their need for insight into their previous difficulties and somewhat cognizant of the nature of the procedures to be used for that purpose. Sullivan says they became not only ready but prepared for (psychoanalytically oriented) treatment.

Without going into further details and complications of treatment that Sullivan deals with, I wish to mention the following. As the patient improves and as his acceptance of the need for help increases, the physician attempts a more direct and thorough treatment, chiefly in reconstructing the actual chronology of the psychosis. He discourages all the patient's attempts to smooth over, or glide over, relevant past experiences, and he employs free association techniques when apparent failures of memory occur. The therapist emphasizes the role of significant persons and their doings in the patient's life. Sullivan tried to impress the patient in therapy with the principle that, however mysteriously the pathological occurrences originated, everything that has befallen him is related to his actual living among a relatively small number of significant people, in a relatively simple way. In this treatment situation, psychotic phenomena recalled from the patient's more disturbed periods are subjected to study in regard to their relation to those significant others. Sullivan studied the patient's dreams under this principle. In this fashion the dynamics of the individual's difficulty become apparent to the physician whether or not they were grasped by the patient. The physician scrupulously avoids forcing interpretations on him and preferably offers none except as "statistical findings." That is, if the patient seems to be gaining insight at a considerable pace, the therapist can *occasionally* offer that "thus-and-so" has, in some patients, been found to be the result of "this-and-that," with a request for the former's associations to this comment.

Sullivan claimed that one of perhaps three situations now develops. The family may insist on taking the patient home, if he is doing very well, while generally ignoring advice as to further treatment. Or, in certain circumstances, the patient is discharged into regular treatment by a suitable psychoanalyst, experienced in the psychiatry of schizophrenia, who is not too rigid in devotion to technique. Or, in certain other circumstances, the therapy is shifted gradually to follow Sullivan's "liberal variant" of the Freudian technique.[38]

But I have gotten a little ahead of my story as it gradually unfolds and must return to the beginning as it appears in Sullivan's first published paper.

He claimed (1924) that in the light of his clinical observations schizophrenia is not to be regarded as a primary disease entity such as that which one may visualize when mentioning *dementia praecox*, a term that has been used by psychiatrists synonymously with schizophrenia. He also saw no profit from pondering on an "organic substratum" that could not be demonstrated in the patient who comes for treatment. Instead, the dynamic viewpoint of Adolf Meyer, and the work to which it supplied impetus, according to Sullivan, proved vastly more cogent to the life problems of the patient.

Sullivan alleged that his investigations led him to the conclusion that schizophrenia is to be characterized as a series of major mental events, always attended by material changes of personality but in itself implying nothing of deterioration or dementia. The disorder is said to be one in which *the total experience of the individual* is reorganized, with a great eruption of "primitive" functions. In addition there is said to be at least temporarily profound alteration of the egoistic structures, what older psychologists called the sentiment of self-regard, and what Sullivan subsequently formulated as the self-dynamism, self-system, or self.

Schizophrenia, according to Sullivan, is a disorder that is determined by the previous experience of the individual regardless of whether it is excited by emotional experience (psychic traumata), by the toxemia of acute disease, by cranial trauma, or by alcoholic intoxication. When he wrote "Schizophrenia: Its Conservative and Malignant Features," he felt fairly certain that there is an hereditary predisposition to the schizophrenic dissociation—a view he seems to have eventually abandoned, or at least vastly modified. He also thought then that it is not the *outbreak* of schizophrenic mental content and behavior that bears upon the individual prognosis but the *dynamics* of the several regressions that seems to be of final importance in determining recovery, chronicity, or a dementing (deteriorating) course.

Sullivan asserted and emphasized that schizophrenia must be recognized as a mental process. It is a disorder of mind (in the inclusive sense), and is manifested as disordered behavior and thinking. The "primary disorder" in schizophrenia is of mental or personality structure, which is of course intimately related to function. It is or becomes manifested as a disorder of motivation, which is in turn reflected in "the thought content" and purposive activity of the person. The mental structure is said to be dissociated ("split") in such a fashion that the disintegrated portions (the part of the mental structure split off, so to speak, from the self-conscious personality) regress in function to "earlier levels of ontogeny," that is, to historically earlier levels of the person's development.

Over the years Sullivan seems to have had difficulty formulating the occurrences of dissociation rigorously, so I shall attempt to clarify them in subsequent chapters. The main point about dissociation of a major system of motives is that certain experiences, due to the history of the individual, are foreign or antithetical to the self and have to be ejected from or kept out of consciousness. If the individual fails to accomplish this, or if, because of certain experiences, he can no longer accomplish it, panic may ensue with grave danger to the personality. Or, in other instances, there may be a gradual, insidious separation, so to speak, of the patient from "reality." Thus, an understanding of the self and its relations to dissociated impulses and experiences is vitally important.

For a whole generation, in various papers and lectures, Sullivan strove to formulate and clarify the nature of schizophrenia. In his first published paper he wrote that the *disparity* of depths (or levels of functioning of the various aspects of the personality) seems to be the essence of that which is schizophrenic as distinguished from other mental disorders. He believed that the "depths" of regression in this disorder greatly exceeded those in other forms of mental illness, which, he said, may be another essential feature of schizophrenia.

Perhaps I can help clarify these statements by mentioning some relevant statements made in "Regression: A Consideration of Reversive Mental Processes." Sullivan asserted that the psychoneuroses represent states in which relatively little of the total mental organization is primitive in its structural organization and the greater part is relatively adult. In contrast, schizophrenia is said to be a state in which decidedly the greater part has relapsed to, if it was not already in, a state of primitive organization. Again in another paper, "Tentative Criteria Of Malignancy In Schizophrenia," he said that the outcome of schizophrenic psychosis is a function not of the general level of behavior but rather of the disparity of depths of regression of the various phases or parts of personality.[39] "And the importance for outcome of this factor of disparity of depth in the regressions is significant only in so far as it implies disorganization of the personality, of the individual's interaction with and within the social environment, and of therapeutic access to the life experience of the sufferer."[40]

One may formulate the contarast in personality organization and behavior between the person suffering one of various possible kinds of neuroses and the person suffering schizophrenia, at the risk of oversimplification, roughly as follows. The neurotic person, as a rule, is less immature. Even if he suffers severe conflicts and anxieties, he still retains a personality organization that as a rule makes possible an adjustment, however inadequate, to the real social and physical environments. His thoughts, feelings, motives, fantasies, and overt behavior patterns are in varying degrees less childlike or infantile, usually, than those of the schizophrenic. It seems that the latter's "ego" is less well structured and less well developed. Hence he has less ability to control his impulses and behavior in a fashion considered suitable in his social milieu than does the "neurotic."[41] In addition, the schizophrenic's ability to communicate, owing to his regressed state, becomes seriously impaired, which in turn makes psychotherapy an especially difficult affair, since among other things an exchange of information is vital. The impaired ability to communicate is connected with his fragile social relations.

However, Sullivan thought that there is no sharp dividing line between the psychoneuroses and psychoses. "The more one learns of what is going on in his patient, the less faith he can retain in the alleged types of anomalous and perverted adjustive reactions. The field of mental disorders seems to be a continual gradation, in which little of discrete types is to be found."[42]

A conclusion expressed in "Schizophrenia: Its Conservative and

Malignant Features" is that the conservative (constructive) aspects of catatonic states (traditionally classified as a type of schizophrenia) in particular, and of early schizophrenia in general, are to be identified as attempts by *means of regression* to genetically older thought processes—to infantile or even prenatal mental functions—successfully to *reintegrate* masses of life experience that had failed to be structuralized into a functional unity—in other words, had failed to be assimilated into a functionally unified personality. This failure of structuralization had entailed multiple dissociations of personality in "the field of relationships" of the individual not only to the external world, including his social milieu, but also to his personal reality, to his experiences of himself as a self-conscious individual.

Sullivan claims that just as the "primitive" thinking in more normal sleep (dreams) solves many a problem and, in the remembered dream brings up for "assistance" (presumably, by a therapist) many an unsolved problem with which psychiatrists feel able to deal, so do these (dreamlike or nightmarish) primitive processes in schizophrenia, insofar as they can be comprehended and turned to some purpose in reorganizing experience that had not been integrated, offer a field for promising direct therapeutic activity.

Dissociation in catatonic schizophrenia, however, is said to be of a genetically more primitive nature than ever appears in a remembered dream. "The regressive processes go deeper in the mental structures; and the functions appearing in content and behavior become lower and lower in the scale of psychologic ontogenesis. Thus it is here that we see that really marvelous demonstration (by regression) of the intrauterine mind—the prenatal attitude, sometimes with makeshift uterine environment (tightly enwrapping blanket, darkness, wetness, etc.). Here we see the unmistakable evidence of prenatal experience."[43]

There are some pretty obscure statements in "Schizophrenia: Its Conservative and Malignant Features" and some ideas expressed, especially those pertaining to an alleged intrauterine mind, which now more than forty years later, seem of doubtful validity and which, in any event, Sullivan soon discarded or modified. In other words, in subsequent years, Sullivan would say that the deepest, most primitive, possible level of regression is infancy, or behavior characteristic of infancy, the first stage of personality development.

I wish to remind the reader that at this time (1924) Sullivan was attempting to employ the Freudian framework. Freud had held for a time that the fundamental urge in man is a striving for pleasure and for the avoidance of pain or unpleasure, though coupled with an instinct of self-preservation. In other words, he theorized that human behavior is governed by sexual instincts and self-preservative instincts. The sexual instincts have a qualitatively special kind of energy at their disposal called libido. They manifest themselves at the beginning of life and develop through manifold stages or phases: oral, anal, urethral, phallic (which in boys is contemporaneous with the oedipal phase), and genital. Personality development is closely linked up with these various phases. In fact, Freud believed that the basic framework of personality structure is laid down during the first five or six years of life, that is, roughly by the time when the Oedipus complex is normally resolved (in boys).

It has been said that infants sometimes seem to be all mouth. Sullivan, following the Freudian paradigm, found that the earliest experiences center around oral behavior. But in one respect he went further and speculated that the baby during the last few weeks *before* birth undergoes experience, has experiences, which are somehow registered and retained. As I suggested above, Sullivan, for a brief period, thought that certain kinds of schizophrenic behavior were proof of this, and even that certain kinds of schizophrenic experience were a recapitulation or replication of the prenatal life, a view he soon abandoned.

Notes

1. *Current Biography* (New York: H. W. Wilson Company), **3**:71, 1942.

2. *Psychiatry,* **12**:435-437, 1949; reprinted in HARRY STACK SULLIVAN, *Schizophrenia as a Human Process,* with Introduction and Commentaries by HELEN SWICK PERRY (New York: W. W. Norton and Company, 1962).

3. FREDERIC C. REDLICH and DANIEL X. FREEDMAN, *The Theory and Practice of Psychiatry* (New York: Basic Books, 1966), p. 1.

4. *Current Biography,* **3**:72, 1942.

5. *Ibid.*

6. *Ibid.*

7. *See* HELEN S. PERRY, "Introduction to SULLIVAN, *Schizophrenia as a Human Process,* pp. xv ff.

8. HARRY STACK SULLIVAN, "Socio-Psychiatric Research," *American Journal of Psychiatry,* **10**:977-991, 1931; reprinted in SULLIVAN, *Schizophrenia as a Human Process.*

9. HARRY STACK SULLIVAN, "Training of the General Medical Student in Psychiatry," *American Journal of Orthopsychiatry,* **1**:371-379, 1931; cf. SULLIVAN, "Socio-Psychiatric Research."

10. Regarding Sullivan's role in the UNESCO Project, *see* OTTO KLINEBERG, "Discussion," in PATRICK MULLAHY (ed.), *The Contributions of Harry Stack Sullivan* (New York: Science House, 1967), pp. 215-217.

11. HARRY STACK SULLIVAN, *Conceptions of Modern Psychiatry,* with a Foreward by the author and a Critical Appraisal of the Theory by PATRICK MULLAHY (New York: W. W. Norton and Company, 1953).

12. HARRY STACK SULLIVAN, *The Interpersonal Theory of Psychiatry,* ed. HELEN SWICK PERRY and MARY LADD GAWEL, with an Introduction by MABEL BLAKE COHEN (New York: W. W. Norton and Company, 1953).

13. HARRY STACK SULLIVAN, *The Psychiatric Interview,* ed. HELEN SWICK PERRY and MARY LADD GAWEL, with an Introduction by OTTO ALLEN WILL, JR. (New York: W. W. Norton and Company, 1954).

14. HARRY STACK SULLIVAN, *Clinical Studies in Psychiatry,* ed. HELEN SWICK PERRY, MARY LADD GAWEL, and MARTHA GIBBON, with a Foreword by DEXTER M. BULLARD (New York: W. W. Norton and Company, 1956).

15. SULLIVAN, *Schizophrenia as a Human Process.*

16. HARRY STACK SULLIVAN, *The Fusion of Psychiatry and Social Science,* with Introduction and Commentaries by HELEN SWICK PERRY (New York: W. W. Norton and Company, 1964).

17. HARRY STACK SULLIVAN, "The Modified Psychoanalytic Treatment of Schizophrenia," *American Journal of Psychiatry,* **11**:519-536, 1931; reprinted in SULLIVAN, *Schizophrenia as a Human Process.*

18. Cf. THOMAS S. SZASZ, "Mental Illness Is a Myth," *New York Times Magazine,* June 12, 1966; reprinted in ROBERT V. GUTHRIE, *Psychology in the World Today* (Reading, Massachusetts: Addison-Wesley Publishing Company, 1968).

19. JAMES C. COLEMAN, *Abnormal Psychology and Modern Life* (3rd ed.; Glenview, Illinois: Scott, Foresman and Company, 1964), p. 193; cf. REDLICH and FREEDMAN, *op. cit.,* chaps. 4, 5, 6.

20. COLEMAN, *op. cit.,* pp. 265-266.

21. HARRY STACK SULLIVAN, "Regression: A Consideration of Reversive Mental Processes," *State Hospital Quarterly,* **11**:651-668, 1926.

22. *Ibid.*

23. HARRY STACK SULLIVAN, "Erogenous Maturation," *Psychoanalytic Review,* **13**:1-15, 1926.

24. HARRY STACK SULLIVAN, "Psychiatric Training as a Prerequisite to Psychoanalytic Practice," *American Journal of Psychiatry,* **91**:1117-1126, 1934-1935; reprinted in SULLIVAN, *Schizophrenia as a Human Process.*

25. *Ibid.*

26. HARRY STACK SULLIVAN, "Schizophrenic Individuals as a Source of Data for Comparative Investigation of Personality," in *Proceedings, Second Colloquium on Personality Investigation* (Baltimore, Maryland: The Johns Hopkins Press, 1930), pp. 43-55; reprinted in SULLIVAN, *Schizophrenia as a Human Process.*

27. HARRY STACK SULLIVAN, "Peculiarity of Thought in Schizophrenia," *American Journal of Psychiatry,* **82**:21-86, 1925-1926; reprinted in SULLIVAN, *Schizophrenia as a Human Process.*

28. HARRY STACK SULLIVAN, "Schizophrenia: Its Conservative and Malignant Features," *American Journal of Psychiatry,* **81**:77-91, 1924-1925; reprinted in SULLIVAN, *Schizophrenia as a Human Process.*

29. HARRY STACK SULLIVAN, "The Onset of Schizophrenia," *American Jour-*

nal of Psychiatry, **84**:105-134, 1927-1928; reprinted in SULLIVAN, *Schizophrenia as a Human Process*.

30. *Ibid.*

31. *Ibid.*

32. SULLIVAN, "Peculiarity of Thought in Schizophrenia."

33. *Ibid.*

34. SULLIVAN, "The Onset of Schizophrenia."

35. Cf. SULLIVAN, *Conceptions of Modern Psychiatry*, pp. 130-167; REDLICH and FREEDMAN, *op. cit.*, chap. 14.

36. HELEN SWICK PERRY, "Introduction" to SULLIVAN, *Schizophrenia as a Human Process*, pp. xx-xxi.

37. HARRY STACK SULLIVAN, "The Modified Psychoanlytic Treatment of Schizophrenia," *American Journal of Psychiatry*, **10**:519-540, 1931-1932; reprinted in SULLIVAN, *Schizophrenia as a Human Process*.

38. *Ibid.*

39. HARRY STACK SULLIVAN, "Tentative Criteria of Malignancy in Schizophrenia," *American Journal of Psychiatry*, **84**:759-782, 1927-1928; reprinted in SULLIVAN, *Schizophrenia as a Human Process*.

40. *Ibid.*

41. Cf. COLEMAN, *op. cit.*, pp. 192-195, 262-266.

42. SULLIVAN, "Tentative Criteria. ..." Cf. SULLIVAN, *Clinical Studies in Psychiatry*.

43. SULLIVAN, "Schizophrenia: Its Conservative and Malignant Features."

2 / The Development of Symbol Systems

I have reached the point in the exposition of Sullivan's early formulations at which I must examine as closely as possible what he meant by mind, or, as he used to call it, mentation, since it is a central concept of interpersonal psychiatry. This problem is by far the most difficult to understand in the entire corpus of extant lectures and published papers. Sullivan conceives of mind from a fundamentally biological point of view. Moreover, he did not think that mind, at least in very rudimentary forms, is confined to man. Mind, in his view, is closely bound up with symbol activity, and the latter is conceived very broadly.[1] The following statement is set forth in "The Importance of a Study of Symbols in Psychiatry":

> In the higher mammals, at least among those organisms possessed of a centralized nervous system, we find an economical adjustive process which consists in the utilization of symbols in lieu of unmeaning realities. We speak of this (in the case of man alone, all too frequently) as mental life. The peculiar effect exerted upon us by our mode of behavior in speech and graphic procedures, and by the implicit use of words and related signs in thought, leads readily to error. Such behavior and thinking is an extremely important variation in the evolution of the mental, but it is far from being the distinguishing manifestation of symbol activity. The use of symbols is probably no more private to *homo sapiens* than is the utilization of locomotive apparatus.[2]

Leaving aside the question of the nature and function of symbols in animal behavior, since it is not vital to this exposition, one can see from a study of his early papers that Sullivan thought that in human experience and behavior there are different kinds of symbols, whose function is different in different realms of experience, as this exposition will attempt to explicate. And just as it requires a specialized education to understand the symbols of physics and chemistry, it requires a specialized education to understand the symbols of dreams, or myths, art, schizophrenia, and the like. Perhaps no one understands these things perfectly in any field. Be that as it may, in psychology and psychiatry symbols are not well understood. Moreover, it is often very difficult to formulate the meaning of various kinds of symbols precisely in ordinary language. Some would say it is impossible because these various kinds of symbols pertain to different universes of thought and experience. Still, one does not wish to adopt an obscurantist attitude regarding these matters, especially since an enormous amount of cant has been—and still is—written about them. It often helps greatly if one can enter into and have the relevant kind of experience oneself.

As a psychoanalytically oriented psychiatrist, Sullivan could not fail to note the importance of symbols and signs for psychology and psychiatry. From his work with schizophrenic patients, he realized more clearly the significance of the fact that the mental life is permeated by representations or "abstracts" of experience, past and present. These "abstracts" of the events of life, including various internal processes of the individual, are symbols in the broadest sense. As such, cognitive symbols are only a part of the symbolical apparatus of the human mind. They are vitally important but still relatively narrow in scope in human behavior. One has only to think of the meanings of symbol in literature, painting, religion, myth, dreams, fairy tales, the thinking of young children, and in much of the waking experience of adults to realize that the symbol is indigenous to the human mind—is, in fact, of its very essence. With the exception of the symbols of logic and science—whose meaning is fixed by convention—symbols do not usually have a universal, explicit, agreed-upon reference to "reality" or to anything else. Often their meaning is, in terms of formal thought, obscure, indirect, and recondite. And they exist in some context, some universe of experience. Until one has penetrated and grasped the nature of that universe, they often are, or seem to be, "meaningless" or "crazy." For example, the symbols employed in the arts cover a vast field, a thorough grasp of which would require a lifetime of study. But it would be fatal to think—as some mediocre philosophers do—that their meaning is merely "emotive." The language of the arts represents a world—a realm of experience—just as real as the language of physics, however different.

Sullivan had learned, apparently from Adolf Meyer, William Alanson White, and Smith Ely Jelliffe, a conception of mentation as the activity of symbols. In "The Importance of a Study of Symbols in Psychiatry," he quotes White and Jelliffe to the effect that in the phylogenetic history of the development that culminated in man all other "tools" had been tried and laid aside in the past and that the symbol developed because it alone offers the means of unlimited development of man's control over nature. White and Jelliffe also are credited with the conception (which seems rather similar to C. G. Jung's) that the symbol is a "source" and carrier of energy. (Consider the energizing power of the symbols of Christianity during the Middle Ages.) They also stress the importance of "archaic" symbols and their relationship to somatic as well as mental illness.

In order to understand the general nature of symbol from a psychological point of view, according to Sullivan, one must keep in mind three fundamental properties of living organisms: (1) a relatively stable organization, including the orderly progression of changes shown in growth, and the more rare phenomenon of reorganization and variation; (2) indissoluble community with their physical environment; and (3) continuous functional activity in and with the environment.[3] For human beings, the environment is not only physical but also sociocultural, a fact that entails the existence of a vast network of symbols of various kinds in speech, myth, art, rites and ceremonies, monuments, and the like.

Sullivan thought that any modification of innate dispositions, instincts, drives, or whatever that are due to learning—a modification that in human beings especially could not occur without some sort of retention of past experience and therefore at some neuropsychic level a representation of past experience—is symbolic. Such learning generally evinces a markedly stable organization. In other words, symbolic representation, however "primitive" as in infants and young children, or abstract and "complex" as in the cognitive learning of older children and adults, generally shows a stable structure. A symbol also has no autonomous existence; analogously to a body cell, it must have, or exist in, a communal "mental" environment, some sort of universe of experience. Finally, while a symbol employed by a human being has a location within the "organism," it is an outcome of a complex physical, psychological, and sociocultural interaction, as in the act of perception or abstract thinking, dreaming, or hallucinating, and can be understood only in terms of the situation or universe of discourse in which it is employed. It is perhaps necessary to add that the evolution of signs and symbols from their primitive beginnings in the infantile patterns of sentience are not yet well understood. Symbolic events constitute experience—which, be it noted, arise from and occur in an organism-environment context. The entire cumulative series of symbolic events culminates in the personality of the moment. In a sense, we are our experience.

Sullivan, in attempting to understand schizophrenic patients, thought they reproduced or replicated experiences going back to the earliest symbolizations.

On the other hand these experiences of adult schizophrenics are to be understood also in relation to the "symbol system" variously called the ego, self-regarding sentiment, or self, which has a long history of development, as I shall try to make clear in subsequent chapters.

Sullivan's early interpretation of symbols is difficult to understand because he did not develop his ideas about symbols systematically. An explication of his interpretation is necessary, however, partly because it sheds light on his theory of schizophrenia, partly because it is an important part of his theory of interpersonal relations. His theory of symbols is essentially different from much current theorizing concerning mental activity. The following quotation suggests a very different approach to mind, while it may illuminate, by contrast, Sullivan's orientation. "Because the brain is largely a neural organ, it would appear that thought is a neural process—some arrangement of differences in neuron sensitivities or synaptic transmissions which always work together, or which, when they do work together, constitute a 'trace' or correlate of a previously sensed external event."[4] Lest there be any misunderstanding about the author's interpretation, he is careful to add: "It is important to keep in mind that the activation of a trace *is* a thought; it does not produce a thought, which would then have to be described as a factor having existence beyond the neural trace itself."[5] Thinking, in this view, is a physical activity. Mind is only a name for a complex set of neural activities. Sullivan explicitly rejected this kind of philosophy. In "Schizophrenia: Its Conservative and Malignant Features," he wrote: "If the element of purpose and means is eliminated, there results sterile brain physiology, psychologization, and that type of hypothesis so well criticized by Henri Bergson, when he wrote of the theory of memory, 'Hence the strange hypothesis of recollections stored in the brain, which are supposed to become conscious as though by a miracle, and bring us back to the past by a process that is left unexplained.' Bertrand Russell, in his *Analysis of Mind,* remarks, 'the response of an organism to a given stimulus is very often dependent upon the past history of the organism, and not merely upon the stimulus and the *hitherto discoverable* present state of the organism.' "[6]

It is probable that the history of every individual human being enters into and influences his life at any given moment. In any case, Sullivan claimed that the *hitherto undiscovered present state* of the organism, including its retention of its past history, is the basic phenomenal explanation that he subsumes in the term *mind.* This state includes a network of symbolic activities.

He never attempted to reduce "phenomenological consciousness," the consciousness of unsophisticated common-sense experience, to something simpler or more elemental. But mind is more than conscious awareness and conscious activity. Mind is a variegated network of certain properties and functions of the "organism," some of which are conscious. The individual, in turn, cannot be isolated from the physical and sociocultural environment. On the other hand, "mental situations" include cognitive, affective, and conative aspects. Psychologically speaking, there is no such thing as pure thought or pure cognition that can be isolated from the emotional, motivational, and volitional aspects of living. Still again, as Sullivan points out in "The Importance of a Study of Symbols in Psychiatry," on the neurophysiological level, it is essential that one rid himself of notions of relatively independent afferent, central, and efferent divisions of the cerebrospinal system, on the one hand, and of functionally independent vegetative systems on the other. Any occurrence in a so-called end organ cannot be envisaged as other than an event throughout the whole organism. In simplest language, a toothache is not literally in a tooth alone; it is "in" the organism.

Before going further with my explication of Sullivan's theory of symbols and their functions in experience and behavior, I wish to call attention to some elementary facts and ideas about sensation, perception, and thought.[7] The human sense organs are the original gateways to the world and to the happenings in oneself. They make possible the sentience infants and adults normally have under various organic and environmental circumstances. Thus it is said that when physical energies, such as light waves and sound waves, impinge on the sense organs, series and patterns of neural impulses are produced. These nerve impulses travel from the sense organs through the nervous system. In the sensory areas of the brain, for example, activities are aroused that, when operating in conjuction with various other activities of the organism, result in one's sensations and perceptions.[8] In the life of every individual, a certain level of maturation and a certain amount of experience must have been attained before *perception* occurs. In other words, one must be able to "interpret" his experiences in order that perception may occur. According to many psychologists the interpreting is done by the brain. The *mind* does nothing. It is in fact a medieval superstition, or an epiphenomenon, as inefficacious as the rainbow on the fountain. To be sure, this notion is dogma. And it raises profound psychological and philosophical problems and difficulties that I cannot discuss in this book. It is of course true that the nervous system is an indispensable instrumentality in sensation, perception, and thought. But the nervous system is not *the* organ of mind, as Sullivan has recognized. Sensation, perception, and thought are outcomes of the total activity of the "organism" operating in a particular environmental setting. In other words, it is the *person* who perceives; it is the *person* who thinks. Further consideration of these matters would take us too far afield.[9]

Perception may be conscious in the sense that it entails recognition; or it may not be conscious. In psychology perception in its most rudimentary form may refer to any action or response that indicates that the individual has discriminated the stimulus (or the stimulus object) from other possible stimuli (or from other possible stimulus objects). But he may not know it. One may say that the perception is subconscious or unconscious without committing oneself to any particular theory of unconsciousness. The fact of unconscious perception has been familiar for a long time, as Shibotani reminds us. Activities of great complexity can be carried out without conscious awareness. "Sleepwalkers perform a variety of dangerous tasks requiring minute coordination. A person may get out of bed and drive his automobile for many miles before awakening suddenly to find himself on a strange highway. Or he may be aroused from his slumber by the screams of horrified spectators watching him tiptoe along a ledge. The fine neuro-muscular coordination is predicated upon precise perception, but there is no awareness until he wakes up. . . ."[10]

Perception may or may not entail a reference to self. A year-old baby may perceive his mother's face, but this may not entail any reference to self because he (probably) is too young to have developed even a rudimentary self. In any case, as adults we know from experience that we often perceive objects without conscious reference to self. But we also often do become aware that we are perceiving. Just as we know that we know, we know that we perceive. We become conscious at times that we are engaging in a particular perceptual process.

Perceptions are meanings, referable to natural processes, but the latter may be internal or external, or a blend of both. In other words, when meanings become "attached" to sensory processes, the latter become perceptions, though it is often very difficult to distinguish one sort of occurrence from the other. Because Sullivan's interpretation of symbols in his early papers is formulated in somewhat obscure terms, I shall attempt a rough translation of the most important part of it—with the usual caveat that no translation can be a perfect reproduction of the original.

In "Peculiarity of Thought in Schizophrenia," Sullivan wrote that thought is organismic activity by the implicit functioning of symbols, which are "abstracts" from the material of life experience, of a living being who acts and "undergoes." Although Sullivan in the first few papers he published postulated the existence of an intrauterine human experience or set of experiences during the last weeks before the individual's birth, I shall postpone a discussion of this matter. When the infant is born he at once, or very soon after birth, undergoes a sort of experience that may be described roughly as a manifold of formless, undifferentiated sensations or sensory experiences that are blind and dumb in the sense that in the beginning they do not know themselves or anything else. Of course, the new-born infant is not as passive as he may seem. Almost at once he, so to speak, begins to take a hand in the business of living, though his first "tool" may be confined to the cry.

In "Regression: A Consideration of Reversive Mental Processes" Sullivan characterizes the meaning of "primitive" as follows:

> The earlier sentience is of a very different nature from the later. The infant becomes aware of items almost utterly different from those with which we are familiar. Their cognitive, conative and affective experiences are not to be envisaged by any speculation having its point of departure in homologous adult experience. Our experience is elaborated from primary sentience which in itself has a complicated background and clear-cut and complex configurations; this in turn falls into relations of an almost infinite ascending complexity, the result of all previous homologous and analogous experiences.[11]

During the first days or weeks of postnatal life the infant's experiences are undifferentiated and uninterpreted. Events impinge on his sense organs, evoking sensations. How much his own actions contribute at first to these experiences is still a matter of speculation. The infant has no notion of the usual distinctions of space and time. As yet, during the first days and weeks, he has no, or almost no, structure or organization of experience that has been retained and is capable of being used for identifying the stream of sensations he feels or undergoes. There is no recognition of a distinction between him and the world in which he lives. He has no specific personality and no self or "ego." But at an indeterminately early age, the global character of the infantile experiences begins to be disrupted and patterns of sensory experiences, some of which are referable to external events, are gradually discriminated. Owing perhaps to recurring infantile activities and recurring sorts of events, a group of more or less differentiated sensations or rudimentary perceptions acquires a reference to some other and previous group of the same kind. For example, the nipple of the mother's breast, or perhaps the nipple of a bottle, gradually becomes an identifiable experience or group of experiences. The infant "prehends" or registers the fact that the nipple is a sign (a "symbol") of previously felt satisfaction, though his ability to "associate" a present pattern of sensory experiences with previous feelings of pleasant experiences may at first be limited in scope to a few hours' duration. In some such fashion, according to Sullivan, the infant "abstracts" constituents of his experiences so that they "remind" him, serve as a sign or "symbol" of some group of experiences previously had and/or of a group of experiences that will presently supervene. One should bear in mind that such symbolizing activities are not separate from the infant's urges, drives, feelings, or whatever. Symbolizing or "abstracting" is a "part-process of a total situation" involving the infant and his immediate environment.

Recent investigation has clarified the function of vision. Kendler has written: "The infant's perception of his mother, for example, seems to depend upon contextual cues rather than solely upon the visual details of her face. The infant recognizes his mother in familiar situations when her appearance is the same as it has been. If she is in an entirely different environment or her clothes or hair style are changed radically, he may not recognize her. In line with this analysis is experimental evidence which suggests that as the child matures his ability to extract details from his global perceptions improves (Mussen, 1963)."[12]

In "Peculiarity of Thought in Schizophrenia" Sullivan wrote that in the "ontogenesis of personality," one can discern two categories of symbols: those that "enter into the mnemic series" and those that are "transitional only." In the first category are those in which "the ontogenetic steps are preserved and become memorial elements." By this Sullivan seems to mean that the particular experiences "abstracted" and, so to speak, embodied in symbols of this class are retained more or less intact and not altered much, if at all, by subsequent experiences. They also do not become "correlates" of symbols at that given time functionally available due to previous experience. Symbols of this sort, whether primitive or more abstract, are "more or less" capable of recall and of functioning in their original state.

This assumption regarding the "timelessness" of certain kinds of symbols provides a logical basis for the conception of regression and of other things as well. Thus, symbols "of lower order of abstraction from multiple experiential data," that is, primitive symbols (while greater and greater numbers of related but more and more elaborated symbols appear), "retain potential activity and may make their appearance in certain special states, such as that of great weariness, profound revery, or in sleep as well as in deep regressive processes."[13]

In the other category of symbols, which embraces "by far the greater number of our innumerable symbol elaborations," the genetic steps disappear completely so that as a symbol of this sort develops little or nothing of its evolutionary stages is preserved. In this category of symbols, nothing of a primitive order of abstraction survives unless the "conative situation" is especially set to preserve them, as in, say, certain almost ecstatic childhood experiences, which every so often are recalled like a haunting melody. Even in the latter case much interpretation is required before such "conative situations" can be revived, unmixed with later elaborations. It is not easy, for example, to revive one's experiences of his first day in school, relatively unmixed and undistorted by subsequent accretions. Perhaps the most famous attempt to do that sort of thing is Marcel Proust's efforts to revivify remembrances of things past. One doubts that recollection is ever total.

Having presented a preliminary survey of Sullivan's formulations of symbols, and their genesis—a topic to which I shall return—I take up next his attempts to describe the growth of symbols from lower to higher orders of abstraction, and from primitive subconsciousness to focal awareness. "The infant is born," Sullivan wrote in "Peculiarity of Thought in Schizophrenia," "with various more or less matured abilities, and with impulses to put these individual abilities into effect. The sensory group of these abilities provide innumerable data which undergo the transmutation into symbols [or mental representations] and which tend to bear a relatively simple relation to the sense data. Needless to say, these particular symbols are neither general, nor even generic; they are quite concrete. Relations grow between them, however, [that is, they become co-related] and a world-representation of a characteristically concrete type evolves."[14]

Our next problem is how do these symbols "grow"? In attempting to answer this sort of question, Sullivan borrowed extensively from the English psychologist Charles Spearman. The growth of symbols from lower to higher orders of abstraction is said to entail processes of finding *relations* and *correlates.* There are three basic activities, three basic kinds of functions, involved in this growth: "(I) the apprehension of experience, the events by which neurophysiological situations eventuate in primitive symbols; (II) the eduction of relations in an indefinitely higher and higher order of abstractness, with correspondingly wider and wider capacity of utilization in the elaborated symbol; and (III) the eduction of correlates of the evolving symbol among the existing available symbols. . . ."[15] It will probably require many years of research before anyone can attempt to provide a detailed description of these activities, though it is possible that any intelligent teacher who has worked with children in kindergarten or the first grade could provide suggestive illustrations.[16]

In regard to the vexed problem of consciousness versus unconsciousness Sullivan quotes the following passage from Spearman, while explicating it: "Every item in the cognitive field possesses some grade of 'clearness.' It stands between two poles, the one of utter obscurity and the other of perfect clarity. ... The clearness would seem as if it were a mental configuration that is only attainable and sustainable by means of some special tension; on this tension being relaxed, the configuration automatically lapses."[17] This clearness is said to be composed of a factor of *intensity* or degree of consciousness and one of *determinateness.* The latter, Spearman says, is a factor pertaining to symbols only since any object or entity or occurrence must be "exactly of such and such a nature and exist at exactly such and such a particular moment." Sullivan says that by this factor of increasing determinateness, differentiation *may* be brought about among already existing symbols; and in the reverse fashion inevitably, a diminution of determinateness, and therefore also of difference, comes about such that symbols tend to be confused. Perhaps the determinateness of symbols in focal awareness in contrast to its relative absence frequently while one is dreaming or suffering certain schizophrenic states is a good illustration. (In regression, for example, the determinateness of symbols is increasingly reduced, with a corresponding spread of meaning, the limit of which is the [subsequently formulated] prototaxic mode of experience. In other words, as regression increases, the symbols "refer to" an ever wider range of objects and occurrences, gradually losing specific determinateness.) Sullivan goes on to say that the intensity factor in itself determines the momentary locus of the symbols, that is, whether they occur in focal consciousness, elsewhere in manifest consciousness (as, say, when a student reads a book in the library while keeping an ear open to the gossip of his less studious fellows), or in the unintrospectible region of the mind called foreconscious, subconscious, or unconscious.[18]

Many of the primitive symbols of the first category mentioned above "escape elaboration into higher order symbols in awareness." As Sullivan says, they remain subconscious because their intensity is below the "threshold of consciousness," thus remaining subconscious. But they are not static and inefficacious. They are not without effect. Furthermore they at least sometimes undergo some elaboration, though perhaps more or less slowly. From the manifold of primitive symbols, other symbols are elaborated that sometimes "erupt and dominate consciousness," as in schizophrenia. Thus, under the influence of a strong desire, the elementary, primitive symbols may contribute a large share in the elaboration of higher order symbols.

It appears that many of these primitive or "primordial" symbols may be considered the source of dissociated processes that exist in the personality, and that may remain forever unknown to, or not understood by, the individual who harbors them.

In any case, by the time the child is able to learn to talk he will have experienced a vast amount of events, which is or may be functionally manifested in symbols and patterns of symbols of a still more or less primitive sort. In *The Interpersonal Theory of Psychiatry*, they are conceived as occurring in the *paratoxic mode*. They provide the groundwork on which subsequent experiences for the most part are built.

In the ever-advancing course of time and the ever-proceeding course of maturation, as the parents talk to one another in the infant's presence, and talk to him, he gradually manifests "vocal productions." The initial vocal productions are purely magical sounds but they soon become a predominant feature of the youngster's "incipient self-consciousness." These "vocal affairs" tend to be substituted for the symbols previously developed because one feels so much more "illuminated" when, for example, he knows the name of an object and can say it. Words, even magic words, including magical names, are powerful tools because they "seem to have such a simplifying effect in the infinite individuality of nature."[19] For such reasons, among others, words are preeminently the tools in "cognitive operations" among human beings.

Nevertheless, a word has generally little true meaning in the sense of being a "correct abstract," a precise representation, of one's experience as it is registered in the more primitive symbols. Words, in so far as they are used in thinking, function as very high-order abstractions. But insofar as "they are correct in relation to a particular person's experiential data, they are as individual as any symbols, and perfectly satisfactory in their place in *his* mental operations. When, however, it comes to communication, there is difficulty. At times, one can depend upon tacit convention as to the meaning of a word to the user and to the hearer; this does all right in commerce. If there is room for any uncertainty, it is necessary for the speaker to attempt to define the implication of his terms as explicitly as is needful or possible. If this is itself impossible, as in dealing with most psychotic patients, then not *your* meaning of a word, but its meaning to the patient must govern its use."[20] To discover this takes skill because its meaning to the patient must be constructed from the contexts in which he uses such a word. In these contexts, the factor of previous experience is vital, not merely in the general sense that meanings are continuous with, have grown out of, previous experience but in the particular sense that the patient's previous experiences have lent his use of language a private and idiosyncratic (autistic) meaning.

In studying symbols and their relation to reality, the psychologist or psychiatrist must take several generic factors into account. These include the interaction of (1) the individual organism and its physical environment, and (2) the individual and his cultural ("symbolic-physical") environment.[21] In other words, throughout the realm of human experience pertaining to "sensory excitations" (that is, pertaining to sensation and perception) the relation between the symbol system of the experiencing subject and a reality sensed or perceived is always a relation of interaction between the two. The nature or the meaning of this reality sensed or perceived is always conditioned by the nature of the subject. The relation, in more familiar language, of subject and object, is always "a quasi-autonomous event made up of (a) some greater or smaller number of characteristics of the event which include the organism-and-environment interaction referred to, and (b) some greater or smaller number of characteristics of the pre-existing symbol systems of the organism."[22]

Take for illustration what one may "see" if he looks at a horseshoe nailed upon a cottage door. "There is, let us say, an initial constellation of the horse-shoe upon or against a ground representative of the wood, vaguely combined with more or less of the neighboring doorway, walls, etc. This constellation grows in richness as the background of the horse-shoe nailed upon the door takes on more and more characteristics, real or analogous, of 'cottage,' and as the combination [of horseshoe and cottage] gains 'meaning' from cultural attributes of the horse-shoe as a 'sign' of good luck in folk-parlance. . . ."[23] "A blacksmith may 'notice' the type, apparent condition of use, and so forth, of the shoe, or the incongruity of the type of nails used to fasten it. What the photographer would 'notice' might be the shadows thrown on the background, the illumination of the unusual nail-holes, and so forth. What the folk-lore expert would 'notice' on the other hand, would include few of these 'simple' characteristics."[24] Thus the group of characteristics of the external object or event that each individual "abstracts" is dependent upon his previous experience and his interests.

Let us imagine one more illustration. Consider what one may "see" if he looks at a tree some hundred yards away from him. "The physicist could use his data and instruments to 'identify the reality,' even to successful prophecy as to possible interactions with it which we might bring about. The neuro-physiologist could interpret in more or less biochemical terms what was transpiring in our receptors and integrative apparatus. The student of cognitive processes ... could show us by what processes our notions of this particular 'external reality' grew from elementary sentience to its terminus in more or less marvellous information."[25] But these studies are all "part-aspects" of the process of abstraction. Another kind of abstraction might result in a different "perception." A schizophrenic person, focusing a presumably identical bundle of light waves, may determine to his satisfaction that he is "perceiving," not a tree, but a gigantic woman with arms extended and hair wideflung to the breeze. He may even rid himself of this troublesome woman by hiring someone to chop down the tree; yet after the tree has been chopped down, sawn into appropriate lengths, split and sold as stove wood, he may still insist that the tree was the aforementioned woman. Evidently, the events making up symbols are occurrences that have their material location entirely *within* the organism.[26] In other words, these events making up the symbol are "autogonous data," which are the result of the communal existence of the person and his environment. Thus the symbol is an event "constituting an abstraction of physiological and morphological events in the organism, and of biological events including the organism and its environment."[27] For such reasons it is practically impossible for anyone to become conscious of an *entire* symbolic event or process.

This analysis is, I think, perfectly sound as far as it goes. But it may leave some readers uneasy. Isn't there any real difference between the perception of the physicist or the psychologist and the schizophrenic? Isn't the latter "crazy"? The point is that symbols are not primarily cognitive at all. They are the outcome of complex internal states interacting with external conditions. The different kinds of symbols are all equally "real" and psychologically significant—but they have reference to different sorts of events and processes. It is the psychiatrist's job to discover what they refer to, for they can inform him as to what is happening in or to the person, or what has happened to him in the past. In regard to the question as to when and how symbols become veridical, the interested reader will find a very illuminating analysis in John Dewey's *Experience and Nature,* Chapter 8.[28] A discussion of Dewey's analysis in this book would take me too far afield. But there is no special mystery about cognitive symbol operations, and they will be discussed briefly in subsequent chapters.

Symbols and symbol systems are hierarchically organized, ranging from the most primitive, preverbal "proto-concepts" to the "master symbol," or symbol system, the self. From very early in life, some symbol systems may be dissociated, split off from the main path of development. These symbol systems may become dissociated from the gradually developing self-conscious personality. Under certain circumstances, the dissociated aspects of the personality may become considerably elaborated. Thus an understanding of symbolizing activities is necessary for a comprehension of the self or "ego" and of dissociated processes, both constituting *personality.*

In "Peculiarity of Thought in Schizophrenia," Sullivan wrote that anything of value in his work came from an intimate and detailed study of particular individuals suffering disturbances of the mental or symbolizing activity. Hence he devoted much effort to understanding symbols of various kinds. The "thinking peculiarities" of the schizophrenic, moreover, make communication with such a person often difficult. Hence the psychiatrist must study the cognitive aspect of mental activity in schizophrenia if one is to achieve an exchange of intelligence, or more simply, to talk meaningfully to the "victim" of this grave mental disorder. However, in "The Language of Schizophrenia," Sullivan wrote that language operations as thought are profoundly different, quite fundamentally different, from language operations as communication and as "pure mechanisms" (such as the rhetoric of politicians or the bedside talk of some physicians) used in dealing with others. He goes on to say that the more completely one becomes "self-centered," the more utterly he becomes cut off from "integrations" with more or less real people; and the more utterly novel, perfectly magical and wholly "individual"—that is, autistic—become the symbols which he uses as if they were language.[29]

Language always begins as an entirely autistic performance by the very young child. When one comes to deal with "terribly significant people," such as parents, one realizes that the sooner one becomes skillful in employing language the better. The more skillful the child becomes in the use of language the more often does he get what he wants and the fewer are the disappointments he suffers. Early in life the child has to operate with the term "I." "We learn quite early in life that our parents can always *refer* to themselves, and we learn to refer to ourselves" (as "I" or "Me").[30] This is how the self-conscious personality or "self dynamism" originates, Sullivan wrote in 1944. This self-system is a great instrument, ordinarily, in getting what one wants, such as satisfactions and the approval or conciliation of significant others, namely, security.

"Throughout life, langue is largely an instrumentality for getting what we want. As we live with other human beings, we are creatures of culture; and as linguistic culture is the most amazing of all cultural ingredients, linguistic symbols—speech—are very important instrumentalities in our getting what we want. So inadequate is the structure of our culture to our needs that language operations have to pertain not only to obtaining what we do want, but also to saving us from experiences, both real and imaginary, which we do not want."[31] According to Sullivan, most children learn to use language more to preserve security than to secure biological satisfactions.

The peculiarities of language behavior in the schizophrenic are said to arise from his extreme need of a feeling of personal security. He uses language more or less knowingly and exclusively in the pursuit of durable security, though he fails because the language he employs lacks "consensual validation." Consensual validation entails a reference to another person or to a group of persons, with whom there is usually an implicit agreement as to the meaning of language. In fact, as Cooley pointed out long ago, language presupposes community. In the schizophrenic the reference to others as potential or actual hearers is tenuous. Without this reference to others, the use of language tends to become idiosyncratic, incommunicable, more or less analogous to the original use of language by the child.

Because Sullivan attached such great importance to consensual validation, for a variety of reasons, I wish to give one of his own illustrations of it.

"If I speak to an audience, I have a fantastic auditor, almost entirely an invention of my own personality, who attends to what I say, notices the more grievous absences of verbs for subjects, prods me gently, as it were, so that I diligently operate this complex neuronic and muscular apparatus in an attempt to say, first, complete sentences; second, sentences of good grammatic structure; and third, good logical sentences. This supervision on the part of a fantastic but realistically constructed auditor is the process of consensual validation."[32]

In this illustration, the fantastic auditor is analogous to a critical audience that one has, in a manner of speaking, internalized. I shall elaborate upon the meaning of "consensual validation" in the next chapter.

Since the schizophrenic is a rather unsocialized, undeveloped personality, his fantastic auditor or "critic" is, so to speak, as immature, undeveloped, and tortured as the schizophrenic himself. What seems to the schizophrenic person an adequate verbal expression is not likely to be meaningful to another person. The schizophrenic himself, when he hears himself utter such neologisms, may become shocked to alertness and review them with chagrin or fear. And no one's security is helped when he hears himself talk "nonsense."

Even though cognitive considerations take precedence over other aspects of "mental situations" in schizophrenic behavior, because of the therapeutic necessities of understanding and communication one must not lose sight of other elements: namely, the affective and the conative. The affective elements, if slight, can be subsumed under the aspect of pleasantness or unpleasantness of mental situations; if they are accentuated, they appear as the principal ingredient of what are called emotions. The conative element refers to what is called impulse, and underlies the phenomenon of desire. In schizophrenia there is a profound disorder of conation and a rather impressive demonstration that thinking peculiarities, peculiarities of cognition, merely follow "in the path of the distorted impulse life."[33]

But before I proceed to clarify these matters, I must now make explicit a few of Sullivan's assumptions employed in the interpretation of data. In "Schizophrenia: Its Conservative and Malignant Features," he formulated three specific conceptions, in addition to the general conceptual basis of science, which he used in the interpretation of schizophrenia and other psychological phenomena. The first of the three conceptions is Freud's "postulate" of the unconscious. Freud believed that the whole psychic life is in the beginning unconscious, and to a large extent remains unconscious, a notion that Sullivan modified and reformulated in his own terms. The second conception Sullivan mentions is a "teleological vitalist" one, though he soon abandoned the notion of vitalism in his formulations while retaining purposivism. Human beings are not machines. They have goals, which they strive to attain whether consciously or otherwise. The third embraces a "genetic hypothesis" of mental structure and functions. This genetic hypothesis is said to imply a vital sequence of experience, an ongoing cumulative stream of experience, the related parts of which are structuralized into preconcepts, complexes, and sentiments that are partly accessible to consciousness. In his initial formulations of schizophrenic processes, and the regressive processes that he thought were typical of such states, he employed such constructs as *preconcept* and *complex* in trying to understand what kind of experience infants undergo.

When the infant is born he has no specific personality. Along with his already more or less matured abilities, he has many capacities that will gradually ripen into abilities as maturation and experience progress. In the beginning, as he starts to register experiences, he will not be able to order them and interpret them in an adult fashion, partly because he has no frame of reference to guide him, no language with which to communicate, no understanding of what is occurring in and around him. In the ordinary sense, he has no ideas to interpret his experience.

However, since early infantile experience is largely a matter of speculation and inference, there is disagreement even among specialists as to its precise nature. Thus, according to Church, "the child from the beginning perceives things in terms of figure and ground, since perception of objects or groups of objects would otherwise be out of the question. But figure-ground organization is dictated neither by stimulus-intensities (except at disruptively high levels of contrast) nor by the formal organizational laws of Gestalt theory. Those objects and those properties of objects stand out which offer some relevance to the child himself in terms of promise or threat or concrete action."[34] In order to avoid misunderstanding, it must be mentioned that Sullivan did not think that figure and ground are perceived from the beginning.

When Sullivan first attempted to formulate infantile experiences, he went one step further and speculated that even before birth the individual has sensations and types of sensations that influence the infant's experiences after he is born. Although these ideas have little or no importance in Sullivan's subsequent formulations I shall presently discuss them in some detail, more for the sake of comprehensiveness than for any particular value they might have. While probably no one knows whether prenatal sensory stimulation influences the infant's experiences after birth, it seems to be well established that the individual does have the following sorts of experiences before birth: "The fetus can and does respond to tactile stimulation, it is capable of responding to other sensory types of stimulation, it can engage in motor responses of head, legs, and even hips, and it can engage in respiratory activities and use its vocal chords."[35]

Returning to the individual's postnatal experiences, I wish to emphasize that the infant's awareness is closely linked up with his needs, drives, feelings, and actions. The experiences he lives or undergoes become organized into constellations or patterns of various kinds, called complexes, which in varying degrees may or may not in the course of time attain the level of consciousness. Complexes in turn, may eventually become more elaborated and "associated" with definite objects, such as the mother. These more elaborated, evolved complexes are called sentiments. Complexes and sentiments are also symbols or symbol systems, in the broad sense in which Sullivan conceived of symbol, as previously described. In fact, for Sullivan, personality structure is a network of symbol systems, hierarchically arranged, which are the outcomes of a long history of organism-environment interactions.

His assumption that the infant undergoes a rudimentary *mental* experience prior to birth, which he formulated in terms of *preconcepts,* further complicates the exposition of his early formulations. These prenatal experiences are somehow retained, and as he wrote in "Schizophrenia: Its Conservative and Malignant Features," "determine the formation of primal complexes of experience" after the individual is born. In this view, the alleged prenatal experience has a significant effect on postnatal experience as it occurs through the various zones of interaction: oral, anal, and so forth.

Apparently Sullivan also thought in those early years that preconcepts not only are retained, making up the earliest kinds of infantile "mental structures," and influencing, directing later experiences, but also that in certain circumstances they can be reactivated, as in schizophrenic occurrences. This idea in turn requires an exposition of the theory of regression. For years Sullivan wrestled, none too successfully, with the problem of regression. It is discussed in considerable detail in "Regression: A Consideration of Reversive Mental Processes." He quotes Ferenczi regarding the paretic to the effect that there is a reversion of the "egoistic requirements," owing to the necessities of regaining self-complacency, to ontogenetic levels at which exercise of the remaining abilities once brought satisfaction to the "organism." Sullivan then offers the following generalization: "If organic abilities are progressively destroyed, the egoistic requirements must be diminished progressively, in order to maintain self-esteem. To that may be added the statement that: organic abilities having developed, by maturation and learning, in close connection with the ontogenesis of the egoistic requirements, their progressive disintegration finds always a comparable historic condition of egoistic evolution, to which it is but natural that the regression takes place."[36]

But what about those disorders in which there is no organic process (of deterioration) as a substrate, so to speak, of the regression? "The first step," Sullivan wrote, "in the extension of the principle consists of the appreciation that while organic abilities, in the example given —paresis—are lost clearly as a result of neurological destruction, *what* is lost is not a neurological matter, but a matter of the abilities of the personality, of the organism as a whole—a mental matter. We can then say, at once: when the abilities of the organism are progressively reduced, regression of egoistic requirements *may* be the effective means for maintaining self-esteem." So Sullivan tentatively concluded that such regression of the egoistic requirements is the only effective means of maintaining self-esteem when the abilities of the organism are progressively reduced.

When Sullivan wrote this, he had not yet begun to work out a theory of the self-system or self-dynamism. Nor had he grasped the apparent fact that the preservation of self-esteem is central to every type of functional mental disorder.

He wrote that there are undoubted reversive changes or regressions other than those of the requirement of self-esteem, applying to all aspects of mental life. One sees the reappearance of affective, of cognitive, and of conative functioning, which are inferior in social ("practical") efficiency, and historically or ontogenetically are of earlier types, replacing temporarily those more highly evolved types, as for example, in alcoholic intoxication. Sullivan suggested that whether or not such regressions can occur without similar change in the need for self-esteem seems to be an individual matter, probably depending on the intrinsic structure of the various sentiments in the given individual. He thought that, in fact, from several groups of data (psychoneurotic, epileptic, and that from alcoholic intoxication), it is to be surmised that very striking regressions of some sentiments may occur without much involvement of the nuclear structure of the sentiment of self-(regard). It appears that more often, when extensive suppression and even dissociation has occurred, there are compensatory developments that make it difficult to estimate the exact situation. "When we turn our attention to the profound psychosis, schizophrenia, we see, indeed, the very greatest discrepancies in this matter of regression of 'individual' psychic structures; as has been indicated elsewhere, disparity of depths of regression seems strikingly characteristic of this disorder." In other words, in the various neuroses and psychoses, one seemingly cannot say that similar psychic structures —cognitive, affective, conative, etc.—are disintegrated in an equivalent fashion, and replaced by earlier types. In the neuroses, the cognitive structures may remain more or less intact while the emotional and motivational patterns become replaced by more primitive ones. This may be contrasted with schizophrenic psychosis, in which there may be a wholesale disintegration of the individual's psychological systems or structures and replaced by those characteristic of late infancy or early childhood.

One must note that regression is not a conscious, voluntary reactivation of previous experience or of whatever has been retained of previous experience. It is not explicable by reference to the processes of recollection or recall. The process of regression, while pertaining to the past of the organism, does not make "referential use" of the past, as in the case of "functional memory" (recall and recollection). Regression entails an inadequate reference to the present and future. Regressive processes "put in action" references as if the present were actually the future while progressive processes extend in their goal from the present to an imagined situation about to arise. They are said to be a moving back of reference to a stage of the past from which the present loses its reality and becomes of the same nature as our ordinary imagination of the future. The investigator discovers that, automatically, the symbol situations that function in the regressive states are of a type historically those of an earlier period in the life of the individual. One may illustrate this interpretation crudely by saying the patient experiences the actual present from the standpoint of his experiential orientation of ten or fifteen or twenty years ago. It is as if the experiences of the intervening years were blotted out, though often not entirely so since elements from recent experience may sometimes become evident. The actual, objective present tends to become a fantastic shadow world. Regression applies to various aspects of the personality: the cognitive, affective, conative, and others. In regard to cognitive regression, for example, the "symbol situations" that function in the regressive states are said to be of a type historically those of an earlier stage in the life of the individual, that is, of infancy and early childhood, frequently.

Sullivan believed regression cannot occur unless there is a certain dissociation of the mental organization, which can be clarified in terms of a study of schizophrenic thinking, which he originally believed entailed a reversion to prenatal mental structures.

A *preconcept,* that is, an alleged type of prenatal mental structure, designates an "experience structure" arising from experience prior to birth, and is contrasted with *complex,* which is a structure acquired during the life of the individual. Preconcept is a particular form of experience that is analogous to *thought, perception, sensation, image,* though more rudimentary, primitive, and inchoate. According to Sullivan, discontinuous events of intrauterine life that follow in time the functional evolution of the foetal sense organs, and are of such nature as to give rise to *sense impressions,* make up the material from which comes the first experience. He claimed that the analysis of clinical data correlated to known biological events leads to the identification of certain major events of intrauterine life, such as the intrauterine activity of the mouth and appendages, structuralized in the *oral* preconcept. As he said in "The Oral Complex," preconcepts, being formed from sense data acquired and structuralized prior to any experience of self and long before the acquisition of the first "symbol," which occurs after birth (and which perhaps is the "clarification" of the nipple of the mother's breast as borne by another person separate from the infant) are not only inexpressible but inconceivable in adult thought.[37]

These unconscious preconcepts function in the form of dynamisms or sets that have an affinity for related postnatal experience, acquired during the life of the individual, and determine the formation of "primal complexes" of experience. In "Psychiatry: Introduction to the Study of Interpersonal Relations," a dynamism is defined as a relatively enduring configuration of energy that manifests itself in characterizable processes in interpersonal relations.[38] Primal complexes are said to be governing unconscious structures fundamental in the personality.[39] The oral complex seems to be regarded as most significant, though anal, urethral, and kinesthetic complexes are also mentioned. It was subsequently reformulated as the *oral dynamism,* an idea of great significance in interpersonal theory. Complexes are constituted of symbol systems previously described.

According to Sullivan in "Schizophrenia: Its Conservative and Malignant Features," the most important of the major systems of complexes so far as influence on personality is concerned is that group making up the *Ego* and *Id* of Freud's theory. This group making up the Ego and Id was formulated as the sentiment of self-regard.

A sentiment is said to be a complex, some part of which is accessible to consiousness. But this distinction between sentiment and complex came to be looked upon soon, as in the Farewell Lectures (1930), as "much more apparent than real." The roots of these complexes and sentiments (or dynamisms, according to a subsequent formulation) are utterly buried, unconscious, but as time passes and more experience is acquired, they achieve some measure of representation in the conscious life.

The oral complex (or, in a later formulation, oral dynamism) is presumed to originate as follows. Immediately upon birth "the recovering neural equipment, and especially the ultraessential autonomic-sympathetic system, reacts powerfully to the oxygen hunger. An extensive chain reflex is initiated, the inception of which leads to the opening of the mouth, the ingulfing of air, and the cry. It is not extravagant to assume kinesthetic and tactile sensory impressions of this event, thus appearing for structuralization immediately after birth. These data are chiefly from the mouth-throat-larynx zone. As such they are attracted to the structure of the mouth [or oral] precon-cept and are not only the first of the postnatal vital experience sequence, but the first experience structuralized in the oral complex."[40] As I have indicated, the latter is a pattern of experiences relating quite closely to the mouth and its appendages. Various experiences following birth, as in suckling, are included in, or assimilated to, this system.

In the field of the so-called abnormal, the oral complex is said to provide an explanation of the oral localization of homoerotic perversions, of the amazing obsessive power of unpleasant interpretations by the patient referring to the oral zone (hallucinations, delusions of certain kinds), of the facilitations of oral sex behavior, either the more normal activities, or fellatio and cunnilinctus, when dissociations of the schizophrenic type have begun. Since the oral complex is a mental (or personality) structure fundamental to other "libidinal" complexes there is no perverse (antibiological) experience that does not indicate the manifestations or workings of this complex. It also sheds light on certain other phenomena, such as mutism and the refusal of food.[41] And, finally, the conception of the oral complex is of help in the analysis of many dream symbols. In *Conceptions of Modern Psychiatry* and *The Interpersonal Theory of Psychiatry* one can learn how Sullivan eventually modified and developed most of these ideas regarding complexes and sentiments.

Chemical necessity is the proximate cause of suckling, for which neuromuscular patterns are prearranged. Sensory impressions from the tactile equipment of the lips are said to lead to protrusion and to the sucking of any suitable object brought into contact. Other tactile stimuli set off the chain reflex already prearranged and practiced before birth. With his characteristic meticulous attention to details, Sullivan writes that the now open glottis is closed and the "deglutition response" proceeds. "Needless it is to emphasize the priority of tactile and kinesthetic sense data from the lips as correlatives of the relief of chemical necessity. . . . At the same time, one must recall also that the purposive activity of food taking is one of the precise tendencies connected with the primal vector ambiguously called the self-preservative tendency."[42]

Though pleasure-strivings are not the only motivational tendencies of infancy, they constitute a major role in the infant's life. In "Erogenous Maturation" Sullivan wrote that for some time after birth there is an increasingly great part of the waking life devoted to the satisfaction of sensory impulses. He claimed that the partition of this sort of activity is determined in part by the degree of maturation of end organs; in part by the efficiency of motor pathways and coordinating apparatus; and in part by the nature of the spatial and other symbols at the time available. For a time, the oral zone is preeminent and the oral complex probably always occupies a position of very great importance in the personality.

The abstraction of visual-spatial aspects of the environment probably follows. Purely sentient and undifferentiated visual aspects are said to begin very early, the primitive elaboration of figure and ground coming distinctly later. Sullivan wrote that in regard to the latter, there is to be considered the "space perception" factor derived largely from coordinated activity of the two eyeballs, whose function may be absent for some little time after birth.

Though the end organs of the cochlear division of the VIII nerve are functionally effective at birth, the middle ear cavity is usually filled with fluid. Therefore auditory stimuli, other than a few stimuli registered through conduction by the cranial bones, "come as a novel form of experience."

At first the infant manifests oral satisfaction of all sorts. Soon he sucks his thumbs. According to Sullivan, not later than the fourth month, in some instances, kinesthetic rhythmical activities provide clear-cut pleasure sources. Spatial-kinesthetic symbols appearing in conjunction with definite proprioceptive functioning of the upper extremities, by the age of eight months, secure the toes for sucking pleasure. Already there have existed procedures of pulling and manipulating anything available. From these observations and inferences, Sullivan thought one could assume an extensive infantile consciousness of sensory input stemming from the upper extremities and, probably, maturation of the finger end organs. The genitals are said to come in for an unusual share of attention at this time though it is not entirely obvious what this attention means.[43]

Following Freud and Ferenczi, Sullivan claimed that it is the clash of reality with the pleasure-seeking infant during those periods neither devoted to food-taking nor covered by the makeshift return to prenatal conditions in sleep that leads to the growth of the sense of reality.[44] The dynamics of this clash is said to be seen in the differentiation of another drive ("vector"), namely, dominance or what he called in later years the "power motive." The goal of this drive toward dominance is the understanding and dominating of the environment so that unlust (unpleasure) may be prevented. "As it arises," Sullivan wrote, "the oral behavior which was initially instinctive in the satisfaction of hunger now takes on added importance as a magical aid to the obtaining not alone of pleasure but likewise of egocentric activity of a part of the environment."[45] This also illustrates how most important experience is added to the oral complex. Apparently Sullivan is referring to things like the cry, which becomes very effective in manipulating the environment, that is, the mother or mothering one.

In the first weeks of postnatal life the visual impressions of the nipple are said to be structuralized as the *first symbol*, described in Levy-Bruhl's terms as a "complex-image" consisting of experience visual, kinesthetic, and tactile. (This notion reminds one of Freud's idea that the mother's breast is the first object of libidinal desire.) The experiences structuralized in this complex-image, according to Sullivan, are held together by the powerful satisfaction feeling derived from suckling. It is "with this nipple-lip image that satisfaction of desire is dealt with in the deep unconscious." This statement seems to reflect Freud's notion of the "primary process." In any case, Sullivan thought that the relation of the infant to the nipple is a matter of extreme importance in the psychic evolution or development of the individual. It is, he says, undoubtedly the lip-nipple disjunction (or differentiation) that forms the basic datum for the evolution of the concepts of objective reality and of self, not the "anus-feces datum," which assumes its greatest importance in aggrandizing distressing aspects of reality. The growing awareness of the "complex-image" or symbol of the lips-nipple due to the increasing ability of the visual apparatus to provide data for tridimensional space perception "is the first step in the evolution of the sentiment of self-regard." The latter is a structure, part of which is readily accessible to consciousness, namely, what Freud called the ego.

In "The Oral Complex" Sullivan claims that it is from the primitive notion of interrupted participation of the mouth as the locus of satisfaction-giving of diverse kinds, there arises the conscious structure of purely hedonistic egoism, which is the "theme" of the early infantile personality. The significance of interrupted participation of the mouth in suckling is considerably elaborated in the *Interpersonal Theory of Psychiatry*.

Sullivan began to formulate a fragmentary outline of the development of personality in "The Oral Complex," emphasizing the great role that the oral complex plays in the evolution of the self or "sentiment of self-regard." He wrote that even before the least effort has been made to teach the infant some measure of control over, and incidentally to create attention and interest about, the sphincters, the adult environment has conveyed to the infant inhibitory experience concerning certain objects of sucking pleasure. From this experience the individual's repressing activities first begin. The original "effector" to any restriction of pleasure-seeking was the dominance vector, with its primitive rage reaction as a consequence of inevitable limitations on the expression of this tendency of pleasure-seeking. At this time the "aversion vector," with emotional concomitants in the form of disgust, is differentiated. Thus experiences structuralized around this "energy path," the oral zone, become a part of the sentiment of self regard, whose direct basis is in the oral complex.

It is not clear to what degree Sullivan had come to realize that disgust reactions are conditioned by the attitudes of parents or their surrogates. In any case he wrote that it is from this field of disgust reactions there come the first vague notions as to negative aspects of the self, that there are certain things, such as feces and urine, which have some connection with the body but are to be kept far from the mouth.

"The infant's observations of auditory impressions, his pleasure pursuit by self-manipulations and the growing effort to achieve tools more useful in the struggle for dominance than is the cry, show by the appearance of babbling and crowing towards the end of the first six months. The vigorous response of the parents to efforts at articulate sounds cannot but emphasize this experience."[46]

While locomotion is an absorbing activity during the early part of the second year, the infant's efforts at oral expression progress to a point at which he can produce real words, generally, by the eighteenth month. But the words do not have the meaning that they usually have for the adults. They are said to be much more related to the "magic words of power" employed not only by children seeking pleasure but by schizophrenics, though such words often have for those people some "primordial awe" attached to them as well.

About the eighteenth month the educational attention of the parent toward the youngster for the purpose of toilet training generally "elevates" the urethral preconcept and the anal zone into the latter's consciousness. At this time a perhaps pernicious anal erotism due to the mishandling of the task of toilet training by the parent may be determined. Sullivan thought that the attachment of disgust ("an emotional experience organically related to the mouth") not alone to the urine and feces but to the excretory acts themselves serves as the

conceptual bridge between exaggerated anal erotic states and copro-
phagia.

There is "much of biting and eating" in the thought of children as
their essays in creative fantasy reveal. "As a carrier of pleasure and
as a prototype of harm to the individual, the mouth and its appendages certainly enjoys notable distinction in the childish generic notions. . . . That we can interpret great sections of adult thought, both
commonplace and abstract, as more related to complex images from
this unconscious structure, then are they to logical conceptualization,
is borne out by contact with cogent analytical material."[47]

In "Erogenous Maturation" Sullivan attempts to analyze the "high
value pleasure from genital manipulations," while developing his
fragmentary outline of personality development. This pleasure is *not*
"a close correlate of adult sexual excitement—those sensory influxes
which have their origin in the end-organs of the prostatic urethra,
vesicles, and ejaculatory ducts. The distension of this part of the
urethra by the extruded urine, originally a stimulus for a lower seg-
ment reflex activity which, at a given threshold value, led to inhibition
of tone of the sphincters, and thus a release of the bladder contents,
has in several of the higher mammals been provided not only with
extensive palae-encephalic but with cortical connections. . . ."[48]

Sullivan wrote that in all the higher mammals studied, as in man,
we see a semivoluntary activity of musculature when the bladder has
been emptied or, for some other reason, the sphincter closed with
fluid remaining in the prostatic urethra. In man, at least, this activity
is usually accompanied by acute pleasurable experience. Sullivan believed there is some evidence that these centripetal nerve impulses
arise as an effect of the contraction of the urethral striped musculature. The same influx is said to be an important constituent of the
sexual orgasm in males. Introspectively this constituent is very difficult to differentiate from the influx of stimuli arising in contractions
of the seminal vesicles and the ejaculatory ducts. This observation is
the source of Sullivan's statement in "Schizophrenia: Its Conservative
and Malignant Features" that the urethral preconcept is the basis of
male genital localization. He thought it obvious how this factor has
bearing upon the evolution of more or less pernicious "urethral erotism," in some cases, and how, if it is unduly the object of attention
from untimely or ill-judged educational influence, it may provide symbols relative to many other impulses, thus constituting the "urethral

character" of Freudian psychology. But he did not find anything in it that bears directly on manipulation of the penis by the fourteen-months-old child.

The bone structures, Sullivan claims, "in their function of geometric fixation, dictate a facility in reaching the genitals and, similarly, the umbilicus." In this statement, he seems to imply manipulations of the penis may occur because the infant's hands happen to rest on the genitals, a sensitive area of the body, so that the infant accidentally discovers they are a source of pleasure, as are the remnants of the umbilical cord.

Another factor, in connection with genital manipulations, which Sullivan discusses in "Erogenous Maturation," is the erectile nature of the penis, which may manifest itself shortly after birth. He surmised that erections occurring in the first months of extrauterine life are in response not to tactile stimuli but to unknown internal situations. If there is any sentience connected with these early erections its nature is "another unknown." "For that matter, the phenomena in awareness relating to such occurrences [erections and keen sentience] even after the functional awakening of the gonads is largely a matter of tactile impressions from the integument of the part [the penis], and tension impressions from the musculature and tendonous appendages. . . . We may dismiss considerations of erection as of any import prior to the evolution of awareness of pleasure from the input of the tactile end-organs of the part. Subsequently to this, erection does assume much importance as it occasions a mechanical heightening of sensory input by bringing the end-organs into their position of maximal efficiency."[49]

The lower chronological limit of real infantile ("juvenile") masturbation, it seems, is approximately fifteen to eighteen months. When the child is not more than three or four years of age, the opposing influence of erection upon relaxation of the bladder sphincter, coupled with erection in response to overdistension, is said to have brought about "a symbol elaboration," which henceforth, barring deep repressive "states of awareness," due to the attitudes of the parent, ties the whole into one system of so-called sexual experiences.

Sullivan wrote that it is against this juvenile "sexual" system that castration fear or other powerful and inhibitory and repressing influences must be brought to bear if the youngster is to be effectively distorted to meet the parental obsessions about sexual sin. "In case the inhibitory influences have been successful in stamping out manipulations of the part *before* the stage of juvenile masturbation, and the processes of maturation do not break down this inhibition fairly early (before the fifth year?) the personality, I believe, is irremediably warped and a fairly normal development of the sexual impulse after puberty is most improbable."[50]

Many "fictive" elements, that is, irrational emotional attitudes and beliefs of the parents, which have been referred to previously in connection with inhibitory and repressing influences, play a significant role in sexual maturation. From the cradle onward, parents, teachers, and social censors are said to combine in impressing on the individual, by gestures of avoidance and words of mouth, their irrational fear of the penis as an object to be looked at. Naturally the infant becomes impressed by the signal importance of this bodily appendage due to the fuss that his elders make about it. Since he cannot understand what all the fuss is about, his penis, or rather the signal importance attached to it, becomes a "primordial mystery." Eventually his native tendency to try to understand this mystery may and usually does (or did, not so long ago) become "swallowed up" in repression. From the later "radiations" of this primordial mystery there may be found the roots of "that obsessing sexuality" so commonly manifested in later life, often surrounded by a lurid twilight of secret fascination and irrational avoidance.

Partly because of this situation the Oedipus complex appears. In contradiction to Freud, Sullivan held that it is not a normal biological development, but a "fraudulant symbol situation," which the child develops because of the cultural attitudes embodied in the personality of the mother and, all too often, in that of the father as well. This warped attitude toward the father (preadolescent sexual competition) originates from the individual's blind efforts to make sense of the world in which he finds himself, especially the mother and the father, amid a welter of fraudulent attitudes, contradictory motives, and domestic infelicities prevalent in his home. When the boy learns about the nature of the sex act and that his father inserts his penis—"hideously sinful object"—into the mother, he enhances the fraudulent sexual symbol situation by assimilating a new and especially destructive addition in the form of disgust, hatred, or other negative affect toward the father. Since this addition to the "symbol cadre," sexual sin, is acquired and assimilated with the aid of the defense mechanism called repression, it creates, or at least facilitates, a wide breach in the coherency of the youth's symbolic representations of people. There are other factors that become assimilated to the kinds of relationships classically designated as the Oedipus complex by Freud: anger at restraints and restrictions, fear of the superior powers of the parent, and wishes to be the center of things. These experiences are much more likely to appear in relation to the father (in the form of childish hatred) than to the sustaining and satisfying mother.

It seems doubtful that Sullivan ever attached much credence in the "allegedly identical Electra complex in girls." In any case he thought that psychoanalysts had thrust upon woman altogether too many conclusions derived from the genetic study of the male.

Even in the early papers, including "The Oral Complex" and "Erogenous Maturation," Sullivan did not literally adhere to all of Freud's formulations about libidinal energy flowing from certain areas of the body to others. In other words, he did not literally accept Freud's theory that "infantile sexuality" manifests in the following preordained stages: oral, anal, urethral, phallic, and (true) genital stages. What Freud called the oral and phallic stages are stressed in "Erogenous Maturation." The so-called anal or anal-sadistic phase is only briefly discussed, and more in terms of stimulation of nervous system structures than in terms of the activation of hypothetical libidinal energy supposedly concentrated at or in particular areas of the body. (While Freud was by no means indifferent to underlying neurophysiological processes, he did not greatly concern himself with them once he became a psychotherapist.) That is, by 1926 Sullivan had abandoned, if he ever literally accepted, the Freudian assumption that there exists a qualitatively special form of energy, the energy of the sexual instincts, though he continued for a while to employ the terms "libidinal energy" and "hormic energy" interchangeably. For example, he wrote: "More or less directly through the sacral nucleus and via paths accompanying the centripetal fibers from that nucleus, there are provided the central basis for symbol elaborations pertaining not only to the penis, the urethra, vesicles, and ejaculatory ducts, but likewise to the anus, the lower part of the rectum, the root of the penis, perineum, and medial surfaces of the upper part of the thighs. All these end organs are more sensitive than the general integument; many of them are exquisitely so. It is therefore no wonder that the cultivation for pleasure of one or other of these areas, in addition to

part or all of the penis, results in the subordination of the oral complex to what has roughly been called anal erotism. This brings about
a great distortion of the total symbol activity, the so-called 'anal personality type.' "[51] Various sexual perversions are dependent upon the
cultivation for pleasure of one or other of the bodily areas mentioned.

In the light of subsequent development of Sullivan's theories, it is
interesting that already in "Erogenous Maturation," a tentative formulation of preadolescent love occurs. It appears, he wrote, generally
late in the seventh or early in the eighth year. Since he knew of no
reason at that time to think this change "in the conative assets of the
individual" was an outcome of previous experience, he assumed it was
the result of physiological maturation, though he had no information
"as to what neuro-glandular development is responsible." At that
time (1926) he thought that the intimacy impulse was a component of
the sexual instinct. "From a strikingly self-centered existence, where
the groups of world representations pertaining to others are quite
without impulses making for a give-and-take attitude, the child is
driven by what has been called a contrectation component of the
sexual instinct to seek intimate contact with others. Play is altered in
its character, and the inner life takes on a greater resemblance to that
of the adult."[52] The repressed early "juvenile" masturbation is said
to be reactivated through talk, example, or actual manipulation by a
playmate. Since the boy's knowledge of the female is severely limited,
(he possesses no "practical symbols", in many cases, of womanhood
other than those of the mother) and often distorted, the intimacy
impulse is directed toward other boys.

"When the gonad function has matured to the state of semen production, and activation of the neural apparatus pertaining to its ejaculation, there comes the adolescent resymbolization."[53] A new
"world-representation" has to be forged. With unprecedented sud-
denness a field of experience of the very greatest pleasure-value
emerges. After the dramatic first appearance of puberty, many of the
old familiar ways, ideas, attitudes break down. Now, with the experience of lust, and all that it normally implies, the adolescent must
rebuild a mass of crumbling symbol systems—secretly and only with
the help of his equally unfortunate peers—which formed the world of
his recent past, despite the beliefs and attitudes about sexual sin that
he has assimilated from parents, teachers, and perhaps others. With
the coming of puberty, sexual sin, formerly a mysterious, vague, wide-

flung influence, now becomes "a rapidly crystallizing symbol system," a set of beliefs including fictions of the past, present and future, of dire consequences, such as hell fire or insanity. Hence arises a conflict between this "gigantic mental fraud" and the indomitable sex impulse, which may spread to almost every symbol, almost every idea providing the "language" or mode of experience of all ill-defined cravings, and of every pleasure source ever inhibited.

If these ideas of Sullivan concerning early adolescence seem extravagant or at least overgeneralized even for the middle twenties to some readers, they may be regarded as starting points of a subsequent more sober and profound analysis of the adolescent era.

In this chapter and in the first, I have several times had occasion to mention the "sentiment of self-regard." This formulation of personality structure by Shand was eventually replaced by Sullivan's "self-dynamism," though the two formulations are not identical in meaning. Sullivan, in "The Oral Complex," tried to reconcile the genetic Freudian approach to personality with Shand's "formal" or "academic" orientation. Thus a part of the sentiment of self-regard is readily accessible to consciousness, namely, the "ego" of Freud. This "mighty system of experience," Sullivan wrote, includes in its functions the groups of phenomena to which such concepts as censor, resistance, dream censor, and ego ideal apply. These are all functions of the ego.

From the point of view of "formal psychology" the sentiment of self-regard is said to be a group of beliefs about the self, about one's own individuality, propensities, and abilities. Sullivan's quotation from Shand is significant since the importance of self-esteem for mental health became evident in his work with patients.

"In all normal individuals, then," says Shand, "there is a love of something to give order and unity to their lives; and the system which is found generally pre-eminent is the great principle of self-love or the self-regarding sentiment, analogous to the chief bodily functions in respect of the number of subsidiary systems which it is capable of containing. ..."[54] He goes on to say that a variety of disinterested sentiments, such as conjugal and parental love, filial affection, friendship, and the like are joined to this sentiment in subtle and intimate ways. Shand mentions that finally there is a "system" of unique importance called respect for conscience, something that is very imperfectly developed in most men and seldom attaining to the warmth and intimacy of love, which is ever contesting both the supremacy of self-love and the attractiveness of the present inclination. In most men, respect for conscience is combined with the religious sentiment. And two other sentiments, self-respect, and respect for others, he adds, closely connected with each other belong to this same class.

In "The Oral Complex," Sullivan also gives a quotation from McDougall that emphasizes the sentiment of self-regard. The latter thought it to be the most important of all the sentiments by reason of its strength and the frequency and far-reaching nature of its operations. McDougall points out that "I" or "me" grows richer in meaning as the child builds up a system of beliefs (of ideas and attitudes) about his own nature and about conduct and character in general.

"This object 'me' thus becomes represented in the structure of the mind," he says, "by a system of dispositions of extra-ordinary extent and complexity, a system also which is associated with a multitude of past events and objects. ... And the conative dispositions of the system, being brought into play so frequently, by every social contact, whether actual or imagined, become delicately responsive in an extraordinary degree, as well as very strong, through much exercise."[55] McDougall also pointed out, as Sullivan acknowledges in "The Oral Complex," the intimate connection in the mind that makes it impossible to think of the self apart from its social setting.

Both Shand and McDougall conceive of instinctive tendencies as hierarchically organized into more inclusive motivational systems and attitudes. The combination or synthesis of more subordinate tendencies and attitudes into sentiments occurs by their becoming attached to the same object. Sullivan adopted the notion of an hierarchical organization of impulses and attitudes and for a brief period the conception of sentiment to explain the motivation of thinking and behavior. In the Farewell Lectures he wrote: "We might take for example the traditional sentiment of love—we might say that in the case of A being in love with B, we have in the A part of the situation very powerful factors arising from the sex impulses, rather powerful factors from the group of tendencies that can be called self-assertive tendencies, sometimes powerful factors from submissive tendencies, sometimes from acquisitive tendencies, sometimes from that group of tendencies which brings about interest in the bearing and the rearing of young, and so on—acting as a vector-addition or vector-sum to hold together all *the experience real and fantastic* which A has of B."[56]

These ideas of Freud, Shand, and McDougall, tested as they were in Sullivan's work with patients, were eventually incorporated, though with considerable modification, in his theory of interpersonal relations and the evolution of the *self-dynamism*. According to this theory dissociation cannot be understood apart from the structure and activities of the self-dynamism, which is a substructure of personality, a fact that will be clarified in subsequent chapters of this book. Nor can dissociation be understood apart from the individual's interpersonal relations. Finally, one must bear in mind that dissociated processes, when the *dissociative* power of the self fails, regress in function to levels of experience similar to, or analogous to, patterns of experience characteristic of experience in infancy and early childhood. This phenomenon is an essential characteristic of schizophrenia.

Notes

1. Cf. SILVANO ARIETI, *The Intrapsychic Self* (New York: Basic Books, 1967), chaps 1-8.

2. HARRY STACK SULLIVAN, "The Importance of a Study of Symbols in Psychiatry," *Psyche* (London), 1:81-93, 1926.

3. *Ibid.*

4. JESSE E. GORDON, *Personality and Behavior* (New York: The Macmillan Company, 1963), p. 142.

5. *Ibid.*, p. 143.

6. Cf. PATRICK MULLAHY, "The Interpersonal Current in Psychiatric Development," *International Journal of Psychiatry*, 2:131-143, 1968.

7. Cf. SULLIVAN, "The Importance of a Study of Symbols in Psychiatry."

8. Cf. MAX L. HUTT, ROBERT L. ISAACSON, and MILTON L. BLUM, *The Science of Behavior Psychology: The Science of Interpersonal Behavior* (New York: Harper and Row, 1967), chaps 3, 4, 5.

9. *See,* for example, T. W. WANN (ed.), *Behaviorism and Phenomenology* (Chicago, Illinois: University of Chicago Press, 1964); JAMES J. GIBSON, *The Senses Considered as Perceptual Systems* (Boston, Massachusetts: Houghton Mifflin Company, 1966); and FLOYD H. ALLPORT, *Theories of Perception and the Concept of Structure* (New York: John Wiley and Sons, 1955).

10. TAMOTSO SHIBOTANI, *Society and Personality* (Englewood Cliffs, New Jersey: Prentice-Hall, 1961), p. 295.

11. HARRY STACK SULLIVAN, "Regression: A Consideration of Reversive Mental Processes," *State Hospital Quarterly*, 11:208-217, 387-394, 651-668, 1926.

12. HOWARD H. KENDLER, *Basic Psychology* (2nd ed.; New York: Appleton-Century-Crofts, 1968), p. 180.

13. HARRY STACK SULLIVAN, "Peculiarity of Thought in Schizophrenia," *American Journal of Psychiatry,* **82**:21-86, 1925-1926; reprinted in HARRY STACK SULLIVAN, *Schizophrenia as a Human Process,* with Introduction and Commentaries by HELEN SWICK PERRY (New York: W. W. Norton and Company, 1962).

14. Cf. L. JOSEPH STONE and JOSEPH CHURCH, *Childhood and Adolescence* (New York: Random House, 1957), pp. 84-91.

15. SULLIVAN, "Peculiarity of Thought in Schizophrenia."

16. Cf. HARRY STACK SULLIVAN, *Conceptions of Modern Psychiatry,* with a Foreword by the author and a Critical Appraisal of the Theory by PATRICK MULLAHY (New York: W. W. Norton and Company, 1953), pp. 33-35.

17. SULLIVAN, "Peculiarity of Thought in Schizophrenia," quoted from CHARLES SPEARMAN, *The Nature of "Intelligence" and the Principles of Cognition* (London: Macmillan and Company, 1923), p. 155.

18. Cf. SPEARMAN, *op. cit.,* chap. XI.

19. SULLIVAN, "Peculiarity of Thought in Schizophrenia."

20. *Ibid.*

21. SULLIVAN, "The Importance of a Study of Symbols in Psychiatry."

22. *Ibid.*

23. *Ibid.*

24. *Ibid.*

25. *Ibid.*

26. *Ibid.*

27. *Ibid.*

28. JOHN DEWEY, *Experience and Nature* (New York: The Open Court Publishing Company, 1929), chap. 8.

29. HARRY STACK SULLIVAN, "The Language of Schizophrenia," in J. S. KASANIN (ed.), *Language and Thought in Schizophrenia: Collected Papers* (Berkeley and Los Angeles: University of California Press, 1944), p. 5.

30. *Ibid.*

31. *Ibid.*

32. *Ibid.*

33. SULLIVAN, "Peculiarity of Thought in Schizophrenia."

34. JOSEPH CHURCH, *Language and the Discovery of Reality* (New York: Random House, 1966), pp. 4-5; cf. ARTHUR T. JERSILD, *Child Psychology* (Englewood Cliffs, New Jersey: Prentice-Hall, 1960), pp. 116-117.

35. HUTT, ISAACSON, and BLOOM, *op. cit.,* Book Two, p. 429.

36. SULLIVAN, "Regression: A Consideration of Reversive Mental Processes."

37. HARRY STACK SULLIVAN, "The Oral Complex," *Psychoanalytic Review,* **12**:31-38, 1925.

38. HARRY STACK SULLIVAN, "Psychiatry: Introduction to the Study of

Interpersonal Relations," *Psychiatry,* 1:121-134, 1938, p. 123, footnote 3.

39. HARRY STACK SULLIVAN, "Schizophrenia: Its Conservative and Malignant Features," *American Journal of Psychiatry,* 81:77-91, footnote 2, 1924-1925; reprinted in SULLIVAN, *Schizophrenia as a Human Process.*

40. SULLIVAN, "The Oral Complex."

41. Cf. HARRY STACK SULLIVAN, *Clinical Studies in Psychiatry,* ed. HELEN SWICK PERRY, MARY LADD GAWEL, and MARTHA GIBBON, with a Foreword by DEXTER M. BULLARD (New York: W. W. Norton and Company, 1956), p. 328.

42. SULLIVAN, "The Oral Complex."

43. HARRY STACK SULLIVAN, "Erogenous Maturation," *Psychoanalytic Review,* 13:1-15, 1926.

44. SULLIVAN, "Oral Complex."

45. *Ibid.*

46. *Ibid.*

47. *Ibid.*

48. SULLIVAN, "Erogenous Maturation."

49. *Ibid.*

50. *Ibid.*

51. *Ibid.*

52. *Ibid.*

53. *Ibid.*

54. ALEXANDER F. SHAND, *The Foundations of Character* (London: Macmillan and Company, 1914), p. 57.

55. WILLIAM McDOUGALL, *Outline of Psychology* (New York: Charles Scribner's Sons, 1924), p. 428.

56. HARRY STACK SULLIVAN, *Farewell Lectures,* Lecture V (italics added).

3 / The Evolution of Sullivan's Theory

Very early in his career, Sullivan became dissatisfied with orthodox psychoanalytic theory. He discovered that, while it contributed many powerful and fertile ideas toward an understanding of the mentally ill, it was in many respects seriously defective. Gradually he began to create a more or less systematized theory of his own, in which less emphasis was placed on hereditary factors and much more weight was ascribed to environmental conditions, especially sociocultural factors. He began to modify Freud's theory of psychosexual development and eventually he discarded it. Fairly soon he arrived at an interactional approach to psychology and psychiatry. Personality and society cannot be divorced. Sullivan began to seek the specific social conditions that foster mental illness, as well as mental health, an orientation that was reinforced by his experiences at Sheppard and Enoch Pratt Hospital. In this chapter and in following chapters I shall attempt to pull together the ideas that gradually evolved. These ideas are set forth in several published papers, in the unpublished Farewell Lectures and in the recently copyrighted *Personal Psychopathology*.

Like McDougall and Meyer, Sullivan stressed a holistic approach in psychology. Man's experience and behavior in this view is a reflection of, or expression of, his unity. He acts as an "organism," or as a person, or "personality." In striving to emphasize man's unity, Meyer, who was influenced by his friend the philosopher John Dewey, rejected the traditional dualism of mind and body. Thus, for Meyer, mind is a function or set of functions of an organized living being in action. Both McDougall and Meyer also stressed purposive behavior or, as contemporary psychologists would say, goal-seeking behavior.

The individual, according to Sullivan, "is an organism including motor and sensory agencies, with extensive neural coordinating, integrating and dissociating apparatus, the activity of which as a whole constitutes purposive effort—behavior."[1] Behavior is a total "reaction" of the human organism and his total experience, innate and acquired, purposively activated by "vital" or hormic energy. This behavior occurs communally with a "relevant environment." The relevant environment, which is both physical and cultural, is correlated with the activities of the organism. For instance, the relevant environment of an infant crying because he is hungry is very narrow and circumscribed while that of a powerful statesman making a speech may be worldwide. Mental life, according to Sullivan, may be restricted in its reference to those higher forms of organisms that have a central integrating system but no further. And the activity of a central integrating apparatus, which is an occurrence throughout the organism, as the Gestalt school held, he wrote in "Erogenous Maturation," must in part at least consist in symbol activity. Mind expresses itself in behavior and thinking, which itself may be considered to be an aspect of behavior.

In the Farewell Lectures and in *Personal Psychopathology*, he elaborated upon certain ideas mentioned in Chapters 1 and 2. Life processes are distinguished into three categories (or generic factors) of organization, "communal existence" and functional activity. In regard to the first, Sullivan wrote: "They are the factors which make a bud from an amoeba grow into another amoeba instead of resolving into less complex defunct organic compounds or developing into a whale or something of that kind. They are the factors that determine what happens after a suitable spermatozoon and an ovum have become confused."[2] Among those factors are "innate determiners," such as genes contained on the chromosomes. The relationships between these factors also make for organization so that if one can displace a gene to a new position on a chromosome one gets a marked change in the development culminating in the adult organism. Recent research in genetics throws doubt on the old formulations existing in Sullivan's day. The following passage illustrates the newer thinking in this field:

Each chromosome is made up of strands of deoxyribonucleic acid (DNA), complex protein molecules that are elementary transmitters of hereditary influences. These protein molecules provide the chemical blueprint for the developing organism.

Modern biochemists are beginning to unravel the code by which DNA transmits information. Before the discovery of DNA as the biochemical transmitter of inheritance, genetecists discussed the passing on of specific hereditary traits in terms of *genes*. Thus a gene is a construct, a hypothetical structure, which was used to account for the fact that specific traits are inherited. Now scientists are discovering that the properties hypothesized for genes can be accounted for by the activity of DNA.[3]

Even in those hereditary factors there are said to be second-order factors due to the relations existing between the primary factors, that is, interrelations between processes.

Sullivan stressed the interrelations between processes because there are no processes in an organism that are "reasonably isolated" from other processes. "The whole organism is a bundle of processes the relations of which are quite as determining as are the processes themselves."[4] For this reason, any event that occurs in a living entity affects, sometimes in a trivial fashion, sometimes in a vital fashion, the entire life process of that entity. In the field of psychopathology, interrelations between processes are likewise of incalculably great significance.

Factors of genetic organization, besides determining the type of organism and its individual innate peculiarities, also are said to fix the general course that its development must follow, that is, the orderly sequence of maturation, set up limits as to possible developments, and are represented in the mental field by a "peculiar group" of factors of intelligence. According to Sullivan, others of these factors are reflected in the primary emotions, "whatever they may be." Still others are reflected in the general urges, drives, or impulses of the organism, which are organized expressions or manifestations of hormic or libidinal energy, and which in most animals are called instincts. Finally, it is by "peculiarity" of these factors that congenital mental deficiency occurs; or, by another "peculiarity," the possibility of genius is determined.

The second category of factors, communal existence, is factors made up of processes connecting the organism and its environment.

In the human organism there are highly specialized zones of interaction between "that which is certainly human organism and that which is certainly environment." But the boundaries between the organism and its environment are not sharp and clear-cut. Nor is the former self-contained. Sullivan points out that it is impossible for any life process to go on solely within that which is clearly the organism. There is always interaction. Communal existence in mental life pertains to the most complex phase of psychopathology. "For the communal environment in the realm of mind is made up of other selves and those monuments and ghosts of other selves, the institutions, the traditions, the mores, the economic-social situations, and so on, which go to make up culture, however simple."[5] In other words, communal existence in the realm of mind depends on interpersonal relations, though mind is "a particular aspect of organism."

The third category of factors or processes characterizing the living is called functional activity. From a broad philosophical point of view, functional activity in and within the environment is aimed fundamentally toward the accumulation of "free energy" and the maintenance of life. In the realm of the mental the factors of functional activity are said to be the mental processes *per se:* sensing, perceiving, thinking, learning, imagining, desiring, and the like.

Mind, for Sullivan, is not a substance. It is, he says, that aspect of life processes that represents total actions of the living organism in and within total situations in which it exists. The discussion of symbolizing activities in Chapter 2 suggests the sort of total actions he was referring to. *Total actions* are distinguished from *local actions,* though the difference is not absolute. For practical purposes, one can say that many events expend their noticeable effect on very limited aspects of the whole organism. Thus a hot cinder falling into one's eye exerts marked effect upon certain conjunctival cells, as it does on certain nerve endings. From the standpoint of the person these effects can be called *local action.* Nevertheless there is also total activity since, owing to the irritation of the nerve endings, the organism as a whole is made aware of pain, and of the location of the pain. And certain behavior, integrated activity, follows to relieve the pain. "In so far as the person is aware of pain," Sullivan says, "and thereupon suspends everything else he is doing to make some gesture toward relieving the pain or removing the cause of it, to that extent we have encountered total activity in and within a situation including the cinder-falling-in-the-eye event."[6]

A total situation is difficult to characterize. It includes both the organism and the relevant environment. The term "relevant" is used because only certain factors in any particular situation have a bearing upon, are relevant in a practical way to, what is going on in that one spot of the universe. (Thus the "events" occurring on the planet Venus have no bearing on the activity of writing this page, while the temperature of the atmosphere outside the window and of the air in the room does. The summer heat makes it more difficult to sit at a desk and write.) The total situation is defined as *that complex of the organization of the living organism, the relevant environmental factors and the relations between them, including particularly the changing relations that are being brought about by the organism.*

But how can an organism of great complexity and subtle differentiation perform anything? How can it act as a unified whole? Integration is a key concept here. Sullivan observes that in passing from the unicellular type of organisms to the highest ones, one finds in the phylogenesis of life increasing specialization of "dynamism" for keeping the complex organization of tissue systems and the varieties of functional activity tied together. In other words, the human organism is made up of millions of smaller structures that carry on numerous activities. All of these diverse activities accomplish the one all-encompassing function of the organism—survival. The only way many units can be made to function as a single unit is by organization, controlling their numerous activities so as to coordinate and integrate them. This means there has to be some way of getting "information" to and from the component units; there has to be "communication." In the human organism, nerve impulses and chemicals are the two kinds of so-called communication devices. (For the purposes of this book, Sullivan's somewhat "dated" references to various nervous system structures and functions as well as his discussion of the endocrine system seem to be of minor value.) At the same time the human organism is functioning in and within the environment and so, with the aid of such things as the respiratory system, sense organs, nervous system, symbolizing activities, and the like, is in constant interaction and communication with it. At all times there is a complex interchange between the two.

The psychopathologist or, more broadly, the psychobiologist, namely, the student of processes of living, whether in a healthy or morbid fashion, of actual, mundane persons, in and within more or less commonplace social situations, must revise his orientation. He does *not,* as it used to be thought, observe the mental (and other) processes and malfunctions of an individual with a mind, taken in isolation from everything else. He deals with an "organism-environment complex," and their relations. And he is always, according to Sullivan, observing phenomena that are properly related to the complex rather than merely to the organism part of it.

From any standpoint, mental disorder concerns total activity. In the higher animals, some of this activity is implicit in the sense that it gives no clear-cut objective signs. Because of the speech apparatus in man, one can frequently get clues to total activity by listening intently to a person.

Thus far in this book I have written about the individual's total activity in and by means of the relevant environment while he is in a waking state. Sullivan thought that the "activity type" called sleep is vitally important as well for the understanding of human thought and behavior. In the Farewell Lectures and in *Personal Psychopathology* he speculated rather freely about various "activity types" and their (imagined) connections with behavior in forms of life much lower (simpler) than the human organism. Much of this speculation seems of doubtful value. Just the same there are some ideas about activity-types set forth that seem important enough to be reviewed briefly. The activity-types that are emphasized are sleep and dreaming, twilight behavior, that is, behavior while one is in a reduced state of consciousness (as in certain schizophrenic conditions), consciousness, and self-consciousness. These are all aspects of or factors entering into the "personal-environmental complex." The activity types are formulated in an ascending order of complexity, and Sullivan thought it important to study them as clues to the sorts of total situations with which the psychiatrist deals.

Sleep pertains to a "relatively simple body of factors," though they are of great significance for the study of schizophrenia and perhaps other kinds of mental disorder. At least forty years ago Sullivan had learned a good deal from his investigation of schizophrenia about the psychological significance of what is now called "sleep deprivation," as one can see from a perusal of Chapter 9, "Sleep, Dreams and

Schizophrenia," in *Personal Psychopathology*. Furthermore, he was a careful student of various phenomena that, in addition to dreams, may occur while one is sleeping. For example, certain dissociated processes may become manifest under cover of light sleep. They are described in some detail in *Clinical Studies in Psychiatry*.

As already mentioned, certain phenomena of so-called waking life are said to be understandable only when the total situation is recognized to be not of the type that we call consciousness but rather that of a state of reduced consciousness, approaching or actually constituting a "twilight state." Sullivan believed that the "elucidation of sleep" and thoroughgoing work on "animal consciousness" or animal psychology would secure much greater insight into the problems of schizophrenic changes, including "twilight phenomena."

Consciousness is an activity-type whose meaning is more or less self-evident and taken for granted in *Personal Psychopathology*. It is said to accompany and to be a part of "these peculiarly comprehensive integrations" (the operation of distance receptors) of the organism in and within its complex. The analyses of consciousness by such philosophers as William James and George Herbert Mead might be suggestive in this context but a review of their ideas would take us too far afield.[7]

At least many forms of animal life seem to manifest a rudimentary awareness or consciousness, though any speculation about it at this stage of knowledge seems idle or at least unnecessary. In any event, it is generally agreed that animals lack self-consciousness. Self-consciousness, according to Sullivan, entails actual or easily accessible awareness of the human organism's own part in the "organism-environment complex." The point of origin of self-consciousness lies in "the evolution of tools of intercommunication prevailingly symbolic in type." From the latter a great "context" of personal experience is subsumed in a verbal symbol "me." The "me" in turn is part of the larger, more comprehensive "approving reference-system called the self."

A variety of pseudoproblems are said to arise from overlooking the fact that the activity-type in the given total situation is not that of a self-conscious organism but instead an organism that is merely conscious, in which the more complex processes arising from self-consciousness are in abeyance. For example, Sullivan believed that techniques peculiarly suited to the self-conscious individual produce absurd or "meaningless" results when applied to a total situation of the activity-type of sleep.

From a point of view different from the "schema" that embraces activity-types, Sullivan distinguished the following two classes of experience and behavior: mental processes, which are implicit or covert, and actions, which are explicit. These kinds of mental processes and acts are "required" in the resolution of situations and problems stemming from the organism-environment complex. The mental processes are of several types: primitive, fantastic, reality-controlled, of either an adjustive or creative sort. Analagously, actions are labeled reflex, impulsive, whether innate or learned, and consciously chosen.[8]

There is no need, for the purposes of this book, to dwell on reflex or "reflex-instinctive" acts, which are on the borderline between local and total activity.

Impulsive actions are characterized by a good deal of antecedent, often implicit, process showing much more clear-cut distinctions from local action. Impulsive acts are either innate or learned. Sullivan observes that a study of innate impulsive acts would have to be made very early in life because the innate patterns of activity, especially in human beings, are increasingly subject to change by experience, and are mostly very plastic tools that are easily pressed to conformity with the particular ends to which they chance to be applied. Sullivan says they tend to disappear among the rapidly learned or habitual impulsive acts, insofar as they pertain to the skeletal musculature. Though infants manifest certain clear-cut impulsive acts, and people whose personality has not grown very much past "the infantile character" show some clear-cut impulsive acts, as well, the impulsive acts we ordinarily talk about, though possessing infantile elements, include a vast amount of later development. They are more or less habitual acts. However, Sullivan claims that the manifestations of innate impulsive acts in the activities of the unstriped, involuntary muscles continue clear-cut much longer, and, particularly in those personalities that have encountered serious warp in the earlier stages of development, may persist conspicuously throughout life.

Consciously chosen activity is in general much more slow in "adjustive execution" than is the impulsive. Consciously chosen activity presupposes education, in the broad sense, and self-control and self-discipline. It is a much more recent evolutionary acquisition, and is a "field," a form of behavior, in which inefficient resolution of the total situation is most frequent. Man has come to live in the kind of environment in which impulsive acts have to give way to consciously chosen activity. Any combination of habits, conditioned motivations and what not, could not possibly enable one to deal with the complexities of a sociocultural environment. Intelligence, however inadequately or unwisely employed at times, is a condition of human survival and growth.

Actions and mental processes are not separate occurrences. They both constitute behavior in the broad sense—total activity.[9] For purposes of discussion and explication, it is necessary to separate them, so to speak.

Primitive mental processes represent an evolutionary very early form of something that occurs within the organism without "primary objectively observable features." This sort of mental process is inferred entirely from the course of events that it precedes—as in, say, the observation of infants and the interpretation of dreams. It can be experienced directly, though infrequently. In the Farewell Lectures Sullivan mentions, as an example, dreams in which "something like" a mystical, religious experience occurs. This is an early statement of what Sullivan eventually called the prototaxic mode of experience. In *Personal Psycopathology,* primitive mental processes are said to be the exclusive "mental content" of early infancy, being rarely experienced after early childhood. "Excepting for the occasional dream of cosmic participation, and some related semiwaking experiences of religious mystics, such a content seems to be the rule only in panic states and during the most profound schizophrenic disturbances."[10] Thus the later appearance in vivid awareness of implicit primitive processes is said to produce the impression of a vague but extremely important something like a transcendental experience, which is most difficult to relate to the self.

Revery or fantasy processes cover a broad scale between the primitive and the highest type of implicit process, called reality-controlled or externally controlled mental process. "At the 'lower' end of this broad band we find implicit processes barely distinguishable from the primitive; and at the 'upper' those all but fully adjustive."[11] Revery processes are "fantastic" rather than primitive because they manifest some evidence of the organism-reality disjunction that Sullivan at one time thought begins to be learned during the first hours or days of extrauterine life. In the really primitive processes, organism and environment are experienced as one; they lack "reality-experience" character, in which many distinctions between self and world have to be forged. Revery processes may be, and often are, profoundly nonrealistic or unrealistic but at the upper level they can be adjustive.

The third type of implicit process constitutes fully adjustive implicit processes that are "valid." This adjustive thinking pertains to features of the organism-environment complex that are perceived or conceived. In other words, adjustive thinking has to do with the perception and understanding of oneself, his relations in and within, his environment, and of various features of the world at large. Adjustive thinking includes "reduplicative memory" or "reintegration." Thus when a person encounters certain factors, there may be a rather prompt "reproduction" or recall of a situation in which such factors had previously been experienced.

Sullivan points out that from birth onward learning includes the accumulation of correct information about the world and about the self. The universe, he says, includes two kinds of information: "the personally valid and the consensually or interpersonally valid." The personally valid [an unhappy, ambiguous term] is that which has a unique relationship to oneself; it has distinctive "meaning-value" to *one's self.* For example, a particular dollar, because of its mint-date or some other characteristic, may have distinctive meaning, an *autistic* valuation, for an individual—and for no one else. The meaning-value does not inhere in the dollar, and can scarcely be communicated to another person.

The second kind of information is *consensually* validated information, which is the result of a conscious *eduction* of relations. Consensually valid information is derived and discriminated from multiple bases or sources of experience with other people and things.[12]

Because this now famous formulation of Sullivan has sometimes been misinterpreted, I wish to quote a fairly long statement about it.

> Thus, in scientific research, data are accumulated under the inspiration or direction of some particular notion that the worker has evolved; when these data have become fairly abundant, they are generally classified on the basis of some alleged characteristic that seems to be conspicuous throughout them; and the individual then attempts to deduce certain incipient relations. If he is relatively competent, having deduced a few of these, he tries to introduce some novel notion, and having introduced this, he

formulates a series of experiments with which to find whether it is correct or false. If it proves to be correct, he presumably has discovered a consensually or interpersonally valid insight into a body of data to which he has been "applying his mind"—with which he had been occupied in a total situation demanding an adjustment in and within similar situations.[13]

In later years Sullivan put great stress on the necessity of checking and counterchecking one's information with others as part of these conscious rational processes. Moreover he believed that there is much evidence in favor of the view that these conscious rational processes rest invariably on an extensive series of reverie processes. He surmised that the eduction of consensually valid information is the next step that occurs in some few fully adjustive reverie series, without which it could not have occurred. Hence, contrary to the usual interpretation of scientific method, he thought that the account of scientific research given above needs a very considerable revision before it becomes "really illuminating," because most of the mental work done by the scientist goes entirely unnoticed. The "logic" of inquiry includes much more than the logic of proof, or, in Sullivan's language, consensually validated information.

Another type of thinking that Sullivan mentions in the Farewell Lectures but does not discuss directly is creative thinking. No one seems to know much, if anything, about creative thinking, though a torrent of words on this subject has issued from various writers.

Primitive implicit processes seem to be hard to become acquainted with because they are quickly overlaid by "fantastic elaborations" due to the individual's experience. Fantasy is said to occupy, still, the greater part of the waking life of most individuals, and dreams and other phenomena not usually of the type of adjustive thinking occur a good part of the time during sleep. Despite the enormous "life-value" of adjustive thinking, most people do vastly more reverie than any other form of thinking.

One must bear in mind that life-experience and the individual personality begin in primitive processes the basis of which is sentience. In the course of time they evolve and become overlaid by a great development of impulsive acts and fantasy thinking. Impulsive act and fantasy thinking become "sprinkled over" by consciously chosen acts and adjustive implicit processes, that is, rational implicit processes.

Primitive and rudimentary revery processes continue throughout life to be evoked in total situations of great simplicity. Sullivan believed in 1930 that customary life situations require only the impulsive, habitual, and fantasy processes. The fact that "new" and complex total situations require the best that the individual has evolved in the way of consciously chosen activities, implicit and overt, and is not forthcoming, is one obvious antecedent to maladjustment and nonadjustment. In situations of maladjustment, the individual seems to be going about resolving them in a peculiarly cumbersome, energy-consuming, and inefficient fashion. When one engages in behavior and thought that have no useful effect in carrying out the processes of life, he is engaging in nonadjustive processes.

In harmony with the emphasis on total activity of an integrated personality in a relevant environment, Sullivan believed that the notion that mental life can be separated into distinct entities of the generic nature of thinking, feeling, and willing is erroneous. Hence the alleged separation of the thinking, the emotional, and the motor life in schizophrenia is misleading. To say that an experience ("anything lived, undergone, or the like") is *prevailingly* affective or cognitive or conative simply means that the most impressive feature of the experience to the observer, and generally to the subject, is in the specified realm.[14]

Sullivan could find no distinctive cognitive or affective features of mental life that could provide criteria of the presence of schizophrenia. "Schizophrenic thinking," he wrote, "shows in its symbols and processes nothing exterior to the gamut of ordinary thinking, including therein that of reverie and of dreams. Even its extra-ordinary symbol situations have parallels in the extravagances of dreams. Neither is its occurrence explicable on the basis of any novel cognitive processes. It is, as a whole, a peculiarly inadequate adaptation of the cognitive processes to the necessities of adult life: This can be analyzed into a characteristic dissociated condition and a reversive (regressive) change within the dissociated systems."[15]

In "Regression: A Considerationof Reversive Mental Processes," Sullivan gave a tentative formulation of regression that I summarized in part in the previous chapter. It is, he said, a process such that the thinking and behavior of the individual "return" to an earlier stage in his historic development, wherein there is at least temporary more or less complete functional loss of intervening acquisitions and developments. The standpoint or orientation from which the individual at some period or stage in the past was related to his environment is somehow reactivated. And all that he experienced and learned since then seems more or less completely obliterated. The reality of the present thus becomes "deformed" and rendered practically meaningless owing to the functional loss of much experience from which the present has ensued. Thus, a reorientation occurs by which the present is treated from the reactivated past standpoint. Regression seems to depend, for its occurrence, upon a certain dissociation of the mental organization.

An explication of the dynamics of dissociation and its relation to schizophrenia will have to be postponed. Invariably Sullivan discovered that schizophrenia culminated in a situation in which the sexual adequacy of the individual according to the standards ("ideals") that he had acquired was acutely unsatisfactory. More specifically the inadequacy pertains to the sexual act and to the securing of a cooperative love object. In Sullivan's case histories this inadequacy is revealed again and again with poignant intensity, though the inadequacy is apparently to a considerable degree an outcome of an unfortunate early life history that had gravely undermined any realistic possibility of emotional intimacy, especially with a member of the opposite sex.

Also, Sullivan observes, one must have regard to the peculiar facility with which more or less "frankly sexual symbols" are brought into relation (are linked up) with the individual's strivings or conative dispositions, which are otherwise susceptible of only the vaguest cognitive treatment (cognitive formulation), though these conative dispositions in themselves are but indirectly tributary to the sex impulses. In other words, these conative dispositions, which are related to the person's past history, may be manifested in thought by means of a "sexual paradigm," providing a language in terms of sexual symbols for disturbed adolescents. More simply put, adolescents who have suffered many distortions from infancy onward, at puberty are able to express many needs and tendencies only or chiefly in the language of sex. The inability of the adolescent, and especially the disturbed adolescent, to employ adequate adjustive (reality-controlled) thinking goes back to early life when the parents inculcated "a truly awe-inspiring collection" of magic words and concepts. And the culture provides many magical concepts and symbols regarding sexuality that parents have learned and employ in their education of the young.

In addition, "childish representations of people" that youngsters learn are of significance for psychiatrists since serious mental disorders and difficulties pertain chiefly to contact with others. What psychoanalysts call the Oedipus complex, for example, is prone to develop in "our type of society."[16]

Regarding the affective features of the mental life of schizophrenic patients, Sullivan claimed, on the basis of "crude observation" and detailed study of facial expression, that the alleged indifference, apathy, and emotional disharmony of those people are more a matter of impression than a correct evaluation of the patient's inner experience.[17] For instance, if a patient says he knows his throat is going to be cut and yet grins cheerfully in the telling, there appears to be a disharmony or incongruity between the affective expression and the content of thought. What Sullivan found was that there is disagreement between what the schizophrenic *thinks* and what he feels called on to say.[18]

It was in the *motivational* sphere that Sullivan gradually focused his interest. Schizophrenia was tentatively considered to be an evolution of the life process in which "some certain few motivations assume extraordinary importance to the grave detriment of adjustive effort on the part of the individual concerned."[19] This disturbance of adjustive effort is said to appear as an interference in the realm of social experience. The phrase "social experience" designates anything lived, undergone, or the like in a person's adjustive or maladjustive contact with at least one other person or with surrogates of persons. "It includes cognitive, affective, and conative phenomena pertaining to persons and groups and to animate or inanimate objects which for various reasons may have magical or religious relationship to the individual."[20] The phrase "social experience" also designates other aspects, including the subject's behavior in the social situation and the response of others to that behavior, as well as such factors as social motivations, tendencies or impulses, which give rise to the actions of the individual, and indirectly govern the content of his more passive or reactive experience.

Sullivan claimed that the problem of psychiatric prognosis is *the prediction of the future adaptability of an individual within some more or less clearly envisaged milieu composed principally of people.*[21] In reaching a prognosis the psychiatrist accumulates facts with regard to (1) the personality of the patient, (2) the morbid processes he is suffering from and their effects on his personality, and (3) the significant factors or variables in the social environment to which he may presently be returned.[22]

Sullivan's study of *onset* of disorder in male patients at Sheppard and Enoch Pratt Hospital seemed to reveal two generic factors preliminary to schizophrenic psychosis. The schizophrenic disorder made its appearance late in a long series of subjectively difficult adjustive efforts. But Sullivan was not successful in his attempts to discover and identify precisely the factors that cause milder maladjustive efforts to evolve or pass over into schizophrenia. In other words, if there are uniquely determining factors he could not discover them. Second, schizophrenia seemed never to occur in people who had even briefly achieved a definitely satisfying adjustment to a "sex object." But Sullivan did not think, even in 1927, that sexual motives and their distortions provide a central explanatory conception of mental disorder. His views on the role of sexuality in human life and the vexed problem of its causative connection with mental disorder will be elaborated in subsequent chapters.

He felt little reason to doubt that in general "cultural distortions" provided by the home are of prime importance. He said he had not seen maladjustment that was without the foundation of erroneous attitudes thrust upon the child by parents or their surrogates. All sorts of maladjustments were found in the history of patients who suffered the "grave psychosis" but "regardless of vicious influences subsequently encountered, the sufferer had acquired the tendency to such an illness while in the home situation. Interpersonal factors seem to be the effective elements in the psychiatry of schizophrenia."[23] For example, Sullivan wrote that an individual cannot develop normally in the formative years unless he shall have as the significant persons to whom he adjusts himself, wittingly and unwittingly, in infancy and childhood, people who are free from certain destructive attitudes and beliefs. The individual himself otherwise "will infallibly grow up a personality warped in the direction either of direct or of compensatory maladjustment to sexual considerations."[24]

So Sullivan came to believe that progress in the direction of practical understanding of the schizophrenic disorders in particular and toward the formulation of preventive and hygienic measures in general cannot occur until an extensive revision of prevailing conceptions is made toward an increased attention to social factors in human life.[25] From the earliest days there is a potent influence brought to bear upon the evolving organism through activity of the relevant adult environment. Therefore, since, among other things, the notion that the patient is a "victim of hereditary factors" will not withstand critical examination, everything favors the view that environmental influences have a tremendous role in determining the growth (and deviation) of human personality.

Schizophrenia gradually came to be conceived as a name for a large and variegated group of life processes manifesting (1) "a regressive preponderance" of fantasy that has replaced reality-controlled thought processes; (2) "a regressive preponderance of overt total activity of the type of irrational ritualistic and magical behavior"; and (3) "an underlying extraordinary preponderance of certain motivations "which normally get only occasional expression in life."[26] These three generic factors were illustrated in the summary of E. W.'s "case" in Chapter 1. This interpretation is said to direct investigation toward mental content, conscious and unwitting; toward a thorough investigation of activity of the total kind mentioned above; and toward exhaustive inquiry into methods of study of human motivation.

Sullivan searched for clues to the etiology of schizophrenia in the life history of the person. Gradually he constructed a theory of personality development and its "distortions." The significance of personality development for an understanding of the etiology of schizophrenia may be suggested by the following.

Infancy, or rather the emotional development that occurs during infancy, does not, of itself, as far as Sullivan could discover, provide any useful key to the evolutionary explanation of schizophrenia. All that one can say is that infantile maladjustments result in a fundamental warp of the personality and load its development heavily in favor of later disaster.

Nor does childhood, the era ushered in by the appearance of articulate speech, provide the key. It is true that, for example, in this epoch one discovers a group of abnormalities arising from incoherence in the sentiment-formation pertaining to the two parents and can trace from this certain grave personality developments, such as obsessional neurosis. In this era there appear infantile deviations now developed in the field of feeding disorders and speech disorders. Clear-cut beginning of psychopathic personality may be evident. Maladjusive dependence on various defense reactions may be inculcated. And, in general, one finds that childhood manifests much of the psychopathology of the adjustment to imposed authority, but little that is "directly illuminating" in the study of the development of schizophrenia.

According to Sullivan, one comes upon factors in abundance pointing toward the evolution of schizophrenic illnesses first in the juvenile era.[27] This phase of personality growth is said to be ushered in by the appearance of true socializing tendencies, manifested as strong motives making for adjustment in and within an environment of other juveniles. Powerful curative processes occur in this era against "malindividuation," which may have developed during childhood. But if some influence prohibits the fulfillment of the juvenile socializing tendencies, grave "warp" of personality of the kind that seems to be rather clearly related to the appearance of schizophrenia is said to ensue.

When family tradition, for example, dictates the exclusion of juvenile playmates, and requires the use of tutors, and the like, a satisfaction of the socializing tendencies by recourse to imaginary playmates and by other forms of highly organized fantasy occurs. But this does not provide an adequate foundation for the adjustment to other people, which will be subsequently required. Vicarious socialization, while better than nothing, is woefully inadequate. Sullivan claims that it makes for a great prolongation of "early adolescence," that is, preadolescence.

In the juvenile era, the sentiment of self is said to be evolved in one of several fairly distinguishable types from the continuum of previous experience to some measure of clear-cut differentiation of (1) things characterized by objective reality of the physical kind, (2) things characterized as purely personal subjective reality, and (3) things characterizable as socially valid.

Preadolescence (the "gang age") begins when impulses making for intimate adjustment with one or two other children of (about) the same age and the same sex appear. Sullivan believed the preadolescent phase begins when the youngster is eight or nine years of age, though it may be delayed. Such interpersonal adjustments may be made impossible by warp in the juvenile era. Sullivan surmised that when that happens hebephrenic deteriorating processes will follow the occurrence of schizophrenia, and that if any measure of true interpersonal adjustment is achieved in preadolescence, hebephrenic deteriorating processes occur, if at all, only after prolonged illness. During this era, motivation that makes for the development of true sentiments for others first appears. True sentiments, as contrasted with sentiments that are highly fantastic, "individualized," and unrealistic, are those that may be characterized by "a new degree of realistic approximation, consensual character and objectively effective influence over behavior and thinking."[28] In other words, one's thoughts, feelings, motives, attitudes, and overt behavior are more nearly governed by the nature and requirements of the real world, including other people. The individual now "so organizes his experience, real and fantastic, occurring in the total situation including the other person that the other person becomes signally important to him."[29] This is a way of saying that the capacity to love matures. Love does not mean lust or the sublimation of sensual desires or a bleached out derivative of some allegedly more basic drive, motive, or instinct. In preadolescence, intimate interpersonal adjustment with a member of the same sex is said to become the great problem of human life.[30] During this era sexual repression becomes clearly manifest (partly because this phase tends to overlap with true adolescence) as does the effect of social forces.

The transition to true adolescence occurs with, or shortly after, the appearance of frank sexual (genital) impulses. There evolves a "growing prepotency of the sexual impulses with consequent adjustive effort." A later phase of adolescence begins with the establishment of habitual sexual behavior. In subsequent years Sullivan also stressed the importance of a shift in the intimacy need, such that it begins to be necessary to get to know and respect a member of the other sex. In his studies of schizophrenia, he found that adolescence was a crucial period, as I have suggested in the previous chapter.

He claimed in 1929 that in every case of schizophrenic illness there is to be found in the history of the individual a point at which there had occurred what might be called a disaster to self-esteem.[31] Subjectively, such an occurrence is often attended by the experience of panic, a grave though temporary complete disorganization of personality, which customarily results from the utterly unexpected collapse of something very important in the life process of the individual.[32]

Of course, probably everyone now and then experiences some temporary loss of self-esteem. A frequent device that people resort to for mitigating the "unpleasantness" is to appeal in some more or less plausible manner to some principle, explanation, or interpretation with the aid of which one conceals from consciousness the true nature of the situation that confronted one, thus providing or restoring a comfortable appraisal of one's self—a stratagem traditionally called rationalization. But in a good many life situations, contrary to the person's assumptions, expectations, and implicit beliefs, the self of the individual proves inadequate for a stress to which he has subjected himself. Failure may be followed by panic. Should this state continue for any length of time, one has, it seems, taken the first great step toward schizophrenia. In fact, schizophrenic processes may follow immediately as the "resolution" of panic.

In "Schizophrenic Individuals as a Source of Data for Comparative Investigation of Personality," Sullivan wrote that, apparently, if one is sufficiently uncertain about life, one loses the cognitive assets that serve us in distinguishing products of autistic reverie from products that include important factors residing in so-called external reality.[33] To put this in more simple language, if one becomes sufficiently demoralized, one can no longer distinguish fact from fancy. And when one loses the cognitive assets that people ordinarily employ in order to separate subjective fantasy from reality, one begins to sink into mental processes significantly like those one experiences when he is asleep. When this happens, there is a partition of experience such that one is unable to distinguish what is true and "consensually acceptable" from what is purely personal fantasy. This dichotomy entails a "peculiar disorder" of social activity and even of nonsocial activity as well. According to Sullivan (in 1929) it is these pecularities that seem to constitute the essence of schizophrenic behavior.

In some situations panic is said to pass over into a chronic feeling of insecurity or inadequacy. "In these cases there has occurred a grave break in the solidarity or dependability of the frames of reference which the individual possessed concerning the synthesis or complex of his self and the world (especially other people)."[34] A vaguely formulated but clearly and poignantly felt uncertainty in the cosmos appears as a symptom of this failure. And one can no longer proceed with the same unthinking directness, once one's conviction of the goodness or meaningfulness of the world is undermined, toward the further elaboration of life experience. Sullivan says that a number of typical chronic maladjustments in interpersonal relations may be "referred to" such a break or failure. At least in the history of a schizophrenic there is always a collapse of that "cosmic security" derived, perhaps by every one, from a very early developmental period.

Sullivan also expressed the belief in "The Relation of Onset to Outcome in Schizophrenia" that the onset of schizophrenia can often be divided or distinguished into two stages. The collapse of the individual's "world synthesis" occurs in the first. There is a rapid loss of faith in the self and the universe. (But it is not "in any necessary close association" with the events that contribute to insidious illness.) A considerable number of people are said to experience the first step a considerable time before the psychosis appears. Normally, individuals reach a certain age possessed of a considerable body of assumptions about themselves and the rest of the world. Everyone depends on a large number of things—beliefs, convictions, expectations, attitudes—that he really is not always justified in depending on, but he has never had any cause to suspect their validity. Thus a great body of assumptions—which one begins to acquire in infancy—provides the foundation upon which the individual's life processes rest. Most people, perhaps, never modify these assumptions in any profound sense as long as life lasts—though the second half of the twentieth century seems less favorable than ever before toward the continued acceptance of unexamined ideas and beliefs. However, in the experience of a great number of adolescents there comes a time when their faith in a body of assumptions about their own abilities or about the consistency, meaningfulness, or goodness of the universe is shattered. These adolescents become terribly upset; yet they cannot fall back upon the stratagems and defense mechanisms that more normal people employ to heal the wounds they periodically suffer to their self-respect or to banish their misgivings about such things as, say, political or social progress, the reign of law and justice, the fundamental decency of people, and the like. These unfortunate adolescents are "different from what they were before"; they manifest various more or less severe maladjustments. Whether they then reach the second stage seems to depend largely or wholly on situational factors. At least some of them remain mired in the first stage for the rest of their lives. They suffer; but they do not become psychotic. A relatively fortunate few may obtain psychiatric assistance.

In the second stage, the individual progresses into a state in which the dissociated aspects of his personality are the effective integrating agencies. More precisely, he *alternates* between a condition of life to which he has been accustomed, that is, one that is under the domination or control of the egoistic structures (the self dynamism, in a subsequent formulation), and a state of being that is dominated by the dissociated systems that may be momentary or prolonged. This condition is called *incipient schizophrenia.* Should it continue, it becomes or evolves into *catatonic schizophrenia,* a state that may go on indefinitely.[35] But following upon "appropriate experience" at least three possible changes may be envisaged. A synthesis or integration of the self and the dissociated may begin, in which case the individual proceeds toward recovery. Second, there may occur a "massive transference of blame," in which case the individual progresses into a chronic *paranoid state.* Or, third, there may occur a dilapidation of the dissociating system (which is a function of the self), and regression of interest and impulses to the level of early childhood or infancy, that is, to a state of *hebephrenic dilapidation.*

Sullivan believed that a sudden, acute dramatic divorcement from more or less commonplace living is of good prognostic omen.[36] The sudden onset, he says, implies a personality that has grown farther toward adulthood than is the case with insidious illness. In other words, the acute onset signifies that one is dealing with a personality integration that has gone a long distance in spite of the dissociated (abhorrent) homosexual cravings or the "masturbation conflict" from which the schizophrenic illness has finally taken origin.

Sullivan's description of the masturbation conflict is rather complicated.[37] He wrote that in those boys who have grown past puberty without any direct contact with mutual genital interests one often finds a dissociation of some of the erotic tendencies, usually including the sexual. In these boys there is apt to be delayed pubescence and their personality warp is frequently of the type that culminates in homoerotic interests. An important factor in their deviation may have been primitive genital phobia. Or other factors may have contributed to their deviation, such as dissociation of the genital (phobic) or other erotic tendencies during late childhood or the juvenile era. It may happen that such a boy, as a juvenile, reported some sexually motivated behavior of an older boy or some vulgarism heard or seen around school, or some precocious experimentation, to one of his parents, who then reacted in such a fashion that the youth suffered so painfully that he excluded the "related interest" of his own from the self. Sullivan relates that as the sexual tensions increase there come nocturnal emissions with or without remembered dreams, and an involuntary reactivation and interest by the youth in data previously acquired and currently available as to sexual matters. He may take into consideration "trying masturbation to see what it is really like." He may harbor other conscious preoccupations with sexual topics. He may even enter into discussions of sex when they are started by another boy.

But on various pretexts he delays overt sexual behavior, displaying enough unwillingness to discourage opportunities "for mutual performances." When finally he starts autosexual behavior, he suffers much self-condemnation and exerts his "willpower" in an attempt to overcome the practice. Not only is he unsuccessful. Generally he has experiences in which he is remarkably free from conflict and self-condemnation in satisfying the sexual drive. Sullivan relates that in retrospect the youth is disconcerted at realizing how "depraved" he can be in states of sexual excitement. This may bring on great self-reproach, causing him to make extreme efforts to lift himself up from the degradation. He may seek help from the church or his family doctor. He may resort to Spartan habits of life. All to no avail apparently. So he often progresses into "a sad state," entailing numerous somatic and mental symptoms.

An insidious onset is of much graver prognostic omen because the growth of the personality has failed long before the hospital admission. Hence there is said to be relatively much less that is useful for a reintegration of anything like an average life situation. In this case there has been a gradual detachment from reality, occurring rather early in the development of personality, a detachment that follows "an ominous course" quite distinct from that of the more dramatic type.

The insidious onset does not arise out of an "excitating situation." Therefore the latter is "wholly irrelevant" to a consideration or study of patients who are insidiously "separated from reality" in schizophrenic illnesses.

A brief mention of the inner dynamics of schizophrenia may help to clarify this psychosis a bit more. Schizophrenia cannot occur unless there is a waking (in contrast to dreaming) dissociation of some one powerful tendency system of or in the self, say, the sexual motivation, by the drive for status. Sullivan claimed that "a continued dream-state," schizophrenia, cannot occur unless there is continued an approximation to a dynamic balance between the tendency (or motivational) system manifesting in the conscious self and the one dissociated from such manifestation.[38] Any event that destroys the balance of forces, of opposing tendency systems, either by enfeebling the *dissociating* system of the self or by strengthening the *dissociated* tendency system may result in schizophrenia, if there has been a chronic dissociation of a powerful motivational system in the personality. In this connection, physiological maturation (of the sexual apparatus which, given certain conditions of life experience, would strengthen the dissociated system) and toxic-exhaustive states (which again under certain conditions would significantly enfeeble the power of the dissociating system of the self) are mentioned as frequent factors.[39] It will be obvious, I think, that the psychiatrist's efforts will be directed toward measures that strengthen the self and, given certain favorable conditions, enfeeble the pressure of the dissociated tendencies, or eradicate the pressure by assisting the patient to become conscious of his dissociated drives in such a fashion that they are assimilated to, or integrated into, the self, thus making it possible for him to engage in more healthy interpersonal relations. In any case, Sullivan believed that the restoration of balance in favor of the dissociating system of the self-conscious personality is achieved by some adjustment of interpersonal relations.

It is clear that dissociated processes constitute one set of significant conditions that, under certain circumstances, bring about, or eventuate in, the onset of schizophrenic states. And one may wonder what these dissociated factors are. Sullivan is frequently not as direct and explicit as one would wish. In general terms, his view is that they have to do with powerful motivational tendencies that are *abhorrent* to the self-conscious personality. Specifically, it appears that "homosexual cravings" or powerful homosexual tendencies, which many persons who entertain them regard as loathsome, abhorrent, and the like, were frequently the dissociated factors. This does not mean that they will be found universally to be *the* tendencies in dissociation. It appears that traumatic heterosexual experiences can be dissociated and serve a similar role perhaps especially in women. In another type of society some other group of experiences and behavior patterns might be regarded as abhorrent. Perhaps it is safe to speculate that whenever any group of personal tendencies, for either cultural or individual "reasons," constitutes a potential disaster to self-esteem, to the realization of personal worth and security, it can serve a function analagous to abhorrent homosexual cravings. This idea is, I think, directly implied by Sullivan.

In any event, Sullivan found that homosexual manifestations were apparently conspicuous among incipient and catatonic male schizophrenics.[40] But he warned that it is unsafe to think loosely of homosexuality. He rejected the Freudian conception that *all* human beings are by nature *bisexual,* and that in normal human beings the homosexual aspect is unconscious. Since there is still a good deal of loose thinking about homosexuality, it seems advisable to relate Sullivan's conception of it. The actual appearance of a homosexual type of behavior in certain individuals (frequently those who have "oral erotic" personalities) is the direct outcome of personality deviations that have their nucleus in abnormal attitudes and beliefs cultivated in the parent-child relationship combining with later extrafamilial experiences. In the absence of certain personality deviations (such as those referred to in which the oral zone continues to chronological adulthood as the zone prepotently gratifying in the individual's relations with the human environment), no amount of homosexual experience will fix a homosexual *modus vivendi.* It is a well-known fact, that, for instance, some men who are perforce cut off from the society of women carry on sexual relations with members of their own sex, but, when females are again available, revert to a heterosexual way of life. Sullivan claims that when, and only when, behavior and thinking are motivated by impulses more or less specifically sexual in nature and tend to be carried out in situations including another person of the same sex, the homosexual designation properly applies. In such instances the individual is not cut off from the society of females by external restraints, such as prison, isolated military stations, and the like. Under Sullivan's formulation, he says, so much of a person's life is homosexual as consists of fantasy, thoughts, and witting and unwitting behavior directed toward the securing of more or less obviously sexual satisfaction from an individual of the same sex.[41] He did not conceive of homosexuality as "a static entity" characterized by a degree of frank sexual activity with members of one's own sex. Thus, he claimed one readily finds a distribution among individuals that amounts to a continuous gradation between what might be described as the ideal pole of purely homosexual personality and the equally ideal pole of purely heterosexual personality.[42]

Even though Sullivan did not subscribe to Freud's notion of a universal bisexuality in human beings, nevertheless he for a while adopted from Freudian psychoanalysis the notion, which seemed to be reinforced by his experiences with schizophrenic patients, that adolescents go through a homosexual phase in the evolution of personality beginning in the "gang age." Furthermore, he believed that under certain circumstances homosexual activities of a "frank sort," when engaged in during the period of personality growth he subsequently called preadolescence, contribute to the growth of personality. He thought that such activities have a beneficial effect in bringing "conceptualization and fantasy of a sexual nature within the frame of real criteria." Thus many youths would acquire a more realistic grasp of the possibilities and consequences of sexual behavior. However, certain indivduals possess ideals, acquired in the home, that render any sexual activity unholy or sinful while their character is so organized that they do not "dissociate" these ideals rather completely from *unconsciously* determined behavior and thought. In such instances any sexual activity, or persistent sexual fantasy, may bring about depreciation of self-esteem and resulting psychopathological phenomena that are liable to grave consequences. Secondly, certain persons have ideals that dictate that only some particular form of sexual gratification is the accessible (permissible) one, and lack any real regard for the methods of attaining the approved goal or for adjusting to compromises in this connection.

Sullivan hypothesized two poles of moral behavior, one at which the ideals ("superego processes") are childish or interfamilial in type rather than socialized and very powerful; and the other at which ideals are very highly evolved, fully socialized, and of a fully "rationalistic," realistic type, and as powerful as those at the other pole. The average among schizophrenics is said to approach the first type of moral ideals, while the average among the frank homosexuals tends slightly toward the second. Again, the average among psychoneurotics is said to tend noticeably toward the first pole, in contrast to the average among normal adults who tend noticeably toward the second pole.

Sullivan believed that attitudes about sexual activity are especially significant, since schizophrenics become "sick" because their self-esteem has sunk to a very low ebb. This is related to the fact that the self-esteem on which most adolescents depend for mental security must survive the eruption of the sexual impulses with resulting resymbolization of ideals and purposes. Apparently those who become schizophrenic are unable to accomplish this resymbolization (rationalization, compensation, substitution, etc.). Their thinking and their attitudes about sexual activity (and especially about homosexual experience), and about other phenomena of life as well, are immature or downright "primitive" (infantile). For example, Sullivan wrote that he discovered in certain cases a group of manifestations clearly pointing to the inculcation of *primitive genital phobia*, an "ideal formation" derived from infantile experience that can be abstractly formulated as a powerful feeling of terror about manipulation of the genitals. This type of phobia is a product of the empathic linkage that existed between the significant parent and the offspring. Such an occurrence is an illustration of how deeply unconscious motivations are gradually built up in the infantile mind by direct "emotional contagion."[43]

So Sullivan advocated "sex reform" in institutionalized attitudes and beliefs that individuals learn in the early stages of personality development. It is not at all clear how extensive this reform should be, in Sullivan's writings, or what precise direction it should take. Since such a reform would perhaps directly affect the family, it immediately raises very profound and far-reaching problems of family life, institutional arrangements generally, and very difficult problems of general (in contrast to merely sexual) morality. While no sane person would advocate irrational attitudes about sexuality, such a powerful force in human life cannot be divorced from other aspects of personality. In short, sexual reform raises many grave issues of a psychological, social, and moral character.

Sullivan eventually abandoned the notion that young people go through a homosexual stage. Homosexuality is incidental to distortions of personality acquired from early life onward.

Since self-esteem, or damage to self-esteem, with the attendant partial or, in extreme cases, more or less total demoralization of the individual is so significant not only for understanding schizophrenia but various other sorts of mental disorders and difficulties, Sullivan turned his attention to the study of its evolution and characteristics, and to the investigation of "correlated types of events" that can result in the disintegrations of personal security. There is, he claimed, within the personality, a system of experience that one may call the ego or self. The self is developed from, or made up of, the factors in which *significant* other people respond to him. "In other words, our self is made up of the reflections of our personality that we have encountered mirrored in those with whom we deal."[44] It is important to note that the people we "encounter" are those who are significant to us from infancy onward to maturity, and, though perhaps to a lesser degree, throughout life. Significant people are those to whom we are related in some meaningful fashion, whether positively or negatively. In subsequent years Sullivan elaborated his theory of the self, which he then, as a general rule, labeled the "self dynamism." It seems to have many similarities to Mead's, though it is very doubtful if Sullivan at this time knew Mead's work at first hand. Mead has formulated the self as follows:

> The individual experiences himself as such, not directly, but only indirectly, from the particular standpoints of other individual members of the same social group or from the generalized standpoint of the social group as a whole to which he belongs. For he enters his own experience as a self or individual, not directly or immediately, not by becoming a subject to himself, but only insofar as he first becomes an object to himself just as other individuals are objects to him or are in his experiences; and he becomes an object to himself only by taking the attitudes of other individuals towards himself within a social environment or context of experience and behavior in which both he and they are involved.[45]

Personality is to a "great extent" a product of culture. In other words, personality, according to Sullivan, is chiefly composed of experience with people and with the traditions, customs, and fashions produced by people. "In the first months of extrauterine life, . . . the infant will learn a great deal of the most pervading culture of the parents, particularly the mother. In the first three or four years, he will have acquired so much of this that he is apt to be from thence on a 'typical American,' or an 'Italian,' or an 'East Side boy' or whatever."[46] The part of the cultural heritage that has been "built into him" during the first three or four years is said to be of a primitive and infantile character, which is not likely ever to be the subject of rational deliberation. (Sullivan also claimed that the infant is born with a great many potentialities, most of which he will never have opportunity to develop.)[47] Some of this has "high emotional value." The parents or their equivalents have transmitted it with much expressed and "empathized" feeling. (By empathy Sullivan means "an emotional linkage existing between the mother and infant" such that certain feelings are "communicated" to the latter in some very obscure fashion.)[48] Later cultural acquisitions—for instance, those acquired in the school or playground—are susceptible to more or less conscious consideration and of some degree of valuational appraisal. These later acquisitions are not nearly in so fixed and final a form within personality as are those of infancy and early childhood. Nor are they of "such extreme import" as are the earlier ones. School and playground experience can be reorganized more easily during later phases of development. These matters will be further clarified and elaborated in subsequent chapters.

The most primitive and perhaps most important part of the self is "contributed" by the mother and/or her surrogates. Very important and complementary "parts" are said to be contributed by the father and/or his equivalents. Insofar as the "parts" contributed by the parents remain infantile in character, they are, according to Sullivan, extremely inaccessible and resistant to change. When they are "too far removed from resemblance to later accretion to the self," when, in other words, they are so incongruous with subsequent experience that they cannot provide a solid basis for personality development, the growth of the personality will be severely distorted and the individual may have the type of organization called psychopathic personality. Sullivan says that if the deviations of growth are less severe, they may take, in boys, the form of a continuing rather childish or juvenile appraisal of the self as it is reflected by the mother. And it is very difficult to wean such people from an attitude of unique dependency on the mother. Usually they have incorporated her value attitudes. "A progression of values," Sullivan says, "to a proper placement of girls as objects of interest does not occur," normally at adolescence.[49] It may be that the mother only, of all women, is eligible or attractive for interpersonal intimacy; it may be only older women who are elgible. Such a boy cannot progress smoothly "to the biologically ordained heterosexual goal."[50] When he reaches the preadolescent period ("the time of outcropping of the need for close interpersonal relations") he may be unable to integrate interpersonal relations with other boys, a development that is required for a normal "gang life."

However, some morbid youths who are likely to suffer a schizophrenic illness may often succeed measurably in the preadolescent socialization, and may achieve great intimacy with another youth. Even so, quite frequently such youths achieve only a mediocre degree of preadolescent socialization. But it is in the next stage, the progression to heterosexual activity, that handicaps in the development of personality appear most restrictively. Morbid ("warped") youths to whom schizophrenic illnesses are likely to occur begin to have serious troubles after the coming of frank genital sexuality. If they have succeeded in establishing good status with their peers, they are now, at adolescence, required, if only by "dint of social pressure," to become interested in girls. But their personality organization precludes the development of interest in girls. As a result their status is imperiled. Being thereby compelled to do something to preserve their self-respect, they have to adopt an extensive subterfuge, Sullivan observes, of the nature of a fictitious sexual life; they have to separate themselves from the general gang and continue nonheterosexual social relations with other youths similarly handicapped, with the result that, because of the increasing pressure of sexual drives, they are apt quickly to assume an homosexual way of life; or they have to "get out of it all," that is, give up any efforts at intimacy with people of their own age group, and regress toward an earlier type of interpersonal living, wherein they resort to a new dependence on the parental and related adult environment.

All schizophrenics seem to belong in the group of people who cannot progress toward a satisfactory sex life. As I have already said, in many instances of schizophrenia Sullivan found that it had "finally taken origin" from dissociated homosexual cravings, that is, upon the eruption into awareness of intense desires to engage in homosexual performances that the person regarded as abhorrent. So he concluded that in "peace times" no one becomes schizophrenic who has achieved a really satisfactory integration with another person of relationship primarily sexual in motivation. Thus, during adolescence, in the ensuing satisfaction of the sexual impulses, he thought that the individual makes a long step toward adulthood and achieves a great measure of safety from the sort of processes that eventuate in schizophrenic illness. Such an individual has "convincingly demonstrated to himself his competence at the 'technics' of interpersonal intimacy necessary for comparative mental health."[51] In all likelihood, Sullivan claims, he will be able to deal with most of the problems that life brings him with adequate self-respect.

When a warp of the personality of the sort previously discussed occurs, and the progress of adolescence includes a severe rebuff in, or, a traumatic experience connected with, interpersonal relations, there is likely to be an "outcropping" of schizophrenic processes. Sullivan held that if the personality is rather well developed in fields other than those making for sexual intimacies of the fully adjustive or equal status kind, it will be rather abrupt and acute in type; and that, on the other hand, if there has been grave warping, such, for instance, that the boy has retired from the realities of interpersonal relations to the juvenile world of "authoritarian" adults, then the schizophrenic processes are apt to appear insidiously and an acute outcropping of psychosis is not seen.

Even after the schizophrenic processes are clearly in evidence, there is said to be *continued striving for self-respect, for status reflecting to the self from other significant people.* The struggle for status goes on in incipient and catatonic schizophrenia. Sullivan believed that the course of the illness is largely a product of the personal relations into which the patient enters voluntarily or in which he is compelled to participate. The patient "recovers if the schizophrenic processes lead to a repair of the personality warp, an escape from the old deviations toward a more normal evolution. If he is of a certain history, or if the persons dealing with him particularly facilitate such a development, the true schizophrenic illness progresses into a paranoid state, in which only so much of schizophrenic processes continues to be in evidence as deal with those drives of the patient that he cannot project by transference of blame. If there is nothing to which his bizarre interpersonal processes seem to attach, or if he is brutally discouraged by those who have come to be significant to him and yet cannot discharge the situation by exteriorizing blame on them, then a profound regression of interest takes place, and he becomes preoccupied with early childhood or late infantile activity-patterns and we call him hebephrenic."[52]

This outline of Sullivan's theory of schizophrenic processes offers only a preliminary statement of his theory of schizophrenia, which I will elaborate subsequently. As I have already indicated, he had also begun to create a theory of personality and of interpersonal relations, which he expanded over a period of twenty years. At the same time he worked toward the creation of a general theory of functional mental illness, and of more specific theories of various mental illnesses—a task he did not have an opportunity to carry very far. Since he was dissatisfied with almost every phase of psychiatry as it existed thirty-five to forty years ago, he tried to reformulate its philosophical assumptions, its methods of inquiry, and its therapeutic technique. In the remaining part of this chapter, I will summarize his ideas on the philosophy of psychiatry, its mode of investigation, and what he considered to be the most fruitful therapeutic technique.

The first point I will take up is Sullivan's philosophical orientation in psychiatry as he formulated it around 1933. He claimed that mental disorders are always defined by reference to an implicit or explicit formulation of personality that sets limits to the manifestations of human individuality.[53] Behavior that deviates from the norm in a given social group is regarded as aberrant and, depending on a "large number of secondary definitions" (evaluations) that "fix" one's relations with his fellows in the group, is considered genius or crime or mental disorder.

The significance of this orientation may be made clearer by contrast with various other conceptions of mental disorder. Sullivan mentions "prenaturalistic" views of human personality that consider mental disorders as the results of manifestations of the "victim" by transcendental agencies, as in the instance of belief in demoniacal possession. He classified naturalistic interpretations into, first, naïve mechanistic doctrines, such as "those which regard mental disorders as the results of medical diseases and attribute them to lesions in the nervous system, the endocrine glands or in other organs of the body."[54] He mentions also, under the naturalistic classification, "the more sophisticated biological doctrines which conceive mental disorders as more or less rigidly determined by the person's genetic constitution or by his environment or by a combination of the two."[55] In these categories, he says, belong most psychological theories of mental disorder, including conditioned response behaviorism, the psychoanalytical doctrine of libido fixation, and other dynamic explanations. Finally, there is the anthropological interpretation that regards mental disorder as the result of unduly complicated interpersonal relations arising from innately conditioned but culturally directed tendency systems. The latter is Sullivan's conception.

He conceived the person as the "resultant" or outcome of physiological, psychobiological, and situational factors.[56] Among physiological factors are listed native endowment, the interplay of nutrition and needs, and disease and injury. Psychobiological factors are said to comprise the evolution of differentiated (individuated) personality, acculturation or education in a broad sense in successive epochs of personality growth; inhibitions and facilitations historically effective (in the development of the person) and manifesting themselves in the present in conflicts of motivations; characterizing drives, energy partition in activities (that is, the amount of energy distributed among or available for one's various activities); sensitivity to events; ease of personal contacts; speech and gesture, including emotional expression. In regard to situational factors, Sullivan says they include the actual interpersonal opportunities and handicaps, which in turn reflect the interplay of culture and its participants, the changing institutional setting of life, and the abundance or restriction of opportunity for new experience.

Mental health, which, according to Sullivan, is meaningful only when it refers to interpersonal adjustment, is that equilibrium or balance among those various factors already mentioned that permits "a positive progression," a progressive and dynamic adaptation to life, in terms of the total situations through which the individual lives. Mental disorder can result from factors in any or all of the categories I have mentioned. Sullivan points out that defective endowment can limit or arrest growth of personality or bring on premature senescence, that defective nutrition may halt development or lead to recessive changes, that disease may disable the organism. In regard to psychobiological factors making for mental disorder, they arise from specific warping experiences bearing upon the person at any time from birth onward. These warping influences may bring about such imbalance or disequilibrium of growth by experience that unfortunate motivation may develop. Explicit and implicit interpersonal relations may cause lack of self-esteem, dissatisfaction with life, chronic anxiety, or persistent fatigue and inertia; these may manifest themselves objectively in symptoms of mental disorder. As for the situational factors, they are said to be involved most simply in the case of defectively endowed individuals subjected to excessive demands and of superior individuals subjected to privation. Sullivan says situational factors are present more objectively in instances in which the adolescent finds himself incapacitated for the demanded adjustive growth because of powerful inhibitions incorporated in him beyond his remedy. Mental disorders arising from situational factors appear to be few as long as the "cultural configuration" of a group is relatively static and the young do not leave its area. However, Sullivan believed that in the contemporary scene (1934), particularly in the case of those who come from remote parts to the great urban centers or who undergo abrupt change of social status, the consequences of personality warp and the new situational factors may be "disastrous." In addition, problems of adjustment of both heterosexual and homosexual motivations assume singular importance for psychiatry because of factors in the "culture complex."

Since some of the problems with which the psychiatrist deals arise primarily from the difficulties of gifted individuals in an unsuitable milieu—problems that are sometimes insoluble because of conditions inhering in the contemporary social and economic organization; and since it is often impossible to correct personality warp in the less gifted because there is nothing attractive to offer the sufferer, the psychiatrist primarily concerned with needless wastage of human ability "cannot but envisage a changed social order under which these problems will no longer exist."[57]

I do not think that Sullivan had any clear idea as to what kind of social order would circumvent the wastage of human abilities. (In any event he explicitly rejected totalitarianism of any kind in the lectures, which have been published in *Conceptions of Modern Psychiatry*.) In the meantime, the psychiatrist and his patients are limited in their efforts by the status quo.

Despite the numerous formidable obstacles enumerated above, Sullivan held that many disordrers can be remedied by competent psychiatrists, though the process of therapy is difficult and the costs are often prohibitive. The two most effective techniques, he thought, were psychoanalysis and his own variant of it, in the treatment of functional mental illness.

Over the years Sullivan was extremely critical of the various psychiatric orientations of many of his colleagues. He condemned those psychiatrists who wrote of psychiatry as a branch of brain physiology. He seemed to think that such "materialistic twaddle" and succeeding mechanistic explanations were the outcome of efforts to eliminate *mind*, no more helpful, perhaps, than Watsonian behaviorism or "spook research" varieties of psychology. The old doctrines of mind-body antitheses had led to new superstitions. Thus many psychiatrists were either "physicians of the soul," lamentably detached from biological viewpoints, or they were "hell on focal infections" or "cortical degenerations" or "endocrine failures," and the like.

Turning to the methodology of psychiatric research, Sullivan found the situation not encouraging. He quoted the experimental psychologist Knight Dunlop to the effect that in planning ("designing" is the fashionable term at the moment) an investigation the most frequent mistake into which experimenters fall is making the scope of the problem too wide, to include too many problems. In some instances, this scattering of labor results from lack of grasp on the real problems involved. Then the fundamental small problems that ought to be investigated cannot be determined with clarity. There is the additional fact that the lengthy and copious working out of a small problem is extremely tedious, "and nobody," Dunlop says, "likes tedious work. The covering of a large topic superficially is much more thrilling."[58]

That, according to Sullivan, expresses the most regrettable truth about much would-be research in psychiatry, as he observed it a generation ago. Large topics are said to have been covered most superficially and thrilling "discoveries" and reports made. "So huge a field as that of the schizophrenic is charged across by our enthusiasts, and 'retreat into narcism,' 'regression to archaic unconscious,' 'dilapidation of the gonads,' 'disorder of the basal ganglia' or what-not of bushwa is 'discovered' as etiology."[59] Then the enthusiast can see nothing but evidence of his correctness. His disciples, who rediscover and rediscover his genius, amass "evidence" in support of the enthusiast's theory. In general, there is no real evidence for such speculations. Here and there you find merely an occasional uncontrolled observation as cornerstones for huge arches of speculation. Take, for instance, C. G. Jung's concept of the archaic (collective) unconscious. Sullivan claimed that the so-called facts on which it is based were culled in the library by dilettantes from the garbled accounts of untrained and prejudiced missionaries "who had about the same contact with primitive culture that the writer has with equine conceptualization."[60]

Unwarranted generalization, which in the more restricted sense means passing from a few particular instances to universals, is a prime evil of psychiatric research. It is the "most vulnerable weakness" of psychoanalysis. "Once a proposition has been universalized, the observation of negative instances dies a natural death."[61] Sullivan asserted that, then, because of our native reasoning ability, relations spring up, correlates are taken for granted, new and ever-extending propositions grow like fungal hyphae and we have a plausible "system," ever ready, like the astronomy of Ptolemy, to receive a new crank to "explain" a stubborn fact that intrudes itself. In psychiatry, where misinterpretations can be disastrous, *ad hoc* propositions are pernicious.

Observation is said to be the touchstone of psychiatric research. Sullivan believed that pure research would probably be observation under rigid and carefully controlled conditions susceptible of ready duplication by another. In psychiatry such conditions are impossible of realization since, for example, no human being is ever quite the same on a series of occasions. And no schizophrenic "is apt to respond in even approximately similar a way to a series of observers."[62] So it requires rather uncommon gifts on the part of an observer who arranges the setting of observational situations, and rather unusual facilities for his work. Fortunately Sullivan was able to approximate those conditions in the special ward he was able to set up at Sheppard and Enoch Pratt Hospital, with spectacular results by him and his successor, Dr. William V. Silverberg.

Regardless of their therapeutic usefulness, many of the conceptions of Freud and other psychoanalysts, for example, are not true scientific hypotheses. Sullivan held that the utility of a conception may be said to hinge on its providing a ground for successful *prediction* of events and for the construction of crucial experiments. "Its plausibility of application to facts of observation already at hand is not a scientific sanction if the hypothesis cannot be *tested*. The therapeutic 'test' is no test at all; witness chiropractic and Eddyism."[63]

Another, and still greater, difficulty facing the psychiatric researcher inheres in the nature of the subject matter, namely, human thought and behavior. A vital part of observation in psychology and psychopathology is experiential report. This pertains to the subject's statements of what he thought, felt, wished, intended. Not only is such a report liable to direct "complications and interferences" (such as defensive stratagems and inhibitions) but it introduces a "great variable" in the form of speech. Words do not have inherent, objective meaning universally applied by everyone. No word in common use can be depended on to mean or communicate precisely what it means to a particular person who uses it. A teacher, for example, no matter how alert he may be to the ambiguities of everyday speech and to the difficulties of communication, may often be startled when he learns what his students "heard" him say. When it comes to reporting subjective situations (what one thinks, perceives, feels, intends, etc.) that are important to the narrator's self-esteem, or to reporting situations for some other reason definitely tinged with emotional experience, verbal reports *"are but mediately available as scientific data."*[64] In such instances, Sullivan said, there must be rather elaborate contexts that include not only verbal report, but, if possible, also extensive data about the situation and (mental) state of the subject, his relations, real or fancied, to the observer and others.

For many years Sullivan was preoccupied with the difficulties pertaining to communication in human relations, and he made substantial contributions toward a better understanding of those difficulties.

Finally, among the problems and difficulties facing the psychiatric researcher, is the factor of previous experience. Previous experience, or the effects of previous experience, have to be taken into account as a fundamental characteristic of the living. Indeed it would hardly be an exaggeration to say that one's history enters into every moment of the individual's life. Mental disorder, and the individual "phenomena" of mental disorder, are said to have, as an essential, contributions from certain past experiences. Objective, detailed observations and the subject's reported experience at the time are necessary, but they are not sufficient. On this issue Sullivan differs radically from such psychologists as Kurt Lewin and Gardner Murphy, who neglect the fact that man's nature is historical. One must discover as completely as possible the genetic background, the cogent material of the subject's life experience *"as experienced,"* that is, what he *actually* felt, perceived, lived or underwent.[65] For this purpose free-associational investigation helps to correct and expand data ordinarily secured in history-taking. In this connection, one must carefully avoid suggestions, gratuitous interpretations, leading quesions, and the like. Moreover, the physician, in the end, must accurately arrange the genetic data so that it represents the "true life-series."

Sullivan believed that the common field of research and clinical psychiatry is to be found in the observation of patients. Though he thought that experimental techniques (involving observation under "rigid" and carefully arranged conditions), which are a commonplace in the study of animal behavior, had to be ruled out, he also thought that "the arranging of several crucial experiments" would be possible if an "enlightened social background" permitted it. Just what sort of experiments Sullivan had in mind is not specified. One suspects he had in mind a modification and elaboration of the Special Ward set-up at Sheppard and Enoch Pratt Hospital. In any case, he concluded (in 1927) that research psychopathology must depend for its greatest aid on ever more nearly perfect observation of human thought and behavior.

Observation of patients is itself a difficult affair, requiring rigorous "criteria" and specifiable general rules of interview technique. For example, negative instances must never be ignored. Precocious interpretation and explanation must be carefully avoided. The patient must be allowed to talk without needless interruptions. The psychiatrist must give close attention to what can be seen and heard. "The ideal interview is one in which the physician offers only the orienting questions to cover the most recent activities of the patient, mention of the particular topics on which he desires the patient to talk, and such provocative interjections as 'and—,' 'and then,' 'continue,' 'which seems to mean what,' and the like. With comparatively inaccessible schizophrenics it is often possible to obtain two or three thousand words in an hour without supplying the patient with anything of 'explanation' or 'interpretation.' In favorable cases it has been possible to secure about as complete a record as that secured by the psychoanalysis of a psychoneurotic from quite paranoid schizophrenics without offering them any interpretation or explanation whatsoever. Needless to say, the impression had been given in these cases that frank discussion would do no harm and would probably accomplish much good. It seems scarcely necessary to invite your attention to the fact that frank discussion does do good by bringing the genetic background and the subconscious motivation of the patient's peculiar thoughts and behavior into the region of his logical consideration and volition."[66] Not least in importance is the necessity to put as much value on the "little details of life" as on the larger issues if one is to elaborate anything even crudely approximating a situation of sympathy.

Of course, Sullivan's techniques with psychoneurotics were more flexible, much more elaborated, much more systematic. These matters will be expounded in Chatper 5.

In Chapter 1 techniques and strategies of therapy with schizophrenics was portrayed in summary outline. No one knew better than Sullivan how quickly all the skill and effort of the psychiatrist could be undone when the patient returned or was returned to an unfavorable environment, usually a "morbific" familial environment. So he looked forward to the day—which so far has never arrived—when convalescent camps and communities might be established for those still more or less seriously ill patients on their way to a potentially full recovery after their stay in the hospital had brought them to some measure of insight and personal security.

Thus far I have merely brushed Sullivan's elaborate variant of psychoanalysis. In the remaining part of this chapter I shall summarize his formulations of Freud's procedures, which he refined and supplemented over the years.

Sullivan claims that the meaning of the free-associational material, the formulations that the psychoanalyst can offer to assist the patient, in the last analysis come entirely from the interpersonal relationship in which the physician participates and which permits the patient to integrate with him. "There is nothing else in the activity of man that approximates the complexity and subtlety of the psychoanalytic situation. No one can know all about this type of relationship as it exists today, and it is unthinkable that anyone can delineate the psychoanalytic situations that will be integrated with people in the future. Culture grows and the human personality is an expanding series. Techniques of therapy must grow in the same manner."[67]

Since some readers may not be familiar with the psychoanalytic process, it seems advisable to summarize those features of it that Sullivan incorporated in his own studies and modified as his knowledge of people, and especially the mentally ill, increased over the years. In Chapter 5 I will explicate his modified psychoanalytic technique. He distinguished three categories of the psychoanalytic "method." The first category pertains to processes of free association, which were briefly discussed in Chapter 1. In free association, the patient more or less freely, uninhibitedly, verbalizes the reverie processes that appear in the psychoanalytic therapeutic situation. He is encouraged to verbalize whatever comes to mind, no matter how nonsensical, or shameful, or irrelevant his "thoughts" may seem to him. In this fashion the patient is gradually led along the path of association to deeply buried and "forgotten" past experiences, which then in the course of therapy become conscious. Such a procedure is by no means as easy as it sounds, because very frequently the patient's internal misgivings, doubts, anxieties, and the like interfere with his efforts at a free flow of reverie. So, unless the therapist is sufficiently skillful, the patient may engage indefinitely in a kind of pseudo-free-association, wherein he verbalizes anything but what he actually feels, thinks, or imagines. Because free association tends inevitably to lead to the uncovering of painful conflicts and anxieties, the patient often unwittingly resists any approach to a conscious awareness of them, so that the free flow of the associational stream is halted or superficialized. In other words, he tends to resist an expansion of clear awareness of self.

This latter consideration takes us to the second category of psychoanalytic processes, namely, *timely interpretation.* The psychoanalyst "must offer timely interpretations because otherwise the stream of reverie processes remains superficial, and the reconstruction of the personality and the obliteration of maladjustive processes cannot be accomplished."[68] Wise and timely interventions or interpretations are required to influence the associational stream in order to circumvent the various defensive stratagems of the patient and to help clarify obscure phenomena that are appearing in the life of the patient both in and out of therapy. Of course this is an enormously detailed and frequently complex and subtle process and one that cannot be described briefly.

The third category that Sullivan distinguishes is transference, which he eventually expanded and reformulated in terms of parataxic (illusory) me-you patterns. According to the classical psychoanalytical interpretation, in transference the patient unconsciously attributes to the analyst variously acquired feelings and attitudes, both positive and negative, which he had observed or experienced in his dealings with people, especially his parents, in the course of his upbringing. In other words, the analyst ideally is a mirror reflecting back the patient's own unconscious attitudes, feelings, motives, and so forth. This becomes revealed through the process of free association. Aided by suitable interpretation by the analyst, the patient gradually becomes conscious of these unconscious forces, which have hitherto so largely dominated his life and bedeviled him with various inexplicable conflicts, anxieties, and symptoms. Transference phenomena constitute one of the great psychological discoveries; yet Freud's formulation is defective because he looked upon it as largely a one-way process. Sullivan interpreted transference as an interactional process. Although Freud was aware that transference entails an interactional phase in "countertransference" and is not solely confined to psychoanalytic therapeutic situations, he did not carry these insights far. Sullivan reinterpreted transference in a fashion that I will explicate in Chapter 5. Summarily, he wrote: "By transference the patient manifests interpersonal processes that open the gates of memory sealed by dissociations, reorients his experience, and facilitates the development of arrested or distorted systems of motives so that he moves forward toward the conditions of adult personality organization."[69] The meaning of this statement can perhaps only be understood from an explication of the *personal interview*.

Notes

1. HARRY STACK SULLIVAN, "The Oral Complex," *Psychoanalytic Review*, 12:31-38, 1925.

2. HARRY STACK SULLIVAN, *Farewell Lectures*, Lecture I.

3. WILBERT JAMES MCKEACHIE and CHARLOTTE LACKNER DOYLE, *Psychology* (Reading, Massachusetts: Addison-Wesley Publishing Company, 1966), p. 72; cf. ADRIAN M. SRB, RAY D. OWEN, and ROBERT S. EDGAR, *General Genetics* (2nd ed.; San Francisco, California: W. H. Freeman and Company, 1965).

4. SULLIVAN, *Farewell Lectures*, Lecture I; cf. HARRY STACK SULLIVAN, *Personal Psychopathology*, copyright 1965 by William Alanson White Psychiatric Foundation, Washington, D.C. (unpublished).

5. SULLIVAN, *Farewell Lectures*, Lecture I; cf. SULLIVAN, *Personal Psychopathology*, p. 11.

6. SULLIVAN, *Personal Psychopathology*, p. 13.

7. Cf. MAURICE R. GREEN, "Prelogical Processes and Participant Communication," *Psychiatric Quarterly*, October, 1961.

8. SULLIVAN, *Personal Psychopathology*, pp. 28-34.

9. Cf. DONALD H. FORD and HUGH B. URBAN, *Systems of Psychotherapy* (New York: John Wiley and Sons, 1963), chap. 14.

10. SULLIVAN, *Personal Psychopathology*, p. 29.

11. SULLIVAN, *Farewell Lectures*, Lecture II; cf. SULLIVAN, *Personal Psychopathology*, p. 29.

12. SULLIVAN, *Personal Psychopathology*, pp. 30-31.

13. *Ibid.*, p. 31.

14. HARRY STACK SULLIVAN, "Affective Experience in Early Schizophrenia," *American Journal of Psychiatry*, 83:467-483, 1926-1927, footnote 3.

15. HARRY STACK SULLIVAN, "Peculiarity of Thought in Schizophrenia,"

American Journal of Psychiatry, **82**:21-86, 1925-1926; reprinted in HARRY STACK SULLIVAN, *Schizophrenia as a Human Process*, with Introduction and Commentaries by HELEN SWICK PERRY (New York: W. W. Norton and Company, 1962).

16. *Ibid.*

17. SULLIVAN, "Affective Experience in Early Schizophrenia."

18. *Ibid.*

19. HARRY STACK SULLIVAN, "Tentative Criteria of Malignancy in Schizophrenia," *American Journal of Psychiatry*, **84**:759-782, 1927-28.

20. *Ibid.*

21. *Ibid.*

22. *Ibid.*

23. HARRY STACK SULLIVAN, "The Onset of Schizophrenia," *American Journal of Psychiatry*, **84**:105-134, 1927-1928; reprinted in SULLIVAN, *Schizophrenia as a Human Process*.

24. HARRY STACK SULLIVAN, "Archaic Sexual Culture and Schizophrenia," in NORMAN HAIRE (ed.), *Sexual Reform Congress* (London: Kegan Paul, Trench, Trubner and Company, 1930), pp. 495-501; reprinted in SULLIVAN, *Schizophrenia as a Human Process*.

25. HARRY STACK SULLIVAN, "Research in Schizophrenia," *American Journal of Psychiatry*, **86**:553-567, 1929; reprinted in SULLIVAN, *Schizophrenia as a Human Process*.

26. *Ibid.*

27. *Ibid.*

28. *Ibid.*

29. SULLIVAN, *Farewell Lectures*, Lecture II.

30. The distinction between preadolescence and mid- or true adolescence is curiously blurred in "Research in Schizophrenia" but is quite clear in the Farewell Lectures.

31. SULLIVAN, "Research in Schizophrenia."

32. Cf. HARRY STACK SULLIVAN, "The Relation of Onset to Outcome in Schizophrenia," in SULLIVAN, *Schizophrenia as a Human Process*, pp. 236-244.

33. HARRY STACK SULLIVAN, "Schizophrenic Individuals as a Source of Data for Comparative Investigation of Personality," in *Proceedings, Second Colloquium on Personality Investigation* (Baltimore, Maryland: The Johns Hopkins Press, 1930) pp. 43-55; reprinted in SULLIVAN, *Schizophrenia as a Human Process*.

34. SULLIVAN, "Research in Schizophrenia."

35. SULLIVAN, "The Relation of Onset to Outcome in Schizophrenia" (Discussion).

36. SULLIVAN, "The Relation of Onset to Outcome in Schizophrenia."

37. SULLIVAN, *Personal Psychopathology*, pp. 192-199; reprinted in SULLIVAN, *Schizophrenia as a Human Process*, pp. 330-338.

38. HARRY STACK SULLIVAN, "The Modified Psychoanalytic Treatment of Schizophrenia," *American Journal of Psychiatry*, 11:519-536, 1931; reprinted in SULLIVAN, *Schizophrenia as a Human Process*.

39. *Ibid.*

40. SULLIVAN, "Archaic Sexual Culture."

41. *Ibid.*

42. *Ibid.*

43. *Ibid.*

44. HARRY STACK SULLIVAN, "Environmental Factors in Etiology and Course Under Treatment of Schizophrenia," *Medical Journal and Record*, 1931.

45. ANSELM STRAUSS (ed.), *Gerorge Herbert Mead on Social Psychology* (Chicago, Illinois: University of Chicago Press, 1964), pp. 202-203.

46. SULLIVAN, "Environmental Factors in Etiology. . . ."

47. HARRY STACK SULLIVAN, "Socio-Psychiatric Research," *American Journal of Psychiatry*, 10:977-991, 1931; reprinted in SULLIVAN, *Schizophrenia as a Human Process*.

48. SULLIVAN, "Environmental Factors in Etiology . . . ," footnote 2.

49. SULLIVAN, "Environmental Factors in Etiology. . . ."

50. *Ibid.*

51. *Ibid.*

52. *Ibid.*

53. HARRY STACK SULLIVAN, "Mental Disorders," *Encyclopedia of the Social Sciences*, 10:313-319 (New York: The Macmillan Company, 1933); reprinted in SULLIVAN, *Schizophrenia as a Human Process*.

54. *Ibid.*

55. *Ibid.*

56. HARRY STACK SULLIVAN, "Psychiatry," *Encyclopedia of the Social Sciences*, 12:578-580 (New York: The Macmillan Company, 1934); reprinted in HARRY STACK SULLIVAN, *The Fusion of Psychiatry and Social Science*, with Introduction and Commentaries by HELEN SWICK PERRY (New York: W. W. Norton and Company, 1964).

57. *Ibid.*

58. HARRY STACK SULLIVAN, "The Common Field of Research and Clinical Psychiatry," *Psychiatric Quarterly*, 1:276-291; reprinted in SULLIVAN, *Schizophrenia as a Human Process*.

59. *Ibid.*

60. *Ibid.*

61. *Ibid.*

62. *Ibid.*

63. *Ibid.*

64. *Ibid.*

65. *Ibid.*

66. *Ibid.*

67. HARRY STACK SULLIVAN, "Psychiatric Training as a Prerequisite to Psychoanalytic Practice," *American Journal of Psychiatry,* **91**:1117-1126, 1934-1935; reprinted in SULLIVAN, *Schizophrenia as a Human Process.*

68. *Ibid.*

69. *Ibid.*

4/The Evolution of Personality in Interpersonal Relations

Psychopathology, a branch of psychobiology, is the study of processes of "mundane" persons in and within more or less commonplace social situations though it puts considerable emphasis on the side of the inefficient and harmful behavior of people.[1] Sullivan wrote that, as we are all much more simply human than otherwise, psychopathology deals chiefly with matters of common experience, but it deals with matters whose personal significance is in each case veiled from the person who is caught up in each "unfortunate complex of social living." In other words, it deals with those processes of living that are unusually inefficient, productive of tension and unhappiness, and contributory to failures of the individual as a self-respecting being. Moreover, "there are numbers of our contemporaries in the case of whom the maintenance of some measure of self-respect is a never-ending task and one entailing great cost not only in personal effort but also in interferences with the comfort and success of others. It may be said that whenever the maintenance of self-esteem becomes an end instead of a consequent of life, the individual concerned is mentally sick and a subject for psychopathological study, finally to be understood by the same formulae that we must work out for understanding the 'neurotic' and the 'insane.' "[2]

Since such partial or total failures in living are very widespread, a reflective individual may wonder why persons endowed with intelligence experience so much suffering, sorrow, and failure. In *Personal Psychopathology,* Sullivan gives the following answer: That "our people, peculiarly favored by natural resources, possessed of linguistic and political solidarity and wealthy indeed in technologies in a great many lines; that this offshoot of the Occidental civilization should be almost primitive in many of its current practices regarding interpersonal relations; [that] such a situation [exists] is surely unnecessary. The current culture adaptive of man to man is sadly deficient, far indeed behind the development of our technologies and the accumulation of material advantages."[3]

However, it seems to be almost universally agreed that many current practices in interpersonal relations are deficient not only in the United States of America but throughout the world. But there is no general agreement about the causes of this unhappy state of affairs, though theories abound.

Sullivan surmised that it is by "misdirected application of some of his abilities" that man has continued to live in a rather primitive interpersonal adaptive culture—an idea that seems almost truistic. However, he did specify a seemingly important variable: language and the difficulties of communication. Language has not proved to be an unmixed blessing. By verbal behavior man can communicate many sorts of things: things false or fanciful as well as true. Moreover, "verbal operations that include symbols standing for *inner* activities, thoughts, feelings, desires, have ever been equivocal, and man's growth in skill at the task of intercommunicating his inner life with other men has been pathetically slow."[4] Still again, man has been handicapped by witting and unwitting interference with his life by the relatively few who are particularly apt at verbal performances, some of whom exploit their relative advantage in the pursuit of short-sighted personal gain (until, in the words of the historian Christopher Dawson, "the very face of nature is changed by the destruction of the countryside and the pollution of the earth, and the air and the waters"),[5] while others "function unfavorably" by their resistance to man's emancipation from error.[6]

Thus, the accumulation of the material culture of the United States is proceeding at a high rate but the achievement of substantive culture (language, customs, moral codes, law, religion, etc.), particularly culture adaptive to the pyramiding material advantages, is proceeding very slowly. In the face of this lamentable—if not potentially disas-

trous—state of affairs, Sullivan offers a program for social meliora-
tion very reminiscent of the social philosophy of John Dewey. Sullivan
put his faith in what Dewey called "intelligence."[7] "The fact of *change*
throughout the universe," Sullivan claims, "is the nuclear conception
that must be grasped. Nothing is timeless, and this is peculiarly true
in the most active area of the world, the living. Everything human
changes inevitably. Change has to be accepted as one of the given
characteristics of reality. Attitudes intolerant to the new or to the old
are morbid, and only a broad tolerance fits one to deal with people
as they are. Man has enough inherent distaste for any marked novelty
to insure him from disastrous innovation—except when he is rendered mentally sick by artificial stabilities to which he is required to
conform. . . ."[8]

Sullivan wrote that we must school ourselves to true tolerance for
inventions in adaptive culture, a tolerance requiring a novel appreciation of the intrinsic value of knowledge concerning the underlying
realities of man and of group life. He asserted that such a tolerance
implies a warmly receptive attitude to the discovery of how the marvelously adaptive human creature, the newborn infant, is converted into
a product of family and school culture, and, secondly, the processes
by which the adjustment of this individually cultured youth to life as
a person among the complex personal and superpersonal entities
making up the modern world occurs. The discovery of the ways and
processes of acculturation requires a wholly unprecedented variety of
open-minded inquiry and experimentation. The "magical power" of
the traditional, formulated mores must be called in question, and the
"inviolate durability" of emotionally toned customs has to be shattered. Not till then can the group advance rapidly to new levels of
achievement by way of a better, clearer understanding of its problems.

Sullivan tempered this strikingly optimistic outlook with the following considerations. The "bohemian attitude" that tolerates nothing
that is not new is as archaic as the "conservative attitude" that per-
petuates in us the errors of our grandparents. The new, he says, may
well be worse in its consequences than the old. Both individual and
social continuity of experience has to be maintained.[9]

For a time, at least, in the life span of the individual and the history
of a society, Sullivan believed, the crystallized prejudices of a person
and the mores of a group serve a function. During that time, the

prejudices of the individual and the mores of the group are each a valuable though imperfect formulation of experience. Social living could scarcely occur without a large body of customs, a tradition of stereotyped behavior, thought, and valuation, to nurture and sustain it. If a person had to reach "good formulations" for most of his interpersonal experience, he could scarcely find the time and energy necessary for dealing with novel situations. Within limits, decidedly real limits, the more of life that is channeled by custom ("stereotyped"), the greater the freedom of the individual. Therefore any notion "that wholesale destruction of prejudices and mores, were it feasible, would in itself represent a great progress is everywhere contradicted in the present situation."[10]

When Sullivan wrote *Personal Psychopathology,* studies of child psychology were scarce, despite the pioneering work of a few men. Since there was relatively little material available, he gradually constructed a rudimentary outline of child development that was in the main very different from the Freudian theory. Since man is essentially a social being, one must try to understand his development in terms of his interpersonal relations as defined and structured by the individual's culture, along with the gradually unfolding maturational pattern of the growing child. One should also bear in mind that human societies, in varying degrees, tend to encourage the development of some human capacities and to discourage or suppress others.

From the very moment of birth, the youngster is exposed to cultural influences. A recent writer has expressed this in a succinct and revealing fashion. From the first moment of birth "a human baby begins to feel the impact of culture—in the way it is delivered, and the mode in which its umbilical cord is cut and tied, the fashion in which it is washed and handled, and the manner in which it is swaddled or clothed."[11]

In the primary group, the family, composed principally of "materials" and two people, the parents or their surrogates, life begins. During the first eighteen months of his life, the infant develops a "marvelous relationship" to the materials of his environment. At the same time, as maturation proceeds, he is developing facilities for communication with his parents. Sullivan claimed that soon after birth the infant responds to emotional conditions in his mother. There is said to be a "primitive interchange," or emotional intercommunication, between parent and offspring wherein the latter "prehends" the signs made up of facial postures, gestures, and the like. This emotional intercommunication, called empathy, is stated in *Personal Psychopathology* to be a factor of great importance throughout life.[12] Everyone "knows," in some unclear fashion, a great deal about some other people who are really of importance to him ("significant people," in a later formulation), though the communication of this body of fact occurs quite exterior to his consciousness. Before the youngster is three years of age, he will have acquired a great many of "the deep unconscious man-ways." Meanwhile he has begun to acquire the great tool of primary communication, the spoken (in contrast to the written) language of his parents. As he begins to acquire language, he now begins the long, intensive, unremitting education in the folkways and mores, the customs, the "fashions," or traditions of his society as they are represented in his primary group.

When the child learns to read, the confines of the family group begin to expand. He now acquires information from people who are not physically present to his senses, and his imagination may be kindled or enriched by fable and story. To this extent he is said to be capable of entering into secondary group relationships, and of receiving information from the great world. Sullivan claims that as soon as the young one has learned to write, he is equipped with the basic tools for our fullest type of group living. In the course of his formal education, he normally acquires the knowledge and skills required for life in a complex urban industrial society.

Sullivan has a somewhat pessimistic view of the early education acquired in the home; at least he seems to stress the shortcomings of the family group unduly when he wrote:

"If it were not for the unyielding primacy of the experience that he has received by empathy, the child would profit greatly from novel experience coming toward him in the secondary group interchange of reading. If it were not for this primacy, the defects and deficiencies of the home group would slough off in subsequent education, in the school."[13] But the emotional processes are said to be more anciently established than are the intellectual. Sullivan thought that growth of the nice discriminations by which one comes to apprehend the novel in the manifold of the accustomed tends to be almost as rare as genius. The emotional stereotypes, which are more anciently established than intellectual abilities, destroy budding tendencies to originality step by step throughout the several epochs of personality growth. It is not possible to guess the range of individual differences in potential abilities possessed by the newborn. There are good reasons, however, for assuming that the "proportion" of these abilities that reach some degree of fruition in adulthood to inherited capacities is "exceedingly small."

Before presenting a more or less systematic account of Sullivan's theory of personality development as outlined in *Personal Psychopathology,* I wish to give a summary account of it. In (early) infancy, he says, besides breathing, the prevailing activity is sleep, and, in order of importance, the taking of nourishment, and that group of events connected with relieving forms of distress not primarily related to hunger. Then, according to Sullivan, there is that group of activities and local action, growing in importance day by day, called play, representing in part an inherent tendency to exercise the parts of the organism as they are elaborated; that is, to give a sort of "trial run" to each new neuro-muscular-glandular apparatus of the organism.

There is also another kind of activity apparent from infancy, which may be called oral behavior. For example, the elaborate apparatus ("nutriment-securing apparatus") evolved for the satisfaction of the nourishment need (hunger) requires at all times the discharge of the energy partitioned to it, which is manifested as a desire to suckle. The oral behavior entailed in the discharge of this energy may also be called play, though it is related to an already existing need. Hence the need for oral activity may be called a "secondary" or "psychological" need. Oral activity is a form of total activity that ultimately becomes extremely important.

As the infant progresses in the use of the voice apparatus to the point at which differentiation of vocalization rather abruptly occurs, and crying is superseded at least occasionally by a new sort of vocal activity, babbling and cooing, articulate speech rapidly develops. This appearance of articulate speech is said to lead to so great an acceleration in the velocity of change in the organism, that is, in the acceleration of the development of the personality, that it should be regarded as marking an epoch in personality growth, ending infancy and initiating childhood. Sullivan claimed that the principal partition of activity in childhood continues to be sleep, though its importance is diminishing and its character is showing some change. The appearance of new sorts of total activity ("that which the whole person does") brings about important modification in all the other activities characteristic of infancy. Consciousness has developed in quality and character to a point at which ideals and ambitions can gradually be inculcated. In other words, because of the behavior of significant adults, the great, controlling power of cultural forces is beginning to make themselves felt.

When the child develops a definite need for other children as playmates he reaches another level of development, called the juvenile era. This is said to be the period of growth of egocentric sociality and of the elaboration of social personality. If real playmates are not available, the youngster creates imaginary playmates. "Previous to the outcropping of this need, the imaginary constructs of the child have all sorts of marvelous patterns. From this time on, however, the child has playmates real or imaginary, and playmates that are like himself."[14] His implicit (or covert) processes are said to begin to take on "an objectivity," so that he manifests a rather rapid development of appreciation, not only of his own wishes and abilities, but also of the other person's wishes and abilities. This is the beginning of true socialization—in contradiction to the quasi-social adjustment to authority and parental "prejudices" characteristic of later childhood. The "total situations" of the juvenile's life, chiefly interpersonal situations, change very fundamentally in character. There is a marked growth of the self, partly because of the increasing appreciation of the general importance of other people of comparable status. Events are said to move swiftly in the juvenile era and the recall of experience had during this period is no mean task.

Sooner or later, the juvenile, in play and in social life, manifests a beginning attachment of a unique type to some other person. If one is a boy, the attachment is to another boy; if one is a girl, the attachment is to another girl. This unique attachment, if it flourishes, is love. It is characterized as follows: "The individual now begins so to organize his experiences, real and fantastic, occurring in the total situations including the other person, that the other person becomes signally important to him."[15] This development brings about a rapid modification in the youngster's life, including the type of total situation (interpersonal situation) he sustains. This "love factor" is said to change the fundamental character of the individual, bringing about a need for interindividual affection. The egocentric sociality of the juvenile is superseded—if only temporarily for many people—by a new interest in the other fellow. With the appearance of the ability to love, the personality, according to Sullivan, has proceeded into its "ultraimportant phase" of growth because henceforth, barring very unfortunate experience, there will always be one or more persons of great importance in the individual's life, or, more concretely, in the total situations through which the individual passes. "True personality is born, and intimate interpersonal adjustment now becomes the great problem of life."[16] During this phase numbers of boys who have progressed to this level of development constitute themselves into more or less highly organized groups or "gangs." An analogous phenomenon appears in girls.[17]

Sullivan called this period the earliest phase of adolescence (or preadolescence), though in subsequent years he modified his formulation slightly.

One should bear in mind that if personal or social circumstances do not allow for the preadolescent development it will not appear. Perhaps that is why many people cannot understand Sullivan's ideas on preadolescence or think they are idiosyncratic. An individual or a group may never experience love as conceived by Sullivan if the conditions of life are unfavorable. Indeed, it appears that current social conditions are frequently adverse to the experience of love at any time of life.

True adolescence ("midadolescence") is ushered in with the appearance of frank (genital) sexual impulses, which entails another alteration in the character of the person's total situations. Coincidentally, processes appear making for intimacy with a member of the other sex, a phenomenon that will be elaborated upon in a subsequent chapter. When one has arrived at an habitual form of activity more or less directly adjustive to the sexual urges he reaches late adolescence.[18]

Adulthood is the last step in Sullivan's schematization of personality development. He characterizes adulthood as a total situation including another person (or conceivably two other persons) in a total activity, prevailingly sexual in character, the resolution of which is complete, in the sense that it does not proceed into disturbing situations, which in turn would require resolution. In other words, one becomes adult when, after having successfully passed through the previous stages, he can establish a durably satisfying relationship with another person, a relationship in which the sexual drive or desire is the conspicuously effective integrating motive. When he wrote *Per-*

sonal Psychopathology Sullivan believed that marriage "and other durable interpersonal relations involving sexual adjustment" is the test of
personality evolution.[19] There is, of course, a great deal more than
this to adulthood, and I shall elaborate upon it at a more convenient
place in this book.

Summarily, "we see the person as a nexus of processes in communal existence with a physicochemical, a social, and a cultural world. He
integrates total situations [primarily interpersonal situations] of various complexities in part on the basis of his previous experience with
appropriately related series of events. He *learns,* shows some measure
of profit from the experiences of life."[20] Also, following upon the
gradual maturation of various capacities combined with the accumulation of appropriate experience, he progresses along a more or less
definable path from a wholly nonrational parasitism to some large
measure of understanding and adjustment in and within an extremely
complex world.

Sullivan wrote that the clearness with which these stages of personality growth may be distinguished diminishes—owing to various complicating factors that may intervene—as we proceed from the
intrauterine condition onward. For example, individuals in each succeeding stage are said to show more or less striking differentiation
because of dissimilar experience. Thus each person, as he grows,
becomes progressively more individuated.

In *Personal Psychopathology,* Sullivan has arrived at a more or less
systematic theory that diverges radically from Freud's. He no longer
thought that it is sound theory or practice to "see" manifestations of
sexual impulses in the individual from birth onward. Freud's theory
of psychosexuality is largely abandoned, though certain of his ideas
on "infantile sexuality" are retained and reformulated in the Sullivanian system. While in Freud's great pioneering works biological
inheritance is emphasized at the expense of an adequate recognition
of the role of cultural determinants, in Sullivan's theories, to a much
greater degree, social inheritance is stressed, though he is by no
means indifferent to what he called the biological substrate of the
human individual.

It is true, of course, that Freud did not entirely ignore interpersonal
relations—how could he?—but his understanding of them is far more
limited than Sullivan's. Though the latter emphasized the importance
of cultural transmission and communication, he did not ignore the

"determining power" of heredity. He acknowledged that inborn factors of organization, the organization of the chromosomes and genes in the fertilized cell, fix the limits of life opportunity in certain ways. Unlike Freud, who thought that direct sexual satisfactions were largely gained at the cost of cultural achievements, or, to put the matter differently, who thought that advances in civilization were, *in the very nature of things,* largely gained at the cost of individual instinctual frustration, Sullivan saw there could be no basic dichotomy between the individual and society. Along with this, he stressed the fact that one cannot adequately study the maturational pattern apart from the social-cultural environment of the developing child. No human organism, it seems safe to say, can have a chance to live, let alone become a fully human being, without the support and nurture of the social environment.

Sullivan formulated his ideas on the course of personality growth with an eye to the "morbid deviations" that may come to characterize the various "stages" or epochs. It would be wrong, I think, to interpret this to mean that a particular kind of neurosis, for instance, is "caused" by the deviations occurring at a given stage but rather that such deviations may be the starting point of a long train of unfortunate events in a person's life. By tracing the course of this train of events back to its beginnings, one has a clearer understanding and broader perspective on how the patient got to be the way he is. Thus one also may be able to learn what necessary experiences the patient *missed,* failed to have, as well as those pathogenic experiences he had to undergo.

Sullivan did not take over the Freudian notion of a mechanical repetition of the past, of a so-called repetition compulsion. As he emphasized, there is always change, which does not occur haphazardly and aimlessly, but in a particular "direction," toward outcomes, fruitions, fulfillments, and realizations, or, especially in cases in which the person has suffered a great deal of unfortunate experience, toward frustrations, defeats, and partial or total failures. Change in a given direction is said to have "velocity"; the change may be increased in speed, slowed down or in certain vital respects practically halted. For change alters, according to Sullivan, in regard to direction and speed, thus at times attempting to follow physical analogies that can be misleading or confusing. While perhaps all change includes a quantitative factor, the changes that the student of interpersonal relations is primarily concerned with are pervasively qualitative in character, and cannot merely be formulated quantitatively without doing violence to the facts of human experience. In other words, one cannot formulate or "measure" the direction and speed of change in an individual's experience and behavior in mathematico-physical terms (in terms of vectors, for example) without caricaturing the facts. The "direction" of change for instance, is "measured" or estimated in terms of goals or ends, or purposes, that is to say, in terms of some implicit or explicit philosophy of experience. Of course Sullivan was well aware of this, but he seems to have been at one time overly fond of physical analogies.

Change, or rather the direction of change, may be "reversed," in which case we have the phenomenon known as regression. As I mentioned in a previous chapter, when this happens the more adult or more recent patterns of behavior are abandoned or disintegrated and patterns of behavior that resemble or are more or less similar to patterns of behavior acquired or learned at an earlier period take their place. Thus it seems as if chronologically earlier patterns of behavior are reactivated, though it is difficult to understand how chronologically earlier patterns of behavior can literally be reactivated. The "reactivation" seems to be of types or kinds of behavior acquired earlier in life.

I turn now to an exposition of Sullivan's ideas on personality development. The first quesion to be considered has to do with heredity. "What we *cannot* develop because there are no suitable organizatory factors in our inherited make-up," Sullivan says, "I am quite willing to accept as determined. Anyone with a mind open to experience, however, must come to see that experience has a tremendous influence on the development of the individual. . . . I prefer to believe that post-natal experience exerts a marked influence on the time interval required for the appearance of latent determining influences, and in some cases an absolute control over their maturation."[21] For example, he thought that a particularly deviated environment may delay the socializing tendency until the age of eight and the appearance of the genital sexual impulses until after seventeen. Even so, he believed, when he wrote *Personal Psychopathology,* that certain impulses, such as the "socializing impulse" or the "intimacy impulse" *normally* appear at relatively fixed chronological stages or "eras," despite occasional statements that would discount such an interpretation. That is to say,

Sullivan appears to think they have a relatively fixed "hereditary determination." They are manifestations of a foreordained evolution or
inherited predisposition, and they normally appear at a certain stage
of development.

However, experience has a "tremendous influence" on the development of the individual. Just how much influence experience has, in
Sullivan's view, is a matter to be discussed throughout several chapters of this book. But despite the great role he ascribed to experience,
he assumes an underlying biological determinism, in the sense illustrated above. But it is not a "rigid" biological determinism; it provides rather broad or elastic limits within which it operates, and it can
easily be modified if further research requires it to be altered. This
"biological" determinism also provides an intelligible though not
necessarily adequate basis for his notion of "distortions" of personality, which are brought about primarily by failures and inadequacies of
acculturation. This can best be shown by a discussion of the various
epochs, "eras," or stages of development.

One has no reason to believe that the neonate has any notion of his
own individuality. But, Sullivan believed, there was much in the "mental state" of the newborn that pertained to himself, constituting the
rudimentary basis of his subsequently elaborated self-consciousness.
This mental state is not limited, bounded, or circumscribed by the
distinctions that are later developed: distinctions of "I" and "Thou,"
of time (before, now, after), of place (here, there), and so forth. Sullivan assumed that in the first few weeks of life the infant cannot
conceive the nipple as anything but a more or less independent and
uncontrollable part of his own "more or less cosmic life." Such a
mental state is said to be approximated later in life only in certain
dreams, experiences of persons progressing into acute mental disorder, and in mystical experiences.

Against such an undifferentiated background, the infant experiences needs leading to or indicating extensive disturbances of the
organism. The needs are expressed by and manifested in the use of
the cry and in changes of the "facial expressive postures." The highly
elaborated oral apparatus (consisting of the motor equipment of lips,
tongue, palate, swallowing mechanism, glottis, salivary glands, etc.)
that is ready at birth is the principal point of contact with the environment, "together with the sensory apparatus including that by which
stimuli applied to the face and the lips are effectively correlated with

activity." This highly elaborated apparatus is used often. "The mother puts the infant to the nipple, or the nurse gives the infant a bottle with a nipple on it, and activity ensues in the case of all those that are to survive."[22] The particular total situations, including contact with the nipple, in early infancy, are said to constitute extremely important experience, to a large degree because there is satisfaction of the chemical necessities of the body. The felt coincidence of suckling and the disappearance of hunger-discomfort, among other things, gradually forms or builds up a kind of experience that is "central" in the "conscious series" (series or progression of representations of events in the awareness) of the individual. In other words, Sullivan believed that (what adults conceive of as) the hunger-nipple-lips satisfaction sequence of events, which is accompanied by various sorts of sentience, is somehow represented in the infant's developing mind—however rudimentary and undifferentiated this mind may be in the first months of life—forming a foundation for subsequent experience. To put this idea as simply as I can, the infant gradually catches on to the fact that when, for example, he has a certain discomfort (hunger) and he cries, satisfaction will supervene, including pleasant sentience connected with the oral activity of suckling.

This recurrent experience, or type of experience, like others, becomes memorially represented in an increasingly effective fashion, such that subsequent experiences are affected or "colored" by it. The "roots" of many "categories of reality" are said to originate in the felt hunger-nipple-lips satisfaction sequence, providing a beginning of the gradual discovery that events have a serial order, of distinctions of sensation and feeling, of the conditional nature of pleasure as it is connected with "reality" (that is, that pleasure cannot be simply hallucinated by arbitrary wish), of the stability of matter or of something that persists unchanged when manipulated and recurrently encountered, of motion, of power to assuage needs, and the like.

When writing *Personal Psychopathology*, Sullivan claimed that the growth of "life techniques" arises in "the successful escape" from pain, unpleasure, and the felt needs of the organism thus adhering rather closely, in this respect, to the Freudian view. In later years he introduced a vital modification, or additional assumption, to the effect that the "pursuit of security" is equally compelling and fundamental. This assumption, which will be explicated subsequently, establishes an intelligible basis for understanding various activities of people, but above all their efforts to attain and maintain self-respect and the respect of significant others.

Quite early in postnatal life—just how early Sullivan apparently did not think he could safely surmise—the nipple and its attributes take on distinguishing marks; and the latter are said to be the first of the long series of marks or signs by which we recognize the external world. With the aid of an "analytic segregation" or rudimentary differentiation of some factors intimately associated with the nipple, an external phenomenon gradually gets defined and distinguished as something distinct from what will subsequently be recognized as "me."[23] It appears that throughout infancy there is continual elaboration and functional improvement of the distance receptors (eyes, ears, etc.). The infant becomes more and more able to notice phenomena that occur outside his own body, including the comings and goings of the nipple, which Sullivan thought are, or provide, the first of the "building blocks" with which we are forced to structuralize our conceptions of the world. In later development there is a separation of the nourishment-satisfaction-sequence from the sucking dynamism itself.

Another thing to be mentioned is that the intimate relation of expressed need, as in crying, to suckling, "has probably been powerfully influential in buttressing the *unconscious* dependence on verbal magic," a "magic" to which most of us resort perhaps more often than we realize.

And now I begin a more detailed discussion of the origins of interpersonal relations: the infant's experiences of the *mothering* one. Originally, according to Sullivan, the experience of the mother, or her surrogate, is had by a sort of rudimentary perception, called prehension, a type of experiencing that is much more primitive and undifferentiated than adult perception with its refined distinctions and available storehouse of long previous experience.[24] Sullivan claims that from the appearance of the first prehension of the person associated with the more or less unmanageable doings of the nipple a variety of experiences are occurring to, or "in," the infant, experiences that are of prime importance in the development of every personality. It is the mothering one, the gradually more and more realistically prehended person, who is the source of practically all the satisfactions obtainable, except those from play. "All the needs which arise that are not simply a call for the exercise of neuro-muscular-glandular apparatus require in the human young some activity on the part of the environment."[25] And the "environment" is not an environment at large; it is chiefly the one who mothers, and this is pretty generally consistently the same person. The infant is not capable of making an adult, rational appraisal of this person, forming instead a primitive or rudimentary conception of a more or less omnipotent being, which gives rise to a primitive mother sentiment; in other words, a mental structure built from experiences with the mothering one, which subsequently in late infancy and childhood undergoes much differentiation and refinement.

The mother-of-infancy, that is, the "primitive mother sentiment," an ideally good and powerful figure, who satisfied all wants, gradually evolves (in the youngster's experiences, of course) into the mother-of-childhood, a much less perfect figure, who is not only inadequate at times but troublesome at others, for her presence and activities give rise not only to pleasure but also pain.[26] From this, Sullivan believed when he wrote *Personal Psychopathology,* originates the first great body of disappointments in life. In other words, as the infant grows he is taught inhibitions, if only because the mother cannot satisfy all his wants and demands, which in a manner of speaking may be expressed in the phrase that he cannot have the full moon. The infant's constantly developing needs and "specialization of needs" also have to be curtailed in certain respects as to their satisfactions, and gradually channeled along socially approved or permissible lines. As the youngster progresses into and through the childhood era, he is deliberately "trained," an experience often fraught with displeasure.

Sullivan points out that the greater part of the infant's time is spent in sleep. He says that one must recognize in the state of sleep a group of processes, a considerable number of activities, rather than merely quiescence and central inhibition. In sleep there often appears the first objective evidence (unspecified) of processes that are not effecting a satisfactory resolution in the "organism-environment complex." "Crying, fretting, and other manifestations occurring while the infant is awake may well indicate unsatisfied needs, may mark ineffective activity in the infantile total situation"[27] (which, as a very significant factor, includes the one who mothers). However, such manifestations may or may not have to do with matters that are sources of important experience.

Sullivan claimed that as a result of the geometric function of the bones, coupled with the gradually maturing nervous system ("the growth of meyelin"), and the functional completion of muscles and glands, the play activity of the hands tends often to localize itself in proximity to the genitals. In play these "appurtenances" are found to be "peculiarly useful." But many parents regard the manipulation of the genitals by the infant or child as obnoxious, as evidence of sin or some other repellent tendency in the youngster. Since there apparently is an "emotional linkage" between the infant and the adults who habitually care for him or deal with him—an emotional contagion said to be often manifested while the infant is nursing—the upset state of the mothering one is communicated to the infant. In Sullivan's view, empathy plays a very important role in early life experience. Through this obscure process the young one is made to feel (or somehow experience) the "emotional upheaval" that some parents undergo when they observe him carrying on certain activities of which they strongly disapprove, such as masturbation or thumb-sucking. Sullivan does not attach nearly as much importance to masturbation as Freud. For the former it *never* of itself has any efficacy in the etiology of mental illness. He regarded it as a minor incident in the life of a youngster except when the parents give it special significance by their disapproving or horrified attitudes, in which case it may result in "primitive genital phobia."[28] Sullivan's interpretation of thumb-sucking also sharply differs from Freud's: it is one of the means by which the oral apparatus discharges energy not used in the securing of nourishment, and has nothing to do with Freud's hypothetical libido. Again, on Sullivan's view, morbid attitudes on the part of the mothering one toward the anal sphincter functions, or toward any "tinkering" by the offspring with the anus, may have serious consequences.

For the sake of clarity I must emphasize Sullivan's rejection of Freud's notion of infantile sexuality, which allegedly develops by manifold stages into adult sexuality.

He wrote that autoerotism, homoerotism, and heteroerotism may be taken to refer to modes of securing satisfactory sensations, pleasurable sensory contents within awareness, by manipulatory procedures including, respectively, parts of one's own body, parts of a body like one's own, and parts of a body in a peculiarly significant fashion unlike one's own. "An attempt should be made to maintain a distinction between erotism and the more specific sexual satisfactions, the latter having the relation to the former of a part to the whole. Pleasure-seeking is evidenced from birth onward; not so, the seeking of sexual pleasure. I do not find any virtue in clinging to the generalization by which all pleasure is identified as a part of a libidinal input, as expressed by Freud."[29]

In the development of personality the three zones of interaction that seem to be especially significant are the oral, anal, and genital, though Sullivan thought the oral zone is of preeminent importance at least for many years. Owing to morbid attitudes on the part of significant others, especially the mothering one, any of the three may seem to the youngster to have "preternatural" importance. I must once more stress the fact that the *reactions of significant others,* in Sullivan's view, are among the things to which one must give careful heed in endeavoring to understand the evolution of personality, and its distortions, including the functions of those part-aspects called zones of interaction. The latter function as canalized outlets (partly owing to somatic structure, partly because of experience) of the important tendencies organized in the sentiment of self. Consider, for instance, the transcendant significance that many people ascribe to talking, and how handicapped they would feel or be if the capacity for oral expression in words were to be seriously impaired. Such an eventuality might seem or be a grave peril to the self.

Before I begin a discussion of the self, I wish to mention that not only do some tendencies that are developed from the mutual interplay of inborn potencies and experience become "distorted," but some "dully activated in early infancy" are said to be so deviated by experience undergone in early childhood that their further development is slight and lack representation in the self-conscious personality. They do not become a part of the self. Should these tendencies that, probably through the instrumentality of empathy, have been shunted off from the main line of personality development manifest themselves in waking life they are not noted or are regarded as mysterious accidental physiological occurrences. One significant consequence of this state of affairs is that the "richness" of the personality is diminished. Another result of this is that there is in an individual who has had such an unfortunate experience a "dangerous substratum" of absolutely unconscious integrative tendencies (motivational systems) wholly unsuited to "socialized living" and to anything other than early childhood behavior. This substratum is the "immediate source" of impulses manifested in nonadjustive phenomena discussed in previous chapters.

These wholly unconscious processes, Sullivan claims, are entirely different from those of repression and dissociation.[30] The latter are processes, he says, that occur withn the self-conscious part (or aspect) of the personality, and they have to do with experiences and tendencies that have or once had "reality value" and meaning to the self. Why they are entirely different from those of repression and dissociation is not too clear in *Personal Psychopathology*, especially since repressed and dissociated processes may be assimilated to them, but the distinction is clarified in *Clinical Studies in Psychiatry*. The main point is that they were not incorporated into the early, rudimentary self, and therefore lack reality value and meaning to the self. Under certain extraordinary circumstances, when these unconscious processes, which are unknown and incomprehensible to the self, along with later additions and accretions from "repressed" and dissociated processes, are powerfully activated and cannot be dealt with or assimilated by the self-conscious personality, panic supervenes.

Sullivan appears to have thought that dissociation first takes place in the main during the juvenile era, when tendencies inacceptable to the self are *denied* conscious appreciation. According to this formulation, dissociation is not so much a positive exclusion from consciousness as it is a development exterior to the appreciated self, a development "in the region of unconscious processes," namely, as dissociated systems. But in other contexts, his discussion seems to imply that dissociation represents a positive act of the self rather similar to repression. However, Sullivan appears to think that repressed processes are less deeply buried than dissociated processes, that is, not so effectively and permanently excluded from the self. There is danger here that one may interpret unconscious, dissociated, and repressed processes as "regions" or "psychic localities" in the manner of Freud. But they are not. They primarily indicate that psychological processes occurring outside consciousness are of varying degrees of inaccessibility to self-conscious awareness. I shall come back to these problems subsequently.

There is then in *Personal Psychopathology* a more or less explicit distinction between unconscious processes, and dissociated processes that have been denied conscious appreciation or excluded by the self from conscious awareness. This suggests Freud's distinction between those processes that have always been unconscious and those that have become unconscious by repression. Sullivan later abandoned the notion of repression, retaining dissociation. But he uses dissociation to designate (1) an activity or function of the personality by means of which experiences or their meaning are excluded from conscious awareness, and (2) a functionally distinct aspect or part of the personality that cannot normally be accessible to the self. In regard to the latter, certain "complexes" and acquired tendencies are said to be thrown out of gear, so to speak, with the increasing experience of the youngster and to continue to function without much relation to the general evolution of tendencies operating in the self-conscious personality.

The question naturally arises as to which factors influence, regulate, or determine the operation of the two "systems," the self and the dissociated, in interpersonal situations. According to Sullivan, two factors have to be considered in this connection: (1) "the partition of energy to the two systems," and (2) "the measure of awareness of the dissociated system that the individual retains or develops." He goes on to say that, as long as the self is so constituted, owing to its evolutionary or developmental history, it insures a considerable measure of recognition of the dissociated activity as of personal origin, and that, because of unknown but real factors in the total situation, the necessary snythesis (or, in the language of some writers, integration) of the self is secure from *grave* dissociation. In other words, the personality is secure from being gravely "split" or fragmented. But if one is unaware of, or not able to note, the situational conditions leading to, or provoking the operation of, the dissociated factors or motivational systems, but also the resulting activity itself, wherein one lacks evidence of it, then the way is said to be open for most unfortunate developments. Why? Sullivan wrote that this state of the self reflects the early side-tracking of important tendencies, such that there are in the personality profoundly unconscious powerful emotional tendencies of which the individual "knows" nothing. In addition, Sullivan asserted that while in any case of major dissociation the individual is at the mercy of motives that can carry him toward consummations with other people, not only without his wish, but distinctly in opposition to his ideals and conventions, and he can never be sure when he will be threatened with conflict, the individuals in whom the dissociated systems are associated with deeply unconscious tendencies are even more unfortunate in that they come often to suffer anxiety, the sources of which are impossible of discovery by the self. "In any case, the more of the personality there is in a state of dissociation, the greater the probability that it will 'take over' the somatic apparatus, when it is activated by a suitable situation, and the more deeply uncertain the individual must become as to all interpersonal situations."[31]

Sullivan had not worked out a systematic theory of the self when he wrote *Personal Psychopathology*, but his somewhat sketchy outline will serve as an introduction to ideas much better formulated during the later years of his life. The oral zone plays a major role in the development of the self and, more generally, enters into especially close relations with the relevant environment of the youngster. The "mouth-nipple combination" is said to provide the root experience for a separating of the "me" and the "not-me," namely, the external world, while the oral play provides the first or root experience of autoerotism. Moreover, the activity of the "vocalizing equipment," though indistinguishable from the mouth in the infantile consciousness is the basis of "omnipotence by magic cries." It is also, in the words of McDougall, the principal instrument of the "instinct of appeal." Vocalizing is said to be the tool of domination most generally effective for the organism in its complex relation with another personality, until the time arrives when the individual learns to enter into secondary group relations. But even following that time—and perhaps throughout life—so great is the relationship of the oral apparatus to thought, even to written expression of thought, according to Sullivan, that it might still be considered to be the principal instrument of "domination." In writing and in otherwise communicating with persons who are not physically present one is still doing the same sort of thing one would be doing in talking to them except that one has to imagine more extensively than if they were in one's immediate environment or elaborate rationally how they might respond to one's words.

"This instrumentality of the oral zone, beginning at the very beginnings of conscious life and being of such extreme importance in the consciousness of the organism, may be regarded as fundamentally distinctive in the elaboration of tendency groups [tendency systems, motivational systems] within the personality. The sentiment of self might be said to take its origin in experiences connected with the oral activity."[32]

Throughout childhood the manifestations of this sentiment in the growth of verbalizations about the self may be studied "most effectively" in the child's talk about himself and the fantasies he can be persuaded to express about himself. In the next era, the juvenile "picks up" the experiences of others about him, "incorporates," them and fits them into what Cooley called the "reflected self." In other words, he is "incorporating" the reactions of others to him, their statements, actions, and attitudes toward him, and assimilating them as best he can into a meaningful, coherent self-structure.

The earliest experiences having the characteristics of self-consciousness, though of a rudimentary sort at first, emanate from the oral zone. This is said to be insured by the recurrent rapid dissipation of discomfort synchronously with the activity of nursing. Nursing provides various sorts of experience that gradually prepares and awakens the dawning self-consciousness, though Sullivan did not attempt to work out a precise explanation of this until several years later. "The particular event," he says in *Personal Psychopathology,* "which happens to be the first that is prehended as of a *personal* nature is neither capable of prediction nor ordinarily of being detected. Once having transpired, however, there is something new in the more or less cosmic consciousness of the infant, and a something that grows rapidly and reduces the primitive consciousness to a thoroughly secondary role."[33]

In 1932 Sullivan thought that development or growth of personality occurs from a "long circuiting" of primitive tendencies. To the primitive "vector qualities," fear, rage, and satisfaction, experience adds components of two general kinds. One kind has to do with "increasing specificity" in the integration of situations that will not lead to pain or discomfort. One may contrast this development with the mass action and global experience of early infancy from which the increasing specificity of function evolved. The other kind of component pertains to the discovery of interpersonal situations that will lead to new opportunities for the securing of future satisfactions of diverse sorts.

The infant is treated by the parents as a person—"even if a sadly rudimentary one"—and their attitudes to a significant degree are soon conveyed to him. They provide experience ("sentience"), or enable him to have certain kinds of experience, some of which is "colored" with pleasure and some with pain. Increasingly this experience becomes meaningful in the sense that "it includes enough of previous experience to stir memorial recall," though this recall should not be confused with adult recollection. Experience does not simply happen to the developing infant; because of what has already occurred to him, it has retrospective and prospective reference, which is a way of saying his experience is becoming meaningful. More and more of it is becoming personal in the sense that it is becoming organized around, and integrated into, the developing sentiment of self. In other words, the sentiment of self, however rudimentary in the first two or three years of life, increasingly becomes a center of reference, a reference-frame, in terms of which, or with the aid of which, experiences are had, organized and made meaningful. To state this in the language of adults: things do not simply happen; they happen to *me* and to *you.* Meanwhile any "deflection" of primitive tendencies into the nonconscious substratum of personality previously mentioned is in considerable part due to personal influences.

In the first years of life the body and its zones of interaction provide a groundwork for the elaboration of the self largely due to experience, so that by the third year the schematization of the self is to a considerable degree somatic. The somatic schematization of the self is at first extremely crude and ingenuous, though subsequently it becomes more refined and realistic. In later years this early schematization of the self may frequently become active in fantasy processes, especially in the service of dissociated systems. One must never overlook the fact, however, that the growing infant is more and more in communication with the world, experiences various facilitations and thwartings of impulse, empathized disapproval, and the like. The interpersonal character of what is happening must be constantly kept in mind. "The morbid mother who, under rationalization of the 'necessity of keeping the penis scrupulously clean to avoid irritation and masturbation,' devotes herself month in and month out to an obscure way of exciting the child's genital zone, is contributing exaggerated genital representations to the 'somatic self' and making the genital zone prepotent 'in response to' interpersonal situations marked by positive tendencies."[34] Sullivan claims that when the morbid maternal drive works itself out in scrubbing the anal zone, this region and its functional activity are exaggerated in representation, and a body of "manifestations of anal erotism" appears in later interpersonal relations. Thus the exaggerated emphasis on some part of the body, the anal or genital zones, for instance, is not mainly, if at all, a result of inherited predisposition but of interpersonal experience. More generally, the experiences of the infant become more and more channeled by and structured in an interpersonal context.

Sullivan wrote that thwartings of impulse either with empathic disapproval or with the more complex sentience arising from quasi- or actually sadistic "play" by the parents, facilitations of impulse also "similarly simply or complexly colored" or conditioned, and specific zone stimulation, such as that mentioned previously—all these and a great many other sorts of experience pour in and add to the self-conscious prehension of the world.

He says that unless the personality growth of all those intimately relevant to the "subject-child" has been relatively unwarped, there will be a good deal of this vicariously displaced pleasure and discomfort incorporated into the youngster's personality. The latter "is all too apt to be a plaything of the unsocialized tendencies of both parents and his elder siblings; and sometimes of those of one or more grandparents. . . . *Each and every individual habitually or frequently incorporated in the family group has an inevitable part in the child's evoltuion of personality,* but the role of each significant person often requires for its elucidation insight, in turn, into the courses of his personality."[35] The significance of this statement for therapy will be stressed in the next chapter, in which the collateral interview is outlined.

The primitive mother sentiment, which evolved in midinfancy, ceases gradually to "pertain directly" to anyone actually in contact with the youngster, and, having faded away, is succeeded by a more realistic awareness of flesh and blood embodiments of authority. He has experienced disappointments of various kinds. Pain, again and again, has had "its educative effect." The privations enforced by life may arouse a variety of maladjustive phenomena. The succession of flesh-and-blood embodiments of authority accompanied by various discomforts and privations, which arouse various maladjustive phenomena, is said to contribute much to the "reality" underlying the so-called castration fear. The notion of castration fear often has been mistakenly used by Freudians as an explanatory principle for *various states of insecurity actually arising from various interpersonal experiences.*[36] The reader will recall that Freud resorted to extremely complicated speculations, including the notion of phylogenetic inheritance, in order to save his concept of castration dread, which for him meant primarily a fear by male children of three or four years of age of losing the penis, of having it cut off, and which he thought furnished the most potent motive for repression of the Oedipus complex.

Sullivan offers alternative interpretations of the "Oedipus guilt" and the Oedipus complex. They are not universal, innately conditioned experiences. He believed that the former is understandable by an appeal "to the infancy and childhood experiences that include individuals vested with authority."[37] In this connection he refers to certain works of Malinowski.[38]

For Sullivan, the Oedipus complex was not the outcome or result of an hereditary disposition or of some racially transmitted disposition (going back to the events of a primal horde). Nor was it, he thought, a sexual phenomenon. He explains its origin as having to do with infantile frustrations or loss of satisfactions, experienced at the time "of the primitive mother-child symbiosis," which the child may be expected, as Sullivan puts it, to discriminate poorly in distributing unpleasant characterizations. In other words, infants and young children cannot make nice discriminations or analyses of events when it comes to locating the sources or causes of their loss of satisfactions. Even adults cannot always make nice discriminations or refined analyses of events leading to the loss of satisfactions (or of security). It is a familiar fact that sometimes we "blame" the wrong fellow for some loss; it may even be that no one is to be "blamed" for the loss of something that to us is precious. So it is no wonder that a youngster under five years of age cannot make such nice discriminations.

For the child it is more difficult to "characterize" events, to sort them out, so to speak, and see how they are related. And furthermore, he too, if I may loosely formulate his behavior in the language of adults, will find a scapegoat. As Sullivan puts it, negative (or hostile) valuations originating in the loss of satisfaction experienced at the time of the primitive mother-child symbiosis will scarcely tend to "segregate" upon the person most closely identified with the satisfaction of needs. And so, in the case of the little boy, they tend to "segregate" around the father.

But in order to account for the so-called Electra complex, Sullivan introduces an additional point in his attempt to explain it and the Oedipus complex of the boy, a consideration that is "rather contradictory to the expectation from the satisfaction of infantile needs." In the case of both boys and girls the primitive mother sentiment is the same, which is followed by the differentiation of the mother as more and more of a person instead of a godlike figure. At this stage the girl also tends to "segregate" painful impressions on some one other than the mother. But then a complicating factor arises, "an extra link in the chain of processes," because of empathy.[39] Parents are said to adopt a more authoritative attitude toward the offspring of the same sex.

"Empathy seems to function in childhood to produce a linkage of male to male and female to female. The son comes to be to the father, and the father to the son, a sort of personality-extension quite different from the linkage continuing between the mother and son. Similarly, there arises this new sort of linkage of the mother and daughter."[40] Sullivan surmised that there enter into these phenomena culture elements in the shape of traditional attitudes of the man as to woman and of the woman as to man, these being empathically prehended by the child. He wrote that the factor [of empathy] seems to show as an unwitting prehension by the man of his son, and by the mother of her daughter, such that the actual behavior, expressive and other, of the father to the son and of the mother to the daughter, is more direct and authoritative than is it in the other cases. Sullivan surmised that the distressing aspects of reality are "most" forced on the child by the parent of the same sex while the other parent retains a more prolonged approximation to the "old all-satisfying divinity" of infancy. And so in the child's partition of positive and negative feelings the son is said to become more antipathetic to the father and the daughter to the mother. If the parent of the same sex is oversensitive to the growing antipathy of the juvenile, the so-called Oedipus hatred and guilt will appear.

In the era of childhood, which is introduced by the maturation of the capacity for language behavior, the training of the child gathers momentum and a great deal is learned, including the "incorporation" into the sentiment of self of "stereotypes" or subcomplexes (subsentiments) of the character of dominant and submissive individuality. One finds that there is much obedience to authority but also attempts to evade it, along with the seeking of means to escape and relieve thwarting and frustration. There has to be a "long-circuiting" (sublimation) of tendencies in accordance with cultural prescriptions as they are embodied in the parents, immediate gratification being frequently denied. Not only the parents but other members of the family group play a role in the "evolution" of the child's personality. The disappointments that he suffers at the hands of parents and elder siblings, are often passed on in some form to younger siblings, pets, or inanimate objects.

In brief, the development of personality entails, stage by stage, an increasing recognition of the "superiority" of certain situational demands to one's own immediate needs and wishes. The future looms larger and larger in the widening horizon of the growing child. More and more, the prospective future interpenetrates the momentary situation. There is a long-circuiting of tendencies increasingly in the interests of remote and mediate ends. The life of fantasy, as a rule, slowly yields and crumbles beneath the pressures of the "real" world. More and more play in general must give way to the demands of "reality." In short, the growing person must adapt himself, as Sullivan puts it, to the demands of the world situation, a task that normally becomes easier as one grows.

Sullivan says that as the growth of reality-prehension—that is, the ever-increasing grasp of the rudiments of the environmental world— might be taken to be the principal of many accessions to personality during early infancy; and the prehension of interpersonal necessities of the type of submission to authority (parents or their surrogates, chiefly), by which a great body of the parental culture complexes is incorporated, that of late infancy and early childhood; so in the next era, the juvenile epoch, there will be the learning of social techniques. He believed that *each stage of development must prepare the personality at least for the principal development of the next era.* Thus failure to achieve significant "accessions" to personality during a given era may have grave, if not disastrous, consequence for subsequent personality development, seriously limiting the individual's chances for a normal and successful life. Sullivan thought, when he wrote *Personal Psychopathology,* that grave disorders of growth in childhood, which will tend to disqualify one for the juvenile socialization, may be classified, in the main under the rubrics of *psychopathic personality* and the *obsessional personality.*

Among the things that may happen during the childhood era and obstruct a realistic "prehension" of the world and facilitate the development of "dynamisms of difficulty" are the following: "If the mother was quick to respond to the infant's cry, and now the child finds that oral procedures are efficacious in securing all satisfactions, his growth of manipulative techniques is apt to be arrested at the level of verbal behavior. He continues at the stage at which certain combinations of words, expressive postures, and gestures possess magical power in securing pleasure and avoiding pain."[41] Instead of finding himself in a challenging environment, he discovers that the situation merely calls for the production of the necessary formulae. His symbolic techniques do not lose their magical investiture. And so when the significant others having "preternatural respect" for verbal techniques allow them to take precedence over less symbolic behavior, the child does not "long-curcuit" his tendencies further in this connection. He fails to learn vital aspects of interpersonal reality, and to develop the necessary foresight, maintaining fantastic patterns (or "images") of people as foci (objects) for symbolic acts considered "useful" in having his own way. There is, in other words, a failure or lack of opportunity to profit from experience.

The psychopathic child's failure applies only to interpersonal relations for he may learn in an average fashion something of the stubborn complexity of inanimate nature. He continues to apply expressive techniques of the late infantile and early childhood stages in dealing with distressing aspects of life, and is increasingly unable to be "*personally real*" in interpersonal situations. "It is as if he lived in a world in which people are significant from moment to moment only in the course of his pursuit of pleasure, and then only in so far as they momentarily demand prompt expressive gestures. They are appraised neither in terms of avoiding unpleasant consequents to action, nor with regard to the enhancement of opportunity for future gratifications."[42] The development of the self is chiefly manifested in the form of improved techniques of expressive, mostly verbal, gesturing. Whatever elaboration of interpersonal experience occurs is split into a restricted growth of personal "prehensions" (unformulated perceptions) within the self, and a fairly large development of complexes manifested as peculiarly irrational positive and negative emotional tendencies toward others. The psychopathic child never learns techniques of consensual validation in interpersonal relations, and so fantasy processes continue to predominate. His emotional tendencies toward others are unrealistic and irrational.

The first evidence of handicap to socialization is said to appear in the beginning of the juvenile era, when he suffers a series of failures in his social efforts. Owing to a deficiency or immaturity of self-formulation, he is incapable of correcting erroneous actions in interpersonal relations, and thus he fails to profit from experience so that unpleasant experience tends to be repeated. The self is truncated, and so many of his interpersonal tendency systems operate extra consciously that he is, so to speak, an uncomprehending victim of inevitably recurring disappointments. The latter add very little to his "adjustive improvement." And whenever any psychopathic person encounters the need for really intimate interpersonal relations, his difficulties are said to become acute. Thus he stumbles through the years, often adopting a cocksureness of attitude to others that only seems to hasten the unpleasant denouement of each new contact.

Despite the fact that in later life the psychopath is often considered to be a great liar, this judgment is unsound since there is little or no conscious determination to deceive. Sullivan claimed that even in the case of the individual who cannot give an authentic account of any of his doings, that is, the pathological liar, the intention to deceive is less conspicuous than is his inability to believe the facts he has experienced.

The development of the self, like all other growth of personality, is largely by way of increasing speed in the acquisition of attitudes, motives, feelings, ideas, and behavior patterns that are relevant and efficacious in the series of total situations, chiefly interpersonal situations, through which the person lives. Normally one acquires facility at logical (verbal) thinking by learning to validate propositions "consensually." In strictly logical thinking, propositions are verified according to certain rules to be found in logic texts. But everyday "logical" thinking rarely approaches such rigor; nor is it usually necessary. In any event it happens in the growth of the individual that words as such are very late in losing "magical investiture" and standing forth as merely symbols for use in abstract thinking as well as being efficient aids for the intercommunication of intelligence.[43] If the acquisition of chiefly verbal techniques are emphasized over other aspects of "interpersonal reality" by the parents, then the growth of the self is severely truncated. The child's interpersonal relations remain immature and distorted while he fails to acquire fairly realistic conceptions of what other people are like, having instead incorporated fantastic patterns of people. Thus the psychopathic self of such an individual is said to continue to be of an astonishing simplicity, while the reality that can be ascribed to other people and their doings is equally limited.

Summarily, Sullivan claims that the psychopathic self continues to be of astonishing simplicity, and one's perceptions of the reality of other people and their doings are similarly limited. Whenever the motivation of the psychopath in an interpersonal situation miscarries, the predisposition or set is usually dissipated by grief or anger and his impression of the unpleasantness is replaced in consciousness by a fantasied success. The handicap to socialization is enormous. Very soon after the beginning of the juvenile era, the psychopathic juvenile begins to sense a difference from others, which is subsequently enhanced by a series of failures in his social efforts. The singular deficiency of the self-formulation makes it impossible for him to correct erroneous actions in interpersonal relations so that his unpleasant experiences tend to recur without any evidence of profit from his behavior. Some psychopathic juveniles become thoroughly embittered and act in such a fashion that they offend the very people with whom they should be on good terms. Some, having become masters of verbal techniques, learn to exploit gullible people. Not only is the psychopathic person incapable of intimacy, he is incapable of a sound sexual adjustment; instead, his sexual behavior is an unfailing source of trouble for himself and his very temporary "mates." Generally he is inadaptable in situations requiring submission to authority, except regimented groups such as the armed forces.

Another childhood deviation that is the result of morbid parental interests and attitudes is that of the obsessional child. He tends to express doubts and uncertainties about everything. The device with which he "handles" significant peoples is "thought." Since the obsessional child is apt to be of superior native intelligence, he has no difficulty with "actually adjustive implicit processes." He can learn easily, manifesting excellent ability to profit from experience, save that pertaining to significant people in interpersonal relations. Again and again he finds *"estimable"* considerations with which to perplex himself and his parents. Among other things, questions of right and wrong, good and bad, are a fertile source of "problems," and those in contact with him may be favorably impressed or moved to compassionate efforts at assistance, whose results are thoroughly disappointing.

Sullivan believed that the parents' loveless marriage complicated by "hypocrisy" and imposture are the prime sources of the obsessional deviation. Without going into all the details of Sullivan's explanation,

I may mention the suppressed contempt and hatred in one or both parents for the other, their lack of love and their intolerance for the child, which make the growth of antipathetic tendencies in him a great trial to them. These tendencies are sidetracked out of the self-conscious personality, continuing, though entirely unconsciously, in a complaisant martyrdom "in search for Truth."

The parents' emphatically proclaimed love of him is spurious. They both try to play the mother role, which neither of them sustains. The child is said to be their most effective tool for malicious efforts, for whose allegiance each parent strives, and concerning which both are uncertain. "As long as he shows positive responses to one parent, the other strives to secure his affection."[44] When at times he does not manifest positive behavior, he is of little interest to either. And so he learns to stretch out the period of suspense; he has found he is most interesting to others when he is hesitating. A "thought-ridden" hesitation becomes his outstanding characteristic. The spontaneous, prompt integration of interpersonal situations disappears gradually, while the manifestations of emotionally colored behavior become obscure. His thoughtfulness is specious, turning all the virtues "into instrumentalities of aggression and aggrandizement of the self." Everything he does takes on "preternatural gravity," and he requires constant reassurance that he is doing the right thing. If the reassurance is not forthcoming, he redoubles his efforts; if it is secured, the giver is of no further importance in this respect, and he "comes up" with a new problem. The self of the obsessional child never abandons its original "omnipotence *anlage*." He acts and thinks as if people in his environment were but shadowy selves tributary to his unconsciously driven obsessional self.

The behavior of the obsessional person may be characterized superficially as marked by an excess of uncertainty and scrupulosity in interpersonal relations. But the obsessional person does not actually suffer from a timorous uncertainty. Usually he is tenacious and stubborn to a degree, especially in doubting. Thus the "anxiety" of the obsessional child to do, think and say just *the* right thing, the many problems or difficulties found by him to exist in selecting the right thing, the punctilious, overcareful scrupulosity of every action, the "undeviating thoroughness" of every preoccupation—all these signs and symptoms combine to make the life of his parents or other significant people constantly in contact with him "something rather less than paradisiacal." Added to these is the fact that he must "explain" his acts, lest there be any probability of misinterpretation. So he demands reassurance, even though he was reassured but a few hours ago on these very same matters. Thus the intolerant parents, who have rejected him, are "hoist by their own petards."

Summarily, the obsessional child has sidetracked (dissociated) anger and rage tendencies, often finding rather complete satisfaction of them by his obsessive-compulsive aggression.

Sullivan wrote that childhood is peculiarly characterized as an era of tendency systems integrating the individual as an organically feeble, easily punished (relatively impotent) person, with other individuals prehended not as comparable persons but as embodiments or sources of pleasureable and discomforting activities. Childhood "passes over into the juvenile era, in which an effort must be made to bring compeers among these entities into pleasureable cooperative activities, and some measure of success initiated in dealing with other individuals who deviate in various measures from the childhood stereotypes of similar more or less adult entities."[45]

Children do not engage in interpersonal relations with other children who are their "compeers" on anything like a uniform basis. Regarding gross activity in social relations Sullivan quotes Dorothy Swaine Thomas, who worked in the Columbia Child Study Institute. Thomas had observed three prevailing types: (1) "children who consistently show certain patterns of behavior; who consistently talk in certain terms, say, who consistently use nouns that refer to objects or consistently are playing with material objects rather than persons"; (2) "other children who will spend say ninety percent of their time consistently in groups where groups are forming, whose language will, to a predominant extent, concern other persons"; and (3) "others who are disproportionately withdrawn from those overt forms of activity . . . they are neither concerned with material objects to any extent as shown by these techniques nor with other persons, but their activities seem to center around their inner life."[46]

Having indicated how, from the Sullivanian view, some difficulties in living may take their start in infancy and childhood, I shall end the discussion of childhood with a few summary observations. According to Sullivan, during the childhood era the self is mainly evidenced in relations of domination by and submission to older people. The child uses most of his energy in quasi-realistic activity. By and large he is not yet able to employ implicit processes of the fully adjustive type. The interpersonal relations of the child customarily eventuate in one of three outcomes that entail, respectively, three valuations of the other person concerned in situations, and contribute in one of three ways to the growth of the self.

In one outcome, the impulses of the child are said to progress easily to complete satisfaction, the adult being compliant and pleased by the child. In this event, "the feeling-tone of the child's related self-consciousness is pleasant."

One finds another sort of situation, in which the impulses of the child are directly thwarted and in which the adult is disapproving of or is displeased with the child. In this kind of situation, the feeling-tone of the child is said to be either a hateful feeling appearing as a tendency to primitive (infantile) rage or one of antagonism "originating by differentiation from the primitive rage."[47] Such interpersonal occurrences, involving active thwarting by an adult, became "dissolved into emotional implicit processes"; that is, the child has recourse to fantasy or play as a means of outlet for anger or antagonism.

Again one finds a third typical set of conditions in which the impulses of the child are met by studied or accidental indifference by the adult. "The total interpersonal situation, which has been integrated to include this adult, thus tends to fail of resolution."[48] The situation is said to persist and its persistence is accompanied by a felt interest, in this instance, in the other self. Sullivan does not elaborate on this sort of occurrence. It may be that he had his own childhood experience in mind. His father, whose affection Sullivan yearned for, may have been, or seemed to have been, uninterested in him.

Before turning to a discussion of the juvenile era, I wish to mention the following. During the first two eras, the life of the youngster is lived chiefly in the home under the supervision of adults and older siblings. The personality is said to grow during infancy and childhood from the intrauterine state to one characterized by a clear-cut self-organization. The stereotypes or subcomplexes (dynamisms) that constitute this self-organization generally remain "prepotent" throughout life. Rarely are they fundamentally altered by subsequent experience. The stereotypes embody "culture entities" imposed on the growing personality "*from above*," that is, from authority figures. Among these culture entities are the superego processes made famous by Freud.

Sullivan claims that "at the same time" (a phrase I take to mean *during the period when* the three kinds of experience mentioned above occur) there is a new measure, an enhancement, of consciousness of the child's self and of his needs for a response by the other person. Sullivan's meaning, though obscurely formulated, seems to be that the need for an audience response is a normal development of childhood, and that this need is enhanced, not created, by any indifference of the significant other. In any case, it is in such situations, Sullivan goes on to say, that the need, subsequently manifested as the seeking for status, arises in the child's self-consciousness. This need is defined as "an enduring organization of the self and its appurtenances such that at least indifference will not be the outcome of situations including other persons, and preferably that the outcome will be favorable appraisal and approbation."[49]

The development of the drive for status is said to be one of the clearest manifestations of beginning socialization. A sort of crude hedonism might be said to be the major preoccupation or guiding principle of the child's life until this time. Henceforth the successful resolution of interpersonal situations includes or requires evidence of favorable attention. And in instances in which disapproval has been much more frequent or effective than compliance the striving for status by hateful or antagonistic activities is "almost to be expected." To such children being bad, as Sullivan observes, is at least being something, for it brings attention and recognition, however unfavorable. Thus even when the status that is being pursued has a negative social value, it is nevertheless "urgently necessary."

As time passes, the self becomes "exteriorized" on animate and inanimate objects, on people, animals, material objects. Some of those who have passed their youth in some one locality and then departed will recall how the familiar ground that one has walked upon, the sights and sounds and odors experienced over and over thousands of times, become so intimate a part of one's life that abandoning them entailed a wrenching of the self. Then, too, there are the people one has known: one's family, as a rule, first of all, friends, neighbors. In varying degrees, they have contributed toward the priceless gift of self. And, to a degree, one returns the gift in kind. In leaving them, one, so to speak, leaves a part of oneself with them forever.

In a passage strongly reminiscent of William James's famous discussion of the self in his *Principles of Psychology*, Sullivan asserted that not only does the sentiment of self grow along the paths of assertion, domination, and submission, and a variety of perhaps subordinate factors, from all the experience in which an appraisal by another person has made its appearance in a social situation, but also it grows by a peculiar "extravasation" of selfhood upon material and immaterial objects in varying degrees attached to or associated with the individual. The clothing worn by a person is said to be usually intimately related to his self. "His home, his parents, the family car—all these are represented in a self-context. Any contribution of a positive or negative valuation to any of these objects also contributes to the self, and to the satisfaction or the reverse of the status-seeking."[50] Sullivan adds that it is only a matter of time until verbal expressions of opinions by the juvenile, too, come to be precious parts of the self, and their good or bad reception a contribution to positive or negative self-feeling. "This factor often becomes so important that an individual will go to great lengths in defending his expressed opinion long after he has become convinced of its falsity."[51]

In the juvenile era, the extension in range and "enlargement" of interpersonal relations greatly augments the importance of social tools that are, according to Sullivan, primarily the expressive apparatus. "Not only do daily contacts with many now take the place of hourly contacts with a particular few, but the zones of interaction tend to become more strictly those of the visage, the voice, and the posture and carriage."[52] The importance of the face is said to grow rapidly, especially since perceptual experience of other faces is chiefly visual. The consensual validation of information acquired from auditory experience is less frequent and probably essentially much more difficult. All the interpersonal expressive equipment is said to be subject from midchildhood onward increasingly to moulding influences of two major categories. These two categories embrace the self-esteemed tendency systems, including the idealizations of the self, and, second, tendency systems chronically dissociated from the self. Sullivan claimed that the changes wrought by the latter tend to become conspicuous and persistently characteristic in the course of the adolescent epoch.

In the juvenile era and in all subsequent periods there is not only "an augmentation of the self by more direct accessions of status," there is also an increase or growth "in the spread of relevance" of experience because the range or extent of the significant, meaningful world becomes greatly expanded because of the development of secondary group relationships. In other words, the significant world, the world that has meaning for one, is no longer confined to the home, neighborhood, or school. Gradually, through the agencies of storybook, school discussions, radio, television, the horizon of one's meaningful world expands. One may become interested in, say, the governmental affairs of one's own country or even in faraway places and far-off things. Increasingly one wonders what India or China is like, or the people of such countries, with their "strange" languages and customs. Unfortunately, teachers, at least in the recent past, have harbored some curious superstitions about foreigners. Nor was the latter's essential humanity stressed. Thus the pupil combined the information and misinformation he had acquired with a measure of personal fantasy. The upshot was "*a sentiment the object of which is an hypothetical (person or) group of people*"—a sentiment that was energized by diverse tendency systems.

As the self grows, one slowly, gradually becomes less parochial. The speed and direction of self growth of course depends on a number of variables. The development of the self may be slow, tortuous, and quickly truncated. It may, in very fortunate circumstances, be for many years rapid and harmonious, continuing though with diminishing speed, as long as life lasts. And the "direction" of self growth may be such that one's experiences become emotionally thin, imaginatively bare, increasingly restricted by anxiety or hostility or conflict. In other instances, of course, the self may continue to grow indefinitely and in such a manner that some individuals achieve great emotional capacity, imaginative power, and intellectual penetration. The social determinants of all such outcomes, operating through native potentialities, include the home environment and the community in which one lives, first of all; but as one grows other influences become more and more important.

It is necessary to emphasize the importance of school if only because secondary group relationships arise, as Sullivan puts it, in part in the more formal education, though their initially most important source is said to lie in the expansion of direct primary relationships. "They," that is, the people outside of past, present, or immediate future, direct sensory experience, take on various measures of reality and relevance, whether "they," as he says, be the semimythological parents of the playmates, or other children of whom the teacher tells, or yet even more remote folk about whom stories are read; "they" become more or less significant in a fashion quite distinct from the objects of direct action. One becomes aware of much that is new and exciting.

The juvenile makes questioning a major concern. "Everything is liable to investigation." He discovers inadequacies in the family group stereotypes. If he still possesses "comparative mental health," the more accessible (more conscious) aspects of the stereotypes that he has learned undergo refinement and modification, or, in Sullivan's phrase, extensive differentiation and resymbolization, along with gradual change in the pertinent or related tendencies of the juvenile. It dawns on one that his parents are no longer to be regarded as almost godlike figures, and that their ideas, attitudes, and actions fall something short of perfection. There is a gradual change of orientation toward the family and the larger world, and along with it a gradual change in motivation and attitude. The teacher and the parents of playmates play a significant role in this change if only because certain aspects of their behavior are observed and consciously compared with those of the parents.

A beginning of active emancipation from some of the limitations of the family group and from some of one's own limitations in the child role may thus arise from the juvenile's observations and conscious comparisons often taking the form of questioning the "central prejudice" (unspecified) of the parent. To this juvenile procedure many parents react in an unhealthy fashion, and the youngster must then attempt to adapt his efforts accordingly. Sometimes the parental reaction to their offspring's questioning and challenging may be violent, with very unhappy consequences to the latter.

"In the family group where the maturation and final emancipation of the offspring are most bitterly opposed—always 'unconsciously'—and the juvenile for that very reason, if he is not already whipped into submission, is the more anxious to secure experience that will help him, we find a situation that is prone to eventuate either in active hostility or in the cultivation of fraudulent behavior towards the parents."[53]

If the latter outcome occurs, the juvenile, who rarely has a capacity for conscious hypocrisy that would deceive the parents, is compelled to resort to morbid dissociation. In such a case, unwitting use is said to be made of the somatic expressive apparatus in the interest of motivations that are incongruous with the major integration of personality, that is, with the self-system. And so he will manifest a striking, though entirely unwitting, "metamorphosis" when he comes into "the zone of influence" of the parental environment, where he remains for the parents what they desire him to be, in contrast to his behavior in the school, playground, and elsewhere, where he manifests a fair approximation to an average growth of personality.

What about the juvenile who engages in frank hostility to the parental codes and valuations? According to Sullivan, even if such a youngster is successful, he still suffers considerable damage. The reason for this is not explicitly stated. Apparently such a rebellion involves too great a wrenching of parental attachments, leaving an empty void, for Sullivan claims that there still clings to the parents much of the aura from the time when they were God, that is godlike figures. In any case, he says, parents who are inadequate enough to desire the complete subordination of their child are hardly likely to maintain a benevolent attitude in the face of a losing struggle. "The issues are joined again and again. Appeals to sympathy, vituperations, threats and gloomy forebodings—these are a few of the devices used against the rebellious juvenile."[54] The latter is said to "prehend" that there is no going back to a friendly status for him, and he discovers that whenever he tries it he is immediately imposed upon. Usually, like the "quasi-hypocritical" youngster, he must resort to morbid dissociation.

In some instances, the juvenile is frustrated in all his efforts at emancipation from the child role, and so he remains in it without material growth of personality. In his further dealings with authority, he maintains the child-parent pattern or his experience with authority occurs exterior to self-consciousness. In the latter case, his experience becomes "tributary" to the tendency systems dissociated as a result of his submission to the continuing immature role. Sullivan calls such personalities chronic juveniles. In the ordinary sense of the word, they fail to become "socialized," and were it not for the existence of certain elders "to whom their veneration is sweet," they would almost certainly suffer grave mental disorder at the period when others enter adolescence. But many of these people find a series of "foster parents" from whom they are said to receive encouragement and the necessary adjustive opportunity, provided any such opportunity does not allow of any overshadowing of the patron person.

So far in the discussion not much has been said about the juvenile's experiences in school. There is one thing, in particular, that I want to mention: the fact that a great number of "adjustive suppressions" are required. More generally, every juvenile encounters "innumerable relevant factors" or happenings in situations that he does not clearly notice or ignores or avoids. In the interest of more satisfactory performances, he suppresses these, or his experiences of them. Sullivan claims that even from midinfancy each "organically average individual" has exercised some selection of factors in the integration of each total situation. This selection is effected chiefly by suppressing rudimentary awareness of factors that would be distracting and, given one's personality structure, might interfere with satisfactory performances in situations. But when some motivational tendencies are very powerful, whose suppression is required, as in the instance of warped children, their suppression, if it can be effected, is said to be done at the cost of so great inner stress that little else can occupy such children. And "complications" usually appear. For example, the frustration may release a more or less directed hostility toward authority figures.

To speak generally, the school provides not only opportunities for growth but also makes certain demands on the pupils that involve limitations on the expression of impulse and on overt behavior. The enforced limitations are "modified" however by a growing social conformity; "the common practice of all the children encourages a modification of the various suppressed tendencies in the direction of sublimation and conforming compensatory satisfactions."[55]

But the juvenile is subjected to interpersonal demands that transcend the situation in the classroom. Often these demands are encountered in the schoolyard or playground. To a degree, every juvenile becomes more widely acquainted with "various vicious and discomforting aspects of one's fellows." Such things may be encountered, for example, on acquaintance with the sadistic bully and the sexually precocious. And these considerations bring us to a discussion of sadism and masochism.

According to Sullivan, sadism, "the securing of pleasure by inflicting pain," has its great inning in the juvenile era, the time of its most "frank manifestation." But he did not think that it, along with its so-called opposite, masochism, "the enjoyment of inflicted pain," is a universal feature of human nature. He speculated that sadistic tendencies are chiefly manifested by juveniles who have been subjected to much irrational and/or malicious thwartings by one of the parents. The more general Freudian usage of sadism and masochism designating activity and passivity or aggressiveness and submissiveness, he believed, contributes to confusion and unwarranted generalization.

Although Sullivan did not think that there is an inherent connection between sadistic, masochistic, or sadomasochistic, tendencies and sexuality, he observed that there is a "curious interrelation" in many persons between them and the "later acquired" sexual impulses. "Individually and socially, this combination is of no small moment," he said, "as it seems that a large part of the sexual drive can be dissipated through the channel of cruelty or the undergoing of abuse."[56] Thus in contrast to Freudian theory, sadomasochistic impulses are not regarded as inherently connected with sexuality or as an outcome of a fusion of Eros and the "death instinct."

To the majority of juveniles a defense by hysteroid incapacitation to bullying is repugnant to the self. But there are those who resort to this sort of behavior pattern. According to Sullivan, as a rule they come from homes in which one of the parents employs the defense of incapacitation and in which the child has not been so fortunate as to grow up "in rough-and-tumble" with brothers and sisters near enough in age for such give-and-take. "When such a one comes in contact with the school bully and has an entirely unexpected very bad time, he may show a facile recourse to incapacitation reactions and incorporate an unwitting attitude somewhat to the effect that in certain interpersonal relations one's reaction is that of becoming sick, feeling faint or whatever."[57] Actually, one can see the building of the hysteric or hysteroid way of dealing with interpersonal difficulties even in the kindergarten. But in the course of adolescence the attitude of the boy's fellows usually "deflects" such hysterical tendencies to some different kind of morbidity, such as hypochondriacal interests. Sometimes a combination of hypochondriacal preoccupations alternating irregularly with paranoid states may be established.

No matter how little a particular youngster may have encountered aggression or sadism until he reaches the school years, he will experience them in the schoolyard or playground, if not in the classroom, as well as elsewhere. According to Sullivan, when juveniles are discomforted by the aggression or sadism of a schoolfellow, and the "unsatisfactory" or inappropriate tendencies that they manifest, the tendencies, in other words, that provoke aggressive or sadistic behavior, are not susceptible of suppression, such juveniles may have recourse to repression, often with an ensuing dissociation. Now, suppression or repression or dissociation of any impulse, drive, or tendency cannot occur by an act of pure reason; the motivating force or "motor" has to include the operation of another more compelling, more powerful impulse, drive, or tendency. For example, if one is motivated both to anger and to conciliation, the anger behavior cannot be suppressed unless the conciliative impulse is more powerful or more powerfully energized than the tendency to anger is. Outbursts of rage or anger or "irritation" by many children are found to be effective tools in situations threatening them with frustration so that this sort of behavior is reinforced by recurrent experience. And so this utilization of anger can scarcely be suppressed when the youngster encounters different situations, even though it evokes hostile reactions from other juveniles. Very powerful tendencies toward conciliative conformity that are stirred by danger and accompanied generally by fear are said to be effectively employed during the juvenile era in the teaching of conciliation and abnegation. Since the utilization of anger or childish tantrum ensues in a "fear-provoking event," it is usually highly repugnant to self-esteem. After a few of such experiences, the juvenile generally represses them, with the result that there is in such instances little profiting from experience. The anger-provoking situations therefore recur, and they tend to identical unpleasant outcome. But a whole series of such incidents make repression impossible. One must, perforce, either modify the tendency to outbursts of anger, rage, or irritation, for behavior which is more realistic and healthy or resort to dissociation of the tendencies whose manifestations are disastrous. In the latter case the related sub-complex or stereotype is dissociated from the self.

Dissociation of any impulse or of any tendency system of course does not make it inoperative. According to Sullivan, while one may continue to manifest anger in various situations, the anger tendencies previously evoked by the situation in point disappear from consciousness, finding expression instead in some unrecognized alterations in postural tensions of the skeletal muscles or the viscera, or in unnoted symptomatic acts. Should the dissociated system be frequently energized by situational factors, its expressions may be manifested as tensions in the muscular equipment that tend to persist except in deep sleep. The expressive apparatus centered in the face is said to be often concerned in this, "lines" in characteristic patterns appearing as evidences of the chronically recurring tensions. "The facial movements develop characteristic peculiarities that are manifest whenever the complex situation including activity of the dissociated system arises. Interferences with the freedom of the cheek muscles and the movement of the jaw and with the freedom of movement of the lips, as well as interferences with tension changes in the larynx and even in the diaphragm, may manifest the dissociated system in characteristic alterations of the voice."[58] Sullivan adds that quality, intonation, emphasis, rate, and precision of syllabic articulation, and several other elements of speech, may undergo both persisting change and this sort of automatic activation.

In the beginning of this and the previous chapter I mentioned the now familiar fact that inborn factors of organization fix the limits of life opportunity in certain ways, though these factors of course provide the biological potentialities of experience. Within the limits imposed by innately determined potentialities, and by the sociocultural environment, the individual gradually acquires or develops a personality such that it facilitates the acquisition of some kinds of experience and behavior while it partially or totally excludes others. But this acquisition is not made by a perfectly unified or integrated organism. To put this loosely, one may say that anyone's personality is not all of one piece. Usually we tend to think of our personality as coterminous with those experiences and behavior patterns that have become meaningfully organized, what Sullivan calls the self-conscious personality or, in a later formulation, self-dynamism. But there are in addition tendencies or drives that, dating from infancy, are "profoundly unconscious," unmeaningful, and inaccessible to conscious awareness. There are, also, later acquired tendencies that have been excluded by the self, called dissociated tendencies, which, according to a formulation subsequent to *Personal Psychopathology,* "attach" themselves to those other deeply unconscious processes, the whole forming a more or less organized, structured "system" functionally disparate from, or antithetical to, the self-conscious personality. Just how elaborated this "unconscious" or dissociated aspect of the personality is, or becomes, depends on the course and quality of postnatal experience.

How, then, can two (or more) frequently hostile strangers, the self and the dissociated, dwell under the same roof? Sometimes they cannot, and one, the dissociated, overpowers the other, the self. But usually the two systems exist without disintegration of the personality, even though the person may sometimes endure considerable strain. In order to account for the fact that most individuals as they grow develop a certain degree of harmony in their lives, Sullivan in *Personal Psychopathology* introduced the notion of a controlling or directive agency that, in fortunate circumstances, limits the elaboration of dissociated processes, channels the development of the self, and at the same time maintains personal integrity. But this concept is obscurely formulated because one cannot see in detail what its precise connection is with the two "systems," though it appears in connection with or as a function of the self.

Within the overall developing personality structure there grows a "prepotent vector pattern" or "deeply unconscious configuration" whose time of probable formation is said to be past before the end of childhood. The "evidences" of this constituent of personality are called *character*. It is said to control the freedom of personality growth and to delimit the field of relevant experience. For example, in the pursuit of status this selective factor, which "shows" chiefly in the motivation of the self, ordinarily ensures that only certain situational conditions are permitted to become relevant, and only certain possibilities of interpersonal adjustment acceptable. The character factor limits the growth of tendency systems exterior to the self. This is said to be its chief import. According to Sullivan, the less effective it is, the more the ongoing series of interpersonal situations that are experienced contribute to a polymorphous growth of the personality and to the appearance of various maladjustive processes. There tends to be, in other words, a lack of integration of the various suborganizations of personality. When the character factor is weak or lacking (if it is ever completely lacking) then the person is relatively helpless in the face of a plethora of interpersonal circumstances, as may be seen in the case of obsessional and psychopathic juveniles in whom it seems to be missing.

Its manifestations, which appear chiefly in the motivation of the self-conscious personality, when present, are said to become increasingly significant in the juvenile and subsequent stages of development. Sullivan surmised that character, or the learned predisposition that a healthy person possesses to function in certain ways, is a "normal evolution" in personality development, and that only when it is well developed is mental health to be presumed. He speculated that character is a stereotype founded "in the first differentiation from the primitive mother sentiment, and integrating in it the subsequent *experience of consistent manifestations of enduring constructive attitudes towards the child* on the part of either or both parents and others relevant in the early situations."[59] Character is thus an outcome of consistent fortunate experiences beginning in infancy with the mothering one, as the infant begins to make elementary discriminations between himself and the environment—discriminations that he accumulates and refines over a period of years. Sullivan says that all that is fully adjustive in the relationship of the individual during infancy and childhood with significant others, and only that which is fully adjustive, is tributary to character. And its operation or functional activity "seems to depend on a fairly comprehensive grasp on the reality both of the self and of other selves." Apparently Sullivan conceived of character as the unifying, integrative aspect of personal life.

Character is not to be confused with the Freudian notion of a superego, or of "conscience," a notion that Sullivan adopted for a time, and which in the *Personal Psychopathology* remains in essentials rather similar to Freud's conception. "Successful man-ways begin to be incorporated in the first days of infancy, and the integration of the character-stereotype is all but finished by the time that unsuccessful, biologically subversive, and incoherently contradictory tendencies can be inculcated."[60] Character is said to root in the "deep unconscious" while the superego or conscience is much nearer the "level" of late childhood, that is, much more accessible to consciousness. "Conscience is a differentiation in the self, composed of self-conscious experiences in which the parents (and analogues) function as theocrats, as agents of transcendental power, and one by which a self-tendency is created to function theocratically. Its explicit manifestations take the form of inhibitory tendencies, failure of which is attended by the appearance in consciousness of a *feeling of guilt,* peculiarly antithetic to self-esteem. . . ."[61] Threatened loss of status among others is said to be so potent in many people that a life of maladjustments results. If one is brought up to believe in the tenets of religion, the "loss of status with God" is said to be an even more serious matter, and has to be remedied.

While character represents that part of the cultural heritage that worked satisfactorily in the lives of the parents and has been transmitted to the offspring, conscience, according to Sullivan, seems to embody that aspect of the cultural heritage transmitted to him that did not function wholly adjustively in the parents—presumably because of its irrational nature. In general, the satisfaction of frustrated conscience, including "discharge" of the sense of guilt, is said to be accomplished variously, sometimes by implicit processes, rationalization, penitential thoughts, prayer, and the like, though usually by witting or unconscious penitential acts, the motivation of which is called a need for punishment. Again, while character exercises powerful control of relevance, powerful control over what shall and shall not become significant, and therefore efficacious, the major stereotype or dynamism called conscience, representing one's moral systems of beliefs, exercise feeble control.

(Before leaving this matter of the superego, I should like to raise the question as to whether Sullivan has not equated the superego of the mentally ill with the characteristics of people's moral experience generally, at least in American society.)

The juvenile era is said to be peculiarly the period for the appearance of compensatory programs apt to be carried on thenceforth throughout life. At least among boys in American society, athletic compensations are greatly cultivated. Athletic prowess is apt to secure a large measure of self-esteem even if, for example, one is a dumbbell in the classroom, for it is highly applauded by one's playmates and frequently by someone in the home such as the male parent. It is likely to earn the warm regard of some of the older boys and some of the younger teachers. "It is thus built into a number of people during the juvenile era that if they are good sportsmen—and into a still larger number that if they are any sort of sportsmen—many shortcomings in other lines will be overlooked."[62] And so, if nurtured, compensatory overdependence on athletic prowess may continue to the senium without any very direct disapproval from others. Since athletic performances are conventionally regarded to be related to masculinity, they may facilitate a beginning of adolescent socialization with the opposite sex; but they often get to be a form of compensations for dissatisfactions and frustrations in the sexual sphere, as well as a mark of a perennial adolescent attitude. During midadolescence, when frank sexual activity should appear, the athlete, according to Sullivan, often fails.

A juvenile is often encouraged to study by parents occupied with other children or with other interests. At least they may give him every opportunity as far as time and place are concerned and perhaps frankly encourage his being out of sight. It may be that, sometmes, in the school or on the athletic field he is encouraged further in this direction by being taught that it is best for him not to be under foot. Juveniles thus encouraged to keep out of the way, while they are not provided with a constructive program of activities, generally sustain the childhood recourse to fantasy and to daydreams in lieu of other activities. Many of them having learned that they are under no more pressing necessity than to kill time discover that time can be eliminated with minimum effort by attending the moving pictures [or viewing television]. From these juveniles who have adopted a superficial sort of life process in the place of constructive thought and action, according to Sullivan, come the typical inadequate childishly compensatory people who never quite get around to doing anything since they never have had to develop any special urge. Their motivation is said to be drained off in the earlier types of satisfaction.

While the psychopath develops fantastic *depreciatory* illusions of other people, the person who comes under the class of juveniles under discussion tends to escape from the socializing process by the development of fantastic compensatory illusions. Again in contrast to the psychopath who, owing to the kind of unfortunate experience mentioned above, from childhood fails to develop any correct appraisal of himself and others, in the juvenile who is facilitated in drifting into compensatory substitutions, there is a beginning of socialization, the development of "fairly correct" appraisals of himself and of other people. Thereafter there is said to be a discharge of the socializing urges, and most other urges, by the childhood method of daydreams and mild amusements. "The day-dreamer crosses the line into adolescence unarmed with improved prehensions of his own and other selves, but, instead, filled with pleasing fantasies of prowess, charm and wit. Not only does he tend in general to avoid the tests of crude reality, but now that interpersonal intimacy is a necessity, he is likely to drift in an extremely unfortunate direction."[63] Lacking adequate knowledge of people, he may seek out friends on the basis of an orientation embodying woefully fantastic appraisals of the other person, with succeeding disappointments. After such a disappointing sort of experience, or perhaps from the beginning, he may resort to fantastic "friendships" with a movie star or with some other inaccessible and "unwitting" object. He may write letters (which he may or may not mail) to this remote and inaccessible object. This is said to be one of the most ominous of the preludes to adolescent disaster.[64]

Another and somewhat "more blessed" form of compensatory personality developed in the juvenile era is said to be that of the "student." Many juveniles who are either handicapped by physical inferiorities or are not able to earn esteem by athletic activities and the like discover that by cultivating their intellectual abilities they can avoid much of the criticism and contempt of other juveniles. In school they receive considerable encouragement from their teachers. Hence, the encouragement of a one-sided development is enhanced. Such a juvenile often becomes a "grand student," while discharging his socializing tendencies in a childlike relationship with elder teachers and with a select few of his compeers who are similarly one-sided in their development and compensating in the same manner. Though this constitutes an unfortunate deviation of the socializing tendencies and is poor preparation for approaching adolescence, it is said to be a sort of existence that can be eked out indefinitely within the walls of a university. In a genuinely healthy development, the experience provided by the parental milieu merges with the experiences in and out of the schoolroom in such a fashion that the growing youngster gradually becomes capable of dealing adequately with the situations and problems of the real world. "Unfortunately, the schoolroom experience is provided in large measure by persons engaged in such work because of their own difficulties and the satisfaction that comes to their needs from the peculiar quasi-parental role in which they stand with juveniles."[65]

In the juvenile era, the need for social approbation becomes "newly important" in the pursuit of which sublimatory processes play an important role. The role of the latter in the juvenile era is "somewhat obscure." Sullivan surmised that all growth of tendencies or motivations from their childhood status toward accommodation to the group standards, when unwitting, might be, by definition, regarded as sublimatory. He says that many instances of self-modification in unwitting pursuit of group approbation are certainly of this character. But there are also instances that are not of this character. The latter instances are said to be maladjustive processes of more or less evil omen for the personality.

It would appear from Sullivan's discussion that underprivileged compeers frequently suffer damage or injury in attempting to accommodate or adjust themselves to the standards and demands of the more privileged. As a class juveniles are said to be unkind to underprivileged compeers—though their behavior is obviously influenced profoundly by the attitudes and values of the adults around them. And here Sullivan marshals that bitter eloquence of which he was so thoroughly a master. He wrote that while in the early years of the juvenile era actual demonstrations of superiority in skill, strength, and the like are more effective factors in establishing status, this presently gives over to the growing respect for caste marks. The latter part of the era is said to come to be the very heyday of snobbery and crass social discrimination. "Social inequalities are fabricated from all sorts of expansions of the juvenile selves, including the trappings of power and position that parents seem so happy to hang on their offspring. The 'outs' are given barbarous demonstrations of the value of being 'in' with the privileged group, and find themselves the butt of scandal-mongering, defamation, and the cruelest of malicious mischief. Perhaps largely by virtue of home training, the members of the 'in' group become expert at making much ado about nothing, propitiating the elect, and flogging the fallen. The juvenile is taught that the most vile accusations may be flung at the outsider, without any warrant for the opprobrium other than the social inferiority. He learns also that the most obvious viciousness of the elect is not only not to be discussed critically, but is best applauded. . . ."[66]

Though a "legion" of defensive processes appear in the juvenile era, in juveniles who have already undergone considerable unfortunate experience, as in the case of the psychopath, one type of defensive process is discussed, the transference of blame dynamism. Some juveniles have recourse to this dynamism under the necessity of finding relief from distressing situations involving loss of self-esteem and anxiety, conflict, and feelings of guilt. The juvenile who suffers the psychopathic deviation very often resorts to blaming others. When this tendency of certain people to transfer blame appears thus early in the evolution of personality, it is said to eventuate in an individual (or sort of individual) who is alert to anything that could be interpreted as unfriendly to him, and competent at so rationalizing interpersonal occurrences as to show that others are handicapping him, harming him, or denying him opportunity. If such juveniles fall in with similarly paranoid companions, as they are apt to do, they learn more and more perfect ways of "rationalizing" the world's doings such that the rationalizations or spurious interpretations provide an "explanation" of their own more or less vaguely perceived inadequacies. Such activities provide a very poor foundation for the development and modification of tendencies or motivations in subsequent eras. Sullivan wrote that either in situations integrated by powerful tendencies requiring interpersonal intimacy, or in those characterized by conflict and the feeling of guilt, the transference of blame dynamism requires the integrating of strong antipathetic attitudes, sentiments of hatred. "It then becomes essential to the person thus maladjusted that there be a supply of personal objects capable of being blamed and hated. It is both remarkable and fortunate, however, that much of human value is accomplished by many prevailingly paranoid individuals, who have insured themselves a few 'really worthwhile' objects of hatred."[67] But the latter may be of only "tenuous reality."

Although there are several ways of exercising "virtuosity" in the expression of antipathetic tendencies, in general they involve the displacement of a hostile or aggressive tendency from a person in a primary relationship with the subject individual to some other persons who stand in a relationship of a secondary group: religious, racial, national, and so forth. Sullivan says this may occur as a more or less direct and healthy growth of tendency, often forming an adjustive sublimation of hatred; or as an accompaniment of suppression, repression, or dissociation. In the latter instances, the tendency system is said to arise usually from a discomforting stereotype some few characteristics of which are elaborated into, or ascribed to, the object group (the Catholics, the Masons, the Negroes) of an antipathetic sentiment. By subjecting the people of such a group to certain kinds of behavior and thought, the motivational tendency that has been suppressed, repressed or dissociated is drained off in a manner more or less satisfactory to the individual. And if this "secondary tendency system" is still somewhat repugnant to one's self, one may rationalize it by an appeal to some principle, such as love of humanity and become actively engaged in combating this or that "evil."

Before turning to a discussion of preadolescence, I want to mention another development that is greatly constructive, called self-idealization, which incidentally should not be confused with the meanings assigned to it by certain other writers. In contrast to the largely negative role that Sullivan assigns to conscience, he claimed that there is a "character factor" that is potent in the "preservation" of personality in the face of great handicaps. This is the *"idealization of the self as the person shall presently come to be,* the formulation within awareness of an intended role from increasingly realistic prehensions of personal abilities and limitations."[68] This idealization of the self, according to Sullivan, is not apt to appear in verbal formulation of a particularized goal, such as that of scientist, artist, teacher, physician. It is the envisagement of a general development of personality, embodying "an implicit assurance of ultimate worthy achievement that colors thoughts about the self and other selves, and emphasizes the future as prepotent over current disappointments and misfortunes."[69] Though this idealization, when it occurs, cannot work miracles, it can and does reduce in significance or relevance many situational factors or circumstances that would otherwise warp growth. By thus reducing the relevance of otherwise harmful circumstances and by "creating" new and more favorable situations, it protects and fosters growth. Self-idealization is very different from the pseudo-idealizations discussed below.

In *Personal Psychopathology* Sullivan divided adolescence into three phases: preadolescence (which in his later work he named a separate era following the juvenile) said to begin with the appearance of an urge to true interpersonal intimacy and to extend through physiological puberty; midadolescence, starting from the appearance of sexual desire tending to integrate a situation or type of situation of interpersonal intimacy with a representative of the other sex; and late adolescence, which extends from the *patterning* of sexual behavior to the consummation of adulthood.

A warning must be given to the reader that the "isophilic" interests of preadolescents should not be equated with "homosexual," though in at least some instances such interest in persons of the same sex may be extended to involve sexual behavior. As I shall show in some detail, in Sullivan's usage sexual pertains to the genital apparatus, its type or quality of sentience, and to activities directly related or connected with it. But Sullivan did believe that the real chums and the more closely knit gangs often manifest processes of a decidedly sexual character, in his own sense of the word. "Fantasies, fables, and actual facts about the genitals become common property. . . . Co-operative or mutual sexual behavior is quite frequently an important part of the gang life."[70] And as a result, an enfeeblement of inhibitions frequently occurs, which, for many boys, is said to exercise a *curative* influence, since this enfeeblement facilitates subsequent heterosexuality. In any event, Sullivan believed that a successful preadolescence is necessary for the socialization of the personality, "particularly in our culture," partly because the gang life is an experiment in cultural adaptation.

A boy is said to enter the preadolescent phase when he first experiences tendencies making for intimate relations with some one or other two boys of similar age. Sullivan wrote that when this happens some one particular person becomes of peculiarly distinguished interest, a new type of sentiment is developed, and there is a new development within the sentiment of self. Thus the preadolescent is no longer content that the other one contribute reflections favorable to one's self-esteem. It becomes more important to him to contribute to the self-esteem of the other, so that one's own pleasure becomes secondary to the satisfaction experienced at causing pleasure to the friend. "There is an augmented tendency to identification with favorable attributes of the other boy. The two, who are never so happy as when they are together, unwittingly but assiduously cultivate each other's characteristics, develop identical or complementary interests, and so alter their social values that they come to be in more or less complete agreement one with the other. Peculiarities of the home life of the one tend to lose their further effectiveness because they fall into unfavorable comparison with similar factors in the home life of the other. Mutual 'suggestion' becomes potent. In other words, the two personalities tend to become closely knit to each other."[71] A great impetus is said to be given to the consensual validation of the boy's behavior and thought in these interactions while all that is subsumed in adaptive culture tends rapidly to become significant.

Juvenile ideals become transmuted such that a new and, humanistically speaking, a higher level of interest is achieved, centered in people as intimates. "Abstract groups now require personal embodiments. Concrete groups lose the differentiation of their members into family and similar classifications."[72] But this entails no loss of "personal differentiation," of individuality. Each boy remains a "carrier" of values different from the other. But the values that the boys who have reached this phase share in common, the values that "remain" when due allowance is made for the personal differentiation of each, are said to function with increasing directness and effectiveness. Despite the individual differentiation of each, the boys of the school class become organized into a more significant unity than the individuality of its members would seem to justify. In contrast to what occurs in the juvenile era, various invidious social distinctions—the trappings of wealth, family background, the deference of the teacher to certain members, and the like—no longer provide the main criteria of personal evaluation. According to Sullivan, the widest social distance between two families may be surmounted in the friendship of the boy and his chum, a friendship that may circumvent various extrinsic divisive factors. When divisive factors that are intrinsic in the two chums exist, the influence of the group may have a more potent conjunctive effect, thus tending to preserve the friendship.

From the interaction of the two-group a conscious formulation of an idealized object of intimacy occurs. The two seek a concrete embodiment of the ideals growing out of their mutual experiences, usually some person in the immediate environment on whom their aspirations may be centered. Thus the drive for concrete representation of the two-group's ideals often is fulfilled in some "well-equipped" boy in the same school or neighborhood, who must be able to demonstrate concretely by performance the attributes that they cherish. The relationship of the two-group with the third boy provides a new outlet for the intimacy urge, while it also gives rise to the problem of personal loyalty in intimate relations. This difficulty is accentuated by the fact that the new boy usually has a chum: a "four-part arrangement" of intimacy is said to be even more of a problem.

In addition, the new boy who approximates the chums' ideals is in all likelihood similarly admirable in the eyes of other boys. A larger group composed of two-groups focused in the leader arises. "The chums now take comparable or complementary parts in the activity of a social unit, the more or less organized *gang,* the first autonomous societal process into and within which the boys' personalities are integrated as part of a whole."[73]

The two-groups and the more inclusive gang are said to manifest the incorporation into their personalities of behavior patterns and standards satisfactory to the group as a whole. Once learned, such behavior patterns and standards constitute potent norms of conduct.

Up to preadolescence, the prime motives of the individual have to do with the furthering of "individualized" interests or "causes" by sundry techniques. Normally, in preadolescence, according to Sullivan, the securing of direct satisfactions in furthering the group causes constitute the prime motives of the individual, frequently in behavior at variance with, or divergent from, preexisting personal patterns. Thus many motivational systems become redefined, reorganized as indicated by altered patterns of experience and overt behavior. Devotion, allegiance, and loyalty to one's group and the group members are said to become a more or less powerful system of tendencies in the personality. Sullivan thought that this new tendency system, the maturation of which initiates preadolescence, and the satisfaction of which requires interpersonal intimacy, is therefore in a nuclear fashion the basis of social processes.

Sullivan also thought that the two-group and the gang have very great significance for the growth of personality. There is a powerful reinforcement of every individual tendency that meets with acceptance by the group. Therefore personal conflicts tend to be resolved since one or another opposing element of a conflict is reinforced. The other element of the conflict may also find an outlet in group action, or may be sublimated as a result of the acquisition of new social values, or may be developed with increasing experience into a rational synthesis of motives on a more mature level. Thus the "gang sociality" fosters increased mental health among its members. At the same time the more the preadolescent had previously approximated to mental health the less of mediocre stereotyping he is apt to undergo in the new relationships.

Sullivan claims that preadolescence seems always to begin some time before the puberty changes have made their appearance and continues to a time well past this somatological landmark. Just how long preadolescence lasts will vary among individuals. Sooner or later a rather rapid change is said to occur in the character of the impulses in the growing boy: he experiences an increase in fantasy about adults and a marked decrease in the satisfaction derived from his chum and from the relationships with and in the gang. The "reality" of the gang and its standards is gradually displaced by hero worship on a new level. The pattern of heteroerotic interests manifested by the "hero" furnishes a model to which it becomes important one should adapt oneself.

As the interest in the chum and in the gang declines, it begins to be important to be thought by others to have "intimate association"

with some certain girl. Woman now takes on a certain "quasi-impor-
tance." And the "impulses making for interest in securing the esteem
and submission of the girl grow to be prime causes of behavior."[74]

It will be clear, I think, that to every adolescent on the threshold of
heteroerotic or heterosexual interest, previous experience with members of the other sex, especially those belonging to the family group,
have a potent effect in determining the ease, difficulty, or impossibility
of the heterosexual change. Sullivan, in *Personal Psychopathology,* absolutely rejects the notion that homosexuality is inborn. On the other
hand he assumed a definite heteroerotic drive in everyone that
"shows" at the "appropriate stage" of development even though it is
in some "distorted" or otherwise prevented from manifest activity.
Hence one must carefully examine the course of postnatal experience
if one is to discover the causal conditions of homosexuality. For instance, the mother's influence, in regard to boys, is said to be of
incalculably great importance.

The initial objects of the impulses making for the heterosexual
change are often girls or women chronologically older than the boy:
the sister of a friend, fairly young school teachers, the young mother
of another schoolmate. There is thus frequently a transitional step
from admiration of more mature women to girls of the boy's own
age-group. (One imagines that this is less true today.)

Certain mothers provide such pathogenic experiences that the boy
is unable to make such a transition. A preadolescent boy who has been
tied to the mother—having been used perhaps as a substitute for her
disappointment with her husband—may find himself in a difficult
situation when he reaches adolescence. A classical source of such a
deviation is said to be the somewhat homoerotic divorcee who has
one child, a son, and who secures her principal pleasure in life from
discussing with other unhappy women the fatuous character of men,
from whose unholy embrace she has succeeded in extricating herself.
According to Sullivan, in these boys, who are often reared in an
almost exclusively feminine environment, and who are sometimes
tediously instructed as to the general worthlessness of the male, with
the appearance of preadolescence and its negative feeling-tones regarding the other sex, there is very much the same "phenomenology"
as in other boys. . . . However, when their peers reach the threshold
of midadolescence, these youths begin to diverge from the average.
"If their experience has not delayed the process of physiological

maturation—their developmental age is equivalent to that of the other boys—the heteroerotic drives appear at the same time, but the initial impulses making for interest in older women are generally continued, often accentuated by disappointments in girls. . . . If the heteroerotic impulses [of a youth of this sort] focus on a frank incestuous object, the mother or an aunt, then either the object finally recoils when unable longer to deceive herself as to the nature of the impulse, or a woefully maladjustive life is initiated for the boy."[75]

It may also happen that he has already suffered serious genital or sexual inhibitions, from which experiences in the gang life have provided only a partial liberation. In fact a whole series of unfortunate life experiences may have such cumulative and dynamic consequences that a boy may have already suffered considerable damage (by way of sexual inhibition, dissociation, inadequacy of socialization) as he progresses rather belatedly to the threshold of midadolescence. Sullivan believed that this was the case in regard to a "considerable number" of boys who, he said, constituted a large proportion among schizophrenic males.

One reaction of preadolescent maladjustment to any sort of persisting, unresolved sexual situation is said to be manifested in recourse to compensatory daydreaming. Many of those who fail to develop an "interest" in the other sex, or in Sullivan's phrase, who have not succeeded in stumbling along into this interest, begin the development of sexual fantasies. This outcome is very unfortunate for two reasons: first, the recourse to fantasy provides a "discharge" or outlet for "the most important" group of impulses making for interpersonal intimacy, and second, it is profoundly enfeebling to the day dreamer's self-respect or self-esteem. In regard to the second point, though fantasy is, at least to a large extent, a satisfactory "tool" in childhood, it can but rarely take the place of real interpersonal relations for a boy on the threshold of midadolescence. Fantasy can be a wonderful thing if one has a store of real experience to "work over," but there are said to be few of the type of boy under discussion who have experience that can be worked over in constructive fantasy. In this instance, the compensatory fantasy has to be "elaborate" and usually associated with some kind of autosexual procedures. But one cannot carry on elaborate fantasy in intimate contact with others (except in situations in which considerable emotional rapport, understanding, and sympathy exist). Those others break in on one's dreams, spotlighting innumerable discrepancies and points of conflict between the inner processes and events in the world. Thus people may ask one how things are going and various other questions, which point up the harrowing discrepancies between the coldly real and the warm, vivid world of fantasy. And since such questions easily become embarrassing, one tends to avoid people who might ask them. This tendency to seclusion makes the already small chances for fortunate experience still smaller. The boy's (or girl's) loneliness increases the need for fantasy, and he thus becomes entrapped in a vicious circle that is accentuated by a growing consciousness of inadequacy, guilt, shame.

Before leaving the discussion of preadolescence, I want to take up some of Sullivan's ideas on the "topic of the isolated boy," of whom there are several classes. In one class—"the most unfortunate"—are those boys who because of serious deviation or warp of personality growth are excluded from gangs and chumship. In contrast to the psychopath, for instance, some of them made fair progress into the juvenile era. This type of boy is usually aware of being "different" from other boys, of being an "outsider," of being distrusted, if not despised by the so-called regular fellows. Such a boy will frequently receive cruel treatment at the hands of his peers. Still, since the drive toward integrating isophilic relationships has not been diminished despite unfortunate experiences, he cannot easily abandon the quest for companionship and intimacy with them. Since his efforts in this respect fail, his self-respect is or becomes gravely impaired. His authority attitudes are said to be upset. His studies suffer. If possible, he becomes "loosely associated" with some other boys who are having similar difficulties, or who are, like him, so-called failures. Such a group is frequently under the "quasi-leadership" of an older, "badly beaten" boy. Sullivan wrote that in this "crowd," which possesses but vestiges of the true social organization of the gang, cooperation is reduced to the level of "hookey" playing, general truancy, and the like. . . . "Learning his rudiments of social action from others who can but observe its superficial manifestations, rather than participate in it, he may grow a crop of definitely antisocial ideals, achieving a truly criminal plan of life."[76] Or, since the returns from the group with whom he has associated himself are meager, for its members are filled with hatred arising from the defeat of their efforts at true socialization and belonging, a boy may then "approximate the ideal" of the lone wolf. Driven to seek self-sufficiency of a sort, a completeness in himself, he may live thereafter in bitter isolation, an enemy of society, with his hand turned against all groups and all group living.

A second category of isolated boy has to do with the solution ensuing upon sociogeographic location. Because of the death of a parent or some other cause, perhaps having to do with economic misfortune, a family group, including a boy approaching preadolescence, may move from a "good" (advantaged) neighborhood to a "bad" (disadvantaged) one. For example, such a family group may perforce remove themselves from a satisfactory suburban area to one of severe social disintegration. Unless the boy's character factor is strong, he may adjust to the new environment in much the same way a feebly inhibited boy adjusts to gang pressure. "He merely sinks from a conformity at a superior social level to one at a lower level."[77] But if he has developed a strong character factor, a large part of the new, personal environment remains irrelevant to him. "He is incapable of manifesting many of the integrations and activities that characterize the new area."[78] He remains aloof from the boys of his new neighborhood or school. The other boys are themselves discomforted by him. Even if he tries to be "one of the fellows" and even if they are attracted to him, he retains a singular inability to cooperate in some of the gang behavior. Whether he becomes a detached leader, or merely a stranger nonetheless respected, or the peculiar enemy of the gang, will depend on combinations and permutations of various factors, some of which pertain to him and some of which belong to the "tendency integrations" of the gang. His personality growth is said to approximate, in significant ways, that of the geographically isolated boy.

Another class of human isolation during the preadolescent era is called geographical. A classical example is said to be the only preadolescent in a sparsely settled rural community. Of course his isolation is not absolute for during the hours of the country school he may secure some preadolescent socialization. However, his situation as a whole (the inaccessibility of his home, his family's ignorance of his significant needs of the preadolescent era) tend to isolate him from gang life if not to prevent him from having a chum. He always has a prolonged adolescence, usually acquiring superficial behavioral patterns of "a preternatural maturity" since the elders are much more attractive to any preadolescent than are children and juveniles. But his maturity is specious. "The working out of isophilic tendencies is not satisfactory and is spread over years of experimentation . . . usually with caution learned by disappointing, if not actually painful, experience."[79] He resorts to fantasy and to the personification of subhuman objects. A development of loyalty occurs to abstract ideals that are more or less embodied in fanciful figures rather than being invested in concrete groups. The boy's loneliness stimulates the capacity for sympathy that is also directed toward fanciful objects.

In some instances there finally emerges from this kind of experience a person who is well above the average level of achievement, the more so since he is an individual who tends to integrate interpersonal situations in which he is more of "a participant observer than a unit merged in unthinking cooperation."[80] Sullivan claimed that the force of public opinion on such a personality may remain relatively unimportant.

On the other hand, such an isolated boy has to pay a price for his hard-won superiority. Thus he "lacks the practice that ensues in unthinking accommodation of oneself to others with whom one has sympathy. His interpersonal relations are not easy, and, despite the effort entailed, tend often to superficiality. Possessed of capacity for intimacy of extraordinary depth, his experience of fraudulent folk may early drive him into a skepticism about people that is extremely annoying to more socialized personalities."[81] And he misses the liberating effects of chumship and gang life on sexual inhibitions.

Adolescence, in the broad sense in which Sullivan uses it in *Personal Psychopathology,* beginning near the age of nine, is that period in one's life during which he develops or tries to develop techniques for living intimately with other persons, a period that nearly always in our society extends into the twenties, "and frequently to the end of life." Sullivan also characterizes adolescence as the epoch during which one achieves or attempts to achieve full membership in his particular community, "enjoying its permissive and its facilitating aspects, and successfully adapting himself to its prohibitions and restrictions." He wrote that adolescence is initiated by the coming of the urge to intimacy, and the beginning of preadolescence, progresses through collaborations with members of one's own sex, through the full awakening of the sexual impulses, through midadolescence, the era of patterning of one's sexual behavior, and late adolescence, the era in which the individual seeks his place in the world as shaped by his needs for interpersonal relations.

A person is said to become adult when he achieves a thoroughly satisfactory interpersonal integration, particularly in the field of sexual situations. Sullivan in later years modified this notion. However, even in the earlier years of his professional life, he did not ascribe to sexuality the transcendant importance that Freud and some of his more "orthodox" followers have. The former emphasized the factor of emotional intimacy in interpersonal relations and incorporated it into his theories and therapy. Perhaps the following discussion will make this clearer.

"Interpersonal relations are matters of ultimate importance in life. One may survive and surmount almost any other sublethal difficulties. Success in intimacies with another, however, requires a personality that is comparatively free from limitations or deviations of growth. One individual, at least, in any two-or-three group must approximate to mental health, or the collaborative actions of the group will fall short of complete resolution of the situational complexes encountered in the course of the group life."[82] Sullivan claimed that incidents of stress or the accumulation of interpersonal tensions finally destroy imperfect social integrations, or interpersonal relations, of adolescents often with more or less of a resulting conviction on the part of the members that human collaboration is an unattainable ideal, and that society is essentially a predatory, a mercilessly competetive, or a nonsensical aggregation that occurred without rhyme or reason. . . .

In mid- (or true) adolescence relations between persons not only of similar developmental stage but also of similar social status are the psychobiologist's principal concern. As the "typical intimate interpersonal relations" of the chums begin to recede with the "awakening" of adolescent sexuality, a transitional phase of several years develops. The typical interpersonal relation is said to tend more and more definitely as growth progresses to become one between a young man and a young woman of comparable personality development and status. "If this is finally and fully achieved, we discover that the individual has passed through adolescence and is a young adult. Of the years that follow puberty, however, several may be spent in patterning various social behavior units, and many in getting into shape to enter into full intimacies including sexual situations."[83] But first attention has to be devoted to the patterning of sexual behavior since disorders in this area of life are "ruinous" to other developments.

Partly because Freud assimilated many different activities and various qualitatively diverse experiences to sexuality, claiming a common libidinous source for them, great theoretical and practical problems arose.[84] Sullivan carried out a careful analysis of the notions of erogeny and sexuality.

Let us consider erogeny, the "securing of pleasure-giving sentience" by manipulation of the various zones of interaction between the individual and the environment, as Sullivan puts it, which are called erotogenic zones by classical psychoanalysts. Freud claimed that the pleasure obtained from manipulation of all of these zones was sexual in quality. This was no mere matter of terminology. In each instance the pleasure is the result of libidinal excitation, or in other words, the result of the activation of charges of libidinal energy (allegedly existing in the various tissues and organs of the body), which may be brought about by self-manipulation or by the agency of some person or thing in the environment.

Sullivan rid himself of a good deal of this psychology by abandoning the notion of a hypothetical and unverifiable libido, and by insisting on a close scrutiny of the facts of experience and overt behavior while giving up unnecessary speculative concepts. Thus he classified erogeny from the standpoint of "environmental agency" under three rubrics: autoerotism, homoerotism, and heteroerotism. And he included an interpersonal, mental component in erogeny, namely, "the prehension of pleasure given to another" along with the pleasure derived from activities connected with the erotogenic zones. In fact, he seems to have regarded this as a necessary condition of genuine homoerotic or heteroerotic activity, in contrast to autoerotism.

Autoerotism signifies the securing of one or more of the various forms of "pleasant sentience" from the zones of interaction of one's own body. Not every form of bodily pleasure is classified as sexual. The pleasure-giving sentience "arising directly or mediately (by reflection) from the genital zone is *sexual*; just as that from the mouth is oral; and that from the lower end of the alimentary tract, anal."[85] Thus behavior in response to autoerotic interest directed to the excitation or stimulation of one's own genitals is called *autosexual* activity. The latter is not necessarily brought about by self-manipulation, as in self-masturbation. Often what seems "objectively" to be a normal heterosexual act is for one party, if not for both, *autosexual* because one or both are using the body, or rather the genitals, of the other as a machine or instrument whose function is analogous to the function of one's own hands.

Analogous distinctions are made concerning the other two classes of erogeny:

"The conceptions of *homoerotic* and *heteroerotic* interests similarly refer to the desire to secure pleasure, but now by prehension of the pleasure of another derived from the manipulation, by the subject individual, of some zone of interaction of the object individual's body. The homoerotic interest manifests as inclination to the pleasure-giving manipulation of another person of the same sex; the hetero-erotic, one of the other sex. *Homosexual* behavior is then the manipulation of the genitals of a member of the same sex, for the pleasure experienced in his enjoyment. *Heterosexual* behavior is the manipulation of the genitals of one of the other sex, for the satisfaction derived by prehension of the other's pleasure. In the homoerotic and the heteroerotic interests we see, obviously, much more elaborated interpersonal tendency systems than in the autoerotic."[86]

Sexual pleasure, like almost any kind of pleasure, is profoundly "conditioned" by acculturation. Much more is involved than somatic maturation, or maturation of the "genital lust dynamism." Since sexual activity is largely conditional on the general structure of personality, it is profoundly dependent on the latter. This is where one's ability for intimacy "comes in"—and also the ability of the partner. Indeed, it seems fairly obvious that various actualized capacities are involved: of feeling and emotion, of imagination, of sensibility, of esteem for others as well as of oneself. All such capacities are involved in any mature heterosexual relationship. Since intimacy entails an affirmation of the other as well as of oneself—a fact that Sullivan has made clear in his discussion of preadolescence—it requires the realization and exercise of such capacities as those mentioned above.

The "nuclear problem" of erogeny characterizing midadolescence is said to be the patterning of the "sexual habits." To all the other forms of pleasure-giving behavior and thought, to all the other "fields" of erogeny that have been previously developed, there is now added the genital. Sullivan claimed that, though there has always been a distinctive character to sentience arising from the region of the genitals, the pubertal change greatly enhances or accentuates this difference so that sexual pleasure then becomes "entirely unlike" any other type of pleasure. With maturation of the genital dynamism comes sexual desire, lust, impelling one toward the integration of situations suitable to its satisfaction. This "inspires play, revery, and more elaborated activities to this end. If it is denied any satisfaction, the tension of accumulating lust can finally suspend any other integrating tendency—excepting physico-chemical hunger and acute oxygen need."[87] Its power is said to be so great that it can be used to energize almost unbelievably complicated processes. Compensation and sublimation cannot be completely successfully utilized for the full satisfaction of sexual motivations. "No action of merely implicit character" can replace lustful satisfaction. Moreover, according to Sullivan, the pleasure arising in the organismic acme is so distinctive that once consciously experienced, it cannot be excluded from recall except by the dissociation of this very powerful motivational system. If the dissociation can be effected it will be at the cost of great danger to the personality synthesis unless ample satisfactions of the dissociated components are available, as, for example, in major hysteria. However, the initial consciousness of orgasm can be greatly delayed by strong inhibitory tendencies. Sullivan thought that many women a generation or two ago seem never to have been aware of it. Analogously, a boy entering midadolescence may be unable to have any waking recall of the dream experience attending nocturnal emissions.

The customary course of elaboration of the sexual tendencies is said to begin with autosexual experience, which is certain to be important at least for a brief period. Sullivan asserts that the initial orgasm may be regarded as anything from the most pleasant experience of life to something terrible that has happened to one.

In some fashion, sooner or later, every adolescent "meets sex; and having met sex, every adolescent finds the world altered. The partly formulated world-view of his earlier years is strangely refracted, and all but the most primitive of the realities he has known and trusted may become shifting uncertainties, the inadequate apperceptions of a child."[88] This adolescent "upheaval" is said to be partly the effect of "newly erupted" sexual tendencies and desires but much more a result of acceleration of the physiological developmental rate. One wonders if some of it is not due to the discontinuities and inadequacies of "cultural patterning."[89]

The defects and inadequacies of previous personality development now "complicate" the integration of those interpersonal situations that have been "newly required" for the maintenance of status. A strong desire for the role of an adult appears. Previously ridiculed conformities become appealing. The adolescent is now concerned about the approbation of people to whose valuation of him he had been indifferent. Self-consciousness is said to be the "dominating content" of the boy's waking hours, and he may become extremely sensitive to approval and disapproval. There is what has been more recently called a search for self-identity. The self is said to grow rapidly and frequently very irregularly. "Sensitiveness to manifestations of the expanded self may become extreme. The least approval or disapproval of one's remarks may stir powerful pleasure or give severe discomfort. One's clothing becomes important. One's companions are no longer simply attractive; they now achieve values in accordance with the reception given them by others whose opinions are temporarily very important."[90] These others are older folk whose fancied approval or disapproval may break up even the affectional relations of an isophilic (preadolescent) friendship that has survived puberty.

Partly because of the rapid "spread of relevance" of experience, which now includes the adult world, and partly because of inadequate or unfortunate previous experience, when inadequate foundations of self-appraisal were established, one's self may become incomprehensible to one, such that one does not know who or what he is. The self, or rather the incomprehensibility of the self, requires "rationalizing": one seizes upon some role or roles that provide an artificial and unstable self-identification.[91] Though he is eager to receive the approbation of the older folk, his expression of whys and wherefores is apt to amuse rather than impress them—an experience that discourages confidences. "The adolescent may begin the 'life behind a mask' that tends to characterize numbers of our urban denizens. The mask, however, requires so much energy for its successful maintenance that personality growth is apt to end with its successful construction. As the necessities for masking certain motivations varies from one to another interpersonal situation, it may be easier to *avoid further integration of the self,* and to develop from this point onward, specialized accommodations and interests for various groups, without the growth of a synthetic self-consciousness," that is, without the development of an integrated self.[92]

This is the customary outcome of midadolescence when the character factor is feeble and the personality is already warped, an outcome in which there come to be "almost as many selves as there are important interpersonal relationships—with a juvenile or childhood self as the consistent nucleus."[93] Such persons, called chronically late-adolescent, may do very well in various affairs of life, unless and until, in conformity to the folkways, they undertake durable relationships requiring intimacy, such as marriage and parenthood.

These late adolescents adapt very well when the sexual tendencies can be satisfied in relatively unintimate situations. They do very badly if, in conformity to the folkways, they attempt to live like more healthy persons. Then their motivational systems are discharged in fantasy processes of the general type of *idealization.* In idealizing one is said to project upon another personality a body of desirable characteristics that exist within oneself as a stereotype in a fashion analagous to the paranoid transference of blame process. How this comes about is explained as follows. Normally experience progressively modifies the various sentiments elaborated and synthesized in personality. Then the organization of sentiments and stereotypes develops dynamically in such a fashion that the outgrown ones are relatively impotent. The tendencies that were associated with the outgrown ones, having been modified by experience, are satisfied through the activity of the current personality organization. But whenever "the experience connected with some sentiment is incoherent, there is apt to be a disintegration of the sentiment, owing to tensional states arising from unsatisfied tendencies included in it."[94] However, the related stereotype (subcomplex or subsentiment), remains and frequently retains considerable power, "at least as a potential nexus of tendencies" or an impulse system that in turn tends to become active. On the frustration or dissolution of any sentiment (such as love of friend or father) the related stereotype that remains, built into the overarching sentiment of self, functions as a tendency to reestablish a sentiment of the same dynamic type as the one previously experienced, of which it is said to be a memorial element.

> The *stereotype* is to be understood as a particular component or subcomplex (subsentiment) entering into the formation of the sentiment of self. It is, as it were, the *self-centered* complement of an "externally" conditioned sentiment—of one the object of which is another person—but of one that is quite subordinate in its manifestations to those of the stereotype. A stereotype remains, built into the sentiment of self, on the frustration or dissolution

... of any sentiment. The conception may become clearer if we express it more loosely as the emotionally toned pattern of experienced reflections to the self associated with a particular person who was once important to the self. Major or even minor (even really irrational) attributes of the person incorporated in the stereotype, when reencountered in another, tend to stir mnemic recall of the emotional and other tendencies embodied in the stereotype.[95]

The activity of the stereotype is said to be manifested as a tendency to reestablish a sentiment of the same dynamic type as the one previously experienced, of which it is a memorial element. This occurs in states of regression. In general, previous disappointments and frustrations of sentiments, according to Sullivan, have led to the organization of a self that includes powerful stereotypes taking precedence over a new situation in such a fashion as to project into it the older pattern of relationships and reactivate ("reechphoriate") an old, perhaps very immature, sentiment with a new object individual.

Thus in idealizing one projects upon another person a constellation of desirable characteristics that exist as a stereotype or "complex" within the self. This process, as I have mentioned, is analagous to that occurring when, in order to rid oneself of characteristics regarded as unfavorable, one resorts to the paranoid transference of blame.

A review of matters previously discussed may be helpful in understanding idealization. Sullivan commented that the drive for intimacy and affectional linkage with another is naturally influenced by the preexisting organization of personality and of the self. From early infancy the individual has participated in a series of relations with other people. ... "The whole body of human tendencies has been manifested through sentiments elaborated with these various other persons as objects, or as sources of the sentiment of self. The pursuit of satisfactions and the even more fundamental avoidance of discomfort, through the periods of growth, has always been intimately associated with one or another of these sentiments. If now these developmental sentiments have not undergone growth, but have instead disintegrated under the force of incoherent experiences without the intervention of grief or related phenomena, their potent stereotypes energize fantasy processes, and tend to integrate situations with perhaps very nearly irrelevant people."[96] For example, an adolescent boy in a mental hospital may form a quasi-attachment to, and have an imaginary "love affair" with, a nurse or female patient with whom in fact he has a bare acquaintance. Consider, again, the numerous "romantic" attachments that an immature young woman may sustain with men, seemingly forever to seek a lost childhood parental love. Or an adolescent college student, who is constantly at war with his teachers, may caricature them as hateful authority figures. Sometimes the "object pattern" (object image) energized by the stereotype in some respects more or less approximates the characteristics of people encountered in reality. In other words *some of the characteristics* of the object pattern are more or less congruent with those of actual people one encounters. The characteristics of the object pattern are not wholly illusory. But the reactivation of the stereotype is apt to occur as a sentiment of the old (immature) sort applying to a particular object individual perhaps utterly unsuited for this kind of integration. The unsuitability of the immature sentiment when applied to the object individual may be hidden, submerged, by the projected characterization. Thus the projected characterization may permit the "prehension" of the person's perhaps single characteristic shared with, or common to, the derived object pattern and the object individual, or actual person who may become invested with various other features he does not possess. "Only gradually, however, does the personal reality escape from the idealization thrust upon it; and the unwitting victim of the projection stands forth a sadly disappointing person."[97] In the meanwhile, during the course of the relationship, some more "valid," more authentic, more realistic interpersonal relations, involving him and the idealizing individual have occurred so that the "total situation has become very complex." Often the situation cannot be resolved because of conventional demands and expectations. So another unsuitable marriage is celebrated. In subsequent years Sullivan formulated such relationships in terms of illusory me-you patterns. It seems hardly necessary to add that idealization is a formidable obstacle to the normal profiting from experience.

Sullivan wrote that there are many family groups in which the personalities of the parents have become all but submerged, for each other, in shifting idealizations, positively or negatively affectionate, enduring through life courses of unnumbered disappointments of ill-founded attachments, hopes, and dreams. These people are said to live, as it were, in a world peopled with unstable patterns of folklore, a fairy scene in which the roles of others can undergo the most remarkable metamorphoses as a result of trifling actions, though the idealized roles attributed to them can "deny" the most obvious evidence to the contrary. While children of this kind of home develop the universal human tendencies, the older they grow the more their sentiments "find merely cultural objects"—or merely idealized role-bearers. Sullivan claims that the parent-child relationships come to be almost exclusively of this type. The (neurotic) parental influence on each child distorts what might otherwise be far more realistic and healthy relationships between the siblings. In other words, since parents are, among other things, models after whom young children tend to pattern themselves, the latter can find no secure anchor in the shifting idealizations of the parents; they are constantly exposed to the distorted, inconsistent behavior patterns of the significant adults from whom they first learn how to live. Their "sentiment formations" will reflect the traditional dualistic character of the folkways, wherein people are either good *or* evil, loving *or* hateful, healthy *or* insane, blessed *or* unholy, and so forth. "All object-individuals are one or another of some certain few cultural patterns; that is, the individual personality to whom any sentiment is applied is lost as anything more than the carrier of a system of fantasy."[98]

Sullivan claims that the *only way* to deal with individuals as culture-carriers is by positive and negative (paranoid) idealization. The person is said to "love" a complex of "traits" that is for all practical purposes embodied in, say, one's spouse, while one suppresses conscious consideration of defects in the submerged person. Thus one or both partners are forever engaged in transactions of shadowy selves. However, one can sustain such sentiment formations with spectacular success only in a society in which the mores prohibit individual variation in interpersonal intimacies.

Since this chapter is meant as only a preliminary introduction to Sullivan's more mature formulation of personality development, I shall not take up various other problems that may become paramount during adolescence.

Despite the fact that Sullivan possessed keen insight into feminine psychology—as several of his former students can testify—he was diffident about writing down his thoughts on women. So he enlisted the help of his friend Clara Thompson, with whom I once collaborated in the writing of a book. His choice was not perhaps too wise. No one knows better than I how theoretically superficial she was.

This lack of theoretical sophistication shows in her "Notes on Female Adolescence," and in various papers she published.

In *Personal Psychopathology* Thompson contributed seventeen pages on "Female Adolescence." Though she attempts to adhere closely to Sullivan's theoretical formulations, she lacks the power and depth of insight of Sullivan. Hence I think her summary of typical problems of female adolescents as those problems appeared in 1932 is of minor value and will not be explicated except for the following observations. Thompson wrote that there are many points of similarity in the development of the two sexes, though there are many points of difference as well, which in the main she did *not* discuss. As for the points of similarity, regarding male and female adolescence she wrote:

> The changes brought about in the girl approaching adolescence in many respects might be said to differ but slightly from those in the boy, later showing a gradual divergence. The preadolescent girl also normally chooses a chum, becomes a member of a gang, and has a period of hero-worship, usually for an older woman. Largely through her gang activities, she acquires sex knowledge and undergoes experience of an homo- or autoerotic nature. In all the important aspects of these things her reactions do not vary greatly from those of the boy, and failure to become incorporated in group life brings similar types of tragedies.[99]

However, Thompson adds that there is marked difference between the interests of the two groups. Athletic activities have less interest for the girl group. Their preoccupation with sex is not limited to the sexual act. For girls sex has a more broadly biological significance in connection with menstruation and pregnancy. "Often, therefore, the girl group engaging in sexual activities finds satisfaction in curiosity about anatomy, and may miss entirely the discovery of orgasm."[100]

Thompson wrote that demands for the maintenance of prestige in the group life make it necessary for the girl to supplant part of her activities with interest in the other sex. Having "dates" and being seen with boys becomes essential. Ideally the change from preadolescent to adolescent relationships progresses to a point where the girl develops embryonic feelings of affection for friendly boys, culminating in the choice of one particular boy as a "love object." Normally a satisfactory, stable partnership with one of the other sex is the final goal. The successful progression of the female through adolescence is by no means identical to that of the boy. "The female must be viewed as possessing different points of physiology, under different social pressures, and distinguished by peculiar psychic and emotional characteristics resulting therefrom."[101]

I shall conclude this chapter by recommending to the interested reader Jersild's, *The Psychology of Adolescence,* Hurlock's *Developmental Psychology,* and Bernard and Huckins' *Readings in Human Development* as excellent supplements to the ideas of Sullivan and Thompson set forth more than a generation ago.[102]

Notes

1. HARRY STACK SULLIVAN, *Personal Psychopathology,* copyright 1965 by William Alanson White Psychiatric Foundation, Washington, D.C. (unpublished), p. 1.

2. *Ibid.,* pp. 1-2.

3. *Ibid.,* p. 2.

4. *Ibid.*

5. Cf. ANDREW HACKER, "A Country Called Corporate America," *The New York Times Magazine,* July 3, 1966.

6. SULLIVAN, *op. cit.,* p. 3.

7. See, for example, JOHN DEWEY, *Human Nature and Conduct* (New York: Henry Holt and Company, 1922), and *Logic: The Theory of Inquiry* (New York: Henry Holt and Company, 1938).

8. SULLIVAN, *op. cit.,* p. 7.

9. Cf. ANSELM STRAUSS (ed.), *George Herbert Mead on Social Psychology* (Chicago, Illinois: University of Chicago Press, 1964), pp. 20 ff.

10. SULLIVAN, *op. cit.,* p. 7.

11. MISCHA TITIEV, *The Science of Man* (New York: Holt, Rinehart, and Winston, 1963), p. 484.

12. Cf. GORDON W. ALLPORT, *Pattern and Growth in Personality* (New York: Holt, Rinehart, and Winston, 1961), chap. 21.

13. SULLIVAN, *op. cit.,* pp. 9-10.

14. *Ibid.,* pp. 38-39.

15. *Ibid.,* p. 39.

16. *Ibid.,* p. 40.

17. Cf. KURT HAAS, *Understanding Ourselves and Others* (Englewood Cliffs, New Jersey: Prentice-Hall, 1965), pp. 36-40.

188 : *The Beginnings of Modern American Psychiatry*

18. Cf. *ibid.*, pp. 42-69.

19. Sullivan, *op. cit.*, p. 41.

20. *Ibid.*

21. *Ibid.*, p. 81.

22. *Ibid.*, p. 82.

23. Cf. discussion of this point in Harry Stack Sullivan, *The Interpersonal Theory of Psychiatry*, ed. Helen Swick Perry and Mary Ladd Gawel, with an Introduction by Mabel Blake Cohen (New York: W. W. Norton and Company, 1953), chaps. 7, 8.

24. Sullivan, *Personal Psychopathology*, p. 8, footnote 4; Sullivan says to *prehend* is to be understood as a step toward conscious apprehension, in the sense of having at least capability of verbal formulation. That is, the initial sentience had by the infant is or becomes usefully elaborated because of further experience but not to the point of being communicated by speech, writing, or the graphic techniques. Sullivan thought that many "prehensions" occur without the person's being conscious of them.

25. *Ibid.*, p. 84.

26. In his later work, Sullivan assumed an original bifurcation of infantile experience symbolized in terms of a good mother and a bad or evil mother.

27. Sullivan, *Personal Psychopathology*, p. 85.

28. Cf. Harry Stack Sullivan, *Conceptions of Modern Psychiatry*, with a Foreword by the author and a Critical Appraisal of the Theory by Patrick Mullahy (New York: W. W. Norton and Company, 1953), pp. 59-61.

29. Sullivan, *Personal Psychopathology*, p. 92, footnote 11.

30. *Ibid.*, pp. 119-120, footnote 3; Sullivan here comments on the notion of *repression*, which he later discarded, as follows:

"From the broader biological viewpoint the consideration of repression as an actual process of living receives such limited support that I must deny it much importance in human life, even entertain chronic doubt as to the validity of the conception. It is retained in this treatise solely because (1) there *seems to be* a gap between manifest suppression and manifest dissocation, which it fills; and (2) actual human manifestations of repression so *greatly* exceed anything apt to happen in the sub-human phyla without prompt death of the animal concerned, that one cannot reason too surely about human limitations from mere *lethality* of a process."

31. *Ibid.*, p. 125.

32. *Ibid.*, p. 93.

33. *Ibid.*, p. 100.

34. *Ibid.*, p. 101.

35. *Ibid.*, p. 103.

36. *Ibid.*, p. 102.

37. *Ibid.*, p. 130.

38. Bronislaw Malinowski, *The Father in Primitive Psychology* (New York:

W. W. Norton and Company, 1927); *The Sexual Life of Savages in Northwestern Melanesia* (New York: Liveright, 1929).

39. SULLIVAN, *Personal Psychopathology,* p. 131.

40. *Ibid.*

41. *Ibid.,* p. 108.

42. *Ibid.,* p. 109.

43. *Ibid.,* p. 103.

44. *Ibid.,* p. 112.

45. *Ibid.,* p. 106.

46. *Ibid.,* pp. 106-107; cf. L. JOSEPH STONE and JOSEPH CHURCH, *Childhood and Adolescence* (New York: Random House, 1957), chaps. 6, 7; and ARTHUR T. JERSILD, *Child Psychology* (Englewood Cliffs, New Jersey: Prentice-Hall, 1960), chaps. 6, 7, 8, 9.

47. For a discussion of rage behavior and its differentiation, see SULLIVAN, *The Interpersonal Theory of Psychiatry,* pp. 54, 211-213.

48. SULLIVAN, *Personal Psychopathology,* p. 114.

49. *Ibid.,* pp. 114-115.

50. *Ibid.,* p. 115.

51. *Ibid.*

52. *Ibid.,* p. 120.

53. *Ibid.,* p. 123.

54. *Ibid.,* p. 124.

55. *Ibid.,* p. 117.

56. *Ibid.,* p. 118.

57. *Ibid.*

58. *Ibid.,* p. 120.

59. *Ibid.,* p. 127.

60. *Ibid.,* p. 128.

61. *Ibid.,* p. 129.

62. *Ibid.,* p. 132.

63. *Ibid.,* p. 133.

64. Cf. SULLIVAN, *Conceptions of Modern Psychiatry,* pp. 100-102.

65. SULLIVAN, *Personal Psychopathology,* p. 138.

66. *Ibid.,* p. 134.

67. *Ibid.,* p. 135.

68. *Ibid.,* p. 140.

69. *Ibid.*

70. *Ibid.,* p. 152.

71. *Ibid.,* p. 147.

72. *Ibid.*

73. *Ibid.,* p. 148.

74. *Ibid.,* p. 154.

75. *Ibid.,* pp. 155-156.

76. *Ibid.,* p. 159.
77. *Ibid.,* p. 160.
78. *Ibid.*
79. *Ibid.,* p. 161.
80. *Ibid.*
81. *Ibid.*
82. *Ibid.,* p. 163.
83. *Ibid.,* p. 164.
84. Cf. KAREN HORNEY, *New Ways in Psychoanalysis* (New York: W. W. Norton and Company, 1939); CLARA THOMPSON and PATRICK MULLAHY, *Psychoanalysis: Evolution and Development* (New York: Hermitage Press, 1950); FRIEDA FROMM-REICHMAN, *Principles of Intensive Psychotherapy* (Chicago, Illinois: University of Chicago Press, 1950); LEON SALZMAN, *Developments in Psychoanalysis* (New York: Grune and Stratton, 1962); ABRAM KARDINER, AARON KARUSH, and LIONEL OVESEY, "A Methodological Study of Freudian Theory," *International Journal of Psychiatry,* 2:489-541, 1966.
85. SULLIVAN, *Personal Psychopathology,* p. 165, footnote 3.
86. *Ibid.,* p. 166.
87. *Ibid.*, p. 167.
88. *Ibid.,* p. 179.
89. Cf. RUTH BENEDICT, "Continuities and Discontinuities in Cultural Patterning," in PATRICK MULLAHY (ed.), *A Study of Interpersonal Relations* (New York: Science House, 1967).
90. SULLIVAN, *Personal Psychopathology,* p. 180.
91. Cf. "Joseph Kidd, Business Assistant," in ROBERT W. WHITE, *Lives in Progress* (New York: The Dryden Press, 1952).
92. SULLIVAN, *Personal Psychopathology,* p. 180.
93. *Ibid.*
94. *Ibid.,* p. 181, footnote 19.
95. *Ibid.,* pp. 102-103, footnote 24.
96. *Ibid.,* pp. 181-182.
97. *Ibid.,* p. 182.
98. *Ibid.,* p. 183.
99. *Ibid.,* p. 220.
100. *Ibid.*
101. *Ibid.,* p. 221.
102. ARTHUR T. JERSILD, *The Psychology of Adolescence* (2nd ed.; New York: The Macmillan Company, 1963); ELIZABETH B. HURLOCK, *Developmental Psychology* (2nd ed.; New York: McGraw-Hill Book Company, 1959); HAROLD W. BERNARD and WESLEY C. HUCKINS (eds.), *Readings in Human Development* (Boston, Massachusetts: Allyn and Bacon, 1967).

5 / The Modified Psychoanalytic Method: Types of Personalities, Typical Situations

In order to elucidate Sullivan's ideas on the personal interview, I must now provide an exposition of his "method" of inquiry and techniques of therapy as he summarized them in *Personal Psychopathology*. The study of personality, as I suggested previously, is an enormously difficult and complex affair.[1] Sullivan wrote that there is an essential inaccessibility about any personality other than our own. We cannot, so to speak, get inside the other fellow's skin and observe the world through his eyes. Though we may gain a great deal of knowledge about the other fellow's experiences and behavior, we can never become acquainted with his experiences in a fashion analogous to our direct, immediate acquaintance with ourselves and our "inner" experiences. That is why years of intimacy with another person does not, and cannot, enable the most devoted friend to be in a position in which he can predict every act of the other one. Moreover, even if the other one should make a gigantic effort at self-revelation, he cannot convey the whole unique totality of his personality. An ample residuum remains that escapes analysis and communication. And even when the other person acts in the best of faith, a good deal that he seems to communicate is fictitious. Only in the works of great novelists such as Stendhal, Joyce, Dostoevsky, Proust, Tolstoy, can we glimpse a personal world that is more or less analogous to what a perfect understanding of another person might bring. However, the empirical study of personality is far different from the realm of art, and inherently subject to very real limitations. Hence, as Sullivan says, no one can hope fully to understand another human being; that, in fact, one is very fortunate if he approaches an understanding of himself.[2]

But these considerations furnish no rational grounds for pessimism about human understanding. Sullivan claims that for the greater part of life the individual activities of any one of us are very similar indeed to well-known, widely spread human acts. "One's way of doing any particular thing is apt to be very well precedented, including but little that is novel."[3] The great body of one's information and belief is said to approach the content of one's fellows in that particular culture. However, the "great part" of an individual's explanations for his behavior is "stereotyped" and must be treated with caution and reserve by the inquirer. Even so, these explanations when skillfully interpreted and related to the individual's personal history and present situation are "always illuminating."

Psychobiology (or psychology) is a very young science; so it is no wonder that the inquirer is beset with all sorts of problems. But even the relatively much older natural sciences have at least one "problem of personality" to deal with, which might be called the "personal equation," namely, the limitations of our special senses. There is, first of all, the relatively trivial fact that the "distance receptors," for example, vary somewhat from individual to individual in quality and range. But this limitation, especially with the aid of various instruments and techniques, can, apparently, be overcome.

(But philosophers have pointed to a far greater and apparently insuperable problem. If man's sense organs were more powerful and more numerous, might he not perhaps perceive a world very different from the one we know?[4] This question immediately raises problems as to the nature and limitations of scientific method, and of the very nature of reality in the metaphysical sense. These matters are, or at least used to be, among the most vital and controversial problems for philosophers. However, they are of little interest to most psychiatrists.)

Turning to the social sciences, Sullivan claimed (around 1932) that they have many problems of personality. He mentions that workings of personal bias and inexperience are everywhere evident in their brief course. Not only do they share the defective instrumentality of which the physicist long since became aware; they are said to be at the great disadvantage that a refining of their instruments means a refining of their selves. This observation would or did perhaps conspicuously apply to the anthropological field worker. However, since the time when *Personal Psychopathology* was written, social scientists have learned a good deal about problems of personality.

Freud, with good reason, had insisted that a self-understanding (achieved through a "didactic" analysis) was a necessary condition of a sound understanding of others. Even the interpretation of observable human behavior is said to be measured as to success by the formulated experience of the observer. It was approximately this point that Freud reached in his development of the psychoanalytic "method." And it is approximately at this point that Sullivan began to expand, modify, and improve upon Freud's great pioneering work.

According to Sullivan, the study of individual personalities is a form of social interaction, as he originally learned apparently from his work with schizophrenic patients. When the psychiatrist attempts to accumulate information about the "subject individual" from other individuals, he is always engaging in interpersonal relations possessing many complexities. The notion of an hypothetical detachment of the "observer personality," the psychobiologist or psychiatrist, is not only erroneous but gravely misleading and destructive of serious therapeutic effort or of any attempt to understand the other one. Even when the student of interpersonal relations interprets written and similar records of the subject personality, he is not a purely detached "objective" observer of such materials, since he is hampered or restricted by not only his own "experience limitations" but by the nature of the materials and their effects on him. In a manner of speaking, the observer and the materials at hand "interact" in the student's act of interpretation. In any face-to-face relationship the interaction constitutes a much more complex and dynamic interchange. "No two people have ever talked together with entire freedom of either one from effects of interaction of the other."[5] This fact is an essential component of human *being*.

Sullivan also points out that when, as is so often the case in personality study, the subject individual, on whom a report from a second person is desired by the investigator, is a friend or foe, a son or a parent, of the subject or patient that when the purpose of the investigator as envisaged by the second person informant may include almost any or all the prevalent "value superstitions"; that when the very language of the two persons conversing may be so differently evolved that identical verbal symbols stand in but remote relations of meaning—how all but certain it is that the truth will remain unknown, while the "detached" investigator will come away only a little more certain of his preconception as to the "facts."

Thus it follows that the most productive informant is at the mercy of the interviewer's "experience limitations" and personal bias. Sullivan discovered that an interviewer's report may show nothing in the (actual) discontinuity of narrative, of the many occasions on which he has turned away from important clues, garbled the temporal sequence of events (of the patient's life), and discouraged the flow of information. It so happened that the interviewer may have acquired a "specious state of complacency." Hence the report of an interview is said to be often unsatisfactory not only by reason of imperfect development of the relevant information, but also by reason "of unwitting fraud" in the shape of its finality and completeness. Sullivan wrote that he knew many so-called explanations of personality disaster (schizophrenia) to collapse into sheer nonsense on discovery that the "explanatory events" *followed* the disaster, or occurred in a sequence otherwise divorcing them of their supposed relationship to it. Incidentally, these are some of the reasons that Sullivan quite early in his career made use of a recording machine. During his leisure hours he could then "listen back" to such recordings in an attempt to understand more clearly what had gone on between him and the patient. Also, as Otto Will, Jr., has pointed out in his Introduction in the *Psychiatric Interview,* Sullivan in 1927 proposed the photographing of interview sessions, with the goal of obtaining a good look at the nonverbal gestural components of communication. Sullivan did in fact make such an attempt with some of his schizophrenic patients.[6]

Every student of personality must learn that any personal interview or any psychiatric interview he is involved in is a part of an interpersonal situation, and that recognition of factors in the interpersonal situation should be the central problem. According to Sullivan's interpretation, in "transference" one has almost everything of the direct interaction of personalities. The phenomena of transference seem strange only to those who are singularly incapable of intimacy. The direct remedial effect of transference is said to arise in its at least brief provision of that kind of interpersonal situation that is the most needed by people of the current scene. "The terrible isolation of the many is the peculiar characteristic of our people, the nucleus of their mental disorder."[7] The technique of the personal interview is devised to overcome the effects of the processes that result in the maintenance of an unnecessary and harmful "isolation" of personality from personality, and to detach or isolate their manifestations. This technique is said to be based on an assumption that the subject individual is more or less willing to enter into some degree of intimacy with the interviewer. This, of course, entails communication. But it must be realized that the self of each individual mediates in most attempts at communication. However, communication is not simply a matter of two people talking together and uttering "verbal combinations" more or less self-consciously. Sullivan says that the two personalities *integrated* into the total situation within which this self-to-self conversation is occurring communicate more or less, as it were, under cover of the verbal interchange. A penumbra of "personality meaning" (unique, personal meaning) is said to be attached to the culturally standardized words, being conveyed from one participant to the other in the degree that there is an empathic linkage from similarity of personality. "Penumbrae of personality-meaning attach to culturally standardized inflections, gestures, postures and other *expressive dynamisms* used in and along with the conversation."[8]

The intercommunication of personalities occurs in many ways that *cannot* be adequately described in words. If there is genuine, successful communication of information about some event to the auditor some of the meaning is conveyed exterior to one's capacity for verbal communication. The culture provides a framework through which much that is unformulated, unverbalized gets communicated, though it is incapable of complete objectivation. "We have improvised in words, syntax, intonations, postures, and unknown ways culture-patterns that have brought correct 'response,' in the shape of that which was within us, in the 'other' personality."[9] The exchange of information between people about themselves and their experiences by means of speech, gesture, and the like is never perfect. Thus, at some certain moment, Sullivan points out, a glance of the eyes may have completed a task beyond our power of words. For such reasons, among others, the student of personality must learn to be aware of the activity of his own participation in each social situation in which he seeks knowledge of another person.

Sullivan wrote that experience taught him that personality studies should begin with direct contact with the personality to be studied. All that one has available in his personality (all his human resources) is said to become effective in a deliberate situation of intimacy with another. In this connection, Sullivan claimed that one's "first impression" is among the most valuable points of departure that can be conceived, though it is the most in need of refinement of any of the technologies available to the psychobiologist or psychopathologist. People generally are prone to like or dislike at sight, or even at hearing over the telephone. The student of personality must become as deliberately conscious as possible of the valuations he so swiftly makes of every person who becomes a subject of study. "He needs to develop a social psychology of empathy."[10] Sullivan surmised that for every student of personality his first impressions are his nearest approach to another personality, that from the occasion of initial contact to the end of however extended a series of contacts, the drives for interpersonal imtimacy and other tendency systems in him and his subject will be functioning to *restrict* and *distort* the interpersonal relationship and a clear-eyed understanding of it by the participants. The Stranger comes to the psychiatrist "uncatalogued." But as soon as familiarity is established, one's systematizing tendency, "especially in these days of innumerable superficial contacts," reduces the Stranger to a more or less "mediocre bundle of characteristics."

The social psychology of empathy is said to begin in an appraisal of the roles for which "liked" people on the one hand and "disliked" people on the other are "intended" ("determined") by one's personality. It is not enough that the investigator convince himself that he has a desire to understand his subject. In integrating the interview situation he must understand the forces at work within him, a requirement that will initially take years of study, a personal ("didactic") analysis, and ideally, perhaps a rich and varied experience of life. "In these times of interpersonal superficialities," Sullivan wrote, "the adolescent drive toward intimacy is frequently projected into a lifework of personality study."[11] Unfortunately, all the shortcomings of the investigator tend to operate in his work and limit or destroy his effectiveness. Thus, Sullivan relates, he had known students who sought only subject individuals "who burnt incense to the self-regard of the investigator."

When the investigator has learned all he can from the initial impression, he proceeds to help the other person to formulate verbally as much as possible of the latter's life history and current interpersonal relations, employing whatever skill that his training and experience have provided. But there are great obstacles to the success of such a task. The "most vicious" obstacle is said to be the preconceptions about the other one (the interviewee) communicated from the investigator or interviewer to the subject individual. Among such preconceptions are valuations, especially ethical valuations, which are a "curse" in therapy if only because they make the patient feel guilty, or more guilty, and anxious, and hinder or destroy meaningful communication. The investigator or therapist has no business playing a Godlike role, and no divine right to sit in moral judgment. To the extent that the therapist or investigator is in the grip of the mores, to that extent he is inadequate for his purpose. A "relative" view of culture is needed. Every personality has a system of valuations, usually derived from his culture, and which as a rule are more or less taken for granted, and every other individual who comes to engage in intimate relations with him is driven to acquiesce more or less unwittingly in this "system." Worse still, from a scientific point of view, besides such valuations as are incorporated in the self-system, there are valuations, often contradictory, of which the investigator personality is unconscious. If one is working with schizophrenics, for example, such unreflective or unconscious appraisals can—and apparently often do—play havoc. But the situation is essentially no different when one is dealing with any form of mental illness.

So, once more, self-understanding (which is closely allied to an understanding of sociocultural processes) is a necessary condition of effective therapy but, as Freud long ago discovered, self-understanding is not primarily an intellectual achievement. As Sullivan says, it is primarily a work of intuition, that is, of grasping the "whole" of a configuration though it should ensue in rational formulation. And such an intuition does not come easily. It does not occur in a blinding flash of illumination in the absence of a great deal of preparation and hard work. Freud's free-associational technique is (or was in or about 1932) the only tool available to the investigator-therapist for the comprehensive exploration of personality by which unguided intuition may be converted into *rational insight.* It follows that "the method of statement" in therapy by the patient, if unsupported by the method of free fantasy (free association) cannot provide rational insight no matter how much the insight of the therapist or questioner may assist the securing of intuition of the subject individual. It follows, further-more, from all that has been said that the rational insights of the interviewer, however penetrating, cannot of themselves be sufficient to discover and reveal the totality of human personality. "There is always interaction between interviewer and interviewed, between analyst and analysand, and from it, both *must* invariably *learn* if sound knowledge of the subject-personality is to result."[12]

Once the interview begins, there is said to be a great deal in favor of making verbatim records of the initial statement of the problem or "situation" as presented by the subject individual. Sullivan asserts that everything that can be recorded of the patient's initial communication about his troubles, as he sees them, and/or the "facts," is apt to prove most highly significant, though most of it will require many hours for elucidation. Usually it will take a long time for some of the clues given in the first interview to recur—if only because the defensive stratagems of the patient are not so likely to be mobilized during this first interview. On this first occasion the patient is "set" toward some broadly conceived purpose. His presentation is therefore said to be more general than will be any subsequent discussion. According to Sullivan, this is peculiarly the case when the patient has sought the interview, though it is also true of any initial contacts between persons. One may regard the comprehensive recording of these phenomena of the initial encounter between therapist and patient as but an objectivication of some of the materials entering into one's "first impression" of another. It seems necessary in this connection to stress the fact that the skill of the investigator must grow toward a *noninterfering facilitation* of the initial communication. "The first great step toward success has been taken if the patient has been *permitted* to say and otherwise express whatever he wanted the investigator to know."[13] Even if the patient, or interviewee, is ready to attempt the creation of deliberate fraud, the story he tells is still well worth minute attention.

And now we arrive at an issue concerning which there is, and long since has been, acrimonious controversy. As is so often true of controversial issues, there are many arguments that can be marshaled for either side of this controversy. Sullivan wrote that there is a great advantage for personality students in the possession of fundamental medical training. In *Personal Psychopathology*, he favored a "prolonged training" culminating in the degree of Doctor of Mental Science or perhaps Doctor of Science. He believed that to inquire into the life situation of a person without being able to obtain firsthand information as to the sort of "somatic apparatus" the latter has to utilize in living, and without being able to appraise relative physiological handicaps and facilitations, is to work under considerable, and sometimes very great, limitations. Moreover, he thought that not to investigate personally the physical conditions of the patient is to forego the aid of some factors potent in the building of a sound situation of benevolent intimacy. Still again, he said that one should certainly make a *physical inventory* of the patient, to discover the "disease history," the state of physical health, the constitutional features of the patient, and so forth. Sullivan thought that clues may be obtained from tensions, gestures, and comments of the patients undergoing such an inspection that lead easily to highly significant material, whose existence may otherwise remain long unsuspected. The act of exposing the body to the scrutiny of the physician is said to be in more ways than one an auspicious beginning in the revelation of one's personality. A physical examination always entails a great deal of personality interchange—partly because it is a unique and more or less intimate sort of interpersonal situation—and should be fully utilized by the investigator. In this situation, the latter should be "extremely observant" of his patient, of himself, and of the inevitable intercommunication.

Sullivan wrote that then one considers the patient as an "apparatus" for functional activity in communal existence in the physicochemical world, inquiring into the zones of interaction, the sensory apparatus and projection fields, the neuromuscular characteristics—such as coordinations, finer adjustments, strength, endurance, and the like—and the more complex integrative ("neuropsychic") processes more or less measurable by performance and other "mental" tests. In this fashion, the investigator studies the patient's equipment of social tools, proceeding, by means of educational and occupational history-taking, to learn as much as he can of the patient's language development and various other of his assets and liabilities manifested in his interpersonal relations, including his utilization of culture patterns.

After the inventories mentioned above have been carried out, the next concern of the investigator or therapist is the patient's "exteriorization of the self." He seeks a comprehensive inventory of the person's current dealings and relations with others: his kind of work, play, his activities in important "interim situations," that is, periods of leisure when he is not engaged in recreation. In other words, one seeks to acquire significant data on the person's occupational and recreational opportunities, his preferences, enjoyments, successes, and failures. Sullivan goes on to say that one progresses easily—and methodically—into the accumulation of historic data on parents, significant relatives, teachers, personal family, such as wife and children, friends, employers, subordinates, colleagues or associates, and on broader issues of the economic, political, racial, and religious type.

Some readers may wonder why those "broader issues" concerning one's economic, political, racial, and religious affiliations and connections are relevant in the context of the interview. Sullivan in the context of "A Study of Personality" in *Personal Psychopathology* does not explain what he has in mind. One may surmise that something like the following considerations have to be taken into account. It is, I think, a generally accepted fact among social scientists that one's economic situation affects not only one's general outlook on life but many details of one's everyday living. A man who by force of economic circumstance is compelled to live in an urban slum area is likely not only to have a different outlook on life from that of a man who can afford to live in an "exclusive" suburb but also to engage in qualitatively different social relations from day to day, if not from hour to hour. Within limits, the "rules of the game" that we may call life are very different, in many respects, in each case. Perhaps this point can best be briefly illustrated from works of fiction. Consider how differently the "characters" in James Farrell's or John Dos Passos' or Theodore Dreiser's novels live and experience the world from those in the novels of Louis Auchincloss, John O'Hara, or Edwin O'Connor. Of course, other than economic factors have to be considered, but these are patently of major importance in the lives of the imaginatively portrayed men and women.

To be sure, economic, political, racial, and religious factors are not always independent, if ever. They intertwine in various complex ways that cannot be specified rigorously. But that all these generic factors, operating in various combinations and permutations, do affect not only one's general outlook on life but one's day-to-day living can scarcely be denied. In fact, to a great extent these generic factors, among others, combine in numerous subtle ways to mould the human personality.

The use of the (Meyerian) "life chart" or life record is said to be a considerable aid in final synthesis of much of this and later material.[14] Sullivan stressed the value of an accurate chronology in assembling factual data about a personality, claiming that every thing should *date*. By this attention to such details, by this careful effort to pinpoint the data chronologically accurately in the life record, important effects of the maladjustive process of retrograde (retrospective) falsification are frequently revealed. "Gross errors of interpretation are prevented." In this fashion, also, "a sound philosophy of life" is encouraged, since it implies that the growth or emergence of human tendencies and abilities depends on an orderly, coherent sequence of innate and acquired factors; that is, in other words, that the maturation of innate tendencies and learning follow an orderly sequence and are mutually interdependent. This latter point is significant, since many people who are mentally ill have some very unrealistic notions of their actual and imagined abilities, the manner in which they are acquired, and the avenues of life that are or might be opened to them.

Sullivan had not yet (1932) fully clarified his conception of the self-system or self-dynamism, so his use of Freudian terms can be confusing, as the following discussion may indicate. Following upon his brief outline of a comprehensive inventory of the person "as objectively manifesting functional activity in communal existence with other people," which has been summarized in the previous paragraphs, he turns to a discussion of the "more direct investigation" of the personality. This investigation pertains to the "formulation of the self or *ego*, of the ideal system or *superego*, and of the repressed and the totally refracted tendency systems, the *id*."[15] In the first paper Sullivan published (partially summarized in Chapters 1 and 2 of this book), he made no clear-cut distinction between self and personality: thus he says in that paper that the self includes the ego and id of Freud's theory. Ultimately, his conception of the self, in a manner of speaking, came to include the ego and superego of Freud, while his conception of the dissociated systems is more or less similar, though by no means synonymous, with the *id*. But, in *Personal Psychopathology*, *self* and *ego* are more or less synonymous terms. Lest the differences in formulation seem a mere matter of terminology, one should bear the following in mind: (1) Some of the processes that Freud categorized under repression, according to Sullivan, properly belong under what he subsequently formulated as *selective inattention*, which has to do only with the control of consciousness, not with the inhibition of motives; and (2) the "contents" of Sullivan's self are by no means identical with the "contents" of Freud's *ego* and *superego,* just as the "contents" of the *dissociated* systems are not synonymous with those of the *id.* There is a third very important difference, though it is not absolute, between Sullivan's "self" and Freud's "ego" and "superego." For Sullivan, the self, though "colored" by unique genetic endowment, family experiences, and the like, is the dynamic organization of relatively enduring and meaningful patterns of recurrent interpersonal relations that characterize an individual's life. The self, according to his mature formulations, originates and operates in interpersonal situations. Freud's "ego," of which the "superego" is a subsystem, is more self-actional. It was not formulated by Freud as an interpersonal dynamism. Despite Sullivan's great indebtedness to Freud, his theories diverged more and more from those of the latter as the years went by. His casual use of Freudian terms, such as *ego, superego,* and *id* in *Personal Psychopathology* apparently suggests that he still hoped for a meaningful communication with Freudian psychoanalysts and with those whose thinking occurred within a Freudian framework. I believe he eventually abandoned any such hopes. If the reader will keep these things in mind, he need have no great difficulty with Sullivan's use of Freudian terms. But one should also bear in mind that we are really no longer in the same universe of discourse as Freud's. We have already in many respects traveled far from the latter's theoretical system, and we still have a long way to go. All these matters will become clearer as we progress from chapter to chapter in this volume.

To return to Sullivan's ideas on the direct investigation of personality, he wrote that the total situation integrated by the patient and the investigator should now develop toward a more frankly expressed purpose of *discovery.* The first phase of this work is a *reconnaissance* of the self. "This should be directed to three formulations: The person as he *wishes and has wished to be; as he has suspected and now suspects* what *he actually is*; and as *his 'enemies' have seen and now see him.* "[16] These three aspects are said to be fairly comprehensive of the experience incorporated in the self. Sullivan wrote that in eliciting the easily accessible data along the three paths mentioned, one encounters innumerable leads toward the foreconscious fringes of awareness, and many clues to processes of which the patient is but vaguely conscious. Also, the investigator elicits or provokes a running account of new interpersonal contacts, experiences that vary from rudimentary to very close interpersonal relationships. One should carefully note each new individual as he is revealed in the patient's life, who is, directly or indirectly significant, being scrupulous in placing them in the correct chronological order on the life chart.

Throughout this phase of the inquiry, aside from dating people and events chronologically, the investigator should limit active interference to a minimum. His business is said to be to observe closely the phenomena that are occurring, both the information that is being produced and omitted, and the manifestations of tendencies operating in the interview situation. But when the data readily accessible for verbal communication ("report") are running low, one reaches a stage at which it is well to start systematic questioning. By sustained inquiry, the investigator extracts the patient's characterizations of all the persons of high significance in childhood and the juvenile era insofar as such characterizations have been retained and are available for recall. (Of course, the patient's experiences during infancy are not available for recall.) Furthermore, in the instance of each person of high significance during one or more of the various developmental eras, especially that of the parents, the investigator should secure whatever data he can chiefly from *other sources* about the people who in turn played an effective role in the shaping of those significant people's personalities. In "Psychiatry: Introduction to the Study of Interpersonal Relations," Sullivan gives a brilliant and humorous account of how one might procure such (collateral) information.[17] On this point what he seems to have in mind is this: The persons who were significant in the patient's life were throughout their lives themselves caught up in intricate networks of interpersonal relations. Data about such relations may provide not only information that the patient lacks regarding his parents, brothers and sisters, friends, and others, but it may also provide a corrective to the necessarily limited standpoint of the patient and/or the significant others from whom one seeks information. The more relevant and significant information the investigator can obtain, directly or indirectly, about the other people significant in the patient's life, the more accurate is his picture of the interpersonal influences that molded the patient's life.

Date from informants, which, insofar as it is possible, should also be dated, are said to vary greatly in value, and should never be regarded as of the same order of relevance or importance as the patient's reported experience. But the data can fill gaps in the patient's recital, especially of the earlier years, and can confirm or correct his personal account of the events of his life. The investigator wants to obtain collateral information from the persons who have been significant at each developmental stage of the patient's life. "One strives to concentrate the recollections of each informant by following particular periods of growth, and attempting to orient him toward recitals *as if* from the patient's viewpoint at that time."[18] In other words, parents (who "should be treated much after the fashion of patients"), friends, siblings, can report "what he said and did," while offering their own surmises as to what the patient was experiencing. There is one qualification to be made about such recitals. The informants' data on the infantile and early childhood eras have to be "objective," because no one can surmise or imagine what goes on in the infantile mind, though one may make inferences about it from a study of an infant's overt behavior. One can also create certain reconstructions more or less in the manner of Freud, from the patient's and other people's reports.

Sullivan wrote that not only should parents be treated much after the fashion of patients—one of them may be quite as mentally ill as the particular patient—but that both of them are so deeply involved with him in the presenting of difficulties that a detached technique of interview is inappropriate. One should permit each parent to "tell the story" very much as he wishes. The investigator should resort to systematic questioning in a step-by-step manner only after the required amount of sympathetic listening with keen attention not only to information and misinformation but also to the processes appearing in the interview situation. The therapist should in general interview the parents separately because one needs all the information one can get "of the personality of each." Afterwards it may be desirable to check some doubtful points with them together. Then their interaction becomes quite illuminating and does not endanger a full report.

The problem of dealing with parents suggests certain other aspects of interview technique in connection with the investigator's attitude toward recitals "but strangely related to the facts," and about his attitude regarding fraud and deception by informants generally. Their demonstration of "complex motivation" in dealing with facts in the interview manifests important phases or aspects of their personalities. Should one or both parents appear to have a low appraisal of the investigator's intelligence, that in itself is but "a part of a customary interpersonal activity" in regard of "their child." The explanation of their attitude is just as "human" and intelligible as are its consequences on their offspring, the patient. The investigator must not engage in prestige performances in order to sustain his self-esteem but instead be alert to develop their underlying self-appraisals and motivations, which are or may be manifested in their distorted reports.

Sullivan wrote that one reads in many records of interviews that the subject individual "admits" this or that. "This is all wrong. The method of cross-examination is frequently necessary but it should never be used in the fashion of our legal brethren, to secure admissions and to impeach veracity. The good interpreter is mildly astonished when his informant shows strong feeling of negative valuation over a fact. He exteriorizes his principles that facts exist, that they are very useful in understanding the patient, and that they have no more of good-or-bad connotation than have a mechanic's tools. He is free of prejudice, but he is not exhorting others to that freedom; he wants the facts [that is, an accurate report] of prejudices that have been of importance, and he discourages by his realistic attitude the interposition of prejudice in the way of his getting the facts."[19]

There is one more topic to be explicated briefly before I leave this phase of the interview. Since Sullivan desired to have collateral information on the persons who were significant at each genetic stage of the patient's life, he employed what he called the collateral interview. Regarding the latter he said the general scheme is to "sketch" the patient as a personality at the beginning of the informant's acquaintance with the patient; to "develop" significant facts of the genetic or developmental stages covering the period of acquaintance; to elucidate the actual integrating tendencies of informant and patient manifested from the beginning to the end of their relationships; and, finally, to attempt a "sketch" of the patient's personality as it has developed during the period for which the informant knew him. Whatever data are discovered should, if possible be "dated" and people "named," that is, identified. Sullivan states that he found it was a good plan to request of every informant a supplementary report by letter of any thing relevant that may occur to him subsequent to the interview for it is apt to be worth having if one can get it.

After the investigator has (1) exhaustively inquired into the material readily accessible to the patient's self, (2) secured most of the collateral information available, and (3) combined the two bodies of data into a synoptic view, he is ready to proceed with the more technical processes of exploration. If the preliminary work has been carried out in a competent fashion, the patient will already have developed an often extraordinary and wholly unprecedented trust in the benevolent purposes of the therapist-investigator, and a conviction that he possesses a wise tolerance and broad knowledge of people. Perhaps the patient will already have experienced a wholly unaccustomed security in intimacy, that is, a perhaps undreamed-of realization that it is possible to be intimate with another person and still have a previously unexperienced security in such a relationship. Parenthetically, one may add that in this first phase of the inquiry, the reconnaisance, the tyro investigator is sometimes so clumsy that he, so to speak, steps painfully heavily on the patient's toes, that is, provokes so much anxiety in his patient that the latter abandons the relationship for good, perhaps refusing ever again to have anything to do with a therapist. (That is one of the reasons that the work of a psychiatric or psychoanalytic candidate-in-training should always be supervised by one or more seasoned therapists.) The rule is that one never unnecessarily provokes anxiety (insecurity) or enhances it, if one can, acting without clear foresight of what one is about. (In treating schizophrenics, Sullivan held there is no room at all for such "stupidity." Schizophrenics, he said, are people with whom the physician must never make a serious mistake. Because their trust in people is minimal the psychiatrist is perhaps the last best hope of the schizophrenic patient. If he injures the fragile trust and security of the patient at a particular stage in therapy he may destroy forever any remnant of hope the patient sustains, and thus unwittingly abandon him to despair.)

In any event, the physician, having carried out the initial reconnaissance, has recourse to the communicational freedom traditionally labeled *the analytic situation.*[20] Pointing out to the patient the incomplete character of the latter's report, he explains the necessity or at least the utility of free fantasy, free association, in establishing connections with lost memories or faded associations. The vagueness that may characterize the initial fantasies are emphasized as the physician begins to reinforce the patient's readiness for actual freedom of communication. "The patient is instructed to express in words, sounds, gestures, grimaces, smiles, tears, intonations—in short in any suitable way—as much as possible of whatever comes to mind, in the periods of repose into which he is to relapse as often as possible during the interview. In order to relax the interference of his accustomed waking 'sets,' he is to abandon any purpose other than that of expressing his 'thoughts.' "[21] He can depend on it that the physician will listen alertly to the flow of material he expresses—material that will be apparently incoherent, often irrelevant, sometimes fraudulent, and at first, to a degree, seemingly inconsequential or trivial. Sullivan claims that the design or pattern of meaning that gradually emerges from the flow of fantasy and the life processes concerned in the fragments of recollection will presently appear to the patient. Though an occasional summary by the therapist of what seems to have been in progress may, to an extent, facilitate this process, in general, only the patient has the facts. The physician's skill is said to be useful only insofar as he may recognize *incompleteness* of recall, obscure manifestations of processes that are hindering recall, and the like.

The instruction provided by the therapist regarding communicational freedom and the free flow of fantasy is at best given piecemeal. The therapist instructs the patient to relax "vigilant effort" at recollection to fill some gap in his memory, and to adopt instead an attitude of undirected attention to his mental processes. But the general rule is "useful recall," provided too significant a group of facts is not under scrutiny or sought after. This sort of experience, recall, is said to encourage the patient, to whom otherwise the dynamics of free fantasy might seem absurd, or esoteric, or actually mysteriously dangerous. Even so, the unhindered "exteriorization" (expression) of free-flowing fantasy ultimately is to be required.

Before I take up Sullivan's ideas on the application of "dream interpretation" as they are outlined in *Personal Psychopathology,* I wish to repeat his warning emphasized many years later: There is an impossible barrier, he said, between covert operations when one is asleep and overt operations and reports of them when one is awake. "What one actually deals with in psychiatry, and actually in a great many other aspects of life, are recollections pertaining to dreams; how closely, how adequately, these recollections approximate the actual dream is an insoluble problem."[22] All that one can deal with is the *remembered* dream and the patient's waking associations to it. Since the remembered dream is *of the person,* an expression of his personality, it is important because it may provide clues as to what is occurring in the person. Hence dream analysis may be of great value, though it is not in the least esoteric.

In *Personal Psychopathology* Sullivan wrote that at the first occasion either of a dream fragment occurring in the stream of communication, or of the appearance of a "dreamlike thought" (once the reconnaissance is completed and the analytic situation is adopted), the therapist informs the patient regarding the utility of the dream as an aid in reaching those aspects of one's life situation that one habitually excludes from one's workaday world. He made it a rule, he said, to postpone all dream analysis until a time is reached when free fantasy is suspended by "phenomena of resistance." The *first* dream that occurs after the patient has learned or been informed that dreams may prove useful should be recorded with great care. At the time that dreams are discussed, the physician or therapist may well instruct the patient to develop a habit of recording dreams each morning, *"immediately upon awakening."* Sullivan advises that the dreams are to be recorded both in the order of recollection, and with a final note as to their probable order of occurrence, dated, and given to the physician at the beginning of each interview. It is insignificant whether any of these dreams serve an obvious function during a particular interview since the purpose of the interview is *the growth of awareness of the patient as to his personality and interpersonal relations*; that is, self-understanding. Self-understanding, in turn, enhances the "primal function" of the person, namely, *to live as completely (or fully) as possible.* This is, in the long run, the acid test of the interviews and their results: the degree to which the patient's awareness of himself and his problems is expanded to the end that living is facilitated and enriched.[23]

Sullivan claims that the very act of systematically recording the dream experience may be all that this phase of the patient's life will require, for weeks on end. But why? Apparently because they provide certain information to the physician. Sullivan says that if there is an important situation manifested in the dream, the stream of fantasy will bring it up. The notes that the patient accumulated about his recollected dreams provide the physician with information by which he may check the fantasy productions. He has no cause to intervene actively by means of dream interpretation unless the development of the analytic situation is obstructed.[24]

Though most of my readers will probably be thoroughly familiar with Freud's pioneering work on the interpretation of dreams, some probably will not. Since Sullivan, up to a certain point, adopted Freud's ideas on dreams, I shall very briefly summarize some of the latter's discoveries and hypotheses on their meaning and interpretation.

According to Freud, the function of dreams is to protect and maintain sleep. Sleep may be considered to be, among other things, a refusal to face reality; and there is a withdrawal of psychical energy from the interests of life. In characteristic fashion, Freud believed that our relationships with the world, which we entered so unwillingly, seem to be endurable only with intermission. Moreover, in sleep we withdraw periodically into a condition similar to that prior to our entrance into the world, namely, into a condition similar to that of intrauterine existence. As one withdraws from reality one regresses to more primitive (infantile) modes of activity, and the controlling forces of the conscious mind are more and more reduced. Furthermore, since all "the paths to motility" are (usually) blocked, less energy is needed for repression of instinctual drives, of internal excitations, which are active during sleep. In other words, there is (ordinarily) no possibility that one will give manifest expression to such drives by acting overtly. To anticipate somewhat, dreams are a reaction to stimuli frequently though not always originating in the unconscious (in the id). Dreams effect a discharge of excitation so that the stimuli are removed and sleep can continue.

Before going further, it is pertinent to mention parenthetically that recent psychological research has substantiated the notion that dreams serve a very important psychological function—regardless of one's particular interpretation of dreams. What has been called "dream deprivation" apparently can have serious consequences.[25]

"Just what are the tendencies and desires which express themselves in sleep? They are the evil, primitive and infantile impulses and desires which remain in the unconscious (or in the id) of every adult. In fact the unconscious (or rather the id, according to the later formulation) for Freud is the infantile in mental life. In dreams we regress to the infantile level of development. Since incestuous desires and wishes to destroy rivals are said to be so prominent in early life, they will be markedly in evidence in our dreams."[26] One may also discover that hate rages unrestrainedly, along with frequent wishes for revenge and death wishes against parents, brothers and sisters, husband or wife, or one's own children. Thus, libidinal drives are shorn of all inhibition in dreams, while aesthetic and moral considerations are discarded.

In regard to Freud's theory of instincts, which provides the basic assumptions for his interpretation of dreams, one has to add that the conceptions of ego instincts and sexual instincts were reformulated. The "contrast" between the two generic drives was abandoned. They both, in Freud's last formulation, fall within the bounds of Eros, or life instinct. That is to say, according to Freud's final theory of instincts, both the ego instincts and sexual instincts are categorized under the more inclusive rubric called Eros. In contrast to Eros is Thanatos, the death or destructive instinct, which may operate internally against oneself as an impulse to self-destruction or be directed outward as an instinct of destruction of others. Just how the two, Eros and Thanatos, mingle or fuse in the vital process, is, in Freudian theory, entirely obscure. The following views expressed in Freud's *Civilization and Its Discontents* will perhaps suffice: He wrote that men are not gentle, friendly creatures wishing for love, who simply defend themselves if they are attacked, but that they possess a powerful measure of desire for aggression that has to be reckoned as part of their instinctural endowment. "As a result, their neighbor is for them not only a potential helper or sexual object, but also someone who tempts them to satisfy their aggressiveness on him, to exploit his capacity for work without compensation, to use him sexually without his consent, to seize his possessions, to humiliate him, to cause him pain, to torture and to kill him. . . . Who, in the face of all his experience of life and of history, will have the courage to dispute this assertion?"[27]

This dark side of man's nature, as Freud pictured it, will, he thought, also manifest itself in one's dreams.

There is an additional point to be mentioned regarding Freud's interpretation of dreams. Sometimes, the impulses, demands, or wishes arise in the preconscious, and are "residues" of the day's activities while one was in a waking state. However, this should not be taken at face value. Freud explicitly says that a desire left over from waking life, a preconscious train of thought with all the conflicting impulses belonging to it, obtains reinforcement during sleep *from an unconscious element.* Thus, according to Freud, dreams may arise either from the id or the ego. But it seems to be that it is the repressed, or deeply unconscious drives, clamoring for an outlet while one is sleeping, that are stressed. Thus, demands or wishes arising from an unconscious source, or from a preconscious allied to an unconscious source, make up the latent content of the dream and they are expressed in the manifest dream as wish fulfillments, however disguised or distorted. According to Freud, the mechanism of dream formation is the same whether the dreams arise from the id or from the ego.

Thus Freud held that dreams represent demands or wishes stemming from the unconscious or preconscious. However irrational and nonsensical the remembered dream may appear to be, it very frequently, if not always, ultimately represents unconscious processes that the dreamer does not know about in the waking state. These unconscious processes are very frequently "infantile," that is, stemming from a very early period in the life of the individual, and are usually repugnant to the waking ego, with its values and awareness of the demands and restrictions required by reality, that is, society.

Since the ego has the task of maintaining sleep in the face of these imperious, ever-active unconscious wishes or drives, which tend to disturb sleep, the sleeping ego resorts to the stratagem of allaying them by a seeming act of compliance. It provides an outlet or satisfaction by means of a ("hallucinated") fulfillment of those drives in the manifest dream. Perhaps a fairly superficial illustration will help to clarify this point. A young child who longs for a particular object, such as a toy train, or yearns for a certain trip to the mountains or the seashore, or craves the love of a particular person, may in his dreams, so to speak, possess the desired physical object, go on that joyful journey to the mountains or the sea, secure the warm, sensuous love of the adored person. Since his wishes are innocent, or at least in his eyes are innocent, he does not have to disguise them. While in the waking state he is perhaps more or less clearly conscious of those wishes, though he cannot have them, in the dream he so to speak gets what he wants.[28] But gradually the child learns that certain of his wishes are not innocent, at least in the eyes of his parents, and, through them, in the view of society at large. Whether implicitly or directly, deliberately, he is taught that certain wishes are forbidden; so he gradually represses them. But they at least often remain in his unconscious (in the id) still active, charged with energy, seeking an outlet. In the course of later childhood and adolescence, various instinctual (frequently infantile sexual or aggressive) tendencies are more and more subject to repression. By the time one reaches adulthood one no longer is conscious that he has such drives; they become "forgotten." In other words, the development of the ego and superego reaches a point where they will no longer countenance them, because one has incorporated the values of society and learned one must adjust to conventional modes of gratification, whether the latter are completely satisfactory or not. Thus during the evolution of personality, forbidden impulses normally are repressed and "forgotten." And they have become antithetical to one's whole outlook on life, including one's values and ideals. Nevertheless they still exist in the unconscious, in the id, actively striving for an outlet. So they have to be dealt with somehow. Because the ego somewhat relaxes its vigilance during sleep, they are allowed a mode of gratification through dreams—a sort of hallucinatory fulfillment. It operates through the manifest dream, the dream we remember. It is this dream—or component of the dream—that constitutes the wish-fulfillment, though it is often unrecognizable as such. The latent content, which is mainly repressed material, thus gains an outlet through the "conscious" manifest dream.

So between the latent dream thoughts and the manifest dream or remembered dream, there has to occur a very elaborate process of disguise called the *dream-work.*

"The *dream-work* transforms the unconscious or preconscious wish, which is the *latent* dream thought, into what the dreamer perceives, that is, into *manifest dream content.* To use Freud's example, if a doctor has to wake up in the morning to be in a hospital on time, which is a case of a preconscious wish, he may continue to sleep and to dream that he is already in the hospital as a patient who does not have to get up early in the morning. The latent dream material is the [source of] conflict about getting up. The sleeping ego protected the sleep by means of the *dream-work*, which transformed the wish into the manifest dream content of being already in the hospital as a patient, thus disposing of the conflict."[29]

Since this example is based on an occurrence in what is only temporarily unconscious, namely, the preconscious, it does not convey the full meaning of latent dream thoughts and their vicissitudes, but it is sufficient, I think, for purposes of exposition. In Freud's *Interpretation of Dreams,* the reader will find a thorough exposition of his theory of dreams. The impulses in the unconscious proper tend usually to be much more powerful, conflict-provoking, and threatening to the conscious mind. The ego cannot prevent the unconscious thoughts, drives, and sensations, that is, the latent dream content, from forcing their way into consciousness, in the guise of the manifest dream. But through the dream work (condensation, displacement, etc.) it can and does make the manifest dream unrecognizably distorted and unintelligible.

There is one more point I wish to mention, namely, secondary elaboration. The ego attempts to mold the manifest dream content into a semblance of logic and coherence. Traditionally this has been interpreted as part of the dream-work.[30]

Freud's interpretation of dreams is enormously complicated in detail. Aside from Freud's own work, the reader may find Brenner's *Elementory Textbook of Psychoanalysis,* for example, suggestive since he has incorporated many subsequent refinements of Freud's interpretation.[31]

It is obvious that in Freud's view, a dream or the two aspects of a dream occur on two levels, one of which, the latent dream thoughts, are strictly an inferential construction. Whether or not the latter exist in a separate compartment of the mind, Sullivan came to believe there is an impassable barrier between these (hypothetical) latent thoughts and the remembered, manifest dream. This observation, however, does not entail a rejection of unconscious processes. But it does dispense with Freud's "topographical theory" of the mind. The same unconscious content may be expressed in different ways and in different kinds of symbols.

Several years before he began to systematize his theories in *Personal Psychopathology,* while he still remained and formulated his ideas more or less within the classical Freudian framework Sullivan wrote in "Peculiarity of Thought in Schizophrenia" that we know that a wealth of detail is lost from most dreams in a few minutes following upon awakening; that the so-called mechanism known as secondary elaboration, by which logical incongruities as a result of the intervention of the self are altered towards greater correctness, functions in the waking interval, so that the "remembered" dream undergoes falsification from hour to hour. Such occurrences suggest that the waking associations to the alleged latent content are of *the whole person* rather than to inaccessible and hypothetical latent dream thoughts. In the same paper he said that if we assume that symbol activity always occurs under the influence of and directed to the securing of an end that was more or less clearly foreseen; that if we assume that those "dynamic situations" termed condensation, displacement, dramatization, and secondary elaboration do similarly exist; and also if we assume that certain "adaptation methods," such as defense reactions, compensation, and perhaps sublimatory reformulation, do likewise occur—if we assume all these things, then, with this "somewhat awe-inspiring foundation," we can bring dreams into line with the recognizable impulses of the organism, and, moreover, understand them as intimately allied to the manifestations of events in waking life, without assuming the existence of latent dream thoughts.[32]

According to Sullivan, sleep is also necessary for the maintenance of the *waking* dissociation of powerful tendency systems. Its contribution to the success of the dissociative dynamics is said to take the form of the release and *fantastic satisfaction* of the dissociated systems in the activity of sleep. When an attempt at resolving a "conflict situation" suspends sleep as it may in the case of an individual on the verge of schizophrenia, the psychiatric importance of sleep privation clearly stands out. When the individual's preoccupation with a conflict situation is one concerning the to him gravest matters of his life, it "confirms" his sleeplessness. So his condition passes from bad to worse. "The connection, therefore, of a period of disordered sleep with the onset of a schizophrenic illness is intimate, and of a nature such that one might well believe that an intercurrent 'good night's sleep' would often postpone the disaster."[33]

In the deeper levels of sleep, symbolic processes will tend to be of the type characteristic of childhood or the early juvenile era. On occasion they may even approach or include the primitive or infantile. Remembered dreams are often couched in symbols from the period of childhood, and thus are far different from the type of symbol activity the dreamer is accustomed to in his waking life. These remembered dreams have considerable significance in therapy. "While there are activities throughout the period of sleep, the occurrence of a dream sufficiently impressive to be recalled is always to be considered as a part of the activity in some situation of real importance to the individual—that is, one including so strong a demand for resolution that it cannot be entirely dissociated during the maintenance of the intercurrent sleep situation."[34]

By conceiving principles of dream interpretation in terms of the symbolic activities of infancy and childhood in *Personal Psychopathology*

—not to a preordained form of mental activity called by Freud the *primary process* or primary process thinking, Sullivan made a beginning reformulation of dream interpretation but he never worked out a reinterpretation of dreams. Yet the germ of a new formulation is there. (In a recent lecture, "Maturational Factors in Children's Dreams," Maurice R. Green has formulated a paradigm of dream interpretation that seems to follow some of Sullivan's ideas.)[35]

While employing Freud's free associational "method" in dream interpretations and various principles of dream interpretation discovered by him, Sullivan fitted them into his own gradually emerging orientation, modifying them to suit his own synthesis of psychoanalysis, certain ideas of Meyerian psychiatry, and his own ideas on, and discoveries about, interpersonal relations.

Returning to the exposition of the psychiatric interview, I will mention next that from time to time the interpersonal intimacy of patient and physician is altered. The tendencies integrating the situation are said to vary with personality factors active in either one or both. "Because of its purpose to free the patient from handicaps, if for no other reason, the drive to exteriorization deals chiefly with memorial elements charged with considerable emotion. Innumerable frustrations, disappointments, injustices, impositions, mistakes, misunderstandings, misjudgments, reprisals, sadistic aggressions, slights, and slurs—all manner of truncated situations once disintegrated through the instrumentality of emotion and maladjustive processes—are reintegrated in a sort of *as if* drama during the free-fantasy exploration."[36] In order to achieve such free expression and communication any necessity for rational thinking by the patient must be avoided. In free association, the patient must not, does not, have to *report* the "memorial elements" to the physician; he must *merely express* the momentary content that, in a manner of speaking, wells up in his mind. He must feel free to do this without subjective appraisal of its effect on himself, on the therapist, or on their interrelationship.

Sullivan asserts that the patient must come to realize the role of the physician as an object for the momentary application of any and all interpersonal tendencies that appear in the course of the free fantasy.[37] And the physician, he adds, must facilitate this transient objectivication (projection) of tendencies and attitudes in his person. In the course of this process he encounters what Freudian psychoanalysts call the management of the transference. Although ideally the investigator or physician should "flow" easily from each "object form" to the next as dictated by the uncovered tendencies of the patient (facilitate an unhindered though transient objectification of a whole series or stream of what Sullivan later formulated as more or less entirely illusory me-you patterns originating largely from the patient's past experiences), the real—in contrast to the falsely personified—physician restricts the patient's ideal freedom to "project" in at least two ways.

First, the physician is said to be the actual object (not an illusory personification) of a sentiment that has grown out of or formed after "the pattern of older sentiment elaborations," during the patient's previous experiences in relationship with him: from expectations based on the reputation of the physician, from reading, from fantasy about consulting him, and from the first impression the patient had acquired (presumably during the first interview). Sullivan asserts that this sentiment acts as more or less of an obstacle to the free objectivation on him of tendencies connected with memories recalled in the flow of fantasy. On the other hand, the activation of powerful but previously buried hostile impulses may gravely distort the patient's perception of the investigator. The patient may then experience him more or less after the fashion of a brutally domineering father figure. So the sentiment formed after the pattern of previous sentiments elaborated during the relationship with the physician is very necessary since it must bear the brunt of powerful antipathetic tendencies (originating usually from experiences the patient had with others in his past life) and still sustain the intimacy needed for continued progress if the analysis is to be continued. The sentiment must bear the brunt of what classical psychoanalysts have called the negative transference. If not, the work is interrupted, unfinished. Sullivan stated that the contributions that the physician has himself made to this configuration, this sort of relationship during the preanalytic interviews, are the determiners of possible success or certain failure in his work with each patient.

The sentiment of the physician is said to follow, usually, one of two generic patterns. In either case, he is in danger of an exalted idealization, wherein he becomes either a "God-the-father or a God-the-primordial-mother." To Sullivan, who, when he wrote *Personal Psychopathology,* had worked chiefly with male patients suffering schizophrenic and related disorders, the latter idealization was the more promising. In any case, the physician must restrain the degree of idealization lest it seriously interfere with the freedom of fantasy. And the extent to which the therapist can accomplish this restriction effectively is dependent on his own freedom from personality warp. Sullivan states that insofar as the physician is capable of real intimacy in the situation with the patient, to that extent he can inhibit idealization of the sentiment; and that every patient readily intuits or empathizes the measure of this capacity and its characteristic limitations in the person of the therapist.

> After the fashion of classical psychoanalysts, Sullivan speculated as follows regarding beliefs in God-the-father or God-the-primordial mother:
> I surmise that an All-father belief, found among some of the most primitive of peoples, is a commonplace of personality evolution. I believe that this comes about somewhat as follows: *A manlike being is made to serve as the idealized object of the disappointed primitive mother sentiment,* sadly unsatisfied by the mothering ones encountered after the birth of personal consciousness. Each child learns that the male is more capable of carrying a generalization of positive attributes than is the female. ... and the Good Goddess progresses into masculine habiliments as the All-father who *demands nothing,* but is prior to all lesser gods, in their turn invested with more or less highly anthropomorphic demands, authorities, spleens, venoms, and so forth. The physician who approximates this nondemanding and all satisfying primitive All-father, otherwise the primitive mother-of-infancy (to use a psychoanalytic expression) "works with the mother libido."[38]

The physician must be eternally alert to the fact that each individual patient, with his unique qualities and characteristics, tends, to some degree, to evoke unique responses from the physician. To put this idea in Sullivan's own formulation, he stated that the physician must be eternally alert to phenomena within himself arising from the specific differential tendency system operative in the case of each individual with whom he deals. In this connection, there is one "general factor" that every psychoanalyst, whether Freudian or Sullivanian, must guard against, namely, an idealization of some particular patient or patients *by the physician.* In a fashion analogous to the behavior of the patient, a physician may thus "deflect" a tendency system from a real object, possibly someone once significant in his own past life, into the energizing of a fantasy. In traditional psychoanalysis this sort of occurrence is an extreme example of what has been labeled *counter-transference*. From empathic linkage with the patient, the physician integrates the former into a situation whose resolution is impossible because of his "technical or other taboos." In other words, the therapist has more or less unwittingly gotten himself into an awkward emotional entanglement with his patient and cannot extricate himself. "The frustrated tendency then evolves in a fantastic sentimentalization of the patient, with nonadjustive anxiety "lest he mismanage the case"—often an anticipatory guilt of taboo-violation from breaking of the barriers."[39] Not only does this anxiety seriously hamper his work with the particular patient, it depletes his supply of interest for working with other patients, a lack that they will be quick to sense so that the necessary intimacy situation with them becomes disordered.

It is clear, however, that "Freud's conception of countertransference is to be distinguished from the present-day conception of analysis as an interpersonal process. . . . That is, the analytic situation is essentially a human relationship in which, while one person is more immediately detached than the other and has less at stake, he is nevertheless an active participant."[40] Sullivan conceived the interviewer's role as that of a participant observer.

He claimed that the second restrictive factor of an ideal use of the physician as a "carrier" of the patient's "tendency objectivation" is the occasional positive action that the therapist is called upon to take. Now and then he must intervene to redirect the flow of fantasy. The old conflicts of (positive and negative) tendencies appear and the two motivational systems have to be separated into two streams of fantasy. Apparently Sullivan has in mind chiefly positive and negative tendencies that originated in the parental milieu.[41] The "old rationalizations" (presumably those connected with the two motivational systems) may continue in a higher-level fantasy process that does little toward clarifying the tendency that is being avoided (possibly over a long stretch of time). It may be difficult to disintegrate the "old projections" of blame and of positive "attributes" (attributions). Sullivan states that the active repressing of tendencies has to be remedied by picking out of the stream of fantasy, for further elaboration, certain vague fancies and "half-remembered dreams" that are the first evidences of escape of tendencies from complete repression. He adds that dissociated systems must be brought to effective awareness instead of being permitted to drain off in symptomatic acts and in streams of fantasy that are not brought into meaningful relationship with obviously related materials (also brought up in the free associational stream). However, this activity of the physician requires considerable skill, timing, and a clear consciousness of what he is about. Only a close perusal of Sullivan's papers, some of which have been republished in *Schizophrenia as a Human Process* and *The Fusion of Psychiatry and Social Science,* might provide a detailed insight into this reintegrative process of assimilating dissociated tendencies with the rest of the personality. But I think the general picture of Sullivan's modified psychoanalytic method will gradually emerge.[42]

While interfering as little as possible, the physician must play altogether too directing a role in therapy to allow his complete subordination to emotional objectivation by the patient. In more traditional language, the physician, in the very nature of his work, must play too active a role to permit his complete subordination to transference phenomena. Given an appreciation of this fact, along with his understanding of the sentiment of which he is the object, he can, and must, when necessary, actively interfere when an "antipathetic impasse" occurs. For example, Sullivan states that when perhaps in reactivating a long-dissociated hatred of the father, the patient is so dominated by his hatred, and by the rage born of his unresolved guilt about the hatred, that he devotes himself to a fury "at" the physician, "at" the treatment, or "at" anything else that comes in handy, then the therapist must intervene in representing the reality of the situation, also sometimes giving an indication of means for "working off" some of the excessive emotion. Otherwise, if he allows the patient to "blunder away," blinded by intense emotion, he is gravely derelict. At any time, when the patient is in the grip of intensely sympathetic or violently antipathetic emotion, he is in no shape to deal with his fellow man without help from the therapist. Quitting the treatment is said to be perhaps but a minor one of the unfortunate performances of a patient unassisted in a period of rage.

Despite whatever limiting factors may exist to hinder an ideal use of the patient's tendency objectivations, Sullivan asserts that the principal role of the physician using the free-fantasy technique is that of a keenly observant individual on whom the reactivated tendencies of the patient (which usually have their origin in some earlier phase or phases of the person's life) find "temporary object." The procedures of dream interpretation, to which the therapist resorts when necessary, are said to be but a modification of the general role of alert passivity. (If it becomes an active performance, dream interpretation can become an interfering handicap.) The therapist, for example, may invite the patient to develop a stream of fantasy—to verbalize his so-called free associations—in elaboration of, or from a beginning in, a dream recollection. "One need not assume that the fantasy will give the latent meaning of the dream-fragment."[43] There is no way of discovering whether such a latent meaning exists if there is an "impassable barrier" between it and the remembered dream. However, Sullivan says that it often happens that streams of fantasy occurring in response to well-chosen aspects of a given dream will synthesize in the patient's awareness, as the so-called meaning of the dream. (In classical Freudian theory, it is the latent content that provides the real meaning of the dream as remembered.) He suggests that it may be that, on the first few occasions of work with dream fragments, the physician will see a clear pattern in the fantasy streams, and that he will be sufficiently certain of the relevance of this pattern to the patient's temporary difficulties to present a *tentative* formulation. But Sullivan judged it much the better practice always to regard the dream as *a meaningful action,* from fantasy about which other, and probably closely related, meaningful actions will arise within consciousness than to regard it as an action capable of exact interpretation in the manner of Freud and his followers.[44] The notion that dreams can be interpreted without the help and cooperation of free fantasy of the dreamer is said to be absurd and unfortunate. One can be certain that the dream is a valid process in furtherance of the general tendencies of the dreamer, though subject to the disintegrative effects of secondary elaboration *as a result of intervention by the self.* "One wishes, therefore, that the patient shall note and record all his dreams, immediately, on awakening. And that, once noted, recorded, ordered, and dated, the dream material receive no further attention until the record is in the physician's hands, and the analytic hour is under way."[45] In personality investigation, the utilization of the dream, which is at best an extraordinary adjustive effort, should be kept thoroughly subordinate to the much more commonplace method of waking fantasy.

Perhaps I should also, once more, call the reader's attention to the fact that since Sullivan did not for long adhere to Freud's ideas on infantile sexuality and the existence of a universal, innate instinct of aggression (death instinct), he very frequently arrived at an interpretation of a dream or dream fragment that would differ markedly from the interpretation of a classical analyst, as one can see from a study of *Personal Psychopathology*. This is partly due to the fact that even in 1932 Sullivan had already developed a more or less systematic theory of personality that is essentially different from Freud's. One's theory of personality—the interpretive framework within which one tends to appraise the "meaning" (the motives, goals, etc., that "lie in back") of overt human behavior—tends to guide one's appraisals and judgments of the other person. Furthermore, one's theory of personality tends to determine, within limits, what one consciously or unconsciously *looks for*. The day is seemingly far distant when a universally accepted synthesis of Freudian, Sullivanian, and other theories can be effected. Meanwhile, an ever-increasing amount of research goes on that will, presumably, in the end, achieve an overarching synthesis.[46]

In the course of an expert psychoanalysis, there is bound to be "a growth of awareness of personal tendencies; but from beginning to end, the growth is automatic, after the fashion of all experiencing, and the *patient must naturally do the profiting* from what he produces."[47] The principle that one learns for himself applies to the process of free fantasy. The physician, when he inquires if there has not been something omitted in a certain stream of fantasy, must know that neither he nor the patient can "know" (immediately). As in every other form of inquiry, knowing has a temporal dimension in psychoanalysis. "The free-fantasy exploration is not comparable to a hunting for fossil trilobites." The patient must learn that such questioning is not evidence of the theapist's esoteric knowledge but results from genuine uncertainty, which can be resolved—*not* by answering queries in a Yes or No fashion—but by cooperative investigation, that is, by a continuation of fantasy from the indicated point of departure under the alert observation of the physician.[48] Thus the free-fantasy exploration is a wholly dynamic reorganization of processes, with which and from which there is only an incidental increase in clarification of the formulation of the self (as characterized above). "The *personality* changes." Most personality change may occur in the free-fantasy exploration without any immediate consciousness of alteration, and is perhaps exactly the most fortunate course. The rational formulation of insight is said to *follow* the progress in reorganization of personality. Conscious insight should not be the goal of the free fantasy. There should never be an essentially frivolous verbal brandishing of the patient's fantasy in the sleeping embrace of this or that "mechanism." "The facts of personality have to crystallize out of the substance of fantasy, in which they are but phantasmagorically manifested."[49]

In connection with such matters, it has been emphasized throughout this chapter that the physician, or psychoanalyst—terms used interchangeably so far—is an investigator or investigator-therapist. The student of personality may well ask himself how or whether he can separate a therapeutic from a "purely research" interest in the subject individual. According to Sullivan, such "problems" are pseudoproblems. He held that it is impossible to do good work toward understanding a particular personality without being of benefit to that personality, though it is quite possible to do bad work with harm to the patient while at the same time learning little about him. The student of personality can be "certain" only of what the patient has demonstrated to be correct. Moreover, any increase in self-knowledge is profitable—a statement that seems to apply generally to people. The investigator doing "pure research" into personality, as distinguished from the therapist, may want to carry his inquiry "further." The former may wish to avoid the vitiating effects of intimacy with the subject individual, or to employ only objectively verifiable procedures. But it is impossible to carry inquiry further than the patient will carry it. "The undue weighting of certain material—dream-fragments, for example—disorders that flow of fantasy material and creates a pseudo-importance for processes relatively insignificant."[50] The outcome is more misinformation.

Perhaps the following needs to be emphasized at this time, when psychologists and some psychiatrists try to outdo one another in the use of impersonal methodologies. Sullivan claimed that the specious ideal of nonpersonal intimacy, or rather, of personal nonintimacy in personality investigation, is sometimes achieved in the "use" of free fantasy by an obsessional individual possessed of a reasonably high intelligence factor. At every point such a patient will cooperate in the avoidance of emotional complications. The freedom of the resulting fantasy is said to be just this freedom from emotional validity ("spontaneity") needed for real intercommunication. An intellectualized "inquiry" of this sort may be very productive—"of words, figures of speech, imagery; also of ennui." This sort of inquiry, insofar as it (ostensibly) pertains to an interchange of information about the personality and its tendency systems, is somewhat less useful than is ordinary conversation. "It is motivated, usually, by a deeply unconscious hatred-system; it generally functions toward a stultification of the physician-investigator."[51]

Regarding objectively verifiable techniques, Sullivan thought that when it has been discovered *what* is to be observed and measured then one may look to making measurements.

Finally in each successful investigation of a personality, the physician reaches a third phase of therapy, namely, reevaluation. Just as the use of *free fantasy* should be introduced gradually toward the end of the *preanalytic* inquiry, so *reevaluation* procedures should be encouraged gradually toward the end of productive free fantasy. In other words, though there is a period, of indefinitely specifiable duration, when free fantasy is productive of highly emotional material closely relevant to the developmental history of the patient, one reaches a time when such material has been exhausted—has "run out." At this stage, the free fantasy, which is now that of a much more unified personality, has to do with relating *recent and current events with newly discovered tendencies.* The subject individual is now concentrated on what has been called the *management of tensions* and the integration of situations that accomplish *the fulfillment of* personality.[52] Briefly the patient has reached a point at which there is a rapid growth to adulthood, of progress toward maturity. This implies, frequently, a considerable alteration in the kinds of interpersonal relations in which the subject individual will henceforth engage.

A detailed specification of this culminating phase must be postponed. Summarily, Sullivan held that marriage and other relatively durable interpersonal relations involving sexual adjustment is the test of personality evolution.[53]

Sullivan briefly describes three sorts of *incomplete exploration of personality* or the exploration of a limited aspect of personality. In these, the inquiry is focused on a more or less clearly delineated tendency system within a particular person. Thus the incompleteness is intended in contrast to personality investigations that are interrupted or aborted. Well before the second stage of free-fantasy exploration—in fact, from the first hours the interviewee spends with the physician—the interview situation is integrated with a limited rather than a general, comprehensive goal. Sullivan relates that one frequently encounters personalities showing, in addition to profound warp, the continuing evil consequences from more recent misfortunes. He discovered that the latter may be removed or attenuated without recourse to the prolonged series of interviews required for complete reorganization of personality.

The first "mode" of the limited inquiry has to do with intelligent people "encompassed with the modern strenuosity," who lack the opportunity for reflection and meditation necessary for formulating one's life situation. These "folk" are said to be often greatly benefited by a brief series of interviews with the physician trained in integrating situations of intimacy. In some instances, such a person finds that the intuited sympathy provides the needed opportunity for self-affirmation ("avowal"). In others, exhortation by the physician regarding the worthiness of the patient's objectives "aids a little." But such exhortation is sound only when and so far as it expresses "in a formula" a sound appraisal of the patient. Sullivan thought that suggestion, namely, the use of formulae to be accepted uncritically by the patient because of unrecognized factors in the intimacy situation, is a dangerous practice. Should the patient accept the suggestion, it merely adds to his "already too complex life situations," presumably because he has achieved no new understanding, resolved no conflicts, rid himself of no anxiety tensions. Should he reject the suggestion, it is said to "carry" or entail a negative appraisal of the help that one can derive from those presumed to be useful in personal difficulties.

The state of *hypnosis* is a special case of suggestion. Hypnosis, according to Sullivan, may be characterized variously but mainly by the subject's passive acceptance of complete subordination to another personality in a situation of great dependency. "The patient permits the integration of his personality into the total situation nucleating in the physician. An approach to the infantile relationship to the mother is reestablished."[54] Hypnosis is said to imply a marked rapport in an interpersonal situation of great intensity, involving aspects of the hypnotist's own personality of which he is apt to be completely unconscious, and which in certain circumstances may arouse conflict in the patient.[55] In any event, Sullivan counseled the utmost caution in the use of this procedure, in which the dissociated systems within a personality are given a measure of freedom from resistance by the self, as occurs in sleep when the watchfulness of the self is relaxed. Thus the posthypnotic integration of the material recalled during the trance may be a very difficult or impossible task.

In "Regression: A Consideration of Reversive Mental Processes," Sullivan reveals that he had on occasion employed hypnosis with schizophrenics.

He used another mode of limited inquiry, in which therapy proceeds through the first stage of interview into the second. Free fantasy techniques are employed to explore the most characteristically maladjustive processes, such as the discovery of important tendencies frequently active in conflict. If all goes well, the third stage of personality study, namely, the working out of these tendencies "in comfortable forms of activity," then proceeds. But this mode of limited exploration is a "ticklish business." Suppose the patient has powerful tendency systems existing extraconsciously. Primitive genital phobia, for example, may exist in dissociation. Sullivan wrote that in such a state of affairs work started as a brief inquiry has to be reoriented to a prolonged study, or the end state of the patient is but little better than before.

There is a third form of limited inquiry, pertaining to the treatment of some promising patients already suffering incipient schizophrenia or related disorders. In these cases, Sullivan says that the investigation of the intimacy situation between patient and physician often cannot proceed *without mediation of a third person* because of their strong homosexual cravings that may become intolerable, leading to panic, occasionally ending in suicide. The principle is said to be to give this kind of individual protection by way of the three-group, instead of working with the patient alone. "The physician distributes his functions between himself and a clinical assistant, striving thereby to effect a distribution of emotional objectivication such that he can always have a positive balance at his disposal to carry the patient forward."[56] In this fashion the therapist enables the patient to achieve a partial socialization so that he can live for a while comfortable in a suitable special group. Subsequently he may be able and willing to enter into a more thorough investigation.

I shall conclude the review of Sullivan's ideas on psychoanalysis with the following: He taught that the study of personality depends on the "elevation" into consciousness of the tendency systems characterizing the subject individual or patient. This study includes many insights ("glimpses") into personality disorder. From these insights he formulated the "disorder types" that he has discussed in *Personal Psychopathology*. Thus, while always subject to a considerable margin of error, the investigator becomes expert at surmising from certain behavior and a certain amount of historical data the probable deviations entering into any given morbid personality. In these "diagnoses" of personality the student never knows whether he was mostly right or mostly wrong until he has actually studied the personality by the interview method summarized in this chapter—up to the point that the disorder itself has disappeared. One must add that this point of view would today be vigorously contested, especially by those who lean toward an experimental approach. For example, Holt, who is an experimental psychologist in a very broad fashion, has discussed the various factors, and the pros and cons of each, that enter into the study of personality.[57] In this connection, one must call attention to Allport's seemingly eminently sensible attitude. He says personality is so complex an affair that every legitimate method must be employed in its study.[58] Time is a stern critic. The never-ending process of free inquiry will eventually pronounce judgment on all "methods" and techniques. But the physician-investigator or clinician cannot rest content with a "long view." He is faced with the *problems of the here and now.* Hence he must employ the best methods and techniques available. Sullivan wrote that it did not seem to him to be quite beyond the bounds of possibility that no great improvement in personality study is to be expected until students of personality will have made a much more extended exploration of the field along the lines he indicated. "When properly trained students—now very few—have been integrated in a broadly conceived investigation of various personalities existing in some few disparate social situations and culture-complexes, we will be actually on the way."[59]

In recent years, the interview itself has been subjected to a searching criticism. The readers may find Matarazzo's essay on this subject enlightening.[60] If I may venture an informed guess, I predict that psychoanalysis and related forms of psychotherapy can never be replaced adequately by other forms of therapy currently in fashion though it may continue to be refined and supplemented by various promising kinds of "tests and measurements." As an instrument for the study of personality, psychoanalysis, in the hands of a Freud or a Sullivan, has proved to be extremely powerful. Who can rival them? And one should not forget that an excessive emphasis, in the field of personality study, on methodological rigor may in the end result in a form of scientific rigor mortis.

The sorts of psychoanalytic interview employed by Freud or Sullivan are very different from the types of interview developed during the past generation by social scientists. There are many reasons that the latter may give for their types of interview. Among such reasons are: the purpose of the interview, the explanatory systems either covertly or overtly assumed, and the variety of techniques employed.[61]

So far in this chapter I have attempted to present a broad outline of Sullivan's modified psychoanalytic method as he had developed it on the basis of "Freud's great pioneering work when he wrote *Personal Psychopathology*. In the ensuing fifteen or sixteen years of his life he carried this refinement much further in connection with the ever-growing elaboration of his theory of interpersonal relations. After I shall have given an exposition of subsequent theoretical developments, I shall return in a later chapter to the exposition of what he subsequently called the psychiatric interview.

Sullivan believed that a provisional typology may be helpful to the student of personality.[62] Life processes of individuals, he said, tend to an almost infinite diversity of late adolescent and adult personalities. But among this diversity, he thought, there are some sorts of life processes that are fairly distinctive around which the continuum of variety might be said to "concentrate." Thus there are said to be types of personalities and typical situations. Although each life situation manifests a "unique character," the physician nevertheless systematizes his procedures on the basis of a more or less conscious schematization of recurrent interpersonal relations in which he is involved in his work.

Sullivan, in *Personal Psychopathology*, mentions various formulations —various kinds of typologies—without discussing most of them, which may be helpful to the student of personality. The significance of such a procedure will, I think gradually become clear. On the basis of *temperament* the following are distinguished: sanguine, choleric, phlegmatic, and melancholic. According to Allport, temperament, which is perhaps largely determined by glandular secretions, might be considered to be the underlying raw material of personality, along with intelligence and physique. It seems probable, he says, that a primary factor or basic dimension of temperament "relates to *drive and vigor* or its opposite, apathy."[63] Temperament is not absolutely fixed from the beginning of life. Within limits, it may be altered by various factors, such as nutritional influences and life experience.

A second classification pertains to intelligence factors or "integrative abilities": idiot, imbecile, borderline intellect, normal, superior.[64]

To the combination of these two categories Sullivan added subdivisions on the basis of degrees of acuity in and prepotency of imagery, after the fashion of E. R. Jaensch, of the following: visual, auditory, tactile, olfactory, and other special sensory fields.

In summary fashion Misiak and Sexton relate how Eric R. Jaensch, along with his brother Walter Jaensch, investigated eidetic imagery or perceptlike imagery. The latter postulated two biotypes, the B-type and T-type, which are, supposedly, related to endocrine function. "The B-type, a very vivid memory image subject to voluntary control, was associated with a hyperactive thyroid gland. The other biotype, resembling an afterimage and not under voluntary control, was associated with underactivity of the parathyroid gland. Jaensch not only described the characteristics of eidetic types, he indicated their relation to clinical psychology and anthropology. . . ."[65]

The morphologist, also, may achieve a typology of gross biophysical organization. Thus, in the manner of Kretschmer, he may subdivide men into the leptosomatic (or asthenic, referring to a frail, linear build) and the pyknic (referring to a fat, rounded bodily structure).[66] There is a third major type, which Sullivan neglected to mention, called the athletic. Such personality traits as extroversion were associated with the pyknic; energy and aggressiveness with the athletic; and a tendency toward introversion with the asthenic. Sullivan writes that the student of disease processes may be astonished to find, as has Draper, that this gross morphology of the body can be correlated with "something of potential morbidity."[67] However, Kretschmer's classification has not stood up too well under further investigation.

At this point one might consider Karl Abraham's classification on the basis of "prepotent zone of interaction," seeking people showing organizations in analogy to the: sucking oral, biting oral, expulsive anal, and retentive anal. There is an additional type, the genital, in Abraham's classification, which is not mentioned.[68]

Having considered the physicochemical and the biophysical level of man's communal existence, the typologist may then turn to a classification on the basis of cultural factors, such as Spranger's, who set up divisions on the basis of certain fundamental "value orientations." Sullivan mentions four: The economic, the theoretical, the artistic, and the religious. There are two other orientations in Spranger's typology, namely, the social and the political, which are not mentioned in this context.[69]

Parenthetically, Allport has used this typology in a very productive fashion.[70]

A different kind of classification, based on a prevailing attitude of the personality toward the cultural heritage itself, was worked out by W. I. Thomas, who thought people might be distinguished by their characterizing attitudes into the three following types: the philistine, the bohemian and the creative.[71] For example, if a man comes under the heading of philistine, he is contentedly conventional in his ideas and attitudes. Thomas carried his analysis further, trying to find a formula concerning the desires underlying attitudes, and gave us his famous four "wishes."[72] These wishes pertain to new experience, security, recognition, and response.

These various classifications, in Sullivan's view, provide *ways of looking at a subject individual* rather than exclusive distinctions between species and varieties of individuals. Or, more simply, in McCurdy's words, "A compromise between the view that all people are alike and the view that every person is different" from every other.

Following upon the discussion of these formulations, Sullivan reviews Jung's ideas on the extrovert and the introvert. While he is by no means inclined to accept such ideas uncritically, in typical fashion he provides a thought-provoking analysis of them, observing that a large number of students have regarded a division of humanity on *the basis of attitudes toward events* as a valid enterprise. He states that there seems to be a more or less perfectly justified dichotomy of actual people between polar or modal types of habitual or enduring "ways" of interacting with events—personal, interpersonal, or social. It seems to be true, for example, that to some people "presenting" events take on a relatively simple relationship with the self; to other people events must be apprehended in a *series* of references to the self. People of the latter class (introvert) manifest an analytic (reflective) tendency that remains relatively undeveloped in people of the former class (extrovert).

It may be stated, provisionally, that the extrovert is the person who takes things as they initially impress him, while the introvert is a person who subjects them to a more or less extensive series of appraisals on the basis of their diverse significance to him, with his particular outlook on life. "The extrovert falls into many total situations including others, most of these being relatively simple. The introvert falls into relatively few total situations with people, and of these most may be of great complexity."[73] Elaborating upon this characterization, Sullivan states that the extrovert personality is capable of manifesting in a unitary fashion various sets of its incorporated (acquired) tendencies, in total activity for direct satisfaction, while, in contrast, the introvert personality in integrating an interpersonal situation on the basis of any of its groups of tendencies is but initiating a series of processes leading to much more complex total situations and decidedly less direct satisfaction. On this view the introverted person participates and commits himself emotionally in fewer interpersonal situations, though often of great complexity, while he gains much less direct satisfaction than does the extroverted person.

Not only does the life experience of the introvert greatly "augment" the elaboration of the self, it also apparently fosters the capacity for "suppressing relevance"—for "suppressing" information that does not fit his particular world view, his particular personality orientation with its rich, complicated subjective processes. Somewhat after the fashion of a child, the extrovert, on the other hand, allows events to "flow by with little evidence of increasing self-awareness," taking things more or less for granted, while maintaining a continued naïve sensitivity to more purely environmental factors—a sensitivity that the introvert often lacks, or loses or suppresses. To the extrovert, everything in the world may be assumed to be understood. From the point of view of the introvert, the world of events has "multidirectional meaning-implications." That is, the introvert tends to be aware that the world has numerous aspects, and can be viewed from various angles: philosophic, scientific, aesthetic, religious, and the like. Piaget's comment regarding the understanding between children applies rather closely throughout the social life of the extrovert: "If they fail to understand one another, it is because they think that they do understand one another." Thus the extrovert is immersed in a naïve egocentrism, in which there is no serious problem of communication or understanding of others. In contrast, the introvert has learned early that others not only do not "read" his thoughts correctly, but that they have somewhat of a faculty for misreading them. "If he fails to understand or to make himself clear, it is because he has too complex a conception of the individual with whom he is communicating, owing to an overly sophisticated egocentrism."[74] He is somewhat like a philosophy teacher who forgets that his freshman students are not skilled in modern philosophical analysis; or a parent who when his child asks: "How can Spirit be everywhere?" tries to answer the question in terms of Plato or Aquinas. It is no wonder that the extrovert likes to work with other people—"even though he hopes to be spared much contact with introverted folk"; while the introvert may find that working with others can become so difficult and annoying that he "as much as possible eliminates them, and contents himself with interest in less recondite data, machinery, engineering practice, or natural scientific research."[75]

Sullivan claims that the possible social and unsocial aspects of extroversion and introversion lead easily into a consideration of persons on the basis of their prevailing attitudes to others: social, unsocial, and antisocial.[76] But he does not elaborate on this suggestion, though he thinks that the possible social and unsocial aspects of extroversion and introversion may also lead into a consideration of persons and their attitudes on the basis of the preferred ordination or ranking of them in relation to others, namely, as *dominant* or *submissive*. Thus in the "dominant ordination" one arrives at a division into three "attitude variations," namely, dominant-social, dominant-unsocial, and dominant-antisocial. The "submissive" or subordinate ordination entails three analogous attitude variations namely, submissive-social, submissive-unsocial, and submissive-antisocial. Sullivan thought these rubrics could be of value to students of politics and criminology.

Another classification that he mentions is the familiar formulation on the basis of erotic interest: autoerotic, homoerotic, and heteroerotic. Each kind of interest may combine with other factors such as dominant or submissive attitudes, and with social, unsocial, and antisocial trends. One must bear in mind the nonsexual factors in human organization also. In this connection a division on the basis of *overt* sexual behavior is made. The autosexual, the homosexual, the bisexual, the heterosexual, and the perverted sexual. The latter division, perverted sexual, pertains to the sexual behavior of people in whom the sexual tendencies have been seriously warped by inclusion of fetishistic, sadistic, coprophagic, urophagic, necrophilic, urolagnic, and other interests.

Finally, Sullivan lists a classification of Adolf Meyer, along with a rather esoteric nomenclature, which I omit.[77] However, I wish to mention that Sullivan quotes with approval Meyer's idea that the best medical standard of typology is that of adequate or efficient function —a standard he adopted and employed in his own attempts at classifying mental disorders.

Because an enormous amount of research has been carried on since Sullivan wrote *Personal Psychopathology* in the fields pertaining to the formulations briefly described above, I should like to interject that an excellent survey of much of this work can be found in Allport's classic *Personality* and in his recently published *Pattern and Growth in Personality*.[78] The relevant chapters in these two works may greatly expand and enrich an understanding and appreciation of most of the types and divisions listed in the last few pages of this chapter. In this connection also, I should like to recommend Hall and Lindzey's *Theories of Personality* (previously referred to) and their more recently published source book, *Theories of Personality, Primary Sources and Research*.[79]

Finally, we arrive at an additional grand "scheme" of Sullivan, which covers several sociological and psychological categories. This scheme is presented mainly in outline form, which can be filled, so to speak, from the relevant sources in contemporary social science, psychology, and psychiatry. To be sure, Freud and Jung, in the early years of psychoanalysis, also sought help from the social sciences, but they had a penchant for a speculative anthropology that Sullivan, especially in the latter part of his career, would not countenance. As he says, "volumes" have been written on the various matters that come under the various "rubrics."

The first major division is kinship, covering several subcategories.[80] As Sullivan points out, the first kinship relations (mother-son, mother-daughter, father-son, father-daughter, etc.) are those from which the "very buttresses" of personality are derived.

"Subrogative" relationships—characterized by clientship to one in the status of expert—is a second division. On these matters, the author of *Personal Psychopathology* is somewhat ironic.

> As a very crude approximation to a most imperfect rule, it may be stated that experts are inclined to a dubious practical socialization.

Whether, as some would have it, one becomes an expert in order to escape an especially keen sense of personal insecurity, variously energized, or, as seems more probable, conscious superiority in one line is taken to grant one a certain leeway in other matters, the fact seems to be that experts as a lot are rather difficult people. They live in part in a world of extraordinary preconceptions, a world more scientific in some of its aspects than is that of their clients. They are approached by people who come to them as allegorical figures, rather than to one having information. If they resist the role thrust on them, their Philistine clients suspect their expertness, and go elsewhere. If they accept it, they find themselves committed to a rather transubstantial sort of living, in which various outworn traditions must be followed while the luminosity of their genuine superiority is expected to suffuse their every notion, including subscription to these archaic folkways. Since one's expert advisors are of *one's choice,* just as in the juvenile era one's parents had to be defensible against any invidious comparisons, so these new authorities are often required to reflect the most variegated credit on one's judgment; the possession of a good office—at the right sort of address—a collection of art objects, and evidences of patronizing a good tailor may be taken to be necessary accoutrements of the experts of today.[81]

A third division is friendship, said to be characterized principally by a wholly intrinsic durability. It may exist between members of the same sex, and with people of similar age, or those who are younger, or older. Analogously, it may occur with members of the other sex, and with people of similar age, or those who are older, or younger. Still again, one may have friendly relations with people who are "mixed," that is, couples, whether married or otherwise. Even when he wrote *Personal Psychopathology,* Sullivan did not agree wholeheartedly even in 1932 with the idea that friendly relations are simply aim-inhibited sexual relations. Perhaps they sometimes are. But they may also be necessary fulfillments of nonsexual tendencies. To insist, for example, on the exclusively sexual motivations of men's and women's clubs is to ignore relevant facts of human social organization.

A fourth major division covers "accommodative" associations. These are characterized by relatively durable adjustments arising from a mutuality or interdependence of ends. Such associations may be occupational, recreational, or of some other kind.[82]

The fifth division is called ordinate. It signifies certain human associations based on relations of superordination and subordination (such as liege-vassal, master-servant, boss-worker); and of hierarchical regimentation (as in the armed forces of any country), and the like.

The last major division, the "formal," which is based on "temperospatial contact," contiguity, coincidence, and so forth, suggests that accidental, unplanned, unanticipated events apparently play a much greater role in human life than perhaps most people would care to admit. Furthermore, those accidental, unforeseen events may at least sometimes have a significant cumulative effect. In any case, under the "formal" Sullivan places "routine-social" affairs, "occupational" occurrences, "recreational" events, and the like. To illustrate briefly, everyone has heard that many girls marry "the boy next door." Occupational contacts sometimes provide an opportunity for the development of friendships of varying degrees of intimacy—though one doubts whether it is often the case that the boss marries his secretary. A casual meeting of two people at a summer resort may result in a brief "love affair" or a lasting friendship. On a somewhat different level the accidents of war have resulted in many American young men's meeting and marrying English or German or Japanese girls, whose existence they might otherwise scarcely dream of. One could multiply indefinitely examples of such happenings, and of others, as well.

Summarily, the greater the knowledge an investigator-therapist has of the forces governing human life, the more profound his understanding of his patients may be.

Notes

1. Cf. GORDON W. ALLPORT, *Pattern and Growth in Personality* (New York: Holt, Rinehart, and Winston, 1961), chaps. 20, 21, 22; FRITZ HEIDER, *The Psychology of Interpersonal Relations* (New York: John Wiley and Sons, 1958).

2. Cf. HAROLD GRIER McCURDY, *The Personal World* (New York: Harcourt, Brace, and World, 1961), chap. 6, "Consciousness and the Conscious Self."

3. HARRY STACK SULLIVAN, *Personal Psychopathology,* copyright 1965 by William Alanson White Psychiatric Foundation, Washington, D.C. (unpublished), p. 4.

4. In HARRY STACK SULLIVAN, "Socio-Psychiatric Research," *American Journal of Psychiatry,* **10**:977-991, 1931, reprinted in HARRY STACK SULLIVAN, *Schizophrenia as a Human Process,* with Introduction and Commentaries by HELEN SWICK PERRY (New York: W. W. Norton and Company, 1962), this thought is mentioned in passing.

5. SULLIVAN, "Socio-Psychiatric Research," in SULLIVAN, *Schizophrenia as a Human Process,* pp. 292-293.

6. See HELEN SWICK PERRY, "Commentary," in SULLIVAN, *Schizophrenia as a Human Process,* pp. 137-138.

7. SULLIVAN, "Socio-Psychiatric Research," in *Schizophrenia as a Human Process,* p. 294.

8. *Ibid.,* p. 294.

9. *Ibid.,* p. 295.

10. *Ibid.,* p. 296.

11. *Ibid.*

12. *Ibid.,* pp. 297-298.

13. *Ibid.,* p. 298.

14. For a detailed understanding of the life chart see ALFRIED LIEF (ed.),

The Commonsense Psychiatry of Dr. Adolph Meyer (New York: McGraw-Hill Book Company, 1948), pp. 418-422.

15. SULLIVAN, *Personal Psychopathology*, p. 300.

16. *Ibid.*

17. HARRY STACK SULLIVAN, "Psychiatry: Introduction to the Study of Interpersonal Relations," *Psychiatry*, 1:121-134, 1938; reprinted as "The Data of Psychiatry," in HARRY STACK SULLIVAN, *The Fusion of Psychiatry and Social Science*, with Introduction and Commentaries by HELEN SWICK PERRY (New York: W. W. Norton and Company, 1964).

18. SULLIVAN, *Personal Psychopathology*, p. 301.

19. *Ibid.*, p. 302.

20. For an introductory survey, see SIGMUND FREUD, *Therapy and Technique*, ed. with an introduction by PHILLIP RIEFF (New York: Crowell-Collier Publishing Company, 1963).

21. SULLIVAN, *Personal Psychopathology*, p. 303.

22. HARRY STACK SULLIVAN, *The Interpersonal Theory of Psychiatry*, ed. HELEN SWICK PERRY and MARY LADD GAWEL, with an Introduction by MABEL BLAKE COHEN (New York: W. W. Norton and Company, 1953), pp. 331-332.

23. SULLIVAN, *Personal Psychopathology*, p. 304.

24. Cf. SULLIVAN, *The Interpersonal Theory of Psychiatry*, p. 332.

25. BERNARD BERELSON and GARY A. STEINER, *Human Behavior* (New York: Harcourt, Brace, and World, 1964), pp. 174-176.

26. PATRICK MULLAHY, *Oedipus Myth and Complex* (New York: Hermitage Press, 1948), p. 75.

27. SIGMUND FREUD, *Civilization and Its Discontents*, trans., ed. JAMES STRACHEY (New York: W. W. Norton and Company, 1962), p. 58.

28. Cf. SIGMUND FREUD, *On Dreams*, trans. JAMES STRACHEY (New York: W. W. Norton and Company, 1952), pp. 29-39.

29. BENJAMIN B. WOLMAN, *Contemporary Theories and Systems in Psychology* (New York: Harper and Brothers, 1960), p. 218.

30. A. A. BRILL (trans. and ed.), *The Basic Writings of Sigmund Freud* (New York: Random House, 1938), pp. 319-468.

31. CHARLES BRENNER, *An Elementary Textbook of Psychoanalysis* (New York: International Universities Press, 1955).

32. Cf. SULLIVAN, *The Interpersonal Theory of Psychiatry*, chap. 20, and HARRY STACK SULLIVAN, *Clinical Studies in Psychiatry*, ed. HELEN SWICK PERRY, MARY LADD GAWEL, and MARTHA GIBBON, with a Foreword by DEXTER M. BULLARD (New York: W. W. Norton and Company, 1956), pp. 179-181 *et passim.*

33. SULLIVAN, *Personal Psychopathology*, p. 240.

34. *Ibid.*, p. 252.

35. Delivered at A Symposium in Celebration of the 25th Anniversary of the William Alanson White Institute of Psychiatry, Psychoanalysis, and Psychology, October 19-20, 1968.

36. SULLIVAN, *Personal Psychopathology,* p. 304.

37. For a brief summary of Freud's technique, see SIGMUND FREUD, *An Outline of Psychoanalysis* (New York: W. W. Norton and Company, 1949), chap. 6.

38. SULLIVAN, *Personal Psychopathology,* pp. 304-305, footnote 8.

39. *Ibid.,* p. 305.

40. CLARA THOMPSON and PATRICK MULLAHY, *Psychoanalysis: Evolution and Development* (New York: Hermitage House, 1950), p. 108; cf. LEO BERMAN, "Countertransferences and Attitudes of the Analyst in the Therapeutic Process," in MABEL BLAKE COHEN (ed.), *Advances in Psychiatry* (New York: W. W. Norton and Company, 1959).

41. Cf. FREUD, *An Outline of Psychoanalysis,* pp. 65-70.

42. See also MARY JULIAN WHITE, "Sullivan and Treatment," in PATRICK MULLAHY (ed.), *The Contributions of Harry Stack Sullivan* (New York: Science House, 1967).

43. SULLIVAN, *Personal Psychopathology,* p. 307.

44. Cf. CALVIN S. HALL, "A Cognitive Theory of Dream Symbols," in DAVID C. McCLELLAND (ed.), *Studies in Motivation* (New York: Appleton-Century-Crofts, 1955).

45. SULLIVAN, *Personal Psychopathology,* p. 308.

46. Cf. CALVIN S. HALL and GARDNER LINDZEY, *Theories of Personality* (New York: John Wiley and Sons, 1957), chap. 1; DONALD H. FORD and HUGH B. URBAN, *Systems of Psychotherapy* (New York: John Wiley and Sons, 1963).

47. SULLIVAN, *Personal Psychopathology,* pp. 308-309.

48. *Ibid.,* p. 309.

49. *Ibid.*

50. *Ibid.,* p. 310.

51. *Ibid.;* cf., for example, T. W. WANN (ed.) *Behaviorism and Phenomenology* (Chicago, Illinois: University of Chicago Press, 1964); JOHN COHEN, *Humanistic Psychology* (London: Allen and Unwin, 1958; republished New York: Crowell-Collier Publishing Company, 1962); BENJAMIN B. WOLMAN (ed.), *Handbook of Clinical Psychology* (New York: McGraw-Hill Book Company, 1965), Part I.

52. SULLIVAN, *Personal Psychopathology,* p. 311; in the footnotes Sullivan refers to L. K. FRANK, "The Management of Tensions," *American Journal of Sociology,* **33**:705-736, 1928, and HORNELL HART, "Family Life and the Fulfillment of Personality," *American Journal of Psychiatry,* **10**:7-17, 1930.

53. SULLIVAN, *Personal Psychopathology,* p. 288.

54. *Ibid.,* p. 313.

55. Cf. the discussion of hypnosis in HARRY STACK SULLIVAN, "The Modified Psychoanalytic Treatment of Schizophrenia," *American Journal of Psychiatry,* **11**:519-536, 1931.

56. SULLIVAN, *Personal Psychopathology,* p. 314.

238 : *The Beginnings of Modern American Psychiatry*

57. ROBERT R. HOLT, "Experimental Methods in Clinical Psychology," in WOLMAN, *op. cit.*

58. GORDON ALLPORT, *op. cit.,* chaps. 17, 18, 19.

59. SULLIVAN, *Personal Psychopathology,* p. 315; cf. BERT KAPLAN (ed.), *Studying Personality Cross-Culturally* (New York: Harper and Row, 1961); WARREN G. BENNIS, EDGAR H. SCHEIN, DAVID E. BERLEW, and FRED I. STEELE (eds.), *Interpersonal Dynamics: Essays and Readings on Human Interaction* (Homewood, Illinois: The Dorsey Press, 1964).

60. JOSEPH D. MATARAZZO, "The Interview," in WOLMAN, *op. cit.*

61. See, for example, ELEANOR E. MACCOBY and NATHAN MACCOBY, "The Interview: A Tool of Social Science," in GARDNER LINDZEY (ed.), *Handbook of Social Psychology* (Cambridge, Massachusetts: Addison-Wesley Publishing Company, 1954), Vol. 1.

62. Cf. McCURDY, *op. cit.*, chap. 10.

63. GORDON ALLPORT, *op. cit.,* p. 34.

64. For an introductory survey of this field, see, for example, NORMAN L. MUNN, *Psychology* (5th ed.; Boston, Massachusetts: Houghton Mifflin Company, 1966), chap. 5.

65. HENRYK MISIAK and VIRGINIA STOUDT SEXTON, *History of Psychology* (New York: Grune and Stratton, 1966), p. 111; cf. GARDNER MURPHY, *Personality* (New York: Harper and Brothers, 1947), chap. 16; see also ERICH R. JAENSCH, *Eidetic Imagery,* trans. OSCAR OESER (London: Kegan Paul, Trench, Trubner, 1930).

66. Cf. HALL AND LINDZEY, *op. cit.*, chap. 9.

67. SULLIVAN, *Personal Psychopathology;* in a footnote, reference is made to GEORGE DRAPER, *Beaumont Foundation Lectures* (Baltimore, Maryland: Williams and Wilkins, 1928); *Diseases and the Man* (New York: The Macmillan Company, 1930).

68. KARL ABRAHAM, *Selected Papers on Psychoanalysis* (London: Hogarth Press, 1927).

69. EDUARD SPRANGER, *Types of Men,* trans. PAUL J. W. PIGORS (5th ed.; Halle, Germany: Max Niemer Verlag, 1928), Part II.

70. GORDON ALLPORT, *op. cit.,* 296-299.

71. EDMUND H. VOLKART (ed.), *Social Behavior and Personality: Contributions of W. I. Thomas to Theory and Social Research* (New York: Social Science Research Council, 1951), chap. 9.

72. *Ibid.,* chap. 8.

73. SULLIVAN, *Personal Psychopathology,* p. 280.

74. *Ibid.*

75. *Ibid.*

76. Cf. HARRY STACK SULLIVAN, *Conceptions of Modern Psychiatry,* with a Foreword by the author and a Critical Appraisal of the Theory by PATRICK MUL-

LAHY (New York: W. W. Norton and Company, 1953), pp. 83-84, 209-211.

77. ADOLF MEYER, "An Attempt at Analysis of the Neurotic Constitution," *American Journal of Psychology,* 14:90-103, 1903.

78. GORDON ALLPORT, *Personality* (New York: McGraw-Hill Book Company, 1937).

79. GARDNER LINDZEY and CALVIN S. HALL, *Theories of Personality: Primary Sources and Research* (New York: John Wiley and Sons, 1965).

80. For a discussion of kinship, see, for example, KINGSLEY DAVIS, *Human Society* (New York: The Macmillan Company, 1949), chap. 15; ARNOLD W. GREEN, *Sociology* (New York: McGraw-Hill Book Company, 1952), chaps. 17, 18, 19.

81. SULLIVAN, *Personal Psychopathology,* p. 291.

82. Cf. ROBERT M. MACIVER, *Society* (New York: Farrar and Rinehart, 1937), for an explanation of various kinds of associations.

6 / *Dynamisms of Difficulty*

In this chapter I will discuss some of Sullivan's ideas on "Dynamisms of Difficulty," as outlined in *Personal Psychopathology*, which the psychiatrist encounters in his work with patients. The dynamisms of difficulty are not regarded as diseases in the sense of medical entities like scarlet fever. They pertain to "difficulties in living," to problems and handicaps in interpersonal relations. As previously related, they are processes that develop in the course of the person's efforts at adjustments in organism-environment situations, processes of living that are unusually inefficient, productive of conflict, strain, and unhappiness, and contributory to failures of the individual as a self-respecting person.[1]

Sullivan employs the notion of "successful living" as the criterion of mental health. From a psychobiological point of view, the successful life is said to be one that is principally characterized by a series of adjustments in the "organism-environmental complex" as the individual progresses in time from conception to death. Mental health may be said "to consist in the continued resolution of total situations to such effect that the growth of personality is neither arrested nor materially deviated as reflected in ensuing sequent situations."[2] Thus "adjustment" designates the type of resolution of "interpersonal situations" as they occur in connection with the activities of the individual in his daily living. In contrast maladjustment designates a group of processes and activities that, while they may resolve the situation, accomplish this only with wastage of energy, often increased complexity of processes, and "unwonted" extension of the situation in time, wherein the individual undergoes stress and experiences varying degrees of unpleasantness. Since these ideas have often been misinterpreted I shall attempt to clarify them further after I have presented Sullivan's "scheme of classification" of total activities. Mental health, for Sullivan, has an essential connection with self-esteem or, what is practically the same thing, self-respect. The person who has developed a high degree of self-respect will ordinarily have the psychological integrity, the initiative, and the competence to resolve most of life's problems, that is, problems of interpersonal relations, without extraordinary waste of time, energy, and effort, and without getting endlessly bogged down in personal conflicts, irrational fears, anxieties, hostilities, and misunderstandings. For the mentally healthy person time provides an opportunity for mental growth, for self-development, for new experience, an opportunity that is often prodigally wasted by the mentally ill.

In Chapter 4 it was pointed out that there are many for whom the maintenance of some measure of self-respect is a never-ending task, which entails great cost not only in personal effort, strain, suffering, and failure but in interference with the comfort and success of others. And this fact led to a general statement by Sullivan about mental illness: Whenever a person is forced to make the maintenance of his self-esteem *an end in itself* instead of a consequent or result of life activities that he engages in he is more or less mentally ill. Accordingly, dynamisms of difficulty are intimately related to the state of one's self-esteem.

The self, in Sullivan's view, like personality, which includes the self, should not be thought of subjectively since it is all tied up with interpersonal relations—as is self-esteem. Personality is said to be the moving (or dynamic) locus of particular life processes; it is a "manifestation of the total organism in and within its series of total situations." It should not be envisaged as a fixed entity within the organism periodically emerging or radiating outward in smiles, tears, thoughts, and acts of kindness or cussedness. Personality is a relatively enduring pattern or structure of life processes that *evolves in the course of years* and comes to characterize each human individual. In this sense, one is not born with a personality anymore than one is born with the love sonnets of Shakespeare on the tip of the tongue. I want to call attention to the fact that the dynamic configuration of processes called personality pertain to "imaginary people" as well as to those who have or have had actual existence, to people with whom one lives in intimate, durable face-to-face association, and to those who are usually, though not always, physically remote, that is, to the larger groupings of society, to whom the individual is related by indirect communication (by the newspaper, radio, etc.), and by "impersonal" and contractual ties.

Personality is said to be the relatively enduring configuration of life processes characterizing all of the person's total activity pertaining to such other persons, real or fantastic, as become from time to time relevant factors in his total situations. The "other ones" may be present to the senses, as they are in the family and neighborhood school, in which case one speaks of processes within primary group relations; or they may be exterior to the ordinary range of one's sense organs —effective by virtue only of the individual's faith in their past or present existence elsewhere—in which case one speaks of processes within secondary groups. Traditionally, primary groups comprised community as the latter was once conceived.[3]

The life processes by which personality is characterized include relatively static or "low-velocity" qualities of the individual, such as physical build, visage, and the like. It includes such things as the "functional activity of the expressive apparatus": intonation, vocabulary, play of facial postural tensions, and so forth. While such qualities are capable of rapid change, they manifest a persistent patterning over relatively long periods. And, finally, personality includes qualities such as the individual's "life-plan" and hierarchy of values, which as a rule change but slowly.

The following classification of types of processes are said to appear alike in success and in partial or total failure of adjustment. There is nothing unique in the unsuccessful processes. (As Sullivan subsequently expressed it, it is a matter of the accent and timing, the prominence and misuse of certain things that distinguish the mentally ill from the healthy.) He wrote that uncommon adjustive ability is apt to be manifested in considerable measure in an invariably well-directed application of processes that in other cases form persisting patterns of less fortunate outcome. As I have indicated in previous chapters, the recurrent manifestation of certain unsuccessful processes may generally be understood by reference to some "warping" influences brought to bear during the course of personality development.

*Human Dynamics**

Scheme of classification of total activity on the basis of the degree of resolution brought about in an Organism-Environment Situation.

I. Adjustment: Total resolution of the configuration so that there is no remaining stress, but only results, including experience

II. Partial Adjustment: By which stress in the organism-environment situation is more or less reduced but the configuration is not resolved directly

   A. *Compensation:* By which simpler activities and implicit processes are submitted in lieu of resolutions of the configuration, which is more or less disintegrated by changes in the tendencies concerned

      1. Daydreaming in lieu of constructive thought or action

      2. Sport, theater, reading and the like instead of effort

      3. Seeking and preying on sympathy

      4. Unsocial lying, pathological lying of idealizing type, etc.

   B. *Sublimation:* By which more complex activities and implicit processes that are in conformity to systems of ideals, social or derived, are unconsciously substituted for more direct adjustive processes, which if carried out will create new organism-environment situations because of the disapproval of others

      1. Altruistic activities

      2. Religious practices[4]

      3. Other ritualistic behavior of positive social value

   C. *Defense Reactions:* By which more complex activities and implicit processes, often without close conformity with the systems of social and derived ideals, are unconsciously substituted for more direct adjustive processes that are blocked by *conflict* within the personality, the stress of the conflict being avoided or reduced thereby

      1. In which the "inner" aspect of the situation is the more impressive:

*The following table is a slightly modified version of one that appeared in Harry Stack Sullivan, "Research in Schizophrenia," *American Journal of Psychiatry*, **86**:553-567, 1929-1930.

    a. Forgetting
       i. Suppression
       ii. Repression
    b. Rationalization
       i. Elaborative
       ii. Retrograde falsification
       iii. Detractive
    c. Transfer of blame
       i. Impersonal—luck, fate, etc.
       ii. Personal—"my sickness," "my views," etc.
       iii. Paranoid—suspicion—blame—persecution
  2. In which the "outer" aspect is the more impressive:
    a. Negativism
       i. Passive
       ii. Active
    b. Incapacitation
       i. Special
       ii. General

D. *Dissociation:* By which some of the systems of experience and some of the somatic apparatus are disintegrated from the rest of the personality and engaged in overt and implicit quasi-adjustive processes not in harmony with those of the rest of the personality

  1. "Psychogenic" tics, mannerisms, and stereotyped movements
  2. Automatisms, including automatic writing, crystal gazing, etc.
  3. Mediumship, etc.
  4. Hallucinosis
  5. Multiple personality and the like

E. *Regression:* By which more recent experience, and the resulting elaboration of complexes, sentiments, and tendencies, are disintegrated in such fashion as to remove them as factors in the organism-environment situation; this resulting in the reappearance of adjustive efforts of a chronologically earlier state of personality

III. Nonadjustive Processes: By which stress in the organism-environment situation is not reduced and no resolution of the configuration is brought about

A. *Panic:* In which the acts are reflex and of a primitive impul-

sive order, and the implicit processes primitive
B. *Anxiety:* Varying from more or less frank attacks of fear to extremely obscure "physical" illnesses, more or less episodic in character
C. *Excitement:* Including many "abnormal sublimations," reformers, etc.
D. *Obsessive Preoccupations:* Including morbid doubts and scruples and pessimistic worrying
E. *Morbid Grieving*
F. *Depression*

Before going further I must try to clarify Sullivan's concept of adjustment or biological adaptation, an idea that takes on various meanings in different writers. As one progresses in time, one faces problems from day to day, if not from hour to hour, which have to be settled, resolved in a more or less satisfactory manner if one is to remain tolerably content with life or at least not miserable. Some of these problems are minor—perhaps most usually are—while others may involve decisions that will influence the whole course of one's future life. The resolution of a particular situational "complex" so that it is no longer existent is said to be adjustment. What is meant by a successful resolution can only be gleaned from the context of Sullivan's writings since he did not work out a logical philosophy or systematized general theory of problematic situations. But the general drift of his thought in regard to the resolution of problems in interpersonal relations is clear. The successful resolution of a situation, as well as failure, leaves "traces" or effects that influence behavior in subsequent situations. Even apparently trivial outcomes of situations because of their cumulative effects over a long period of time may exert a vital influence on one's life history.

In Sullivan's usage, as he explicitly says in *Personal Psychopathology*, adjustment, maladjustment, and nonadjustment do not designate statistical norms, and he assumes that the individual is caught up or involved in objective states of affairs (physical, biological, psychological, sociological) that cannot be transcended and that cannot be slighted or ignored without danger to or loss of health and happiness or contentment. In his view "intrapsychic" processes do not occur and cannot be understood apart from the environing world.

In trying to understand human behavior one must study the individual's acts piecemeal while at the same time viewing them in a larger context of the individual's life history and social situation. One must learn what the individual is striving for in particular situations, how he acts, succeeds, or fails. Life is lived—or in some instances simply endured—from hour to hour and from day to day, though normally sustained and made meaningful traditionally by some life plan, of which the individual may not even be clearly aware, and which usually, though not always, is adopted and perhaps reworked from the set of values obtaining in one's community or society. Thus adjustment does not take place at large but in particular situations, in given times and places. And so the phrase action toward adjustment designates "specific activity in a particular total situation, and not to an enduring condition."

Every individual must in varying degrees bring to any situation a number of powers and characteristics that *partly* determine success or failure of adjustment: intelligence, imagination, feeling, knowledge derived from past experience, personal security, and the like. Of course, different situations may, partly or entirely, "demand" the exercise of different powers and qualities. One cannot properly exercise gentleness, for instance, with certain kinds of aggressive, domineering people who would take it for weakness. Delicacy of feeling and graceful behavior may be entirely lost on those who are coarse or obtuse. And these considerations take me to the second point. In any actual interpersonal situation, the powers and qualities that the other person brings to the situation play an equally important role, usually, in determining whether the situation will be adjustive or not. Stated in another way, if in any actual interpersonal situation adjustment is to occur, or the resolution of any problem, it must be as an outcome or result of an *interaction* of the two, or more, people directly involved in the situation. Or again, to put this matter in still another way, human behavior is not self-actional.

In regard to the concept of adjustment, Sullivan says that if the particular action actually in progress in a given interpersonal situation is proceeding in a manner such that the situation is being changed in the direction of resolution, the person (or subject individual) is regarded as manifesting more or less fully adjustive processes. The preservation or enhancement of self-respect and the respect of others, along with the satisfaction of various other needs in interpersonal situations, seems to be what Sullivan primarily meant by resolution of a situation.

When action is "continuing" or maintaining the situation without material change, the person is said to be engaged in nonadjustive processes. Although almost any form of activity may be more or less adjustive in some or most situations, Sullivan claims, there are kinds of activities such as depressive ruminations and worry, which very seldom accomplish much and are therefore quite generally nonadjustive. These activities, which accomplish little as a rule, besides the extension of a total situation in time, are directed toward a preservation of the *status quo*.

According to Sullivan, it is considerations of the ease and difficulty, of directness and indirectness, of "simplicity" and "complexity," not of possibility in contrast to impossibility, in achieving "implied" (or inferred) goals that distinguish adjustive and maladjustive processes. There are, I think, hidden valuational elements in these "considerations." In the context of the discussion in the manuscript, some goals are avowedly "good" or desirable; others are not. Furthermore, the "considerations" mentioned above imply some means of achieving goals are efficient ("simple"), while others are not, which implies an evaluation of means as well as of goals. The concept of adjustment is itself value-laden, if only because a sound, logical judgment about adjustment entails an evaluation of means and ends. As far as I can see, there is no way by which psychiatry can escape or avoid such evaluations of means and ends, though it need not, and of course should not, be *moralistic*—a quite different matter. Accordingly, from the side of theory, as well as practice, psychiatry cannot avoid the use of norms or standards of mental health and mental illness, whether mental health be conceived in terms of adjustment, self-realization, or something else, even though it must eschew moralizing if it is to be a science.[5] On the other hand, I think it will be generally agreed that a psychiatrist who in his professional capacity *condemns* a patient on moral grounds is therapeutically incompetent. Furthermore, the patient usually has to learn for himself what is healthy or "sick," good or bad. Subtle indoctrination by the psychiatrist normally has to be avoided. He must not play God.

In discussing maladjustive processes, Sullivan emphasized the fact that the means employed to achieve goals are inadequate with unhappy consequences for the person (and often for others) mainly because of unfortunate life experiences and personality "warp," while in nonadjustive processes the goals are emphasized as defective or "wrong" or otherwise inadequate either from the point of view of the sufferer's efforts to achieve happiness or contentment or that of society's welfare. But on both philosophical and psychiatric grounds, one cannot make this distinction between maladjustive and nonadjustive processes sharp or "absolute." Philosophically speaking, one may say that means enter into and modify ends. In psychiatry this latter point is often abundantly—even poignantly—made evident. As Sullivan has often observed, maladjustive processes may "evolve" or eventuate in nonadjustive processes.

Maladjustive processes are frequently, if not always, marked by inner tension, emotional disturbances, difficulty in concentrating, and the like. One may be uncomfortable even when one is physically alone because of inner tensions, apprehensive ruminations, and so forth, or as a person among other persons, that is, when one is in the company of one or more other persons. In either instance, the discomfort has to do with interpersonal relations. This becomes clear when it is realized that though one may be physically alone one may in imagination and thought be related to others, whether the latter belong to, or are connected with, one's past life, or the present or the anticipated future. And one relates not only to people who are, or once were, real, existing persons but also to imagined persons who are creatures of fantasy and dream. For no matter how "alone" or isolated we may be, we live in a world of memory, belief, hope, expectation, which may sometimes become transformed and, for us, lose its joyful aspects, leaving us to dwell in anxious misery, deep sadness, painful boredom, fear, paralyzing depression, or despair. Not only oneself but environing people may suffer since we live in a world of people whom we affect while being affected; and even if we could retire from the world indefinitely, our withdrawal would in varying degrees often affect others still.

In maladjustive processes usually the person's at least dimly foreshadowed goal is reached only under undue stress, difficulty, and discomfort if it is reached at all. This will be amply illustrated in the discussion of dynamisms of difficulty.

The question arises: What is a simple, "uncomplicated" situation? As Sullivan observes, a situation that is relatively simple for one person may be very "complex" for another, depending on the previous experience, native endowment, and the like, of the persons involved. Thus for a mentally defective person an algebraic formula with which he is presented may be impossible to understand, something that would be well within the grasp of an average high school student. If such a mentally defective person, seeing he is unable to "handle" such things, merely "gives it up" without further ado, he does not suffer. But suppose now he is made to feel that others will think less of him if he fails, having been led to anticipate scoffing on failure to handle algebraic formulae. A new and powerful "demand" is then introduced into the situation: the preservation of his status and his self-respect. The situation is now definitely becoming "complicated." Though realizing his inability to understand the algebraic formula, he is compelled to act in such a way as to seem not to have failed, while abandoning the problem. Now he suffers.

It may be that if he perceives that failure will be attended by loss of some (to him) extremely desirable factor (such as the respect of his peers, or a desired promotion), then realization of his impending defeat may be accompanied by a blocking of activity: he frets or grieves or does nothing about the problem. This is nonadjustive activity. The problem situation is not even partially resolved.

Sometimes in such a situation the person engages in random activity or in rage behavior. His suffering is in this instance "exteriorized" and actively involves others.

Again, especially if the situation has ensued on a long series of rebuffs, thwartings, frustrations, he may "ignore" the complex demands of the situation (demands for not only solution of the formula but maintenance of status and self-esteem), and resort to a simple apathetic self-absorption, or "childish" amusement, in the course of which environing people and their activity cease to be "relevant" to him, or, if they are still "relevant," it is on the basis of processes more or less exterior to his conscious awareness. (Thus, there seems to be no universal rule by which one can characterize simple situations.)

It is clear, I think, that most human activities either directly or indirectly significantly involve one's self-respect, which is so intimately bound up with one's self-confidence when one encounters new situations or difficult situations generally, whether novel or familiar. That is why, or at least one potent cause of the fact that, it is so frequently difficult to approach new situations with, say, the cool detachment of a skilled mechanic faced with a difficult mechanical problem. All too often interpersonal situations cannot be appraised with a calm intellectual or rational appraisal of all the factors involved, which they frequently, though not always, require, especially in an industrial urban society. The preservation of one's status and/or self-respect in interpersonal relations enters as a "complicating" factor though one may sometimes be unaware of it. This in turn is intimately related to one's life history, to the contemporary social order and one's position or "place" in it. Yet one may say that in general the more secure one is or feels, the more self-esteem one has, the more overall self-confidence one possesses, the less anxious personal concern will he feel about status in interpersonal relations.

Almost from the moment of birth onward, as Sullivan has said, the "factors" of prime significance in situations are other people, and because of various social and personal conditions, people, or an understanding of people, very frequently remain beyond the grasp of intellectual processes, as does an understanding of one's own self in relation to them.

If that be the case, how then do most people get along in life as well as they seem to? Our "marvelous adjustive potentialities" are said to be realized for the greater part outside conscious awareness so that we are left more or less free to deal with the complexities of the material world and of "schematized" society, of standardized social norms and customs, with at least the possibility of unemotional, rational analysis. It happens, however, that people "depend" at the wrong time or in the wrong situation on extraconscious dynamics, and when they should be employing the best analytic tools that they have are in the grip of emotional upheavals. More often than not they do not lack capacities to deal with situations in contrast to the person in our illustration who was deficient in one of the most important human qualities. It is the task of the psychopathologist generally to discover those extraconscious processes, and their mode of operation, which tend to baffle the individual when they operate in interpersonal situations, constituting or resulting in maladjustive or nonadjustive processes. In searching for and elucidating such extraconscious processes, one must study the development of the personality from which, or during the course of which, the personally unrecognized or un-understood processes originated. This is one reason that the psychopathologist must have or acquire a grasp of the course of personality development: a general theory, however crude in the beginning, to guide him in his researches, and, with its help, he must make a careful review of the life history of the person before him, a search of this past "as it continues to exist" in the personality of the patient and its numerous ramifications and effects. If the psychiatrist is to understand a particular personal event in the life of his patient, for example, he must identify certain frequently abundant relevant factors that are more or less completely unrecognized by the latter. These unrecognized factors are said to arise generally in close relation to past experience of the person concerned. Sullivan thought it necessary to warn the student against assuming that, because the momentary situations of two people seem alike, the experience each is undergoing resemble each other. On numerous occasions he pointed out that the factor of past experience enters into every total situation and enters so effectively that sometimes the true character of the situation may actually be beyond the power of the observer to conceive.

It is important to note that Sullivan does not set up standards of mental health that for most people have only an abstract possibility of realization at this stage in human history; standards that only serve to stigmatize the great majority of people who get along fairly well in these times of troubles and perils almost beyond one's ability to imagine. These lofty standards may provide their authors with a delightful feeling of superiority or possibly, in some instances, a temporary alleviation of their own feelings of anxiety and inferiority but such standards tend to have a malicious effect, since many naïve readers of books wherein those standards are eloquently expounded tend to believe they are damned if they fall short.

Sullivan wrote that it should be clear that one who would be useful to those whose life course is bringing them and their associates a "measure of unhappiness" and dissatisfaction with life is called upon to achieve a practical understanding of human individuals functioning as persons among persons. "The fact that there are limitations in the possible completeness of this achievement no more justifies him in oversimlifying his conceptions of himself or his fellows than it justifies a pessimistic solipsism that does violence to the common-sense observation that people *do* carry on a considerable measure of understanding cooperation. On the other hand, the persons concerned in each situation possess some measure of uniqueness which may or may not require his appreciation. He must school himself from the beginning never to seek in the individual alone the explanation of a psychobiological phenomenon. In this realm, all effective understanding is to be sought in a relevant complex including the individuals principally concerned, and having practical limits."[6]

We are now in a better position to peruse the outline of dynamisms of difficulty that was given above. One can see at a glance that compensation, sublimation, the defense reactions, dissociation, regression, come under the heading of partial adjustment. They are names for various groups of *maladjustive* interpersonal processes, most, if not all, of which may under certain circumstances evolve into, or facilitate, *nonadjustive* processes. As Sullivan emphasized, there is nothing holy or absolute about this classificatory scheme. Like all classifications, they were constructed for a purpose, which may be modified when circumstances warrant, as indeed they were in Sullivan's later work. Although these categories of dynamisms of difficulty are taken chiefly from Freud and certain other psychiatrists who were influential forty or fifty years ago, they are organized, formulated, and interpreted rather differently—that is, from a contextual, interpersonal point of view. Thus as psychiatric theory changes and develops, so do classifications of mental disorder.

In the following summary discussion one may note the great emphasis that Sullivan puts on the person's strivings to attain or maintain self-esteem rather than on needs and efforts at finding an outlet for libidinal urges or destructive drives as is the case with Freud. Sullivan's emphasis is a logical outcome of his interpersonal orientation, which in turn originally grew primarily out of his work with schizophrenics. The libido theory (as it is often called) and the concept of an inherent destructive instinct (as well as much else in Freud) are abandoned as not only artificial and cumbersome but gravely misleading when applied in therapeutic work. Sullivan's innovations are radical, and only now, more than thirty-five years after he wrote *Personal Psychopathology,* are beginning to be thoroughly understood, with great and beneficial consequences for therapy. Another thing to note is that anxiety does not yet appear as a central explanatory conception in interpersonal theory. Hence Sullivan's explanations fall short on several crucial points of what he could accomplish ten years later. For instance, he had not yet grasped the apparently pervasive connection of loss or lowering of self-esteem with the susceptibility to anxiety.

All of this does not imply that Sullivan slighted sexual and other needs and drives, though he emphatically claimed that sexuality is not to be regarded as a central explanatory conception of mental disorder. He believed that they must be viewed from a broader or at least different perspective, from the point of view of the person's striving for and concern with self-esteem and the esteem of others in an interpersonal context, a context that cannot be fully understood except in the light of a long-range, developmental history.

There is no need, I think, to review Sullivan's formulations and explanations of the dynamisms of difficulty in every detail. The following discussion is designed to communicate in a general way Sullivan's ideas and formulations and to promote the reader's insight into the interpersonal theory of psychiatry. The stratagems and reactions that are explicated are more or less typical of people's behavior when they encounter difficulties in living—or, as the popular jargon has it, "problems." The first sort of stratagem, *compensation,* is now more or less familiar to most people.

As an example of compensatory substitution, take that of a boy who starts out bright and early to seek work, encounters some rebuffs and as attention to "duty" flags, wavers and finally lapses, or as the passage of time has made job-seeking for the day officially futile, presently wends his way to a theater, where he passes some hours enjoying the performance. Both working and the theater are means to an end: "The experiencing of novel features of living." Of course, working might enable one to achieve such experiences directly rather than vicariously, but the former goal is remote and job-seeking is dispiriting, while enjoyment of the theater is immediate and does not entail any rebuff, even though it provides only a vivid fantasy of participation in the life and goings-on portrayed on the screen.

For the time being, the duty-to-work impulse disappears from consciousness because one or more than one powerful tendency system becomes active while the duty-to-work tendency is drowned out or put in abeyance. Working is an acquired, learned means, in the main, to an, as yet, far more "fundamental" end, the gratification of some powerful tendency (or motivational) system, even though eventually the need to work may itself become powerfully implanted in the system of needs and tendencies characterizing personality. But the boy feels compelled to do something only indirectly satisfying to some one or more already existing powerful tendency systems from which the duty-to-work tendency has been elaborated. Perhaps all goes well: his conscience does not nag him; nor will his wife because he has no wife.

It may be, however, that if "sufficient energy" is not "drained off" from the duty-to-work tendency (for whatever cause Sullivan does not say), the duty to look for a job persists in harassing him while the boy is trying to enjoy himself in the theater; in which case he suffers a minor variety of conflict though he may hit upon a formula (a rationalization) to justify the recreation.

Let us consider another example, that of a "high-pressure executive," who when faced with a particular complex problem gets the notion that he must go to the links for eighteen holes of golf. A situation of this sort is somewhat more complex. "This good man," says Sullivan "is scarcely to be taxed with evading an unpleasant task by simple compensatory activity." If he were told that he is engaging in compensatory activity he would have a neat rationalization to offer: that he must keep fit in order to deal effectively with the problems of his difficult job. Moreover, he has discovered that sometimes an interruption of conscious preoccupation with a problem may facilitate its solution.

Sullivan thought that athletic performances may be a form of compensatory activity. Imagine a man who goes bowling, when in an angry mood. In this fashion he substitutes a simple performance for the difficult effort required to resolve directly his "antisocial" tendencies. His throwing a ball at the pins may also be considered a substitution of a socially approved, *more* complexly motivated performance for direct action, such as throwing stones at any enemy. This man's behavior seems to be a sort of compromise between sublimation and compensation. In fact, certain athletic performances are said to serve both a compensatory and a sublimatory substitution synchronously.

This illustration points up the fact that compensation can be so broad and diffuse a category that under it one can subsume almost any human activity except sleep. Some psychiatrists, according to Sullivan, used to interpret all behavior except that in accordance with their own prevailing interests as, among other things, a compensation for a feeling of inferiority. In this fashion one can plausibly appeal to the alleged principle of compensation—that is, use it as a rationalization—for one's inadequacies, while also disparaging an unadmitted antagonist by this reference to one's suspicion of his inferiority. Thus some people may engage in vicious interpretations to degrade socially approved behavior, "including a great body of useful sublimations."

Eventually Sullivan abandoned compensation as an explanatory principle.

Leaving the topic of compensation aside, I take up Sullivan's discussion of *sublimation,* which is said to be frequently the most nearly adjustive activity in which people can engage, that is, people who are insecure in some area or areas of living, and where direct action would imperil self-esteem or some other vital interest. Within limits, it is an "excellent dynamism," though Sullivan does not ascribe the transcendent importance to it which Freud did. According to the former, sublimation "functions satisfactorily for a great many in the case of whom a direct satisfaction with social disapproval would be either intolerable to self-esteem or economically disastrous."[7] A great many things other than sexual drives can be sublimated: hostile tendencies or cruelty impulses, for instance. But Sullivan believed that if sublimation is employed to handle the "sexual integrations," it is liable to result in lamentable failure or nonadjustive excitement, "a sort of random occupation in which *anything* but the really essential factors are given relevance."[8] Sublimatory processes are unwitting and "essentially unconscious." They are effective in adjustment only as long as the components of the particular integrating tendency are in "a certain relationship." Sullivan claims that when the enhancement of self-esteem by the "accrual" of social approval is definitely subordinate to the satisfaction derived from direct fulfillment of the sublimated tendency, the sublimation is unstable. In other words, if direct gratification of the tendency that has been sublimated is more satisfying than the enhancement of self-esteem that sublimation of the tendency gains, the sublimation is unstable and is prone to fail entirely or partially at intervals. The term "subordinate" seems to imply a less forceful motivation in some hierarchical organization of needs. As I have mentioned, Sullivan has emphasized the difficulty as well as the instability of sublimation of sexual drives, especially during the adolescent years. When "the reverse is true," when the satisfaction to be gained from the augmentation of self-esteem from the "accrual" of social approval, which is gained by sublimation of the tendency, is greater than the satisfaction or fulfillment to be gained by direct gratification of the original, unsublimated tendency, then the sublimation is said to be relatively stable. There is then, at least in fortunate circumstances, a dynamic equilibration between the fulfillment of the need to maintain self-esteem and the satisfaction of various other needs of a person, with his particular personality structure, in a given social order with its accepted social and moral codes. And the condition or state of one's self-esteem is intimately related to one's own past interpersonal experiences, to one's education or acculturation from birth onward.

Certain types of people may advocate "social reform" as a sublimatory solution of their own life situations. The unreasonable and illogical features of their behavior tend to betray their real, unconscious motivation. "The 'vice' to be remedied is not subjected to a rigorous analysis; no careful estimation of the facts is engaged in; no inquiry is made into the virtues of the opposition. The 'movement' is highly emotional. The formulation of the 'cause' is such that it is propaganda, an appeal to prejudice. Facts are transmuted to suit the purpose, and anyone not readily converted is subjected to the darkest suspicions—the least that he can be is an enemy of progress."[9] More likely he is a tool of the wicked capitalists; in short, a fascist. In such cases—which incidentally point up some of its weaknesses—if sublimation fails excitement or a defense reaction ensues.

Sublimation, or the *unwitting* "combination" of a pursuit of, or striving for, social approval with that of a more "individualistic," private goal "pertains" to very many things.

Sullivan surmised that there exist in each of us a great many fantasy processes dealing with the direct satisfaction of each tendency that we have developed in the course of life. The socialized person permits only such of these processes as are in agreement with the accepted social code to receive focal attention. His selective attention does not efface the unacceptable fantasy processes though it does facilitate the sublimatory resolution of situations. Imagine a "well-socialized man" who is angered by a situation in which he thinks "unfair" advantage has been taken of one of his weaknesses. He cannot resort to a direct resolution of the ensuing situation because it would violate his social code. But his situation is so urgent, however, by reason of its connection with his self-esteem, that the frustrated tendency "causes" in him an angry *mood*. By visiting a bowling alley and playing a series of games he sublimates his anger. The success of the maneuver is said to be indicated by the disappearance of the forementioned mood and the becoming irrelevant of most of the details of the anger-provoking situation. "The 'ten-strikes' that he has made have perhaps defeated the competitor with whom he put himself in primary relationship at the alley. . . ."[10]

Defense reactions are said to be the most frequent solution of conflict. Conflict should not be equated with the mere selection from alternative possibilities and the exercise of choice. To be human is to have the ability to choose, though this ability is fostered or limited by various conditions: individual, social, historical. Life, as Charles Horton Cooley put it, is always a give and take with surrounding conditions. These "conditions" have multiplied in scope, and in range now include the far corners of the world, so that an educated person may avail himself if he wishes of the thoughts and ideas of many peoples all over the world. Nevertheless, while this possibility has brought opportunity for wide-ranging choice and personal growth for some people, it at the same time has brought a good deal of tension and moral confusion partly due to the loosening of traditional beliefs.

Despite the fact that conflict is related to choice, since there would be no conflict if there were no choice, the two are not synonymous. Tendencies that can be satisfied seriatim are not likely to eventuate in conflict. And many times in our lives we have to postpone the resolution of some long-felt need or problem, as well, in order to satisfy some urgent, intercurrent need. This is a commonplace of life, however regrettable it may sometimes be. Nor should one confuse conflict with a momentary indecision. Conflict is characterized as *"a total situation so integrated that two or more disparate resolutions tend synchronously to occur."*[11] There must be two or more competing, mutually exclusive highly desirable goals presented, one of which cannot be secured without the person's relinquishing any hope of attaining the other.

In the person undergoing such a conflict, torn as he is by the pull of competing motivations, the traditional unity of consciousness is lacking, while concentration is destroyed by the continual shifting of attention from one to another content. It is no wonder that he is acutely and often terribly unhappy. Such a person is at one moment keenly aware of the ultimate necessity of conforming to some one of the mores even though he is impelled by some inner drive to violate it, to commit a violation that would greatly lower his self-esteem, since, it may be, the other person or persons concerned in the situation would immediately make an unfavorable valuation of him or of his behavior. And at another moment, despite the fact that he has just considered the consequences that his action, if he carried it out, would entail, he is filled with desire to engage in it, and he is a prey to fantasies of such a course of action. As a result of the baffling of one integrative tendency by another, there is a piling up of tension. "Such

a state," Sullivan claims, "endangering as it does the very maintenance of life, is invariably of brief duration."[12]

Three possible outcomes are mentioned: (1) a maladjustive process
that represents a substitute for resolution of the opposing tendencies
may appear; (2) one of the tendencies that are in conflict may be split
off from access to consciousness (dissociation); (3) panic may appear,
and from this extremity regression or suicide, among other things,
may result.

One form of defense reaction is *forgetting*, though not all occurences
of forgetting are instances of defense reaction. Sullivan claims that
from birth onward we manifest ample evidence of a native talent for
forgetting. But in the case of certain events (unspecified) this talent
does not apply though one has a great conscious willingness to be rid
of their unpleasant recollection. These events are said to be unpleasant owing to the inability of the person concerned to accept the reality
and personal significance of the incident, and he cannot do so because
such acceptance would entail painful embarrassment, shame, guilt, or
anxiety. What such events are will vary with different people, of
course. They might have to do with sex or hostility or some humiliating experience or something else. The retention of such recollections
is due to their relevance in a "perduring situation." The unpleasantness combined with the persistence of the recollection may be so
troublesome that a defensive process that Sullivan calls *suppression*
(not *repression)* may be applied to the situation concerned, or the
events in it, which tend to provoke the unpleasant recollection. Avoidance of any "reduplicative recall" of the "central unpleasantness" is
primary owing to the necessity of protecting self-esteem. If the person could actually verbalize this, he might say, "I don't want to go
through *that* again; I don't even want to think about it."

Avoidance "is achieved by a negative activity by which perception
is suppressed and by positive action in the shape of unwitting alertness for and avoidance of factors apt to be relevant to the suppressed
situation."[13] The meaning seems to be that (1) the perception of some
relevant factors in a situation (relevant because they pertain to the
satisfaction of some need or tendency in a situation or in recurrent
similar situations) or their significance is not noticed or slurred over
by some negative activity, an activity of avoidance, which Sullivan does
not specify but which, I think, may at times be almost as crude as
looking the other way; and/or (2) there is "positive action," which

takes the form of *unwitting* alertness for and avoidance of the relevant factors because they provoke recall of the "central unpleasantness" that was and remains hard on the self-esteem. Both (1) and (2) are conjunctive aspects of one process. The "central unpleasantness," to repeat, has to do with the loss of self-esteem or self-respect or with the threat of such loss. I think it is clearly evident that people will go to great lengths generally to preserve self-respect, and this, be it noted, is always, either directly or indirectly, connected with interpersonal relations.

If the suppression has to do with a major tendency system (for instance, sexual motivation), an ever-present sense of danger lurks in the fringes of consciousness; and one is constantly fearful (anxious), the more so since the suppressed tendency persistently eludes one's efforts, impelling him to integrate at least abortive relevant situations through so-called accidental occurrences, slips of the tongue, awkward entanglements, and the like. Furthermore, though one may have fairly effectively suppressed the tendency from conscious awareness, one's "expressive mechanism" (the expression of one's face, the tone of voice, etc.), and even one's overt behavior may give one away to an actually or potentially interested second party, thus advertising the tendency and acting to integrate the relevant situation.

The difference between suppression and repression, which I wish now to discuss, is not "absolute." There are certain experiences the memory of which cannot be recalled except by special procedure. Neither by recurrence to the conscious mind nor by continuing effort at suppression is there any manifestation of recollection. Such experiences have aroused some tendency in the person whose manifestation he regards with profound dread, loathing, or horror. In other words, when a previously all but unsuspected tendency becomes awakened and creates an intense conflict regarding some situation or type of situation, some people are able to efface from consciousness the memorial elements connected with an occurrence and therefore awareness of the tendency; that is to say, they are able to repress the experience. In this process, or as a result of this process of repression, something like a divestiture of reality occurs to the repressed incidents: they become subsequently associated with or regarded as belonging to the never happened or to the mythological. But repressed experiences are not rendered absolutely inefficacious: their effects are evidenced in a modification of some related tendency or tendencies. If a person who has carried out such a repression is presented with a factual, ungarbled account of the context of the occurrence, he is apt to deny in all honesty that such was the case. Taxed with the facts, he may develop a vague uncertainty, which is in turn readily forgotten.

Repression has its limitations, bringing with it certain consequences: "Others are not given to acceptance of the repression of factors concerning them; they take it as weird or fraudulent."[14] So they distrust one. This distrust by others is enhanced by the fact that the repressed experience often leaves its mark in the form of changes in the tendency system or network of tendencies of the personality. Also, other people's responses react back or "repercusses" on the self, leading to a deterioration of self-assurance. To be distrusted or otherwise to meet with unfavorable response is an experience that is hard on self-esteem and on an already shaky self-confidence in such cases.

Nor is this all. As Freud claimed, repression involves a quantitative factor. When "too much" has been repressed or when the tendencies or motivational system constitute a powerful component of the personality, the defensive network (of the self) breaks down, manifested as either "frank failure with a flooding of consciousness" of the "forgotten" material, or dissociation.

I take up next the concept of *rationalization,* which has been adopted by the general literate public in such a fashion that its misuse takes on high nuisance value in parlor conversation. Rationalization, like so many other things, is connected with our efforts to maintain self-esteem and the esteem of others. Hence it is "rather closely related" to suppression and repression. "Each of us," according to Sullivan, "constructs from the perceived reactions of others to us, a body of beliefs as to our personality, this going to make up the self."[15] But he did not think the statement applies to the personality as a whole. The construction or body of beliefs includes principles of right conduct, and of right opinion regarding thought and behavior (which in Sullivan's formulation belong to the self while in Freud's they belong to the superego); and we pride ourselves on some of these principles. Even so, it is possible for a dispassionate observer to note that we are "decidedly emotional" about these principles, concerning some of which we pride ourselves, and that we are expert in appealing or "referring" to them to "explain" actions that in fact are or may be rather incongruous with such standards. If called upon to account for some deed or expression of opinion, our self-esteem requires us to give a plausible "explanation" or "reason," and one which is calculated to cast no unfavorable light on the self. This does *not* necessarily mean that the person is clearly conscious of what he is doing. As Sullivan and others have said, conscious, deliberate hypocrisy is much more infrequent than one might assume. In any case, the "plausible pseudo-explanation by a facile appeal to principle" is called rationalization.[16] Whether one's behavior is "good" or "bad," he tends to "explain" it, either to himself or to others, if required to do so, by an appeal to principles that are congenial to the self, or to one's so-called self-image.

Furthermore, when they are observed ("caught") doing something contemptible and have a chance to create a neat rationalization of it, "many people many times succeed in losing the reality of the act, and have remaining a transmuted precipitate suited more to the angels than to denizens of this mundane plane."[17] This kind of process often works retroactively on "memorial elements," on memory, so that a speciously exalted motivation is ascribed to one's past doings; and the actual placing of them in the correct temporal sequence is "wonderfully falsified," with the result that owing to the false temporal sequence any evidence of the unworthy course of one's life is completely destroyed. Sullivan called this process retrograde falsification. In addition, whether the rationalization be "current" (that is, pertaining to, or operating on contemporary happenings) or "retrograde" (operating retrospectively on past happenings), it often comes about that the "other fellow" undergoes a considerable depreciation. An "indirect rationalization" by "direct detraction" from the esteem enjoyed by the other fellow may be attempted, perhaps mainly when a direct rationalization entails little chance of success: One has done something unworthy because the other persons involved are the sort of people who understand only abuse, or for other reasons. The appeal to a principle in this case is said to approach somewhat to the use of the *paranoid dynamism*.

The person undergoing a "paranoid development" escapes from conflict by blaming or finding fault with something outside himself. The appearance of conflict, to the potentially paranoid, in any interpersonal situation, is said to lead to a suspicion that all is not good in the attitude of the other person. One activates the paranoid process by *projecting,* into one's appraisal of another, "of those features of himself for which, if he accepted them as of unqualifiedly personal origin he would be much ashamed." Whether or not such a process "works" depends to a large degree on the importance of the tendencies connected with the threatening conflict. If only what Sullivan calls "secondary tendencies," for example, "the socially approved drives for self-respect," are involved, some people, he says, may achieve a measure of complacency by putting the blame for failure on luck, Fate, or on disastrous coincidences. (The notion of secondary tendencies seems to imply a dichotomy of primary and secondary drives, motives, or whatever, which Sullivan was to correct in his subsequent formulations.) Such processes, which are characterized as a sort of exterior rationalization, are usually accompanied by "rationalistic procedures" and compensatory appeals for sympathy. "If the latter is a conspicuous element, we often find blame for personal inadequacies and failures passed over to a more or less real sickness, a more or less unnecessary identification with 'some lost cause,' or something else that is both personal in its application and yet allegedly beyond control by the individual."[18] When and only when a powerful tendency or motivational system is not involved, such processes are fairly successful in bolstering up a limited self-respect.

And even when conflict that is connected with a powerful tendency threatens, a transference of blame onto one *impersonal* "object" may be considerably effective in preserving self-respect. Heredity may be blamed. But the success of this operation is said to depend to a considerable degree on an unwitting blame of the parents, and through them, humanity at large. As long as the people of importance ("significant people") to the subject respond satisfactorily, the process provides a neat escape from painful conflict and loss of self-respect. However, the transference of blame processes, if resorted to in dealing with really powerful motivations, tend generally to a grievously unfortunate outcome, namely, a paranoid state or paranoid schizophrenia.

Paranoid attitudes are numerous and socially far more "important" than paranoid psychotic conditions. There are said to be a great many people who can get on quite well in resolving all sorts of situations in which conflict is threatened if and only if they can lead the person concerned into making the first move. The other one may then be blamed for any consequences, real or fantastic. But a great many people do not need to blame the other overtly; they simply "know" it was his fault, so the guilt lies with him. There is also a considerable number who must "complete the resolution" of a situation by expression of overt hostility, punishing the other one for his cooperation. A fairly common example is that of a psychopathic man who "loves" one "loose woman after another," whom he entices into making the first move. After he has engaged her in the sexual act, he immediately loathes the partner, openly expressing his "disgust with her," and usually advertises her loose morality.

Sullivan has emphasized the fact that human behavior is not "self-actional," occurring, as it does, in an interpersonal context, and that the "more competently socialized" person recognizes that his behavior is a "result of himself and the other one, scarcely to be credited as to causality to either person."[19] Actually, there is a very real sense in which one's behavior is a "result" of all the significant people one has known as well as of oneself, though this conception is too unwieldy for many purposes. This fact does not imply that the more competently socialized person is "overdependent." On the other hand, the only "person" who is independent of a social group, and, more specifically, of "significant others" is a corpse. "We are always on the alert for the approving and disapproving reaction of [significant] others to our acts and expressed opinions."[20]

There are people who, as Sullivan pointed out, grow to depend greatly on favorable appraisals and who also develop a marked concern with techniques for pleasing the other person, putting great emphasis on "what the other one wants." But if a serious "deviation" in the evolution of the personality of such a one does not occur, which would distort his preoccupations with the desires and wishes of others, the course of events will gradually reassure him. Outside the real intimacies, he will be a success in interpersonal contacts, "at least at the customary superficial level." "Given some measure of genuine satisfaction of the sleep, the nutritive, and the sexual needs, such a person usually progresses through life, a delight to business associates, an economic success, and a good citizen. As a salesman, he may be phenomenal. As a politician, he may be one of the least vicious. . . ."[21]

There are many individuals ("inadequately developed personalities") who have acquired a similar overdependence on the reactions of others *along with* the development of ideals or values that are inhibitory to any direct satisfaction of the "primal interpersonal drives," such as the sexual. Many youths, for example, while they have been taught to overvalue favorable personal appraisal, have also learned to regard sexual behavior as uncouth, vulgar, or sinful. These youths (though they may not be as frequent as they were a generation ago) lack any ability for action toward adjustment in intimate interpersonal situations involving sexual behavior. Suppose that such a "morbidly virtuous person" integrates a situation in which the other person, so to speak, exerts sexual attraction on him. Conflict appears, unless it happens that his sexual desires are not strong, enabling him to "handle" the situation before conflict has a chance to develop. But if conflict in situations in which sexual drives, for example, are the most potent integrator, does arise, the relative mental health of the person is always imperiled. A grave defense reaction, dissociation, or regression may ensue. Of course, the previous experience of the person is a significant generic factor concerning such possible outcomes, though psychiatry has not yet advanced to the point at which one can say what follows what with precision. The "variables" in mental illness are multiple, and their interrelations cannot yet be mapped out with anything like rigorous exactness. Sullivan claims that whether a defensive process will take the form of a "paranoid state" or manifest itself as a negativistic or disablement reaction is dependent on the previous experience of the individual in regard to the relations in which he stands to other people.

On the appearance of conflict, the potentially *paranoid* person feels a suspicion that there is something wrong in the other person. He suspects the other person of possessing those features of tendencies in himself that are in conflict with his self-esteem. To express this in another way, the paranoid process begins when one unconsciously attributes to ("projects" on) other people tendencies of one's own which harass one, and which, if recognized as part of oneself, would make one feel ashamed, guilty, and the like, which is a way of saying that one would suffer painful damage to one's self-esteem. Since some powerful tendency system, usually the sexual drive, is impelling him to integrate situations with the particular persons who interest him, he can hardly avoid entanglements. "No matter how many individuals he has shunned or driven away by his suspiciousness and peculiarity; no matter to what great lengths he has cultivated an austere and forbidding manner; no matter, in fact, if he has actually become so repellent that casual strangers automatically avoid him; there is no escaping the drive that integrates him into new situations, frequently including utterly unsuspecting people."[22] Moreover, his attitude of suspicion may interfere with satisfaction of the need for companionship.

Like some other needs, the need for sexual satisfaction, when ungratified, can become all-pervading. And the paranoid dynamism represents such a poor adjustment that one is driven, pushed, more and more wildly. He may be in the grip of such an intense state of tension that overt acts of hostility ensue, and he is judged insane. Or if the person is fairly able to conform to convention, he may engage in legal and other actions against those he takes to be enemies. Still more frequently it may happen that, along with the development of hostility to unfortunately attractive people, wedded to increasing tension of unsatisfied desires, the person becomes so clearly conscious of the conflict that he is forced to resort to dissociation. That is to say, the "abominated features" of the personality, the intolerable cravings, are overtly dissociated by the self-regarding system, becoming *"as if* they were autonomous," hounding one in the guise of devilish thoughts, which are "forced on his mind," hallucinated voices, and the like.

Without going into various other paranoid attitudes and developments, I turn to Sullivan's discussion of *negativism,* where "a feeling of privation of the self-esteem" is said to be the "energizing component," rather than a feeling of guilt. A long historic development has resulted in a conviction that one's importance as an independent person is always being minimized. "People are always overlooking one's importance, ignoring one's rights and prerogatives, demanding things to which one is solely entitled, or expecting returns from acts insufficient in payment for one's cooperation."[23] Feeling that he must protect himself from such inroads on his self, such a one has the notion that he must become "automatic" in refusing cooperation until a situation shall have been so altered that it is, as Sullivan expresses it, his "will" that action take place. There are said to be many grades of the negativistic organization of defenses in the face of actions that threaten conflict. In one instance it is enough that every "demand," to use Sullivan's phrase, is transformed into a polite request; in another, it is sufficient if it takes the form of a subservient plea. In still another, a "demand" must never appear: there must only be provided an opportunity for one to choose a course of action.

Negativistic people feel that only by such ritualistic performances is their importance protected from fancied slight, along with ensuing action toward its demonstration, a conviction based on tenuous self-esteem. Owing to unfortunate childhood experiences, they have learned, so to speak, that status is more easily acquired if one is an "obstacle" than if one is compliant. For them, domination is a great virtue. Their emphasis is on superordination and subordination of selves, with a corresponding failure of appreciation and valuation of other kinds of experience in interpersonal relations. Their selves are so constituted that they require or provoke "reflections" of their importance in order to have respect. And so it is no wonder that any interpersonal situation tends to arouse conflict between the drive to reaffirm self-importance as indicated above and some other drive whose satisfaction requires cooperation. Since the negativistic person has great difficulty in relationships with superiors, he tends to seek satisfaction among people who are in some respect inferior, intellectually or socially or economically or physically (or in some other way). In certain instances, such a person is driven to behavior that leaves him seriously disorganized, owing to his inability to gratify powerful impulses, with an ensuing dissociation.

Defenses by incapacitation are in many ways, according to Sullivan, the opposite of negativism. The threat of conflict between the necessity to preserve self-respect and to satisfy some other motivating tendency whose gratification is not in harmony with the self-regarding impulses is handled by the development of a physical illness that provides a way out. In some instances the person is so enfeebled that interpersonal relations are greatly simplified, most tendencies being worked out by "compensatory preying on sympathy." Major tendencies or motivational systems, like the sexual motivation, thus become so "distorted" by suffering that their otherwise morally repugnant character is lost in the intense suffering. Another and much more common result is that the incapacitation defense eliminates any physical sensations that lead to pleasure, the individual becoming, as it were, "a passive and rather martyred vehicle for the satisfaction of the mate." Occasionally defense by incapacitation is employed in securing convenient lapses of consciousness, during which the disapproved motivational tendency is satisfied.

Before discussing dissociation, I must raise some considerations regarding the notions of repression and "the unconscious."

What happens to the "material" (thoughts, feelings, fantasies, impulses, tendency systems) that gets repressed? Freud postulated an "unconscious" system in order to account for the indubitable fact that psychological processes almost from the beginning of life occur outside conscious awareness, or have been ejected by the ego from consciousness, and still operate as shown by their effects on thought, feeling, imagination and overt acts. Among other things, "the unconscious" was conceived as a "psychic region," a sort of mental locality. Can we say, then, that what is repressed is pushed "into" this psychic region, the unconscious? If we could legitimately do so, our next question, would be: *Where* is the unconscious? And to this question, Freud has no ready answer. Accordingly, we really seem to have reached an impasse. And when, on further reflection, we ask, what can a *psychic* region be, the case is still worse. Psychic regions are admittedly metaphorical. To think of them as otherwise is a manifest absurdity.

But we are still faced with the stubborn fact that psychological processes take place outside conscious awareness, the evidence for which has long been familiar. They cannot be explained away. And we must guard ourselves as best we can against relatively easy, quasi-mechanistic formulations in the manner of John B. Watson and Company.

At times Freud writes of the unconscious as a *separate psychical system,* which is analogous to the one we know or know something about, what we ordinarily think of as our mind. At any given time most of the latter is "latent" or "potential" and tends to operate only, or chiefly, as the necessities of life demand. But our thoughts, feelings, sensations, fantasies, do not fall from the blue. Nor do they ordinarily appear in a haphazard or chaotic fashion. Within certain limits, they manifest themselves in a more or less orderly manner, connected or related in a significant and meaningful way. There is available to us a store of memories, without which we would not be able to recognize anything, or to know anything—not even to recognize, let alone understand, ourselves. Somehow and somewhere we register or "record" experience in such a fashion that, willfully, deliberately, or not, we can usually draw upon it when the occasion requires. There have been many speculations as to where our experiences are "recorded," stored up, as it were, in some unknown way. A view widely held at the moment is that they exist as impressions in nervous tissue. Instead of speculating about this, I shall simply note that it is an empirical fact that we do have available an orderly representation of past experiences that appear in the shape of ideas, feelings, fantasies, and so forth.

The philosopher John Dewey has expressed this point so well that I wish to quote his words: "When we read a book, we are immediately conscious of meanings that present themselves and vanish. These meanings existentially occurring are *ideas*. But we are capable of getting ideas from what is read because of an organized system of meanings of which we are not at any time completely aware. . . . Change the illustration from reading a book to seeing and hearing a drama. The emotional as well as intellectual meaning of each presented phase of a play depends upon the operative presence of a continuum of meanings. If we have to remember what has been said and done at any particular point, we are not aware of what is now said and done; while without its suffusive presence in what is now said and done we lack clue to its meaning. Thus the purport of past affairs is present in the momemtary cross-sectional idea in a way which is more intimate, direct and pervasive than the way of recall."[24]

The "psychical system" that we are conscious of, or which is capable of becoming conscious, at least to a considerable degree, is the Deweyan "mind," though it might be said that "mind" in Dewey's sense may have some unconscious aspects. For the purposes of this book I ignore the latter possibility. The Dewayan "mind" is close enough to Freud's "preconscious system" (especially if we ignore Freud's "mental typography") to suggest what the latter was trying to formulate, however loosely and awkwardly, when he spoke of preconscious and conscious processes—except that Dewey was keenly cognizant of the "communal existence" and social nature of mind, while Freud was not or at least much less so.

Dewey has summed up the difference between mind (regarded here for the sake of illustration to encompass the Freudian preconscious system, though the correspondence may not be strict) and consciousness as the latter ordinarily appears:

> Mind is more than consciousness, because it is the abiding even though changing background of which consciousness is the foreground. Mind changes slowly through the joint tuition of interest and circumstance. Consciousness is always in rapid change, for it

marks the place where the formed disposition and the immediate situation touch and interact. It is the continuous readjustment of self [of personality, in Sullivan's language] and the world in experience. . . ."[25]

There are, however, significant factors to be recognized in this connection that hinder certain extraconscious aspects of mind from becoming conscious at appropriate moments, and often seriously limit one's efforts at readjustment. Some of them have been explicated and others will be discussed.

So we still have to deal with those aspects of the self, and of the entire personality, that are ordinarily incapable of becoming conscious, at least some of which may be repressed and dissociated. Before I discuss this point, I have to introduce some further ideas.

One of the most important things to notice about the self is that it is definitely organized. In other words, our thoughts and feelings, for instance, manifest a certain pattern or structure, however loose, topsy-turvy, or frayed this pattern may seem at times, when we are extremely tired, conflicted, fearful, anxious, or alcoholic. Without such a determinate pattern we would have no mind at all, no self, no personality. This pattern of psychological processes can be noticed and understood, at least to a considerable extent, if we are willing to make the effort.

Organization is a pervasive feature of life and of human personality. For the moment we may consider the personality as the most inclusive organization of processes with which we are concerned. It is "made up" of an indefinite number of suborganizations, such as the self. The self in turn has its own network of substructures.

The notion of a separate unconscious psychical system indicates or suggests that personality is not all of a piece. In other words, one or more suborganizations of the personality are not articulated functionally with the rest. It (or they) exists and operates as if it were a separate structure, analogous to the self, but functionally "split off" or dissociated. To state this from an experiential angle, certain thoughts, feelings, overt acts, and the like that may occur do not fit into the more or less familiar pattern of psychological processes. They often seem strange, incomprehensible, foreign in so far as they, in certain circumstances, or their disguised "derivatives" appear in consciousness. They do not ordinarily make sense to us. Such occurrences are manifestations or indications of *dissociated* processes. How extensively elaborated or developed such an ordinarily unnoticed and unnoticeable structure may be depends largely on the course of one's life history. The relation of the self-system to these dissociated processes is none too clear in detail. In summary fashion, one may say that the pattern or network of processes in which tendency systems cohere, which is "foreign" to the self, is dissociated, its manifestations ordinarily inhibited or disguised by the self. In some circumstances, dissociated processes become too powerful to be contained: too much has been repressed and dissociated (if we express this matter in terms of Freud's "quantitative factor") or the dissociated tendencies are powerful, extremely urgent components of the personality that can no longer be inhibited and kept from conscious awareness. They may "emerge" to "flood" consciousness, clothed in a strange and terrifying "meaning system." Their meaning or meanings are largely derived from certain long buried (unconscious or dissociated) symbol systems that were explicated in Chapter 2. Perhaps from childhood onward these symbol systems are manifested in dreams. In schizophrenia, along with their correlates and derivatives, they become overt.

Sullivan thought of the various levels of personality structure and their operation or functional activity in terms of dynamisms instead of the Freudian mechanisms because mechanisms are likely to call to mind electric washing machines, automobile engines, or television sets. *Dynamism* includes any psychological agency or means that operates, along with other dynamisms, to bring about change, or to preserve, protect, or maintain some aspect or function of the personality. It designates a characterizable and usually recurrent pattern of processes. A dynamism is a conceptually distinguishable but not actually, literally, a distinct "part" of personality, whose functioning must be viewed as a whole, not as a sum of parts. In his later work, Sullivan gives the name *dynamisms* to the self-system and the dissociated processes, but I think it would be less confusing to say they represent a network of dynamisms, leaving the notion of a single dynamism for more subordinate processes, though this is an issue which depends on the perspective from which one is operating and the problems to be dealt with. In other words, any configuration or pattern of processes is always a part aspect of a wider context, situation, or "field"; and such a configuration in turn embraces a number of "elements" or subordinate processes. Consider the self. It is a "part" or aspect of a larger, more comprehensive configuration, namely, what Sullivan calls *personality,* which is related to still larger organizations of events, namely, family, class, community, and the like. The self, on the other hand, embraces numerous substructures, what Sullivan subsequently called "me-you patterns"; and the latter, of course, can be analyzed further. And as one studies the different "levels" of organization and different classes of interacting processes one finds that different qualities "emerge." The individual has many more characteristics than his conscious self. The family or community has many new and different properties when compared with the individuals in it.

People sometimes ask how many dynamisms there are "in" personality. This is somewhat like asking a person how many habits he has —God only knows. The significant thing is to learn which ones are important, and this, in turn, largely depends on the problems one is dealing with, and what one wants to find out.

Freud failed to give an intelligible account of "the unconscious," though this is partly concealed by his frequent resort to elaborate metaphor. Of the fact, however, there can be no doubt. But we need an intelligible "explanation." In attempting such, we have to discard the Freudian metapsychology, and resort to a functional point of view.

Examples of *multiple personality* offer the most dramatic instances of the empirical fact that a person may function as if he had two or more "selves." At a given moment he acts (carries on various activities) as if he had one sort of personality while the "other" is largely, though not necessarily entirely, in abeyance. The most plausible formulation seems to be that his personality is so organized that one or the other of two (or more) incompatible aspects (or networks of symbol systems) operate at a given time, these incompatible aspects having been developed to an extraordinary degree, a development that is to be understood in terms of his life history. It is also quite true that even "normal" people have had to resort to minor dissociations, that is, they have been forced through certain life circumstances to "segregate" less powerfully motivated aspects of their personality than those that are "in" the self. Seen from another point of view, what is conscious and what is "subconscious" or "unconscious" (suppressed or repressed or dissociated) are to be gauged by their ease or difficulty or accessibility to conscious elaboration and communication.

These matters cannot be understood without considering the relation of the individual to the environment. We often conceive of personality as if it were a self-contained and more or less private possession of the individual. In the case of some aspects of the individual, it is easy to show that this is not so, and cannot be so. Try to breathe without the environing atmosphere, to walk without a ground to walk upon, to gaze upon another person in the absence of light waves. To suggest such things is to point up their absurdity. We cannot exist apart from the environing world; in fact the phrase "environing world" may be misleading because we live communally with or by means of the environment. This is as true of the social as it is of the physical aspects of life; it is true of all aspects of life. For instance, try to think without the use of the language or languages one has learned, or to live for even one day without resort to the techniques of keeping alive and in good health (eating, dressing, recreational activities, and the like) that one has learned. One of the things that Freud did not sufficiently understand is the "communal" nature of mind, its social or interpersonal organization and functional activity. This is one of the major differences between his atomistic, individualistic orientation and that of Sullivan's much more culturally oriented viewpoint.

And so the mind, or personality itself, while it has its own unique pattern, cannot be divorced from the wider social organizations from which it developed, and from those in which it functions. There are no sharp dividing lines here because the world of "reality" shades imperceptibly with the world of creative imagination and thought. (Indeed, there is a very real sense in which we "create" the world.) With the aid of modern communication, wedded to scientific technology, the easy access to books and the like ("mediate acculturation," Sullivan used to call this), the social environment to a considerable degree has indefinitely expanded.

And therefore we cannot understand human experiences and activities until we grasp the significance of the fact that man is a social being. The individual's problems, fears, anxieties, cannot be divorced from his social nature and existence. They do not suddenly appear full-grown in some deep, dark cavern of the personality. This applies equally to such a spectacular "dynamism" as that of *dissociation*. In this connection, one must also stress the person's developmental career.

In the case of a major dissociation, the individual is said to be at one moment a self-conscious person and at another a quite different individual engaged in activity intolerable to the self. Some powerful, unsatisfied tendency system "has been able to dissociate the self, so that the individual functions *as if* the self were not any part of him."[26] In such instances, the dissociated dynamism is in the saddle, having usurped the "place" or function of the normal, familiar self, that part or aspect of personality that represents a meaningful organization of life experiences and, at least to a considerable degree, is capable of recall and recollection on appropriate occasions. The condition in which the dissociated dynamism usurps the function of the self may be very temporary or it may not. There may be periods in which the person alternates between the two states of being. There is sometimes temporarily, sometimes permanently, a grave disintegration of personality structure, owing to intolerable conflicts and anxieties, with the result that in some cases a reintegration on a much more "primitive" or "childlike" level has to be effected in order that one may escape or minimize unbearable suffering.

According to Sullivan, such "extraordinary integrations of total situations" as occur in the phenomena of major dissociations, where the self is not a part, or in regard to which this aspect of the personality functions in the shape of an unwilling and detached observer, may include various activities. He mentions somnambulism, some trance phenomena, some hysterical behavior, automatic writing, mediumistic speech, hallucinosis, crystal gazing, shell hearing, tics, and stereotyped movements. During the course of such affairs the "traditionally unitary organism becomes the moving locus of two (or conceivably more) streams of total activity; integrating and being integrated into two (or conceivably more) coexisting and mutually exclusive total situations."[27] The personality is "split" such that one aspect, the self, integrates one sort of relationship to the world, and the other aspect, the dissociated, a quite different, competing relationship—and this at the same time, or period of time.

Sullivan calls attention to interpersonal situations in which the projection field of a special sense rather than the whole somatic apparatus is at the disposal of dissociated tendencies operating in the various hallucinoses, such as the auditory hearing of voices. The special sense affected (speaking very loosely, since much more than a special sense is involved if only because the senses do not function apart from the rest of the personality) "functions toward the self-conscious personality *as if* it [the special sense affected] were in the service of another personality, the embodiment of the dissociated tendencies."[28]

The conceptions of personality disintegration, and reintergration on a more "primitive" level coming on certain occasions as an aftermath to the failure of the defensive network of the self in the face of some major dissociation may serve to introduce the conception of *regression,* which is a very difficult one. Is it legitimate to say that one somehow reinstates the experiences, or rather the kind of experiences, and activities of early life? And if so, how can such a thing be done? Great changes have taken place in the adult human being, for example, since childhood. How can they be discarded, either temporarily or permanently, as if they never existed? How can things that have apparently been outgrown, and thus apparently gone out of existence, be recovered? In what sense, if any, do early life experiences leave a "record," "trace," or "memorial element" such that they can be activated or reactivated?

Sullivan was aware of such problems and many times expressed misgivings about the traditional notion of regression. But he held, nevertheless, that as a result of certain unfortunate situations, such as conditions of starvation, fatigue, and the like, more recently elaborated adjustive processes tend to disappear and "chronologically earlier" processes that are reactivated take their place. In certain "complex" life situations also (such as in certain psychotic states) it appears that recent experience "tends to become as if it were not." Furthermore, in regression, or what is called regression, the whole "interest system" is said to have shriveled to an historically earlier stage in the person's growth, and things formerly interesting seem no longer to have any interest for him. In any event, regardless of difficulties of logical formulation, it seems to be a well-established fact that people do (1) overtly abandon more elaborated patterns of behavior and (2) manifest kinds of behavior that are similar to those of an earlier stage of development when they experience intolerably great stresses of living.

I take up next the topic of *panic.* Panic is a state of total disorganization even though of brief duration. It occurs in situations gravely imperiling one as a living organism or as a person and is said to be perhaps the most appalling experience that man undergoes. In certain interpersonal situations something fails with utter unexpectedness and contrary to an implicit assumption, long taken for granted, about some essential aspect of the universe; that which fails is the self-system, or as it is elsewhere expressed, the dissociative power of the self. Such an occurrence is followed by panic, also called *primordial fear*.

While I shall postpone a detailed discussion of Sullivan's account of such failures, I want to indicate that these things are not as remote and recondite as they may seem to some, at least not in Sullivan's view.

> Nearly everyone can recall an occasion on which there was an easy progression into a situation, the denouement of which came as a sudden and very embarrassing surprise; the withdrawal from which remains none too gratifying a recollection. Sometimes when the facilitation of the unwitting involvement is the result of powerful dissociated tendencies, the shock of belated discovery as to "what one has let oneself in for" includes the reintegration of the previously dissociated system and the appearance of violent conflict. In some cases, panic is particularly apt to supervene. Once one has undergone this experience, the paralysis of behavior and thought while one is a prey of utter, formless terror, followed by collapse or by blind random action, one is not what one was before this experience. In some, there is a gradual recovery from the shock, and the development of adjustive processes tending to insure the personality from a recurrence of the horror. In all too many, however, the panic episode is prelude to an immediate outcropping of schizophrenic processes amounting to an acute psychosis. ...[29]

Anxiety states and "equivalents" and the *phobias* are said to be more adult forms of "primordial" fear. In the anxiety states, the object feared is unknown ("unconscious"), while in the phobias it is "irrational," that is, lacking any justifiable reason (though it is not uncaused), such as, for instance, a constant dread of, say, canned food. The phobia is an obsessional substitution of one object of fear for another, the "proper" object, and one that is often very hard to discover. Each occurrence or specific instance of the phobia is to be viewed as a formula substituted obsessionally for action in a situation.

Obsessional substitution is said to be peculiarly the disorder of the "thinker." Sullivan's account in *Personal Psychopathology* is summary, though in subsequent years he made considerable contributions to the understanding of the obsessional dynamics.[30] "Varying from low-grade ruminative preoccupation, a considerable part of which is derived from the revery subordinate to adjustive thinking in connection with some fairly complex situation," Sullivan observes, "to a preoccupation of awareness by logical or pseudo-logical formulations so intense that adjustive thinking appears only in crisis situations, the obsessional dynamics covers a broad field of processes."[31] The obsessional person may be consciously preoccupied with dreads, phobic fears, doubts, and unending scruples. Corresponding overt activity may take the form of countless socially useless rituals, time-destroying "habits of complexity," speech disorders, "an awesome array of systems, procedures and precedences." Though these things have a history—have some "relevant historic justification"—they have become "meaningless."[32]

As I said previously, when he wrote *Personal Psychopathology,* Sullivan had not worked out his theory of anxiety. He mentions *anxiety states* as being among the most frequently encountered of the nonadjustive processes. A person experiencing "major anxiety" is said to undergo attacks of intense fear, such as fear of immediate death, in connection with no very evident cause and manifesting such signs and symptoms as tachycardia, tremor, blanching, perspiration with "subjective feelings" of cold, disturbances of the breathing rhythm. Sullivan observes that an anxiety attack is of the nature of a threat but one never attended by a context of meaning in terms of interpersonal relations. "It is an an expression in consciousness mediated by the affected somatic apparatus of incomprehensible danger to the self."[33]

An "even more important" group of occurrences called *anxiety equivalents* are also mentioned, and said to have equally recondite cause, that is, in comparison with major anxiety states, in which the person undergoes a seizure with some one or more of the signs and symptoms that accompany anxiety states. Some people who suffer from certain of the anxiety equivalents (unspecified) may seek and secure extended medical treatment "for alleged morbidity." In contrast, some others undergo mild anxiety equivalents so often that are taken to be personal idiosyncrasies such that they are only to be endured and perhaps outgrown. Excessive perspiration of the hands whenever one is faced with a difficult interpersonal situation is mentioned as a common example.

A number of so-called hysterical conversion symptoms are "in the middle distance" of frank attacks of fear and "physical" illnesses. Examples of conversion reactions are *globus hystericus,* characterized by peculiar choking sensations, transient impediments of speech making one unable to utter a sound, and pains, especially in the region of the heart or "in the head." Sullivan claimed that the delineations of the disablement reactions, of the autonomous manifestation of dissociated systems, and of nonadjustive attacks of fear of an unknown cause are overlapping. They are all aspects of a "nuclear process," namely, *conversion.* "When an autonomous system takes over a major skeletal unit, the individual suffers a symptom which may or may not function as a specific disablement. When some part of the expressive apparatus is affected, we must question whether the more appropriate formula is one of unwitting expressions of a dissociated content, of interference by tensional modifications required to suppress an expressive impulse, or of the complete or partial expression of fear of known or of unknown origin. When some part of the deeper visceral apparatus is affected, we have generally to deal with anxiety, but again may be encountering a hysterical compromise—a specific or general disablement."[34] One must look to the consciousness of the individual concerned for clues to the correct classification of these things. For example, the sufferer of anxiety attacks finds them unalloyedly troublesome since he has not experienced any unpleasantness that they have eliminated. In contrast, the person prone to defense reactions has avoided at least vaguely threatened conflict so he grants them a sort of right to exist.

Another "emotional situation" is grief. "Whenever, in the course of a total situation, a person relevant in it becomes either literally or practically disintegrated, before the resolution of the total situation is complete," there always appears in the subject individual a group of emotional processes called grief. A total situation is left, including powerful tendencies now without "a real object of application." Sullivan surmised that it was an inherent necessity of the organism that grief phenomena be experienced in the course of the dissolution of the subject individual's sentiments for the lost one. During the manifestation of such phenomena, there is normally a reorganization of the subject individual's tendencies. In sum, grief "may be said to apply to a fantastic construct of the lost person, which as it gradually disintegrates releases the tendencies concerned from the preceding configuration [from the preceding interpersonal relationship] and makes them again available for interpersonal adjustment."[35] Grief is concerned not only with the literal death of some one significant to the subject individual, but also with the disintegration of, among other things, certain intimate relationships such as marriage.

But some people "grieve and grieve" over the lost one, and in various ways seem to protect the substitute sentiment of grief from dissolution by enhanced interest in its fantastic object. This is morbid grief, wherein there is an abnormal extension in time of the "disadjustment" brought about by the loss of the loved person. Sometimes morbid grief is made possible because the sympathy bestowed on the bereaved has an "unwonted sweetness"—and thus serves a form of compensation. In other instances it may be seen as a defense against the possible institution of new interpersonal relations.

Excitement appears in persons of a certain type when one has put too great a burden on a sublimatory process. The fantasy directly related to the motivational system to which an underlying complex (sublimatory) resolution involving social approval has unwittingly been attempted is said to make appearance at least in the fringes of consciousness. Then one is faced with the threatening possibility of conflict and anxiety that compel the individual to an almost uninterrupted series of "screen activities." The latter confines consciousness of the disturbing fantasy at a minimum while tending to ward off anxiety. Sullivan asserts that by plunging rapidly through acts and ideas, one, so to speak, prevents the development of situations to the point of consciously activating the negatively evaluated tendencies, and also minimizes anxiety. The social results of such a random occupation, in which anything but the really essential factors are given relevance (as well as the wear and tear on the individual), entail thoroughly unfortunate consequences. The constant flight from consciousness of the underlying threatening tendencies renders any constructive thought impossible. Since his acts constituting the excitement are not informed by any judgment and entail a glaring disregard of consequences, the sufferer becomes a menace to himself and to others. So the fully developed excitement process constitutes one of the major psychoses, requiring custodial care.

Sullivan points out that in some of those who are susceptible to morbid excitement there may be prolonged periods of life characterized by a low-grade excitement labeled *hypomania*. This state may not "progress" if, for example, sexual gratifications are not so complicated that the sexual drive does not contribute an important component to the threat of conflict. In some other instances hypomania is a "prelude" to psychotic excitement. It may be that the hypomanic becomes an extreme social nuisance who engages in unreasonable performances of many kinds, as in the case of the "reformer" type previously mentioned. If he has unwittingly included too powerful a group of tendencies in his "sublimatory substitutes" he may, as Harold Lasswell[36] pointed out, become a "complacent demogogue, appealing in an unprincipled fashion to the lowest prejudices in alleged furtherance of his elevated aims."[37]

The fully *manic* development of excitement is said to be characterized by extraordinary distractability and exaggerated activity, with attention shifting rapidly from object to object, "flight of ideas" and "pressure of behavioral activity." As often as possible the person attends to something new: he seizes upon every available triviality. As quickly as possible he abandons each train of thought that occurs to him by means of outer distraction or inner transition by rhyming, punning, distortions of word syllables, and the like. Every so often he changes his behavior. There is said to be great volubility and a considerable display of emotional signs. "The mood is more or less persistently elevated, the elation continuing in spite of showers of tears at more or less suitable occasions. The attention and response of others is demanded, being literally fought for if otherwise unattainable. At the same time, the integration of any intimacy has to be avoided, and the most frequent manifestation of manic interpersonal relations takes the shape of more or less malicious mischief."[38] In such a phase of excitement, the individual augments his behavior in primary group relations by a fervid activation of the instruments of intercommunication; "the manic individual going into action like a nation at war." His turmoil increases toward fury. Though his observable ideas and acts are individually rather simple and direct, they are hopelessly truncated so that the total pattern of his behavior is lacking in any but accidental meaning except in so far as it suspends activity in any significant interpersonal situation. Even sleep has to be reduced or temporarily abolished.

Excitement frequently gives way to *depression.* Moreover, there is "unhappy excitement," wherein the individual's facial postures indicate sorrowful longing or fear, while he shouts his joy in song.

In depression, there is said to be a preoccupation of consciousness with a small group of grief-provoking ideas that recur again and again. Though the distractibility of excitement is wholly lacking, the same function seems now to be served by a resolute concentration of attention "on a formula," a state of affairs that is as unproductive as was the excited preoccupation with distractions. Both overt activity and inner processes are few and slow. Sullivan claims there seems often to be a marked and facile flow of inhibitory impulses opposed to any intrusion of sentience, alteration of the ideational content, or behavioral acts. The mood is said to be as persistent as that of excitement. "The more massive skeletal movements are especially inhibited. And the physiology seems to be so adjusted that anobolic processes are at a minimum and the emunctory activities greatly handicapped."[39]

In Chapter 1 it was mentioned that there are schizophrenic illnesses whose initial phenomena give the impression of a rather "pure" depression. Sullivan claimed that there are some young patients in whom the gloomy preoccupations for a time mask the serious distortion of thought, "queer" beliefs, and delusions of schizophrenia. It seems desirable to mention these things owing to their possible diagnostic significance. Some young psychiatrists have been known to confuse manic-depressive psychosis and the initial stages of schizophrenia.

Sullivan claimed that depression can often be seen as a sort of false sublimation, also, for destructive tendencies integrated into a sentiment of hatred. The object of the hatred is made to suffer by the persisting depression of the subject individual. Even suicide may serve the function of injuring the hated object since it may leave a permanently painful scar in him.

I shall conclude this chapter with a brief summary of Sullivan's comments on certain differences between maladjustive and nonadjustive processes. The former, despite an excessive "complexity" of most of them that hinder personality growth or at least are not "in the direction" of personality growth, represent activities that, in the given circumstances, contribute to self-esteem and tend to be regarded by the person (by "his self," in Sullivan's language) as good. But the nonadjustive processes are said to be all opposed to interpersonal relations, that is, they are designed to destroy interpersonal relationships and/or actual significant persons, though the sufferer is unconscious of this motivation. Such a motivation is not to be regarded as the manifestation of an inherent destructive instinct but represents grave distortions of personality development and unbearable thwarting and painful failures of effort at interpersonal adjustment.

Until the developmental history of such nonadjustive processes is understood, they tend to be incomprehensible. That is the reason, or at least a major reason, that one must study the course of the person's early life. Although he later modified his views of the dynamics of nonadjustive situations, in *Personal Psychopathology* Sullivan claimed that they pertain to tendencies that are presocial, to processes that lack any of the characteristics of selfhood. These tendencies are said to date from late infancy and early childhood, at a time when self-consciousness is lacking or rudimentary. "Their later manifestation in the form of the non-adjustive states is indicative of their non-incorporation into the self in the stages of childhood and the juvenile era. . . . If they had been incorporated into the self-conscious personality, no matter how severely they might ultimately have been suppressed or how completely dissociated, they would have acquired at least a personal reality, and would have undergone some favorable modification by application in interpersonal relations either in higher level fantasy or constructive thinking, or both."[40]

Notes

1. HARRY STACK SULLIVAN, *Personal Psychopathology,* copyright by William Alanson White Psychiatric Foundation, Washington, D.C. (unpublished), p. 1.

2. *Ibid.,* p. 45 (pagination imperfect).

3. Cf. CHARLES HORTON COOLEY, *Social Organization* (New York: Charles Scribner's Sons, 1909).

4. The reference to religious practices in the text are brief and almost a caricature of religion.

5. Cf. SIDNEY HOOK, *The Quest for Being,* Part One (New York: Dell Publishing Company, 1961).

6. SULLIVAN, *op. cit.,* pp. 20-21.

7. *Ibid.,* p. 50.

8. *Ibid.,* pp. 53-54.

9. *Ibid.,* p. 51.

10. *Ibid.,* p. 52.

11. *Ibid.,* p. 56.

12. *Ibid.,* p. 57.

13. *Ibid.,* p. 58.

14. *Ibid.,* p. 59.

15. *Ibid.*

16. *Ibid.*

17. *Ibid.,* pp. 59-60.

18. *Ibid.,* p. 60.

19. *Ibid.*

20. *Ibid.,* p. 61.

21. *Ibid.,* p. 62.

22. *Ibid.*, p. 63.

23. *Ibid.*, p. 65.

24. JOSEPH RATNER (ed.), *Intelligence in the Modern World* (New York: Modern Library, 1939), pp. 814-816.

25. JOHN DEWEY, *Art as Experience* (New York: Minton, Balch and Company, 1934), pp. 265-266.

26. SULLIVAN, *op. cit.*, p. 67. Cf. JAMES C. COLEMAN, *Abnormal Psychology and Modern Life* (3rd. ed.; Glenview, Illinois: Scott, Foresman and Company, 1964), pp. 214-217.

27. SULLIVAN, *op. cit.*, p. 68.

28. *Ibid.*

29. *Ibid.*, pp. 71-72.

30. See PATRICK MULLAHY (ed.), *The Contributions of Harry Stack Sullivan* (New York: Science House, 1967) chap. 2, and HARRY STACK SULLIVAN, *Clinical Studies in Psychiatry*, ed. HELEN SWICK PERRY, MARY LADD GAWEL, and MARTHA GIBBON, with a Foreword by DEXTER M. BULLARD (New York: W. W. Norton and Company, 1956), chap. 12.

31. SULLIVAN, *op. cit.*, p. 75.

32. *Ibid.*, p. 75.

33. *Ibid.*, p. 74.

34. *Ibid.*, p. 73.

35. *Ibid.*, p. 76.

36. HAROLD LASSWELL, *Psychopathology and Politics* (Chicago, Illinois: University of Chicago Press, 1930).

37. SULLIVAN, *op. cit.*, p. 54.

38. *Ibid.*

39. *Ibid.*, p. 75.

40. *Ibid.*, p. 79.

7/Personality and Interpersonal Relations

In the decade following the writing of *Personal Psychopathology*, Sullivan greatly refined and expanded his theory of interpersonal psychiatry. "Psychiatry: An Introduction to the Study of Interpersonal Relations," which was originally planned as chapter one of a book, shows how he was working out his ideas.[1] Before this time he had already envisioned psychiatry as a study of interpersonal situations, rather akin to social psychology.

At this point I wish to mention that a controversy has arisen as to whether Sullivan's theortical orientation and therapeutic method can legitimately be called psychoanalytic. He himself in the later years of his life did not regard his "views" as psychoanalytic, while he acknowledged his indebtedness to Freud. In a sense, this "controversy" represents a struggle for power and prestige within the psychoanalytic "movement." Anyway, it raises rather nice questions as to what psychoanalysis is, theoretically and therapeutically.[2] It has been suggested that, in regard to subject matter, Freud was dealing (or thought he was) with *intra*psychic processes while Sullivan concerned himself with or studied *inter*psychic or interpersonal phenomena. From an historical point of view, this distinction has merit. Freud held to the notion that, psychologically, the individual may be studied as if he were a self-contained and self-enclosed entity. Witness his "metapsychology," including the idea of mental topography. He thought of the "psyche" as a private domain peopled by numerous and frequently incompatible psychic forces, some of which are not only walled off from one another but from the world outside. These "forces" are thought to be instinctual. Freudian psychology is primarily "self-actional," not interactional or transactional.[3]

Insofar as such notions helped Freud in his researches, they served a purpose. But it is doubtful if they serve any useful purpose now. In any event, from a scientific point of view, the distinction between intrapsychic and interpsychic processes no longer seems useful for reasons that I hope to make clear. Sullivan assimilated the notion of intrapsychic processes into a more inclusive framework that emphasizes community rather than singularity and separateness. For Sullivan we are not islands in a common sea though in an "impersonal" industrial, urban society we may think we are. In fact, feelings of isolation and loneliness serve to emphasize the interpersonal character of human life and human experience.

This does not imply that there is no "psyche" with "laws" of its own. A general psychology text such as Hutt, Isaacson, and Blum's *The Science of Behavior/The Science of Interpersonal Behavior* describes and explains numerous such "laws."[4] Furthermore if there were no psyche, no personality, there could be no interpersonal relations. The problem at issue is one of understanding. As Sullivan used to say, the "material location" of psychological processes is within the organism but they cannot be *understood* as self-contained, isolated, intrapsychic processes. There is simply no way of separating the human organism from its physical and sociocultural context. From the moment of birth, the survival and the physical and psychological development of the infant depend on the interactions or transactions of the organism and its environments. And this development is due just as much to the environmental settings as it is to the organism. Stated in another way, there are both inner and outer determinants of psychological processes, which, so to speak, interact. It would make no sense at all to write of sensation, perception, feeling, and the like apart from the environing world. The two sets of factors, the one inner, the other outer, play an equally important role, forming what Sullivan called the organism-environment complex. They unite or combine to bring about interpersonal relations. Because many of the organism-environment transactions are covert, it is easy to confine oneself to the "intraorganic" side while ignoring the environmental with which they are indissolubly connected. What could seemingly be more subjective than a dream? Yet its connections with the social relations, both past and present, of the dreamer are so intimate that they make no sense at all until they are interpreted in the light of such relations. Thus the psyche is always part of a larger, more comprehensive whole ("integration") and cannot be understood apart from the "total situations" to which it belongs and which it exists.[5]

In the *Conceptions of Modern Psychiatry* Sullivan has clearly stated the problem of explicating his ideas in the familiar, "individualistic language" of traditional psychology.

"When we speak of an impulse to such and such an action," he said, "of tendency to such and such behavior, of striving toward such and such a goal, or use any of these words which sound as if you, a unit, have these things in you [as if they were fixed, self-contained entities] and as if they can be studied by and for themselves, we are talking according to the structure of our language and the habits of common speech, about something which is observably manifested as action in a situation. The situation is not any old thing, it is you and someone else integrated in a particular fashion which can be converted in the alembic of speech into a statement that 'A is striving toward so and so from B.' "[6] This implies that B is a very highly significant element in the situation. But it is the situation that one studies; or rather the action that "indicates" the situation and the character of its integration. Such a situation is never static: The participants are engaging in a transaction extending in time during which "some dynamic component" in each of the people usually is resolved or discharged. And it is resolved in such a fashion that it eventuates in a change that is satisfaction-giving or tributary to security.

Actually, more than one dynamic component in each of the two people may be operating, of which they may not even be conscious. If the additional dynamic components are complementary, or conjunctive they may also become resolved. Otherwise, if they are disjunctive, they will not. This is where the self-dynamism of one or both may intervene to provoke difficulty, conflict, anxiety, and the like.

Except for students of the social sciences, educated people generally have had difficulty in trying to understand what Sullivan was driving at. Indivualistic modes of thought are still pervasive; they are deeply fortified by the structure of the language and a long philosophical and psychological tradition. For Sullivan, the domain of psychiatry includes more, much more, than the study and treatment of the mentally ill. He claims that it seeks to discover and formulate the laws of human personality. But these laws are not to be found "in" the person. This is where the difficulty starts. One must realize that personality is made manifest in interpersonal relations, and not otherwise. And any interpersonal situation is made up of, or involves, two or more people—"all but one of whom may be more or less completely illusory." Illusory or fantastic "people" are symbolic representations of previous experiences with people and/or anticipated experiences. The influence of significant people on us exists and can be very potent when they are remote in time and space, or even dead, people who have been significant in our past experiences with them in regard to certain needs and drives and aspirations. Their influence may be so powerful that it may completely overshadow or negate the behavior of a flesh-and-blood individual with whom we are ostensibly "integrated." This applies not only to the "transference" of psychoanalytic therapeutic situations, but to everyday relationships and affairs, and it is possible primarily because we have minds, which include memory and foresight, not because, as some might say, we have been "conditioned" like dogs or rats.[7] In other words, a good deal of human behavior is, or includes, abstract symbolic behavior—something that is beyond the capacity of any animal. Despite the efforts of some psychologists, one cannot, in theory, assimilate the behavior of a Newton, a Da Vinci, or a Beethoven to that of a chimpanzee or a rat without doing violence to the facts of human life.

The "laws" of personality referred to above pertain to interpersonal relations and can only be discovered in such relations. It is primarily behavior, including verbal reports of "subjective" or "inner" experiences that the psychiatrist "observes" or studies. The student of interpersonal relations has no mysterious faculty of reading the other fellow's mind. So he never "observes" personality, according to Sullivan; he observes behavior. This does not mean that personality is a mere convention or an illusion any more than Newton's Law of Gravitation. Personality, for Sullivan, is a unifying principle that helps to make human behavior intelligible and to enable one in the course of inquiry to relate in a more or less systematic fashion the manifold interconnections and ramifications of subjective experiences, as they are related to him, and of overt behavior.[8] Despite his occasional reference to it as an "hypothetical entity," he did not really believe this, as his detailed discussions imply.

The conception of personality is something about which controversy can go on indefinitely. Gordon Allport has distinguished "fifty representative definitions." In due course, I will indicate as precisely as I can how Sullivan conceived of it. But there is no royal and easy road to the twin goals of communication and technical precision. For most of this journey I must travel the common highways and byways of commonsense language if I am not to travel alone.

In the paper I mentioned above, Sullivan gives an exquisitely detailed illustration of what he meant by saying that personality is made manifest in interpersonal relations. In order to communicate the meaning of this statement, Sullivan discusses a fanciful example of a man who consciously experienced weariness as a veiled ("unconscious") expression of resentment. In this illustration, the experience of weariness followed upon a derogatory remark made by this man's wife a short time previously. In other words, the resentment provoked by the lady may be said to exist outside his conscious awareness. A verbal report by the person of what he had undergone would not state that he felt resentment or hostility. Are we to assume he is lying? No. What justification, then, in such an instance, is there for saying that he is motivated to punish or harm—which is what resentment signifies —though it is denied recognition by him, by his "self"? The answer is that it is by observation of the husband's *continued* behavior toward his wife that one may "demonstrate" such a motivation.

For the purposes of illustration one may assume that this observation is carried on with, among other things, the aid of various instrumental devices. As is the case in psychotherapy generally, and elsewhere, the "observation" or study must be conducted with the help of inference. In this respect psychotherapy is no different in principle from scientific work in various other fields. Freud resorted to an extensive use of inference. The trouble was that his inferential constructions often rested on inadequate assumptions, due in part to the fact that he had relatively little data to work with, especially in the earlier part of his professional life.

In the fanciful example we are discussing, the man in question, when he talks about "I" (as for instance were he to say, "I feel tired") includes in its reference only those motives of which he is conscious. But there is more to the self than is covered by the reference to "I," the latter being what Sullivan later called the personified self. But the self-system that includes the personified self is in turn less inclusive than the "hypothetical" personality. There is more going on "in" the fanciful gentleman under the Sullivanian microscope than is included in, or designated by, the self. There are, for example, dissociated needs and impulses, and these are "included in" the more comprehensive *personality*. But there may also be feelings, needs, and motives that are a part of the self, neither "repressed" nor dissociated, which are selectively inattended. They are not relegated to some fanciful subterranean level of the psyche. One fails to attend to them; so they are not noted and apprehended. They are overlooked.[9]

Suppose one were to claim that the "I," the personified self, is synonymous with his personality.[10] Then, unless one is given to mechanistic interpretations of behavior, he must assume that, in the illustration, Mr. A (as he is named), if he is motivated by resentment will or would in this sort of situation behave in such a fashion as to punish the other person without resort to elaborate self-deception; that he is more or less clearly conscious of an occurrence that provoked the motivation; of the state of being resentful or of wanting to punish his wife; of the punitive activity; of the activity of the other person, that is, of his wife's response to his behavior; and of the satisfactory resolution of the situation when his wife is discomfited. But he is not conscious of any of these things. Evidently there are things going on "in" him of which he is not conscious. In other words, he is not conscious of some aspects of his behavior. One must also note that his behavior would be unintelligible to us without taking his wife's actions into account. And conversely Mrs. A.'s behavior does not make sense except in relation to the "other person." And furthermore, to anticipate somewhat, the previous history of both must be taken into account. Also their relationships to certain others, such as their friends. But I am getting far ahead of my story.

If, say, a close friend with whom he feels at ease were to offer this interpretation to Mr. A, that he is resentful, he might vigorously deny it while insisting vehemently that his wife meant nothing by her remark. Let us assume that the friend persists, skillfully challenging and questioning Mr. A.'s self-deception. It may be that finally, after a series of unsuccessful rationalizations, he reaches a point at which he becomes somewhat conscious of or admits the fact that he was hurt by his wife's remark. Still, in all likelihood, if only because his self-esteem is involved, he will maintain that she meant nothing by it: that was her way since that's how people where she was brought up treated one another. Mrs. A, as she is represented in her husband's awareness, does not manifest hostility toward him. In other words, consciously he "pictures" her as uniformly friendly, at least to him, even though on some occasions this idyllic notion can scarcely be sustained. And this self-deception is intimately related to the part or aspect of his personality that Sullivan calls the self or self-dynamism. In other words, owing to the structure of Mr. A's self, which represents a meaningful organization of his life experiences, he cannot recognize certain aspects of his relationships with Mrs. A.

But much more occurs or may occur in this sort of situation, and in order to indicate this without at this point going into details of psychiatric research, let us assume the following: Suppose one were to observe Mr. A in the focus of a slow-motion camera when his wife made the derogatory remarks.

> He glanced sharply at her and looked away very swiftly. The postural tensions in some parts of his face—if not, indeed, in other of his skeletal muscles—changed suddenly, and then changed again more slowly. . . . Yet farther, let us suppose that, some time prior to the event, we have caused him to drink some "barium milk" and that we are observing the tone of the muscles in his alimentary canal by aid of the fluoroscope at the time that Mrs. A disturbs him. We have noticed that the shadows cast by the barium in the fluid that fills his stomach and small intestines is of a certain character. The insult comes. We observe, from change in the shape and position of the shadow, that the tone of his stomach walls is changing. His pylorus is becoming much more tense, may actually develop a spasm. The lumen or internal diameter of the small intestines is diminishing; their muscular walls are now more tense. . . . One might surmise, from all these data, that the impulses which appeared in Mr. A as he prehended the hostile action of Mrs. A tended first to the ordinary expression of anger by changes of facial expression, and tensing of some of the other skeletal muscles—perhaps clinching a fist. It would seem that the impulses had very quickly been deflected from these objectively detectable expressive postures and movements, and that they had then discharged themselves by increasing the tension in the musculature of the alimentary tract.[11]

Nor is this all. Suppose, in this illustration, one had provided a device for phonographically recording Mr. A's speech and other vocal phenomena. A series of phenomena would appear, perhaps beginning "with an abrupt sub-vocal change in the flow of the breath. There might appear a rudimentary sort of a gasp. A rapid inhalation may be coincident with the shift in postural tension that we observed in the skeletal muscles. There may have been a respiratory pause. When Mr. A speaks, we find that his voice has changed its characteristics considerably, and we may secure, in the record of his first sentence, phonographic evidence of a continuing shift of the vocal apparatus, first towards an 'angry voice' and then to one somewhat expressive of a state of weary resignation."[12]

There is, then, an inhibition of a direct, relatively simple action, such as an angry retort, and one that would be presumably effective because the resentment would have been discharged instead of "swallowed." Instead there occurs a series of processes that may "represent" or constitute an indirect complicated and only obscurely effective discharge of the resentment: Mr. A's "weariness" may interfere with some prospective action or plan of his wife, say, their going to the moving pictures, while he becomes withdrawn and preoccupied with his "weariness." In other words, he is *continuing,* though unwittingly, a complicated and dubiously efficient act of retaliation. Instead of collaborating toward the achievement of a common goal or goals, Mr. A and his wife are working at cross purposes, engaging in self-defeating activities.

There is not only an inhibition of direct action. An "inhibition" of consciousness occurs also such that Mr. A does not know in the usual sense of the word, has no information, of his wife's hostility to him. He is conscious of an illusory or "parataxic," uniformly affectionate Mrs. A. In fact, if challenged on this score, Mr. A would insist he has an ideal wife. However, he is consciously aware that Mrs. A is not uniformly friendly toward others, for example, toward his friend Mr. B, whom she cannot abide.

So one can see that Mr. A's conception of *himself* as his wife's husband is quite unrealistic, is "sadly awry." Equally illusory is his conception of Mrs. A as his wife. In sum, with an illusory Mrs. A (or Mrs. A[1]), a lady who is full of amiability and devotion there goes an illusory Mr. A (or Mr. A[1]), a gentleman who is never slighted or hurt by this paragon of wifely devotion. The interpersonal situation experienced by Mr. A may be said to be parataxic or illusory in the sense that (1) he has an unrealistic conception of himself as husband of Mrs. A, (2) has an unrealistic conception of Mrs. A as his wife and (3) entertains a false idea as to the character of the interactions between him and his wife. The misconceptions that Mr. A has of himself *as husband* and of Mrs. A *as his wife* are instances of what Sullivan called "parataxic me-you patterns." It must not be thought that these me-you patterns are necessarily fixed or static. They may change in the course of time, say, a day or a week or longer. Even in a situation in which there is no change of place or interruption of time, in which, let us say, husband and wife are spending an evening together at home, the me-you patterns of either or both may also change.

It should be noted that we have dealt with the situation from the side of Mr. A. Mrs. A may also entertain one or more illusory me-you patterns concerning herself and her husband. Hers may or may not dovetail or be "congruent" with Mr. A's in the sense that they facilitate an approximate agreement of mutual illusion. For instance, Mr. A's conception of himself as husband of the embodiment of amiability and devotion is congruent with Mrs. A's conception of her role as that of tolerant wife-mother to a "rather incompetent, absurdly conceited, but devoted husband." Yet Mr. A may sustain for a time the same "illusion-pair" or illusory me-you pattern in the face of another and *incongruous* me-you pattern of Mrs. A, to the effect that she is the disillusioned victim of an utterly selfish man who thinks women are inferior creatures. For a time Mr. A, in such circumstances, may think that he is misunderstood and, owing to the structure of his self-dynamism, for reasons that are *not* to his wife's discredit.

Such an incongruous "integration" may however grow to a point at which the husband suspects that there is something wrong with his wife and consults a psychiatrist about her. (Of course the psychiatrist may suspect that there is something wrong with both.)

One must not assume that the existence of illusory me-you patterns of or "in" one or two (or more) people integrated in a situation occurs only to those who are "neurotic" or "psychotic." In Sullivan's view, it is a quite normal, in the sense of a usual or everyday, affair. "The series of me-you patterns," he said, "and their more or less congruous me-you patterns in the awareness of one's intimate are seldom, severally or collectively, of much value as objectively verifiable descriptions of the two personalities concerned."[13] In fact he claimed that "the average person magically stripped of his illusions about his friends and acquaintances would find himself surrounded by strangers."[14]

To return to Mr. A, he will admit that he has a tiff with his wife once in a while, saying that in this respect he and his wife are no different from other couples. After all, people do not agree on everything. Suppose, then, for the sake of illustration, one is invisibly present at one of the family quarrels, possibly about Mr. B. Let us start at the point at which Mrs. A has just complained about the number of evenings she has had to shift for herself recently, because, she says sarcastically, of her husband's devotion to his cronies. This is where Mr. A loses his previously maintained equanimity despite his wife's slightly veiled hostility. "Now abruptly, he takes a deep breath, glares at her, flings down the newspaper, and in a frankly angry voice says that at least he does not have to listen to crackpots discussing art when he is with his friends." (Mrs. A has "accumulated" artist friends.) His wife retaliates in kind, telling her husband not to judge her friends by the fools he spends his evenings with. After this come sundry extravagant abusive statements about each other's apparently all-embracing shortcomings and the imbecility of each other's friends. The climax is reached when Mrs. A shouts that if she ever sees that swine B around anymore she will tell him to his face what he is, and Mr. A what he is also, to go around with Mr. B. Mr. A undergoes an abrupt alteration. His color changes, his loud-voiced anger is replaced by low-voiced rage. He is clearly conscious of a desire to strike, to kill the *illusory* Mrs. A. who is now before him, a woman who is the epitome of malicious persecutions whom the law protects. The things he says now would shock him if he were to recall them later when he is calm. As he leaves the room to get his coat and hat in the hall closet, his wife laughs at him.

There is then an A^1-and-Mrs. A^1 pattern or interpersonal "configuration," which is characterized or represented in perduring Mr. A's consciousness by mutual respect and affection. There is also in his consciousness an A^{11}-and-Mrs. A^{11} configuration, which is characterized by mutual contempt and hostility. In this sort of relationship, investigation might reveal a third, a fourth, a fifth of such illusory me-you patterns in Mr. A's interactions with Mrs. A and in Mrs. A's interactions with Mr. A in an analogous fashion as they go on living together. If an inquiry were carried out therefore with the aim of presenting *Mrs. A's conscious experiences* of herself and her husband, a series of congruous or complementary configurations or illusory me-you patterns would usually appear.

The question may arise as to whether there is any limit to the number of such me-you patterns in a perduring interpersonal situation such as that of Mr. and Mrs. A. There is a limit, and this limit is a function of the self-dynamisms of Mr. and Mrs. A as the two go on living together. The "weaker," the more poorly integrated and immature the self, and in fact, the entire personality, the more susceptible one is, in other words, to anxiety, conflict, doubt, indecision, the more is one likely to be a prey to a plethora of illusory me-you patterns and awkward entanglements. Since so many factors or variables enter into such situations, it is impossible to speak of such relationships and their outcomes with precision. But one may say this much, that they entail harassment, strain, conflict, and frustration that nurture difficulties in living to a point at which they sometimes become almost or entirely unbearable.

Illusory me-you patterns can be clarified by tracing their origins, which usually or at least often go back to early life. They originate in experiences with significant others in the past, especially the mothering one. At times Sullivan writes as if all subsequent experience has some connection, even if remote and attenuated, with the facilitations and deprivations and satisfactions and insecurities experienced in infancy with the mothering one. But this is probably not always true.

In any case the child does not develop a completely new reference-frame in connection with the father. It may be different but it is still "conditioned" in varying degrees by previous experience with the mothering one. Thus when a child begins to encounter others, his experiences do not, as it were, make a fresh start. New experiences may sometimes radically alter but rarely if ever completely obliterate the original reference frame, or perhaps I should say reference frames, since the youngster usually experiences a good (satisfaction-bringing, tender) mother as well as a bad (anxiety-provoking) mother, which in the course of time become "fused" into a more or less realistic "prehension" of the flesh-and-blood individual who takes care of the offspring. Under severe stress, the individual may manifest the original bifurcation.

Parataxic me-you patterns or parataxic distortions result from unresolved difficulties originating chiefly from the past. According to Sullivan, they constitute the "underlying reality" of Freud's notions of *transference* and the *repetition-compulsion*. But they do not constitute mechanical repetitions of the past. As already stated, parataxic me-you patterns also are *not* confined to the psychotherapeutic or psycho-analytic situation. They may and frequently do to a degree operate in almost any sort of relationship. And so it is gravely misleading to equate Sullivan's concept of parataxic distortion with the classical Freudian notions of transference and countertransference. Me-you patterns are fluid, dynamic transactions both in and outside of therapy.

Nor can the content of parataxic me-you patterns be located in or traced back to an unresolved Oedipus complex. Sullivan for one thing did not subscribe to Freud's conception of the Oedipus complex. There is no one nuclear complex, which is universal in scope and biologically ordained, occurring at a given stage of personality development, which in certain instances has to be revealed and resolved in the process of psychotherapy. Instead, according to Sullivan, there is a *career,* a line of development starting from the time one is born and progressing through various significant interpersonal relationships —including of course the vitally significant relationship with the mothering one—in which and with the aid of which personality grows and manifests itself. In certain circumstances this developmental process may be greatly retarded or gravely disrupted. And in such unfortunate outcomes, where subsequently serious "difficulties in living" arise, Sullivan stressed his belief that *anxiety* and its effects must be carefully studied.

He believed that it is "a notorious fact about personality problems that people act *as if* someone else were present when he is not, as the result of interpersonal configurations which are irrelevant to the other person's concern, and do this in a recurrent fashion without any great difference in pattern. . . . A person, for example, may be said, with considerable justification, to act towards his wife as he did towards his mother. Now it is true that there are many differences in detail, but the general patterns of emotional relationship of conscious versus unnoticed motivation, of intended versus experienced acts, are very much those that the person first developed in manifest behavior with his mother."[15] Nevertheless, in the *Conceptions* Sullivan warned against the notion of a mother fixation as a sort of "master symbol" in thinking. He had learned, he said, from every male patient, new depths of meaning in the pattern of the mother-son relationship. An approximate identity of significant features was not discovered.[16] He did not discover, for example, a fixed pattern of mother-son relationships as outlined in Freud's formulation of the Oedipus complex.

The reader will have observed that Sullivan is using the word "un-noticed" where Freud might, in many instances at least, say "uncon-scious." What, then, is the status of "the unconscious" in Sullivan's more matured theories? It is not a mental realm or psychic region; it is an "hypothetical" construct. (Many psychitarists and psychologists believe that the existence of unconscious mental processes is an es-tablished fact. Sullivan himself most of the time took it for granted. In this respect he reminds one of Freud, who once wrote that "in-stincts" are "mythological.") Without the assumption of an "hypo-thetical unconscious," Sullivan claimed, psychological events are or appear to be erratic and unpredictable. It fills all the "gaps," the discontinuities that are present in mental life, and in theory, at least, restores orderly continuity. Now, what are "in" those gaps or discon-tinuities that the conceptual or hypothetical unconscious can account for in plausible fashion? It is said to include (1) much that has been conscious but preverbal or subverbal, (2) a great deal that has never been attended to and therefore may have been or may not have been on the margins of consciousness (selective inattention), and (3) some experience not represented in consciousness, including "a great de-velopment of processes" side-tracked from the self-system in the course of socialization but which appear or manifest variously: as remnants of previous endowment, previous experience, and previous behavior (dissociation).[17]

No matter how verbally articulate one is, it seems safe to say that there are a good many experiences never expressed in words. Some of them, for all I know, may be psychologically continuous with experi-ences in late infancy and childhood before verbal skills appeared or at least were much developed.[18] In addition, regardless of origin, some experiences do not lend themselves to verbal expression. How could one verbalize the rapture one may enjoy listening to a particular symphony or the enchantment of a particular play that one has at-tended? But that does not necessarily mean that they are not a part of the self-system. Subverbal processes, unless they are connected with a certain extremely anxiety-provoking set of experiences, called "not-me processes," usually belong to the self.

In regard to (2), Sullivan has in mind selective inattention, primarily, a process in which one overlooks certain "obvious" things that would be awkward or anxiety-provoking if one perceived them.

In the very nature of the case attention is selective; one ignores things that do not matter to one and in which one has no interest. But there are many times when one ignores things that *do matter*. Because no way has been found of being secure about them, of feeling at ease with them, one excludes them from awareness as long as possible, especially from focal awareness. This is selective inattention, a process not to be confused with what is called concentration, although Sullivan does not always clearly differentiate them.

Experience not represented in consciousness, including that which has been side-tracked in the course of socialization, has been discussed in previous chapters. However, Sullivan's formulation of dissociation requires further elaboration. The difficulty of "explaining" dissociation is enhanced by the fact that over the years he did not always maintain an identical formulation. In the *Conceptions,* dissociation is overemphasized at the expense of selective inattention, which he had not yet worked out.

Now, the question arises as to what carries on such processes as selectively inattending or dissociating so that one does not notice or perceive certain things. The logical answer would seem to be the *person,* though we must not conceive behavior self-actionally. But Sullivan often uses a sort of shorthand formulation, ascribing the processes of selectively inattending and dissociating to the self or self-dynamism. In the *Conceptions,* except for one or two references to it and in subsequent lectures, "repression" has been dropped. Selectively inattended processes belong to, are a part of, the self. They are not nearly as inaccessible to consciousness as dissociated processes, which form a functionally distinct aspect, or subsystem, of personality.

The self-dynamism often employs anxiety as an instrumentality by means of which experiences that are incongruous with its current organization and functional activity tend to be ignored, selectively inattended or, in extreme cases, dissociated. How extensively this instrumentality has to be employed depends on the structure of the self and the person's current life situations. The origins of anxiety can often be traced to infantile experience, a topic that will be explicated in the next chapter. Anxiety is said to be the product of a great many significant people who disapproved of one's behavior, chiefly perhaps owing to their own inadequacies and irrational attitudes. It often gets represented in one's personality by certain symbolical manifestations called "imaginary people" who disapprove. Some of these "abstract personifications" are so tenuous that they may assume the form of ideal statements taken originally perhaps from religion or from ethical philosophy. On the other hand, some "imaginary people" may be "almost phenomenologically evident," that is, they almost seem to be present to the senses.

Anxiety, in a manner of speaking, "shoos us this way and that," diverting us from some thought, feeling, or overt action to a different one more congenial to the self. Therefore it may cut us off either temporarily or permanently from a good deal of experience, including a good deal of initiative. It may also "shoo" one into many actions that wisdom, if one had it, would have warned against. It may prevent one from perceiving many things a knowledge of which would make possible the correction of many shortcomings.

Very frequently anxiety comes finally to operate so suavely and smoothly that very few people have the vaguest idea that a great part of their lives is influenced by it. In such a case, it often manifests itself as selective inattention wherein one just misses, fails to observe, all sorts of things that would cause one embarrassment, things that, many times, it would be very profitable to perceive. "You don't hear, you don't see, you don't feel, you don't observe, you don't think, you don't this, and don't that, all by the very suave manipulation of the contents of consciousness by anxiety."[19] When anxiety does not work smoothly, it becomes a psychiatric problem "because then it hashes our most polite utterances to the prospective boss, and causes us to tremble at the most inopportune times."[20]

The self is the part or aspect of the personality that is "central" in the experience of anxiety; the latter is, in other words, a function or instrumentality of the self. So that when one says anxiety does this or that, or even when one asserts that the self does something or other, it must be understood as a shorthand phrase. Ultimately, the only thing that ever does anything is the person, however much anxiety, sometimes allied with something else, may influence behavior.

And so it comes about that one's consciousness of one's performances and those of others tends to be permanently restricted to a part of all that occurs between him and others. Year after year this limitation may be maintained by one's experiencing anxiety whenever he tends to overstep the "margin" of the self. Sometimes one does not actually experience anxiety, save perhaps momentarily;

instead one feels tired or angry or engages in some activity by which one unwittingly forestalls the experience of anxiety.

Not everything, therefore, that is materially relevant in situations and is not perceived can be said to be dissociated. When Sullivan published the *Conceptions* he made no mention of selective inattention. As he afterward admitted, there is too much emphasis on dissociation to the neglect of selective inattention. Since the latter operates so as to restrict consciousness, it serves, among other things, as a means by which dissociated processes are kept out of conscious awareness.

When a person, owing to unfortunate life experience, has had to *dissociate* a considerable number of powerful and durable motivational systems, he will be markedly vulnerable to mental disorder. Dissociation is not by any means restricted to the "lust dynamism" or to any broadly conceived sensual motivations. Sullivan says that, for example, some of the power processes that the infant and child, perhaps even the juvenile, found effective may come under stern disapproval at a subsequent stage of personality development and have to be dissociated. There are a great many things, such as negative, hostile motivations, or positive, affectionate ones that can be and in some more or less extraordinary circumstances may have to be excluded from the self-system.

Lest I be misunderstood, I wish to state explicitly that impulses, drives, tendencies, motivational systems, are shorthand terms for particular states of the organism conceived as a whole. These states, or at least many of them, have become differentiated, molded, structured, in the process of acculturation, though their origins may be traced to the "instinctive" tendencies and activities of early life, at least in the mature person. They have developed out of, "emerged" from original, primitive conditions, and have acquired new and distinctive qualities. In the case of the mentally ill, such a development remains conspicuously incomplete. Complex "arrests of development" have occurred. Various "symbol systems," explicated in Chapter 2, have remained more or less primitive. To a minor extent, this may be true of even mature people. But this does not preclude the development of new tendency systems, emotions, thoughts, imaginative creations, subsequent to the various developmental stages.

But any state of the organism occurs only in connection with and in relation to the world in which one lives, whether, for instance, one speaks of hunger, thirst, sexual desire, loneliness, or love. It is the person, the individual, nonetheless, who is hungry, thirsty, lonely, or "on the make." One can often define such states behaviorally, in terms of what the person does with and to other actual persons. Sullivan held that they have to be conceived in terms of interpersonal situations, that is, as "integrating tendencies." The unit of study, he insisted, is a person-integrated-with-another-person in a situation, though the latter may sometimes be imaginary. Moreover, some covert processes have only an indirect or remote and recondite relation to the world, which do not appear as imaginery people but as thoughts or complex symbol systems. These may or may not be autistic.

Since behavior is interactional, the other person or persons with whom one is "integrated" also play a causal role in it. For example, the "other person" may say or do something that makes one angry, anxious, glad, or whatever. The behavior of the other person reacts back or "repercusses" on one's own. His mere presence may be enough to alter one's state of mind or to modify overt actions. This works both ways. The other person also reacts to what is done with or to him. There is, in other words, a dynamic interchange or "transaction."

Because of the character of the self-dynamism, and of the entire personality of one or more of the people involved or integrated in a situation, interpersonal relations are sometimes extraordinarily complex. There are many factors or variables that have to be taken into account, both overt and covert. For example, a person may "express" or "discharge" not only a known, witting motivation but also one that is unnoticed or at least not perceived and possibly quite unknown, that is, dissociated. In such a case, besides the interpersonal situation as defined within the consciousness of the person, there is a concomitant interpersonal situation quite different in regard to its principal integrating tendencies of which the person is more or less completely unconscious, whose origins, at least in many instances, can be traced back to an earlier period, giving rise to an indefinite and shifting group of illusions and impressions about the other person, to the illusory me-you patterns explicated in this chapter.

Sullivan has claimed that if it were not for the "parataxic concomitance" of unresolved interpersonal situations of the chronological past that survive in and complicate temporally present interpersonal situations, the study of human relations would be much less recondite than it is. In other words, if it were not for the hostilities, conflicts, anxieties, frustrations, that are provoked in certain kinds of interpersonal situations because of the illusory personifications that each participant has of the other, chiefly owing to their previous life situations, the study of people would be much less difficult. The trained investigator, therefore, must be relatively free from the serious inhibitions of his alertness when he interviews a patient or interviewee. He must also be free of unconscious tendencies that would give rise to parataxic concomitances in his study of the other person. Needless to say, he must be able to detect the illusory personifications or parataxic distortions of his patient.

Every person is to some degree different from every other owing to a variety of conditions both innate and acquired. He has a unique and relatively durable constellation of traits or characteristics that constitute his personality. In order to understand another person, one must be alert to the specific differences, whether great or small, that mark him off from everyone else. To think that one can apprehend the personal traits of another as easily as a teen-age boy can distinguish a Corvette from a Cadillac is terribly naïve. Unfortunately, the less secure one is, the more lacking in self-esteem he is, the greater is the comfort he derives from a facile classifying of other people—which may amount to a pattern of projections of one's presumptively static traits, and their verbal opposites.[21] Even so, one should never forget Sullivan's famous dictum that, despite all our differences, we are all much more simply human than otherwise.

The previous statements have to be qualified by further considerations such as the following:

> The traits with which one believes one's self characterized are often amazingly fluid, if one's serious statements are to be taken as evidence. Discussing one's self with one person, one reports one perhaps only moderately consistent set. In an equally serious discussion with a different auditor the account is different. Some people are consistent in referring to certain outstanding traits about which a consensus could be obtained; some are consistent only in the breach—the traits that they generally claim are those which come near being merely ideal; the statements express wishful rather than factual data. Some know that their accounts vary with different auditors and can even rationalize noted differences —usually on the basis of the attitude of the auditor and one's wanting to make as good an impression as possible. The traits

with which we endow others are also of varying certainty and sometimes subject to radical change under pressure of divergent opinion. The shift may not appear in the course of the particular controversy but may become evident in subsequent discussions. About all that seems perfectly certain about personal traits as subjects of opinion is that the having of such opinions seems important.[22]

The interpretation of behavior is said to be generally regarded as of a higher probability of correctness than is the analysis of conversation about one's own self. "It is easier to say the right thing than to keep on doing the right thing." Yet this should not be taken too seriously. Some people can consistently maintain a role that they believe is incongruous to them because it is demanded by the other person. However, the role may be a clearly noticed instance of something that has been occurring from very early years. Thus a professor may claim his scholarly research to be too valuable to be interrupted by the petty routines of administrative work. Yet when the Dean offers him the position of chairman of the Department he accepts and maintains the role without any apparent conflict of interest or unhappiness for a period of several years.

All these things—everything described or explicated in this chapter —can be understood only by a study of the individual's personality structure and functional activities in relation to the personality structures and functional activities of other individuals with whom he has been significantly involved in situations. Some of these situations may have been very "simple" in the sense that there was an unhindered, direct fulfillment of mutual or complementary needs. Other situations that the individual "integrated" with one or several persons over the years may have been very "complicated" wherein the fulfillment of mutual or complimentary needs did not occur or occurred only with considerable effort, anxiety, conflict, or whatever.

Interpersonal relationships that are or become "complicated"— and these are the sorts of relationships with which psychiatrists, in the main, have to deal—can be further clarified by a summary of certain emotions that frequently are destructive of satisfaction or intimacy in a person's dealings with his fellows. These emotions or feelings include anxiety, fear, anger, rage, hatred, guilt, pride, envy, and jealousy.

For the first time, in this chapter, much attention has been paid to *anxiety*. Only late in his career did Sullivan realize its full etiological significance and arrive at a thorough understanding of it, though he seems always to have had an intuitive familiarity with its manifestations in his patients. Anxiety is closely related to self-esteem. In fact, the two are more or less inversely related, at least after the infantile stage of life. In other words, to suffer anxiety is to experience loss of self-esteem. In a given situation it tends to be provoked by the disapproval of someone who is significant to one, whether positively or negatively, or by one's own self, owing to the values and ideals one has learned or developed. The "roots" of anxiety go back to infancy, but a discussion of that will be postponed to the next chapter. Sullivan eventually came to the conclusion that it is a central explanatory conception for the understanding of mental disorder. In fact, he theorized that the self comes into being in order to evade or minimize anxiety—seemingly an extreme or at least overgeneralized view.

It is impossible to enumerate all the things that are "caused" by anxiety. First and foremost, it inhibits awareness; that is to say, it restricts it. One becomes less alert to various relevant factors in an interpersonal situation. Therefore anxiety interferes with the refinement and precision of action related to the resolution of situations. Loss or lowering of self-esteem is more or less synonymous with loss or lowering of self-confidence and therefore a serious obstacle to the exercise of various abilities. Intense anxiety, if prolonged, may lead to a gradual demoralization of the individual. For reasons that will be made clear in the following chapter, it is frequently a woeful barrier to intimacy. It may cause temporary sexual impotence or frigidity. Intense anxiety may make one nauseous, or temporarily deaden one's appetite. According to Sullivan, it is "central in understanding the ever more widespread vicissitude of peptic—and, probably, duodenal —ulcer, and the symptom picture related to it as well as I know not what others of the so-called psychosomatic disorders."[23]

When an individual has been considerably exposed to and influenced by anxiety from significant others, his ability to learn and understand many phases of living will be greatly reduced. Thus his ability to profit from experience will be lessened. As I have written elsewhere, anything, such as the use of a word or a thought, having a particular feeling, or an overt act, when it becomes heavily invested with anxiety is then automatically inhibited or distorted or somehow made "complex" by the intervention of the self. When the other person in a situation provokes anxiety in oneself, one's "personification" of that other individual tends to change rapidly and very likely in a negative or hostile direction. Otherwise, as Sullivan has observed, if this more or less automatic function did not occur there would be much less mental illness in the Western world. Learning to live happier, healthier, more productive ways of life would, for many, be far less difficult.

While anxiety directly or indirectly always pertains to interpersonal relations, fear may also, at times, or it may not. Sometimes, both fear and anxiety occur together. In general, fear is a very different affair. Fear is often aroused by "too great novelty," which cannot be exactly specified, in an external situation, while anxiety is often a warning signal that there is danger from within; that is, a warning signal not to do something that would cause one's interpersonal security to sink suddenly as a result of the actions or attitudes of significant people or as a result of provoking in one's self significant ideas that are incongruous with the current organization of the self. Fear is also aroused by threats to the biological integrity of the organism, by something in a situation that is dangerous, or by something that will cause pain or severe discomfort.

In contrast to anxiety, fear causes increasing alertness. There is intense concentration on the fear-provoking situation and on the means of escaping it. In contrast to anxiety, also, fear entails an increase in the supply of available energy for muscular action.

Sullivan also distinguished what he called "abnormal fears"—which are *not* anxiety equivalents. In some people the self is so organized that situations that are essentially harmless make them fearful. The self-system somehow interferes with the recognition of an essentially harmless situation. The person is never able to get acquainted with it so that when it recurs it retains an ominous novelty. This is quite different from the sort of situation that is genuinely novel: one's first day in school, one's first trip in a jet plane, one's first ride on a motorcycle, one's first "date," one's first public lecture, or one's first marriage. In the case of the recurring situation that remains ominously novel and strange, Sullivan surmised that it usually pertains to some past interpersonal experience in which the individual's security was concerned and in which there was a "coloring" of anxiety. But he does not specify any. Perhaps Sullivan's own fear of taking a horse over a jump is a good illustration. When he was young, he enjoyed horseback riding but he and his horse for a time could not get over a wall or a hedge together.

Both fear and anxiety may become so extreme as to amount to terror. Sullivan thought that the psychiatrist should be extremely alert to this distinction. When the latter encounters a person in a state of terror, he should determine whether the terror is a result of, or an extreme form of, anxiety, or whether the patient is "terribly afraid" of something that is objectively real and actually threatening. If the frightening situation has objective reality, the more the psychiatrist can introduce clarity into the formulation of what it is that is fear-provoking, the more apt the person is to improve. There is said to be then a diminution of the relatively blind tendencies that accompany extreme terror. The terror born of anxiety—which may verge on panic—cannot be dealt with in the same way. Let me assure you, Sullivan asserted, "that a careful discrimination between what could easily appear to be actually threatening and what is more purely projection on the part of the patient is often absolutely necessary in order to calm a terrified psychotic patient. As long as you do not discriminate, then what you have to say means nothing to him."[24] The reason is this: When one is able to perceive the true state of affairs, he becomes less frightened or ceases to feel fear. The psychiatrist should encourage the patient to observe the fear-provoking situation more carefully and to consider alternative hypotheses about the character of the "personal environment" that seems so threatening. If the patient can do this he may be able to discover that the situation is essentially harmless and merely novel. On the other hand, the psychiatrist cannot explain anxiety or terror born of anxiety away. The patient's self system is very seriously threatened with failure. He is terrified over what he feels impelled to do to others or over what (he believes) others are impelled to do to him because he is "projecting part of his conflict of motivation"; and because he so misinterprets "certain movements" (unspecified) that they are in his eyes threatening physical violence. If the psychiatrist attempts to talk away anxiety when the self is threatened in this fashion, he is "encumbering the field with meaningless jargon" and destroying what little contact he may have had with his patient.

Anger is part of the "biological equipment." Sullivan surmised that its purpose is to enable us to destroy threatening and injurious objects or situations or to drive away the threatening objects and be rid of the obnoxious situations. But the anger Sullivan believed to be most psychiatrically significant is "caused" by anxiety. When one begins to feel anxious, he minimizes it, so to speak, by getting irritable, bad-tempered, or angry so that the person provoking the anxiety is stymied, intimidated, or goes away. This way of "handling" anxiety is said to have been learned at the time of the young child's empathic linkage with significant adults before there are any particularly analytic thought processes. Sullivan speculated that this comes about as follows. A significant adult makes the young child anxious by mistake; that is, the adult is wrong. Then the child almost invariably feels abused and angry. So he starts to look for whatever it is that affected him in this fashion in the surrounding world; and he discovers anger is one of the things in his environment that has always been conducive of intense anxiety in himself. "In this way the child learns [from human example] the given pattern of being angry, the social expressions of anger, in the mild degree that parents show it toward people in late infancy. Thus anger takes on the beginnings of social conditioning."[25] At the same time he discovers that it spares him anxiety. The child is said to need only a very little random experimenting with this new discovery to find that if he gets angry he does not suffer much anxiety. Thus various degrees of anger may be employed to ward off anxiety, except when one is involved with people that it would be dangerous or unwise to become angry with.

Rage is frustrated anger. Perhaps often the earliest appearance of the dynamism of rage is the tantrums of children. "The central core of the definition of rage," according to Sullivan, "is that it is a symbolic discharge of a high degree of anger, when the direct purpose of anger—that is, the destruction or driving away of the endangering thing—cannot be accomplished."[26] A great deal of energy is discharged in random activity. The great significance of rage for psychiatrists pertains to its relation to hatred, a very important, complex integrating tendency.

Before these matters can be clarified, one must reiterate the following. A person gradually gets to dislike people who can provoke the minor degrees of anxiety in oneself that one promptly meets and evades by getting annoyed or angry. A tendency to develop cooperation in some situation with another person would certainly be undermined by such experiences. In short, anything approaching recurrent insecurity with a cooperating person would tend to discourage the

maintenance of the situation wherein the other person tends to provoke anxiety. The bad temper or anger that appears recurrently as a
disguise or escape from anxiety amply serves its purpose: one merely
moves out of further contact with the cooperating person simply by
employing some stratagem of avoidance, which includes repelling the
other fellow. In this fashion the original biological function of anger
—the preparation to drive away or destroy the troublesome person or
object—need not be employed. But the situations that evoke rage
cannot be dealt with by repelling the other person, since rage cannot
accomplish the obliteration or avoidance of the object by destruction
or driving away of the other person in the situation. Sullivan claims
that rage has to be sidetracked into a relatively symbolic discharge.
He says it must be sidetracked because the person who calls out the
rage is either of such extreme significance or of such power that it
would be extremely risky to attack and very harmful.

Sullivan asserts that recurrences of that type of situation are almost
bizarrely different from recurrences of the situations that evoke minor insecurities, irritations, and anger. In the former case (instead of
effecting the gradual withdrawal of the person who provoked the
anger or irritation, or avoiding him) he often if not invariably integrates a situation with another person that is rather "firm," rather
fixed, and perhaps long-lasting. In this situation one finds two people
who are bound to each other by the bonds of *hatred* and whose main
interpersonal activity may best be characterized as mutually destructive. These integrations of hatred are said to be almost the parting of
the way (or perhaps the point of no return to normal living) for an
obsessionally rational person. Though he cannot make any sense out
of his need for becoming involved in such a relationship, he continues
in it. Since he apparently cannot procure anything except frustrated
anger from this relationship, the other person becomes anathema to
him. Yet even though this is what he consciously thinks, the other
person becomes strangely necessary to his living. Generally the situation proceeds "in the direction of deterioration"; things go from bad
to worse—unless the paranoid dynamism becomes activated.

How, then, is one to make sense out of these situations of hatred?
Thus, Sullivan asserts that when one studies one of these hateful
integrations, one finds that the only thing that both parties have any
real enthusiasm for is damage to the prestige of the other. The hateful
person thinks he has accomplished something satisfactory only when

he can hurt the other person's feelings, only when he has made him feel small and humiliated. According to Sullivan, the explanation must have a great deal to do with the self, though this durable, destructive integration of hate is not in the service of satisfactions or genuine security. The person is conscious of a certain motivation, though he cannot accept it as proper, right, and rational. He cannot sublimate it since there is no socially approved outlet. It cannot be dealt with by "the relatively easy magic of the obsessional neuroses." It has not caused a schizophrenic dissociation. Nor can it be dissociated in any nonschizophrenic fashion. For example, one cannot fall back on the hysterical type of dissociation. Such a tendency, namely rage, and/or hatred, is part of the self—"unavailingly and eternally part of the self," because it has been closely allied to the experiences in which the self was "born."

Sullivan surmised that this sort of person had as a child experienced so much of this motivation in his relationships with early significant adults that it became a part of his self. In other words, "this emotion of rage was a relatively frequent part of the interpersonal processes that bore on the child."[27] Just how rage manifested itself in the early relationships with significant adults is not made clear in *Clinical Studies in Psychiatry*. But in other lectures it is. In punishment situations in which pain is to be inflicted there is said to be invariably an element of restraint of freedom of movement. And physical restraint in the very young tends to produce rage behavior when certain types of physical restraint that produced terror were imposed. In punishment situations, the significant adult deliberately attempts to interfere with the child's efforts to escape the physically enforced pain. Sullivan thought that in any very young child who had escaped disastrous experience up to then, the punishment situation tends to arouse so much fear that rage behavior is provoked.

> But rage behavior doesn't have any particular value in this situation. And so, since the possibility of analysis and discrimination, and the exercise of foresight are already fairly well under way by now, instead of rage itself occurring as a frequent eventuality, what might be described as a version of its felt component— namely anger—comes to be quite important. Especially in circumstances in which children are punished by an angry parent—but in all cases sooner or later, if only from improving discrimination of the progression of forbidding gestures in the authority-invested

adults—everyone learns the peculiar utility of anger. . . . But when one is around the age of thirty months, it may or may not be that one is well trained in the use of anger with the authority-carrying adults; in the more unhappy parental situations, one does not get very much encouragement that way, in partial result of which it comes about that in certain unhappy homes, children well into the school years have tantrums, which are in essence unmodified rage behavior.[28]

In this manner, rage becomes a powerful dynamism of the self well within consciousness at the early stages of personality development. In subsequent eras, the weight of social censorship and disapproval become "so borne in on" rage behavior that additional elaborations of the self-system are evolved in order to get rid of this source of insecurity. Since these elaborations of the self-dynamism are part of the "machinery of getting security," rage and the much more elaborated motivational system of hatred cannot be dissociated. One does not, and cannot, unless one becomes schizophrenic, dissociate "machinery" designed to foster or protect security. Nevertheless, one strongly disapproves of this unfortunate rage dynamism, which is a misfunction of the self because it causes insecurity. And so one inhibits it as best he can.[29]

One of the "neatest" ways of disposing of something in one's self that one strongly disapproves of but cannot eradicate is by the development of specious ideals. This elaboration is almost like a second self; it operates in many ways like a duplicate self-system though it operates in a very restricted area of life. The person who has developed these specious ideals becomes very sensitive to, and extraordinarily critical of, the behavior patterns in others that one is constantly fearful of revealing in one's own behavior. In other words, one's rage quite frequently becomes "converted" into an extreme sensitivity toward and intolerance of rage performances by others. (Many "ideals" are said to follow more or less the same pattern.) When such a person encounters marked anger in others he adopts a disapproving and forbidding attitude toward such behavior so that he "carries away" a derogatory appraisal of them. By means of this stratagem he avoids a great many situations that might otherwise lead him into rage. At the same time he feels superior to such unworthy individuals. Having detected the danger of situations in which he might feel angered or enraged he has warned himself away and thus feels more secure.

This secondary elaboration in the self interferes with any progressive development of a constructive integration with another person. An individual who is secure and fairly well integrated senses difficulty, trouble, and awkwardness in a relationship with such an unduly complex person, and is fended off. Now, suppose an "unfortunate" in whom the rage dynamism is an outstanding feature meets another individual who is very like himself with respect to the secondary elaboration concerning anger but who in other respects has a "peculiar suitability" for intimacy. Here we can see a really "complicated" interpersonal situation. The suavity with which the "overcomplexity" of the secondary dynamism (secondary elaboration) works has a doubly thwarting effect. First, it enables the unduly complex person to "approach" intimacy because it thwarts the usual stratagems for avoiding it. That is, both individuals are "so disapproving and so sensitive to the possibility of anger that that trait in both of them tends to ward off the performance that they would ordinarily derogate in another person."[30] Since the familiar barriers have been circumvented, the road to intimacy is open. But there are too many roadblocks ahead. As the constructive integrative tendencies act to bring the two people together toward collaborative effort, events occur that tend to provoke anger. Of themselves, in almost any situation approaching intimacy, such events are likely to occur on occasion. As Sullivan says, the development of intimacy "is not entirely without its cares, its experimentation, its rebuffs, and one thing and another." But more normal people tend to accept these difficulties as part of life. They will be able to surmount many obstacles in their path, some of which they will probably have anticipated. So they do not become unhorsed at the first jump. But the unfortunates under discussion have neither the resources nor the experience to be able to surmount the ordinary barriers and difficulties that the elaboration of intimacy in American society often entails. As "intimacy thickens, injury—in the sense of that which calls out anger and particularly rage—also thickens." Sadly, sadly, now that one is really feeling close to another person perhaps for nearly the first time in his life, the other one (so one may rationalize) manifests an incomprehensible and perverse tendency toward rage over one's most innocent words or well-meaning acts. As Sullivan says, that works both ways. The outcome is a "horrible miscarriage of human intimacy." Nor is this all. Along with the poignant failure at intimacy, there rapidly comes about "an almost omnipotent struggle" between the two as to who will hurt the other fellow worst. Now the doubly thwarting consequences of the overcomplexity are complete. The hopes for and efforts at achieving human intimacy have amounted to little except sorrowful misery. The never adequate defenses against raged have failed.

Nevertheless, our story of such unfortunates is by no means complete. Underlying their rage and their rage defenses possibilities for two such people to collaborate together in real intimacy still exist— in the rest of the personality. "Thus in the rest of the personality," Sullivan held, "one finds great longings for warmth and lust and love and all sorts of things that are gruesomely truncated and grimly caricatured in the waking intimacy."[31] Processes can be observed by which the person strives to diminish or assuage the constructive tendencies that are unsatisfied in the waking hateful lives of the two people as they go on living from day to day. The impulses that would make for simple collaboration are said to exist in what has traditionally been called the unconscious, manifesting themselves in unwitting, unnoted behavior, such as automatisms or other dissociated behavior. Sullivan taught that in this behavior the person sometimes seems to come very close to manifesting a deep love for the other person, who is always being tortured and who is in turn torturing the partner. Any impulses tending toward love must otherwise be dealt with in sleep. The dreams of hateful people include symbolic operations that serve to release the tension of positive, constructive drives. However, the stresses of this way of life may become too great. One may simplify matters enormously by including certain primitive operations (parataxic thought and perceptual processes) in his appraisal of reality so that he becomes paranoid.[32]

Grief is said to be the way by which we detach our integrating tendencies from a lost significant person. It is a series of psychological processes by which the fantastic consequences (illusory personifications, idealizing memories) to serious emotional loss is erased so that the integrating tendencies that had been involved in the relationship now forever ended are gradually released for a new attachment. Otherwise, the ability to live would be seriously impaired. Anyone who has not reached the level of preadolescence does not truly grieve because the ties between developing personalities who have not reached preadolescence are transitory in regard to the ability for closeness. However, this does not preclude a sense of loss or of loneliness in a juvenile.

It is no secret that human beings are extremely vulnerable to the evil consequences stemming from the accidents of nature, such as illness and death, which destroy people we love or who are in some other way valuable to us. It is also no secret that human beings are peculiarly susceptible to the consequences of other people's stupidity or of their evil behavior. The satisfactions and security we need are dependent, directly or indirectly, on others. So, in addition to the dangers and catastrophes to which nature exposes us, the culture is in so many ways irrational that any attachment to any other person exposes us to another set of dangers: that in some way our incompetence, or our diffidence or the malice of someone who is comparatively irrelevant to our lives or some act of a faithless friend or relative may also destroy the "real effectiveness" of a relationship that has become very important or even vital to us.

Sullivan claimed that when we are deprived of a valuable relationship by accident or design we are in great danger of translating a more or less real intimacy into a wholly fantastic intimacy. People learn only slowly to separate their idealizing expectancies about persons to whom they are close from what is justifiable expectancy. It is extremely difficult for a great many people to discover the consensually valid character of a person who is strongly liked or strongly disliked. "Thus you can realize," Sullivan asserted, "how shockingly probable it is that even two or three years of intimate life as husband and wife may leave relatively untouched a large body of illusion in each person as to the character of the mate. Very real and objectively demonstrable interaction has been unable to brush aside this great body of illusion about the other person. . . ."[33] So it is not difficult to understand that there is a danger when a valued person dies that the loss will deliver the other person over to a life with a fantastic illusion of the person who is gone forever. The surviving person builds the preexisting illusion further. Normally, grief gradually eases these attachments, which are a menace because they tend to leave us transfixed in an illusory life, a sort of fantastic existence.

Only a gifted writer like James Agee in *A Death in the Family* can describe the shock and grief that the survivor may experience when a loved one dies. In Sullivan's formula it can be stated: "He is lost; this is horrible; he is lost." Yet this almost "obsessional repetition" of the expression of grief gradually neutralizes the tendency to continue the preexisting pursuit of satisfaction and security with the now purely fantastic object. It emphasizes the fact the loved one is forever lost, however hideously painful this realization is at first. Moreover, there is a conscious diminishing preoccupation with the references or associations that events have to the lost one—though some people grieve so profoundly that they border on despair, consciously cannot accept the loss for a long while, and will at times call out to "him" who is supposedly in the next room. "The first day after the loss," Sullivan says, "since intimacies interpenetrate so much of life, it is almost impossible not to be reminded of the loss by any little thing—even the position of the saltcellar on the table for instance. But each time this happens, you might say, the power of the particular association to evoke the illusion of the absent one is lessened." The very clarification of the link with the lost one gradually lessens the object's power to be reminiscent. In this fashion one tie after another is gradually loosened and finally broken. Eventually little or nothing is left of the once familiar associations save perhaps an occasional poignant memory when, say, a childhood acquaintance of the lost person is encountered or some story is reread or some aria is reheard that was cherished by the person one had loved and lost. As the months or the years go by, bringing unavoidable changes, the old ways, the old habits of life, the once intimate sharing of life's activities, are irretrievably transformed or forgotten. The experiences connected with grief processes are, of course, extremely painful, but the pain also diminishes day by day or week by week.

Moreover, Sullivan claims that aspects of the individual's personality now appear that it would have been rather hard to find any understandable evidence of during the real relationship with the other person when he was alive. It is said to be extremely difficult in this culture to find a companion so perfect that all of one's personality is "expanded" and more easily fulfilled through collaboration with him. Even among very happily married couples there are certain needs that are not met by one of the partners, and there are things he at least occasionally does that are not conducive to the security of the other one. During the period of grieving itself there is a fairly evident new development and assimilation of aspects of the personality that have been selectively inattended, sublimated, substituted for, or dissociated. New interests are discovered. Thus, during the period of grieving, the rest of the personality not involved in this dynamism is, in a manner of speaking, renewing its youth and looking with new hope at possibilities for the future. Previously unsatisfied needs are therefore giving the grieving process a helping hand. Even early in the period of grieving, despite the desolation one experiences, sleep "can be magnificent and untroubled" so that one's energy is renewed for new grieving, which, however, gets to be less and less as time passes.

There is also a dynamism called *morbid grieving*. In such a case, grief "becomes an adequate [acceptable] mode of life." In some fashion the security of the person is said to be involved in the maintenance of a position of loss. Besides whatever satisfaction and security the relationship had contributed in a normal manner, it had also contributed "mightily" to some morbid, neurotic way of life. So the "erasing function" of normal grieving cannot be carried out for it would entail the abandonment of the complex pattern of life that the live couple had sustained and expose the survivor to a more grievous insecurity. Instead of abandoning the associational links described above, one becomes obsessively preoccupied with them. "We find that, instead of progressively losing its power to evoke tragic recollections, the salt-cellar is now surrounded by a very elegant doily, or is in some other fashion enhanced and made a symbol, extravagantly fortified in its power to evoke the lost one."[34] Certain statements are "rattled off" over and over to the effect: "I cannot live without John. John is with me, in spirit if not in fact." But, in fact, a close study of the relationship with John would reveal that it was interpersonally "criminal." By this Sullivan means that the relationship was always much more important in a never-formulated way than it was in the ostensibly formulated [conscious] way, and that to lose this love object means that the person would stand convicted of something tawdry. Tawdry unhappy performances may range from marriages of convenience to facilitations of death. (The novels of John O'Hara contain many accounts of such tawdry relationships.) So the self-system is utilizing this morbid dynamism of grief in order to cover up the true state of affairs and maintain a relative security. But the ordinary processes of grief cannot be utilized as an effective and constructive dynamism for the furtherance of life.

A purely fantastic relationship with a dead person cannot be an adequate substitute for the really substantial relationship that existed when he was alive. The morbid use of grief serves as a barrier to any possibility of a new and actual interpersonal relationship. Hence the needs once satisfied are now being thwarted, and they cannot be eradicated by magic. So conflict outside the area of the self, in the rest of the personality, arises. Sleep becomes disturbed. The person has recourse to "operations" in dreams in an attempt to still the unsatisfied, clamorous impulses once fulfilled in an actual relationship with the person who is now dead. The actual sharing of thoughts, observations, feelings, recreations, is no more. Instead, the person is trapped in a forlorn and lost "entanglement" with the once existing person. The fantastic continuation of that person is said to be resolutely used as a barrier to life, to change, to further progression on the path of life's experiences, to new interpersonal relationships. As Sullivan taught, over and over, isolation from actual interpersonal relations is most disastrous to the human personality, resulting in human deterioration. That tends to be the fate of the person who persists in morbid grief. Regression begins to set in; that is, the elaboration of needs for satisfaction and of behavior for the securing of those satisfactions and the security obtained in healthy relationships begins to disintegrate, becoming of an earlier type. Social sanctions are said to begin to lose their power to refine behavior and simply disappear. The range and depth of interest in others shrink. One of two things now may happen. The person may "cross the line" into the very dangerous condition of depression. Or one may become an "unhappy wreckage" of life by the slow deterioration process brought on by the fantastic life with the lost "love object."

Guilt is the experience ensuing upon some violation of one's moral code or "ideal system." In such a case the person is justifiably and properly shaky at having "fallen down on his own standards of life." In other words, guilt is "a drop in euphoria" because one has not lived up to his most important convictions of what he is good for and how he should live. According to Sullivan, guilt is "a function of behavior in central awareness; that is, it occurs in circumstances in which people know just what they are doing or at least know what they have done an instant after having done it—and it is the only form of anxiety, I suppose, that most people ever experience in which there is such clarity."[35] This notion of guilt seems to imply the existence of an "ideal system" that is different from Freud's superego because Freud held that the superego, in part, functions unconsciously.

When a person is properly shaky at having violated his moral code, there is no great therapeutic problem. The psychiatrist has to find out what the circumstances were under which the violation occurred. A person with a strong ideal system does not ordinarily let things that violate it happen. What was it that permitted the unusual to happen? The psychiatrist expects to find this "something" to be outside the purview of the self and to be by no means easily accessible to consciousness. Its ultimate elucidation will probably entail great anxiety. Something in the personality—probably some dissociated tendency—conflicts with the most valued ideals in the self-system. Hence it represents a great threat to security unless and until it becomes elucidated. This is so because one is "trained," educated, fairly early in life to feel insecure when he fails himself just as he is trained to feel insecure when he antagonizes, distresses, or disturbs significant others, such as parents and teachers.

There is also what Sullivan calls "crazy guilt" or spurious guilt. Crazy guilt is a rationalization of anxiety, pure and simple, by means of which the person escapes any clear awareness of his anxiety. Sullivan claims that one may "rattle off" a great deal about his feelings of guilt when it is quite clear from any calm, objective study of his behavior that he is controlled by no elaborate and obviously highly valued ideal in the area in which he allegedly feels guilty. But he does something that will, say, violate the rights of another person and is made mildly insecure. One might say that he suffers a mild feeling of pseudoguilt that functions as a rationalization. This is somewhat analogous to the behavior of the pseudoreligious person who does something wrong according to the tenets of the religion to which he pays lip service, and then sorrowfully asserts he has committed a sin. The "joker" in this kind of situation, as Sullivan might say, is that he continues to lie, or steal, or whatever. But since he has rattled off a few verbal formulae, which he calls prayers, to "atone" for his sin, combined perhaps with some pseudoexplanation as to why he does these things, he feels he can continue to cultivate the sport of lying about his neighbors or engage in a bit of shoplifting for the sake of the children. The person who professes crazy guilt gets "all wound up with a flock of moving thoughts about guilt feeling," thus avoiding the anxiety and the additional insecurity of perplexity as to why he feels anxious. But he never consciously experiences much, if any, genuine anxiety and cannot imagine what the psychiatrist is talking about if he mentions it. The person may gradually decide that he "must have felt a little guilty" about something or other. But for therapeutic purposes, the overcomplication must be "traversed" and gotten rid of. This is usually accomplished by an appeal to other similar occurrences by which the person has violated some alleged principle with utter impunity and lack of anxiety. In this fashion the rationalization is disintegrated and the possibility of discovering the actual cause of the underlying anxiety is accomplished.

Sleep is not particularly disturbed in the case of crazy guilt. Should it happen that sleep does become disturbed, it is because of what is being covered up. The "symbolic operations recalled as dreams" do not reveal anything related to the alleged guilt but they do reveal (to the skilled psychiatrist) the events connected with the underlying insecurity. On the other hand, in the case of the person who suffers real guilt there is said to be a very great disturbance of sleep, because the violation of ideals means that there are powerful impulses that are not represented in conscious awareness. As Freud discovered long ago, sleep may provide an outlet for unfulfilled drives. So it is possible, sometimes, that the pressure toward satisfying the unconscious impulses can be toned down in sleep by the person who violates his sincerely held moral code.

I come next to the dynamism of *pride*. Some people regard pride as a sin; others, as a virtue; and still others, as unadulterated conceit. Very probably the three groups are not referring to the same thing. In any event, Sullivan conceives pride in a specific psychiatric sense: that it is the presenting aspect of an elaborate self-deception. When the organization of the self is unable to meet some of the recurrent requirements for security, one may employ various security operations or defense mechanisms, and/or resort to very extensive stratagems in an attempt to ward off anxiety and at the same time conceal some inadequacy. Pride is the façade—the stratagem—that excludes from awareness some inadequacy in the self. Therefore, in Sullivan's conception, the person is *always* proud of something that is not so. For example, one may be proud of his lack of competitiveness or of his love of people. In actual fact the person may be intensely competitive but he does not know it. Or an individual's professed love of people may be entirely spurious though he may often manifest a seemingly great "preoccupation" with the ills of humanity, and may even write books about them. So pride may be said to be a dynamism that is based on a fictitious self-appraisal, which was unwittingly developed to conceal something that is not adequate in the organization of the self.

One might ask, how can they get away with it—this elaborate self-deception? The answer is, at least in part, by means of selective inattention, wherein vast numbers of negative instances are ignored. And if selective inattention does not work, some other more elaborate stratagem may be employed.

The pride dynamism has at least two unfortunate aspects. Sullivan claims that when security depends on any striking use of the pride dynamism a great deal of selective inattention is inevitable, with the result that the person is going to be poorly acquainted with the particular aspect of reality in which this pride is centered. Also, such a person is vulnerable to a direct, frontal assault. Someone may confront him with a specific test: "Show it; demonstrate it." And so he is made intensely insecure. The profound humiliation that he suffers for months afterwards carries with it a fierce hatred of the person who put him "on the spot."

Sullivan thought that *almost anything* can be humiliating to some one or other. Like a great many other things, humiliation probably is very largely a product of early acculturation. The pride dynamism probably grows out of something that happened during the early school years, a perhaps too simple example of which might be failures at learning mathematical skills. But one generally cannot divorce such things from the total situation of the juvenile, nor, probably, from the course of his previous experiences. Sullivan has pointed out that a person may respect himself for things he does not have or may respect himself for his essentially trivial attributes rather than for certain real greatnesses that he apparently never realizes he has. (Bertrand Russell did not know he was a particularly bright fellow until he went to Cambridge University.) These things are not astonishing when one realizes that the self develops through the process of acculturation from infancy onwards in interaction with significant others, to whose appraisals one is subjected year after year from infancy— appraisals that largely "determine" the character of the self, at least until one is well into adolescence, and to a greater or lesser degree throughout life.

But it is in the juvenile era that a great many acquire rather realistic data on where they are "good" and where they are not. In the school society, competition is an outstanding trait. The juvenile performs a good deal of actual exploration, making rather careful comparison of how he rates with other people who seem to matter. Sullivan claims that by and large most of the things that the juvenile builds into his self as guides as to where he stands in comparison with others in particular fields function pretty well. But in some fields his valuations of himself are unduly high and in others a juvenile's valuations may be unduly low. In certain areas the juvenile's appraisals may be very much warped by certain circumstances, emotional disturbances, specific taboos, and the like. The abnormal use of the pride dynamism is observable only in cases in which the valuations are strikingly and unduly high. But by and large the solid core of the self-respecting system is said to be based on fairly well-evaluated real experiences built up to a considerable degree from interactions with others.

Sometimes the juvenile's valuations are unduly low because of special circumstances. It is the peculiarities that occur in the instances in which the valuations of the self-respecting part of the self are unduly low that are of major psychiatric importance. Pride is perhaps one of the most subordinate of the dynamisms of emotion. As a morbidity the operations of pride have to be rather restricted because they can get one out on a limb that is easily rotted. Pride cannot be overloaded without falling of its own weight to the ground.

Though the low appraisal of one's self generally does not mean that one is really inadequate for life, it does imply that certain dynamisms of difficulty have become quite effective during the period of the individual's personality development. Low self-appraisal entails a chronic vulnerability to being made anxious, a chronic insecurity, a chronic aching void, which may have so seriously interfered with the processes of normal self-appraisal that the person never could get a very clear idea of what he was good for—or perhaps what he might be good at. The significant others from an early stage of his development will have inculcated in him a conviction of near worthlessness, so he constantly suffered because again and again he was no good at something that it was terribly important for him to to be good at. He did not, and could not, shake off this kind of misery by resort to the magic of pride. In some cases in which significant others keep telling a youngster, directly or indirectly, year after year, that he is no good at this and that and the other, or simply behave toward him in a fashion that conveys such attitudes, it tends to become a self-fulfilling prophecy.

Conceit is a feeling that arises from an *overvaluation* of certain things at which one may be very good. The conceited person derives a feeling of superiority on being able to demonstrate average, or more likely, better than average abilities in certain immensely overvalued traits. These overvalued "traits" cover a wide range in American society. The conceit of a radio announcer, a gossip columnist for a tabloid newspaper, a popular singer—these are but a few illustrations of how the "culture" fosters and "validates" this spurious feeling of superiority. But Sullivan seems to have some more common garden varieties of conceit in mind: that of the more successful sales clerk in a department store, a popular though not really skillful teacher of the first-grade pupils in the local grammar school, the small-town "banker" or the most highly paid salesman of ladies underwear in the Bronx.

Somewhere in the earlier experience of the conceited person, his demonstration of ability in some particular field—such as that of the salesman—was so powerful in assuaging anxiety that it began to take on rather magic power. It convinced him that as long as he was good at a particular activity or line of work, he would be "all right with people." It represented a virtue of which he was the lucky possessor, and he assigns "preternatural importance" to it as a dependable source of security. Even though his conceit may make him a chronic bore or an irritating companion he remains unperturbed. It works. But how? Not by means of selective inattention, as one might guess. Sullivan claims that the very organization of the self-dynamism, or those elements of the self-dynamism that explain conceit, also implies that the course of interpersonal events that the person experiences must fit this pattern of the self or be relatively devaluated as instances of bad taste, bad upbringing, bad manners, and the like on the part of the other people who are not unduly impressed or who are amused, bored, or whatever.

Sullivan, as well as others before him, has pointed out that in "our considerably irrational social order" a great many of the material and adventitious trappings of life have significance in the shape of pres-tige and deference from others. These "trappings" become a part of what William James called the "material me." For those who suffer "an uncertain security," they become important props to a shaky convic-tion of personal worth, and so become awfully important. An individual of this sort cannot derive adequate fulfillment in his direct, face-to-face, interpersonal relations. Hence he has to fall back upon the trappings of material possessions and the prestige and perhaps power that they bring for the sake of interpersonal security. There seems to be a widespread craving for such things in the United States—and in other parts of the world as well. This craving is fostered by every resource of the "business community" and its hired minions for we are told the "health" of the economy rests upon the multitudes' desires to purchase more and more. And so if a man has only one automobile while his neighbor possesses two, if his neighbor's wife owns a mink or a sable or a leopard coat while his wife has to make do with a couple of last year's cloth coats, if his friends can afford a trip to Europe while he can afford to travel no farther than Maine, he often becomes envious. "Envy," according to Sullivan, "is an acute discomfort caused by discovering that somebody else has something that one feels one ought to have."[36] It is however, not confined to invidious distinctions of material possessions and the social prestige that they usually entail; it often applies to invidious distinctions of intellectual or artistic achievement. It pervades the university like a bad odor in a subway station lavatory. It is a constant companion in the world of professional musicians and in the world of the theater. It blooms in governmental circles. (Imagine the tragedy of not being invited to one of Perle Mesta's parties.) And it is by no means absent in the world of the common man who can afford to buy a car only by grace of the local banker who like the local undertaker always awaits you with outspread hands.

Sullivan asserted that the insecurity that leads to *envy* is not specifically related to any particular need for satisfaction. A very markedly envious person may enjoy lots of good food and lots of bad women. Envy is the outcome of inadequacies of the self-system pertaining to the pursuit of security, though one may lack many complete satisfactions in interpersonal relations that are only slightly related to envy. A study of the history of the development of the self-system of the person who is very vulnerable to envy reveals that he has learned to appraise himself as an inadequate human being. In some instances he has been taught, both in the home and in the school society, in a simple, direct, and comphrensive way that he is inadequate: he does not rate; he is not the sort of person that others would wish they were. He is the kind of person who has disappointed his parents' hopes and expectations for him. Sometimes he has rather slight gifts; but his parents had expected them to be larger. So the contrast between his actual and hoped-for talents has brought their smallness very keenly to their attention.

In other cases of the envious individual, the personal background is very different. The parents provided him with an irrational and extravagant picture of himself as a child and as a young juvenile. School brings poignantly bitter disappointments since he cannot live up to expectations. Constantly experiencing the disappointments and dissatisfactions of others in his attempts to approximate the standards that his parents have inculcated, he suffers keenly from inevitable humiliations. Though he is intelligent, his continuous failure to demonstrate how much he is worth, how gifted he is, adds up to a very intense if never quite formulated conviction that he really does not rate.

Thus the envious person looks elsewhere for a means of attaining or restoring his self-esteem. He invests with importance all sorts of things that carry prestige or approval. He believes he must add to whatever abilities, skill, prowess he possesses in order to be on an even footing with others. For a male teenager, the possession of a Corvette may serve the purpose for a while. For a high school girl, possessing the most expensive clothes of any girl in the school may serve an equal purpose, though being the recipient of expensive jewelry from boys probably always helps. Of course, as one proceeds toward adulthood this level of aspiration rises gradually as a "compensation" for one's "failures" in other areas of life. There seems to be no need to discuss the unremitting striving of many adults for wealth, power, and status and prestige.

When there is an exceptionally continuous, prolonged insecurity and the driving need for various irrational personalized props, the pursuit of satisfactions in interpersonal would-be intimacies is said to be apt to be poisoned and overcomplicated by efforts to remedy the insecurities. Because of the grossly exaggerated reliance on property, prestige, and the like as means of attaining security, which can go to fantastic and self-revealing lengths, the actual pursuits of satisfactions are always badly complicated. Sullivan illustrates this by the example of a boy who while attempting to get on really intimate terms with a girl may have so much to say about himself, his family, their properties, his expectations, and so forth, that he becomes to be regarded by the girl as a fearsome bore. She grows tired of constantly hearing about his activities as a student at Princeton or Yale and how someday he will take over his father's business and expand it to fantastic heights. He puts her under a demand to say that everything about him, such as his clothes, his sports car, his family, his school record, and so on is unusually or spectacularly good. Therefore, however physically attractive the young lady may regard him, the necessities of her own security and considerations of reputation cannot allow her to become a "sex object" for him since she correctly surmises that, just as he brags about other things, he also will have to brag to men about his sexual conquests. His ideals about discretion or secrecy concerning his so-called intimate life, and the perhaps rapidly fading ideals of being a "gentleman" in contemporary life, are much less potent than his attempts to assuage insecurity as manifested in his envious attitude toward all sorts of things. Moreover, having had sexual intercourse with a girl is "a little counter" of prestige in a prevailingly juvenile society, he will advertise the fact; and this kind of information about a girl tends to travel far and fast. And even in 1968 when college girls are allowed to visit young men students in their rooms, a young woman who is not a "hippie" or a certain other kind of deviant will probably wish to exercise some discretion.[37] So the markedly envious person is apt to manifest many evidences of the thwarting of satisfactions due to the ubiquitous envy operations.

Since there is always a lot of unfinished business, which carries over from the day, unless it happens to be a very unusual, atypical day, the sleep of the envious person is only occasionally of a deep and utterly restful character. The exceptional days are those when there are no superior people around or people endowed with a greater panoply of wealth, power, and prestige than he. A wholly novel situation, such as a vacation trip, where people cannot be easily categorized, may serve a similar function. Then, provided they are not too prolonged, vacations may make the envious person quite comfortable. So he has a wonderful time and sleeps like a baby. If the vacation lasts too long, the novelty wears off, and the envious person begins more and more to feel the need for the prestige marks on which he ordinarily relies so heavily. This is said to occur partly because envy represents a deficiency of the self, with a corresponding alertness that the self controls, so that he begins to observe the evidences of his losing ground with strangers and similar failures.

By and large, the dynamism of envy, which is rather frequent, especially in America, Sullivan held to be "a fairly poisonous ingredient of the personality," much more destructive than some other dynamisms, such as pride and conceit. He thought that envious people quite frequently die of the results of hypertension. In their later years, envious people tend to develop a paranoid attitude. In order to clarify this one must realize that envy is a very unpleasant experience. It conflicts with traditional moral teachings. It reminds one that the other fellow is better at acquiring those so-cherished props—which makes one feel even more insecure. Elaborate rationalizations are called for. Thus some sort of atrocity has been committed against one: an injustice has been perpetrated against one by society whose rules have so unfairly deprived one and favored the other fellow who is a scoundrel. But this is not good enough, since the "paranoid business" is risky. Once one resorts to it, he must "go whole hog" or often find himself in extremely awkward positions with the processes within awareness: one may become conscious of extremely unpleasant things in oneself. (This will become clear in a later chapter on schizophrenia.) The thought that: "If he wasn't a scoundrel, he wouldn't have any more than I have" is not very satisfactory. It needs a little more verisimilitude by getting it more or less tacitly accepted by others. The only way such bitter derogatory statements of others, which are expressions of envy, can be made freely is by saying them of people who do not matter to the person to whom one is talking. To his interlocutor the envious person implies that present company is excepted from the general derogation. Of course it is perfectly clear to anyone that the envious person is excepting present company only for the purpose of communication. Present company is really no different from the other so-and-sos, who, in a just world, would be beneath one's notice. Yet, because of the driving need for props to his security, he goes through this performance perhaps as long as he can find a listener.

The envious person's derogation of others is said to reflect those aspects of American culture that have been most disastrous to the evolution of an adequate self in so many. There is a singular dearth "of good prescriptions" for intimacy and accommodation to other people coupled with staggering success at exploiting natural resources. Sullivan tried to explain these things by reference to American history—an idea that was not completely new. He pointed out that the American population is the outcome of one massive wave of immigration after another, made up of groups of people who for the most part possessed different languages and ways of life. (See Oscar Handlin's *The Uprooted,* for example, or Marcus Lee Hansen's *The Immigrant in American History.*) Since it was the "Anglo-Saxons" who succeeded in establishing their culture in this country, for purposes of exposition I will ignore the French and the Spaniards. The English immigrants settled this country, or at least a large part including what is now called New England, cleared the forests, and in one way or another, with some help from the mother country, established their own economy and culture. After a couple of centuries, when they had built up a prosperous civilization, the Irish (along with the Germans), who lacked almost all the Yankee virtues, came to this country in droves. Naturally they were looked down upon by the Americans. (Edwin O'Connor's *The Last Hurrah* gives one a glimpse of how it happened.) And it may be of interest to some readers that Sullivan was familiar with the rich lore that had been handed down probably by his grandparents and other Irish immigrants about the arrival of the Irish in this country who were fleeing from the Great Famine. Then came other waves of immigrants, such as the Italians, the Poles, and the Jews. Meanwhile a very interesting thing had been happening. The descendants of the original immigrants were hostile and contemptuous of the Irish.[38] And in a generation or two, when the latter had struggled one step up the social ladder, they looked down with hostility and contempt on the more recent immigrants, such as the Italians, who incidentally were steadier workers because they were not inclined to go on periodic sprees like the Irish. And so it went. The situation of the Negroes of course was much worse owing to their having been brought over to this country from Africa on Yankee ships to be sold as slaves.[39] Anyway the foreigner became especially useful, as Sullivan says, as a target for enhancing one's prestige—"by the somewhat treacherous route of seeing one's faults in others." Successive waves of immigration provided plenty of targets.

The other factor that Sullivan mentions has to do with the exploitation of natural resources, the spectacular accumulation of wealth and upward mobility. Without going into details, I wish to mention his condemnation of advertising—"that vicious misuse of human credulity"—which stimulates people to buy more and more. "So the business of making things as conspicuously different from each other as possible, and grading these differences in terms of cost, has become an extremely successful way of accumulating other people's money. As a result, the material trappings with which one frantically tries to relieve one's envy—and therefore magnifies it—grow apace."[40]

I should like to mention in passing that Sullivan's interpretation, while psychologically valuable, seems sociologically inadequate. It needs to be supplemented. G. William Domhoff's *Who Rules America?*, for example, provides considerable insight into the folkways of the rich and the powerful in American society.[41]

But an understanding of the essential factors in life has been profoundly retarded, partly because so much energy, time and talent have been employed by the various groups in the upward climb, generation after generation. The evolution of a culture that would include the growth of "charming ways of human intimacy," as well as the understanding of the essentials of life have lagged.[42] So Americans have learned many erroneous prescriptions and few correct orientations in living for the achievement of human intimacy. On the other hand, they are mightily impressed "from all sides with the importance of the kind of paint they have on their houses and the number of horsepower in their cars." So it is not very surprising or mysterious that Americans are not a really friendly people, though they can be polite and genial as long as there is no strong demand for intimacy. Similarly it is not strange that they are "so horribly afflicted" with a driving need for status symbols that so often culminates in envy. In the United States of America envy is said to be a very widely distributed dynamism of difficulty of which everyone is ashamed but which a great many people cannot avoid betraying since it is built into the self-system.

While competitiveness is not the same thing as envy, it seems likely that there is a significant correlation between them. In any event, competitiveness is a marked feature of American society. Intensely competitive adults are said to be people who continue to live at a relatively juvenile level, namely, people who live as if they always have to prove that they are better than the other fellow. A specific trait of a continued juvenile organization of personality is *morbid ambition.* Sullivan claims that the morbidly ambitious are extremely impatient, and sometimes horribly insecure under the impatience, about the speed at which they ascend to a greater social position. Though they strive to get the other fellow down, it is simply because he is in the way. Ruthless though their behavior is, it is more nearly adjustive than is the gnawing, clumsily disguised suffering of envy.

The last dynamism of emotion to be discussed is *jealousy,* which is often confused with envy, and is a "horribly unpleasant mental state." It always occurs in a context of three people, though if there are larger numbers of people involved, they will still be entangled in or break down into a three-group relationship. "Jealousy appears in its most obvious and understandable form in the rather rare circumstance where person A, the person who is going to be jealous, is on terms of comparative intimacy both with person B and with person C. Persons B and C are at first relatively unacquainted with each other. But then some unhappy event brings B and C close together, and they immediately manifest a tendency to develop a situation of intimacy. At that time the person in the central position has the poignant and horrible experience of jealousy."[43]

In other words, suppose a person is capable of only partial intimacy with another individual, the former will still have unsatisfied components of personality that tend to integrate relatively identical situations of intimacy with still other people. Jealousy is said to occur under those circumstances when the other two people (B and C above) involved with the subject person (A above) in one of these truncated and relatively abortive intimacies manifest, or are fantasied as manifesting, greater capacity for satisfaction with each other than with the subject person. On such occasions the devastating dynamism of jealousy appears, and the subject person becomes abysmally unhappy. Supplementary processes in the latter, due to his excruciating misery, are apt to appear, processes very close to the appearance of the paranoid state.

Freud thought that jealousy indicated the presence of a component sexual impulse, namely, homosexuality. Sullivan disagrees. Granted that jealousy is a rather common phenomenon, and that intimacy among Americans is perhaps "preternaturally related" to sexual "intimacy," the explanation of Freud appears to be, in general, invalid nevertheless. A person who has matured without serious warp, who has in other words matured in a sequence of situations that were rather rich in experience so that he has developed a fairly well-rounded personality, free from any serious handicaps to obtaining satisfactions—such a person, possessed of considerable self-respect and security, will suffer jealousy only under the most extraordinary circumstances. Sullivan claimed that the more adequate a person's preparation for a theoretically complete satisfaction of needs in interpersonal intimacy, the more impossible it will be for him to stand in such relation to two or more people that he will pursue the same satisfactions in each of these intimacies. Very few mature people escape the impression that interpersonal relations, at least in American society, increase in demands, risks, complexities, risky misses, awkward entanglements, and the like in direct proportion to the magnitude and profundity of the needs they fulfill. Thus, when a person has a fairly well-developed personality, enjoys thoroughly satisfactory sexual relations with his partner, he will not be inclined to indulge any surviving curiosity as to whether a similar intimacy with another person might not be even better in the face of the ordinary considerations of life's difficulties and hazards. So the chances of one's becoming involved in a potential jealousy situation are said to be in inverse proportion to the degree of maturity one has achieved.

Although in American society jealousy often centers around sex, it is not the nuclear explanatory conception of the dynamics of jealousy. The real explanation is as follows: The person who is prey to jealousy suffers a fatal defect in the self, to the effect that he suffers a deep conviction of relative unworthiness. He believes that he is to some extent "getting away with murder" when he enjoys the friendship of others. He is convinced he does not deserve the regard of others because they are better than he is. In no matter what situation, in no matter what field of human needs, they are more capable than he. He feels inferior in some significant respect to the people to whom he is related in various types of cooperation or collaboration in the pursuit of satisfactions. Thus one feels he is not up to the level of people in whom he is interested. According to Sullivan, there is a feeling of relative emptiness of worth or value in the interpersonal field. Suppose it is affection or love—which is *not* necessarily connected with sexuality—that he wants. A will still suffer this wretched feeling of jealousy vis-à-vis B and C even when the latter like him just as much as they do one another. So, whether the conjunctive force between B and C has to do with sex or intimacy or love, A will think to himself: "They can really love each other, whereas I have not really been up to that standard." In this case, all sorts of rationalizations or irrational referential processes are likely to occur, sometimes of the more or less schizophrenic type. Sullivan thought that jealousy and a definite paranoid development may frequently be singularly closely related.

Almost inevitably, in the individual who is a prey to jealousy, there is a barrier to the development of intimacy or love, wherein the satisfactions and security of the partner are at least as significant as one's own. Therefore the jealous person, even when he values the partner, does not honor the partner as much as he does himself. This leaves open the possibility of attempting to minimize his insecurity by means of "love affairs," which are additional entanglements, with the sometimes fairly explicit thought, "Well, if this person finds out about me, I'll not be utterly without harbor—there'll be the other one." And so by this very stratagem of attempting to bolster his self-esteem he leaves himself open to jealousy "if some of these personal entanglements tangle with each other." (What would American "Soap Operas" do without these triangular entanglements? And what would the American housewife do without the Soap Operas?)

Sullivan claims that the state of the personality in this situation can be of several orders of complexity. He mentions that among them is the type of barrier toward sexual intimacy with members of the other sex that fosters homosexual interests after the preadolescent period. Moreover, since "we are the sort of people we are, and particularly since the emancipation of women has proceeded at a rather staggering pace in the comparatively recent past of the American development, it is probable that a great many people do reach chronological adulthood and set up homes without having achieved freedom for integrating love with a member of the opposite sex."[44] A person who does not reach maturity cannot even approximate love, especially with a member of the opposite sex. And since there is a barrier to love, from which flow many of the consequences previously mentioned, given suitable circumstances jealousy is apt to appear and wreak havoc upon the person who suffers it and sometimes upon all concerned. This is often one of the consequences of "our superficial type of living."

Since the jealous person can manage only a none too adequate satisfaction of needs, he suffers a certain amount of tension and has to resort to various stratagems: sublimations, substitutions, dissociations, and the like. Such an unhappy, problem-laden individual manifests a difficult life situation in the form of uncertain sleep, sleep disturbed by terror dreams, and so on. But that part of his life is, in a great many ways, not related to the actual incident of jealousy. It is a reflection of his total life situation.

Symbolic operations in sleep, which may appear to be the very essence of jealousy, are not necessarily connected with jealousy. They are said to be frank schizophrenic phenomena. Imagine a man who has sustained a rather comfortable relationship with his wife, but a man who is probably rather self-centered and completely lacking in ability for real intimacy with his wife. In various ways he has been under increasing pressure and tension so that he is becoming increasingly disturbed. "One night he has a dream in which his wife is eloping with a colleague of his, and this dream ushers in a schizophrenic episode."[45] This man's wife and his colleague were merely casual friends, and the man himself had no experience of jealousy.

I shall end this chapter by calling the reader's attention to the fact that the dynamisms of emotion discussed above could no more be adequately described or explained by reference to "intrapsychic" processes than that human behavior generally can be explained by reference to the Transcendental Ego of German philosophy. The psyche is always a part-aspect of a total situation that is more inclusive and more complex: "the organism-environment complex" or "field." Since traditional Freudian analysis emphasized the "intrapsychic" to the relative neglect of the interpersonal, it is not very surprising that a number of psychiatrists have become disenchanted with classical psychoanalysis.

Notes

1. HARRY STACK SULLIVAN, "Psychiatry: Introduction to the Study of Inter-personal Relations," *Psychiatry*, 1:121-134, 1938; reprinted in HARRY STACK SULLIVAN, *The Fusion of Psychiatry and Social Science*, with Introduction and Commentaries by HELEN SWICK PERRY (New York: W. W. Norton and Company, 1964).

2. Cf. JUDD MARMOR, "New Directions in Psychoanalytic Theory and Therapy," in JUDD MARMOR (ed.), *Modern Psychoanalysis* (New York: Basic Books, 1968).

3. Cf. ABRAM KARDINER, AARON KARUSH, and LIONEL OVESEY, "A Methodological Study of Freudian Theory," *International Journal of Psychiatry*, 2:489-541, 1966.

4. MAX L. HUTT, ROBERT L. ISAACSON, MILTON L. BLUM, *The Science of Behavior/The Science of Interpersonal Behavior* (New York: Harper and Row, 1967).

5. Cf. PATRICK MULLAHY, "The Interpersonal Current in Psychiatric Development," *International Journal of Psychiatry*, 6:131-143, 1968.

6. HARRY STACK SULLIVAN, *Conceptions of Modern Psychiatry*, with a Foreword by the author and a Critical Appraisal of the Theory by PATRICK MULLAHY (New York: W. W. Norton and Company, 1953), pp. 50-51.

7. I have discussed this point in "A Philosophy of Personality," *Psychiatry*, 13:417-437, 1950; reprinted in HOWARD BRAND (ed.), *The Study of Personality* (New York: John Wiley and Sons, 1954).

8. Cf. JOHN DEWEY, *Logic: The Theory of Inquiry* (New York: Henry Holt and Company, 1938). chap. 14.

9. See HARRY STACK SULLIVAN, *Clinical Studies in Psychiatry*, ed. HELEN SWICK PERRY, MARY LADD GAWEL, and MARTHA GIBBON, with a Foreword by

DEXTER M. BULLARD (New York: W. W. Norton and Company, 1956), pp. 38-76.

10. Sullivan did not make use of William James's famous distinction between the "I," the knower, and the "Me," the known, as two aspects of the self.

11. SULLIVAN, "Psychiatry: Introduction to the Study of Interpersonal Relations."

12. *Ibid.*

13. *Ibid.*

14. HARRY STACK SULLIVAN, "A Note on the Implications of Psychiatry, The Study of Interpersonal Relations, for Investigations in the Social Sciences," *American Journal of Sociology,* 42:846-861, 1936-1937; reprinted in SULLIVAN, *The Fusion of Psychiatry and Social Science.*

15. HARRY STACK SULLIVAN, "The Illusion of Personal Individuality," *Psychiatry,* 13:317-332, 1950; reprinted in SULLIVAN, *The Fusion of Psychiatry and Social Science.*

16. SULLIVAN, *Conceptions of Modern Psychiatry,* pp. 90-91.

17. SULLIVAN, "The Illusion of Personal Individuality."

18. Cf. HARRY STACK SULLIVAN, *The Interpersonal Theory of Psychiatry,* ed, HELEN SWICK PERRY and MARY LADD GAWEL, with an Introduction by MABEL BLAKE COHEN (New York: W. W. Norton and Company, 1953), pp. 184-185, for a discussion of nonverbal processes.

19. SULLIVAN, "The Illusion of Personal Individuality."

20. *Ibid.*

21. Cf. HARRY STACK SULLIVAN, "Dissociative Processes," in *Clinical Studies in Psychiatry,* chap. 8.

22. HARRY STACK SULLIVAN, "A Note on Formulating the Relationship of the Individual and the Group," *American Journal of Sociology,* 44:932-937, 1938-1939; reprinted in SULLIVAN, *The Fusion of Psychiatry and Social Science.*

23. HARRY STACK SULLIVAN, "The Meaning of Anxiety in Psychiatry and in Life," *Psychiatry,* 11:1-13, 1948; reprinted in SULLIVAN, *The Fusion of Psychiatry and Social Science.*

24. SULLIVAN, *Clinical Studies in Psychiatry,* p. 94.

25. *Ibid.,* p. 95.

26. *Ibid.,* p. 98.

27. *Ibid.,* p. 101.

28. SULLIVAN, *The Interpersonal Theory of Psychiatry,* p. 212.

29. SULLIVAN, *Clinical Studies in Psychiatry,* p. 101.

30. *Ibid.,* p. 103.

31. *Ibid.,* p. 104.

32. Cf. HARRY STACK SULLIVAN, "The Paranoid Dynamism," in SULLIVAN, *Clinical Studies in Psychiatry.*

33. SULLIVAN, *Clinical Studies in Psychiatry*, p. 107.

34. *Ibid.*, p. 110.

35. *Ibid.*, p. 114.

36. *Ibid.*, p. 129.

37. Cf. ARNO KARLEN, "The Unmarried Marrieds on Campus," *New York Times Magazine*, January 26, 1969.

38. Cf. MARCUS LEE HANSEN, *The Immigrant in American History*, ed., with a Foreword, by ARTHUR M. SCHLESINGER (New York: Harper and Row, 1964), p. 161:

"Tradition has little pleasant to say regarding these Irish immigrants. They were regarded as stupid and dirty, superstitious and untrustworthy, diseased and in despair. They were viewed as beggars and thieves, the overflow of Irish poorhouses and outcasts from overpopulated estates."

39. This statement is not entirely accurate. See CHARLES and MARY R. BEARD, *The Rise of American Civilization* (New York: The Macmillan Company, 1930), chap. 3.

40. SULLIVAN, *Clinical Studies in Psychiatry*, p. 135.

41. Cf. ARTHUR KROCK, *Memoirs* (New York: Funk and Wagnalls, 1968), and GEORGE F. KENNAN, *Memoirs* (Boston, Massachusetts: Little, Brown and Company, 1967).

42. Cf. IRVING KRISTOL, "The Old Politics, the New Politics, the New, New Politics," *New York Times Magazine*, November 24, 1968.

43. SULLIVAN, *Clinical Studies in Psychiatry*, p. 139.

44. *Ibid.*, p. 142.

45. *Ibid.*, pp. 143-144.

8 / The Development of Personality

Conceptions of Modern Psychiatry and *The Interpersonal Theory of Psychiatry* contain Sullivan's most elaborated ideas on the evolution of personality. Since they were embodied in lectures, not in books, they constitute little more than a general framework for the understanding of personality development. Nevertheless, what Sullivan's theory of development lacks in detail is more than compensated for by its originality and power. Today, twenty years after his death, those ideas are markedly influential, even in general psychology texts such as Hutt, Isaacson, and Blum's *The Science of Interpersonal Behavior*, in child psychology texts such as Jersild's *Child Psychology*, and in social psychology texts such as Krech, Crutchfield, and Ballachey's *Individual in Society*.

From Sullivan's point of view, personality development constitutes a history of interactions or transactions of the "organism," and the psychophysical-social world. Personality is not preformed at birth, though the distinctions of different stages or eras of development may easily give one that impression. Genetic structure provides the raw potentials of personality. No one is destined by heredity to become any specific kind of person, though *temperamental* differences may appear at birth or soon after.

In *Conceptions,* the transactional point of view on the biological level is stated very clearly in the following passage:

> Let us consider the beginning of anyone, the fecundated ovum in the uterus. This cell manifests the basic categories of biological

process. The cell carries almost stupifying potentialities. It exists as a demonstrable entity. It lives, however, and starts the realization of its potentialities, not as a unit organism surrounded by a suitable environment. It lives communally *with* the environment. Physico-chemical factors, substances, plentiful in the uterine environment flow into the cell. They undergo changes while they are within the describable cell-area. They return presently as other physico-chemical factors, to the environment. The cell dies if the continuous exchange is interrupted. Progressive changes depend utterly on the communion; retrogressive changes appear swiftly on its restriction.

From a relative position in time and space, the environment flows through the living cell, becoming of its very life in the process; and the cell flows and grows through the environment, establishing in this process its particular career-line as an organism. It is artificial, an abstraction, to say that the cell is one thing and the environment another. The two entities thus postulated refer to some unitary thing in which organism and environment are indissolubly bound—so long as life continues.[1]

Sullivan goes on to say that there is *organization* in the cell-medium complex, before there has been a single division of the fertile cell, such that a vital balance is maintained in the more purely organismic part of the complex. Thus he defines an organism as a self-perpetuating organization of the physicochemical world that manifests life by functional activity in the complex. On every level—physical, biological, psychological, sociocultural—organization is a key conception. *Functional activity* and *communal existence* are other basic conceptions in Sullivan's theory of interpersonal psychiatry. All three add up to a transactional interpretation of human living. Human life is a history of transactions of the human organism and the psychophysical and social environments. Thus the human organism, like any organism, is a "bundle" of interrelated processes. Physicochemical and biological processes may, in the main, comprise animal life but not human life.

As the new-born begins the long journey of life, he is almost utterly helpless if unaided by others. He is far too immature to live by his own functional activity. But this very helplessness is a necessary condition of human development. As growth and maturation proceed, the long stretch of postnatal existence required by the human young for the attainment of independent competence to live, acculturation, or education in the broadest sense, is "inevitable." The human infant has to be cared for by people. Significant people, especially the mothering one, at first unwittingly but soon, in a matter of months, deliberately begin to educate him in "select excerpts" of the culture of her community or society. Anyone who has ever engaged in caring for an infant knows how marvelously cooperative and eager he is—long before he can talk or utter a word.

So the infant is by no means a passive creature. Sullivan has pointed out in the *Conceptions* that almost from birth the infant begins to attend to movements and objects about him. He is impelled by various kinds of physiological drives. In harmony with the psychology of his day, Sullivan stressed such drives as hunger and thirst, pain, and the need for sleep. More recent studies indicate that other kinds of drives are very important, such as activity, manipulation, and curiosity, though Sullivan was by no means unaware of them. It has to be emphasized that the manifestations of all such drives occur in an interpersonal context. Drives are molded, structured, take on "meaning" only in such a context. The more or less periodic interchange between mother and infant makes this possible.

Toward the end of his life Sullivan explicitly formulated "tension" in a very broad sense: as a potentiality for action, for the transformation of energy in the various activities of life. Logically, the tensions of need and of anxiety may be regarded as components of this tension —except that the young infant has no ability to relieve anxiety tension.[2]

Sullivan thought that the "object" that satisfies the hunger and thirst of the infant provides the first vivid perception of a person relatively independent of the infant's own being. Strictly speaking, it is not the mothering one as a separate, independent object who is first perceived. The nipple is said to be the first vaguely prehended perception—a "complex image" or symbol with very broad reference. Hence this perception cannot be conceived to be nearly as clear-cut as the perception of figure and ground; the latter comes later, and is first experienced in the parataxic mode. The "clarification" or recognition of the nipple as borne by another person instead of being a part of one's own undifferentiated ("cosmic") experience is said to be the first step in shrinking to life size.

This leads to a discussion of the three "modes" of experience: The prototaxic, parataxic, and syntaxic. During the first months of an infant's life his experience is undifferentiated, unformulated, uncircumscribed by any of the distinctions adults take for granted. This experience begins as pure sentience. Elsewhere I have formulated the prototaxic experience of the infant as follows:

> Some psychologists regard the period from birth to about 1½ years of age as the "sensorimotor stage," wherein the infant receives impressions and reacts without the intervention of a mediating self. Hence, there is no distinction between the self and the external world. Piaget called this state of affairs an undifferentiated absolute of self and environment. . . .
>
> Sullivan's notion of the prototaxic, or "primitive," mode of experience is similar but more elaborate. It forms the basis of memory (retention), although it ordinarily defies formulation and, hence, discussion. The infant has not yet learned how to differentiate and categorize experience. Thus, distinctions in terms of "now," "before," "after," "here," "there," "I," "you," and the like are lacking. Of course, he undergoes and registers experience, perhaps from moment to moment, but he is apparently unable to discriminate the order of events impinging on his senses. Sullivan thought that all the infant "knows" are momentary states, merging and vanishing like raindrops into the vast reservoir of memory. He may register earlier and later states but without discerning any serial connection between them. The alternation of need and satisfaction is first experienced in the prototaxic mode. But, within the flux of experience, the infant gradually "prehends" or discriminates a recurrent pattern of events—such as the nipple-lips sequence—which serves as a sign that the state called satisfaction is about to supervene. Sullivan inferred that anxiety tension also is first experienced in the prototaxic mode.
>
> The prototaxic mode is not confined to infancy. Sullivan "presumed" that from the beginning to the end of life individuals continue to undergo these momentary prototaxic experiences. If Sullivan's assumption is valid, it may be that all differentiated experiences occur in connection with, and rest on, the prototaxic mode. He thought that some dream processes, certain schizophrenic episodes in which he held that the person's experiences are "cosmic," and perhaps some experiences that are classed as mystical occur in the prototaxic mode. . . ."[3]

In Chapter 2 it was pointed out that the infant undergoes a rudimentary awareness, owing to the impressions he responds to, which originate in either the external world or in his own body. Apparently he can sense and he can feel but his responses tend to be "global." As soon as he begins to make some discriminations among his impressions or his experiences he is starting to be capable of the second mode of experience, the parataxic. Sullivan thought that the infant's distance receptors, eyes and ears, for example, are of a quite different order of relationship from things that his tactile or gustatory receptors encounter. "That which one has in one's mouth so that he can taste it," Sullivan said in *Conceptions of Modern Psychiatry,* "while it may be regurgitated to the distress of everyone is still in a very different relationship than is the full moon which one encounters through one's eyes but can in no sense manage." If there were no obstacles in the world, no pain, or unpleasure, no lacks or needs presumably one might, in theory, remain forever in an undifferentiated, global state of bliss.[4]

In order to clarify Sullivan's formulation of the parataxic mode of experience, I shall enlist the aid of a child psychologist regarding certain experiences of the infant. Soon after birth the latter manifests another aspect (along with sense impressions and feelings) of the mind:

> The ability to respond to cues—to respond to a part of a past total stimulus situation as he once did to the total stimulation. We see this when the child who previously stopped crying only when picked up and held to his mother's breast now ceases his crying when his mother touches his cheek, or when he hears the sound of the door latch as his mother enters his room. The touch, the sound, which were earlier but a feature of the total situation of being fed now (for the moment at least) have the quieting effect that originally was produced only when he was actively fed. A process of *association* has occurred, so that now a part of a situation functions for the whole. Here, in a rudimentary form, is a situation analogous to what happens when a driver applies the brakes upon seeing a red light: The light is a symbol of danger and of society's laws. Even though no visible danger lies ahead, and no one orders him to stop, the driver stops.[5]

Jersild's statements put us in a better position to understand the parataxic mode. The infant gradually begins to make some discrimination between himself and the world as maturation and learning proceed. The original global experience is broken up into various aspects or parts, which, however, are not logically connected. These diverse aspects of experience, or some of them, may or may not occur together, depending on circumstances. In traditional psychological language, the sundered aspects of experience may, when circumstances (which may perhaps to some degree be categorized in terms of laws of association) permit, become associated. Thus the varied experiences that occur in the parataxic mode are lived or perceived as concomitant but not yet—if ever—recognized as being connected or related in any sort of orderly manner. Because of his limited store of knowledge and experience, the offspring takes this mode of experience for granted and, as it were, the natural way of things.

Suppose a child is beaten or otherwise mistreated for no evident cause by a parent. Imagine, further, that soon after he is subjected to "sweetness" and "love." Let us assume that the parent is a somewhat immature and neurotic mother who subjects her child to this incongruous sequence of events rather frequently—it is perhaps a daily occurrence. An objective observer might interpret the mother's inconsistent behavior as senseless and destructive. But the youngster, limited as he necessarily is by his experience, does not perceive any inconsistency or senselessness in his mother's behavior. That is how things happen; that is the way life is though he may wish things were different or strive to circumvent them. Often a recurrent pattern of this sort will be assimilated by the child into his growing self-system. In fact, numerous analogous irrational patterns may be assimilated into the developing self since it is likely that for many years he will be subjected to the incongruous attitudes and irrational inconsistent behavior of a parent without his ever questioning such attitudes and actions. He has learned that life is like that—at least for him. Moreover, even in more normal homes children are, in varying degrees, subjected to various kinds of irrational attitudes and behavior patterns since the parents usually reflect the inadequacies as well as the virtues of their society, community, or social class.

The activity of selective inattention occurs in the parataxic mode. Illusory me-you patterns, which facilitate various kinds of other distortions in interpersonal relations, occur in this mode. Parataxic distortions, such as illusory me-you patterns, often manifest themselves when one is dealing with strangers, or acquaintances, sometimes with friends, often in "romantic attachments," and probably always in difficult marital situations. Roughly, it is often anxiety that stimulates or arouses these illusory me-you patterns (and various other kinds of distortions as well). However, experience in the parataxic mode is often a normal in the sense of usual or very frequent occurrence in everyday affairs. Perhaps the major part of life occurs in, or is lived in, the parataxic mode.

In Chapter 2, Sullivan's early formulation of symbol activity was outlined. Before I take up his ideas on the *syntaxic* mode of experience, I shall, once more, enlist the aid of Jersild. The latter wrote:

> A further property of the mind appears when the child not only responds to cues or signals in the external environment (such as the click of the door latch) but employs symbols of his own. This occurs, for example, when he forms an impression, retains it in the form of an idea or image, "sees" a dog in his dreams or in his imagination plays with a dog that isn't there. In time, the child's mind becomes a treasury of symbols, enabling him to encompass the present, to relive his past, to project himself into the future. He becomes able in his thoughts to deal with countless circumstances of life without actually encountering them in the flesh. By the use of symbols the child is able, in a sense, to detach himself from the world and yet manipulate it by means of thoughts and fantasies.[6]

The symbol activities that Jersild describes may be conceived as occurring in a continuum of experience from the earlier, more primitive forms of the parataxic to the highly organized and more communicable syntaxic operations. *Autistic* symbol activity, as formulated by Sullivan, is a verbal manifestation of the parataxic mode. He describes autistic symbol activity in the *Conceptions* as follows:

> The ability to make articulate noises and the ability to pick phonemal stations in vocal sound—that is, the peculiar ones of a continuum of sounds which are used in the forming of words, which varies, incidentally, from language to language—the ability, as I say, to learn phonemes, to connect them into syllables and words, is inborn. . . . The original usage of these phonemal stations, syllables, words, however, is magical, as witness the "ma" and as wit-

ness, for example, any of you who have a child who has been promised on a certain birthday a pony. As you listen to the child talk about the pony you realize perhaps sadly that twenty-five years from now when he talks about ponies, pony will not have a thousandth of the richness of personal meaning that pony has for him now. The word of the child is autistic; it has a highly individual meaning. And the process of learning language habits consists to a great extent, once one has got a vocabulary, in getting a meaning to each particular term which is useful in communication. None of us succeeds completely in this; some of us do not succeed noticeably.[7]

The original symbol activity of the very young child is literally unique, for the most part untested and unchecked against the symbol activity and knowledge of others. Hence, it is, largely incommunicable. His capacity for verbal communication is only beginning to appear. Up to this point in his career, he lacks the tools necessary for verbal communication. His thoughts or ideas and fantasies are also largely parataxic, that is, occur in the parataxic mode, as illustrated by his various and incongruous conceptions of pony.

Another illustration will perhaps further clarify the significance of the parataxic mode. Imagine the case of a child who has been presented with a picture book containing printed matter. There will be, let us say, a picture of a cat, below which is written what the youngster, who cannot yet read, will subsequently learn as c - a - t. Significant others, such as parents and elder siblings, also call the animal who runs around the house the same name as the colored or black and white pattern in the book. It is likely, however, that the child will notice an enormous discrepancy between the immobile representation in the book and the very active pet who runs around the house. The fact that both are called the same name also may seem very strange. Yet because significant others perhaps every day, sometimes overtly, sometimes subtly, refer to the picture and the animal by the same name the child finally accepts this reference to the picture as "kitty" and to the amusing creature as "kitty" as a useful and "valid" occurrence. The consistency of occurrences can be very impressive and psychologically compelling. This consistency tends to cause one to accept them as factual or veridical.

The child progresses, so to speak, to the printed word from the picture and spoken word, finally discovering that c - a - t includes or designates the animal who runs around the house, the picture of the cat, perhaps a kitten doll, and alley cats seen from the window. No one troubles to point out the sundry "types of reality and reference" that are being experienced. But, as we have already noted, according to Sullivan, there is nothing like consistent experience to impress one with the validity of an idea or of the usage of words. So the possibilities for confusion in handling the various kinds of symbols are said to remain quite considerable. In most everyday affairs, however, this may not be of great moment, since various concrete situations tend to identify the particular usage of a word or a sentence, that is, its meaning. In this fashion the meaning is fixed "consensually," by public (usually implicit) agreement. Group activities, interpersonal relations, tend within certain limits to sort out the various meanings of words, which comprise the language employed in commonsense affairs. And so when the child learns the shared meanings of language he has reached the syntaxic mode of experience. Meanings are no longer primarily "defined" in terms of one's own private world, though not rarely there is considerable overlapping of the private and unique and the public or shared.

The syntaxic mode entails an appeal to principles or facts that are accepted as true or established by the hearer. This is what Sullivan often calls consensual validation. Some critics, with a great flourish and sounding of alarms, have galloped into a verbal fray over Sullivan's "consensual validation." They have, quite correctly, pointed out that popular usage is by no means always a reliable criterion of truth. Assuredly Sullivan knew this. In an earlier chapter of this book it was pointed out that he thought the most rigorous form of consensual validation is located in experimental procedures carried on under carefully controlled conditions. But he also thought that the study of interpersonal relations does not lend itself to such procedures. What concerned Sullivan primarily was (1) a sufficiently precise use of language that his students might learn to communicate intelligently and accurately in order to facilitate a pooling of information; (2) a clarification of the kinds of symbols patients may employ, and of the purposes of these symbols; and (3) the importance of a careful checking of a patient's use of symbols in order that the psychiatrist might learn what the patient was talking about. Sullivan's work with schizophrenics had revealed what extraordinary and bizzare meanings patients may attach to symbols—meanings that can easily be overlooked.

Every kind or form of experience is a form of learning. The native equipment of the infant—sensory, neuronic, impulsive, and the like—provides the necessary conditions of all growth. But without an environment, physical and sociocultural, by means of which the infant lives, all his marvelous equipment would signify nothing. Leaving aside the physical environment, which, though essential to life and development, may be taken for granted in this book, the infant requires a mature social medium in every phase of personality growth. This medium, called culture, is provided first and foremost by the parents or their surrogates.

The infant encounters elements of the culture from the time he is born or even during the period of his birth. From a subjective (inner) point of view, his earliest experience is of tensions and "energy transformations." Tensions are typically of needs, both general and zonal, and of anxiety. Energy transformations are actions or activities (breathing, sucking, and the like) that remedy biological disequilibration or satisfy needs. The human organism is an energy system, and, like all biological energy systems, has *structural,* and *functional* properties. Thus the human organism is one overall structure, supported by the skeleton, an integrated system of various substructures, such as the digestive, circulatory, reproductive, nervous, and other systems. Every living organism may be thought to have a built-in tendency, or "tension," as a potentiality for action, for the transformation of energy on the biological plane, to maintain itself, to maintain a delicate balance between the various inner subsystems, and of the system as a whole and the outer environment. The various activities of the organism serve to maintain, or when interrupted, to restore the "equilibration." On the human level, the "enduring influence of the tensional history" of the organism's living in the present and "near future" constitutes experience.[8]

For the sake of convenience of exposition, one starts with the fairly "obvious" somative tensions and energy transformations. General needs, such as those for food and water, are familiar. So are activities such as breathing, sucking, and (an occurrence that comes later) eating, and the like. But complexities in human experience and behavior that appear very early in life must be recognized and accounted for. For example, there are the tensions of the need for tenderness and of anxiety. There are other tensions that Sullivan merely brushed in theory, such as manipulation and curiosity.

In order to round out the exposition of Sullivan's "postulates," I must take up another basic assumption of his. While Freud for many years had assumed the existence of a pleasure principle as the controlling, directing principle of human life, Sullivan postulated *euphoria* in an analogous fashion. Euphoria is simply *a state of well being,* which in fact is never "absolute." The tensions of physiological needs more or less periodically lower this euphoria, disturb the equilibrium, which stimulate the infant to perform various actions, such as crying. Such an activity of the infant induces tension in the mothering one. This tension, called a feeling of tenderness, motivates the mother (or her surrogate) to perform activities designed toward the relief of the infant's needs. These more or less recurrent actions by the mother are soon experienced by the infant as the undergoing of tender behavior. Hence the infant's needs are said to take on the character of a general need for tenderness. Sullivan seems to imply that this need for tenderness is built into the organism though he is not entirely clear about it. He calls it an interpersonal need since it—like almost all needs of the very young—requires cooperation from another person, usually the mothering one. A normal mother has a complementary and appropriate need, namely, to behave tenderly toward her offspring. From the side of the infant, all needs, actions, and care by the mother are first experienced in the prototaxic mode.

The satisfaction of needs along with the experience of tenderness restores and perhaps enhances the infant's euphoria; though it is not at all clear how the mother's feeling of tenderness first gets communicated. Some would say it is by sheer physical contact but this is uncertain. At one time Sullivan theorized that it is by means of empathy—an obscure mode of communication or emotional contagion that he was once rash enough to speculate may not occur through ordinary sensory channels—that "good feeling" is conveyed. Subsequently, he modified his position. Empathy appears first in connection with anxiety, being most conspicuous between ages six months and twenty-seven months. However, it seems safe to assume that at an indeterminately early age the infant somehow experiences the tenderness of the mother—and with the aid of ordinary sensory channels. Further research in child psychology may reveal how early and precisely in what ways the infant experiences the positive and negative attitudes of the mothering one.

Sullivan theorized that the second "genus" of tensions significant especially for psychiatry, has to do with anxiety. (The first pertains to needs.) Anxiety in an infant is a "fearlike" state that can be inferred only by certain behaviors of his. Once the self begins to develop, anxiety can be characterized as a loss or lowering of self-esteem, a kind of "feeling" that is very different from fear. Not so in the young infant who during the first twelve to eighteen months has no distinctive self. Anxiety in the infant is suggested by certain indices such as certain sorts of feeding difficulties, certain crying spells without discoverable cause (as determined, say, by a pediatrician), somnolent detachment. In fact Sullivan thought that all the performances of the infant are vulnerable to being arrested or impeded, in direct "chronological and otherwise specific relationship" to the emotional disturbances of the significant other person. These emotional disturbances of the mother include anxiety, anger, fear, and the like. They are said to induce a tension in the infant when the mother is physically close such that more or less in a fashion analogous to hunger it lowers the infant's euphoria. Whether the *infant's* experience of this sort of tension is different from his experience of the tension of fear cannot yet be determined. But Sullivan theorized that this tension state aroused by emotional disturbances in the mother develops into the sort of experiences that older children and adults can learn very definitely to identify, and which is *markedly different* from fear or any other feeling-state. If Sullivan's assumptions about infantile anxiety tensions are valid, it follows that parents who are chronically disturbed or neurotic may unwittingly induce chronic anxiety tensions in their offspring, no matter how good the physical care they may provide. It may also be true that some parents under chronic stress during periods of war, revolution, insurrection, religious or racial strife, religious or racial persecution, may unwittingly induce anxiety tensions in their offspring.

In Sullivanian theory, the ramifications of anxiety are great. First and foremost, it is the *fons et origo* of the need for interpersonal security, roughly a need to be emotionally confortable with significant others and to gain or maintain their approval, and to accept and respect oneself. In the young infant, anxiety tension is not manageable; he can do little or nothing about it. In contrast, when he is hungry or in pain because, say, a diaper pin is sticking him, he cries and something happens, something is done to bring relief. But when he cries because he suffers this extremely unpleasant anxiety tension, it is not assuaged. His crying may make his mother more upset and hence his unpleasant feeling is enhanced because of the (assumed) empathic linkage. Some of the very unfortunate consequences of anxiety tension in infancy may be suggested by the statement that it is in "opposition" to the satisfaction of needs and of activities. For example, it interferes with sucking and swallowing. In general, at any time of life, it tends to lower one's euphoria, with concomitant heightening of interpersonal insecurity.

A third kind of tension is the need for sleep. Because we have a long acquaintance with sleeping, we tend to forget that "the *phasic* variation" between waking and sleeping is necessary for the continuation of life. Sleep is necessary for mental health also. Physicochemical needs and especially anxiety are "oppositional" to sleep. Prolonged sleep deprivation eventuates in a marked loss of euphoria.

In the light of recent research a fourth genus of "tensions" may be postulated: those of activity, manipulation, and investigation (roughly, curiosity). Animals and the human young engage in strenuous activities, often called play, though it seems to serve the function of learning to come to grips with the environment. Anyone who has ever taken care of livestock on a farm can testify that the gamboling of spring lambs is no mere poetic phrase. On the human level, activity, whatever its instrumental function may be, has its own careless rapture. Some psychologists claim that these activities demand a *maintenance* of tension in order to sustain "good feeling." It is as if activity tensions—along with others, such as manipulation and investigation—demanded their own continuance. But for how long? And at what level? In any case, Sullivan's assumption (which is an "ideal construct") that there is an inverse relationship of absolute euphoria and absolute tension has to be translated in empirical investigation and perhaps modified. In almost all of living, he said, "there is some tension."

Observation of an infant will reveal that he delights in manipulating things. Thus activity passes over into manipulation. A puppy dog or a monkey acts somewhat similarly. "We give babies rattles and other toys early because we know that they like to hold them, shake them, pull them. We are aware that monkeys do this sort of thing, so much so that the word 'monkey' serves as a verb to describe casual manipulation for whatever satisfaction it brings. That monkeys do indeed like to 'monkey' is illustrated by a number of experiments. If various mechanical toys are placed in the monkey's cage he will begin to take them apart, becoming more skilled with practice, without any evident reward other than the satisfaction of some sort of manipulation drive (Harlow, Harlow, and Meyer, 1950). If he is fed each time that he takes the puzzle apart the behavior changes: the interest in manipulation is reduced in favor of finding in the puzzle a means to food. It appears, therefore, that manipulation is a motive in its own right."[9] Analogously, if one will place his watch within reach of a one-and-a-half-year-old child, he may pick it up, hold it, play with it, drop it on the floor, pick up the pieces and play with them.

Investigation as a motive has been broken down into three elements: orienting responses, locomotor exploration, and investigatory responses. The organism is said to respond by changes in posture and sense organ adjustments that have widespread physiological consequences when a novel or striking stimulus appears. Determinants of the orienting response include intensity, color, novelty, surprisingness, and complexity.[10]

Animals have a tendency to run about when in a new place, investigating and inspecting the environment. Rats are said to spend more time in rooms with greater complexity than in more monotonous ones, regardless of familiarity.[11] While one cannot safely infer anything in particular about the human young from such experiments, I suggest that gross observation will reveal that locomotor exploration is more outstanding in normal children than in animals.

Piaget has been the great pioneer in the psychology of so-called investigatory responses, though the motive to investigate was observed ages ago. Thus Aristotle in the *Metaphysics* declared that all men by nature desire to know. The investigatory responses entail some sort of manipulation that changes an unfamiliar object, by picking it up, tearing it apart, and the like. Piaget has recorded the inquisitive behavior of infants of varying ages.[12]

Activity, manipulation and curiosity as motives, like almost everything else in human life, cannot be clearly understood apart from interpersonal relations. In the case of human infants and children the mothering one encourages, rewards, ignores, disapproves, or punishes them when they manifest such motives. As Dewey pointed out long ago in *Human Nature and Conduct,* impulses and activities of every sort are shaped and moulded by significant adults, who in turn, as a rule, are representative of the prevailing cultural norms and attitudes. Such motives as *activity, manipulation,* and *investigation* in varying degrees become important ingredients of the self dynamism, though like almost everything else subject to enormous distortion in and through experience.

Before explicating Sullivan's maturest formulations of the self, I must take up some other fundamental ideas of his. He paid close attention in various lectures to zones of interaction. In *Conceptions of Modern Psychiatry* he briefly discusses the *oral,* the retinal, the auditory, the general tactile, the vestibulo-kinesthetic, the *anal,* and the *genital.* He thought that the oral, anal, and genital are greatly varied from person to person because of the special cultural influences that operate in their organization and functional activity. One might argue that the retinal (vision) is also varied considerably from person to person because of cultural factors, and, in varying degrees, the other zones as well, but these considerations are not of major importance for the purposes of this book. Since Sullivan attached enormous importance to the zones of interaction, partly because they are the instrumentalities by which we communicate with the world, and the latter, so to speak, communicates with us, I will summarize his ideas about some of them. From one point of view the oral zone, for example, can be subdivided into three types of apparatus: (1) a receptor apparatus that pertains to the organization of special senses, such as sight, special tactile sensations, gustatory and olfactory sensations; (2) "eductors" or, more generally, connectors within the brain and spinal cord that have to do with the reception of stimuli and integration of nervous impulses, and the activation of muscles and glands; and (3) effectors or muscles and glands. The oral zone is said to be the "end station" in the necessary varieties of communal existence with the physico-chemical world, the world of the infrahuman and the human world. Processes in and pertaining to this zone and all other zones have a great deal to do with experience, from infancy onward.

In another context, where "eductor" pertains to mental activity, Sullivan said that when he mentioned the eductor aspect of the zones of interaction, he was referring to *knowing,* that is, the understanding, interpretation, recognition, and contemplation of goals in regard to the lust dynamism. More generally, in regard to mental capacity in this connection, there are facilatory, precautionary, and inhibitory referential (or symbolic) processes. The first of these has to do with processes that facilitate the identifying of situations that might be appropriately integrated. Precautionary measures are said to have been taught us by the difficulties of dealing with tenderness and other motivations that call for the kindly intervention of others. Such measures make it possible for us to conceal the fact, when we think it necessary, that we are motivated by lust, for example, and tend to protect us from making fools of ourselves. Inhibitory processes make it impossible, sometimes, or very difficult, to interpret the activities of the receptor apparatus as an experience of lust. This occurs when "lustful integrations" would collide with the self-system .[13]

Just as receptor, connector, and effector apparatuses are involved in, not one or two, but all zones of interaction, so the "eductor equipment" is involved conspicuously in the major zones of interaction.

Experience relates "backward and forward"—it is retrospective and prospective, as manifested in recall and foresight—to the particular zone of interaction to which it is related. This seems to be especially true of very young infants, though in adults experience is frequently general rather than partial or local. Moreover, experience pertaining to a particular zone becomes "colored" in a unique fashion; it is qualitatively different from the experience had in connection with some other zone, such as the genital, which in preadolescence and especially adolescence contributes a powerful share to various new kinds of experience.

The retinal area or zone of interaction, along with the auditory, is of peculiar significance. Sullivan pointed out, as previously stated, that we learn in infancy that objects that our distance receptors—eyes and ears, primarily encounter—are of a quite different order of relationship from things that our tactile or gustatory receptors encounter. With the help of optical apparatus, the retinal zone enables us to see over unimaginably great distances. But it is also "peculiarly" related to objects within reach. It is closely connected "with dexterity, with our prehensile and manipulative skills shown primarily in the functional activity of the hands."[14]

One can hardly overemphasize the significance of the "strong invasion of culture" into the physiology of the organism: For psychiatrists this is a matter of central importance. Thus the oral, anal, and genital zones become profoundly affected by the processes and procedures of eductional acculturation. The very young, for example, are taught, whether explicitly or implicitly, that certain things must not be smelled, that others cannot be tasted, and still others not touched: Thus it comes about that, for instance, many people's olfactory abilities are seriously impaired. According to Sullivan, the genital is so conditioned by the attitudes, the prejudices, and beliefs of the parents, that it is apt to be forever impaired for its biological function. In the teaching of rather elaborate toilet habits, the anal zone is also strongly conditioned by the culturally derived attitudes of the parents.

Activities that are symptomatic of a "symbolic segregation" of various parts of the body occur. Thus the genital may be so conditioned by the irrational attitudes of the parents that it may be permanently impaired for its biological or reproductive function. Any activity connected with this part of the body may be looked upon as disgraceful, disgusting, and damned. Manipulating the genital may become intensely anxiety-provoking. Such attitudes may be incorporated into the self dynamism, with episodic or periodic lowering of self-esteem. The anal zone may become analogously conditioned and "marked."

Zonal needs may be mentioned at this point. General needs, such as those for food and water, have to do with the requirements of the organism as a whole. But in addition to the fact that zonal needs are instrumentalities of general needs—water, for example, is taken in through the mouth—they are manifestations of more or less localized conditions as well. The need to suck is a classic example. Freud thought that sucking for its own sake was a manifestation of the sexual drive. Sucking provides libidinal pleasure. Sullivan, in the later years with the help of data provided by David Levy, held that pleasure sucking in an infant has nothing to do with the sexual drive; it is a way of getting rid of excess energy. Nature provides more than sufficient energy required for the satisfaction of the needs for food and water. The excess energy begins to be channeled as a need to exercise the oral zone. In general, what Freud called autoerotic activity in infants is interpreted by Sullivan as an expression of the beginning need to exercise a particular zone. The latter emphasized the activities of the oral and genital zones of interaction.[15]

Sullivan not only stressed the powerlessness of the infant—which anyone can see—he inferred several specific consequences of it. However, very soon, crying, as in crying-when-hungry becomes a very powerful tool: When the baby is hungry or thirsty or in pain, he cries and some significant adult "rallies round" and relieves the distress. In fact, the mother may learn to distinguish different qualities of crying. Crying-when-hungry is not quite the same thing as, say, crying-when-frightened. In any case the baby catches on to the fact that the cry brings results, what adults might call remarkable results. But sometimes nothing may happen after the baby cries when he is hungry. Mother may be gossiping with a neighbor next door. Possibly mother left him in the care of a baby-sitter who wants to watch uninterruptedly the current episode in that great American television drama series, "Peyton Place." So when nothing happens the baby may lapse into apathy, a sleeplike state, which finally culminates in sleep. When he awakens and cries again nothing may happen. In normal homes this is a perhaps relatively rare occurrence, the experience of unexpected powerlessness following upon the failure of the cry. (One should not overlook the possibility that it is a frequent occurrence in some homes, with serious consequences for the infant.) The failure of crying-when-hungry can be crudely expressed as failure to produce the nipple—the "good," milk-or-formula-giving nipple: But normally it is infrequent enough to be "quite exterior to expectation."

Thus Sullivan held:

> The accompaniments of these experiences of powerlessness are various. The significance of such experiences of powerlessness probably increases for some time after birth, until one has developed adequate ways of handling such experiences and by adequate I mean personally adequate in the sense of avoiding very unpleasant emotion. The very early experiences would, if they continued long enough, unquestionably produce very marked effects on the developing personality of the infant, but here the intervention of the dynamism of apathy tones off, as it were, these instances of powerlessness. . . . And so the intervention of the apathy processes, to which I have already referred, prevents a serious complicating effect from the relatively infrequent instances of the infant's powerlessness to produce the nipple by the cry.[16]

Frequent success is said to have a very powerful influence in determining the character of foresight, of anticipation, even very early in life. To use a very old-fashioned jargon, the expectation of tenderness gets "stamped in." In other situations something very different happens: Anxiety in the mother in connection with anything at all that is happening in her world induces anxiety tension in the infant when she is nursing or feeding him from a bottle. As she draws near to nurse him, when she is anxious, the infant experiences a sudden drop in euphoria. Now the lips-nipple configuration is something new and different from the satisfying lips-nipple configuration. Mother has, so to speak, presented a different and evil sort of nipple even though there is no visual difference. So he will not hold it in his mouth and suck it. This may, in turn, aggravate the anxiety of the mother, perhaps then further lowering the infant's euphoria.

If the infant suffers prolonged and intense anxiety he may lapse into *somnolent detachment*, which, like apathy, is a sleeplike state. But apathy is evoked by unsatisfied, extremely aggravated needs, while somnolent detachment is evoked by inescapable and prolonged anxiety. Apathy reduces the tension of needs, so that they become markedly attenuated. Somnolent detachment serves as a different kind of safety device; it attenuates one's susceptibility to the interpersonally induced tension of anxiety. In an unpublished lecture Sullivan speculated that if these safety devices have to be frequently employed and unduly prolonged their use may result in permanent physical and/or psychological injury.

The good and evil nipple of infancy gradually evolves into the good and evil mother, who in the infant's experience are, in adult language, two different beings. Meanwhile the infant is developing the ability to differentiate independent aspects of the infant-environment complex though this is by no means an instantaneous affair. Increasingly the infant learns to distinguish differences in similarly perceived objects, just as he gradually learns to distinguish differences in the perceived parts of his own body. The identifying of differences in perceived objects is the precursor of "recognition" (*re*-cognition). This identifying process invariably *antecedes* recognition and it is a precursor or sign in all *acts* of recognition. The infant's identifying is said to progress to the point at which he is able to generalize experience that is marked with the characteristics of several zones of interaction—tactile, thermal, gustatory, olfactory, kinesthetic, visual, aural—as experience pertaining to *one* recurrent pattern of sentience from the distance receptors. In other words, the visual and auditory experiences are taking precedence over everything else in regard to his perception and experience of objects forming a particular rudimentary perceptual pattern. When this happens, the infant has taken the first great step beyond the prototaxic mode and is beginning to perceive things, and more generally experience things, in the parataxic mode. Under the driving necessity to avoid the feeling of anxiety, he can distinguish between the good, tender mother and the evil, anxiety-provoking mother. But how?

Gradually the infant learns to discriminate forbidding (and encouraging) gestures, chiefly those of the mothering one. He does this by means of visual and auditory cues. "This matter of the infant's refined discrimination of what we call forbidding gestures first applies to the mother and thereafter applies throughout life to practically all significant people—that is, those people who come to have an important place in his living, in other words, his interpersonal relationships. The discrimination of heard differences in the mother's vocalization and seen differences in the postural tensions of the mother's face, and perhaps later of differences in speed and rhythm of her gross bodily movements in coming toward the infant, presenting the bottle, changing the diapers, or what not—all these rather refined discriminations by the distance receptors of vision and hearing are organized as indices frequently associated with the unpleasant experience of anxiety, including the nipple of anxiety instead of the good nipple."[17]

Sooner or later these forbidding gestures are generalized, becoming characteristics of practically all significant others, while they themselves have grown to be signs of impending anxiety. Originally they were simply associated with the bad nipple. Eventually they are differentiated as significant characteristics of the bad mother. With increasing age, they undergo still greater refinement, become signs of disapproval. Still later (via a simple statement such as, "*Jane,* you are very *lively* this evening") a mother, by inflection, intonation, articulation, of speech patterns can convey to her early teen-age daughter at, say, a dinner party in her home the message: "You are talking too much, and acting silly. Shut up."

Clearly the infant's personifications of the mother are not the real mother, not the flesh-and-blood embodiment of womanhood known to her husband, relatives, and friends. In later infancy there is said to be a synthesis of experience that more or less obliterates the primary discrimination so that an adequate perception of the mother as a person who is sometimes good (tender and approving) and sometimes bad (frustrating and disapproving or anxiety-provoking) evolves. On the other hand the mother's personification of her offspring is not the real infant, in the sense that her perception of her baby is at least often distorted by various irrelevant factors. For example, part of what he symbolizes to her is her recognition of her social responsibilities with respect to him. This recognition of her social responsibilities in an inexperienced or insecure mother may stir up anxiety in her, thus reinforcing the infant's personification of the bad or evil mother. A mother's personification of her infant, after she has already borne several children, may have more to do with her experience of the first or second offspring than of the one now before her. In any case, her previous experience will influence the way in which she perceives and relates to the infant. Sometimes the second-born may benefit considerably from the mistakes mother made with her first-born child.

Various studies of socially and psychologically deprived children of families living in the slums seem to lend support to Sullivan's ideas on child-parent relationships. A reviewer of a book on such families wrote the following: "In part the authors arrived at the same findings that others have made (Mattick and Malone, Martin Deutsch) concerning the failure to attend, the poor memory, the need for motor discharge, the absence of impulse control, the deficit in internalization, the failure to abstract and differentiate. They go beyond others when they relate the poor communication that goes on in the family, and the patterns of interaction, to the children's inadequate attempts to cope with the world outside the home."[18]

During the earlier part of infancy the mothering one tends to give unqualified cooperation in the fulfillment of the infant's needs. Subsequently, during the latter part of infancy she regards him as educable, to a degree, more and more capable of learning. So he is then increasingly subject to the parent's efforts at discharging her social responsibilities. Mother believes her offspring should start learning certain things, so she begins to restrict her tender behavior under certain circumstances. As a rule, she is an ordinary, average human being, not an embodiment of supernal widsom, the purveyor of the virtues and limitations of her "culture" or subculture and social class. The mothering one teaches her offspring how to eat and drink; or, as Sullivan would say, she provides training in the functional activity of the oral-manual zones. Usually, the society in which she lives dictates the period during which she should teach him acceptable toilet and other habits. Sometimes the period of toilet training of the infant is a bit of an ordeal for an American middle-class mother, especially when she regards his bowel movements as a very messy, if not disgusting, affair. This attitude may be contrasted with that of a peasant woman in an agricultural society, who usually has a relaxed, good-humored, earthy attitude toward the whole business. Moreover, she does not have to worry about expensive furniture or carpets, or dainty clothing getting soiled. Still again the American mother may sometimes become resentful of the time and energy required in the teaching of proper eating habits, toilet habits, and the like. (Imagine the following occurrence at a somewhat later period when mother takes Johnny to the moving pictures. She takes him into the lavatory and places him on a toilet seat. Then there is the following interchange: "Go." "I don't have to go, Ma." "Go!" "But I don't have to go, Ma." "In five minutes the movie starts, and you can't go then, so go now!" In a mechanized world even "natural functions" tend to be regulated by the clock.)

Training entails more or less focused approval and disapproval. Sullivan claimed that very often there is a rewarding tenderness arising from the mothering one's pleasure at sight of the skill that her offspring has learned—in contrast to the universal, unconditional tenderness of early infancy. The rewards for good (successful) behavior become something special, which implies that the awareness of the infant becomes more and more concentrated on particular actions of his own and of the significant other. He enjoys approval and suffers when he encounters disapproval. Unfortunately, some mothers believe that an infant of, say, one year of age, can and does become willfully troublesome and difficult, an attitude that entails disastrous consequences for the youngster, since he will encounter a vast amount of disapproval. However, what is important to emphasize at this point in the exposition is that the infant gradually learns to differentiate approved situations, which enhance euphoria, from those situations that bring a measure of disapproval and hence some degree of anxiety. So with training, grades or degrees of anxiety first become of great importance in learning. Unsatisfactory behavior of certain types brings increasing anxiety, which the infant learns to veer away from, which is a way of saying he learns to alter his behavior in a maneuver that will minimize or counteract the disapproval of the mothering one. Obviously, then, training entails approval of some actions of the infant while it brings various degrees of disapproval of others as the mother or her surrogate proceeds with the task of fulfilling her social responsibilities. To a large degree the cultural norms and patterns that she has assimilated will dictate the manner in which she goes about this, though one cannot ignore her own unique make-up, which is bound to affect the ways she interprets and fulfills her role as mother.

One can scarcely do more than suggest in a general way how the "anxiety gradient" operates in numerous instances to affect and alter the behavior of an infant. Severe anxiety probably does not convey any information—perhaps at any stage of life. It "wipes out" any experience or occurrence that immediately precedes or accompanies it. One simply does not know what it was. (In *The Psychiatric Interview* Sullivan gives several illustrations of such occurrences in adults and their significance for therapy.) However, less severe anxiety does permit a gradual realization of the situation in which it occurs. Thus, if the infant manipulates the genital when mother can observe him, he may suffer some anxiety. Then the genital is no longer manipulated, though the infant may have discovered quite by accident that it is a source of pleasant sentience—at least until mother intervened. He learns perhaps through the instrumentality of empathy or the observation of forbidding gestures that he suffers an unpleasant feeling when he touches the genital. So he stops. In this fashion there is learning of an inhibitory nature, though it does not follow that the infant understands what happened.

Less severe anxiety makes it possible for the infant to discriminate increasing from diminishing anxiety and to alter his activity in the direction of the latter. This Sullivan called the anxiety gradient. He thought that an immense amount of human behavior in any society is learned on the basis of this gradient from anxiety to euphoria, though he believed this is outstandingly the case in American society. Thus the infant who by force of anxiety stops manipulating the genital may discover that it is all right to touch or rub the umbilicus, bringing about a very important alteration of behavior. He has learned that manipulating the genital must not occur when mother is around though it is all right to touch and manipulate other parts of the body. Analogously, he may learn that he must not rub the anal region when mother is present though "fiddling" with it through a blanket (even if he does not recognize the blanket as such) brings much less unpleasant feeling. This is a rudimentary form of *sublimation*: a "long-circulating" of the resolution of situations chiefly those of zonal needs, in the beginning, a long circuiting that is socially acceptable. In other words, the infant has *unwittingly* adapted some pattern of activity, which will partially satisfy a need while it circumvents anxiety.

Sullivan distinguished several other kinds of learning, which appear, at least in elementary form, in infancy. The learning of how to do things by trial and success is one. A fairly simple example is that of the infant's learning how to get the thumb into the proper position in the mouth. Though there are many misses, at first, the "hits" are rewarding and thus the successful pattern gets stamped in. Observation of an infant or young child will reveal how numerous behavior patterns are thus learned.

Another sort of learning is the process of learning by rewards and punishments. Unlike trial and success learning, which has no essential connection with significant others, though it may be encouraged and reinforced by them, learning by rewards and punishments is always an interpersonal affair. Sullivan claimed that the rewards that encourage learning in the very young probably begin with fondling. In general, rewards are said to take the pattern of a change from relative indifference to the youngster to more or less active approval of whatever he seems to be doing. Very early in human life a need for an audience response appears. Even a passive, affectionate observer is very welcome. But babies like to be picked up, hugged, played with, sung to. Normal young infants display a remarkable facility at enticing the parent to become involved and participate in their goings-on. Of course the vicissitudes of family and social life may encourage or discourage the parent in his relations with the child. A peasant woman who works in the fields all day may have only enough time and energy to nurse her baby. An upper-middle-class or upper-class American woman may be so caught up in her important social activities that she has to delegate her job as mother to a nurse—if she can find one. An "underprivileged" mother, who has to go out to work five or six days a week, may have to put her baby in the charge of an elder sibling.

Little need be said about material rewards in regard to any phase of child development. In the United States of America, children are all too often surfeited with various kinds of toys and gadgets—sometimes apparently as a substitute for the affection that the mother cannot offer.

With the exception of the induction of severe anxiety, punishment can be educative, provided it is neither harsh nor cruel nor stupid, that is, ill-timed. Punishments include the inflicting of pain, the refusal to contact or of attention, and the withholding of privileges. Although no intelligent, normal mother will slap a six-months-old baby, a year or two later a hard slap on the hand whenever the youngster approaches a hot stove or tries to break away from mother's grasp when they are outdoors on the street may save him from getting burned or running blindly in front of a speeding car. It is unwise to attempt to explain Newton's laws of motion to a two-year-old. On the other hand, corporal punishment in the case of a ten- or twelve-year-old sometimes can be so humiliating to the youngster that it may be not only self-defeating (because it may engender defiance or stratagems to perform the forbidden activity), it may arouse intense hostility because of the assault on the youngster's self-esteem. Even so, there are times when nothing else seems to work, as in certain situations in which, for example, a youngster is given to beating up a younger sibling or a neighbor's child.

Beginning with the juvenile era, the foresight of isolation, the fear of ostracism, and loneliness become increasingly threatening. Juveniles can be surprisingly expert at punishing one of their peers. Corporal punishment may be a very mild penalty in comparison with ostracism. And so one perforce may have to learn certain things, such as compromise and cooperation. During preadolescence loneliness can be fearsome. Probably few can withstand it for long and most will go to very great lengths to avoid it.

Trail-and-error learning from human example can scarcely be over-rated. Let us take smiling. John B. Watson had the curious idea that it begins at birth and can be aroused by intraorganic stimulation and by contact, for example, by the mother's touching the baby's cheek. On this view, a smile is a more or less fixed face pattern that resembles reflex action. Since Watson professed to believe that mind is a medieval superstition, one is not too surprised. At present, many psychologists would say that the "meaning" of smiling is learned, just as Watson might say it becomes "conditioned." Accidental expressive postures of the face become identified with smiling. A grimace, as it were, becomes a smile.

Sullivan's ideas on expressive postures are so important that I shall quote them at length:

> By mid-infancy, solely because of contact with the mothering one and any other significant people, the infant has learned certain patterns of postural tension of the face that are right and wrong. Among the most important of all these learnings is the coordination of posture and change of posture—that is, the expressive movement—of the face which is ordinarily called smiling. It might be thought, and in fact I am sure that for many years it has been

taught, that we are born with instincts, or something of that general class, for smiling, and, I suppose, for expressing all sorts of things from respectful admiration to frank disgust. But that charmingly simple idea undergoes a little damage when we lift our eyes from our own community and bring them down on the very young in a strikingly alien culture area, such as, for example, Bali or one of the Micronesian Islands in the period before the war and the diffusion of Western culture. In these places, oddly enough, some human beings seem not to have the instinct to smile in the sense that we know it, but instead an instinct to smile in a very different way, so different that you wouldn't recognize it as a smile until you noticed what the others did in a similar situation. The point is that man has an unending, a numerically enormous, number of possible resting states of the face, and a still more enormous number of transitions in resting states of these so-called expressive muscles. Thus a truly astounding number of so-called expressions is possible, and it is by the organization of initially prototaxic experience, later elaborated further into combinations of sentience from various zones, that the infant gradually picks out from this numerical multitude rough approximations to what the culture-carriers esteem as expressions. That is literally the way that a great deal of our facial expression comes into being.[19]

Finally, there is what is perhaps the most characteristically human type of learning: the eduction of relations. It is in essence human intelligence, for it pertains to the ability to grasp the relations or connections of things. Before the infant learns to talk he manifests, in elementary form, an ability to grasp certain rudimentary aspects of his interpersonal relations with the mothering one.

One should bear in mind that the various types of learning mentioned above, and possibly others not known to Sullivan, in varying degrees, occur from infancy to adulthood. Otherwise, the development of personality becomes a very mysterious affair.

It has been pointed out previously that the self or self-dynamism is not coterminous with personality, since the former is a subsystem of the latter. Sullivan defined personality as the relatively enduring pattern of recurrent interpersonal situations that characterize the life of a human being, while the self includes only those that are meaningful. This fact makes the explication of the self more difficult. All that has been written so far in this chapter may be regarded as preliminary spadework for the construction of the theory of the self. A rudimentary awareness of the body, which develops out of self-sentience, is a part or aspect of the dawning self-consciousness. Before the infant is aware that he is an entity different and separate from the rest of the world, he experiences a stream of sensations from various parts of the body. At the same time, so to speak, he is exploring and manipulating what adults know are parts of his body while he also explores and manipulates objects in his vicinity. Sullivan wrote that by midinfancy the hands are exploring all reachable parts of the infant's life space and are encountering a variety of objects that fall into two genera: the self-sentient (which is the ultimate basis of what other writers have called the "bodily me") and the non-self-sentient. Though the self-sentient is not the self, it is "the point of departure" for the development of ths self, a very important part of which is the "me" of everyday discourse. The self-sentient originates as follows: "The mouth feels the thumb, and the thumb feels the mouth; that is self-sentience." Thus as the baby explores with his hands he feels (what he will ultimately recognize as) various parts of his body, which in turn "feel" (are sensitive to) his hands. Other things, such as the blanket, are felt by the hands but do not, in turn, feel the hands. The latter objects are the non-self-sentient that will eventually be recognized as external to "me" and "my body." No doubt visual perception also cooperates in the "prehension" of the self-sentient in contrast to the non-self-sentient.

It would be a mistake to equate the self-sentient with a clear-cut, differentiated awareness of a "bodily me." One must not read adult distinctions into the infantile mind. Moreover, it takes a good deal of sophistication to distinguish any subsystem or part of the self (how often can adults clearly distinguish the "me" from the "bodily me"?). The self-sentient infant interacts with significant others and, as a result, the self-dynamism in late infancy begins to develop. But Sullivan's account of self-development is more subtle than this. About midinfancy two personifications connected with the self-sentient baby develop, namely, *good-me* and *bad-me*, which eventually fuse and become *me*, unqualified. But throughout life during periods of prolonged, intense stress the original bifurcation or its analogue may appear.

Good-me is said to be the beginning personification that organizes experience in which satisfactions have been enhanced by the tenderness of the mothering one. In short, good-me is a function of the love that a mother manifests toward her offspring. It is the *sine qua non* of an individual's self-esteem. Good-me is ultimately the subject of *me, myself, I.* That is, we normally tend to think of ourselves as "good," estimable, worthy—unless parents and/or significant figures in later life have subjected us to prolonged destructive (hostile, cruel, anxiety-provoking) experience. Of course, as the youngster grows, he is normally less and less vulnerable to the psychological inroads that others may unwittingly or deliberately try to inflict.

Bad-me is said to be the beginning personification that organizes experience in which increasing degrees of anxiety are associated with the mothering one. The mother's anxiety-provoking attitudes, including disapproval are prehended ("sensed") by the infant. So the "frequent coincidence of certain behavior on the part of the infant with increasing tenseness and increasingly evident forbidding on the part of the mother is the source of the type of experience which is organized as a rudimentary personification to which we may apply the term bad-me."[20] Although it is impossible to be precise about these matters of infantile experience, it follows that if "bad-me" is more firmly built into the dawning self-consciousness than "good-me," the individual will be starting out in life with fragile self-esteem. It will ordinarily be very difficult for him to grow with the deeply felt conviction that he is a worthy person who can enlist the respect of significant others. This may become very clearly evident during the juvenile era, when, sometimes, a malevolent transformation of personality occurs. In any case, the origins and consequences of bad-me are a very fertile field for future psychiatric study.

When the infant is about one and a half years, normally, good-and bad-me fuse and the me, unqualified, emerges. This *me* is, approximately, the personified self or that to which we refer when we say "I" (in contrast to "You," "He," "They") and forms the core of the self-dynamism. William James made a formal distinction between the "I" or "Knower" and the "Me" or "Known" (when "I," the Knower, take "myself" as object) but Sullivan did not. Sullivan did not attempt to separate the two aspects of the self. The self or self-dynamism is primarily a system or organization of meaningful interpersonal processes, real and "imaginary," or rather a fusion of both. It is a dynamic, more or less consistent, and meaningful pattern of life experiences. It maintains continuity, not identity, of pattern. There is no evidence that this continuity *normally* is ever broken. From late infancy or early childhood to adulthood the self grows and develops. Thus the pattern or structure of the self normally is never sundered. It develops and hence changes, possibly by minute increments, from month to month, though there is no way as yet to measure these things in a fashion analogous to that by which growth of the body can be measured. Sullivan once thought that as the self takes on structure it tends to maintain it.[21] He should have said it tends to maintain *continuity* of structure. That is probably what he *meant* since it is absurd to think of the self of a five-year-old as identical with that of a twenty-year-old. In any event, without self-continuity there is chaos—or schizophrenia.

Once adulthood or maturity is reached the structure of the self undoubtedly maintains itself indefinitely under normal circumstances. Self-system processes become uniform or "recurrent." However, for many people, middle age, with its foreshadowing of declining powers, lost opportunities, limited horizons, brings stress and difficulties in living. How much these things may affect the self is unclear. Probably several factors, some of which would pertain to the individual's previous history, and others to contemporary environmental circumstances, have to be considered.

In ideal circumstances the self would continue to grow until one reached old age. But this book is not primarily concerned with the ideal.

It is a moot question how much weight should be attributed to the first five or six years of life. Freud seems to have thought that the essentials of self-structure are established during those years. This cannot be literally true since a great deal of self-development is overtly manifested during the following ten to fifteen years at least. Yet it is easy to go to the other extreme because the later years are increasingly accessible to investigation. While Sullivan did not agree with Freud, he did attach enormous significance to the early years— almost to the point of self-contradiction in the *Conceptions.* There is no doubt that "early training" and early experience generally have a great deal to do with the character and structure of the self-dynamism, but the latter probably are not as fixed during the early years—in *normal people*—as Sullivan seems to have once thought. In the *Interpersonal Theory of Psychiatry,* the overemphasis on early life experience is largely abandoned. A more detailed analysis of the contributions to self-development during every phase of growth is given. In any event, the first five or six years of life are so crucially important that a great deal of unfortunate experience then (which can be so subtly provided that it escapes the eye of a naïve behavioristic child psychologist) may permanently stunt and distort the development of the self—witness "child schizophrenia." Unfortunately, opportunities for close and prolonged study of the interactions of the mother and her offspring are not readily available. The notion that "child schizophrenia" stems largely from hereditary factors is from a Sullivanian point of view— short of demonstrable inherited organic impairment or defect—erroneous.

The question as to whether the character and structure of the self are more or less permanently established during the early years of life brings up another, and related, problem. Is the self as an interpersonal dynamism constituted of "reflected appraisals" (good-me and bad-me) from the parents and other significant people? If the reflected appraisals are meant to cover only the first five or six years of life, the answer is no. Definitely no. But what if they are meant to cover the period from infancy to adulthood, which is what Sullivan apparently had in mind? There is no ready answer—speculations about freedom, autonomy, self-realization, and the like aside. This is another area in which detailed empirical study is needed. It is possible that Sullivan, and before him, Mead, have overstated their case, but that remains to be discovered.

Since experience functions in both recall and foresight, it seems almost inevitable that the character of the self will reflect or at least be circumscribed by the attitudes of the "generalized other," as Mead might say—that is, a cumulative residue from past and anticipated relations with significant others. But this does not rule out a gradual and partial modification of the self if one has the ability and "drive."[22] In this case the self becomes related to and influenced by new significant others. One must also add that the dissociated dynamism may "contain" elements or impulses that do not conform to the self. Whether or not such impulses can contribute to personal growth and greater freedom depends partly on their character or quality, but also on the, usually extraordinary, circumstances that may permit their recognition and integration. A long time ago C. G. Jung pointed out that some of the "best" as well as the "worst" features of personality may be "unconscious."

There is a third gradually evolving "personification" (in addition to good-me and bad-me) to be explicated, namely, the *not-me*. In essence the not-me pertains to characteristics of the personality that one regards as dreadful and subsequently as loathsome or abhorrent. This personification, which appears in rudimentary form in infancy, evolves very gradually. Its beginning takes shape as a result of intense anxiety, perhaps frequently in connection with some of the infant's "autoerotic" activities. It is also possible, for example, that a young mother's attitude toward her child may change profoundly during infancy or childhood because of some radical change in her life circumstances, such as a divorce. The youngster may come to be regarded as an intolerable burden so that when he seeks affection his efforts are met with intense disapproval and harsh rejection. Gradually, as the youngster grows, any impulse to seek affection from a woman (since the mother tends to be a "symbol" of womanhood) creates a feeling of dread, or, more accurately becomes associated with "incidents" that are attended by dread, loathing, awe, or horror.

The experiences that have been associated with intense anxiety, caused by intense forbidding gestures by the mother, cannot be understood by the "victim." Intense anxiety paralyzes any effort at differentiating causes and consequences. They are said to persist throughout life as relatively primitive, and unelaborated, occurring in the parataxic mode. These not-me (or "not of-me") experiences are not confined to the abnormal. Perhaps everyone in infancy and/or childhood has some intense anxiety-provoking experiences, which manifest themselves in nightmares. The personification, not-me, is "very emphatically encountered" by people undergoing a schizophrenic episode. In contrast to good-me and bad-me, not-me never becomes a part of the self. From very early in life there is a transfer of some aspects of "my body" to the "not-me" aspect of the world. It persists in dissociation. If one wishes to employ traditional Freudian language, one may conceive of the not-me as part of the "deep unconscious." The infantile or early childhood not-me may also be conceived to be the deepest, most primitive layer of unconscious experiences that become manifest in schizophrenic episodes during preadolescence or adolescence, since primitive not-me processes tend to be more or less "fixated" and change but slowly.

It is a profound error to think that the infant is *mindless*. By midinfancy various *covert* processes occur, which, however. can be grasped only through inference, not from direct observation. When "speech behavior" begins to appear, it provides a "wonderfully good index" to the probability of correctness of any particular inference regarding the covert psychological processes of infants. Sullivan thought that the occurrence of delayed behavior also provides evidence for the existence of such processes. Needs manifest a hierarchical organization. An infant may be doing something or other that satisfies some need when hunger supervenes. After the infant has been fed he resumes the previous, interrupted activity, though perhaps with some alteration of its pattern. Symbol operations have been occurring meanwhile "behind a screen," as it were, which carry or bridge the interrupted activity forward after the hunger has been satisfied. Much more elaborated covert processes more or less of this type take place in adults during sleep.

From the end of the first year the "immediately and vastly most important" kinds of overt behavior that are learned are gesture and language. Gesture includes not only facial expressions but vocal tonal patterns, such as the rhythm and melody of speech. A twelve-month-old may already have learned these things—by trial and error from human example ("imitation"). Even earlier he will have begun "syllabic experimentation" as part of his learning some of the important elements of speech. Perhaps he will hit upon an approximation of "ma-ma" or "da-da" during his vocalization, which he may tend to repeat. If the parent regards such a repetitive sound pattern as evidence that the baby already "knows" her (or his) pet name she (or he) will be usually delighted. Hence the baby will receive an increment of tenderness, that is, a reward. In such a manner many sound patterns in the course of time get stamped in, perhaps also reinforced by the youngster's enjoyment of the exercise of his vocalizing ability. Various other vocal patterns are met with indifference. Eventually these vocal patterns disappear from the baby's verbal patterns. They are, so to speak, stamped out. This phenomenon is part of teaching by *indifference.*

Indifference provides the paradigm of the subsequent fear of ostracism, one of the most potent of human fears. In fact, as interpersonal relations develop, indifference or its threat becomes a potent element of socialization. Most adolescents and adults tend to find the accidental or studied indifference of peers, neighbors, associates, colleagues a very unpleasant experience. The bitter tears of an unpopular adolescent girl, for instance, are comical only to the dull-witted or insensitive.

Chiefly as a result of trial and error learning from human example, the baby gradually learns a variety of verbal patterns, which, according to social convention, form words in the language of the parents. Strictly speaking, only when the child learns the socially defined meanings of these verbal patterns can they be called words. Otherwise, by and large, verbal patterns do not make sense, and cannot communicate the experiences of the child. They may have considerable "meaning" for the child but they have no public, verifiable meaning. And when the meaning of verbal patterns continues to be private and idiosyncratic, they can be called autistic since they are incapable of "consensual validation." And it seems to be the case that most people often retain a private, idiosyncratic penumbra of personal meaning to many of the words they employ in everyday speech—especially when they leave the more familiar world of things and concrete activities for the more abstract world of thought.

When the infant has progressed to a point at which he can designate some of his experiences and activities by what adults call nouns, verbs, adjectives, he is beginning to manifest experience in the *syntaxic* mode. That is, he can employ words that have been consensually validated. This implies he is beginning to employ communicative speech so that a consensus of meaning is or can be achieved. "A consensus has been reached," Sullivan said, "when the infant or child has learned the precisely right word for a situation, a word which means not only what it is thought to mean by the mothering one, but also means that to the infant."[23] Of course, during the period under discussion, roughly the end of the first to the end of the second year, the infant still experiences a great deal in the parataxic mode. Nor should one forget that in reverie the youngster carries on a good deal of living in wordless thinking. Moreover, this form of living, in reverie, continues throughout life.

According to Sullivan's formulations, childhood is "ushered in" by the capacity to employ language at least in a rudimentary form. The distinctions between the different "eras" or "epochs" are not absolute. For example, a very bright and emotionally secure youngster may enter the childhood era earlier than most. On the other hand, an older child, whether intelligent or not, if he or she is a very anxious and warped person, may remain transfixed in the preadolescent era indefinitely. Still again there are many chronological adults who marry, bear children, live respectable lives, who have regressed to the juvenile era. They are capable at activities involving cooperation, competition, compromise, social accommodation, and the like, but they have lost the capability for collaboration and intimacy, which first appear during preadolescence.

During the past twenty to twenty-five years child psychologists and psychiatrists have learned a great deal about personality development, that is, roughly from the time when Sullivan's formulations as we know them had been worked out. While it would not be very difficult to incorporate most of this information, I shall not attempt it partly because such a great body of facts would require an additional volume. The most important thing to keep in mind, from a Sullivanian point of view, is that this knowledge is relatively useless until it is interpreted in the light of the development of the self-dynamism; or more broadly in the perspective of the development of the personality (the self and dissociated systems). A mere enumeration of the facts of each stage or phase does not contribute a great deal to the understanding of the person. The present is not merely historically continuous with the past; it employs, via retention, recall, recollection, and the like, an accumulation of past experiences in some more or less orderly fashion.

According to Sullivan, the self-dynamism gradually takes on a tendency or peculiarity that is designed to preserve self-esteem or self-respect at almost any cost. For psychiatric purposes he recast this idea in the "theorem of escape." The self is said to be extraordinarily resistant to change by certain kinds of experience. In other words, the self-dynamism, owing to its structure, functional activity, and environmental relationships, tends to reject experiences that are incongruous with its current organization, relationships to the environing world, and functional activities. Under normal peacetime circumstances, the resistance to change is *not* primarily caused by fear though under highly abnormal, more or less catastrophic circumstances, the self may be radically altered or disintegrate because of fear, terror, and related experiences. If the new is not soluble in the old, it tends to be selectively inattended or dissociated.

Since fear and anxiety are often confused—and since this confusion has unfortunate consequences in psychiatry—an explication of some of their differences is necessary. Anxiety is a product of acculturation and of living with significant people. It is acquired from one's experiences with people. Though the young infant first experiences or feels anxiety tension prior to the development of the self, owing to the empathic linkage of the mothering one and her offspring, it becomes the "mainspring" of self-development. That is, it is the major instrumentality of the self when anything happens that would disturb or alter the latter's current organization and functional activity. The organization and functional activity of the self arise from interpersonal relations. From Sullivan's point of view, the need to avoid or minimize anxiety, due chiefly to cultural norms, is the major experiential determinant of the particular structure that the self takes on. But the self is not only an "antianxiety" device; it is at the same time the power —owing to its organization and functional activity—by means of which the human organism perceives and apprehends the world. Apparently Sullivan assumed that this is "obvious," but it is not. One learns to relate to the world in certain ways because of the necessity to escape or minimize anxiety. But the organization of the self that comes into being for that purpose takes on a life of its own; as Gordon Allport might say, it becomes functionally autonomous. Though Sullivan may have overemphasized the influence of early life experience in the evolution of the self—one is not too sure about that—once the self with its particular structure emerges it tends to maintain it. And this tendency is closely linked up with anxiety (and perhaps fear as well). Thus the "antianxiety" device tends, within limits, to become self-perpetuating. When potentially new and perhaps highly educative experience becomes objectively available, the self, through the instrumentality of anxiety and its concomitants, tends to evade it by such stratagems as selective inattention or, in certain cases, dissociation.

Now, in the lectures compiled in *The Interpersonal Theory of Psychiatry,* Sullivan was careful to say that the delimiting power of the self is itself limited. The only valid question is: Do his formulations allow sufficiently for growth despite the interventions of the antianxiety system? This is for future research to decide. But it seems likely that Sullivan is closer to the truth than, say, Gordon Allport, who, in *Pattern and Growth in Personality,* almost ignores the limiting, controlling aspects of culture. Sullivan was explicit in stating that the lifelong tendency of the self-system to escape profit from experience is not absolute— otherwise growth might seem to be a mystery. "Because of the general effect on personality which accompanies every newly matured need or capacity in the early stages of each developmental phase," he said, "the functional activity of the self system is peculiarly open to fortunate change" by experience.[24] But the occasions, the "setup" for such change to be reasonably expected among people with serious difficulties in living, often have to be elaborate and very considerably prolonged. In therapy so great is the resistance of the self to change, as a rule, that "complexly organized," rather prolonged therapeutic operations have to be performed in order that the patient's self-system may "expand." Otherwise he may flounder indefinitely or become unable to have restful sleep, or become "sicker" or, possibly, abandon therapy and seek out a Guru, native or foreign.

Since more normal people often become pretty skillful at avoiding anxiety, and learn more or less unwittingly to back off from almost any situation that promises to arouse this very unpleasant feeling, it may seem that anxiety has little or no influence on their lives. In general this does not seem to be the case. First of all, there are various feelings that are complex derivatives or associates of anxiety: embarrassment, shame, guilt, "humiliation," "feelings of inferiority," some "irrational fears," and the like. More generally, conformity—at whatever cost—is often enforced by the threat of anxiety or, in other words, loss of self-esteem and the esteem of significant others. This is not to say there are no other powerful determinants of conformity to the rules, the norms and standards of one's community, "set," or social class. Fear, for example, is no mean determinant.

What, then, is fear? And how does it differ from anxiety? While anxiety is ordinarily "called out" by the disapproval of significant others or of one's own self, because of certain supervisory patterns, such as the "censorship" exercised by one's own self over one's experiences and activities, fear is ordinarily evoked either by the great novelty of a situation or by something in a situation that is objectively dangerous or that promises misery or pain. It seems to be inborn, unlearned—though there certainly are learned fears. Morgan and King have summarized some of the work of experimental psychologists regarding this problem in the following paragraph:

> Many fears are learned, but some appear as unlearned reactions to situations in which the individual finds himself. In general, the situations that provoke unlearned fears in animals and children involve strange noises, strange sights, and strange objects. In-

fants less than two years of age tend to show fear when they are presented with a strange object or a loud noise. . . . Young chimpanzees similarly show fear when they first see certain strange objects, even the face of a human being. Rats also are fearful, as indicated by copious defecation and urination when first placed in a strange enclosure, especially if it is relatively large. Hence we can say with reasonable assurance that strange or novel situations are the principal cause of fear in young or naïve organisms.[25]

In regard to objectively dangerous or painful situations, fear is a "very widely distributed device of living things for purposes of self-preservation." Sullivan seems to have thought that great novelty is similarly threatening for human beings. In human beings this may be due to the (presumed) fact that great novelty is too great a barrier to adaptation, failure of which causes injury or death. It appears that one becomes fearful when there is a direct threat to the biological integrity of the organism or an indirect one when one's adaptation to the world may be destroyed. Learning further complicates matters since human beings, as a result of certain kinds of experience, become fearful in situations that, from an objective point of view, are not dangerous or threatening to one's survival or biological well-being. In either case, there is no threat to self-esteem. Presumably one may die of hunger or gunshot wounds with one's self-esteem intact.

There are some indices of fear and anxiety. The former creates increasing alertness in a situation; the latter interferes with alertness. Thus there is an intense concentration on the fear-provoking situation and on a way or ways to escape it. When one feels very anxious there is a tendency to concentrate on anything but the relevant factors in a situation that evoke the loss of self-esteem. Also, fear creates internal bodily changes so that the supply of energy available for action is increased. Anxiety does not create such changes; on the contrary, not rarely there is a subjective feeling of weariness or a lack of élan.

The problem of the differences between anxiety and fear is further complicated by the fact that in some situations one may suffer a combination of anxiety and fear. Still again, extreme instances of fear and anxiety become indistinguishable as in terror. Thus, war often creates terror because of an objective threat to one's survival. The disintegration of the self in schizophrenia, due to an intolerable loss of self-esteem, may also create a state that is indistinguishable from the terror of war or of imminent death.[26]

These distinctions are not "academic." A psychiatrist may encourage a patient to observe the fear-provoking situation more carefully, and to analyze it. But he ordinarily cannot resort to such a simple technique when the patient suffers anxiety, that is, when the patient's self-system is threatened with failure. The psychiatrist must employ more elaborate techniques in the latter case and a more indirect approach. Otherwise he will destroy "what little contact" he has with his patient, especially if the latter's problems in living are very severe.

According to Sullivan, in an "ideal culture" the self would be coterminous with personality. In such a Utopia, all of one's capacities would be fully developed, actualized. There would be no restrictions of awareness, no "inhibitions" save those that intelligence would consciously dictate. Possibly the gods on Olympus enjoyed such a state: Jove seems to have been aware of almost everything that was going on in the world, at least when he was not pursuing one of the goddesses, and to have been singularly free of inhibitions and anxieties.

As things stand in the world of today, the child is increasingly subjected to education—good, bad, and indifferent—in the cultural patterns of society. One very important refinement of behavior patterns and covert processes is sublimation, which has been briefly mentioned previously in this chapter. Sullivan's formulation is much more inclusive than the classical Freudian conception, which pertains chiefly to libidinal drives, though some contemporary Freudian psychoanalysts may conceive of sublimation much more broadly than Freud conceived of it. Aside from psysiological drives (for food, water, sleep, rest, the elimination of waste products), it appears that almost any drive or motive can be sublimated—within varying limits. While it appears first in infancy, though in a rudimentary form, it becomes "conspicuous" in childhood and "very conspicuous," that is, more elaborately refined and inclusive, in the juvenile era, when the youngster directly encounters the wider social world for the first time, as a rule. Behavior patterns of increasing complexity and refinement must be learned. This is brought about, in part, by changes in previously acquired behavior patterns, which sometimes do not immediately and directly satisfy motives.[27] For example, "aggressive" tendencies may be increasingly frowned upon and have to be channeled into more acceptable behavior patterns, though one has to be alert to social class and, perhaps, ethnic variables.

Referential processes (roughly, symbolizing processes or thinking in a broad sense) also are modified as well as becoming more elaborate. Autistic thinking becomes increasingly disapproved of as one proceeds through childhood, and overt verbal behavior patterns become more and more elaborate and refined. The child is increasingly taught the necessity of "consensual validation" by example and precept. But this is not to say that a great deal of covert autistic processes do not still occur. In the infant (inferred) covert processes cannot be conceived of to be within the infant's consciousness in the sense that he has a clear recognition of them. More generally, many covert referential processes occur that are completely unknown to the person who has them, even in adulthood. They are inferred from what the person knows or notices. They usually occur in the parataxic mode, and take place sometimes when one is awake, engaged in some activity. Hence they may serve as an instrumentality of sublimation and the like. Such covert processes are particularly significant in psychiatry since they contain important data the patient is not conscious of. This is consistent with the earlier formulation of symbols summarized in Chapter 2.

These cursory statements may help to make Sullivan's definition more intelligible:

"Sublimation is the unwitting substitution, for a behavior pattern which encounters anxiety or collides with the self-system, of a socially more acceptable activity pattern which satisfies part of the motivational system that caused trouble." [28] Symbol processes occurring in sleep (and perhaps in play) are said to take care of the rest of the unsatisfied need, in more fortunate circumstances. Thus, in childhood, either overt or covert symbolic processes provide an outlet for the unsatisfied residual need—provided they are not particularly associated with anxiety. Child psychologists, such as Jersild, and Stone and Church, provide a great deal of information regarding what Sullivan calls sublimatory processes in childhood. Related to sublimatory processes in childhood is play, at least to a degree, though Sullivan did not stress it, but which seems to be important in the development of the self. On this matter, child psychologists also have a good deal to offer.

In contrast to sublimation, the *disintegration* of behavior patterns and patterns of covert processes may occur, under the force of anxiety, quite early in childhood. Sullivan is referring to a situation in which a pattern of behavior in the pursuit of satisfaction, and the use of recall and foresight in connection with this satisfaction is halted, brought to a stop, by the mothering one. Several possibilities are now open, partly depending on the particular need, and partly on the evolutionary stage of development reached. The child may not discontinue the related behavior pattern—in the face of intense disapproval—so more and more anxiety "piles up" in his personality. Then, it seems, the *"whole of living"* is rather disorganized; or the particular behavior pattern in the pursuit of some satisfaction and the related covert process are disintegrated. Following upon this outcome the disintegrated pattern of behavior and covert process may be recombined in more complex patterns of activity. This recombining of activities in more complex patterns is said to be best revealed in various mental disorders—such as obsessive-compulsive neurosis. Still again, when the particular pattern of behavior and related covert process are disintegrated, regression may ensue.

The "theorem" of reciprocal emotional and motivational patterns provides a very powerful principle for an understanding of (1) the dynamics of interpersonal relations and (2) the course of development and/or disintegration of personality. This theorem is: *"Integration in an interpersonal situation is a reciprocal process in which (1) complimentary needs are resolved, or aggravated; (2) reciprocal patterns of activity are developed or disintegrated; and (3) foresight of satisfaction, or rebuff, of similar needs is facilitated."* [29] In regard to (1), the simplest illustration perhaps is that of the baby who needs tenderness and of the mother who needs to act tenderly. On an adult level, a husband has various kinds of needs that are complementary to those of his wife. In general, from infancy onward, the individual has various needs that are complementary to those of significant others with whom he "integrates" situations. Some of these needs pertain to man's bodily organization, but a great many do not. Hence it would be better, more precise, to use the more neutral "fulfillment of needs," since Sullivan tended to link up "satisfaction" primarily with the gratification of bodily needs.

The discussion of (1) easily leads to (3). The child who is cared for, respected, and loved will tend to anticipate, to "foresee" similar treatment in the future. The "openness," the eager, friendly, "outgoing" attitude of such a child can be very impressive to an adult, who knows this attitude can scarcely survive intact when in the "middle years" of childhood and subsequently he encountes the great world. A college instructor may note, with a feeling of sadness, the marked changes that often seem to occur in students from the freshman to the senior year. The freshmen tend to be more "outgoing," "innocent," spontaneous, while often many of the graduating seniors seem to be more reserved, cautious, and even a shade cynical. The anxieties, fears, and failues that children and adolescents may suffer in their relations with peers and adults apparently often take their toll on the human personality. Even a child of three or four years who has been loved by his parents may suffer a rude shock when he discovers that the neighbor's child is harshly treated or deprived of some of the things he has always taken for granted.

The gradations of unfortunate or malign influence of the mothering one on her offspring seem to vary over a wide range: from instances in which the mother is simply inept to instances in which she is increasingly indifferent or anxious to instances in which she hates her child. In regard to the foresight of rebuff, which, starting in late infancy or early childhood, may become a lifelong painful burden, Sullivan pointed out that the mothering one, for good reasons or bad, as she "trains" her child may withhold tenderness on many occasions concerning which she was previously indifferent or tolerant. When the youngster manifests a particular need, he encounters forbidding gestures, which entail anxiety. Thus, over a period of time, he learns to foresee anxiety when he has such a need so that it becomes aggravated instead of satisfied or fulfilled. For example, a child may learn very early that any manifestation of the need for affection will meet with indifference, forbidding gestures, or even ridicule. A year or two earlier, he may have learned that the need for physical contact has become taboo: his efforts at enjoying physical contact are rebuffed. Soon his need to learn (curiosity) is frowned upon; his questioning and exploring his immediate environment have become a nuisance and so meets with disapproval. If the mother is a shade malicious, she may tell her offspring that he is "stupid" or, in effect, that he is a wretched burden. Such experiences tend to be assimilated to the "bad-me" aspect of the self, or, in extremely anxiety-provoking situations, to the "not-me."

Before proceeding further, one must call attention to the fact that needs are manifested in activities that cover a broad spectrum, beginning with the crying of the infant to talking and playing during childhood. Aside from activities that are outgrown, discarded because they are no longer necessary or useful for the fulfillment of needs, in more fortunate circumstances, most activities tend to become increasingly refined and/or elaborated. But when the manifestation of a need in appropriate activity encounters persistent rebuff, then a previously successful pattern of activity may have to be disintegrated. This will not usually destroy the need, which may then become sublimated, distorted, or dissociated, banished from the developing self-dynamism. Thus, for example, behavior that is an expression of the need for adult participation in play, having met with persistent rebuff, may be sublimated, disintegrated, or reformulated in "mischievious" behavior. The child's expressed need for an audience may suffer a similar fate when the mother withholds tender cooperation and approval.

Perhaps not nearly as frequently as formerly but still fairly often today (especially in working-class and lower-middle-class families) the child is presumed to deserve or require corporal punishment on certain occasions. Sometimes, mothers are observed to whack their child on the buttocks or across the face for the most trivial cause or no discernible cause at all. Chances are in such cases the youngster has no idea of what the "offense" was; so he simply stands his ground, helpless, crying or whimpering. However, these are probably more the exception than the rule. A more benign parent, usually the mother, since the father is away at work all day, may firmly believe that a breach of certain of her rules requires the infliction of pain on her offspring, with no particular anxiety attached to it; she may even regret its presumed necessity or be quite indifferent as though she were training a pet. This is a new type of "educative influence," that is, learning enforced by an increasing discrimination of the connection between violations of imposed authority and pain. However, when the parent is ill-tempered, the administration of corporal punishment may be accompanied by plenty of anxiety, so that it becomes difficult or impossible for the child to identify and analyze the factors in situations that resulted in his getting hurt. Nor can he therefore gain much, if any, insight that he can incorporate as foresight in the future. Needless to say, this sort of thing, if prolonged, does not foster an optimistic world outlook or the development of great self-regard.

In childhood, the increased efforts of the parents to educate the youngster partly in order to discharge their social responsibilities sometimes produce an individual who is "obedient" or, in other cases, one who is "rebellious." It may be that the patterns of obedience and rebelliousness will alternate in the same child, patterns that have a very definite connection with the existent personifications of good-me and bad-me, which are not yet tightly welded into a single, generic *me*. Sullivan thought that in reasonably healthy circumstances, good-me tends fairly early to be associated with obedience, while a considerable measure of freedom for play and other activities is allowed, and that rebelliousness tends to be part of the personification of bad-me.

In early childhood there occurs a "beginning discrimination" by the individual among the authority-invested adults around him, and, somewhat later, a rudimentary discrimination of authority situations. He begins to learn, quite early, who is the more dominant parent, and in what situations. Thus he generally starts to learn when it is very unsafe to disobey authority and when there is a chance to disobey with impunity. If the parents are very inadequate or "overloaded with inappropriate and inadequate ways of life," then the otherwise useful experience for dealing with authority figures in later life becomes very confusing, and the failure to gain insight may already manifest itself in the first grade in school when the youngster has to deal with the teacher. Sullivan held that insofar as the authority figures are confusing to the child and insofar as the authority situations are from time to time incongruous with the result that, within the scope of his maturing abilities and experience, he cannot make sense of them, then perhaps before the end of the thirtieth month the child begins to suffer a deterioration of the development of "high-grade" foresight. In short, he cannot develop much foresight in interpersonal relations if the parents and other authority figures, such as an aunt or an uncle, are so inconsistent and irrational in their behavior that it is beyond the grasp of a child's mind.

A great deal of the education of the child is said to be devoted to teaching him what he *ought* or ought not to do by parents who are uninformed or suffering from "unfortunate peculiarities of personality." "Oughts" and "musts" pertain to the culture prescriptions that are generally required in the socialization of the young. Sullivan believed that these prescriptions are often so glaringly contradictory on different occasions that they require "complex discriminations of authority situations." For a good many years, also, the child is incapable of grasping whatever rational basis these cultural prescriptions might possibly have. But most psychiatrically significant is the fact that the teaching of oughts and musts by means of tenderness and fear and anxiety cause a great many children to conceal what is going on in them. They learn to deceive the authoritative figures. Some of this ability to conceal and to deceive is said to be literally taught by the authority-carrying figures, and some of it to represent trial-and-error learning from observing and analyzing the performances, the successes and failures, of siblings, servants, and others. Already in the first grade a teacher can observe some remarkable instances of the ability to conceal and deceive by warped children.

Sullivan claimed that the growing abilities to conceal and deceive tend very early to fall into two of the important patterns of inadequate and inappropriate behavior that in later life manifest themselves in mental disorder, namely, rationalizations and *as if* performances. Rationalizations come to have power to spare one from punishment or anxiety. They are psychiatrically significant because, operating as a function of the self, they hinder favorable change.

As if performances fall into two categories. One form of such performances is said to be an absolutely inevitable part of everyone's developing during the childhood era. Sullivan called it *dramatizations.* (It may be contrasted with Freud's *identification,* which, if analyzed closely, is hardly intelligible.) They are described as follows: "A great deal of the learning which the child achieves is on the basis of human examples, and these examples are at this phase authority-invested. The child will inevitably learn in this fashion a good deal about the mother, and, as the father personification becomes more conspicuous, about the father; and this trial and error learning by human example can be observed in the child's playing at *acting-like* and *sounding-like* the seniors concerned, and, in fact, playing at being them. Probably the progression literally is that one tries first to *act like* and one tries then to act *as if one were.*"[30]

Sullivan asserted that in the earlier half of childhood this inevitable part of one's learning to be a human being becomes a rather serious concern only when these dramatizations become particularly significant in concealing violations of cooperation and in deceiving the authority-invested figures. In these latter cases these dramatizations evolve into what may be called subpersonifications. "The roles which are acted in this way that succeed in avoiding anxiety and punishment," Sullivan thought, "or that perhaps bring tenderness when there was no performance based on previous experience to get tenderness, are organized to the degree that I think we can properly call them personae; they are often multiple, and each one later on will be found equally entitled to be called I."[31] These personae are me-you patterns or roles that one plays in interpersonal relations, which are often grossly incongruous ways of relating to people.[32]

The other category of such performances is *preoccupations*. In everyday life one may observe preoccupation, in a mild degree, over a wide range of activities, from the housewife who, day after day, works for hours at keeping her apartment spotlessly clean to the professor who cannot eat a meal without a book at his elbow. One becomes so engrossed that many useful or enjoyable activities are excluded or neglected. In potentially catastrophic social situations, one may become engrossed in daily routines to the neglect of any analysis of impending danger. Preoccupation is said to be a way of dealing with fear-provoking situations or the threat of punishment, and of avoiding or minimizing anxiety—a stratagem that one may learn quite early in life. Sullivan claimed that quite often the irrational and "emotional" manner in which parental authority is imposed teaches the child that preoccupation with some particular onetime interesting and probably profitable activity is very valuable to continue as a stratagem to ward off anxiety and punishment. If such a stratagem is not only successful in avoiding unpleasantness but also meets tenderness and approval, it may start him off on a very complex life course: the obsessive-compulsive. Thus it is not correct, from a Sullivanian point of view, to maintain that the dynamics of obsessive-compulsive neurosis pertain to fear alone or primarily to fear. In fact, in a great many of the more severe "obsessional people," their abnormal vulnerability to anxiety necessitates an extraordinary attenuation of relationships with others.

Anger and resentment, which were discussed in the previous chapter, often have a complex relationship to anxiety, though they may also often have a relatively simple connection with fear in various situations. Thus certain people who are said to be chronically angry or, at least irascible, may give one the impression that they are "hostile," "antagonistic," and the like. What really motivates them is not anger or hostility but anxiety. The anger may be an unwitting device to hide from oneself the fact that one is anxious, while at the same time it may serve to protect one from anxiety-provoking situations. Of course such a "dynamism" does not function according to a rational appraisal of situations. It has been repeatedly pointed out that anxiety interferes with the operation of one's critical faculties. But it is, or seems to be, less unpleasant to be angry or irascible than to be anxious.

In childhood almost everyone learns the "peculiar utility of anger." Children are angry with their toys and subsequently with their imaginary companions: Sometimes the anger results from punishment by an angry parent but in general the growing ability to discriminate forbidding gestures in the authority-invested adults seems to provide the occasions for anger. That is, the anxiety aroused by forbidding gestures becomes channeled into the angry behavior. To be sure, anger may sometimes provoke a great deal of punishment; so that in some very unhappy homes the child is not encouraged to employ anger in relation to the authority figures. The partial result, in some cases, is that children for several years have tantrums, which are essentially unmodified rage behavior, analogous to the rage behavior of infants when certain types of physical restraint are imposed that produce terror, particularly restraints that might interfere with breathing.

In a great many other unfortunate homes children are said to develop a complex modification of the facile use of anger when otherwise they would be anxious. Punishment, almost always accompanied with anxiety, was visited upon the child when he was doing something that he could not foresee would be forbidden, so that there is no possibility he can understand what he has been punished for. Or the forbidden activity may be so attractive that he ignores the consequences, even though foreseen. So a great many children in such circumstances, learning that anger will aggravate the situation, develop *resentment,* a complex, indirect modification of anger, which tends to have very important covert aspects. Sometimes these covert processes (thoughts, fantasies) are "complicated" by efforts to conceal even the resentment, lest the child be punished. Concealing resentment constitutes "one of our first very remarkable processes" of the group underlying so-called psychosomatic ills. It may for example give one "indigestion." In the concealing of resentment, the child has to effect the distribution of tension in a way that is different from anything discussed so far in this chapter: for example, the tension is directed into certain areas of the gastrointestinal tract. At the same time, the gradually developing self system precludes one's knowing one's resentment; one "represses" it.

Under certain circumstances, the child becomes neither obedient nor rebellious but malevolent.[33] A reader may doubt that a child can be malevolent but if he saw a three-year-old trying to claw the eyes out of a two-month-old infant's head, he might begin to wonder if some children may not fall short of the angelic. The ways that children manifest malevolence are said to be numerous. Some so-called timid children show it by being so "afraid" to do anything that they always manage to fail to do whatever is most urgently required. A great many children who come under the rubric of the malevolent transformation are "frankly mischievous," who when they get to school give the teacher a very hard time, or the other children in the class. But they should not be confused with the kind of disturbed school child who, when the spirit moves him, will dive through a ground floor window and take off for parts unknown—much to the chagrin of the teacher and principal because parents are more inclined to blame the school administration for Johnny's deviant behavior than to face the fact that as parents they have done a wretched job. Still another kind of warped child may manifest his budding malevolence by knocking over other children when mother takes him for an outing in the park. And when he starts school he may soon earn a reputation as a "bully."

Given a fair chance—chiefly parental love—children are wonderful people for whom one would like to write a paean. So what happens to make some hateful and destructive? It starts with the parents. Sullivan thought that for a variety of "reasons" many children have the experience that when they need tenderness, when they do the things that formerly evoke tender cooperation, they are not only denied tenderness but are treated in a fashion that provokes anxiety and sometimes pain. If warped parents and other authority figures are so minded, they can easily take advantage of a child: confuse him, lie to him, beat him, ridicule him, ignore him, and make him feel wretched. Thus a child may discover that when he manifests a need for tenderness, he is disadvantaged by the potent authority figures, made to feel anxious, laughed at, and sometimes literally as well as figuratively hurt. Even an insecure adult subjected to this kind of treatment by, say, the spouse would soon become bitter and perhaps demoralized. The relatively helpless child has no effective means of protecting himself; so he suffers anguish and perhaps something akin to despair. The most devilish aspect of this kind of situation is that eventually he may become convinced that there is something terribly wrong with him to be treated the way he is. For where can he learn that he is worthwhile? Fortunately, in some of these situations there is an aunt or an uncle or a grandmother who can partially blunt the malicious behavior of the parents or their surrogates.

When a child learns that, owing to the attitudes and behavior of the authoritative figures around, any manifestation of a felt need for affection, tenderness, approval and the like brings anxiety, ridicule, pain, he begins to "show" something else, namely, a malevolent attitude, which embodies the conviction that one lives among enemies. As a result, later on, in the juvenile era, he will make it practically impossible for anyone to be affectionate or kind toward him. He has been so "conditioned" that any show of benevolence is a threat, a signal of impending trouble. So he protects himself, as it were, by a display of his malevolent attitude.

This attitude of malevolence can grow into a basic attitude toward life. It creates a vicious circle. One has less and less experience of benevolence from people because they are repelled by one's attitude. Hence one has less and less truly educative experience with people because in those circumstances one can scarcely learn that there are potentially friendly and kind people who would appreciate one if given a fair chance. The attitude of malevolence becomes a "self-fulfilling prophecy."

Sullivan thought that malevolence is perhaps the greatest disaster that happens in the childhood era. Although one may sometimes learn ways of circumventing anxiety-provoking and fear-provoking situations when dealing with authoritative figures, one never feels exceedingly good or worthy. One often becomes burdened with self-derogatory attitudes, which, in turn, breed derogatory attitudes toward others. For as one esteems oneself so shall he tend to esteem others.

It is generally the mother who plays the major role in the malevolent transformation, because the child lives in her company or under her supervision most of the time. She may not be merely rejecting and harsh. If she is malevolent toward the child, she may, from quite early in his life, subject him to disparagement and invidious comparison with other children. Sometimes, even though the father may be initially more kindly disposed, under his wife's influence he may begin to adopt the mother's attitude and thus "compound the felony." Recent studies of infants and children in the slums are uncovering an array of extremely grave misfortunes visited upon helpless babies and children, a discussion of which is beyond the scope of this book.

Dramatizations, designed to conceal and deceive, obsessional preoccupations, malevolent transformation, and the like, result in a slowing down of healthy socialization instead of the customary healthy development of the repertory of interpersonal motivation, emotion, intelligence, and behavior. This slowing down of the normal progression toward adulthood constitutes an *arrest of development* as well as a deviation from normal growth patterns. The conspicuous evidence of arrest and deviation of personality development is said to be at first manifested by a delay in the appearance of changes that characterize the statistically usual course of events and subsequently in the appearance of eccentricities of interpersonal relations. An arrest of development does not signify a static condition but that the freedom, the potential for, and the velocity of healthy growth are very markedly reduced. In other words, however truncated the self-dynamism may become it does not usually arrive at a complete standstill.

Sullivan taught that telling or reading stories to the child is a strong influence in transmitting certain of the cultural prescriptions. These stories may be socially approved moral tales; or they may be inventions of the authority figure, which may, or may not, be far removed from the socially approved moral stories—that would depend on the make-up of the parental personality. Long-continued stories that the parent recites every night, carrying the imaginary protagonists through new adventures, are likely to impress the child. In this way many children are said to get the impression that they should be governed by certain social values. Values acquired (primarily in the parataxic mode) from hearing stories do not necessarily have much, if any, connection with the observed behavior of parents and their values or with the actual, concrete living of the child himself. But they may constitute rich soil for the production of rationalizations about one's behavior, and, being part of the cultural heritage, have a magical effect in impressing the other person.

Since Sullivan did not live to enjoy the blessings of television, one must add that nowadays in general the child is more likely to be influenced by television programs. It seems that many parents have discovered that positioning a youngster in front of a television screen is a wonderful way of keeping him from getting under foot. Just what the psychological consequences may be for a child are not yet definitely known, though the plethora of violence portrayed via cartoons can scarcely be healthy.

Moreover, the type of story children generally like to hear seems to have changed. *Cinderella* and *Sleeping Beauty* are perhaps much less appealing to contemporary youngsters than *The Cat in the Hat.*

One wonders if the stories that the child, say, a child of three to five, hears or, somewhat later, reads are merely or chiefly a rich source of verbalisms. They may sometimes help to kindle the imagination of an intelligent child, suggesting the possibility of a world that transcends the mundane world of the parents. Analogously, he may see—and hear and taste and smell—things in the concrete world around him especially, perhaps, if he lives in the country, things that are hidden from or ignored by the adults. Hence "the actual living experience of the child" perhaps need not always be confined to the everyday mundane world of adults. In any case, these occurrences become a part of the covert life of the child. He catches on to the fact that there are things one cannot talk about, and there are things to which the parents are mysteriously blind, in contrast to what can be expressed, "demonstrated," shown, or said. So some experiences have to become covert in the presence of authority figures because otherwise one gets laughed at or punished. There is the additional consideration that children only gradually can distinguish reality from fantasy, and this enhances one's vulnerability. It may happen that the child will try to penetrate the barrier that some parents erect against his troublesome curiosity or his "strange" fantasy by asking seemingly pointless questions. Sullivan thought the pointless question is marked in the history of those who do not attain adequate ways of living. In any event, he claimed that when the child has grasped the fact that certain things about which he needs some information are taboo for any demonstration or discussion he begins to ask questions that do not say what he wants to know. Since it is not safe to inquire directly about what he would like to learn, because the threat of anxiety or punishment is too great, he adds an "autistic" element to what would otherwise be a direct question. "The older the child gets, the nearer these autistic elements are to word combinations that actually refer to something, so that the child may make perfectly rational, diligent inquiries about why mother and father are always doing this and that in the morning when he really wants to know why mother and father do not say a word to each other when they wake to join the day?"[34] Analogous behavior by certain kinds of mentally ill adults is not rare.

It has been mentioned that the very young child does not clearly distinguish between fantasy and reality. A good many things that have no objective reality are said to be built up in his mind from the example of authority figures or from the maturing needs of the child himself. These things are of approximately equal "reality" as the objectively real things, at least as long as they continue to be effective in covert processes and in play. These statements pertain to a child under thirty months. An understanding parent, if not an actual participant, will at least be a sympathetic audience as the child lives out in play various fantasies. Children who cannot obtain any cooperation from the significant others around them become lonely and are likely to multiply the imaginary personifications that fill their minds and influence their behavior. Some children speak aloud without intending to communicate anything. But a parent who hears the child's rudimentary ideas may then reward or punish him—to his profound mystification. He does not understand what has happened. But he gets the impression that authority figures can more or less read his covert processes and discover things he is attempting to conceal. This notion may grow and in later life may sometimes result in the conviction that one's mind can be read or at least "be wonderfully accurately suspected." In addition, the child is apt to believe, perhaps because of cultural artifacts about the eyes, that this mysterious ability of the parent is exercised through the eyes. In later life this conviction may appear in the delusion of a psychotic: people can look into his eyes and read his mind.

By the end of childhood, which is chronologically not identical for every youngster, the pressure toward socialization is so great that a child is carefully sorting out what is capable of being agreed upon as real by the parents. Rewards and punishments put "a big premium" on recognizing what is socially defined as real. A country child who confuses a "pet" animal on the farm with a cow of similar coloring whom he has seen contentedly grazing in a churchyard—to the vast amusement of authority figures—may learn a never-to-be-forgotten lesson about how adults define the real. A more intelligent and benign adult may teach him that you do not cut a log into three halves. A child who prefers to believe her cousin is her brother will be rudely disabused of this fantasy when she starts school if the parents have not already destroyed it. Preschool children are said to believe that the people they see on television are quite literally located inside the set. Parents, kindergarten teachers, as well as peers, whether by attempts at rational explanation, or otherwise, teach youngsters that the figures on the screen are not "real." Nor should one forget the operation of the child's developing mind. How is it that Santa Claus—minus the reindeers—can be at Macy's, Gimbels, Alexander's, and Saks Fifth Avenue all within the period of a couple of hours? If the authority figures in the home are indulgent toward the imperfect grasp of the "really" real and the fantastic, when the child starts school, his classmates will not. They will laugh at him for his "mistakes," tease him, or otherwise punish him. Moreover, already in childhood, the child has developed some facility at "syntaxic operations," those symbol activities that make possible a consensus with some one else and work "quite precisely" with other people under appropriate circumstances. These symbol activities work quite precisely because "in actual contact with other people there has been some degree of exploration, analysis, and the obtaining of information." That is how the syntaxic mode of experience occurs. That is, by and large, how children learn what teachers call "socialization skills." But it is not the whole story.

Probably every child retains, in varying degrees, a private realm of covert operations, which may be a source of delight or solace, and which is carefully hidden from others. In fact, adults, as Sullivan pointed out, do vastly more fantasy thinking than consensually validated thinking, which provides an outlet for unfulfilled dreams, aspirations, and wishes of all sorts. If this were not so, mental illness might be as common as the common cold. (Mental illness is common enough anyway, often assuming strange guises that society does not recognize as such.)

There is another point that needs to be mentioned in passing. Parents, teachers, and others are "agents" of society. And any and every society does not tolerate a recognition of certain features of the world, be they social or aesthetic or psychological. Unconsciously parents, teachers, writers, ignore or explain away those unwanted or feared characteristics of the world. Rather early in life, perhaps at the end of childhood and subsequently, some bright and sensitive children who are not overwhelmed by the force of social requirements perceive, however dimly at first, that these features are taboo and perhaps forever after relgate them to a silent, secret world of private rumination.

Sullivan claimed that the lonelier a child has been because of the lack of adequate recognition and appreciation of his needs, the more striking may be the necessity for continuous recall and foresight to "fix" the distinctions between what happened, and what was part of fantasy process. A "lonely child" may enter the juvenile era relatively underdeveloped in the very quick discrimination of what is private and what may be consensually validated. Already in childhood he has had to develop a very rich fantasy life in order to "compensate" for the lack of audience and of participation by the authority figures. In the juvenile phase, if he reports what was lively fantasy as real, he gets laughed at or on occasion punished for "lying." So he tends to acquire "the feeling of risk in life"—which does not mean that he becomes malevolent. It means that he foresees danger and anxiety. People become not so much enemies as unpredictable "sources" of punishment, humiliation, and anxiety when one tries to communicate. Thus the "lonely" youngster's bent toward social isolation may be reinforced during the juvenile era. This loss of faith in the world, and to a degree in one's acceptance as a worthy participant in it at so early an age can be quite shocking to observe for a sensitive adult who can foresee some of the probable consequences. However, the young juvenile's inability to sort out purely imaginary events from the real is probably accompanied by other inadequacies and/or distortions that make the juvenile socialization very difficult. As time goes on, one can observe such a youngster (who may secretly wish he could have remained in, or return to, an idealized childhood) encounter more and more difficulties.

Before turning to an explication of the juvenile era, I must take up the topic which Freud made famous: The Oedipus complex. In *An Outline of Psychoanalysis,* Freud declared that the mother in caring for the child's body becomes his first seducer. He wrote that the phylogenetic foundation or racial inheritance has so much the upper hand in all this that it makes no difference whether a child has really sucked at the breast or has been brought up on the bottle and never enjoyed the tenderness of a mother's care. "When a boy, from about the age of two or three, enters upon the phallic phase of his libidinal development, feels pleasurable sensations in his sexual organ and learns to procure these at will by manual stimulation, he becomes his mother's lover. He desires to possess her physically in the ways which he has divined from his observations and intuitive surmises of sexual life and tries to seduce her by showing her the male organ of which he is the proud owner. In a word, his early awakened masculinity makes him seek to assume, in relation to her, the place belonging to his father, who has hitherto been an envied model on account of the physical strength which he displays and of the authority in which he is clothed."[35] Now his father is said to become a rival who stands in his way and whom he would like to push aside. Freud's formulation of the Oedipus complex in girls (sometimes called the Electra complex) is quite elaborate, though it need not be explicated in this book. It is described at length in the *New Introductory Lectures*.

The chief significance of Freud's conception of the Oedipus complex in classical psychoanalysis is perhaps that he thought the child's failure to resolve it forms the kernel of every neurosis. Some writers employ the notion of the Oedipus complex more loosely, that is, as more or less synonymous with the child's *emotional* attachments to the parent of the opposite sex. Since boys and girls normally do form such attachments, it is easy to confuse this fact with Freud's notion that the boy wants to become his mother's lover and that the girl desires to have an analogous relationship with her father. Moreover, some psychologically naïve readers assume that because incestuous relationships do undoubtedly occur on occasion between an adolescent boy and his adolescent or even preadolescent sister, and between a father and his adolescent daughter or between a mother and her adolescent son, that these occurrences "prove" the existence of a universal Oedipus complex in little boys and girls as Freud had held. Sullivan discovered that in some of the schizophrenics he treated there had been an overt incestuous attachment of the mother for her son, but he did not adhere to the Freudian view for long.[36] *Personal Psychopathology* provides the evidence that he had extraordinary insight into child psychology forty years ago. He rejected Freud's idea that there is a sexual relationship between children and their parents. Sullivan thought that each authority figure or parent of the opposite sex acted in a way that is somewhat favorable to the more rational, insightful education of the child. The father is said to have a feeling of familiarity with boys and is therefore more comfortable with them. So he believes he is justified in making demands and expectations of them that he is less likely to do with his daughters toward whom he has "a surviving, justifiable feeling of difference and of uncertainty." The surviving justifiable feeling of difference presumably originated from his experiences with his mother, while the feeling of familiarity with his sons presumably originated from his experiences with his father. The "contrary" is said to be the case with the mother in regard to the sons and daughters. From this point of view parents tend to be more indulgent or tolerant toward children of the other sex. This is, Sullivan thought, what *normally* occurs. However, in abnormal homes, the variables are multiple and at this stage of psychiatry perhaps not capable of rigorous formulation. Consider the following rather typical Sullivanian description: In a family group "comprised of a domineering and none too successful father, deeply attached to his mother —who lived in the immediate neighborhood—and a gentle, rather incompetent mother (the only girl in a fairly large family, herself gradually progressing into a condition of chronic anxiety as her children grew around her), there were born three sons in succession and then a daughter. The eldest was frequently in conflict with the father and grew into adolescence so warped that he underwent a schizophrenic illness; the middle son came to a markedly paranoid attitude; the youngest became a politic but markedly unsocial sort of unconscious homosexual; and the daughter grew into a remarkably good approximation of mental health."[37]

The end of childhood more or less coincides with one's entrance into kindergarten or the first grade. However sheltered the youngster may have been at home, he now, for the first time, directly encounters "society" in the shape of one of its most potent agencies. But however important the formal instruction in the classroom may be, it is only a part of the juvenile socialization. The interaction of the juveniles in the classroom and in the playground provides enormously important experiences for their further development. As Sullivan stated in *Conceptions of Modern Psychiatry,* the teacher has considerable influence for good or evil. In regard to basic skills, such as reading, math, writing, spelling, the role of the teacher is obvious. But it perhaps should be emphasized that the teacher's attitude towards her pupils, as well as toward her subject matter and toward her own role as a teacher, will influence the manner in which she imparts these skills. Moreover, with the best will in the world and technical competence, she will still be severely handicapped if she does not have at least an intuitive understanding of children and the phases of their growth. Because they come from various sorts of home environments, have reached different levels of personality development, possess greater or lesser degrees of capacity, the teacher needs to be alert to the fact that not all children in the class learn as easily or quickly as others. Hence some of her charges will need more instruction than others, perhaps more attention than others, and more supervision than others. From the point of view of this book, it is vital that the teacher foster the self-confidence and self-esteem of her pupils, within the limits imposed by the educational structure. A teacher who has a negative attitude toward her class—one who never smiles or jokes, who without respite proceeds in a routine, more or less stereotyped fashion, to "instruct" during the allotted or allowable time, who makes disapraging remarks —is bound to be a poor teacher, that is, a person who arouses boredom or hostility. Such a teacher will reinforce negative influences stemming from the home life of unfortunate youngsters. She can scarcely create or sustain a love of learning. On the other hand a pleasant and skillful teacher can do something to counteract the negative unfortunate experiences that some juveniles will have already had with their parents—provided they are not too seriously damaged. A teacher who likes to teach and who likes her pupils will help many unhappy youngsters learn that there is something better in life than what they have seen or lived through at home. In fact, the school, via the teacher, may reveal a new and undreamed-of world for some youngsters who come from emotionally and intellectually impoverished homes.[38]

Another vital task of the teacher is to introduce structure and intelligent routine. Things are done according to some intelligible pattern or plan, not haphazardly or inconsistently. Every youngster needs an intelligible pattern in order to organize his experiences. It does not fall from the blue. When the home situation is "chaotic"—where there is no ordered living—the juvenile may be able to learn in school that he can live more effectively and more pleasantly by introducing a modicum of organization into the hours alloted for work and for relaxation. While disorder may occur at various levels of family life, a few rudimentary illustrations will serve. There are youngsters who come to class wearing their brother's shoes because they could not find their own—and mother does not care. There are youngsters who do not receive regular meals at home because it is easier for mother to give them money to go to a restaurant or a luncheonette. There are youngsters who at home more often find beer in the refrigerator than food; mother is alcoholic and father is not around. In such situations various kinds of deprivation occur. In any event, such occurrences do not provide good preparation for living in a "technological society." In fact it is an anthropological commonplace that in perhaps every society life is organized around some generic pattern, or patterns, often perhaps modeled after nature itself.

From all of this it does not follow that the teacher is also a therapist. Even when juveniles need therapy, the classroom situation is not designed for it. And the teacher is not trained to do therapy. Should a teacher, nevertheless, who fancies herself a therapist, attempt it, she will do no good and very possibly harm.

The juvenile era is the stage in personality development for becoming "social," for learning various techniques or skills that are necessary in order to relate in a satisfying fashion to people. Sullivan thought that this is the first developmental stage in which limitations and peculiarities of the home as a socializing agency begin to be open to remedy. If various eccentricities acquired in the childhood socialization are not remedied during this stage they are apt to survive and "color" or warp the course of development through subsequent periods. The changes that occur at the thresholds of the developmental eras often make much of what has been acquired previously inadequate or at least not fully relevant to the sudden new expanding horizon of the self-dynamism. For this reason the beginning phase of each era may considerably alter and help rectify previously learned and inappropriate aspects of personality. For example, a child who starts school with the conviction that his every wish must be satisfied will quickly learn from his peers that he had better modify that wish or face ridicule, hostility, or ostracism. Juveniles are not tolerant of an unfortunate youngster's personality distortions. The beginning of preadolescence opens up other opportunities.

Two very important contributions to growth in the juvenile era are the experience of *social subordination* and the experience of *social accommodation.* Whether one likes it or not, every society demands an individual's subordination to authority. To be sure the types of authority figures in a bureaucratic industrial society are very different in many ways from those of, say, an agricultural society. The former are more impersonal and governed by a set of formal rules and regulations. In American society, when a youngster starts school he experiences a great change in the type of authority figures. For one thing, the new authority figures tend to be more objective and detached. Although many teachers like their pupils (some teachers do not), in general they tend not to become deeply "ego-involved" with their charges. Thus, the juveniles are more likely to be treated in accordance with their merits, behaviorally and scholastically. This can be a very educative experience for some youngsters whose parents are capricious, whimsical, inconsistent in their attitudes. Moreover, the juvenile may be able to observe the "interrelation of the behavior of his compeers to success or failure with the new authority figures." In other words, the juvenile may learn from observation of his peers what behavior patterns will or will not work with the new authority figures. To some degree some other juveniles may become models for a particular juvenile. Teachers who are not impartial but sentimental ("Johnny is so cute; I could eat him up") are not likely to be the most effective ones.

The more emphatically effective contribution of the juvenile era is said to be that of *social accommodation.* By this Sullivan means "a simply astounding grasp" of how many slight differences in living there are; how many of these slight differences seem to be acceptable, even if new or strange; and how many of these differences do not seem to be acceptable and right, though one would be unwise to attempt to correct them. Some juveniles with a great variety of personal peculiarities acquired in the home are treated with the utmost crudeness and cruelty by other juveniles, though the latter lack the finesse of adults. Juveniles are shockingly insensitive to the feelings of personal worth of others. Nevertheless the opportunity that is provided the young juvenile for learning how other people are looked upon by authority figures and by one another is an "exceedingly important" part of the educative process. He can observe what other people are doing, and how they do it, what they can get away with and what they are reproved for. Because up to the time he started school he had little or nothing but his own experiences in the home, the juvenile can now perceive differences between people he had never imagined.

Some of the progress achieved during the juvenile era is neatly summarized in *Conceptions of Modern Psychiatry* as follows: "One discovers quite suddenly that parents are by no means the worst people in the world; that parents, whatever their faults, take one rather more seriously than do teachers and older boys and girls. One finds that tried and trusted symbol operations—speech, gesture, excuses, promises—are no longer effective. Autistic fringes begin to stand out as barriers to communication. Mediate and immediate acculturation proceed apace. The world begins to spread, the horizons move off. One begins to see that there is a great deal which one had not previously suspected."[39]

As Freud pointed out long ago, young children tend to look upon their parents as godlike figures. According to Sullivan, in the juvenile era there is a beginning differentiation of the childhood authority figures as simply people. From his observations of teachers, and from a comparison of their merits and demerits, and perhaps from observations of some other youngsters' parents as people, which, under more normal circumstances, he discusses with his parents at home, he acquires a more realistic grasp of what they are. But if he is unable to effect this discrimination and continues to regard his parents as the most perfect people on earth, he will have suffered a grave failure in socialization. This failure will be a grave handicap in future appraisals of adults, and in future relationships with them.

In *Conceptions of Modern Psychiatry,* Sullivan held that the child proceeds into the juvenile era of personality development by virtue of a new tendency toward cooperation, which is *not* simply a friendly attitude. Cooperation refers to a particular kind of behavior wherein the juvenile performs with others toward the achievement of a common goal. One suspects that the inner joy that cooperation may sometimes bring is not fully appreciated by American psychologists and psychiatrists, who live in an intensely competitive society. In any event, no society, however competitive, can long endure unless its members are capable of a good deal of cooperation, as well as competition. In *The Interpersonal Theory of Psychiatry* cooperation during the juvenile era is merely mentioned. This is a curious and serious oversight. In any case, cooperation becomes marked in the juvenile era. Its further development probably depends a great deal on the character of one's society. But almost anyone who cannot cooperate suffers an almost crippling defect. Aside from the handicaps it entails for juvenile socialization, it tends to restrict greatly the sphere of activities later on.

Whether children are born with a "predisposition" (a notion that is badly in need of an operational definition) toward cooperation, competition, and compromise is uncertain. In any case, it is widely recognized that learning plays a great role in their development. Jersild defines competiton as follows:It "usually denotes a struggle or contest in which one individual seeks to equal or excel another, or to secure objects, recognition, prestige, attainments, or honors also sought by others."[40] Sullivan claimed that certain provisions for competition and compromise are made in the primary education of all (literate) cultures that value these things at all. In American society, competition often secures very great rewards, especially in the middle and upper classes. The juvenile society itself is said to encourage competitive efforts of all kinds. So do the authority figures. But anthropologists have discovered that in certain societies tendencies to compete are strongly discouraged. However, it would be a great mistake to assume that competition is everywhere and always psychologically harmful. Within limits, it may stimulate an individual to do his best, so that in some areas of life it may foster excellence. Even so, competition often fosters envy, hostility, and sometimes downright destructive behavior. Chronically juvenile people adopt competitiveness as a way of life in which nearly everything that is regarded as important is part of a process of getting ahead of the other fellow. Sullivan taught that if the youngster has suffered a malevolent transformation of personality, *getting the other fellow down* becomes the outstanding pattern in the integration of interpersonal relations.

Juveniles learn to resolve differences, conflicting interests, and conflicting values by a reciprocal modification of their wishes and demands. In such situations, the participants surrender a part of what they want in order to obtain the rest. Compromise is often encouraged by authority figures but it is enforced by the juvenile society. Failure to compromise can result in social isolation: one's peers simply ignore one. Some very insecure juveniles are willing to yield almost anything in order to retain a modicum of popularity; they become compliant. Others leave the juvenile era with the notion that, if verbalized, might read as follows: "I am willing to surrender ten percent of what I want in order to get the other ninety percent." Although this may take some doing, as Sullivan might say, there are individuals who seem to be able to get away with it often.

The juvenile era is said to be the time when the world begins to be complicated by the presence of other people, that is, people other than parents and perhaps elder siblings who care a great deal about one. The strenuous attempt by society during the juvenile era to teach the young to talk well, to read, to learn math, and the like, and to act rightly causes them to suppress, selectively inattend, or dissociate "operations" that were previously acceptable in the home situation. In other words, through the increasing power of the self-dynamism to control focal awareness ideas and operations of childhood are "forgotten." This is said to come about because of the very direct, crude, critical reaction of other juveniles and because of the relatively formulable and predictable manifestations of adult authority. The juvenile normally learns a great deal about security operations, ways of being free from anxiety, as a result of his increasing grasp of social sanctions and their violations. Sullivan claimed that insofar as the norms and sanctions and activities that will avoid anxiety make sense, or can be consensually validated, the self effectively controls awareness. It does so in such a fashion that what does not make sense tends to be ignored, inattended or, if necessary, dissociated. Anxiety controls awareness, in a manner of speaking, so strictly, that consciousness is more and more shepherded into the syntaxic mode of experience. This mode, because it entails at least some analysis of one's experiences, offers a possibility of predicting the novel and of accomplishing real interpersonal communication. A combination of the fortunate and unfortunate uses of selective inattention results from this control of focal awareness. Sullivan thought that this has great psychiatric significance for it is the misuse of selective inattention that very often stands in the way of the patient's profiting from experience as well as being a great hindrance to therapeutic operations. "The sensible use [of selective inattention]," he taught, "is that there is no need of bothering about things that don't matter, things that will go all right anyway. But, in many cases, there is an unfortunate use of selective inattention, in which one ignores things that do matter; since one has found no way of being secure about them, one excludes them from [conscious] awareness as long as possible."[41] (In this context, Sullivan has employed selective inattention in two senses, the first of which means that one ignores what is irrelevant.)

The world of the juvenile is made up of three groups of significant people: the family, the nonfamily authorities, such as teachers and school administrators, and one's peers—other juveniles, or those of them who enjoy prestige for one cause or another. (Some juveniles may be ostracized, forming a subgroup whose members have interpersonal relations with one another.) The life of the juvenile thus alternates largely between the immediate family group and the school, in its "double aspect," which comprises authority carriers and other juveniles. Thirty to forty years ago, when Sullivan began to formulate his ideas on the juvenile era, television was nonexistent. So one must add that television, radio, and moving pictures provide important interests for most juveniles, which are an important auxiliary to the school, in its double aspect. For boys, sports may provide an important source of interpersonal relations, in which competition and cooperation are outstanding. Girls visit back and forth with their "friends." There is, in general, a good deal of social interaction—boys tend to associate with other boys, girls tend to associate with girls—after school hours.

The juvenile educative process "which is tributary to success in living" is said to be very largely a manifestation, not of rational analysis and valid formulation, but of the sublimatory reformulation of patterns of behavior and of covert processes. This conception is much broader, more inclusive, than Freud's for whom it was largely confined to sexual behavior and aggression. Sublimation, in Sullivan's sense, entails the development of a pattern of behavior that is socially approved, which will satisfy a part of a motivational pattern that in its original state is not acceptable to the authority figures and not tolerated or esteemed by one's peers. The approved pattern of behavior is unwittingly substituted for the behavior pattern that is or would be incited in order to satisfy motives that are disapproved or not tolerated. The "remainder" of the unsatisfied need-drive pattern may be dissipated in private "reverie" either while one is awake or asleep. Sullivan claimed that, unfortunately, a very great deal of one's education for living has to be this sort of sublimatory pattern of unwitting processes, which are not well or clearly understood. Usually this "mechanism" or dynamism enables one to have great surety in what one is doing. And so when a juvenile learns some particular pattern of relating himself to another person that is approved, that "works," he "simply *knows* that what he is doing is right." In other words, the culture or subculture reinforces his behavior, providing him with a conviction of the rightness of his behavior. This sort of thing in one fashion or another apparently occurs in every society. The increasing power of the juvenile's self dynamism to control the content of consciousness usually circumvents the possibility that any disturbing doubts will arise. The Platonic Socrates taught that the unexamined life is no life for man but the truth of the matter is that the unexamined life is what most men seem to want. Sullivan claimed that since there is no particular reason for anyone to bring into the juvenile's conscious awareness how he arrived at these sublimatory reformulations, most people reach adult life with a great many firmly entrenched ways of dealing with their fellowmen that they cannot explain. Nor can they envisage any other mode of life that promises the surety and relative content of the one they already "know." "Even in adult therapy," Sullivan asserted, "it is fairly difficult for the psychiatrist to attract enough of the patient's attention to one of these sublimatory reformulations to get him to realize that there's something about it quite beyond explaining. People are not even particularly vulnerable to inquiry in this area, because by the time anybody is apt to be investigating it, they have a whole variety of devices for heading off awkwardness."[42]

It has been pointed out that the ways a person experiences the world, the ways he perceives and interprets the world, are based on symbol systems or "cognitions." Otherwise the world impinging on the individual would be a formless flux, in which stability would be impossible and hence life could not be. The symbol systems by means of which one experiences and interprets the world are embodied chiefly in one's self-system. From infancy onward, systems of symbols, such as images, percepts, concepts, are gradually built up by the growing person in order to survive and make his way in the world, especially the world of people. In the course of time, as the self takes on a particular structure, new experiences tend to be assimilated to the familiar systems of thought, perception, and fantasy. As Gordon Allport would say, the new becomes soluble in the old, the familiar. To a large extent, the various symbol systems constitute the stuff of life, giving it meaning, stability, and order. As one approaches adulthood, the flexibility required for altering one's symbol systems usually diminishes. Moreover, even when certain adults acquire a new and highly elaborate symbol system, it often tends to be external to their everyday lives. Thus it may happen that certain professors are often disappointing to their students. The professors may not be able to practice what they teach—because they have not lived it. A scholar learned in almost every system of thought from the pre-Socratics to Wittgenstein, may, in his personal life, be petty, competitive, envious, and mean. The point is that the individual's avowed "ideology," his professional *Weltanschaung,* may form no significant part of his self, because the latter was already firmly established before he ever entered graduate school perhaps. And now, by the age of thirty, let us say, it is too late to change that much, even if one wished it, because one lacks the courage or the ability.

A great deal of stereotyping occurs during the juvenile era. We learn to categorize the items of our experience in relation to a frame of reference we usually acquire from significant others, from reading, from television. These categories in the course of time tend to become fixed and are assimilated to the self-dynamism. So they are not easily modifiable in the light of further experience. Fixed categories that are more or less immune to modification despite the occurrence of numerous negative instances, or the absence of verifiable experiences, are what are often called stereotypes. They are applied to people and things. They tend to hinder or undermine one's ability to make careful discriminations about people, political and social occurrences, nature's processes. Since they embody a set of assumptions about the world that are part of the self, stereotypes are in general extremely resistant to change.

A great deal of stereotyping, especially about people, is said to be stamped in during the juvenile era. "Since there is so much to be done in this era and so much pressure on the juvenile to take over any successful patterns for doing it, in our type of school society at least, one of the conspicuous outcomes is that a great many juveniles arrive at preadolescence with quite rigid stereotypes about all sorts of classes and conditions of mankind."[43]

Stereotyping occurs not only in relation to other people and to occurrences of various kinds. It characterizes the development of the juvenile's self-system. Supervisory patterns in the already "very complex system of processes and personifications" that comprise the self are a nearly inevitable outcome of the most fortunate kind of juvenile experience. Sullivan taught that these supervisory patterns amount to subpersonalities in certain instances: imaginary people who are always with one. They are said to be only a small part of this very elaborate organization, the self-dynamism, which everyone has for maintaining a feeling of personal worth, for securing the respect of others, and for insuring the protection that positions of prestige and preferment confer in American society. A classical instance of a supervisory pattern that becomes elaborated as a subpersonality would be Jung's *persona*.

In psychoanalysis, Freud made famous a particular kind of moral supervisory pattern, the superego. Sullivan distinguished three, which were briefly mentioned in a previous chapter. One is the *"hearer."* For example, if one gives a lecture, one, so to speak, listens to what one is saying. Does it make sense? Is one using communicable and reasonably precise words? Is what one is saying relevant? Is one's grammar respectably good? If one writes a "paper" or a book, one applies similar criteria. One's *"reader,"* in a manner of speaking, is silently standing at one's elbow. But one may face additional problems. If one has a definite group of readers in mind, one knows fairly well how much he may take for granted. Even then some writers worry unduly about the attitude of the readers. Are they friendly, even if judicious? Or are they hostile, carping critics? This is where one's self-confidence as a writer comes in. If one's "reader" or "writing critic" is "paranoid," then one is unlikely to write very much—or very well. The third supervisory pattern is the *"spectator."* He is the fellow who watches what one does and says in everyday intercourse. Thus the *spectator* tends to be diligently attentive to what one "shows" to others, and does to or with them. If he thinks one is making the wrong impression, he prods one to alter one's behavior or add some "fog" or camouflage" in order to minimize any careless breach of acceptable or desirable actions. As in the case of every supervisory pattern, the person's self-assurance is a very important determinant. The more insecure, anxious, one is, the more "paranoid," one's "critics" tend to be. On the other hand, if one has a deep conviction of personal worth and/or ability, the more indulgent and good-humored one's "critic" in a situation usually is. In such a case, also, one is less vulnerable to hostile critics, real or imaginary.

A good many things may happen during the juvenile era that will seriously handicap the progress of one's development in interpersonal relations. Illness occurring at critical periods may recurrently keep a youngster out of school. An inability to participate in sports or games that carry great prestige in some quarters may handicap him. Social handicap, due to social class prejudices, ethnic or religious differences, may bar one from the society of one's peers. The social mobility of the parents, requiring the juvenile to change schools at frequent intervals, may leave one a stranger time and again in juvenile society. Nor is such a handicap confined to the juvenile era. Since literally millions of Americans move from one part of the United States to another at least once, and in very many instances, several times while their offspring are in primary or secondary school, one wonders what the psychological costs may be. Or do many of these youngsters acquire a preternatural deftness in interpersonal relations suited to the type of life of the "organization man"?

A common phenomenon on the American scene is said to be the employment of derogatory and disparaging attitudes toward others. Such an attitude may be universal or it may be directed chiefly at those who are believed to be in some respect superior or more fortunate. The operation of belittling others may be first learned in the home. One or both parents may resort to disparaging anyone who makes them feel uncomfortable, anxious. If "little Willie" reports that another boy in his class is doing well, mother may promptly "knock the spots off" the other boy. After a while Willie becomes convinced that he is incapable of knowing what is good. No one seems worth emulating. So Willie has no models from whom he can learn anything. Moreover, he may already have got to the point where he is becoming adept himself at disparaging techniques. The other boys are "stupid"; the girls are "stuck-up." Soon the teacher becomes an object of disparagement as well. As Willie's insecurity increases, he can only protect his feeling of personal worth, however tenuously, by disparaging anyone who seems to stand out. Sullivan claimed that when security, of a sort, is achieved in this fashion it strikes at the very roots of that which is essentially human, namely, the utterly vital role of interpersonal relations. Barring extraordinary good fortune in subsequent eras, Willie will never be able to be genuinely friendly or intimate with another human being. Moreover, others are likely to sense his attitude. So Willie then has a lot of experience of hostility from others —or social ostracism. The "disparaging business" becomes a vicious cycle.

One has the impression that Sullivan does not quite do justice to the learning of formal subject matter. Aside from whatever intrinsic enjoyment formal education has for some, it is very often the means by which ambitious youngsters ultimately secure some of the "good things of life," which of course include much more than money and prestige. See, for example, Norman Podhoretz's *Making It.*

By the end of the juvenile era, the person usually has to a degree developed a generic pattern of relating to others, an orientation in living, which will manifest itself in every sphere of life. This is what people who are mentally disordered lack, at least to a large degree, though they may have developed various stratagems to try to hide this lack from themselves and others. *"One is oriented in living,"* Sullivan taught, *"to the extent to which one has formulated, or can easily be led to formulate (or has insight into), data of the following types: the integrating tendencies (needs) which customarily characterize one's interpersonal relations; the circumstances appropriate to their satisfaction and relatively anxiety-free discharge; and the more or less remote goals for the approximation of which one will forego intercurrent opportunities for satisfaction or the enhancement of one's prestige. "*[44]

In other words, one is developing a good grasp on how to live if one knows what one's needs and motives (generally) are; if one also acquires insight into the occasions and situations that are adequate for their fulfillment; and the intermediate (in contrast to the immediate or long-range) goals that one strives to attain, and for which one sacrifices momentary pleasures, and opportunities for gaining prestige. The foundation for a good orientation in living will have been established by the end of the juvenile era, if one has been fortunate, though a great deal still remains to be accomplished during the subsequent eras. Thus the web of human life, of interpersonal relations, is fashioned stage by stage.

It may be well to take an historical backward glance. When the United States was an agricultural society, boys usually worked on the farm after school hours while girls performed various chores in the home. Youngsters of both sexes learned various skills that as a rule have no place in contemporary life. But the removal of human life in America from the rural community has much larger consequences. According to Baker Brownell, John Dewey has, in the words of the former, pointed out the following: "When life in the main was rural, the child came into contact with natural things. He knew the care of domestic animals, the cultivation of the soil, the raising of crops. The home was the center of industry and in it all the child took a functional part. His mental and moral training was here. The development of hand and eye, of skill and deftness, and, above all, his 'initiation into self-reliance, independence of judgement and action' were the stimulus to habits of regular and continuos work." In the city these educative influences are absent. "Just at the time," Dewey says, "when a child is subjected to a great increase in stimulus and pressure from his environment, he loses the practical and motor training necessary to balance his intellectual development. Facility in acquiring information is gained: the power of using it is lost."[45] Of course, the ways of life of the rural community are lost in America, and cannot be regained. But to concentrate wholly on the present is a form of provincialism. It narrows one's vision of the possibilities and hazards of the future. It blinds us to the fact that the rising generation is only one link in what Dewey called the endless chain of humanity.

Some time between eight or nine and twelve years of age in the American culture the growing youngster experiences "the quiet miracle of preadolescence." This miracle of preadolescence is love. Its appearance is not sudden or dramatic, marked by, say, some spectacular physiological change. Like almost everything else in personality development, it appears gradually, flowing out of the past, through the present into a perhaps dimly foreseen future. Love, or what according to Sullivan amounts to the same thing, intimacy, should never be confused with popularity, as Maas has reminded us.[46] A preadolescent girl or boy may be very popular, may in fact be the "leader" of her or his group, with little ability for love. Such a girl, or boy, may continue to be very popular with most members right on through chronological adolescence—proceeding perhaps to a culmination in a psychologically disastrous marriage. Nor should one confuse love with "romantic love," which is essentially romanticized, idealized sex. The latter has been very cleverly exploited by the moving picture industry, the television industry—indeed by American industry in general. Thus the advertisements in the *New York Sunday Times* remind one more and more of *Playboy* magazine. Since almost any man or woman not too seriously crippled emotionally can engage in sexual relations, and since the "culture" seemingly makes love an ever increasingly difficult achievement, it is easy to confuse love and sex. This is consistent with the fact that interpersonal relations are becoming a "game," to be played skillfully if one is smart enough to learn the rules well.

Preadolescence is said to be ushered in by a new type of interest in a particular other person who becomes a close friend or a chum. The relationship between the two is a novel one. Nothing like it has occurred previously. The chum becomes "of practically equal importance in all fields of value." The maintenance of his satisfactions and security becomes as important to one as one's own. In other words, the welfare and happiness of the other person becomes as important to one as one's own welfare and happiness. This is how Sullivan characterizes love or "interpersonal intimacy." *It has no essential connection with sexuality.* This is in marked contrast to Freud's conception of love. For him love is sublimated sexuality. Sullivan's conception of love is closer to Aristotle's, who, in the *Nichomachean Ethics,* asserted that a friend is another self.

Ordinarily love appears under "restricted circumstances." There are many necessary conditions. "Some of these may be called obvious likeness, parallel impulse, parallel physical development. These make for situations in which boys feel at ease with boys rather than with girls. This feeling of species identity or identification influences the feeling involved in the preadolescent change. The appearance of the capacity to love ordinarily first involves a member of one's own sex."[47] Still, it is perfectly possible that the capacity to love never appears, owing to individual and cultural circumstances. One may proceed without it through adolescence, marry, and live a conventionally successful life. The history of mankind seems to testify to this. In the United States, it is often disguised by a patina of "romantic love," which of course is always very temporary. But it does serve society's purpose, however imperfectly. Under the influence of romantic love, many people marry (and remarry), bear children, and thus foster the continuance of society. Without the institution of marriage to regulate sexual behavior, there would be no family life, and children would go uncared for—or be cared for in state nurseries. Whether any society could continue for long under these circumstances is debatable.

Another question arises. Cannot one first learn to love a member of the opposite sex? The traditional view is that love first appears—if ever—in connection with a member of the opposite sex, usually during adolescence. Part of the difficulty over this problem lies with the definition of love. Almost any sort of emotional experience has been conceived of as a characterization of love. If one were to take this attitude seriously—though it often seems to embody a stratagem of self-defense, that is, a security operation—one would have to examine the function of definitions as outlined in philosophical and logical treatises. (See, for example, John Dewey's *Logic: The Theory of Inquiry.*) Summarily, those definitions that serve the purposes of psychological investigation or, in another context, that help clarify some philosophy of experience are the controlling ones. Subjective definitions or characterizations are of no help to anyone since they lead nowhere. Thus the value of a definition of love in terms of sexual behavior, interpersonal intimacy, self-affirmation, or something else is determined by its consequences in therapy or in the course of life itself. It seems safe to say that if one equates sexual relations or "romantic love" with interpersonal intimacy, one will suffer a rude awakening.

The other part of the problem is factual. Is interpersonal intimacy during adolescence or subsequently necessarily preceded by preadolescent "chum" relationships? Sullivan thought that the answer is yes. For example he believed a chronological adult cannot love unless and until he experiences preadolescent love.

How, then, does one concretely characterize interpersonal intimacy? First of all it involves free, uninhibited communication of one's thoughts, fantasies, feelings, motives. This is no mean achievement in a world in which language is often used to hide one's real thoughts, fantasies, plans, motives. It may be difficult for many to recapture the experiences of the lost years of preadolescence when one could spend hours at a time talking freely to a friend and sharing one's thoughts and experiences. One may easily mistake the more or less formalized and often trivial conversations of adults for the spontaneous communications of the "chums." Like juveniles, many adults seem to be preoccupied with saying the right things as well as doing the right things in order to preserve one's prestige or to protect one's occupational position. Expressing oneself freely during preadolescence makes possible a great increase in the consensual validation of symbols and of information, of the data about living and of the world in general one has picked up. This entails a movement away from egocentricity to a more social, altruistic outlook on life. "As soon as one finds that all this [previously acquired] vast autistic and somewhat validated structure to which one refers as one's mind, one's thoughts, one's personality, is really open to some comparing of notes, to some checking and counterchecking, one begins to feel human in a sense in which one has not previously felt human. One becomes more fully human in that one begins to appreciate the common humanity of people—there comes a new sympathy for the other fellow. . . ."[48]

Each one of the two-group affirms and enhances the personal worth and integrity of the other. There is a "validation" or reinforcement of the value of the various aspects of the personality of each. This is brought about by collaboration, that is, what Sullivan calls clearly formulated adjustments of one's behavior to the expressed or manifested needs of the other person in his pursuit of satisfactions and security. Collaboration is a reciprocal affair.

With the preadolescent expansion of personality, learning takes on a significance that it may never have had before. Sullivan claims that it is only when the world expands as a network of meaningful persons and interpersonal relations that knowledge becomes truly significant, and learning becomes a serious attempt to implement oneself for life.

In American society, the preadolescent frames of influence are "about the clearest and most workable ones that we have." They are not complicated by lust, which is, generally, a confusing and misleading element. "Love is new and uncomplicated." Sullivan stated in the *Conceptions* that for a great majority of Americans preadolescence is the nearest that they come to untroubled human life: that from then on the stresses of life distort them to inferior cariacatures of what they might have been.

Preadolescent two-groups tend to interlock. Since the love of preadolescent chums is neither absolutely exclusive nor possessive, it leaves room for some sharing of interests between members of different two-groups so that a linkage of interest among all of them is possible. One or a few preadolescents may be so outstanding in some respect that they become models for the other two-groups, while they themselves remain members of two-groups. They become leaders in certain situations. Some of them can persuade the others to work toward the achievement of common aims. Others, perhaps by virtue of superior intellectual ability, can get their ideas and opinions widely accepted. In *adult life* today leadership seems to be a more complicated affair.[49]

The preadolescent society often has various beneficent consequences. The great remedial effect of preadolescence is said to occur not only by direct virtue of the intimacy of the two-group but also because of the real society that emerges among the preadolescents. Sullivan thought that the world is reflected in the preadolescent microcosm. "The preadolescent begins to have useful experience in social assessment and social organization. This begins with the relationship which the two-groups come to have to the larger social organization, the gang. The chums are identified as such, and are literally assessed by all other two-groups—and this is not in terms of who they are, but of how they act, and what you can expect from them in the social organization. This is an educative, provocative, and useful experience in social assessment. ... And the gang as a whole finds that it has a relationship to the larger social organization, the community, and that it is assessed by the community."[50]

(However, one doubts if the world is reflected in the preadolescent micricosm to the degree that Sullivan conceived it. Interactions between members of one sex cannot adequately reflect the larger world, wherein various kinds of interaction occur between individuals and groups of both sexes. Furthermore, the interactions of the members of an institution are frequently very different from the interactions of the two-groups in gangs—especially in a bureaucratic society. Still again the interactions of different institutions—via chosen representatives—seem to be on a different plane. Psychological paradigms seem to be inadequate for understanding institutional arrangements. That is why Sullivan's attempts at "a psychiatry of peoples" are perhaps of little value.)

Of the several disasters that may occur during preadeolescence, only one will be considered. A preadolescent may be or become a close friend of an adolescent due sometimes to the fact that the former developed a need for intimacy later than his age mates, while the latter may for one cause or another be having difficulty relating to girls. Sullivan surmised that this state of affairs in a number of instances contributed to the establishment of a homosexual way of life or at least a so-called bisexual way of life. In his work he discovered that in a "notable" number of instances schizophrenic disorder was precipitated by one of the chum's proceeding well into adolescence while the other remained preadolescent, partly because the former developed a "very lively" interest in sexual operations with the latter.

Psychologically, it seems, an individual may not progress beyond preadolescence, and this can have very serious consequence , one of which is a homosexual *modus vivendi.*

Before turning to an explication of some important developments during adolescence, I wish to summarize Sullivan's ideas on loneliness, which seems to be a major disorder in any highly industrialized, bureaucratized society. It is possible to be very lonely for many years with little or no consciousness of psychological isolation, especially if it has taken root during the childhood era. Remarkably early in his career Sullivan noted many of the destructive consequences of the isolation of persons from one another, bringing in its train loneliness, and sometimes demoralization and despair. He could not adequately communicate "a really clear impression of the experience of loneliness in its quintessential sense." During preadolescence, it reaches its full significance, he thought, and may continue throughout life relatively unchanged. Full-blown loneliness is so terrible that it "practically baffles clear recall." Very few are willing to make the effort. Existentialists and others who write about loneliness often give one the impression that they are writing from ideological commitment, not from personal experience. The utter isolation that quintessential loneliness entails is almost beyond belief or imagination. In schizophrenia it can be "cosmic." Thus a schizophrenic patient whom Sullivan knew was one day sitting in the lobby of a famous New York hotel. Apparently this person sat facing a window. All of a sudden the physical objects and people around him began to fade away, as it were, to disappear from sight, and he sat there facing a vast blue sky, in a universe that was absolutely empty.

Various "components" derived from infancy onward to preadolescence combine in the culmination of loneliness: the need for tenderness, the need for adult participation in childhood activities, the need for compeers, the need for acceptance. The "final component" that enters into loneliness is the need for intimate exchange with a fellow being in preadolescence. When the web of interpersonal relations by means of which one is related to the world begins to crumble, or when the values of that world seem to be spurious, one becomes "alienated" from that world. A measure of sadness or of fairly mild depression probably often accompanies loneliness. However, Sullivan's description of depression in psychoses is essentially different. For example, in depression there is said to be a reduction of activity and a preoccupation with grief-provoking ideas. Unless one becomes demoralized by loneliness, an isolated individual can engage actively in everyday occupations, especially when he is able to develop a value system of his own. Even so, psychological isolation is always hazardous and often costly.

Ordinarily, one does not allow loneliness to engulf him. In the face of intense anxiety or fear one will seek out companionship, which will, to a degree, constitute a relief from loneliness. However, since he probably has a defective orientation in living, he is by no means yet free of the possibility of subsequent disaster.

Although Sullivan concerned himself chiefly with forms of loneliness derived from unfortunate experiences during the various eras of personality development and their connection with mental disorder, one should like to mention in passing that loneliness seems to be bound up with man's fate. A particular instance comes to mind of a friend in the terminal stages of cancer. Lying in a hospital bed for hours every day alone, during an interval of weeks he suffered not only dreadful pain and fear but apparently anguished loneliness as well. Another instance, that of an eight-year-old boy whose parents died abruptly in an airplane accident comes to mind. Grief and loneliness became inextricably intertwined in a nightmarish existence. So he sets about writing daily letters to his dead parents. He wants to know, he writes, when they are coming home, and how hard it is to be without parents when all the other boys and girls in his class see their parents every day and every night. (Compare James Agee's *A Death in the Family.*) Still again, there is the loneliness that comes from unshared thoughts and experiences that one knows will die with him.

Adolescence is distinguished into an earlier and later phase. As a period of personality development, the earlier phase is defined as extending from the "eruption" of true genital interest, felt as lust, to the patterning of sexual behavior, which is the beginning of late adolescence. Lust and the need for intimacy are "strikingly distinct." Thus, some people develop great sexual virtuosity while they possess little or no ability for intimacy with a member of either sex. In order to make sense of the difficulties and complexities that are experienced in adolescence and subsequent phases of life, Sullivan thought it necessary to distinguish in this era *three* different kinds of needs: the need for interpersonal security or freedom from anxiety; the need for intimacy; and the need for satisfaction of lust, or "the felt component of integrating tendencies pertaining to the genital zone of interaction." Incidentally the adolescent who enjoys intimacy does not suffer "a loss of identiy" because intimacy entails the affirmation of one's identity. Loss of identity is a symptom of failure at intimacy.[51]

As adolescence appears, a change in the "object" of the need for intimacy occurs unless one has previously been very badly warped. There develops a growing interest in the possibilities of achieving some degree of intimacy with a member of the other sex "rather after the pattern of the intimacy that one has in preadolescence enjoyed with a member of one's own sex." The degree to which the need for intimacy is satisfied in America is said to leave very much to be desired. Sullivan thought that the cultural influences that are borne in upon each person include very little that prepares members of different sexes for a fully human, "simple," personal relationship together. He had in mind mainly the traditional barriers between the sexes, the definitions of roles, legal conceptions pertaining to marriage and parenthood, and the like. But what a "simple," personal relationship between a man and a woman may be is not perfectly clear. Such a relationship between a man and a woman who are unmarried can hardly be equated with a relationship between husband and wife. In the former case, the relationship is a more or less "private" matter —provided no children are born from such a liaison—in which society has no direct, immediate interest. Marriage is never a purely "private" matter. By definition, marriage is a social and legal contract. The intervention of society is direct, and its interest never ceases. Marriage confers a new social status on each of the parties concerned and every status entails a social role or a number of social roles. Marriage provides new rights and new obligations. Thus the relationship between husband and wife is a very different matter from the liaison, which may be very temporary or long-lasting. The former is always a very "complicated" or multidimensional affair whether all the parties to the marital contract know it or not.

It is necessary to make the previous points in order to clarify what Sullivan has in mind. Heterophilic or heterosexual intimacy is a situation characterized by a relative absence of anxiety of the partners, an ability to communicate with each other freely and unrestrainedly, and a mutual concern for the welfare and happiness of each. Marriage may —or may not—provide for or enhance such a relationship. Ideally it always does. Actually many people who are ill-suited to each other enter into marriage and find its demands and responsibilities so onerous that it soon becomes a wearisome tedium. Others are so immature and self-centered that they cannot "adjust" to each other; then the daily round becomes an unbearable monotony. Nor are these the only causes of marital difficulties.

At one time many writers put great stress on "sexual experimentation" as a necessary or at least very desirable prelude to any successful long-lasting heterosexual relationship. Actually the "mechanics" of sexual behavior are not difficult for a normal person to learn—otherwise the human race might have perished long ago. Heterosexual behavior may become difficult when there is a serious barrier to intimacy with a member of the other sex. And such a barrier probably almost always arises from an unfortunate life history on the part of one or both participants. On the other hand, sexual virtuosity is no guarantee of intimacy; it may in fact become a substitute for intimacy: one may become so preoccupied with perfecting the various possible patterns of heterosexual behavior with one or several succeeding "objects" that one disguises from oneself the fact that one is incapable of intimacy with the partner. Moreover, it is distinctly possible that the current "dating" patterns of young teen-agers sometimes serve as an obstacle to the development of the intimacy need with a member of the other sex since a preoccupation with sexual satisfaction or the prestige of having numerous "dates" at so early an age may blur the necessity for learning what the other person is like, as, for instance, his intellectual and emotional capabilities or lack thereof.

With the change in the need for intimacy comes a new awakening of curiosity in the boy about girls and in the girl about boys and how one might get to be on as friendly terms with a girl or boy as one has been with his or her chum. His or her fantasies take on a rather abrupt modification. If they are not merely compensatory, they serve a sort of exploring in imagination of possibilities about relating to a girl or a boy, as the case may be. A great deal of trial-and-error learning from human example occurs during this change from preadolescence to adolescence. Previous observations of girls or boys, which had hitherto seemed relatively unimportant, take on new meaning. So do experiences one may have had with them in school or in one's neighborhood. Sometimes an experienced adult can provide valuable information—provided one is wise enough to accept it. An elder sister, for example, may provide a boy with some important clues as to adolescent feminine psychology.

Intimacy is not the same thing as "falling in love," which seems to be generally the romanticized feeling of sexual attraction. But the two seem to be often confused in people's minds. The following quotation from Jersild suggests that "falling in love" has more to do with so-called sexual experimentation than intimacy:

"The average person falls in love not once but several times during early and late adolescent years. In a study of 153 women aged 15 to 35 years, judged to be normal, 109 of whom were single and 44 married, Landis, Landis, and Bolles (1940) found that over a third reported having been in love three to 5 times, and almost half said they had had 6 or more love affairs. . . ."[52] In this context, falling in love seems to be equivalent to being "intensely attracted" to a male or males, a state of affairs in which little or no intimacy may exist.

Apparently adolescence in the psychological sense, that is, roughly, from the standpoint of interpersonal relations, has undergone a considerable change in recent years. Stone and Church write:

"Perhaps most striking is the change in dating patterns. Although young boys and girls have always gone to shows and parties together, the members of each sex were likely to cluster together, with little or no pairing off of boy and girl. The real date used to be considered proper only for later adolescence. Currently, dating at age thirteen or fourteen is not uncommon and, in spite of adult resistance, is becoming increasingly widespread. We keep hearing reports of dating prior to the teens. . . ."[53]

Moreover, Jersild cites studies of one investigator (Ellis) that indicates that "it is not exceptional for girls to be infatuated with two males at the same time."[54] (There appears to be much less information about adolescent boys' "love life.")

One suspects there is less value attached to intimacy than was the case a generation ago. It seems that contemporary society often tends to put insuperable obstacles in the way of its development in adolescents and in adults. Be that as it may, there is no question that many people, whether adolescent or adult, in the conventional sense, still seek intimacy. Nor is there any doubt that a number of adolescents find "lust" a difficult "emotion" to deal with satisfactorily. Furthermore, Sullivan thought that intimacy provides the surest guarantee of mental health. So a summary of some of his ideas on intimacy and lust still seems pertinent and valuable.

If an adolescent is seriously handicapped "for lustful activity," it "promptly collides with a whole variety of powerful dynamisms of personality": The most ubiquitous collision is said to be the collision or conflict between one's lust and the need for a feeling of self-esteem and personal worth. Whether this is as true today as it was a generation ago is questionable. In any case Sullivan thought that a great many people in early adolescence suffer a lot of anxiety in connection with their "new-found motivation" to genital activity. Perhaps the most severe handicap is "primary genital phobia," wherein the genital zone is converted into "something not quite of the body" since any sort of genital activity is disgraceful, disgusting, damned, and intensely anxiety-provoking if one dared to attempt it. Thus, lust may become dissociated, may become a part of the "not-me," and then the consequences are likely to be serious. "It is almost impossible for the adolescent who has this type of warp to arrive at any simple and, shall I say, conventional type of learning of what to do with lust. Therefore, as that person becomes lustful, he has the energy of the genital dynamism added to loneliness and other causes for restlessness; thus his activity with others becomes comparatively pointless, which almost certainly is humiliating and is not a contribution to his self-esteem. Or he may actually have some fairly serious disturbance of personality because of the outstanding power of the lust dynamism and the comparative hopelessness of learning how he, in particular, can do anything about it."[55] Such difficulties are the outcome of an enduring personality warp often first acquired in late infancy and early childhood, when the mothering one becomes very disturbed at the youngster's attempting to "tinker" with the genitals, in which case she may suffer from other psychological problems as well, which affect her offspring.

The shift in the intimacy need also may conflict with the need for security. This may occur when the parents are strongly opposed to the adolescent's "move" toward members of the opposite sex. One or both parents may openly ridicule their son's or daughter's increasing interest in any member of the opposite sex. The parental opposition may not be so blatant. It may take the form of subtly or grossly disparaging any adolescent of the other sex whom the son or daughter brings to the home. In some instances, a parent may compete with his or her offspring for the attention of the prospective boy friend or girl friend. Thus a mother may behave very seductively toward her daughter's friend, who is flattered by the apparent interest of a mature woman in him. Somehow the three of them always seem to be together, with the result that the daughter believes she does not measure up and cannot compare in attractiveness with her "sexy" mother. In extreme cases, a very pathological parent may coerce her or his offspring into relinquishing any overt interest in the opposite sex by threatening to commit suicide. In most of such instances where there is parental opposition it is very difficult for the adolescent to go out on "dates," to go to parties or dances, and so forth. Usually his self-esteem is directly or indirectly threatened by the parental opposition and disapproval.

Conflict may also occur between the intimacy need and the sexual dynamism. Sullivan mentions four common varieties of "awkwardnesses" in this connection, the first three of which make up one group, and are, so to speak, tied together: embarrassment, diffidence, and excessive precautions. It is the "collaborative intimacy," not lust, that threatens one with anxiety. However much one may desire sexual gratification, one becomes "inhibited" and lacking in spontaneity. Anxiety gets in the way of forming a friendship or any kind of real exchange of thoughts and feelings, with a member of the other sex. One's freedom of behavior may become so limited that one does not quite know what to say or what to do in various situations involving a member of the other sex. Sooner or later the other person become puzzled, chagrined, or simply bored so that the incipient relationship ends.

In the fourth kind of awkwardness, one resorts to a "not technique." The person learns that the diffident attitude and behavior do not work. So he resorts to a form of not-diffident behavior, that is, a bold and probably crude approach "in the pursuit of the genital objective." Usually it is so poorly suited to the sensitivities and insecurities of the "object" that the latter in turn is made to feel embarrassed and made diffident especially, perhaps, when the "object" is a girl and the would-be suitor is a young adolescent male. Conversely, an aggressive, insecure girl may offend a young man because he does not want to or cannot deal with this type of female. On the other hand, if he is shrewd and unscrupulous, he may coldly and calculatedly use her to satisfy his lust or his prestige until he tires of her. In any of these situations, in which the adolescent consistently acts in an aggressive, perhaps domineering fashion, the probability of establishing a relationship of intimacy is remote even in cases in which the two adolescents start "going steady."

The dichotomy of intimacy and lust is perhaps one of the gravest problems of intersex relationships in America. Although the more extreme occurrences of this dichotomy are of great interest to psychiatrists, since they may lead to dissociation of lust, homosexuality, bestiality, and the like, it seems to be a fairly common occurrence among people who are considered normal, respectable citizens. The failure to effect the preadolescent redirection of the need for intimacy may be disguised by pseudoheterosexual but security-giving performances, with or without resort to marriage. Although there are several causes of marital disasters, the dichotomy of lust and the intimacy need is probably the most potent.

The "lust dynamism" is a very complicated affair, which is described in *The Interpersonal Theory of Psychiatry,* but which need not be described in this book. A generation ago Sullivan believed that American culture "is the least adequate in preparing one for meeting the eventualities of sexual maturity." In those days he believed that Americans are "the most sex-ridden people on the face of the globe." It seems unlikely that they are less sex-ridden now despite the relatively "permissive" attitude toward sexuality that is coming to prevail. In this connection it is also well to remember that in these people who have suffered disasters in the stages of development prior to adolescence, the lust dynamism may serve to channel the partial satisfaction of a variety of other integrating tendencies so that it may seem preternaturally important. For instance, lustful activities may channel resentment at authority. They may provide an outlet, an instrumentality, for evading the responsibilities and demands of adult life. Sometimes they are taken to be a symbol of "freedom" or of rejection of "middleclass" norms or of any norms. They may provide an outlet for cruelty impulses or of so-called masochistic drives. But all this is now pretty familiar. In regard to what used to be called "free love," or rather its glorification, one might bear Sullivan's dictum in mind: "It really doesn't take much intelligence to use your penis."

According to Sullivan, the traditionally Freudian belief that functional mental illness is the outcome of distortions of sexual development, often reinforced by hereditary factors, is wrong. A person's sexual behavior can provide data useful to the psychiatrist on personality warp since such behavior is a very important part of personality. The crippling handicaps to personality have, in the main, been acquired by the time the person "has plunged" into adolescence and experienced maturation of the genital lust dynamism. (I omit any discussion of handicaps arising from the vicissitudes of middle age since Sullivan has relatively little to say about them.[56]) So Sullivan thought it is a mistake to think one can remedy personality warp by "tinkering" with the sex life of the patient. "When difficulties in the sex life are presented by a patient as his reason for needing psychiatric help," he declared, "my experience has demostrated rather convincingly that the patient's difficulty in living is best manifested by his very choice of this as his peculiar problem. In other words, people don't go to psychiatrists to be aided in their sexual difficulties; but they do sometimes present this [problem about sex] as their problem, and such problems show, when properly understood, what ails their living with people."[57]

Sullivan apparently ascribed little or no value to religion in the life of the adolescent. Yet several psychologists, and a few psychiatrists, take a different view. It used to be fashionable in psychiatric circles and in other intellectual circles as well to regard religion as a "crutch," often associated with reactionary social philosophies. Hurlock, Stone and Church, Jersild, and some other psychologists take a different view, suggesting that, typically, adolescents tend to take religion seriously, though often with a good deal of critical examination. Might not psychiatrists do the same? Likewise, the moral attitudes and behavior of adolescents have received less than a carefully critical study. In all such matters the shadow of Freud, who was hostile toward religion, tends to dim clear thought. George Santayana's *Reason in Religion* and William James' *Varieties of Religious Experience* probably come closer to the truth than any psychiatrist who ever lived. In fact, probably all the great philosopher-theologians also have something important to tell us about man's religious experience.

Late adolescence, in American and "allied cultures," is said to extend from the patterning of preferred genital activity through unnumbered educative and eductive [reflective] steps to the establishment of a fully human or mature repertory of *interpersonal relations, as permitted by available opportunity,* personal and cultural. That is to say, when a person discovers what pattern of genital activity he prefers and the ways it fits into the rest of his life, including the need for intimacy, he enters into late adolescence. Sullivan thought that failure to achieve late adolescence is the last blow to a great many warped, inadequately developed personalities. This failure may be poignantly expressed in a sort of shorthand form by an adolescent when she (or he) says: "If I could only find someone to love me *just once. . . .*" To make matters worse, one's acquaintances are enjoying "dates," conquests, getting engaged (and, if one is a girl, perhaps flashing that diamond-studded ring in one's face if they are females), or married. One becomes convinced that for some inexplicable reason one is inferior and cannot live a normal life. Generally, adolescents find this kind of an experience such an all-absorbing and all-frustrating preoccupation, according to Sullivan, that it often constitutes the presenting difficulty that precedes the eruption of very grave personality disorder in a large number of people. But no such grave disorder may appear. Instead, the individual may be condemned to a life of misery, outwardly going through the motions of a normal existence. One may resort to alcohol or drugs in order to assuage the pain that one dares not mention and the failure that one must hide. Nevertheless, from a psychiatric point of view, the failure to achieve late adolescence is not the actual difficulty. The fundamental difficulty has to do with relating to people in any and every area of life in a fashion that is reasonably satisfying and self-fulfilling.

However, Sullivan, in the later part of his career, became wary of "self-fulfillment" as a category of mental health. It always entails a value judgment. So then one is faced with the question: *Whose* value judgment is valid or at least acceptable? Moreover, some writers have conceived of "self-fulfillment" so rigorously—sometimes in the interest of some social philosophy—that a majority of the population become stigmatized since they do not measure up. Self-fulfillment, on this basis, in the contemporary world, becomes almost as difficult as sainthood. As a psychiatrist Sullivan was wary of criteria of mental health that at best only a tiny minority could approximate. He conceived of self-fulfillment in terms of the pursuit of satisfactions and the maintenance of self-esteem or, more accurately, as necessary conditions of self-fulfillment. Such a view leaves the psychiatrist a broad range of therapeutic operations in his attempts to help the patient. And it does not preclude self-growth on the part of the patient, that is, the development of various capacities. Such a development is always a matter of degree, since every individual is limited by a host of interlocking factors: genetic, familial, sociocultural. In any case, if the psychiatrist can help the patient to overcome major handicaps in living, due in great part to his developmental history and if the patient is helped sufficiently so that he can obtain the satisfactions he requires and realize his self-worth as a person, then the road may be open to achieving a greater measure of self-fulfillment. Then he will have more freedom to choose and to live intelligently, as defined, for example, by Sullivan's *Orientation in Living*.

To the extent that "the long stretch" of late adolescence is successful there is a great development of experience in the syntaxic mode, which entails precise communication with other people. These others may be limited to members of a small, circumscribed community, or may include a large variety of people at a great university. Perhaps the best example of broad-ranging communication is that of a top-notch journalist such as Arthur Krock who can communicate with kings, presidents, prime ministers, and a vast number of more humble people all the way down the social hierarchy to day laborers and those who will not labor at all. Of course, the perfection of such skill probably takes several years subsequent to adolescence. Summarily, Sullivan thought that once a person who is not very seriously warped has got the "sex problem" settled reasonably well whatever he does is bound to broaden his acquaintance with other people's attitudes toward living, the degree of their interdependence, and the ways of handling various kinds of interpersonal problems. Getting the "sex problem" straightened out entails the achievement of interpersonal security in heterosexual relations as well, which normally begins to be achieved during the earlier phase of adolescence. In any long-lasting heterosexual relationship, the drive for sexual satisfaction and the drive for intimacy, so to speak, tend to coalesce. But it would be foolish to ignore the fact that more or less brief heterosexual relationships among late adolescents and adults, which involve little or no intimacy, is a commonplace in contemporary society. A good deal of the learning of the ways of handling the problems of late adolescence and early adulthood is accomplished by trial-and-error learning from human example. So, a generation ago, Sullivan could say that everyone during late adolescence becomes more or less integrated into society as it is. This is no longer true. An indefinitely great number of Negroes are "alienated" from American society as it is currently constituted. Actually this was true when Sullivan was alive too, which he well knew. Charles Johnson in a lecture delivered many years ago, which is published in *Contributions of Harry Stack Sullivan,* related how, at his request, Sullivan took time out from his busy practice to study a Negro community in the South. As Johnson said, in those days such an undertaking brought no prestige to Sullivan and, I believe, no money either. For reasons unknown to me, and without my knowledge, this part of Johnson's report of the undertaking was edited out of his published lecture by persons unknown.[58] A sizable number of affluent white adolescents, for somewhat different causes, are also alienated.

Sullivan thought that human maturity is not a problem for psychiatry, and that in any case an understanding of maturity eludes psychiatrists. The psychiatrist's job is, at the most, to help the patient rid himself of the psychological road blocks on the road leading to maturity. Often he cannot attempt anything as ambitous as that. Either the patient's practically irremovable inadequacies or social circumstances limit him to helping the patient, say, resolve some current major handicap in living—and that is no mean achievement.

People who go to a psychiatrist for help are, almost by definition, in varying degrees immature. So in his practice the psychiatrist gets relatively little data on maturity. As a rule, society itself provides an implicit definition of maturity, which the psychiatrist may or may not accept. But any conception of maturity entails many implicit assumptions and value judgments that psychologists and psychiatrists tend to borrow from disparate sources. On this issue there is no room for dogma. In any conception of maturity, the descriptive and normative are intertwined. In any event, the patient has to learn to come to terms in some fashion with the society in which he lives. There is no escaping that—unless one is willing to become a gypsy or a revolutionary. Even professors who advocate revolutionary doctrine are happy to enjoy the privileges of the university, which largely reflects society as it is.

Even though Sullivan had no fixed, detailed formula of maturity, he "guessed" a few things about it. He surmised that each of the outstanding achievements of the developmental eras will be outstandingly manifest in the mature personality, including intimacy. Ordinarily, the mature person will be quite sympathetically understanding of the limitations, interests, possibilities, anxieties, conflicts of those among whom he "moves" or with whom he deals. Perhaps as a result of widening interests or of deepening interests his life grows in importance, in contrast to the lives of many of those who remain immature. Even when the immature person is able to live an outwardly conventional life, he tends to be handicapped by lack of various abilities, prolonged frustration, painful conflict, or severe anxiety. His life may become increasingly trivialized and boring or spent in the pursuit of goals that bring neither joy nor happiness nor contentment.

Of the many misfortunes that may overtake one in late adolescence, only a few will be explicated. It is mainly certain self-system functions that impede personal progress during late adolescence. These are due to inadequate and inappropriate personifications of the self and of other people. Owing to many misfortunes during one or more phases of development, one grows up, so to speak, with a derogatory picture of oneself. More accurately the structure of the personality is awry: it is maldeveloped. At the level of communication and interaction, one views oneself as inadequate, inferior, not capable of intimacy or love. One becomes intensely anxious if one attempts to reach out to others. This is in marked contrast to the mature person, who is self-confident, assertive without being aggressive and forever trying to impose oneself on others, capable of easy communication with others, capable of judging people as they are, able to establish intimacy with those who are or become significant. In the case of the late adolescent who lacks self-esteem, he often "projects" incomprehensible falsifications of himself in his attempts to maintain interpersonal security. So he comes to be regarded as an "odd-ball" or a "neurotic." In short, because of self-system functions operating in the interest of maintaining security, he unwittingly tends to bore other people, to antagonize them, or to repel them. There are a thousand ways of doing these things. Sometimes owing to the nature of the personality, self-system functions bring about awkward entanglements or even foster dangerous self-destructive relationships.

Sullivan claimed that one could not personify others with any particular refinement except in terms of his own personification of himself, and in terms of more or less imaginary entities, which are related to unconscious or dissociated aspects of one's own personality. (The self-personification is a subsystem of the self-dynamism, which, in turn, is a more inclusive subsystem of personality.) As one "judges" oneself, one tends to judge others. Thus inadequate and inappropriate personifications of the self tend to prevent one from appreciating other individuals as persons of worth and dignity. For example, if one's own self is a "derogatory system," one will, consciously or otherwise, tend to entertain wholesale indiscriminate derogatory attitudes about others. If one has been able to reach maturity without personal warp, one will respect others if and when they give one a fair chance. Limitations in the personification of the self often foster certain stereotypes, certain inadequate and inappropriate personifications of others, which, among other things, give rise to prejudices, intolerances, fears, anxieties, hatreds, aversions, and revulsions. While the mature person tends to judge people on the basis of adequate observation, analysis and consensual validation of data about them, the individual who relies on stereotypes judges people on the basis of little thought and on parataxic distortions.

In general, failure to "negotiate" late adolescence successfully results in serious restrictions in living. Overtly they are manifested as gross limitations on one's ability to relate to others in a satisfactory, anxiety-free manner. Sometimes these restrictions are so severe that one is compelled to adopt a "strikingly isolated way of life." In other less extreme situations, one maintains such great social distance that one of necessity misses a great deal of educative or enjoyable experience. Failures during late adolescence also manifest themselves in restrictions of interest. The range and quality of interpersonal relations become narrowed down. There are people who seem to do little more than arise in the morning to go to work, spend the working day carrying out some dull routine, return home and, after dinner, watch television for a while, and then retire. This mode of living may be occasionally punctuated by a visit with an old high school friend or a gossipy chat with a neighbor. Restrictions in the freedom of living are said to be attended by complex ways of getting at least partial satisfactions for what one's restrictions prevent and by further complex processes in the shape of sleep disorders and the like in order to discharge dangerous accumulations of tensions. There are also a great many less "complex ways" of getting at least partial satisfactions when one suffers restrictions in living. For instance, if one is a girl and knows how to dance well, one may get a part-time job in a school for ballroom dancing in lieu of "dating." Or one may join one of the more innocuous religious organizations that give the more affluent members of society the illusion that they are leading a good "spiritual" life. In such organizations, one can spend a couple of hours "socializing," with a minimum of effort and human contact. If one belongs to the "lower classes" one may spend several evenings a week in a bar and grill, where no problems of intimacy need arise. The more affluent may frequent an elegant and expensive cocktail lounge or nightclub. Though these stratagems are also avenues of escape from threats to one's security they may often help to relieve boredom or loneliness as well.

This chapter, like the previous chapter on the "evolution" of personality, is designed to communicate several ideas. One is that personality does not grow in the manner of an acorn into an oak: it is no mere unfolding of innate traits. It is always a remarkably complex outcome of fulfillment of what is potentially given more or less in the biological organization of the human being with a great variety of contingent factors. Every human being not only has a history; in a very real sense he is that history. And that history enters into present, current living, though one is largely unaware of it. A knowledge of the past illumines the present, though it is no substitute for a careful study of one's current life. Past and present interact in numerous subtle ways. The psychiatrist has to learn as much as he can of both when he deals with a patient, as well as keeping an eye on the patient's prospective future.

Notes

1. HARRY STACK SULLIVAN, *Conceptions of Modern Psychiatry*, with a Foreword by the author and a Critical Appraisal of the theory by PATRICK MULLAHY (New York: W. W. Norton and Company, 1953). p. 31.

2. HARRY STACK SULLIVAN, *The Interpersonal Theory of Psychiatry* ed. HELEN SWICK PERRY and MARY LADD GAWEL, with an Introduction by MABEL BLAKE COHEN (New York: W. W. Norton and Company, 1953), pp. 34-37.

3. PATRICK MULLAHY, "Interpersonal Theory," *International Encyclopedia of the Social Sciences,* Vol. 15, pp. 398-405.

4. Cf. SULLIVAN, *The Interpersonal Theory of Psychiatry*, chaps. 4, 5, 6, 7, 8, 9 and 10.

5. ARTHUR T. JERSILD, *Child Psychology* (5th ed.; Englewood Cliffs, New Jersey: Prentice-Hall, 1960), p. 302.

6. *Ibid.,* pp. 302-303.

7. SULLIVAN, *Conceptions of Modern Psychiatry,* pp. 18-19.

8. Cf. ALBERT MILLER DUNHAM, JR., "The Concept of Tension in Philosophy," *Psychiatry,* 1:79-120, 1938.

9. ERNEST R. HILGARD and RICHARD C. ATKINSON, *Introduction to Psychology* (4th ed.; New York: Harcourt, Brace and World, 1967), pp. 130-131.

10. *Ibid.,* p. 131.

11. *Ibid.*

12. *Ibid.,* pp. 131-132. Cf. ERNEST SCHACHTEL, *Metamorphosis* (New York: Basic Books, 1959), and JOHN DEWEY, *Human Nature and Conduct* (New York: Henry Holt and Company, 1922), pp. 97-99.

13. SULLIVAN, *The Interpersonal Theory of Psychiatry,* p. 284.

14. SULLIVAN, *Conceptions of Modern Psychiatry,* pp. 64-65.

15. SULLIVAN, *The Interpersonal Theory of Psychiatry,* pp. 124-126.

16. *Ibid.* p. 71.

17. *Ibid.*, pp. 86-87.

18. *Psychiatry and Social Science Review,* May, 1968, p. 25.

19. SULLIVAN, *The Interpersonal Theory of Psychiatry,* pp. 146-147.

20. *Ibid.*, p. 162.

21. SULLIVAN, *Conceptions of Modern Psychiatry,* pp. 20-22.

22. Cf. PATRICK MULLAHY, "Will, Choice and Ends," *Psychiatry,* **12**:379-386, 1949.

23. SULLIVAN, *The Interpersonal Theory of Psychiatry,* pp. 183-184. Cf. JERSILD, pp. 305-318.

24. *Ibid.*, p. 192.

25. CLIFFORD T. MORGAN and RICHARD A. KING, *Introduction to Psychology* (3rd ed.; New York: McGraw-Hill Book Company, 1966), p. 217.

26. HARRY STACK SULLIVAN, *Clinical Studies in Psychiatry,* ed. HELEN SWICK PERRY, MARY LADD GAWEL, and MARTHA GIBBON, with a Foreword by DEXTER M. BULLARD (New York: W. W. Norton and Company, 1956), pp. 91-95.

27. Cf. YVONNE BRACKBILL (ed.), *Infancy and Early Childhood* (New York: The Free Press of Glencoe, 1967).

28. SULLIVAN, *The Interpersonal Theory of Psychiatry,* p. 193.

29. *Ibid.*, p. 198.

30. *Ibid.*, p. 209.

31. *Ibid.*

32. Cf. DAVID KRECH, RICHARD S. CRUTCHFIELD, and EGERTON L. BALLACHEY, *Individual in Society* (New York: McGraw-Hill Book Company, 1962), chap. 2.

33. Cf. FRITZ REDL and DAVID WINEMAN, *Children Who Hate* (New York: Collier Books, 1962).

34. SULLIVAN, *The Interpersonal Theory of Psychiatry,* p. 221.

35. SIGMUND FREUD, *An Outline of Psychoanalysis* (New York: W. W. Norton and Company, 1949), pp. 90-91.

36. Cf. KAREN HORNEY, *New Ways in Psychoanalysis* (New York: W. W. Norton, 1939); DAVID E. SCHECHTER, "The Oedipus Complex: Considerations of Ego Development and Parental Interaction," and TESS FOREST, "The Family Dynamics of the Oedipus Drama," *Contemporary Psychoanalysis,* **4**:111-137, 138-160, 1968.

37. HARRY STACK SULLIVAN, *Personal Psychopathology,* copyright 1965 by William Alanson White Psychiatric Foundation, Washington, D.C. (unpublished), p. 105.

38. Cf. RONALD G. CORWIN, *A Sociology of Education: Emerging Patterns of Class, Status, and Power in the Public Schools* (New York: Appleton-Century-Crofts, 1965).

39. SULLIVAN, *Conceptions of Modern Psychiatry,* p. 39.

40. Arthur T. Jersild, *Child Psychology* (Englewood Cliffs, New Jersey: Prentice-Hall, 1960), p. 214.

41. Sullivan, *The Interpersonal Theory of Psychiatry*, pp. 233-234.

42. *Ibid.*, p. 235.

43. *Ibid.*, p. 238.

44. *Ibid.*, p. 243.

45. Baker Brownell, *The Human Community: Its Philosophy and Practice for a Time of Crisis* (New York: Harper and Brothers, 1950), p. 8. Cf. Matthew Dumont, *The Absurd Healer: Perspectives of a Community Psychiatrist* (New York: Science House, 1968).

46. Henry S. Maas, "Preadolescent Peer Relations and Adult Intimacy," *Psychiatry*, 31:161-172, 1968.

47. Sullivan, *Conceptions of Modern Psychiatry*, p. 43.

48. *Ibid.*, p. 44.

49. Cf. Krech, Crutchfield, and Ballachey, *op. cit.*, pp. 432-433.

50. Sullivan, *The Interpersonal Theory of Psychiatry*, p. 257.

51. Cf. Maurice R. Green, "The Problem of Identity Crisis," in Jules Masserman (ed.), *Science and Psychoanalysis* (New York: Grune and Stratton, 1966).

52. Jersild, *op. cit.*, p. 277.

53. L. Joseph Stone and Joseph Church, *Childhood and Adolescence* (2nd ed.; New York: Random House, 1968), p. 442.

54. Jersild, *op. cit.*, p. 278.

55. Sullivan, *The Interpersonal Theory of Psychiatry*, p. 267.

56. Cf. Elizabeth B. Hurlock, *Developmental Psychology* (2nd ed.; New York: McGraw-Hill Book Company, 1959), chaps. 12, 13.

57. Sullivan, *The Interpersonal Theory of Psychiatry*, p. 295.

58. Cf. Harry Stack Sullivan, *The Fusion of Psychiatry and Social Science*, with Introduction and Commentaries by Helen Swick Perry (New York: W. W. Norton and Company, 1964), pp. 85-107.

9 / Clinical Entities

Very early in his professional career, Sullivan became convinced that the traditional categories of what he eventually called "difficulties in living" were a grave hindrance to psychiatric investigation and therapy. He concluded that mental disorders are not fixed medical entities. Many years later, as his experience and knowledge during the course of his career grew, he used to say from time to time, in his lectures, that psychiatrists can often recite long definitions of schizophrenia, manic-depressive psychosis, and other conditions, often being able to apply such labels to patients with a fairly high probability that the future would justify the labeling. But when the open-minded, unprejudiced investigator examined the data on a particular patient the alleged basis for employing the label simply did not exist.

But if this is true—or was true a generation ago—one naturally wonders why psychiatrists did such curious—and self-defeating—things. Part of the answer is historical. One has only to think of the history of science—or of medicine—to realize that traditional notions and procedures often die hard. In any case, in the field of psychiatry, Havens has given an illuminating account of the evolution of diagnostic concepts and psychiatric procedures that resulted, at least often, in the futile work Sullivan so bitterly criticized.[1] Havens' explanation, which I summarize in a somewhat oversimplified fashion, is this. It is true that patients do *present* "with symptoms predominantly somatic, perceptual, cognitive or behavioral." Various psychiatrists, who were impressed by one or another of these kinds of symptoms, tended to classify patients accordingly. In due course, Kraepelin, the famous German psychiatrist, came along. He grouped symptoms *as they occur,* "following their course over time and noting what other features—of frequency, distribution, heredity—accompany the syndromes: this was Kraepelin's great work. Then perceptual or cognitive phenomena became but one element in a clinical entity which comprises much more than the disturbed restlessness indicated by Pinel. ...." Symptoms were grouped into syndromes and with the accumulation of certain facts, the term *disease* seemingly became appropriate. But the Kraepelinian classification soon began to face difficulty, as Sullivan pointed out long ago. Or, as Havens puts it, "Transitional forms appear between syndromes which threaten to engulf the new diagnostic structure." Nevertheless, the psychiatrists shored up their diagnostic structures as best they could—and some apparently still do.[2]

However, Sullivan's animus against neat classificatory schemes was partly due to what he considered to be their misuse. He claimed that psychiatrists may develop a very strong prejudice as to the actual meaning of some symptom or some pattern that they believe themselves to have observed; and once they have applied this label, it becomes involved with their professional prestige. "So they are inclined to fight for it, and sometimes to influence the patient insidiously in the direction that the label requires the patient to move."[3] In such a fashion, the misdiagnosis may become a self-fulfilling prophecy. Meanwhile the psychiatrist misses a lot of highly relevant information, which he might otherwise be able to use in order to assist his patient. Probably something more or less analogous to this occurs in many professions and in everyday life. A professor of, say, mathematics is explaining some problem in a required course in calculus on the blackboard, and, possibly because he is preoccupied with some other matter (maybe a fight he had with his wife that morning), makes a mistake in deduction or calculation. It may be that most of the class will doze quietly on, but, almost inevitably, there will be a bright alert student present, who will immediately "catch" the error—and call it to the professor's attention. Unfortunately, there are professors—few in number, one hopes—who cannot admit to an error in front of a class because they believe their prestige is at stake. So an argument ensues, which the student inevitably loses. By this time the class has become wide awake and delighted to observe the professor's discomfiture—all except the innocent student who had stayed alert. He has now earned himself the reputation of being "difficult." And if he is an insecure person, he may become defensive, carrying a chip on his shoulder for the rest of the semester. In short he has "proved" that he is a difficult person.

Previously formed attitudes may also ensue in pseudoclassifications or categorizations in everyday life. They are often negative stereotypes (in the traditional sense) and are too well known to require discussion. These stereotypes often exert a gravely destructive influence on the victims, so that they tend to become very skeptical of others' good faith, suspicious, hostile, unscrupulous. In *Personal Psychopathology,* Sullivan pointed out how certain attitudes and pseudoclassifications interlock and may reinforce one another, become conspicuous during the latter part of the juvenile era. The following illustration, however, is taken from the behavior of (chronological) preadolescents. In a certain school, in a lower-middle-class suburb of New York City, a certain boy is a pupil in the fifth grade. He suffers from cerebral palsy. Allied to this terrible affliction is his inability to talk. While his previous history is not known—his parents having recently moved into this suburb—it seems safe to assume that at an early age he experienced rage (helpless anger) at the limitations and frustrations that nature imposed upon him. In any event, a cruel fate seems to guarantee a life of unrelieved misery for this youngster. The other boys in his class torment him: they openly ridicule him; they mimic his facial expressions; they mimic his manner of walking on his crippled legs. When the class is lined up and walks to another room where a particular course is taught, it often happens that the boy behind him will give him a push, causing him to flounder helplessly or fall to the floor. The girls in the class leave him alone apparently because they are repelled by him. This youngster, who may have encountered similar treatment from the time he was in the second or third grade, is said to be "hostile." Except for a few highly intelligent and sensitive teachers who have heard about him from their colleagues, the school staff as well as the older boys and girls, who may have acquired the wisdom of their mentors, regard him and treat him as a sort of pariah. Moreover, they believe they are justified since he is "simmering with hostility." His own teachers treat him with cold indifference or yell at him when he falls behind trying to do a class assignment. When he enters junior high school, his "record" will, so to speak, go with him. And part of that record will contain a "résumé" of the youngster's alleged personality traits, including his "simmering hostility." In other words, he will be categorized, branded, as he proceeds to what appears to be an almost certain wretched future. In his situation, psychiatric help seems to be unlikely.

There is another point to be considered in regard to classification —which incidentally is usually considered to mark an elementary stage in the development of science. The culture is said to put great emphasis on diagnosis, and the patient's family, after the pattern of the culture, are eager to find out whether the doctor can label the illness. This is unfortunate because what *can be done* for the patient is the important thing, and that may often be determined without any particular reference to any specific diagnosis.

Still Sullivan did not reject classification wholesale. He advocated two very different "frames of reference" that he believed are much sounder in regard to the question of diagnosis. The first frame of reference constitutes the study of each "case" in terms of the patient's outstanding difficulties in living, his liabilities, in comparison with the degree of ability he has demonstrated to meet complex situations, especially interpersonal situations, that is, his assets. This approach is obviously very different from that of the internist who can tell his patient: "You've got appendicitis"; or "You've got a slight case of pneumonia"; or "You've got a mild case of gout." Of course the average layman does not know anything about these matters, but he tends to feel a little reassured, nevertheless, and so he is grateful to the doctor, whose prestige is enhanced perhaps a bit more. Moreover, after the inevitable day arrives when the patient has to meet soaring medical expenses, he may be a little mollified by the thought that the doctor rescued him when he perhaps thought he was at death's door. But the psychiatrist cannot or should not try to emulate these admirable medical performances.

When the psychiatrist interviews his patient, employing the first frame of reference, and discovers little or no convincing evidence that this person has manifested any capacity to meet difficult or unusually complex situations, and that he has reacted in many situations with a "dynamism of difficulty," then the prognostic outlook is "dim." Of course, other variables, to some extent have to be considered, such as the patient's age. The outlook for a twenty-year-old schizophrenic, whose capacities may be great, is, in general, not nearly as "dim" as is the outlook for a fifty-year-old schizophrenic, whose life history has manifested no evidence of superiority in any field despite his having had a reasonable amount of opportunity.

The other frame of reference is said to be that of determining, on the basis of such information as is available from the patient, what are the grounds for the therapeutic operations, what are the positive opportunities for therapeutic operations, and evaluating the possibilities of a good life after favorable change. For instance, if the psychiatrist discovers that, according to any information he can discover, the patient has never had a continuing friendly relationship with anyone, the psychiatrist insofar as he has got the correct information, has learned that the patient does not have the sort of experience that will readily enable him to have faith or trust in his therapist. In the beginning of treatment, "things have to start for a patient in a quite irrational way." Hopefully, after a degree of therapeutic progress has been accomplished, a modicum of reason will prevail. Meanwhile the therapist tries to appraise the gross characteristics of significant figures in the patient's past, seeking the parataxic distortions or illusory me-you patterns that will undoubtedly characterize any attempt at treatment. As well as he can, the psychiatrist anticipates which people are going to remain significant in his patient's future life, and even whether these people who provide only the antithesis of contentment and security can be eluded or circumvented. Suppose the patient is hopelessly entangled with relatives who are not interested in letting him live as a person—the sort of person, for example, who cannot stay alone in his apartment for one night in the absence of his domineering wife—then this also must be taken into account. "None of us," Sullivan asserted, "is willing to change unless we have the hope of improving our condition; that is, recovery itself is increased facility for contentment and security."[4] He claimed that if the patient and the doctor see that it will be terribly difficult to get the patient out of the entanglements that beset him, so that he can implement the increased facility for a more meaningful life, then they can anticipate great difficulty in undertaking treatment.

All prognostic thinking for any intensive psychotherapy should include these two (very different) frames of reference. Sullivan taught that they are useful in assessing the factors (various distortions, arrests of development, etc.) that can be extricated from a good history of the patient's life conceived in terms of the developmental eras discussed in the previous chapter—and for making some preliminary inquiry with the patient. Considerations of time—one does not want the patient to live out his life in therapy—demand that these frames of reference should be employed before formal psychotherapy is undertaken. For purposes of illustration consider the fact that schizophrenia of sudden onset is usually thought to have a more favorable prognosis than the schizophrenia of more gradual insidious onset. But even in these "cases" of sudden, dramatic onset, if the patient has had no really satisfactory experience with significant persons in his past life, he may be practically beyond redemption. Though he may recover to the extent of achieving excellent institutional recovery, the psychiatrist who expects he can put the patient out into the world without prompt relapse is "daft."

These considerations lead to another important point. Sullivan believed that since all patients at one time or another manifest *various dynamisms of difficulty,* the psychiatrist who is addicted to a static label for the patient's behavior can miss the shifts from one dynamism to another. This is strikingly the case in the kind of patient Sullivan treated in the earlier part of his career especially. Such a patient is said to be typically a fairly young person, usually under thirty; and the data on his earlier career line show that he has had schizophrenic episodes and has been rather strikingly obsessional in between these episodes —even to the point of being a pretty classically obsessional or "obsessive-compulsive" neurotic. In private practice they are seen rather frequently, though Sullivan had "quite a run" of them in institutional (hospital) practice. A close relationship exists between the marked obsessional distortions in such a patient's living and the frank schizophrenic psychosis. When the patient is prevailingly obsessional in his behavior, the psychiatrist must deal with the obsessional dynamism as the principal difficulty. But when the same patient is definitely schizophrenic, techniques of therapy employed in dealing with the obsessional are terribly inappropriate. So the psychiatrist must modify his techniques, not on the basis of a label, but in accordance with the presenting difficulties and peculiarities of interpersonal relations. Although this lack of fixity in more or less normal interpersonal behavior does not usually appear so dramatically as in the sudden changes mentioned above, it appears less dramatically in the behavior of all mankind. Another example appears in the hypochondrical process that may shift to a paranoid process. Therefore it is a wise and rewarding thing for the psychiatrist to remain alert to the manifestations of dynamisms other than the outstanding one, if only because of the time he will save.

Though dynamisms of difficulty shift at different times, Sullivan did not think they also exist as "mixed states," after the manner of the static Kraepelinian classification or its reformulation. He believed that any person may have available and frequently employ "the whole congeries of dynamisms," while the extraordinary accent on one of them will provide a picture or pattern of mental disorder. But he asserted that he did not expect to see a person whose pattern of interpersonal difficulties will be "somewhat betwixt and between." Instead, he expected that anyone will manifest dynamisms of difficulty now and then to meet particular situations of stress; and that the gross pattern of interpersonal relations in situational stresses to be rather outstandingly of a particular pattern. However, the following possibility may occur. A psychiatrist may discover that a patient whom he knows to manifest a particular, usually consistent, pattern or "congeries" of patterns of living, will, wherever a certain type of problem becomes the major problem of the moment, manifest a dynamism that is definitely different from the dynamisms that normally characterize his mode of life. Consider a hypothetical example. Imagine an obsessional neurotic who meets all the tensions and stresses of interpersonal relations by the substitutive type of operation, and who is obsessed with some content of consciousness. Yet it is conceivable that this person might react to a particular type of employer by an hysterical disablement at times when the employer was especially domineering. Under such circumstances, the employer, were he a psychiatrist, might be inclined to think that the appraisal of the person as an obsessional neurotic constituted an error in judgment, and perhaps tend to pronounce him an hysteric. If he did label this person an hysteric he would be mistaken. Sullivan claims that if he attempted to document the prevailingly hysteric character of such an individual's adaptations to life, then he would run into the "obsessional business" because the dynamism that gets to characterize a "sick" person is like almost anything else that characterizes people in their interpersonal relations. It is *more or less habitual*. Thus the special trimmings that one might employ to meet a particular type of problem *will not be carried out consistently over a large area of living*. It is possible that an incongruous dynamism may be very conspicuous in meeting a particular type of problem—that is, incompatible with one's typical patterns of behavior in day-to-day living. In this imaginary illustration regarding the obsessional neurotic, as soon as the psychiatrist broadens the field of inquiry to "anything like" life-size proportions, then the incongruous dynamism comes under the category of the unusual rather than the more or less typical pattern of living.

This sort of thing is more or less analogous to everyday life situations of more normal people. When, for some reason, they are impressed with a particular role they adopt with a stranger, they can play that role quite well for a while (people are often strikingly on their good behavior, so to speak, when they meet important strangers.) But as one's impressions of strangeness wear off, and as one begins to derive some notions, however imperfect they may be, about the other fellow, one also starts to be somewhat worn out with the unfamiliar restraints he is exacting of himself, and, so, more and more, one reverts to one's habitual type of interpersonal behavior. A young woman, for example, who has been rather unrestrained in her relations with members of the other sex since she was a freshman in high school, may find it rather wearing after a time to play an ingenuous role when she starts "keeping company" with an unworldly medical student who has the old-fashioned intention of marrying an innocent and artless virgin. Or a university graduate student who is more or less habitually an aggressive, exploitative individual may for months overtly appear ingratiating to the point of subservience and then after he has become at least superficially acquainted with his professors revert to his more usual and habitual aggressive self.

According to Sullivan's theory of personality any patient will manifest a series of parataxic distortions toward the analyst, which are completely explicable on the basis of the past experiences, including the morbid experiences, of a particular patient. These parataxic distortions are said to reflect undigested experiences of the past, that is, things that could not be integrated into a unitary system of motivation. In his work Sullivan found that these distortions, in the main, have not been very strikingly different, although the people who manifested them and their problems were different. These distortions constitute the basic warp of personality (in traditional language, the disease of the patient), the disorder that "colors" so much of life that it has to be eradicated or at least alleviated if the patient is to improve. However, there are said to be subsidiary (secondary) parataxic distortions, representing more or less crucial experiences that have led to complications or aggravation of the basic distortion or warp of personality. Sullivan inclined toward the view (1943) that the major problems, at least the major presenting problems, that appear as distortions of the relationships with the therapist, differ surprisingly in detail but do not differ strikingly in the dynamisms concerned. (In a footnote, the Editor recalls a subsequent formulation: "I have become occupied with the science not of individual differences, but of human identities, or parallels, one might say. In other words, I try to study the degrees and patterns of things which I assume to be ubiquitous."[5] The latter notion represents no major change but a modification of theoretical formulations in which individual differences are no longer emphasized.) The *presenting problem* in the patient is said to be a disastrous experience, the first disastrous experience he had suffered. The latter establishes a deviation or warp from the conventional patterns of development that facilitates certain "increments of deviation and certain diminutions of deviation" during subsequent eras, though it has no direct effect on a wholly unrelated type of experience. One can hypotheticate a person who underwent a major deviation in late childhood and who then, in the juvenile era, had a very disastrous experience that affected a previously unwarped system of the personality. However, it must not be thought that a disastrous experience at any stage has no effect on the personality as a whole. It does not occur entirely unrelated to other aspects of the personality. Moreover, Sullivan claimed that the tendency to live and to enjoy mental health is the thing that is affected by the initial warp—which does not usually occur overnight—and the initial warp has the effect of leaving a person vulnerable to subsequent disasters in that area, whether it be related to sex, intimacy, or something else. (On the other hand, the longer a person lives the less vulnerable he is, despite an initial warp in some area, to experiences in comparatively unrelated fields.) The patient that the psychiatrist ordinarily sees is said to have suffered a series of disasters, following the major one, which manifest themselves as a more or less characteristic distortion of personality, distortion of communication, distortion of observations of the other fellow, and the like. If these factors are taken into account, then clinical entities have a purely pragmatic utility in psychiatry. With this qualification, Sullivan admitted that they probably are useful in preparing one for what one has to do in appraising the probable difficulties of psychiatric procedure, or even in guessing as to the future course of a patient's life. Nevertheless the facile labeling of patients has to be avoided for it may interfere with observation, thought, and the employment of adequate therapeutic techniques. The most damnable and destructive thing of all perhaps is to go around using labels with which to stigmatize people. Very insecure people—including some very insecure psychiatric residents—are prone to do that sort of thing rather frequently.

In *Conceptions of Modern Psychiatry* Sullivan seems to have overstated his case against the discrimination of clinical entities, though one need not take it too seriously. He employs the term "syndrome," that is, a pattern of phenomena, of signs and symptoms, which is frequently encountered and the abstracting of which from the ongoing conglomeration or "flux" of interpersonal events is presumed to be based on a valid insight into human life. Thus it is with the help of these syndromes that a psychiatrist arrives at a *diagnosis* as well as a *prognosis* of mental disorders or of dynamisms of difficulty in living.

From Sullivan's point of view, it is not only the "momentary" present or the past that the psychiatrist studies; it is a *career* that he studies, the unfolding of personality in time under given sociocultural conditions, involving the past, present, and prospective future. This is why psychiatry radically differs from physics, the history of whose subject matter in a particular inquiry may be disregarded. Only a knowledge of the history of the person can fully reveal the extent and scope of his accomplishments and failures, what sort of necessary experience he failed to have, what necessary experiences he *did* have, his potentialities and limitations, and with varying degrees of probability, the possibilities for the future. Thus the psychiatrist always keeps his eye on the prospective future as well as on the individual's present and past life. As Sullivan pointed out *diagnosis* is inextricably involved with *prognosis.*

Since human beings seem capable of manifesting an indefinitely great number of dynamisms of difficulty, I shall limit the exposition to some more or less typical dynamisms that Sullivan discusses. The first syndrome or clinical entity to be explicated is that of the *hypochondriac.*[6] The hypochrondriacal person has a "preternatural" interest in his ill health, and employs his failing state of health or some specific disease or disability as the principle device for communicating with others. But he may also often use other subsidiary security strategems as well. He manifests an intense preoccupation with the morbidity of his body—a preoccupation that varies directly in proportion to the stress of the situation in which he finds himself. Thus the morbid preoccupation with the body and its functions is the peculiar device of the hypochondriac for maintaining security.[7] His interpersonal relations are said to be chiefly influenced by the need to discuss the illness or disability. In any conversation he always gets around to it. Frequently his symptoms are the only thing in which he has sufficient interest to keep up the effort of talking. This does not mean that he is preying on sympathy. Regardless of the attitude of the listener, who in fact may be bored or annoyed, or who may even delight to hear of his sufferings, the hypochondriacal person *must* discuss his physical ailment. He uses it as a means of augmenting his security. Otherwise he would feel inferior, abased, if he lacked the ailment, and would believe he is devoid of any merit in the eyes of others.

Like every other major dynamism of difficulty, hypochondria takes its toll. Sullivan thought that though the pursuit of satisfactions does occur, it is poisoned by the intrusion of hypochondrical considerations. He suggested that, for example, a preoccupation with ill health and a demonstration of this preoccupation to anyone with whom one is integrated could have a rather desolating effect on the development of a relationship for the satisfaction of lust. A man who, day in and day out, entertains his Lady with a dissertation on his fallen kidneys is not going to be very enchanting or sexually irresistable.

Though one might expect a great deal of disturbance of the *sleep* function because of the thwarting of needs as a result of the distortions in the self-system, that is, a "large amount of unfinished business left over from the period of surveillance by the self system to the nocturnal period of comparative freedom, at least for implicit processes," or dreams, this is far from being necessarily the case. This happens to be true even though it is also true that hypochondriacal patients report that they suffer from the most fearsome insomnia and disturbance of sleep. In actual fact these people sleep very soundly six or seven hours a night. But their insecurity is said to be sometimes so great that they have to wake up every now and then and make considerable noise in order to support their claim of insomnia.

How then, is one to explain the fact that the hypochondriac does not have disturbed sleep? By the occurrence of regression. The integrative tendencies connected with various needs for satisfaction have functionally reverted to a much earlier level, and the experience "in between" has vanished. So there is no piling up of tensions. If the lust dynamism, for example, regresses below the level of preadolescence, the hypochondriac tends to engage in prurient stories and obscene jokes, peering into the neighbor's window at night, and so forth. When a deeper regression occurs, when the person functionally reverts to a still earlier stage, as in the case of the "genito-urinary hypochondriacs," it becomes very closely related to schizophrenia. In some cases, the symptoms manifest the same degree of regression that one observes in certain of the schizophrenic masturbatory activities: "regression to the point of reactivation of urethral components of the orgasm." These people are said to have experience with a drop of mucus, for instance, in lieu of anything that ultimately becomes the genital dynamism. The physiology of this sort of thing was brushed in Chapter 2. In *Conceptions of Modern Psychiatry,* pp. 145-146, this occurrence is elaborated. Occasionally the paranoid state alternates with the hypochondriacal state.[8]

In *Conceptions of Modern Psychiatry* Sullivan claims that the paranoid, the algolagnic, the hypochondriacal, and the obsessional states are probably different patterns of much the same maladjustive processes. Although he did not think there is to be found a "betwixt and between" pattern of interpersonal difficulties, he believed that persons suffering the four so-called types of mental disorder mentioned previously may manifest various "blends" of the four and some patients definitely alternate between one or another of them. Some hypochondriacal people are said to become paranoid, and vice versa; and there may be more than one such transformation.

Perhaps the nonpsychiatric reader will find these disorders a little less incomprehensible after a review of Sullivan's ideas on the "dynamics" of such disorders. Owing to the early experiences of anyone suffering one of these disorders, he has developed a prevailing negative self or, in other words, a pervasive self-derogatory attitude. During the course of his development he did not receive enough "approbation" from parents and significant others, which is a way of saying he got little consistent affection from them. This as time goes on has brought about a sort of vicious cycle. His difficulties, especially his "negative" (derogatory) attitudes toward others (born of his own self-derogatory attitudes) has interfered with, if not thwarted, the securing of satisfactions and esteem from others. In more familiar language, he has projected his own low self-appraisal onto potentially suitable people, who are then made to feel anxious, resentful or in some other fashion repelled by him, with the result that he has minimized perhaps every opportunity to relate in a satisfying way to others. Even when he compares himself with those whom he has already derogated, belittled, he still feels unworthy and inferior—a conviction of unworthiness that he will have tried to conceal. But his attempts at concealment will not have worked for long anyway, especially in the case of those who have some understanding of people. In any event, his unhappy, unsatisfied state, often represented in his conscious awareness more or less clearly as loneliness, at times becomes intolerable. (Sometimes people in this wretched condition resort to deviant interpersonal or other activities that turn out to be seriously self-destructive.) Failure after failure is said to undermine the vestiges of interpersonal security that come from reverie processes of a forward-looking type. The reverie processes lose their utility. The person then endures a state bordering on despair.

Such a person suffers the terrible conviction that he is not fully capable of being "human," that for some inexplicable reason he cannot quite feel and think and act as normal people do. The loneliness of such a condition leaves one in a state of utter desolation. One's insecurity has become so great that whatever remains of adaptive effort crumbles. "One ceases to make positive or negative movements toward others. Random, relatively purposeless restlessness becomes the expression of unsatisfied longings; sleep is disturbed and fatigue phenomena appear. The processes making for consensual validations are entirely suspended."[9] One's reveries become more and more autistic. Although they are oriented to constructive purpose they become more and more autistic, taking the direction of a search of the past. "One goes back, as it were, over the course of one's development, seeking for a time in one's life which was satisfactory."[10] As one regresses, one always reaches something that is experienced as a meaningful way from which one can start over again. There is a change in the regressive direction. The autistically valid but "consensually" (socially) inassimilable pattern of interpersonal relations then unfolds as "an episode of mental disorder." The regressive redirection has initiated a relatively stable maladjustive progression of the individual's interpersonal relations. However, regression is by no means equally "conspicuous" or equally "deep" in all mental disorders. There are degrees of regression, a fact that was described in Chapter 1.

Various degrees of awareness are said to attend these dramatic changes of life direction from a regression in the face of terrible demoralization or actual despair (which perhaps one rarely succumbs to except as the aftermath of schizophrenia) to a progression along the lines of one of the syndromes of mental disorder. Some of the events that "impinge" on the individual are provocative of the reverie processes that pertain to highly illusory or fantastic interpersonal relations manifested during the *regressive course*. As the person was regressing some one of the events impinging on him may "strike off" a vivid alertness. Because of the narrowing of consciousness, due to fatigue, such an event may be all the more impressive. (Even in a normal person the scope or range of consciousness at any given time is very restricted, but he has much more control of what he focuses on than a person who is regressing, while the latter's thought processes become more autistic and fantastic.) This impressive event, which, owing to the regressive direction of the person's thoughts and fantasies, may be perceived in the setting or orientation of an earlier state of development, may also become the very cause of the redirection of the person's behavior in a "forward" movement. For example, as unhappy person who "suddenly sees it all" may emerge from regression into a quickly systematized paranoid state.

In the *algolagnic* state, in contrast to the hypochondriacal, it is the world rather than one's body that is treated as ailing.[11] Algolagnics are said to be possibly the most gifted of all people at taking the joy out of life. Sullivan asserted that they are the people who suffer life: who are always glad to tell one how terrible things are and who only with great difficulty can be led to show any particular interest in anything, except how wretchedly everything is going and how grim the prospects for the future are. They are absorbed with the suffering life has caused them. Sullivan describes the behavior of an algolagnic on his first trip abroad, while riding on the "coronation Scot" from Glasgow to London. "He read a detective story throughout the journey, only thrice glancing out of the window. Finding himself observed he remarked to his companion, 'Isn't the landscape boring?' Asked as to the book in which he had seemed to be absorbed, he said that it was very tiresome. He mentioned in retrospect that the English trains were bad; the food tasteless; the money entirely beyond his understanding. In brief, everything he noticed—or was observed to notice —was bad, wrong, or positively distressing."[12] He could discover a grim possibility behind any piece of good news. In every promise there lurked a high probability of evil. Despite the fact that he was an artist of great talent he did practically no work because he was so distracted with the suffering caused him by life. Like the hypochondriac, the algolagnic must have a hearer. Thus the artist mentioned above had married a somewhat handicapped woman, to make sure, perchance, that he would always have an audience.

Sometimes the algolagnic and the hypochondriacal states overlap. Thus there are people who are chiefly concerned with their ill health but at times they "will gallop into extensive diatribes about the state of the world." Nevertheless, the hypochondriac may not have any necessity to impress others or himself with the idea of how ghastly the world is. Some hypochondriacs radiate optimism about everything but themselves.

Sullivan believed that algolagnia is the outcome of a distortion that begins in the juvenile era or at least rather early in preadolescence, representing an inadequate fruition of the preadolescent development. Nevertheless, the "genital necessities" are not usually met by autogenital behavior or by treating the partner as a mere convenience. In general, regression is not a conspicuous element in the algolagnic adaptation to life. Sullivan thought that the algolagnic process is more a way of handling a good deal of fear and anger, that is, hatred, and therefore appears to reflect what can happen to a person who has been subjected to extremely deleterious influences from a certain point comparatively early in life. Though he must have experienced some affection and security in the beginning, he got bogged down fairly early in life. Then this sort of person discovered he could put others at a disadvantage by recounting how wretchedly he is being treated by the world. Insofar as other people grow discomposed and embarrassed, they serve the algolagnic's purpose, namely, to maintain a measure of security. If they can be milked of not only sympathy but also money, "or some convenience of that kind," then the algolagnic process becomes a very effective security device.

The so-called *paranoid* condition is said to require the algolagnic, in a manner of speaking, as a springboard. Sullivan's statement about algolagnia as a springboard that may speed one on his way to the paranoid condition is not explained. Perhaps he has in mind the fact that the algolagnic is concerned only with the (real or imaginary) unpleasant aspects of life. Moreover, for him "a high probability of evil" lurks in every promise that things will get better. Given a certain kind of upbringing during the first three or four phases of personality development, it is not very difficult to become convinced, in various circumstances, that the high probability of evil's lurking in the world has become a certainty. Then it may be only a short step to the conviction that one is a victim of that evil, especially of evil people. But nevertheless the paranoid state is closely connected with the hypochondriacal if for no other reason than that it can clinically alternate with the hypochondriacal state. For reasons that will be expounded in the next chapter, Sullivan hypothesized two "imaginary poles," one of which is pure paranoia and the other pure schizophrenia. The paranoid condition under discussion is somewhat nearer the pure (ideal) paranoid pole. But in general, paranoid conditions range from a very troublesome attitude such as suspiciousness in interpersonal relations "to very florid developments of persecutory delusions with any amount of impressive documentation and a very considerable feeling of grandeur, accompanied by certain delusional rationalizations."[13] When the hypochondriacal state alternates with the paranoid, as sometimes happens, a very interesting thing occurs. Thus, when the hypochondriacal patient begins to manifest paranoid ideas quite clearly, his health improves markedly. On the other hand, as his health begins to deteriorate, paranoid ideas fade away, wherein one had believed himself to be persecuted, ennobled, and the like.

The central question is said to be: "What becomes of the needs for satisfaction?" "It is quite clear," Sullivan adds, "that the paranoid mechanism works beautifully for security, for how can you avoid respecting yourself if you, the very embodiment of goodness and mercy, have been persecuted and driven by surrounding enemies into a state of impotence. . . . Thus the feeling of worth is as well protected by the paranoid transference of blame as by anything I have ever heard of."[14] But the person who employs the simple stratagem of transferring the blame for all his shortcomings, which have damaged his self-esteem and disturbed his feeling of security uncontrollably for years, by the very technique of protecting his self-esteem cuts himself off from almost any opportunities for the satisfaction of needs. The "paranoid" cannot sort out people so that some become sources of satisfaction and others as sources of persecution. The cause of this lies in the way everyone grows up. The individuals who were the original sources of satisfaction were also the same people who inculcated the need for self-esteem, for a conviction of personal worth. And so the people who are the sources of satisfaction are said to be the only people to whom one is drawn close enough so that they can become a menace to one's security, who can criticize or wound.

The paranoid's needs for satisfaction, therefore, have to undergo a regressive distortion to processes of an earlier type, in a manner reminiscent of the hypochondriac. Yet under certain peculiar circumstances he is able to act in an apparently mature fashion. For example, he may manage to have sexual intercourse with a female, but when one studies the situation one discovers that she is far from being the man's social equal. The paranoid may regard her as an inferior creature, not overly invested with humanness, so that she is perhaps all right for genital experimentation though hardly a menace to one's self-esteem. Or if she happens to be his social equal, she is someone so very different from the women with whom the patient has been significantly related in the past that he can probably invest her with a large element of autistic (and perhaps depreciatory) fantasy and, so far as the paranoid is concerned, she also is scarcely a human being who can be threatening or dangerous to his fragile self-esteem.

The paranoid dynamism is said to be rooted in an awareness of inferiority of some kind, which then necessitates a transfer of blame onto others. But these two occurrences constitute only what Sullivan calls "a paranoid slant on life." In order to reach a "full-blown paranoid state," something else that will be discussed shortly is necessary. So an explication of the first two occurrences seems desirable. If one is bedeviled by a consciousness of inferiority, it entails some chronic feeling of insecurity, of anxiety, or what may be even worse, jealousy. When one is apprehensive that others can disrespect one because of something in him that he manifests and that he knows he cannot "fix" he is always insecure in his relations with others. One might say that there is in the self a formulation that reads: "I am inferior. Therefore people will dislike me and I cannot be secure with them."[15] Because man is a social being this conviction is a terrible burden to carry through life. Hence the person makes increasing efforts to rid himself of this incubus. And these efforts take the form of refined cognitive efforts. The solution to his problems is reached with "all the trappings of a great insight and illumination." And the solution is simply this: "It is not that I have something wrong with me, but that *he* [or *they*] does something to me. One is the victim, not of one's own defects, but of a devilish environment. One is not to blame; the environment is to blame. Thus we can say that the essence of the paranoid dynamism is the transference of blame."[16]

However, before the paranoid dynamism becomes "full-blown," that is, becomes a paranoid state, the person has to take a further step. He must invent "a specific, rather transcendental (in the sense of a thoroughly psychotic [or profoundly irrational]) explanation of why these people do this."[17] Sometimes the explanation is so bizarre that it implies a violation of the laws of nature. Often the cognitive operations are brilliant—except that they operate on false assumptions and result in blatantly contrary-to-fact conclusions. In any event the essence of the explanation is that there is a *conspiracy* against one, which may amount to a most exquisitely built-up plot. In general, the paranoid state appears under many guises. But, as Sullivan might say, to maintain a paranoid state takes some doing. Various stratagems have to be employed, including selective inattention, obsessive substitutive operations, and the like.

Freud believed that homosexuality is the dynamic, motivational component in the etiology of schizophrenia. It is easy to err on this factor because paranoid processes are to "a high degree" the outcomes of incomplete development of personality in the preadolescent and adolescent phases, though this incomplete development did not start during those eras. But the "homosexual formulation" is said to be misleading, and hence dangerous from the standpoint of therapeutic efforts based on them.

When any person cannot maintain a feeling of personal worth in his relations with significant others he will suffer serious "deficits" in the satisfactions that require cooperation from others. Therefore, during sleep he will make an extraordinary effort to employ "symbolic tools" (dreams) in order to diminish the tensions of these unsatisfied needs that would otherwise "unhorse the self," that is, cause a deterioration or disintegration of the self-system. Hence before the appearance of the paranoid development, the sleep function is said to be rather badly disturbed, and during the waking hours, evidences appear of a good deal of dissatisfaction, tenseness, and perhaps more or less aimless or aim-inhibited drive. Somehow or other the person sets out to get something from someone but he does not pursue it because it becomes complicated by his diminished self-esteem: he believes he could not procure it from the other person concerned. Sullivan offers as an example an "heterosexual situation" in which a man evinces many traits that can be identified as an attempt by a man to have a sexual relationship with a woman. But the situation "moves rather unpleasantly into a twilight zone" in which sexual gratification no longer seems to be clearly the purpose of this man's behavior. He begins to quarrel with the woman over such a topic as to whether women are really any good or whether they have a right to take themselves as seriously as they do. This kind of "argument" with a woman is almost a certain guarantee of a quarrel, which can easily grow in bitterness if she believes that her very essence as a female is being attacked. Though, in retrospect, it is hard to interpret the situation, the man in question apparently started out with the aim of heterosexual intercourse, and wound up in a fight. Hence such a person, in interpersonal relationships, is pretty tense because as soon as he starts doing the right thing with the other person, his self-system intervenes to complicate the situation and necessarily spoils any efforts he may try to make in order to remedy the situation. Such a frustrating maneuver is of course unwitting. Summarily, the apparent original, constructive integrating tendency becomes distorted or cast aside. Consequently this man, this unsatisfied person, has all sorts of dream processes "and one thing and another, remembered or otherwise." After that the paranoid development appears.

Though the sleep of the person in the paranoid state can be very seriously disturbed, yet it is not nearly as badly disturbed as it was before the paranoid state evolved. Though a patient may report that his sleep is just as badly disturbed as ever, if the psychiatrist observes him, noting such objective clues to sleep as the lines in the face, he will discover that the patient's sleep is much better. Nevertheless, it is interrupted by dramatic dream experiences every now and then. These dream experiences are "more or less consonant" with the general persecutory beliefs so that the psychotic content manifests itself in dream processes. But because the latter are "of a piece" with the waking processes, the patient identifies them "as real and valid." Since they are not different from his waking experiences, they are said to be just as real and "valid" in the life of the patient as many another of the exquisitely complicated misinterpretations that constitutes his orientation in reality.

The improvement of the sleep function that appears with the paranoid development suggests, among other things, something more of the dynamism of hate. The latter represents a pseudosublimation. In genuine sublimation the individual "combines" an impulse that has provoked intense anxiety, which is therefore very unwelcome to the self, with the pursuit of some socially worthy goal, gaining thereby partial satisfaction. The person who has suffered the paranoid development wants to integrate a particular type of satisfactory interpersonal relationship. But since this kind of situation has always made him intolerably anxious concerning the other person's esteem for him, the only way he can "obtain any peace" for these impulses, whose satisfaction normally requires the cooperation of another, is by combining them with the pursuit of security by means of hostile, derogatory actions. Yet this pseudosublimation provides a partial satisfaction by means of the following sort of process. Originally, the thoughts of the paranoid went something like this: "I want to be close to this person for a feeling of warmth, which I need because I'm lonely; but if I move toward him, he will regard me as inferior and unworthy and will deny me this warmth because he won't warm so inferior a person." This may be said to be the original thought pattern, which then, owing to predispositions built up from very unfortunate past experience, veers, along with a shift of direction and emphasis of needs (a sort of reformulation of needs) toward the following thought patterns: "That person wants me to want to be warmed by him so that he can injure me by refusing. He is a hateful enemy." In a somewhat crude fashion, one might say he has "projected" his own feelings of hostility or hatred. Yet a remarkable amount of time is said to be spent in all but closeness to this person, sometimes in actual physical closeness. Sometimes the paranoid person seeks warmth in a rather subtle way, and he may receive it even though he consciously believes the other person is hatefully derogatory of him. In general the paranoid person secures partial fulfillment of integrating tendencies by means of his fanciful belief that the attitude of the other person is hateful. It thus comes about that in any situation in which he wants warmth from another person, the latter is persecuting him because he is a hateful enemy who wishes to injure or destroy him. Moreover, he is a representative of society. Thus the full-blown paranoid attitudes become generalized. The paranoid person becomes convinced that the social order is personally hateful and destructive to him.

As a rule, no "integration" in a situation involving a paranoid person can last long because of the kind of punishment he "radiates." A good many changes of objects of such integration occur. The partial satisfactions and fulfillments that are obtained often do not suffice because some integrating tendencies are too powerful for one to find adequate relief. Sullivan uses lust as a paradigm. The "eruptions" in the sleep of the parnoid are said to be quite frequently experienced as gross sexual assaults, but which include discharge of genital tensions, fitting into the pattern of the paranoid because they are done in a hateful fashion and by enemies for his detriment.

Summarily, Sullivan claimed that the whole personal organization, the personality structure of the "victim" of the paranoid substitutive dynamism, is characterized by complex, hateful, partial satisfaction of needs and by the maintainance of a newly high level of security by means of constant preoccupation with the attacks from a hateful environment. This phenomenon is a substitutive operation in the sense that it keeps one preoccupied searching for plots, conspiracies or what not, while it keeps consciousness free from a knowledge of the true state of affairs. But the paranoid dynamism has another value. Even though most paranoid people are driven to offering "psychotic" explanatory rationalizations of their importance, their bizarre behavior gains attention, however unfavorable, recurrently from a vast number of people. That is something; it is a lot better than being ignored. Sullivan has pointed out that if one cuts oneself off so completely from intimacies with others that, at the level of verbal communication, the only defendable topic is, say, the wretched state of one's health, as in hypochondria, one is very much more shut out from a moderately satisfactory life than if one restricts communicative and cognitive processes to how wretchedly one is being abused by other people, specific other people as is the case in the paranoid dynamism. If one is restricted to talking about only the "sentient-flux" from the interior of the body, one's personality must be reduced to the level of a much earlier developmental phase. On the other hand, the paranoid person can usually function pretty well because his self-system is so reorganized that he can attribute his shortcomings to others. But the paranoid dynamism is far from being a perfect solution of one's problems. Anyone who resorts to this stratagem cannot for long remain in contact with the people who were (once considered to be) dangerous; they might point out those intolerable weaknesses that one "unconsciously" knows one has. And so if one becomes involved with a newly acquainted person, someone who did not figure in one's past, the self-system of the paranoid continues to function in such a manner so as to "entangle" the other one into the protective system designed to ward off criticism. The person who employs the paranoid dynamism can feel relatively safe only with persons who are not threatening in the sense of reminding him of "what really ails him." With such a person, the paranoid sometimes may become quite physically intimate and sometimes reasonably affectionate within the confines of a relationship that can be pretty fantastic, that is, hedged in by illusory me-you patterns and various security operations.

There is another point to be mentioned. While the algolagnic can make virtues out of juvenile inadequacies, crying to heaven of his incompetence, seeking pity and a helping hand—a behavior pattern that can delight other relatively juvenile but slightly more secure people because it provides them with an excuse for feeling superior—the paranoid can find no such arrangement. No one will take pity on him or offer a helping hand in order to feel superior. The "terrifying hash of life" that is the paranoid state first appears in the preadolescent era. Juvenile behavior patterns offer no hope for a person in this state.

There are different ways of formulating *obsessional* behavior. But since most people in the audience when Sullivan lectured were psychiatrists, he could dispense with the elementary textbook classifications and descriptions. Moreover, Sullivan, as a rule, did not have much use for textbook formulations and classifications, since he thought that in those days they were embalmed repositories of traditional psychiatric ignorance and prejudice. Nevertheless, as a starting point for the general reader I will employ Redlich and Freedman's description. "Obsessive behavior," they wrote, "may be separated into obsessive symptoms and obsessive character traits. Symptoms are divided into obsessive thoughts, feelings and acts. All obsessive symptoms have an ego-alien character; the patient considers them as strange, disturbing, and not compatible with his conscious thinking, feeling and striving."[18] Ego-alien is more or less equivalent to Sullivan's *dissociated dynamism,* though the former suggests a somewhat static conception.

Sullivan's brief summary of obsessional states in *Conceptions of Modern Psychiatry* will serve as an introduction to his subsequent, more elaborated formulations. Unlike the hypochondriacal person, the obsessional, though he may suffer from a variety of bodily ailments, does *not* use them as "simple tools" in interpersonal relations. The latter's physical disorders are employed as instruments in the maintenance of "parataxic integrations," that is, in the maintenance of illusory me-you patterns in situations in which he is related to another person. The obsessional's ailments do not protect him from an "easy attack" on his prestige or self-esteem by the other one. They do not directly forward his pursuit of satisfactions. Sullivan narrated that often enough the physical disorders seriously interfere with bodily health, thus undermining one's euphoria and lessening the possibility of satisfactions. Like others before him, he observed that the obsessional is methodic, ritualistic, punctilious.

Interpersonal situations including an obsessional person are said to be characterized by obscure power operations directed to the maintenance of control over everything that happens. These "power operations" are stratagems designed to exercise control over situations. Sullivan relates that he once had a patient, a good artist, who hated to market his works. One day, coming downstairs from the second floor of a two-story house in which he lived, enroute to a dealer's, he was seized with the thought that he might hurtle himself over the rail, gravely injuring or killing himself. In this fashion further progression toward the dealer's was paralyzed. Having crept back upstairs to his studio he called his wife and told her of his awful experience. It may be that his wife tried to reason with him, pointing out the fact that there was no objective danger. Laymen often try to reason with a relative or friend who is mentally disordered, not realizing that the latter's problems basically have little or nothing to do with his intellect. In any case, the artist in question soon was overcome by his "fear of stairs" to the degree that he became immured on the second floor of his home. His disablement soon reached the point that his wife, who was a rather domineering woman, was reduced to going for his commissions, making deliveries of his works to the galleries, and carrying his food to him upstairs. Though he continued to do good work, the necessities arising from his growing fear of stairs eventually drove his wife to call in a psychiatrist. Upon his removal to a mental hospital he made a rather prompt institutional recovery. That is, his recovery quickly took place on the second floor of the hospital, where little but "good, routine, institutional regimen" was provided. Sullivan says he had reverted to a simply quite obsessional condition, free from the disabling fear of stairs.[19] Once more, for the sake of the general reader, one must emphasize that the phobia ("fear of stairs"), in another instance might have been a "fear" of traveling in any kind of vehicle or public conveyance. That is, the phobias are primarily symptoms of "unconscious" or dissociated processes. Moreover, these phobias are not isolated affairs, insulated from the rest of the personality.

In a lecture delivered some years after those published in *Conceptions of Modern Psychiatry,* Sullivan provides some more information on the "artist" patient. (In the latter account he is referred to as an "engineer.") He saw the latter for a while in order to try to discover what "ailed" him, and, after a number of interviews he could discover nothing suggestive of anything but "classical obsessional processes." At this particular stage in his career, apparently before he went into private practice and carried out a more or less intensive study of obsessional behaviors, Sullivan claimed he was not particularly skillful with obsessionals—a statement that need not be taken at face value since he often played down his own formidable knowledge and superb skills as a therapist. (At a small social gathering composed chiefly of psychiatrists, for example, when he was asked a certain question, he declared he really had little or nothing to offer on that subject—and then proceeded to give an hour-long dissertation on the topic.) Sullivan relates that he "staged some scenes" so that the patient got fairly well out on a limb, that is, by means of certain procedures he had temporarily undermined the patient's usual security operations to the point at which he could no longer ignore some pertinent facts. "I am transferring you to the second floor now," he said, "and issuing orders that you will not be served a tray. And so, I don't know; maybe you will die by flinging yourself over the stairs; I doubt it. Maybe you will starve to death. I doubt that too. But we'll have to see."[20] It worked. The patient was discharged not very long after that from the hospital as much improved, though he apparently had gained little insight. But Sullivan had demonstrated to him that there was a transparent level of profit (secondary gains) he was deriving from his neurosis, which the hospital would no longer tolerate. Sullivan thought that he could recall that two or three years later the patient's wife divorced him, in a sense more or less following after the pattern of the hospital. That is, when she left him, he could no longer (unconsciously) derive any benefit from his "fear of stairs." This does not mean that he was cured of his obsessive-compulsive neurosis, but it does suggest he could no longer easily employ a crippling phobia.

But, the general reader might ask, why could not those psychiatrists in the hospital cure him? The answer, in general terms, is that it is extremely difficult to "cure" such a person. But why? Sullivan claimed that obsessional states, or rather people who suffer them, when threatened by failure of their obscure power operations, often shift to an even more grave disorder of living, frequently to schizophrenia. Hence the psychiatrist has to exercise the utmost skill in order to evade such an outcome. He has to "expand" the obsessional's awareness regarding the activities in which he is engaged, a feat that is extraordinarily difficult and usually enormously time-consuming.

Parenthetically, one must be clear on the fact that no one, however miserable, willfully abandons a familiar pattern of living, which has provided some meaning to his existence, unless he can foresee the possibility of a better, happier existence. Moreover, one does not experience things that have no precedent. Hence it takes a very long time to discover what has happened in a given situation when one has no past experience to which the occurrence can be "attached" or related. Still again, an unprecedented experience lacks the reinforcement that comes from the constant growth of experience that documents the benefit or worthwhileness of past encounters with situations that are more or less similar to one's present mode of life. In other words, the self-system tends to selectively inattend, or, in some circumstances dissociate, whatever threatens anxiety, or sometimes fear that is due to too great novelty or promise of injury. This is one of the great problems—if not the greatest—in therapy. The patient is often somewhat in the position of a man who has been incarcerated for fifty years, having been imprisoned at the age of fourteen; so he cannot be expected to rejoice at a proferred pardon. In all likelihood, he will have lost the ability to enjoy the proferred "freedom" to which he can scarcely adjust. He cannot foresee a better life.

The obsessional's difficulty has arisen from a very early if not lifelong condition of profound insecurity. This is said to have been made endurable by the perpetuation and refinement of personal magic lineally descended from the late infantile and early verbal stages of development. (Magic in Sullivan's usage pertains to relationships that are incomprehensible, having no discernable logical order; to consequences that have no "necessary" relationship to causes; and to events held to be other than "inevitable" sequences of preceding events.) Such a person cannot enjoy the comfort that comes from a feeling of personal worth and the conviction that others are favorably disposed toward one. Though the obsessional has an abiding contempt for himself it is usually much more vividly illustrated as a contempt for others. He is often able to conceal his very low self-esteem by acting the role of a powerful but subtle magician. Sullivan asserted that the quiet grandeur of many of these people is simply too staggering to occur to many people: they are quietly omniscient and omnipotent. An obsessional person will dismiss a manifest error or shortcoming by a casual resort to verbal magic, or reduce a situation that seems to put him in an unfavorable light to insignificance. If a companion pointedly calls attention to any of these things the obsessional may preserve his role with a simple statement: *"of course*, you are right." Or, if the companion deliberately demonstrates that he is much more capable in some field than the obsessional, the latter may dismiss the entire field as of trivial importance.

As previously noted, the treatment of a person suffering the obsessional state is a formidable task. When this state is severe, the therapist can tell him nothing. However, he can provide data from which useful information may sooner or later occur to one's mind. In typical fashion Sullivan often, in suitable situations, would quietly say "humbly" to such a person: "Quite often, when a person experiences such and such a series of events, it means such and such a motivation." Usually the patient dismisses such comment from his attention, but days to months later he has a surmise that there might be such a motivation. Sullivan's comment on this throws light on some of the problems of the obsessional. *"He* has to be the one who knows, discovers, effects. My role, to match his ideal, is that of one who 'only stands and waits'—a sort of admiring slave who never shows any unmistakable sign either of enslavement or freedom."[21] Though an obsessional person can *notice* and report many an occurrence fraught with great possibilities of insight, the report is so garbled with parataxic distortions regarding what the other person in a particular situation was doing that the therapist is led astray. The obsessional person can overlook, fail to perceive, almost anything when he is under stress or he can warp the occurrence unrecognizably so as to make it fit his determination as to what the situation must be or have been. Frequently, in this process of unwittingly falsifying his experiences, he develops severe visceral disturbances that take on the appearance of primary physical disease: as in the case of the man who more or less chronically "swallowed" anger or resentment.

Sullivan asserted that sometimes the obsessional is a tragic figure moving majestically through an awful world of inferior and malevolent people; that sometimes he is a Christlike figure who undergoes tortures in trying to "arrange" things as they have to be for his peace of mind, without interfering with or accomplishing anything for anyone. In the former instance they suffer and make others suffer. Usually any attempt to interfere with the obsessional's arrangements provokes him into withdrawing to an extremely detached, morose, or hurt attitude. Frequently, short of physical violence, one cannot interfere. In the latter instance, in which the obsessional is a Christlike figure, any "integration" in an interpersonal situation with him provides nothing that the other individual might want.

The obsessional state is said to be classically one in which there is great activity of thought. The obsessional person's interpersonal relations are always complicated by great parataxic distortions, by me-you patterns, which can be strikingly illusory. He is always "trying to make himself do this or that," or be this or that which he thinks is desirable. His conscious mind is filled with "oughts." Often, when the obsessional person feels relatively comfortable, he is self-consciously observing his performances. At a party, for example, where he is the host, he may silently think: "Behold me, making my guests comfortable," or "I am really being very agreeable."

Although we have not yet uncovered the roots of the obsessional's problems as Sullivan envisaged them, we have reached a point at which we can begin to dig deeper.

We shall start with another illustration (suitably disguised, as in the previous "case," in order to protect the patient's identity) in order to fix our ideas. Sullivan had a patient who was the son of a hateful, domineering, self-centered mother, who was even more miserly than Silas Marner, and of a charmingly unreasonable and henpecked father. Apparently the son took a rather long and leisurely approach to marriage. At all events, he eventually married a woman who was some fifteen years older—after having had made a good many more socially suitable contacts. The woman he did marry was a lady of great social charm, possessing broad social interests, one of those ladies who get to be known as a philanthropist. The patient's mother had always respected her, and she, herself, treated her husband in a definitely maternal way, and as Sullivan remarks wryly, "very kindly." His wife and his mother had been acquainted for years. (The general reader must be warned against any facile identification of the wife as a "mother-figure." As Sullivan might say, that sort of thing is all right for late evening alcoholic conversations—or the "bull sessions" of psychology majors in college—but it can be gravely misleading.) The patient could not clearly recall how he happened to marry his Lady: perhaps it came about as a result of the death of his father or merely because he realized he was growing old. Although Sullivan does not go into further details, one can easily imagine his mother—unless she was devouringly possessive—telling her son, over and over, that it was time, or past time, for him to marry "some nice girl" of his own social station. Or perhaps he himself began to feel compelled to do what every normal man is supposed to do, according to the cultural mores: marry and raise a family. (If he does not, his men friends—and especially their wives—may start to "wonder." What's wrong with him?) The thought of escaping from his hateful, self-centered domineering mother conceivably could have provided an added incentive. So for whatever cause, he married this charming lady, despite some rather serious misgivings. The consummation of the marriage is said to have been thoroughly unsatisfactory.

As it turned out, the wife was not interested at all in "physical endearments." Not too surprisingly, the patient could not reconcile himself to this state of affairs and often made endearing gestures. For a while, apparently she tolerated the man's lustful overtures, but as the years went by, she did so less and less. Though the patient did not tell this to Sullivan, in the course of his analysis, as data accumulated, it became evident. Sullivan also learned that, some years before consulting him, the patient had developed a gastric ulcer, which had perforated with "grave hemorrhage." Indicative of the sort of relationship that he sustained with his wife was his volunteering the information that at that time he felt quite willing to die. Though the ulcer had healed the patient still suffered many symptoms of gastrointestinal spasticity, which in itself can be a very unpleasant if not frightening experience. He still had to follow, quite rigidly, dietary and other hygienic requirements. It will probably not come as a surprise to any psychiatric reader of this book that despite meticulous care of himself, the patient still suffered quite a few attacks of gastrointestinal disorder. In other words, the tensions due to his unfortunate relationship with his wife were still sidetracked into the gastrointestinal tract.

Sullivan and his patient worked intensively to resolve the severe obsessional state which the latter suffered. After about a hundred interviews, Sullivan progressed to the point at which he could demonstrate—despite any and all the power operations or "magical" stratagems that the patient could muster—that the patient was the victim of an unvarying dislike of him by his wife. (This is a pretty good illustration of how difficult it is to "expand" the obsessional's awareness.) Overtly, at least, she "respected" him, quite successfully maintaining appearances and facilitating his career in other ways. (To the world, that is, the upper-middle-class world of the patient's and his wife's friends and acquaintances, she was probably looked upon as a "good wife." Such a state of affairs, in which husband and wife manifest an unvarying dislike of each other in their private life while presenting a picture of marital happiness to the world, seems to be not rare these days, as most readers will know.) "But she clearly detested physical intimacy." And her husband was still actively seeking it though for fifteen years she was not only uninterested but discouraged any sort of physical intimacy. Gradually, as the patient's security increased and his awareness expanded he began to recall clearly some of the unnumbered occasions in which he pressed for some demonstration of affection from his wife in physical contact. He recalled that he was always rebuffed, and, for several years, had been quite brutally rebuffed, and then after each such occurrence he would withdraw, concealing his hurt and humiliation. Being the sort of person he was, bedevilled by feelings of inadequacy and abysmally low self-esteem, he had to resort to extensive security operations. He would try hard to put such incidents out of his mind by telling himself what a fine person his wife was, how desirable a home he and his wife had, what standing in their community they held. Meanwhile, it also became quite clear to Sullivan that on equally innumerable occasions the patient must have been filled with rage, of which the latter was just beginning to be conscious.

Another warning is perhaps in order for the general reader. He may be inclined to think that this woman was a vicious, puritanical bitch, who wilfully made her husband's life a nightmare. Such an interpretation would be quite foreign to Sullivan's. First of all, for causes unknown (but probably not unknowable), she simply could not enjoy any sort of physical endearment. Her recoil at any sexual overtures was not a pose. As Sullivan might say, the sexual overtures "put her on the spot." It is entirely possible that at some level of awareness she felt inadequate over her lack of sexual responsiveness. Her respect for her husband, according to Sullivan's account, seems to have been genuine. Her dislike of him may have arisen from her being so frequently put on the spot. Moreover, living with an obsessive-compulsive person is no picnic. At any rate, Sullivan would undoubtedly relate his patient's marital difficulties to those of his wife. In other words, a more comprehensive investigation would focus on the interpersonal relationship of the two, never on one party alone. For purposes of exposition of certain aspects of obsessive behavior, Sullivan, in this instance, does not emphasize his transactional orientation.

To continue with the exposition of the obsessional discussed above, when he became able to be conscious of the hopeless campaign to win over his wife, and the supplementary procedures that enabled him to overlook his helplessness and avoid profiting from his rebuffs, he also became clear about the rage and hatred he experienced. The great love and contentment he professed faded away. The husband and wife learned to live on a much less provocative, frustrating, and painful basis. The gastrointestinal spasticity is said to have correspondingly faded away and the patient no longer suffered from the disorder of the alimentary function.

This brief excerpt provides an excellent illustration of the fact that a therapist who approaches mental illness from an "intrapsychic" point of view—if he practices what he teaches—will be gravely handicapped because the patient's difficulties are intimately related to his interpersonal relations. He had to learn that his difficulties with his wife were intimately tied up with her problems as well as his own. Their difficulties masked and reinforced one another. The insight he gained in therapy would probably amount to little if he had not been able to alter his relations with his wife and learn to accept, as best he could, her "intrapsychic" problems. In other words, as he gradually gained insight into the character of their interpersonal relations, and accordingly learned to alter his behavior in such a fashion that he could mitigate her "intrapsychic" problems, the situation improved. This works both ways, once the partner senses the change. And presumably his wife no longer suffered the anxiety and anger that her husband's behavior unwittingly provoked. Their marriage was probably still far from ideal, but both had perhaps still a good deal to offer the other, with much less mutual suffering and a relative absence of demands on each other that they could not fulfill.

Having presented a preliminary introduction to an understanding of obsessionalism, we can proceed with a more detailed explication. In Chapter 4, an outline of the sort of childhood an obsessive-compulsive neurotic generally has was given. So only a few additional comments will be given in this chapter. While it is true that everyone occasionally has recourse to verbal magic—which he would normally have begun to learn during the childhood era—beause of his home life the individual who is destined to suffer the obsessional state or become an obsessive-compulsive neurotic will learn to put an abnormal reliance on it. He learns that when he commits some violation, if he knows the right string of words, some verbal proposition, he at least often escapes anxiety or harm. True, it does not bring the satisfactions or tolerance he needs, but it does save him a lot of trouble. If this sounds obscure to the general reader, he has only to recall that normal adults every once in a while will employ the technique of "I'm sorry" or "I apologize," or "Please forgive me" or even much more elaborate verbal propositions in order to appease some one they have hurt, insulted, unsuccessfully tried to deceive. And such a technique often works in the sense that an individual can thus ward off some threatening retaliation. Still, a more or less normal person knows that this technique has only limited utility and that he had better not overdo it. A woman may enjoy hearing her husband say to her, "I love you" but if he becomes frequently thoughtless and neglectful, his attempts at appeasement by the familiar formula, "I love you. I love you. I love you. I couldn't live without you" will not work indefinitely. Even if he can also at the same time maneuver her into bed for a frolic, all the while telling her how irresistible she is, she will sooner or later catch on to the fact that this too is one of his stratagems, even if a different one. So he has to mend his ways—or else.

The home of the obsessional when he was a youngster fosters verbal magic. No matter what aggression any member of the family perpetrated on another there was always some worthy principle to which the parents and elder siblings could appeal, that is, they would fall back on verbal magic. A trivial example is the case in which mother has suffered one of father's aggressions, and, feeling hurt and angry, seizes upon some pretext to give vent to her anger by walloping "little Willie," all the while telling him "I'm doing this for your own good" —somewhat after the fashion of the "good old days" when a sadistic teacher would wallop one of his pupils with a cane while reiterating, "This hurts me more than it hurts you." It may often be that fifteen minutes earlier, whenever a lofty principle has been enunciated, another and contradictory principle had been evoked. Thus, it is conceivable that not long before little Willie was thrashed, his mother had been teaching him that kindness and love are virtues he should learn to espouse. It is also possible that little Willie's elders can find some suitable quotation from the Bible to justify their aggressions. Of course, their neighbors may call them "damned hypocrites." But Sullivan held that here is a situation in which it has been found that it is better to have this limited verbal magic than to have the only other thing one could have: "an awful lot of fairly open hostility and dislike and hatred."[22] Thus it was unlikely that little Willie's father would do what a farmer whom the writer of this book knew long ago would do: threaten to cut off the legs of his little nephew with a scythe.

In a good many homes like little Willie's, love was perhaps the one thing that was of no significance in establishing the marriage. Convenience was important; and perhaps wealth and social standing as well. Sullivan taught that, in such a home, if one of the partners originally didn't have this knack of appealing to ancient ethical principles for the purpose of excusing all sorts of selfish, domineering, and self-seeking performances, he or she had learned it from the other partner before Willie arrived on the scene. Hence Willie does not get the highly educative opportunity to learn what works with mother will not work with father. Though he learns that a great many things will not quite work with anyone, they are better than nothing. Almost from birth he is surrounded with them—and in his situation he has no chance to learn anything he might contrast them with—so evidently they are a part of the universe and he must learn them. Thus he misses the highly educative value that he might otherwise derive from the sharp failure with verbal magic, for it would impress him how important in verbal operations the hearer is. Instead he has a confused impression that nothing works very well, or if something occasionally does work well, he has no faith that next time it will, too. Sullivan claimed that to the extent that verbal magic operations are better than nothing, the youngster is inhibited from developing some of the most valuable aspects of verbal implicit operations. This seems to imply that his thinking processes become arrested, and, perhaps, distorted. In any serious interpersonal problem he is liable to bog down in his development by concentrating, so to speak, on his half-satisfactory verbal magic operations—half-satisfactory for reasons mentioned previously. They do not really protect him from some degree of anxiety or greatly enhance his euphoria but they do hinder severe anxiety and ward off punishment.

According to Sullivan, the self-dynamism develops by one's learning how to circumvent anxiety, or to avoid anxiety-provoking situations. In the previous chapter, it was described how numerous kinds of potentially educative experiences are distorted or missed by the intervention of anxiety, thus in varying degrees hindering the growth of the self and perhaps warping its development. All of this occurs in relation to significant others. In the process of learning what one should or must do, and what one should not or must not do, the child who lives in a home in which ethical principles are simply verbal magical tools learns to employ the obsessional verbal magic to allay anxiety, to ward off feelings of guilt and shame that represent the critical evaluation or supervisory patterns of the self. Perhaps because he knows that a great many things he has learned do not work perfectly with anyone, he becomes overly conscientious, in a peculiar way, about whether or not he is doing the right thing in all sorts of situations in a home where everyone seems so greatly concerned about moral principles. One should also bear in mind that in his home life the youngster is deficient in models who embody affection, genuinely rational behavior, and the like. The parents, in fact, are quite likely to be thoroughly incapable of love. If the youngster has an affectionate aunt or grandmother with whom he can communicate or at least receive some tenderness from he may be saved from evolving into a "caricature" of a human being.

The translation from the early, clumsy miscarriage of verbal operations to the full-blown verbal magical operations of a chronologically adult obsessive-compulsive neurotic is a matter of very rich detail, which the psychiatrist can discover if he has the time and energy to seek it out. This does not imply that he could find an identical "translation" or evolution of mental content in every case. The niceties and nuances by which particular obsessional mental contents get to be important are as numerous as those contents themselves. Sullivan claimed that almost anything conceivable can "determine" that an obsessional thinks so-and-so under such-and-such conditions. But it is a mistake to believe that as a result of his thinking in that fashion, he, so to speak, magically achieves security. He never does. Obsessional people are said to be definitely insecure. Without the verbal implicit mental operations, a person of this kind would be much less secure. The elaborate ritual of activities to which he is prone serve the same function: warding off dangerously intense anxiety and a feeling in consciousness of abysmally low self-esteem.

The person who is "prevailingly obsessional" may have little skill at implicit verbal operations—quite in contrast to the more normal, intelligent person—which are the instruments of successful communication of novel and complex states of mind. He has difficulty in the most troublesome, hardest field of communication: "trying to get oneself across to someone or to get clear on somebody else," such as his wife, his boss, or his therapist. Sullivan asserted that he is apt to meet all baffling interpersonal difficulties with a stream of verbal implicit processes that have very little relevance to those difficulties and are a continuation of the not very satisfactory business, namely the security operation or "defense mechanism" that characterized his home when he was a child. "It is almost as if the child had learned that you have to have certain things in your mind before you can do certain things—you have to be perfectly ready to spring this hokum if anything backfires."[23] So it seems to him to be perfectly good sense to have the hokum ready—just in case. Subsequently when he becomes rather badly confused in his progression toward adulthood, "the hokum takes over," so to speak, whenever he is threatened with the bafflement or confusion which would lead to an acute feeling of anxiety or inadequacy. Again this is in marked contrast to the behavior of certain normal individuals who skillfully, deliberately employ "hokum" in order to confuse the other fellow, such as some salesmen, some merchants, some politicians, some business executives, and others. Try, for example, to extract a logical explanation from the unscrupulous salesman who sold you your new air conditioner as to why it does not function properly—when perhaps all along he knows his underpaid workmen failed to install the machine properly, neglected to level it at the right angle, or otherwise failed to perform adequately. He may deluge you with more or less plausible, pseudoexplanations, stories of what happened with this customer and that. Unfortunately, this kind of "hokum" works frequently all too well and its purveyors often prosper, perhaps becoming pillars of their communities.

Obsessional behavior is a function "wholly of the self." The "victim" of obsessional states is not aiming to baffle the other fellow for the sake of success; he is trying to maintain his own interpersonal security, and in the process often gets *himself* awfully confused. He often employs selective inattention, and its frequent use is almost a guarantee that one will fail to understand numerous situations in which one is involved. Obsessional behavior is said to have nothing to do with the satisfaction of the impulses that do not require the intervention of the self, complicating them only insofar as they have been made "sources" of insecurity, as the sexual drives often do. For the obsessive-compulsive neurotic sex is almost always badly complicated by rituals of one sort or another, though that does not entail impotence or frigidity. Obsessional behavior has to do with security, which in turn, is directly related to the self; therefore in a "prevailingly sexual situation, the obsessional person provides a lot of nuisance for the other person in connection with his security needs, but is relatively free so far as the actual genital cooperation is concerned."[24]

Like so much else in psychiatry, *obsessional behavior* can be conceived as forming a spectrum of certain behavior patterns, provided one bears in mind that behavior is often covert or implicit as well as overt. (In this book "covert processes" or "implicit processes" have been used to designate various kinds of "inner" experience: emotions, motives, fantasies, thoughts.) Sullivan pointed out that, from time to time, everyone has recourse to verbal magic but some people learn to confine their magic feats to situations in which they seem to be needed and feasible. Thus it is likely that many husbands learn that recourse to a bit of verbal magic can be efficacious with their wives on certain occasions, such as wedding anniversaries, birthdays, and the like. On such occasions, it is needed and wanted—provided that one has a minimum of skill. These reflections lead to the following question: When is a therapist clinically justified in labeling a patient as a "case" of obsessional neurosis (obsessive-compulsive neurosis) instead of labeling him a "prevailingly obsessional personality"? So far we have slurred over this distinction, as did Sullivan himself in *Conceptions of Modern Psychiatry,* in which he discusses *obsessional states,* conditions under which the individual may range in his behavior from the neurotic to borderline psychotic. The criterion for the distinction between a "prevailingly obsessional personality" and an "obsessional neurotic" is anchored in the relative security one can maintain in interpersonal relations. A person may "perhaps" be best said to be described as prevailingly obsessional who does not impress ordinarily intelligent, reasonably observant people he comes in contact with as being at all odd or queer or, in more or less contemporary popular jargon, "kookie."[25] His interpersonal relations are less marked by obsessional mental content and overt behavior because they evoke milder degrees of anxiety—in contrast to the obsessional neurotic who may be often bedevilled by anxiety, particularly when his security operations fail owing to circumstances he cannot control, or foresee, especially in connection with a significant other person. However, the former does manifest a definitely obsessional "stickiness" in relation to those with whom he is *chronically* integrated. In the case of the prevailingly obsessional personality, rather than that of the obsessional neurotic—though this difference is not entirely "absolute"— some fairly useful traits are said to be almost necessarily associated with insecurities that begin as early as the obsessional processes do. Sullivan claimed that obsessional people frequently develop considerable skill at technical operations of a good deal of complexity and a good deal of economic value. A person who does not suffer the insecurities of the obsessional and who finds other people delightful perhaps would not be sufficiently interested to endure the long and exacting regimen required to earn a doctorate in, say, electrical engineering or mathematics. Although Sullivan does not mention it, a cultural element perhaps also has to be considered. For example, the Irish are famous for their poets, dramatists, and novelists but they are not distinguished in the field of mathematics, excepting for a few mathematicians such as Boole and Hamilton. (It is perhaps of interest to note that Sullivan himself apparently possessed some talent for mathematics and physics.)

The person who cannot enter into any actually meaningful relations with a stranger without obtruding this "stickiness" previously mentioned can "probably" be called an obsessional neurotic. Hence the difference between the person who is prevailingly obsessional and one who is an obsessional neurotic is, as previously noted, a matter of degree. The prototype of the stickiness is the functional stutterer who as described in *Conceptions of Modern Psychiatry,* employs language, not for communication, but for defiance and domination. He is said to have found a magic of articulate sounds that really works. Because he can demonstrate an inability to produce a word, and ceases to try, he immobilizes the other person and arrests "the flow of process in the world." This is a formidable power operation going back to the time when "sheerly magic operations" are being abandoned and the child is beginning to learn the consensual validation of language. The stutterer puts forth a tremendous amount of effort, Sullivan claims in *Clinical Studies,* and, in addition, in case you want to go away, or to help out: "almost a compulsion is exercised on you to stick around, until finally you have your information—if you can live that long." The obsessional employs an almost identical process, whose basic purpose is the warding off of acute anxiety, not domination.

An obsessional can be as "maddening" as any stutterer since he seems to lack a grasp of the value of time unless it becomes a life or death matter. Suppose you badly need to get a certain item of information very swiftly that is in the possession of your obsessional secretary. If you tell her to make haste, you may convert her into a "mass of jitters which closes off everything." So in order to obtain the information you want you must wait patiently until she gets through talking at whatever length—even if you are on a transatlantic telephone line. There is no other way. One cannot win in a frontal attack on obsessional obstruction. This—the obscure to obvious resort of the individual to magical power operations—is said to be "the life" of the obsessional in a great many contacts with other people. Despite all his efforts, he is not genuinely secure, and the more anxious he becomes, the more he resorts to the obsessional magical verbal symbols and/or to a vast array of rituals in lieu of simple communicative statements. Summarily the difference between the markedly or prevailingly obsessional personality and the seriously disturbed obsessional neurotic is to be defined chiefly in the success, or lack of it, in the "obsessional process." If the obsessional processes are fairly successful, then he can be called a prevailingly obsessional personality, because, in other words, he very rarely encounters acute and severe anxiety. In contrast, when these processes are much less successful with significant people, then the individual's interpersonal security is so tenuous at best that he is extremely busy utilizing his repertory of rituals in order to ward off severe anxiety. But he lacks the time—and perhaps the facility— to adjust the rituals to the nuances that the "prevailingly obsessional personality" can so easily do. Instead "he becomes very rigid in his adherence to certain magic formulae which may sound as if they referred to something" but the therapist cannot discover what it is. These obsessional formulae, by translation, as it were, can be reduced to a ritualistic type of behavior whose meaning is incommunicable. It will be futile to inquire about these rituals, for the person is unable to communicate anything about them. All that a person who has a compulsive ritual usually knows is that when he carries it out he feels better. Otherwise his relative peace of mind would be disturbed. And it is very difficult for the therapist to learn any more about this behavior. Perhaps the following relatively trivial and oversimplified illustration may help the general reader to "fix" this sort of occurrence in his mind. Suppose one is going out to dinner with such an individual, and that the evening is to be ended by going to a "party" or some other sort of social gathering. Suppose, also, that one stops at his apartment for a drink before going out to dinner. While this individual is preparing the drinks, one may observe that he is going through a lot of seemingly unnecessary motions, and one may begin to wonder if the dry martinis (or whatever kind of drink is being prepared) will be ready before midnight. Finally the drinks are served and consumed. Conversation is difficult though one cannot understand why a simple statement one makes becomes elaborated by the obsessional into a rather long, legalistic type of argument. As the evening wears on, he prepares to leave, but he has to refix his tie, recomb his hair, wash his hands for the second or third time, and make sure that there are no lighted cigarette butts in the ash trays. Perhaps one becomes a little impatient and suggests the hour is growing late—a statement that seems to irritate one's companion. When at length he is ready to leave and heads for the door, he falters in his stride—and then stops. Turning around, he proceeds back into the living room to check the ash trays once more. During dinner he seems preoccupied, saying little, but he may vaguely hint or otherwise indicate that he feels a bit unhappy. What he does not say, and never will say, is: "There is going to be a certain very attractive young lady at that party I have long wanted to go out with, but I feel very nervous when talking to her and in fact I lack the self-confidence even to carry on a real conversation with her." The point is not that he had some such thought consciously in mind. They were "translated" into compulsive rituals. Moreover, it is not the fact that she is sexually desirable and attractive that is threatening *per se* to him. Nor any conviction that he is sexually inadequate. It is the fact that his self-esteem is so abysmally low in significant situations that he anticipates painful rebuffs from any attempts to become friendly with this young woman who may actually have shown some interest in him. Like every obsessional neurotic he has never experienced outstanding success in interpersonal relations. Otherwise he can maintain a low level of well-being. If he has no real interest in the young woman, if there is no conceivable possibility that she can or might become significant to him, he will perhaps be able to engage in a fairly normal, polite conversation—at least until she becomes bored.

That is the idea that Sullivan "harped upon." The psychiatrist, in order to understand the obsessional (or obsessive-compulsive) neurotic must grasp the fact that he has never had the satisfaction or fulfillment of outstanding success, such as intimacy, in interpersonal relations. Sullivan claimed that only people who are involved as necessary to the satisfactions and a measure of security of an obsessional neurotic can unhorse him. As I mentioned above, he cannot be comfortable as to his personal worth and the favorable attitude of significant others to him. A woman who is quite satisfactory as a sexual partner to her husband, may, for one cause or another, start to find fault with her husband in *some other area* of their relationship. That in itself becomes a source of insecurity to him. And therefore, instead of making a careful analysis as to what might have gone wrong with the marriage, instead of trying to discover what the real, actual situation is, he resorts to frustrating magical operations. The latter provide a reason, or at least an excuse, for the wife to intensify her fault-finding, which in turn makes her husband more anxious. Then, perhaps, one of them consults a psychiatrist.

Suppose both husband and wife are rather obsessional. If one of the partners, due to increasing difficulties in their relationship, consults a psychiatrist, he will say something to the effect that the longer the two live together, the more crotchety and difficult the partner gets to be. With increasing insecurity about the relationship they have got to pestering each other more and more, which superficially may seem to be an attempt by each to get the other down. But that is *not* what they are trying to do. Each is trying to negate the other's power to produce anxiety in him. And if in the process of attempting to overcome the other's power to produce anxiety, the "mate" becomes sexually impotent (or frigid, as the case may be), that is a dreadful misfortune to an obsessional neurotic, and he may hasten to a psychiatrist.

It is now time to take up the "unending doubts" that plague many an obsessional. Sullivan thought that the obsessional neurotic prefers to be uncertain about a great many things because the static character of obsessional neurosis is largely maintained by unclearness about anything that is so "oppressively evident" that he cannot treat it with selective inattention. In addition, it has seemed to Sullivan, in some cases where doubts and uncertainties were alleged to be the patient's problem, as if he had at some time or other stumbled upon the fact that a tremendous amount of misery about doubts is one of the most baffling things the American social environment can encounter. In effect, the obsessional who is forever doubting is asking other people to resolve his doubts, that is, advise him, which works very neatly for the following reasons: "Americans, being among the world's most insecure people so far as close approaches to intimacy are concerned, are also the most ready to advise without a moment's hesitation; for if you start handing out advice you don't have to get any closer—you immediately begin disposing of the situation rapidly."[26] Sullivan claimed that all the obsessional has to do is to maintain the most unhappy inability to become convinced, and other people just rattle on with no effort on his part. Certain people who consulted Sullivan about their morbid doubts quite soon got into struggles of the classical obsessional kind with him. At a strategic moment, he would ask a question, deliberately framed to be disconcerting, such as the following: "Well, why the enormous harassment about it? What difference does it make which is right?" He added that on such occasions it sometimes became plain that these doubts are "transparently bunk." The obsessional's behavior is often so exhausting and monotonous that he becomes careless from fatigue. In such situations, when he has been too careless to have a really valid doubt, Sullivan "moved in" and, so to speak, demonstrated to the patient that his doubting was bunkum, a maneuver that in the short run is very shattering to his prestige and intensely anxiety-provoking.

The psychiatrist does not learn much by regarding the doubts as an obsessional process in itself. He must "see around the doubts" in order to learn what the patient is doing, and then give the doubting operation a few jolts when it is rather clear that they are not suitable to the situation or to the therapist as a significant person. After that the classic "obsessional business" takes over. The doubting may become a device to keep the social environment preoccupied so that people are less likely to attack the obsessional very much. It is also conceivable that the doubting makes other people make damn fools of themselves trying to help the obsessional, which may also be a way of enhancing his security a little.

But there is a different kind of patient who suffers from "real, abiding uncertainties."[27] Sullivan claimed that these can be awfully harassing experiences, perhaps as painful mental states as one can chronically have, though they are never expressed in frank doubting. Such a patient is eternally wondering whether he is a "boy" or a "girl," a man or a woman, that is, where in the "masculinity-femininity distribution" he belongs. But there is no rattling off of harassing doubts as is the case with the obsessional neurotic. In the former instance, even though the patient is always preoccupied with them, he cannot confront them clearly. He cannot tolerate his problem but he cannot drop it or forget about it because it has become enmeshed in the whole structure of the prospective future. Unless and until he is able to resolve this problem as to where in the masculinity-femininity distribution he belongs, he suffers uncertainty, insecurity, sometimes suspicion and always caution regarding what people mean by their statements or questions, and what their actions mean. Now, suppose the therapist is able to close in on a really probable hypothesis about what lots of little details are all about and says: "Look, are you unclear as to whether you are mostly a man or a woman?" Then, to judge from the patient's facial expression, following upon this revelation he seems for a moment to believe that someone at last has "opened the gates of paradise," and he says "Yes, I think I have always worried about that."

But in the case of the obsessional neurotic, if the therapist similarly closes in on a probable hypothesis, he gets greatly disturbed. "As soon as you start anything of that sort, the obsessional practically gets up from the couch and throws it at you." He will do almost anything to prevent you from talking. He is warned immediately that the therapist finally has caught on to whatever ails him or at least some of it in such a fashion that he cannot escape it. He makes it very hard for the therapist to formulate the problem. And when he has heard it, despite his efforts to stop the therapist from saying it, he does *not* experience great feeling of relief. But although he gets angry, he also benefits markedly from the confrontation. As time goes on the anger diminishes, and his admiration for the therapist increases. Provided that he really feels secure with the therapist, he is apt to say for weeks afterward, "Oh this—that's my damn what-not that you made me see." Needless to say, before Sullivan "closed in" like that on an obsessional neurotic, he would have carefully explored the field, that is, the latter's mental state, the severity of his insecurities, and the like.

While ultrarefined interpretations of the content of the obsessional neurotic's speech or the particular behavioristic pattern of a ritualistic gesture he manifests seems to have little, if any, therapeutic value, ticlike movements and automatisms represent action necessary to maintain a dissociated system and hence it may be necessary to find out what they stand for or mean—or it may not. But an "attack" on the origin of the meaning of an automatism may not be sound therapeutic strategy. (Moreover, the original meaning of something, such as the original meaning of the autistic speech of the obsessional neurotic, may not have any relevance or significance in the patient's verbal behavior, at least as far as the therapist is concerned.) Sullivan found that even though an automatism has a significant meaning, in treating obsessional schizoid people who had automatisms their original meaning became quite clear as certain of the patient's problems were cleared up. This, in a manner of speaking, occurred automatically without his ever thinking the clarification was taking place, even though it may be sometimes very difficult to get an automatism "to unfold into what it stands for" despite the fact that it may be something very significant. Sometimes the origin, or original meaning, would become quite clear to the patient though not necessarily to the therapist. The former would report "wonderful and sometimes immature types of thinking," which were an adequate explanation to him of the automatisms. But they were not very meaningful to the therapist, which suggests that automatisms are constructed from types of implicit or covert activities that are, or have remained, pretty immature, possibly made of the stuff of certain primitive symbol systems and their correlates mentioned in Chapter 2. Such automatisms, whose meanings seem to become clear to the patient but not to the therapist, resemble what once happened with one of Sullivan's patients who was rather definitely schizophrenic part of the time. For a long time this patient had had the feeling that something, not a fluid, not a stream but "something" went down his leg into the earth. "It was essential that, when this happened, his foot should be in contact with the ground or the pavement or something else that stood for the earth. Thus the arrival somewhere of whatever it was that went down his leg seemed to be a part of his nuisance."[28] Therapist and patient worked up "a lot of obscure business' about his mother's relations with him and his brother. This could have been interpreted as the mother's attempt to castrate her boys but aside from the fact that Sullivan had no use for ideas on "castration complexes" because they did not make good sense to him, what difference would such an interpretation have made to the patient? As the therapy proceeded, the latter "puttered around" in very early experiences he recalled about the mother's getting her boys into bed and, though this was never clearly recalled, communicating in some fashion to her sons that their hands might well be placed so that they were a reasonable distance from the genitals. All this was very hard to recall and "pretty subtle," but very "meaningful." Then one day the patient startled Sullivan by saying: "Well you know, I think I have at last come to understand this obscure thing I've told you about something going down my leg." Apparently he did, but Sullivan did not, and never got any reliable clues as to its meaning.

Before exploring the connections of obsessional neurosis and schizophrenia, I wish to review briefly some of Sullivan's ideas on substitutive processes, dissociation, and the like. Sullivan believed that there is no "clear line" between people who in interpersonal relations employ substitutive processes of the obsessional type and those who suffer schizophrenic episodes of living. Obsessional substitution is an outstanding function of the self for the purpose of keeping something utterly excluded from consciousness, so that there is no possibility of its "eruption" into consciousness. Substitutive activity, almost by definition, is any activity of the self whose function is to avoid "certain conscious clarity" about one's own situation, one's own motivation.[29] Whenever dissociated systems of motives are invoked in one's interpersonal relations there is a relative

Clinical Entities : 467

"suspension" of consciousness as to any effects such systems have. The suspension of consciousness may range from selective inattention to wish-fulfilling fantasies to automatisms (tics, certain more elaborate "muscle-nerve combinations," certain gestures, which are not controlled by the self-conscious personality), whether minor or major. If the automatism is major, one finds oneself, along with very considerable disturbance, in very awkward situations into which one has apparently entered with one's eyes open, as it were, and from which one extricates oneself, usually, considerably shaken. That is to say, some major dissociated motivational system took over temporarily. In *Clinical Studies,* Sullivan gives a detailed explication of dissociated processes and how they may be manifested.

The grave complication that can occur in an obsessional neurosis is said to be that it may progress into schizophrenia. There seems to be "a fairly easy transition" from the one state to the other. In fact there are some patients who "shift back and forth" between the two. The artist (or "engineer") previously discussed was possibly saved by Sullivan and the hospital staff from progressing into schizophrenia although he does not say so. He mentions another patient who apparently suffered from a "compulsive neurosis," that is, an obsessional state with much ritualization of behavior. (Sullivan did not adhere to the current fashion of designating all obessional neurotics as obsessive-compulsive, though it is recognized that in a given instance either "obsessive thoughts" or compulsive actions may predominate.) This patient feared that he would be contaminated by encountering feces. His behavior quite early during his sojourn in the hospital is said to have become marked by his frequently getting into the men's toilet in any way that he could. While in the toilet he alternated between washing "the skin off his hands" and standing under an exposed soil pipe—where he had the greatest opportunity, if there was any leakage, for him to be contaminated by fecal matter. (A Freudian psychiatrist might interpret his behavior in the light of the alleged characteristics of the "anal character" type, reverting back to the period of toilet training.[30]) It became quite obvious to Sullivan that this patient had evolved into a schizophrenic state. He quickly became hebephrenic, and not long after he died with startling speed from a certain form of tuberculosis. Hebephrenia is usually the end of the road, as it were, for a schizophrenic, involving a great dilapidation of human traits and a terrible despair. Sullivan thought that, as a rule, this condition has no promise of even partial recovery.

The following account of another patient, a brilliant young man, provides a picture of how, under stress, a person may shift from obsessional processes to "schizophrenic phenomenology" and then after treatment in a hospital revert to an obsessional state. "This young man's mother had married, not the man she loved, for he was one of her brothers, but instead an extremely ambitious man whose harsh centering on himself and his career was apparent from very early in life."[31] Before very long she too is said to have become extraordinarily ambitious, concerned with the task of being his wife and consolidating a social career for herself, which was facilitated by his successes. In fairly close succession, she bore him four children and, following upon quite a long interval and a disastrous occurrence, a fifth. This disastrous occurrence was the fatal injury in an automobile accident of the eldest daughter, the only child for whom the father had any real feeling. As far as the other children went, they regarded him simply as a man who, when he sometimes got annoyed because they were talking to one another, "cuffed them into silence." Having been absent from home at the time of the accident, the father rushed back home to find his daughter already dead. The mother was reduced to a state of agitated depression by her husband's behavior, a depression that persisted for approximately a year. She bore the fifth child, a son, in the latter stages of this depressed period. This child was the only one who did not turn out to be an "emotional wreck" when Sullivan knew them. Unlike the other children he became normal and extroverted, ignoring the rest of the family. This son was so different from them that they were "unable to get him down." It seems that his mother had become so paralyzed by the "hangover" of her depression that "she just could not get him into harness as she had the rest of the children."

Sullivan related that his patient was the most brilliant of the older surviving children, who was the quintessence of obsessional neuroticism. He had to handle everything very carefully and cautiously, taking an interminable length of time to do anything. Apparently he derived much pleasure from studying mathematics. But he had gotten into a "profound emotional jam" with one of his professors, who had the same "intensely arrogant, contemptuous manner that the father had always shown." So this brilliant young man became tied up into emotional knots when he attended the arrogant professor's class. The poor fellow was unable to hear the professor, or to answer any questions.

In this patient's history there were two rather shocking things. One pertained to some sort of difficulty of bowel functions. This had appeared when he was traveling in Europe one summer in the company of a young instructor at the University who had suggested that the patient travel with him. Shortly after the instructor's suggestion was made, however, the youth began "getting more and more incredibly entangled" in obsessional operations. Finally, after he had got more and more preoccupied with some problem of the bowel function, the instructor realized that they were apparently not doing well together, so he proceeded ahead on his own. Then the patient's symptoms "cleared up somewhat," with the result that he could join the young instructor at the port of embarkation for the trip back to the United States. Though Sullivan heard the story, or some reference to it, a great many times he came to realize that he did not possess even "the foggiest notion" of what the youth was talking about, and that he could foresee no immediate prospect of finding out. The second striking thing in the patient's history had to do with a fellow student, a roommate, when he was an undergraduate at the University. "The situation with this fellow had been perfectly awful; it got worse and worse, and at that point I did actually get the detail that the sun seemed to be involved in some way or another in this thing."[32] This he told under pressure, at which Sullivan was so thoroughly skillful: one must know what one is about and when to apply pressure. As the patient related this item of information, it seemed that he had to be outdoors a great deal under the sun in order to add to his vitamin D supply or for some similar purpose. But he also gave obvious indications that he knew that his explanation was a rationalization and that he was aware there were "lunatic fringes" to his explanation about going out under the sun to add to vitamin D supply or whatever. At times he was mute, unable to make any attempt at conversation.

Sullivan asserted that, as the therapy proceeded, it finally became evident that, in some fashion, the mother had constituted herself an inescapable restriction on the genital function very early in this youth's life. He could recall that it occurred when he was still sleeping with his brother in a cradle. In some fashion—which Sullivan generally in his later work linked up with emphatized anxiety—what with their mother's arranging their hands under the sheets, she became identified as a very serious threat to the youth's perineal region. This occurrence sounds very much like what Sullivan called "primary genital phobia," which is explained in *Conceptions of Modern Psychiatry*.

After making a nearly fatal therapeutic blunder because the latter did not at once grasp the significance of certain of the youth's communications, patient and therapist "puttered along," ultimately, it seems, getting the blunder repaired. Then one summer the father died suddenly, apparently causing the mother to verge on "blowing up with joy," and precipitating the patient into a schizophrenic episode. These occurrences came about when the youth was no longer in treatment with Sullivan. So back he came in this schizophrenic state. He started out by performing some very obscure "operations" concerning how great a danger he was in to work with the therapist, which at face value practically signified that by coming back to Sullivan he was giving up every hope he ever entertained about getting well. Presently, after some more therapy, the patient emerged from the "schizophrenic phenomenology" to the pretty typical obsessional caution that had always been characteristic of his behavior. Whether *any* person who depends principally on the obsessional dynamism will, under stress, become schizophrenic, is unclear.

Sullivan said it is a rare experience to find a markedly obsessional person in a really tender, considerate, and constructive environment. Comparatively comfortable and easygoing persons are not likely to get enthusiastic about obsessionals as potential friends or lovers, so they tend to avoid them. In Sullivan's experience, the obsessional manifests an outstanding tendency to become involved in a situation that may be described crudely as prevailingly hateful. Though, "like everyone else," they are "lousy with good intentions," they tend to become involved in very sticky, awkward entanglements in their interpersonal relations. In therapy they live in fear of being understood, since they believe "a maximum of clarity" would reveal that they are unregenerately bad. The obsessional's attitudes and behavior patterns can easily be interpreted as hostile or malevolent because he is constantly attempting—by very inefficient self-thwarting means—to maintain an uncertain security when anyone who is significant is around. "And when you are trying to maintain a feeling of security, with the constant marginal feeling that the other person doesn't respect you, well, you are not apt to be loving, you see; it *is* a rather hostile performance, so far as the other person is concerned."[33]

Obsessional neurotics are people who frequently, if not always, underwent a desolating childhood. Often they have been subjected to severe cruelty by a parent who masks her sheer brutality. Obsessionals know their parents were not happy and that at least one of them was savagely cruel to the offspring. The thin veneer of convention and sweetness and light was always baffling. The bafflement of the child is said to have taken the form of wondering whether mother, for example, was really cruel to him or whether she was sweetness and light, so that it was just his own cursed perversity that made her seem so cruel. And so, as Sullivan might say, "the thing grew and grew over the years," nurturing various ramifications and security operations, which, among other things, made it impossible to trust any person who was significant.[34]

Before I take up the last clinical entity to be described in this chapter, I shall quote a few pertinent comments from Leon Salzman. "In earlier years the hysterical personality was more widely studied; Freud used the hysteric as the paradigm of his conceptualization of psychoanalysis and therapy. For that reason many psychologists and behavioral scientists were led to believe that hysterical manifestations of disordered personality were more common than they are. There is now good reason to believe that, both for primitive man and for those acculturated to highly developed civilizations, the obsessive defensive mechanism provides the most widespread technique for enabling man to achieve some illusion of safety and security in an uncertain world."[35]

As in most things, Sullivan's interpretation of hysteria is very different from Freud's, though the former did not carry out a very intensive study of this famous disorder. Sullivan thought that the hysteric might be said in principle to be a person who has a happy thought as to a way by which he can be respectable even though he is not living up to his principles. But Sullivan also says it is practically impossible to prove that he has had that thought. However, under hypnosis the hysteric can be led to recall the thought that provides the key to revealing how one can "dissociate" with comparative impunity without employing the elaborate apparatus of the "true dissociated condition." Sullivan claims that in the hysteric one sees the whole achievement of the hysterical dynamism is to prevent the environing people from recognizing and being able to prove the existence of the "dissociated" impulses behind the façade. In contrast, a person who suffers "the great dissociative processes" is not aware at any level of the evaluation that other people might place on the dissociated system of the personality. The self-conscious personality has no access to, no conscious awareness of, the impulses or tendencies that have been "blotted out." But the self-dynamism of the hysteric is said to be so "sketchy," so immature and underdeveloped, that as soon as the other person, such as a therapist, hits on a fairly well-aimed guess as to what the dissociated impulse is, the whole impulse system shifts. "In other words, one particular self-against-impulse process may be abandoned and a new one developed."[36] So hysteria is very much simpler in these aspects than say, "obsessive-compulsive neurosis," in which dissociation may exist in its fully developed form. In the hysteric there is *not* a "highgrade conflict" between a system of ideals one finds in other people and the hysteric's unregenerated impulses. He merely has "the happy thought" of how to get away with something. This happy thought, if true, would exempt him from blame. Thus, in hysteria the symptoms are fairly simple in comparison with those found in other mental disorders. As long as he can get away with it, the person who employs the hysterical dynamism solves rather serious conflicts with "singularly little apparatuses."

Imagine a man with a strong hysterical predisposition, who has married, perhaps for money, a woman who because of her husband's rather dramatic and exaggerated way of doing things soon realizes that he has had a very practical consideration in marrying her and who cannot completely blind herself to the lack of importance she has for him. "So she begins to get even." Perhaps she will develop "a never-failing" vaginismus, which effectively puts an end to sexual intercourse. Yet the husband will not become conscious of the fact that his wife's condition is directed against him, cutting off his sexual satisfactions, since the hysterical process precludes such objectivity. A careful discrimination of interpersonal phenomena would tend to deprive him of his own hysterical behavior. But suffering greatly from sexual privation, he will make great and rather extravagant efforts to overcome the vaginismus. However, his efforts are characterized by a "certain rather theatrical attention" to detail rather than to a penetrating scrutiny of his wife and her behavior. Though he continues actively to seek intercourse, he fails again and again. Then one night when he is exhausted after another ineffectual attempt at physical intimacy—because the vaginismus can overhwhelm the powers of even a lumberjack—and has had perhaps a precocious ejaculation "in his newest adventure in practical psychotherapy" he says to himself, "My God, this thing is driving me crazy." This is the happy thought, or sort of thought, that the hysteric has—though he will ordinarily never remember it.

The hysterically predisposed husband falls asleep after he has had the "happy idea." But at some early hour in the morning, possibly when his wife is in deepest, soundest sleep, he has a "frightful attack of something." Perhaps he awakens with a cry as he clutches his wife in great fear, quivering, stammering, tearing his hair, beating his forehead. His wife, who has been awakened, is very frightened and calls the doctor. Meanwhile, before the doctor arrives, the husband in some oblique fashion will let her know that he fears he is losing his mind. Now his wife becomes reduced to a really agitated state. When the doctor arrives, he prescribes a sedative, which lulls the husband, who finally falls asleep. Now and then the attacks will recur but even if the doctor is a psychiatrist and tries to secure a history of the immediate situation, he will not get the recollection of the thought, "My God, this thing is driving me crazy." He will learn all sorts of details. But he will not hear about the happy idea nor about the difficulties "in the sex life."

The husband has found a way of punishing his wife for an "atrocity" though he is not sure the atrocity is designed to affect him. Still it is an atrocity, for the vaginismus deprives him of satisfaction. He is much too self-centered to study and reflect on what his wife may be suffering. So if he could verbalize this hysterical stratagem and its aftermath it would amount to something like this: "If I went insane because of this vaginismus, that would give her a bad mental state herself." Though he is not conscious of any punitive inclination toward his wife, it is strangely attractive. There is also another element in the situation of which he is not clearly conscious. Since everything he does is *ipso facto* important, because of his self-centeredness, his sexual performances have become "tainted" with his efforts to maintain prestige. So his lust is involved with his security operations in the relationship with his wife. He has found a disguised way of satisfying unacceptable impulses, such as competitiveness, vengefulness, or exploitativeness in a personally satisfactory way that relieves him of blame and social condemnation.

Sullivan said that such an hysterically predisposed man has these attacks in and out of season when the provocation is sufficient, while he remains comfortably unaware of their consequences for others. This comfortable unawareness is due, in part, to the fact that he does not pay much attention to other people, and, in part, to the occurrence of this mysterious and rather awful sickness which abruptly descends upon him at 4:00 A.M. on some particular, unforgettable morning—a sickness that even the doctors cannot understand. As long as he remains unconscious of the happy idea, the mystery of the seizures is maintained without much effort. The connection between symptom and life in general can remain obscure.

The observable interpersonal relations of the prevailingly hysterical person are said to be characterized by an extravagance of emotional behavior ("color"). His "euphoria" is higher than an objective appraisal of his perhaps fleeting situation would warrant, alternating rather vividly with negative emotions that are equally extravagant, so that a drop or increase in euphoria may occur "as fleetingly as summer showers." No close relationship exists between the mood of a particular hour and the most common personal occurrences of that hour. His emotions are highly labile so that his moods swiftly come and go. "The hysteric can be very angry, immensely pleased, very devoted and very hostile in rapid succession. But if these dramatically extravagant emotions effect their purpose, that's the end of it."[37] Thus there is an extraordinary, amazingly sudden shift in "emotional address to other people." In the hysteric the level of motivational and emotional systems is quite incomplete. In many instances, the personality development has not progressed much beyond the juvenile era. Love and intimacy are beyond the reach of such people in everyday life. Competitive motivation deriving from the juvenile era, often manifested with members of the same sex, is frequently predominant.

Ordinarily hysterics live a rather unhappy married life. Depending on personal circumstances, they may advertise the better or worse side of their marriage. A markedly hysterical woman, for example, may inform the neighbors that she has an idyllic home life until a row with her husband occurs, and then she may tell all and sundry that her husband is a beast in his private life. Yet such an inconsistency does not trouble her because she has provided herself with fairly "crude loopholes," such as rationalizations, and returns to her usual tales of an idyllic existence. On the other hand, such a person, even if she (or he) is having a dreadful time with the partner may be briefly "so swept" with euphoria that she will give a "divergent account" to a neighbor, while also providing herself (or himself) with fairly crude loopholes before reverting to the conventionally unhappy state. But anyone who is more extravagant than the hysteric is said to be the bane of the hysteric's life. This competition may sometimes get the hysteric into very awkward positions *vis-à-vis* the more conventional community and its members, a situation that leads, in turn, to new hysterical symptoms designed to cope with his difficulties in interpersonal relations.

With the hysteric "so much goes on in words"—in lieu of healthy interpersonal relations—that some more or less innocent bystander may take his verbal communications seriously or somewhat seriously. To the inexperienced or superficial, he may seem to be a very sociable, warm, outgoing and, perhaps, exciting person. Just as he may employ sex for purposes of manipulation, he will employ language for that same purpose. The innocent bystander may become the object, in a pretty unrealistic fashion, of some more or less dramatic fantasy of the hysteric. If he is "schizoid" and relatively meek, passive or gullible, he may become bound to the hysteric in wedlock, which is not necessarily a consummation devoutly to be wished for by the schizoid person.

Sullivan claimed that the sexual relations of the hysteric are often badly marred by immaturity. He surmised that, since disorders arising from genital impulses are so common among the prevailingly hysteric, it accounts for the *libido* of orthodox psychoanalysis being indistinguishable from a generalized lust. While inquiring into "the trouble with the sex life" of such a person, the psychiatrist encounters the "crudest expression of Oedipus survivals." It is in the field of hysteria that the psychiatrist or psychotherapist may expect to discover the sort of woman who quite intensely hates her mother while almost obviously still very attached, in fantasies, to the father. It is in this field, especially, that the clinician encounters wives who frequently recite invidious comparisons between the husband and father —comparisons that are directly derogatory of the husband. Also occasionally he will hear an hysterically predisposed man make overt, straightforward comparison between the wife he so unfortunately married and his mother who loved him. Thus, if the therapist works with hysterics he will not find it difficult to support the notion of the Oedipus complex as long as he confines himself to "this type of material." Moreover, "the hysteric woman can be a man in a homo-sexual relation with an abandon which is scarcely conceivable in any other type of human organization, and the hysterically predisposed man can act the woman with incomparable thoroughness and lack of cynicism."[38]

It may be well to remind the general reader that Freud himself for quite a while worked exclusively or chiefly with hysterics.

Hysteria is a peculiar distortion of interpersonal relations, such as those outlined above, and frequently marked by "conversions," amnesia, and other symptoms. Freud thought that "conversion hysteria" is a distinct clinical entity, which entails a retranslation or conversion of psychic energy into the somatic language of the body. Sullivan believed that the distinction between conversion hysteria and "other hysteria" is perhaps not very important. Current psychiatry seems to agree. Sullivan interpreted conversions as solutions of conflict by the utilization of some part of the body, with the aid of very simple thought processes, because the conversions are at the developmental level of the juvenile era, when the hysterical dynamism was formed. Thus the bodily symptoms, such as anesthesias, paralyses, and visceral disturbances tend to follow the rather naïve notions of anatomy and physiology that the average juvenile has.[39] However, not every hysterically predisposed person will manifest gross bodily symptoms.

When there is a conversion, which appears "in the major hysterical entity," and which French psychiatrists used to describe with loving care, it has a meaningful function: it occurs chiefly *within* the self-system and serves that self-system. This is markedly different from a major dissociation, which, by definition, does not occur within the self-conscious personality and is *not* a tool of the latter. A conversion is an "almost juvenilely simple type of operation" designed, in a manner of speaking, to profit from the disabling system. For example, a patient may say: "If it were not for this malady then I could do——." Such a statement may often be succeeded by a grandiose appraisal of one's capacities. The disability is said to function as a convenient tool for security operations.

Sullivan claimed that under cover of the hysterical disorder the patient works out, or acts out, dramas that are rather blatantly expressive of what is in his mind. The hysteric performs prodigies of inattention, which is a function of the self-dynamism. By means of inattention, failure to develop refined cognitive processes, and failure to reflect on the details of his performances the hysteric circumvents any clue as to the source of his difficulties from reaching his consciousness.

In *Conceptions of Modern Psychiatry,* Sullivan asserted that hysteria is the distortion of interpersonal relations that results from extensive amnesias. By means of amnesia, the hysteric in certain instances can "wipe out" a whole course of life and bring about highly desirable results. This is in marked contrast to the major dissociations. Amnesia "as such" does not appear in real dissociation. In the real dissociated states, were the psychiatrist to attempt to "juggle" external occurrences that would necessitate the person's accepting the dissociated system as an ingredient of his personality, the psychiatrist would probably precipitate panic. Under similar circumstances, were he to attempt a like tactic with an hysteric, the latter would abandon or shift the symptom or symptoms—and probably come up with new and different symptoms.

At one time Sullivan interviewed a seventeen- or eighteen-year-old boy who following upon a minor accident very quickly developed "a tremendous amnesia." No one could persuade him that he was the person people had known, namely, one of several children of a steel worker. (Several years previously he had been "taken under the wing" of a childless couple and lived in their home.) The youngster did not recognize the members of his own family when his foster mother took him to his original home after the accident. He did not know his name. Nor could he recall "large chunks" of recent experiences. The internist whom the foster mother called in to treat the boy, after a few days, called Sullivan. The latter saw the youth several times and found him genial and ingratiating while at the same time defeating Sullivan's efforts to "cure" the amnesia. But this boy did manage to leave a large element of suffering "sort of free-floating." With the cooperation of the wealthy foster parents, Sullivan employed a stratagem that would make his patient's disorder very expensive to cultivate indefinitely. He arranged that they, and in particular the foster mother, suggest to the youth that since he had lost all recollection of the skills that he had acquired through the intervention of his benefactress, the "lady Bountiful" to his family, he was left with the prospect of returning to a machine shop as an apprentice. In other words, the amnesia would cost him considerable economic and social advantages. The stratagem worked. "And lo! the boy had a miraculous recovery, late enough at night to wake up the whole household. He went shouting through the house his joy at having recovered his memory."[40] Not long after, the youth went away to school. Apparently there was no subsequent recurrence of the amnesia.

The behavior of the hysterically predisposed is markedly different from that of the introverted, schizoid person. The latter, in general, is more alert, more able in his analysis of life situations, even though he may be painfully shy and "appallingly incapable" of handling other people. As Bertrand Russell pointed out ages ago in one of his books, the introvert may have been perfectly comfortable in some Asian societies, but he is at a grave disadvantage in almost any "variant" of Western civilization, where an ability to "handle" people is almost a *sine qua non.* Due to this lack of ability, the so-called introverted, "schizoid" person has to be capable of being eternally forewarned so that he may have a chance of avoiding rebuffs, aggressions, exploitative attitudes, and behavior patterns of many more "normal" people. "The idea," Sullivan asserted, "is to spot the rebuff in time and either protect oneself from it or leave." So he gradually learns to make proper deferential gestures to certain social standards of propriety that other people embody in their behavior. In short, the interpersonal behavior of such a person with a major dissociation can be regarded as the behavior of a highly sensitive, highly differentiated person, even though he may be often quite "wooden" or tense in the presence of certain kinds of people, who may regard him as queer, or "a babe in the woods."

Even though some hysterics are highly intelligent, they usually lack much analytic ability regarding their own life situations. For one thing, they are too self-absorbed. Hence, they tend to be much less objective than the introverted in interpersonal relations. Moreover, the latter do not usually have the "rather deep contempt" for others of the hysteric. The hysteric regards them as comparatively shadowy figures, before whom he plays a role or series of roles. In a sense, he is the greatest of liars, though to no purpose, for he always has to exaggerate a little in speech as well as in overt performance. He twists language in a characteristic manner, describing everything in superlatives. Only superlatives will suffice. Hence mere people as they actually are and mere events as they actually occur are contemned.

How does the hysterical disposition get developed? One finds that

the late childhood and early juvenile phases of the hysteric's development are characterized by fantasies of a "rather crass dramatic type."
This may be clarified by reference to the markedly introverted person
whose fantasies take on an increasing nicety of referential detail, a
growing sublety, as he proceeds from childhood to adolescence. A
mythlike fantasy or daydream of last year, Sullivan asserted, would be
just too crude to be entertained this year. Hence the introvert may
enjoy a rich fantasy life, some of which is compensatory, some of
which may be creative and original—at least until he reaches chronological adolescence when, if he has had to dissociate a major motivational system, he may encounter undreamt of disastrous experiences.
But in the case of a person who is developing the hysterical predisposition, a type of fantasy that sufficed in late infancy may persist for
years except for an elaboration of the fantastic characters in the
crudely organized drama or melodrama through which he lives and
perhaps a concealment of elements of it that are too glaringly fraudulent or socially disapproved. The shifting idealizations of people to
which some are prone, discussed in Chapter 4, seem peculiarly relevant to the hysteric's *modus vivendi*. The hysteric trafficks in superlatives. But real people are relatively unimportant to him. From an early
period in life he acquired an unclarity of connection between other
people and the pleasure or pain he has experienced. Hence he does
not recognize any great necessity for elaborate caution about other
people. He does not feel particularly hostile to others: they "don't
really matter enough." Their main importance lies in their providing
an audience for him: to talk to when one is bored, to notice how well
one does things.[41]

Sullivan claimed that in the case of the hysteric one usually finds a
self-absorbed parent or some other highly significant figure, who
regards the child as something of a plaything, a decoration of her
personality. Though the parent lacks respect and appreciation of the
offspring, the latter does not experience "the direct, carefully
focused, and terribly warping hostility to which a good many pre-
schizophrenic children are exposed."[42] The parent of the hysteric is
herself an instance of the self-absorbed, relatively self-centered type
of personality, tending to belittle reality extravagantly "and to doctor
it up." From her, by rote and example, the child learns that things are
not good enough, very early in life. It is thus he also learns to "improve" reality. But the lack of parental respect for his actual character-

istics and traits fosters the kind of self-development that will deprive him of easy access to others, including direct human intimacy. On the other hand, the self-absorbed parent does not demand any nice show of appreciation of her or of others. So the groundwork of appreciation of others, for a nice discrimination of other people's characteristics, is not laid. It does not become a part of the self, which remains immature and truncated. The youngster lives "in the lotus-land sort of existence surrounding the self-absorbed parent," and learns accordingly. The relatively unrefined mental processes required of this sort of existence hinder the refinement of behavior and the skill necessary to formulate and understand other people's behavior. They progressively fail to foster interpersonal adjustments that entail plasure or pain, joy or sorrow, and refine one's relationships with others. The self-absorbed are said to integrate situations with foggy embodiments (the "stereotypes" of *Personal Psychopathology)* projected upon us from their fantasies of themselves.

Notes

1. LESTON HAVENS, "Main Currents of Psychiatric Development," *International Journal of Psychiatry,* **5**:288-310, 1968.

2. See, for example, OTTO A. WILL, JR., "Schizophrenia and Psychotherapy," in JUDD MARMOR (ed.), *Modern Psychoanalysis* (New York: Basic Books, 1968).

3. HARRY STACK SULLIVAN, *Clinical Studies in Psychiatry,* ed. HELEN SWICK PERRY, MARY LADD GAWEL, and MARTHA GIBBON, with a Foreword by DEXTER M. BULLARD (New York: W. W. Norton and Company, 1956), p. 194.

4. *Ibid.,* p. 196.

5. *Ibid.,* p. 201.

6. See *ibid.,* pp. 77-84; cf. HARRY STACK SULLIVAN, *Conceptions of Modern Psychiatry,* with a Foreword by the author and a Critical Appraisal of the Theory by PATRICK MULLAHY (New York: W. W. Norton and Company, 1953), pp. 76-86.

7. Cf. HARRY STACK SULLIVAN, *The Interpersonal Theory of Psychiatry,* ed. HELEN SWICK PERRY and MARY LADD GAWEL, with an Introduction by MABEL BLAKE COHEN (New York: W. W. Norton and Company, 1953), pp. 355-358, 362-363.

8. SULLIVAN, *Clinical Studies in Psychiatry,* p. 86.

9. SULLIVAN, *Conceptions of Modern Psychiatry,* pp. 122-123.

10. *Ibid.,* p. 123.

11. See SULLIVAN, *Clinical Studies in Psychiatry,* pp. 84-86.

12. SULLIVAN, *Conceptions of Modern Psychiatry,* p. 120.

13. SULLIVAN, *Clinical Studies in Psychiatry,* p. 86.

14. *Ibid.,* p. 87.

15. *Ibid.,* p. 145.

16. *Ibid.,* p. 146.

17. *Ibid.,* p. 148.

18. FREDERIC C. REDLICH and DANIEL X. FREEDMAN, *The Theory and Practice of Psychiatry* (New York: Basic Books, 1966), p. 375. Cf. JAMES C. COLEMAN, *Abnormal Psychology and Modern Life* (3rd ed.; Glenview, Illinois: Scott, Foresman and Company, 1964) pp. 221-227.

19. SULLIVAN, *Conceptions of Modern Psychiatry,* pp. 112-113; cf. GERALD CHRZANOWSKI, "Interpersonal View of Phobias," *Voices,* Fall, 1967, and LEON SALZMAN, "Obsessions and Phobias," *Contemporary Psychoanalysis,* Fall, 1965.

20. SULLIVAN, *Clinical Studies in P ychiatry,* p. 259.

21. SULLIVAN, *Conceptions of Modern Psychiatry,* p. 114.

22. SULLIVAN, *Clinical Studies in Psychiatry,* p. 231.

23. *Ibid.,* p. 234.

24. *Ibid.,* p. 236.

25. *Ibid.*

26. *Ibid.,* p. 251

27. *Ibid.,* p. 252.

28. *Ibid.,* p. 255.

29. SULLIVAN, *The Interpersonal Theory of Psychiatry,* pp. 318-319, 347-348, 353-358, and *passim.*

30. Cf. REDLICH and FREEDMAN, *op. cit.,* pp. 375-377.

31. SULLIVAN, *Clinical Studies in Psychiatry,* p. 261.

32. *Ibid.,* p. 263.

33. *Ibid.,* p. 267.

34. Cf. LEON SALZMAN, *The Obsessive Personality* (New York: Science House, 1968).

35. *Ibid.,* p. vii.

36. SULLIVAN, *Clinical Studies in Psychiatry,* p. 204.

37. *Ibid.,* p. 213.

38. *Ibid.,* pp. 215-216; cf. REDLICH and FREEDMAN, *op. cit.,* pp. 369-373.

39. Cf. COLEMAN, *op. cit.,* pp. 204-212.

40. SULLIVAN, *Clinical Studies in Psychiatry,* p. 219.

41. Cf. SULLIVAN, *Conceptions of Modern Psychiatry,* pp. 78-80.

42. SULLIVAN, *Clinical Studies in Psychiatry,* p. 212.

10/Sullivan's Theory of Schizophrenia

Through the years, beginning in 1924, Sullivan published numerous papers on schizophrenia. Apparently his ideas on this "grave psychosis," as he called it, first began to take shape while he worked at Sheppard and Enoch Pratt Hospital. He went to Sheppard in 1923 as an Assistant Physician. It was there that he established his special receiving ward that became a spectacular success, not only under Sullivan's supervision but under the supervision of his successor, William V. Silverberg.

Many of the papers Sullivan wrote on schizophrenia during the years he spent at Sheppard have recently been collated and republished in *Schizophrenia as a Human Process*, as I mentioned in Chapter 1.[1] Because they were published in various journals, they were probably read by a great number of psychiatrists who belonged to Sullivan's generation. Yet, as the psychiatrist Donald Jackson has suggested in another context, they were probably not understood or at least appreciated then. Sullivan was ahead of his time. In fact, most of the younger psychiatrists I knew twenty years ago had not read them.

Throughout his professional life he continued to develop his theory of schizophrenia as a grave disorder of living. In the lecture series published under the title of *Conceptions of Modern Psychiatry*, it is considerably elaborated and described in a language that, to my knowledge, has never been equaled in any psychiatric textbook.

A major innovation in *Conceptions of Modern Psychiatry* is the conception of anxiety as a dynamic process, first acquired in infancy, and developing through the various phases of personality growth. In the case of potential male schizophrenic patients, it evolves or passes over into terror or literal panic, usually during the adolescent phase, under circumstances that cannot always be exactly specified, though they are amply illustrated. Sullivan believed that in women the onset of schizophrenia often occurs several years later than in men because of cultural factors that he did not attempt to pinpoint.

Anxiety may be characterized variously. In Sullivan's more mature formulations, it is a felt threat to, or actual loss of, self-esteem owing to the actual, anticipated, or imaginary disapproval of significant other people or of disapproval of one's self, owing to the values and ideals one has acquired or developed. Its roots may be traced back to infancy, when various activities of the baby may be intensely disturbing to the mother (or her surrogate). But an emotional disturbance in the mothering one need not arise from her observation of the infant's activities. Apparently any current emotional upset she suffers gets "communicated." Thus, according to Sullivan, various upset states in the mothering one may induce in the infant a tension state that may gradually develop into anxiety, a condition that may generalize increasingly as the youngster approaches the adolescent era.[2]

Concomitantly, various other unfortunate experiences, mal-developments, and distortions that the individual suffers may all combine to render him abnormally vulnerable to the demands and stresses of the adolescent stage in Western society—demands and stresses that he cannot successfully negotiate. It appears that, in such cases, a powerful motivational system exists in dissociation, which is contradictory to the self-dynamism and which is entirely unsuited to the type of life for which the self has been organized.

Sullivan uses the notion of a dynamic balance between the self-system and the dissociated elements or processes of the personality. In people who, owing to the evil effects of their education or acculturation, are destined or predisposed to become schizophrenic, the balance between the two is uneasy, a condition that may have been obscurely manifest for a considerable period. Some specific event may happen that destroys the equilibrium. Hours or days later panic may ensue, an experience that includes extremely unpleasant visceral sensations with a boundless and contentless (objectless) terror.

This may be illustrated by a brief account of one of Sullivan's patients, an only boy with five sisters who led "as sheltered a life as that situation would permit."[3] Soon after having been inducted into the armed forces, he was "prowling around" Washington, D.C., and one day was "gathered up" by a very well-dressed and charming dentist. This man took the boy to his office and performed fellatio on him. The following day he found himself, quite absent-mindedly, returning to the immediate vicinity of the dentist's office, whereupon he could no longer exclude from his consciousness that he wanted to continue to have such experiences as he had had the day before. He became conscious of what Sullivan called abhorrent cravings, that is, increasingly intense, because unsatisfied, longings to engage in performances that are abhorrent to one. Though the day before, his encounter may have seemed to be only a new kind of experience, now the realization burst upon him that he was a prey to homosexual desires, a realization that was attended by all sorts of revulsions and a feeling that it was infrahuman to have such interests. Presumably he then underwent panic for he arrived at (or was taken to) the hospital shortly afterward in what is called a schizophrenic disturbance.

Schizophrenia occurs upon the collapse of the self-system. This collapse frequently manifests itself as panic. Panic, in turn, represents failure of the dissociative power of the self.

The essence of the self, which is determined by its primary functions, namely, the fulfillment of needs and the preservation and maintenance of emotional security (though Sullivan emphasized the latter more and more in the course of his career), represents a meaningful organization of life experience. Roughly speaking, this self includes one's habitual thoughts about the world and about oneself, one's everyday perceptions (and misperceptions), one's more or less recognizable and familiar emotions and motives, one's attitudes about life in general, one's moral code, one's hopes and expectations about the future, and one's philosophy of life, if any. These may be said to constitute the stuff of life. Unless we are inclined toward reflection we tend to take them for granted. And, since we are, as a rule, products of our "culture," others share these meanings too, in the sense that the self of each of us is built up from widely held attitudes, beliefs, ideas, emotional patterns, and norms of conduct until or unless we begin to modify those beliefs, attitudes, ideas, when we reach maturity. Thus, typically, our way of life, which the self-conscious personality structure embodies, is reinforced by the attitudes and behavior of members of our society and social class, aided and abetted nowadays by mass media of communication.

While it is perfectly true that every self, and every personality, is uniquely structured, Sullivan believed that this aspect of the person has been overemphasized and is, in any event, beyond the grasp of science. Science deals with uniformities, with recurrent patterns. Furthermore, personality is not self-actional. Human experiences and activities require the cooperation of the environment, either directly or mediately. No matter how much "ego autonomy" one may possess, he can exercise it only in conjunction with the powers or abilities and actions of other people, who embody widespread uniformities of behavior and dispositions or traits more or less common to people in the culture. Human life is a history of "transactions."

Because man is a social and moral being, nothing in the world is more horrifying to most of us—perhaps not even the prospect of imminent death, which some people, at least, can face with stoicism and unfaltering resolution—than the abrupt or insidious disorganization or disintegration of the self-conscious personality. An experience, or train of experiences, that undermines the structure of the self strikes at the very heart of whatever is meaningful, worthwhile or "good" in one's way of life. The pattern of one's thinking, imagining, perceiving, feeling is abruptly (or sometimes insidiously) torn apart so that the world has become "wholly irrational and incomprehensible."[4]

When panic occurs, all organized activity is lost and all thought is paralyzed. Panic, according to Sullivan, is disorganization of the personality arising from the utterly unforeseen failure of something completely trusted and vital for one's safety;[5] it occurs when some essential aspect of the universe that one had long taken for granted suddenly collapses. The disorganization that follows is probably the most appalling state that man can undergo, and one that is entirely incompatible with life. It is, however, a transitory state.

Consider the experience of one young man whom Sullivan had interviewed. Parenthetically, I shall mention that for certain reasons (discussed in a general way in Sullivan's formulations of personality development and its distortions) this patient had sublimated all recognized manifestations of lustful (genital) integrative tendencies or motives. In general, sublimation is "the unwitting substitution, for a behavior pattern which encounters anxiety or collides with the self-system, of a socially more acceptable activity pattern which satisfies part of the motivational system that caused trouble."[6] In more fortunate circumstances the rest of the unsatisfied need or "motivational system" is discharged through the symbol processes occurring in sleep and in reverie. In dreams, impulses that in waking life are dissociated are said to make their appearance and play out dramas of interpersonal relations with more or less purely fictitious people. (For this reason, among others, one should never forget the immensely significant psychological role of sleep.) Sullivan believed that under certain circumstances the self is able to dissociate lust and the impulses to genital behavior. Even so, one can dissociate the "genital lust dynamism" only at grave risk to effective living. It is so powerful a dynamism that in most people it cannot be dissociated at all. If an individual can dissociate lust, he can accomplish it only by the unwitting development of new and elaborate stratagems and techniques of living.

For the purposes of this exposition, imagine the young man who had sublimated lust having met an extremely attractive and most forthright young woman "who firmly believes that lust should be satisfied and that its satisfaction is unqualifiedly good."[7] Assume also that he is attractive and suitable for "genital integration." Imagine, furthermore, that he, so to speak, succumbs and enters "quite effectively into the integration." In the titillating language of popular discourse, they have "an affaire," though of brief duration.[8] Even though the young man has a "shockingly good time," he does not, like a Hollywood moving picture idol, emerge triumphant and joyful. In the aftermath he suffers self-recrimination and severe conflict because "evil" early life experience has done its work. To make matters worse, a good deal of his distress gets communicated to the partner, who is upset and repelled by his behavior. She may say something that makes him feel that he has not only done the wrong thing but made a fool of himself. His conviction of personal worth has been gravely shaken if not shattered.

One possible outcome of this occurrence is "ecstatic absorption," a transitory state, though one that may result in an "end state" similar to that ensuing upon panic.[9] In ecstatic absorption, Sullivan says, the patient regresses rapidly to a condition in which dreamlike processes pertaining to a Godlike state solve his acute feelings of abasement. One must bear in mind that a person who suffers such a threat to the integrity of the self and such an injury to his already fragile self-esteem has usually, if not always, been subjected from infancy onward to intense anxiety tensions and suffered painful feelings of inadequacy at some phase or phases of his development, for example, isolation from his peers during the juvenile era, overt disparagement from his parents and others, inability to have a close friend, or failure in school or on the job.[10] The fragmentary case histories that Sullivan has published and his illustrative comments on the development of mental disorder are replete with examples of such misfortunes. Puberty brings added difficulties. The young man cannot learn to relate to the other sex in an intimate fashion, or finds it overwhelmingly difficult to effect "genital integrations" with them. Perhaps he is reduced to treating all his female acquaintances like sisters—treatment that not all of them will appreciate. Everyone else he knows seems to be enjoying "dates," conquests, and exciting experiences. What, he may ask himself, is wrong with him? Given the current "obsessional" preoccupation with sex, he is likely to be subjected to intense pressures to go with a girl, if only to prove his manliness, by his parents (who are perhaps dimly aware that they have proved inadequate) and others.[11] The outcome of the encounter mentioned may be the crowning blow to his already shaky feeling of self-worth compelling a regression to an early stage of development. The dreamlike reverie processes pertaining to a Godlike state in ecstatic absorption appear to be reaction to the acute feelings of abasement.

The regression is said to be facilitated by the person's increasingly ineffectual attempts to remedy his interpersonal situation involving the sexual partner by conversational efforts that are becoming increasingly autistic and correspondingly puzzling to her or to others to whom they are addressed. Sullivan asserts that the state of ecstatic absorption has its root experiences in earlier performances connected with falling asleep when one was feeling very insecure. The person's attempts to maintain relations with actual people fail partly because of the increasing inutility of speech (for he has become increasingly incoherent and incomprehensible) and partly because of the "prehended" disconcertion of his auditors, who are likely to be baffled or dismayed; so he abandons all efforts to talk to anyone. "His awareness is now that of a twilight state between waking and dreaming; his facial expression is that of absorption in ecstatic 'inner' experiences, and his behavior is peculiar to the degree that he no longer eats or sleeps, or tends to any of the routines of life."[12]

If one recognizes that the evil effects of early experience have not merely necessitated a "sublimatory reformulation" of all genital drives but have also resulted in a barrier to women, with corresponding homosexual motivation existing in dissociation, the ecstatic absorption can be understood to accomplish a double function by isolating the young man from either woman or man. The repercussion on the dissociative power of the self is what has made the distressing aftermath of his unexpected sexual engagement so dangerous.

The sudden failure of sublimation may follow a different course that bears more directly on the topic of this exposition. Assume the young man leaves his partner without any painful discussion. By becoming preoccupied, he will put the thought of the experience out of mind. The following night he sleeps poorly, tossing and turning in his bed through the night while harassed by unpleasant dreams. The next afternoon, with fatigue increasing due to insufficient rest and mounting inner pressures, he takes a long walk. Wandering with no conscious destination in mind, without warning he suddenly discovers that he is returning to see his sexual partner and burning with desire to repeat the experience. He is terrified. Panic, or a condition bordering on panic, supervenes.

As I have mentioned, panic is disorganization of the personality—a state that cannot last long if one is to survive—involving failure of the dissociative power of the self. "The mental state," Sullivan says, "is best suggested by referring to a sort of experience which may have befallen anyone. If you have walked each day for years across a little bridge in the sidewalk, and it one morning yields under your feet, suddenly gives way and sinks a few inches, the eruption into awareness that accompanies this experience ... *is* panic."[13] It results from temporary total failure of the functional efficiency of the self-dynamism.

The personality in such a situation reintegrates as swiftly as possible; often, according to Sullivan, through a transitory state of terror with extreme concentration of attention on escape from the poorly envisaged danger. All of one's energies are directed to flight. Sullivan asserts that if the flight response is impossible, panic eventuates in circus movements, random activity, and finally incoordination of the skeletal muscles. In terror, he says, the perception of the source of the threat is primitive, having the cosmic quality of the very early (infantile) formulation of the Bad Mother. (The Bad Mother is a "complexus of impressions" of the mothering one by the infant resulting from her interference with the satisfaction of needs and her association with the induction of anxiety.) The sufferer of this dreadful state experiences the whole world as threatening and everyone as dangerous, hostile, and bent on one's destruction. "The terror-stricken person is alone among deadly menaces, more or less blindly fighting for his survival against dreadful odds."[14] (However, this experience is very different from that of "paranoid schizophrenia," to be discussed subsequently, where there is a wholesale transference of blame.)

An extreme restriction and distortion of perception occurs, illustrated by the typical delusionary conviction that one is being watched and followed. After panic has passed into terror, many patients, before they are admitted to the hospital, believe they are followed by people in automobiles. In this delusion, the person walking along the street notices only the cars that are behind him. As a car passes, it immediately disappears from notice and is no longer perceived. Hence no cars are perceived to pass by. And as long as the cars are behind one, and remain behind one, it must be that they are menacing. This is an extreme example of a process Sullivan subsequently formulated as selective inattention. One fails to perceive or to grasp relevant factors in certain situations and to "forget" them instantly even when one may have *noticed* them.

Phenomena that arise from the autonomous function of a specific zone of interaction, such as the auditory or oral, or the oral supported by the auditory, are even more disturbing than the sort of delusionary belief previously mentioned. To say that a zone of interaction becomes autonomous means that it is no longer under the control of the self-conscious personality, serving instead as the channel for the expression of a dissociated "system." The sufferer may notice but does not comprehend such phenomena. Sullivan states that in the phase of terror following panic it is usually the auditory zone that becomes intermittently autonomous. "One hears voices, spoken statements which pertain to the experiential structure of the dissociated integrating tendency."[15] These hallucinated utterances are said to carry with them many indications of the nonexistent speaker's personality. They are, in fact, disguised, symbolic "representations" of the dissociated processes of the patient's personality. Hallucinated statements rather quickly become expressions of particular illusory persons or personifications: God, the Devil, the President, one's deceased mother, and various legendary figures one has learned about (which C. G. Jung might regard as expressions of a collective unconscious). Though initially these hallucinatory experiences are profoundly disturbing, to patients who have suffered them for years the "voices" may become commonplace occurrences, having about the same significance as ordinary conversation.[16]

Other forms of automatism besides hallucination, such as the tic and automatic writing, are of great significance in psychiatry but they do not require an explication here.[17]

Certain stratagems or security operations are used by many persons to handle (though not to comprehend) a dissociated tendency that manifests itself in certain obscure ways *within consciousness*. But in the schizophrenic state ensuing upon panic this is not possible. Not only has the dissociative power of the self failed completely, its ability to employ security operations—which both normal people and, to an even greater extent, "neurotic" persons may employ when their self-esteem is threatened—have largely failed as well. All that remains of security operations ("defense mechanisms") by the self-dynamism is a disowning of the now far too meaningful symptoms. While in all other conditions or states of mental illness the self maintains a monopoly of consciousness, a more or less exclusive control of consciousness, in schizophrenic states there is a functional splitting of the control of awareness, covering that which is part of the self and also that which attends the autonomous activities of the hallucinating zones of interaction. "In schizophrenic states . . . a state of conflict has as it were been universalized, the conflict-provoking tendency systems being accorded independent personality with power greater than that of the self."[18] According to Sullivan, the schizophrenic is unable to accept the manifestations of the dissociated tendencies, disowned through projection as the performances of others. "They" communicate abuses and disturbing suggestions to him, making him experience disagreeable and disgusting sensations, and otherwise (through the hallucinosis) destroying his peace of mind, perplexing and puzzling him, and (by fatigue and other interferences) reducing him to deeply regressed states of being. To the degree that the self functions, the person engages in regressive magic operations in an attempt to protect himself, that is, to regain some measure of security in a world that has become nightmarishly terrifying, irrational, and incomprehensible.

A psychologically unsophisticated individual might wonder why the patient does not accept the dissociated tendency system as part of him, or in other words, incorporate it into his self and learn to live with it. Would not that be better, less harrowing, than the present ghastly situation? One must bear in mind that such a course would entail an extreme change in personality, a reorganization of the sorts of interpersonal relations according to which one has lived and had his being—a prospect that would not even be acceptable to most normal human beings who have maintained a more or less intact personality structure. Because of the limitations imposed by the organization of the self-dynamism—because, in other words, of the limitations imposed or set by past experiences, which act like blinders—the schizophrenic has no foresight as to the direction and extent of such a change. Nor can he foretell that such a radical change would be tolerable. Practically, he has no choice. He is enmeshed in the present course of events and cannot strike out on a course that seems to entail all the terrors and anxieties of the unknown—even if he were able to contemplate such a possibility. And he is bedeviled by an awful driving urgency, always hovering on the fringes of awareness, until sleep brings a respite. But, Sullivan says, it returns when he awakens in the morning and remains until he has again fallen asleep. One might say that "the schizophrenic suffers an almost unceasing fear of becoming an exceeding unpleasant form of nothingness by collapse of the self."[19]

Hence he cannot easily reestablish (reintegrate) a unitary consciousness, and rebuild an integral, unified self. He cannot accept any suggestion that his terrible experiences are no more real than a nightmare or that they arise from his own inner unrecognized needs and desires.

Sullivan claims that if the patient has fortunate experiences with the "more real" people whom he encounters in his disturbed state, the fury of the hallucinosis may decrease, the welter of delusional perceptions may diminish, and a condition approximating a stable maladjustment of a deeply regressive sort may ensue. In these "fairly quiescent" states the regression of the patient's personality is such that he lives in a world and participates in interpersonal relations that are, in varying degrees, dreamlike.

Schizophrenic processes do not always appear suddenly and dramatically. In the *incipient* schizophrenic state they may appear gradually, even insidiously.[20] According to Sullivan's account, a patient may feel unhappy for a long time over his inadequacies, believing that others do not respect him, dislike his company, and perhaps talk about him in a derogatory way. In order to avoid further hurts to self-esteem, he becomes more and more seclusive, which in turn causes him to suffer increasingly from loneliness. His efforts at communication begin to fail. "He appears more and more preoccupied, inattentive, or given to puzzlement, misunderstanding, and misinterpretation."[21] His responses to questions become more and more autistic. Sooner or later he will withdraw from efforts to deal with his peers. He remains more and more indoors, if he is living at home; often he appears to need the company of one of his parents, though he becomes decreasingly communicative and increasingly morose and unpleasant.

At this point, a definite persecutory formula is apt to erupt into the patient's awareness: "His mother has been putting poison in his food; a friend is trying to make him homosexual; people are reading his mind and printing stories about him in the newspaper."[22] Thus, fleeting convictions that one is being subjected to persecutory or destructive influences almost invariably occur in the incipient schizophrenic state. This "paranoid coloring" is found in catatonic schizophrenic states as well, but it is not a true paranoid development because it does not relieve immensely depressed self-esteem nor does it remove chronic and recurrent anxiety. The paranoid coloring is due to the loss of the more refined referential processes; it is a mistaken explanation for puzzling events.

Having presented a general introductory outline of Sullivan's theory of schizophrenia, I shall now give a more detailed exposition of it. Schizophrenia is a *disorder of living,* not of the organic substrate. One becomes schizophrenic for situational reasons, and this may happen more or less abruptly or gradually. The disorder is an "episode," or series of episodes, in one's career among people, a career that begins at birth and ends at death. Such an episode may be preceded by months or years of maladjustment. It is often precipitated by a disaster to self-esteem, resulting in a grave, though tempo-rary, disorganization of the personality. Frequently the "victim" has gotten himself involved in a situation that he entered more or less blindly—without foresight as to its meaning and outcome for him. Increasingly intense—because unsatisfied—deeply unconscious long-ings have caused him to engage in something that is abhorrent to him. He has stumbled into a situation that provoked the eruption of abhor-rent cravings, such as homosexual desires. The conscious realization of such tendencies, as illustrated by the experiences of the patient whose encounter with the dentist proved disastrous, may result in a fateful disaster to the person's self-esteem and collapse of the self-dynamism. "At some particular time which he will never forget, the structure of his world was torn apart and dreadful, previously scarcely conceivable, events injected themselves."[23]

Though some readers may wonder if Sullivan has not overempha-sized schizophrenic disorders of sudden onset, this possibility is not vital for the purposes of this book and will not be discussed.[24]

Sullivan concluded, from his own studies of schizophrenia, that whether one shall or shall not continue to be typically schizophrenic is wholly determined by *situational* factors. Thus he believed—con-trary to received psychiatric opinion, which recognizes at least four types of schizophrenia: simple, catatonic, paranoid, and hebephrenic —that there are *no* "types" of schizophrenia, only some typical courses of events to be observed in schizophrenic conditions. While there are no types of schizophrenia, the latter may be classified as one of several "types" of psychosis.

The prevailing climate of psychiatric opinion in Sullivan's day—an orientation he bitterly fought against—was radically at variance with this approach. The author of a psychiatric textbook published in 1936 wrote that many "cases" of schizophrenia are "youths who are not disposed to accept the social restrictions and the cultural demands of their environment; they resent situations which interfere with their gratification of natural impulses, or which jeopardize their security and restrict their opportunities for gaining recognition and achieving pleasurable satisfaction. Instead of putting forth intelligent and con-structive efforts to unify personality and achieve self-realization in the midst of such difficult situations, they adopt what to them appears to be a more ready avenue of escape and revert to this technique of creating an inner compensatory world of fantasy and romance."[25]

In contrast to such views, Sullivan held that the schizophrenic has not gradually and inattentively drifted into a world of vague philosophizings in lieu of interpersonal relations, or into a world of more or less pleasant fantasy reminiscent of early childhood. He has arrived at his present state by a course that has been fraught with anxiety, "fear, terror, or literal panic."

Sullivan says that if the course of one's interpersonal relations comes to a schizophrenic state that continues without complication, one manifests a peculiar pattern of behavior that may be called the catatonic state. In this state the patient as a self-conscious person is assumed to be profoundly preoccupied with regaining a feeling of security. Since he is in a profoundly demoralized, regressed condition, he pursues the goal of security by means of activities rarely manifested after early childhood, except in sleep. But since an indefinitely great part of the patient's previous experience relevant to the pursuit of security is still in evidence, the picture is complicated. The integrations that the self-dynamism manifests include parataxic illusions on the pattern of the Good Mother (originally a personification of the mothering one who behaves tenderly toward the infant), the Bad Mother (originally a personification of the mothering one who interferes with the satisfaction of needs and provokes anxiety tension), the Good Father (a personification analogous to the Good Mother) and the Bad Father (a personification analogous to the Bad Mother). In general, these illusory personifications or "me-you patterns" are symbolic representations derived from experiences with significant people, chiefly the parents or their surrogates during infancy and early childhood. Additionally, insofar as education subsequent to early childhood continues to be effective, it provides the parataxic illusions with attributes acquired from the myths, folklore, or religion that the patient has acquired. Although the goal of these integrations involving illusory figures is security, the performances in these fantastic interpersonal situations are exclusively power operations (analogous to the magical performances of infancy and early childhood) designed to gain dominance or control over them.

The experience that the patient undergoes in the catatonic state is said to be of the most awesome, universal character. He "seems to be living in the midst of struggle between personified cosmic forces of good and evil, surrounded by animistically enlivened natural objects which are engaged in ominous performances that it is terribly necessary—and impossible—to understand. He is buffeted about. He must make efforts. He is incapable of thought. The compelling directions that are given him are contradictory and incomprehensible. He clings to life by a thread. He finally thinks that he is dead; that this is the state after death; that he awaits resurrection or the salvation of his soul."[26]

Sullivan states that acts and ideas reminiscent of the whole history of man's elaboration of magic and of religion appear in such states, including ancient myths of redemption and rebirth. Though the patient believes he is dead, he "clearly is not through with life." As an explanation for this state of affairs, he may hit upon surviving remnants of religious teachings. He will be absolved from the faults and failures of his past. Then he will be reborn. This "archaic" thinking reflects his deep regression to a state in which only primitive prototypes of "abstract" thought processes can be active, *not* the tapping of a "collective unconscious." The driving force is an "abysmal insecurity."

As Sullivan describes it, in the midst of this dreadful experience the patient is beyond the commonplace necessities of living, taking neither food nor drink, noticing nothing of the excretory processes, silent, uncomprehending of the meaning of others' efforts on his behalf. He may manifest little overt activity, lying nude with his eyes closed, his mouth "finally shut," hands clenched, and most of the skeletal muscles in a condition of tonic contraction. The catatonic may engage in strange motions: often these motions are rhythmical. He may experience sudden eruptions of excitement. From mute catatonic stupor he may occasionally pass into violent excitement with apparently random activity. Though he may harm others or kill himself, there is said to be no personally oriented hostility (directed toward any particular person) and no self-destructive motivation.

Catatonic stupor is said to be related to the vague but driving urgency to do something, combined with impractical referential processes, often causing initial bizarre action of some sort, which often miscarries "appallingly." The appalling miscarriage of action shows the individual that he is crazy. Sullivan relates the story of a patient of his who, after driving seventy miles an hour over dangerous roads, eventually hit a tree, becoming swiftly mute and immobile. He had traveled in this fashion "with a feeling that he was under almost divine protection, alone in a universe without trees and other obstructions." His hitting the tree showed him that he had done a crazy thing, that what he had done made no sense. This is what strikes most schizo-phrenics, as a result of their observations: they are crazy. Thus the discovery by the man who drove his car recklessly and hit a tree forced him to realize that his behavior did not get him any nearer some urgently desired goal. Far from it; it precipitated stupor, in which skeletal activity is tied up, though stupor "is a very active business, and anything but the inhibition of all postural tensions."

Sullivan thought that stupor is precipitated in almost all instances pretty much in this fashion. The patient does something under "unearthly" great pressure, and he fails. He may then attempt to do something else, which also is not effective. So in his more lucid mo-ments, he catches on to the fact that something is terribly wrong—that he is getting nowhere, failing wretchedly in his efforts. "And he ties up the whole skeletal apparatus in what starts out . . . to be an intensely alert readiness awaiting for some motivation, some pattern or activity, to appear, but which gradually settles down to be the thing in itself."[27] Though such a patient relaxes during sleep, the tension recurs as he awakens. It may happen that a patient who has been stuporous for months abruptly awakens one night and does something very active and carefully focused. For example, he may try to strangle someone or try to kill himself.

Stuporous people are said to be extraordinarily alert in their stu-por, though they are not "having any action" because they have had enough of that. However, should they fall asleep, another of those impelling drives may awaken them, spurring them again to action. So then they do something once more, only to be convinced again that it is just crazy, though they do not do much clear thinking about it. "And so they literally tie themselves into immobility." Sullivan says it is as if a *power* fixes them in their immobility. Since the self, in a manner of speaking, has become universalized, stuporous people "are almost a universe of their own" (that is, they have reverted to the prototaxic mode of experience) in which some great cosmic force ties up the skeletal muscles, preventing action.

Sometimes stupor is interrupted by "eruptions of activity," related generally to sleep. Tense inactivity is not sufficient. The driving ur-gency calls for something more. While previously the catatonic felt possessed or hypnotized by a cosmic power, he now *"becomes the power."* Sullivan claims that by gestures of power and magical opera-tions involving the whole body, he seeks to affect the cosmic drama in a desirable fashion. This is said to lead to statuesque posing and all sorts of things. Though this behavior appears to be related to the ritualistic aspects of medieval magical practices, it really consists of intensely meaningful gestures and postures that cannot be described in words. Sometimes these gestures and postures are performed in a remarkably slow type of movement in a manner suggestive of a high-speed camera projected at ordinary rates. At times the catatonic can perform superb feats of balancing to the quiet accompaniment of what appears to be a slow ritualistic dance, involving the expenditure of an enormous amount of energy.[28]

Many catatonics are compelled to use speech by the driving urgency mentioned previously. This speech varies in communicability from the consensually valid to profoundly obscure autistic utterances. Sullivan asserted that because of the disturbance of reference—the shifts in the level of reference—they undergo the oddest kinds of experience with speech in the sense that the meanings of words are as widely distorted as one could possibly imagine. A catatonic may say things that are as bizarre as the incantations of a witch doctor.

In general, according to Sullivan, when the catatonic is stuporous or in a state of excitement, the psychiatrist may assume that nothing but schizophrenic processes are occurring. Otherwise the psychiatrist should entertain the possibility that his patient is not far removed from the capacity for verbal communication.

To return to the subjective experiences of the catatonic schizophrenic, his interpersonal relations are frequently of great "parataxic complexity," that is, they are dominated by, or composed of, numerous illusory me-you patterns, some of which are of an awesome character. Such a patient is unable to relate to real persons for varying lengths of time, being driven to integrate situations with imaginary or illusory others who are endowed with various, and apparently incongruous, attitudes absorbed during an earlier period of life. Hence, little experience or behavior is manifested in a simple, conventional manner. Any impulse may be immediately followed by some negating impulse. In the act of experiencing an idea, a whole series of contradictory ideas may occur, or it may be "blocked," that is, negated or wiped out by a shift in one's level of awareness. Therefore, it is not strange that such a patient often gives up the struggle to communicate or understand what is happening and becomes entirely mute. Nor is it difficult to understand why the stress of this way of life is very great.[29]

The referential thought processes of the catatonic schizophrenic also become "primitive," or analogous to the symbol activity of infancy and early childhood. The earliest type of thinking, or symbol formation, occurs in what Sullivan eventually called the *prototaxic mode*, which is succeeded by the parataxic mode of symbol activity. The infant originally has no self. He may be conscious in a rudimentary sense but he is not self-conscious. Nor has he any awareness of himself as an entity separate from the rest of the world. There is no "I" in contrast to "Thou." His felt experience is an undifferentiated whole; he receives impressions and reacts, as Allport puts it, but no mediating self intervenes.[30] Distinctions of time and place are lacking. His experience is timeless and "cosmic." The alternation of need and satisfaction, of anxiety tension and security, is at first experienced in the prototaxic mode; the infant does not realize any serial connection between them.

The parataxic mode of experience develops during infancy and early childhood. In the parataxic mode of experience, the infant makes elementary discriminations between himself and the rest of the world—he no longer reaches out to touch the moon. The original, undifferentiated wholeness of experience is broken up, but the diverse aspects, the "parts" of experience, are not related or connected in an orderly, logical fashion. They are experienced as concomitant. In the most literal sense, they are *associated* rather than logically connected. There is no logical movement of "thought" from one idea or experience to the next.[31]

The referential processes of the catatonic patient seem to be similar to these early modes of symbol activity. For considerable periods of time, he is unable to employ the communicative, consensually validated speech he began to learn in childhood. His referential processes are of a less focused, less precise character than communicative speech. Hence, a spread of meaning occurs. Many things that have not seemed meaningful since the patient's childhood again "become important ingredients of the relevant universe of the schizophrenic." The boundary between the patient and the universe, particularly the world of people, undergoes a "diffusion" similar to the "extravasation" of meaning because the distinction between *"thee"* and *"me"* no longer exists. The schizophrenic tries to communicate by means of these primitive referential processes. "And when the schizophrenic tries to communicate in this way, it sounds as if he has become involved with the whole universe, or as if he has become involved with vast entities whose performance is, as it were, a cosmic drama which struggles to find the solution for a life problem in the same way that a nightmare does."[32] For such reasons, according to Sullivan, communication between therapist and patient is often extraordinarily difficult.

Another thing that disturbs communication is *blocking*. By this Sullivan means an abrupt interference with what the person planned to communicate, so that it is cut off. Thus a sentence that the person begins is not completed. The schizophrenic is unable to continue and complete the statement in such a context. What has happened is a "shift in the level of consciousness," while a preverbal or extraverbal type of thought has intervened. In such a situation the blocking is not caused by a conflict of ideas but a disturbance of consciousness so that what was being said "is no longer there."

Still another disturbance of communication is schizophrenic perplexity, which is also due to shifts in levels of reference. In contrast to blocking, perplexity is more of a step-by-step affair. "The person drifts from communicative speech, let us say, into autistic speech, and from autistic speech into preverbal use of articulate noises, and from there into some level of wordless thinking."[33] In the process of being stated a sentence sometimes undergoes change. Then an alert and experienced psychiatrist can sometimes actually arouse the patient more or less in the fashion that one might "rouse" someone who is falling asleep. If the psychiatrist can do this, the patient reverts to a communicable level of thinking and continues with what he was talking about. However, further discussion of therapy with schizophrenics must be postponed.

In view of the dreadful kinds of experience outlined above, the elaboration of a *paranoid* distortion of the past, present, and future, for those whose personal history permits it, occurs as a welcome relief. Compared to the exhausting and extremely "embarrassing" flood of the sorts of experience mentioned, the paranoid systematization of experience is relatively firm and dependable for the patient— though it also takes a heavy toll. To systematize a belief is to suppress (selectively inattend, in this context) all negative or doubt-provoking instances, and to bolster an inherently inadequate account of one's experience with rationalizations in the service of an unrecognized purpose. In the paranoid transformation of personality, a massive transfer of blame is made to the (supposedly) evil people among whom one lives. Next the patient invents a specific "transcendental" or psychotic explanation of why people are persecuting him or plotting against him. In this fashion he discovers an "explanation" for his own inadequacies and difficulties. More accurately, since it has become impossible to maintain dissociation, that which was dissociated is now personified as *not-me*, or as *others*. These others now carry the blame for those tendencies formerly maintained in dissociation as intolerable aspects of one's own personality, and they are (in the patient's view) very evil creatures. Thus the paranoid person arrives at the following formula: "I'm a very important person against whom certain more or less devilish people are engaged in a destructive plot."[34]

Many people have a "paranoid slant on life" without being psychotic or schizophrenic. But my main task is to elucidate the differences—which are by no means absolute—between paranoid states and paranoid schizophrenic states. The much more common type of paranoid person is said to be the paranoid schizophrenic. Paranoid schizophrenia is a "mixture" of elements of the systematized paranoid state and of elements of schizophrenia.

Sullivan observes that the onset of paranoid schizophrenic illnesses, that is, *schizophrenic illnesses that are likely to wind up as chronic paranoid states that are in turn more or less schizophrenic,* statistically date from a much later chronological age than the durable catatonic or the hebephrenic states. For the sake of greater clarity, one should bear in mind that he believed absolute "types" of schizophrenia do not occur, only certain more or less typical courses of events characterizing the schizophrenic process. Analogously, the distinctions "between paranoid schizophrenia, paranoid states, and paranoia will not ... stand up under any very intensive study of individual patients."[35] The paranoid dynamism, which was explicated in the previous chapter, is said to be rooted in (1) an awareness of some inferiority—which is a manifestation or expression of insecurity or low self-esteem—and (2) a transference of blame onto others, necessitated by the awareness of inferiority. These two alone constitute merely "a paranoid slant on life," not a paranoid state or paranoid schizophrenia. The awareness of inferiority entails the formulation in consciousness of some chronic feeling of "profound insecurity," either anxiety or, perhaps worse, jealousy. The dread that others can disrespect one because of something one manifests and cannot "fix" entails a constant insecurity in his relations with others. Such a disability represents an almost fatal deficiency of self-esteem for one is unable to disguise from oneself, or exclude from consciousness, a definite conviction or formulation that says: "I am inferior. Therefore people will dislike me and I cannot be secure with them."[36] Such a loss of self-esteem is hardly to be borne for it can bedevil one night and day, depriving one of any happiness or contentment.

Just as unresolved needs for satisfaction and security evoke certain processes in sleep, the failure of the self-dynamism to protect self-esteem causes the person to redouble his efforts to redeem himself from the tortured consciousness of inferiority. Effective efforts follow the precise pattern of the self operations anyone uses in making careful, consensually valid statements that communicate precisely what he means. According to Sullivan it is by means of refined cognitive operations that the self-system develops the group of processes that constitute the full-blown paranoid dynamism, which appears suddenly with all the trappings of a great insight and illumination. One suddenly sees that one is the victim of a devilish environment, which is to blame for all one's troubles. So the essence of the paranoid dynamism can be said to be the wholesale transference of blame. Still, we have not yet arrived at an adequate explanation of the paranoid state.

The operation of blaming others in order to relieve painful insecurity is not "bomb-proof." A psychiatrist can demonstrate to the patient, by skillful interview technique, that his explanation is unsound, not based on solid fact. As yet, the patient has merely arrived at what one might call a "paranoid slant on life," though a formidable one. He is still at the mercy of anyone who is not deceived and can inquire into the true state of affairs, a position that can be very awkward, and threatening for the patient who has not yet achieved an unshakable feeling of power and certainty. He has another fork in the road to choose before he reaches a point from which there is rarely a way back.

The last turning in the road, the final step, toward a grave psychosis occurs when the paranoid person invents "a specific, rather transcendental (in the sense of thoroughly psychotic) explanation of why these people do this."[37] He now "knows" of a conspiracy against him, a conviction he substantiates with a vast amount of introspective falsification. The plot may be an exquisitely built up pattern of delusions, as illustrated in *Conceptions of Modern Psychiatry*. Sullivan one day interrogated a patient at Sheppard and Enoch Pratt Hospital who on entering the office drew an odd diagram on a piece of paper. According to the patient, the diagram symbolized the patient's intricate association with a scientist with whom he had had casual contact abroad on one occasion. "I learned," Sullivan says, "that these two people were about the most important people on earth. They exercised vast powers achieved by command over natural forces through the instrumentality of hypnotism, and were soon to achieve ... hegemony of the world. They were in constant communion, across the continent, by telepathy. Both were imperiled by a horde of secret agents who were all around us."[38] This patient's behavior exemplifies a well-systematized paranoid state, with only incidental schizophrenic remnants in its structure.

At the beginning of the paranoid transformation of personality (following upon the schizophrenic episode), "the only impression one has is of a person in the grip of horror, of uncanny devastation which makes everyone threatening beyond belief. But if the person is not utterly crushed by the process, he can begin rather rapidly to elaborate personifications of evil creatures. And in this process of personifying the specific evil, the transformation begins to move fast, since it's wonderfully successful in one respect: it begins to put the blame on these others—people who are outside of him, his enemies—everything which he has clearly formulated in himself as defect, blamable weakness, and so on. Thus as the process goes on, he begins to wash his hands of all those real and fancied unfortunate aspects of his own personality which he has suffered for up to this time. Under those circumstances, needless to say, he arrived at a state which is pretty hard to remedy—by categorical name, a paranoid state."[39] Sullivan observes in *Clinical Studies in Psychiatry* that a highly systematized paranoid state may appear either under the guise of litigious paranoia, or it may be a nightmare of practically "transcendental" persecution. The paranoid dynamism works because the person has discovered a substitute activity that is a completely adequate occupation of the self: one scrutinizes every event that impinges on him and gains his attention to see how it is part of the plot to injure him, that is, to make him feel anxious or insecure or inferior. Such substitutive activity functions primarily to avoid clear, conscious certainty about one's own situation and motivations.

The term *paranoid* in this context implies the premise that people around one are dangerous and ill-disposed toward one; that transcendental superhuman powers, or persons endowed with such powers, who may be malignant or punitive, are at large. The person who entertains such ideas of hovering malignant power becomes blameless, ennobled, and expanded in worth.[40] In varying degrees and nuances, these are the attitudes and ideas that the psychiatrist encounters in paranoid states and in markedly paranoid schizophrenia.

Since there are certain almost sacrosanct explanations in psychiatric circles of paranoid processes, it may be well to turn briefly to Sullivan's interpretation of their genesis. He claims that the extent to which explanatory "doctrines" that make other people responsible for one's own shortcomings are utilized varies from family to family. One particular family may be very ingenious at discovering how other people are to blame for its members' sins of omission and commission, while another family may be much less clever at finding scapegoats, that is, people whom one can blame for the deeply shameful or contemptible things in one's own make-up. Thus, apparently, the beginnings of the paranoid process are first learned in the family, where a child learns from the adults in his home to make other people a basis for self-ennobling or self-excusing explanations of behavior of his that has no real causal connection with the behavior of the people who are blamed. In a previous chapter, such behavior patterns were explicated at greater length. Subsequently, the child fails to encounter or to benefit from corrective experience, which would demonstrate that blaming others does not work satisfactorily because it evokes hostility, ridicule, or even ostracism, or that there are potentially kind people who will respect him if he can give them a fair chance.

It seems that a paranoid person acquires the blaming strategem as a youngster by first having been the victim of it himself. Significant people blamed him at times, or took out their disgruntlements and shortcomings on him—an experience that certainly lowers one's self-esteem. A more or less cruel parent may enjoy piling blame on the child. Or a professionally inadequate teacher may gain a certain pleasure from making the child suffer for her (or his) embarrassments while concealing her inadequacies as a teacher by blaming—and perhaps ridiculing—the child for being stupid or lazy.

To be sure, the origins of security or insecurity go further back into infancy in connection with empathically experienced significant people. The roots of the self and the primitive origins or anxiety can be traced to infancy and early childhood. But the person cannot reach back that far, cannot recall that period of life and say, "I would be perfectly happy and content if it were not for the significant people in my infancy and their evil effect on me." That is one of the inescapable limitations of human living: the nucleus of the self is established long before one can reason or understand what is happening or why. But one can reach back into late childhood, whether or not one can recall all the attendant circumstances when significant people blamed him unfairly. Even if one was able to attack their unfairness, they "compounded the felony" by defending themselves, claiming that they were not unfair. This, according to Sullivan, is ultimately reassuring because the child eventually perceives that a person who cannot admit a fault is obviously not as secure as he seems and concludes that he is superior to his detractors.[41] So, Sullivan says, the following thought, easily accessible to awareness at any time in the experiences of everyone, occurs to the child: "I wouldn't have this horrible feeling of discomfort with others if *they* weren't there, and if I hadn't been taught the way I've been taught by other people." Another thought, based on real experiences in the person's earlier years under certain circumstances, occurs to him: "I wouldn't have this sense of discomfort if other people didn't treat me unfairly."[42] As I have already pointed out, in some families blaming others for one's own shortcomings becomes a way of life. A child in such a family may be subjected to increasing insecurity and blame as he proceeds, stage by stage, with ever growing feelings of inadequacy, toward adolescence.

But it is not until he has reached the preadolescent era that paranoid developments appear. Paranoid processes result to a high degree from incomplete development in the preadolescent and adolescent phases, which in turn is apparently to a large degree an outcome of previous very unfortunate experiences. They appear "very commonly" in the "midadolescent" stage of personality development, which extends up to the patterning of sexual (genital) behavior. The paranoid person does not progress through a patterning of sexual behavior. He has failed to establish workable sexual habits. In fact this failure, "this final defeat," according to Sullivan, is the situation in which the paranoid state usually appears, though it is generally preceded by a schizophrenic episode. In other words, failure to establish workable sexual relations, constituting the final defeat in a life already pervaded by excruciating thwartings, defeats, and failures, has precipitated a *schizophrenic episode* that may be quickly replaced by a substitutive state traditionally labeled paranoid schizophrenia.[43]

However, this exposition of paranoid processes is incomplete and must be pressed further. They do not appear until preadolescence owing largely to the results of incomplete development of personality in this era continuing into adolescence—a phase of development that in some people may persist into the senium. Sullivan gives an illuminating account of a "paranoid preadolescent" who had had "an appalling life." Very early in his life a distant relative who had been compelled to live in the boy's unhappy home for a time treated him "like a human being" though she finally "escaped." Sullivan says that everything else that happened to him was as unfriendly and frustrating and savagely cruel as one might expect. In school the boy was a holy terror, hated and feared by teachers and schoolmates, and "quite a gifted thorn" at home. Then at preadolescence he discovered that all the available youngsters toward whom he felt any tendency to be friendly shied away from him because they were repelled by his "problem character," which amounted to a lack of humanity. Though he tried hard, by serious application and much self-disciplinary planning, to convince his peers that he *was* human—an acceptable human being—he failed in his efforts. Under some circumstances, an emotionally distorted preadolescent, whose behavior may be obnoxious to more normal youngsters, will team up with other "sick" preadolescents. But in this instance there were no other such people available. The boy soon "came out with a fine paranoid system." Sullivan relates that this unfortunate youth would detail to unsuspecting youngsters a story about how he was really quite an important individual, who had been stolen from a hospital for purposes of blackmail by the woman who now claimed to be his mother, elaborating much alleged evidence for his story.[44]

Some psychiatrists might interpret this boy's situation to mean that he got bogged down by his intense hatred of his mother, who had been extremely thwarting and cruel to him, when he thought of "moving" toward women; in short, that he was paranoid owing to a homo-sexual conflict. Sullivan had no patience with this style of interpreta-tion, which he thought was not only incorrect but destructive of therapeutic efforts. In Sullivan's opinion, the psychiatrist who "at-tacks" a paranoid state on the basis of an attempt to interpret to the patient his alleged homosexuality, where such experience is missing, is effecting an atrocious miscarriage of the therapeutic process. He destroys any possibility of establishing rapport with the patient, for the therapist in effect agrees with or fosters the patient's conviction that there is essentially a revolting difference between him and good, estimable people. Hence the psychiatrist unwittingly strengthens the victim's paranoid state.[45]

Anyway, Sullivan held that what the youngsters suffered from was *an inescapable barrier to intimacy with man, woman, or beast.* He had failed in his almost frantic efforts to achieve intimacy with *someone.* From other people's avoidance of him he was forced to conclude, "they have no use for me." Over and over, he was forced to tell himself, in effect, if not in so many words, "I am too inferior to get what I must have." This driving, poignant, excruciating consciousness of inferiority be-came so intolerable that he at length reached the solution of blaming others, a solution bolstered of necessity by his compensatory explana-tion of why he was persecuted.

Statistically, it seemed to be true that the great majority of "para-noid cases" emerge around the ages of 25, 26, and 27. However, these people are still, psychologically, in early (or mid-)adolescence, the phase that *precedes* the patterning of sexual behavior. They have failed to establish workable sexual habits. And this final defeat has cul-minated in a paranoid development.

In Sullivan's view, while such a final defeat may often be the *present-ing* difficulty in therapy, it is *not* the real difficulty. The real problems, the basic problems, of any patient in therapy have to do with interper-sonal relations, with living as happily as circumstances allow with others.

Sometimes those "midadolescents" (or early adolescents, accord-ing to Sullivan's subsequent division of adolescence into early and late stages) have been able to establish a measure of intimacy with someone during preadolescence. Sullivan says that those who are not too badly warped may have been quite close to some other person for a time. They then have attempted to comport themselves like other young men—"which too often in this culture means abandoning real happiness in favor of heterosexual prestige."[46] But owing to the barrier against women, they are unable to achieve successfully comfortable relations of an intimate nature with them.

Such an adolescent may become convinced that no woman would have anything to do with him. This notion in turn becomes generalized into the conviction that other men know that women would not put up with him, that he is no good with women. The next step is that he believes men think he is sexually interested in them—that they ascribe his failure with women to homosexuality. So his 'perception' of self includes an intolerable consciousness of defect, of inferiority, of not being fully human that can, if no positive experience intervenes, set off a schizophrenic episode followed by a paranoid development.[47]

In summary, Sullivan believed that it is *the need for intimacy*, coupled with the inescapable consciousness of a fatal incapacity for that intimacy, that evokes "this desolating paranoid dynamism."[48] One should also bear in mind that failure to develop workable sexual habits does not lessen the intensity of the genital lust dynamism. Such a failure implies an added burden to be borne. Frustration of the sexual drive itself impairs one's sense of well-being, becoming an additional source of unpleasant tension.

As I have pointed out, under the heading of the paranoid dynamism Sullivan includes those processes that he labels the paranoid slant on life, characterized by a profound feeling of insecurity and inferiority and a transfer of blame onto others for the troubles and difficulties insecurity entails, such as severe anxiety and jealousy. At this stage, a merely intellectual, cognitive transference of blame is attempted. Such people work out a faith, making a "religion" of how wretchedly others treat them, falsely and derogatorily misinterpreting their most benevolent actions. But this operation or strategem of blaming others fails when one attempts to validate it consensually. One cannot employ it effectively since it includes factors he does not understand. The real causes for the feelings of inadequacy and inferiority that spur one on to blaming others originate in late infancy and early childhood, beyond the reach of cognition. Blaming others is a primarily intellectualistic operation that is not sufficiently potent to cope with the deeply buried roots of insecurity. The wretched feelings of inferiority and ineffectuality remain, and they compel the sufferer to redouble his efforts. Then comes the third step, whereby he feels persecuted or conspired against. Typically he engages in such paranoid interpersonal relations as writing bitter, troublesome letters to his Congressman, starting lawsuits, pestering psychiatrists, or intimidating neighbors.

The overt, diagnosed paranoid patient is said to be an intellectually gifted individual whose systematizations make his self-system impregnable to any disturbing influences emanating from his psychiatrist. By his skill at reasoning (though on false assumptions), he is usually able to divest any communication from the therapist of its power to stir dissociated tendencies and thus bring conflict into consciousness. Nevertheless, his is a far from comfortable way of life. His ability to obtain the satisfactions he needs is reduced, sometimes gravely so. As a rule, if not always, warm, intimate relationships are beyond him. Unless he is integrated into paranoid interpersonal relations, wherein he can blame others, real and imagined, for his troubles, the power of the dissociated tendencies of his personality comes to exceed the dissociating power of the self. In the latter case, he becomes prey to anxiety, conflict erupting within consciousness, or panic, followed by the outburst of schizophrenic processes previously described.

Parenthetically, Sullivan believed that it is not much use for the psychiatrist to assume that he has engaged a markedly paranoid schizophrenic in the curative process as long as the latter's history continues to reveal no markedly schizophrenic beginning of the illness. The patient has too much skill at reasoning convincingly against one. Only when he can be induced to admit that he has experienced a phase in living that Sullivan labeled the schizophrenic episode—an episode that the patient *cannot* understand or explain away—is there hope for therapeutic progress. "If the patient cannot be gotten to review a period when he was thoroughly schizophrenic, then I do not think the psychiatrist can do much with any of the later content. Only people who are quite gifted in referential operations, argument, and rationalization can sustain so complicated a distortion of reality as is the paranoid position. And so, when you encounter a person who can do so, there is no use in struggling with his interwoven blend of facts, misinterpretations and slightly fraudulent distortion of events."[49]

Sullivan distinguishes pure paranoia and pure schizophrenia as two absolute poles, never fully realized in actuality. He says that a person who approached pure paranoia would be one who handles all his difficulties by transferring any feeling of blame in any connection out of his consciousness and onto the persons making up his environment. The nearer a patient approaches this (imaginary) pole of absolute paranoia, the more highly systematized his delusions of persecution and grandeur become as an explanation of why he is persecuted.[50] Sullivan believed that the essential schizophrenic condition is catatonia.[51] Although he does not explicitly draw the comparison, it appears that pure schizophrenia is similar to catatonia as previously described. In this condition control of conscious awareness is lost—often following upon a disaster to self-esteem—with the eruption into consciousness of unorganized and primitive referential processes, to the profound mystification of the person affected. These reverie processes and subverbal or autistic verbal operations escape the excluding devices of the self. Control of the *content* of consciousness is lost. A "regressive divestment" of the later acquisitions of personality occurs. The schizophrenic disaster, involving the collapse of the self, may occur hours or days after some event has precipitated very grave conflicts between one's need for satisfactions and one's need for security and self-esteem. If a capacity for intimacy with another person has never been consolidated, the schizophrenic disaster follows a course that quickly eliminates a great many of the more recent additions to the self. If the person has experienced a need for and succeeded in the consolidation of intimacy, regression is not so swift. In the latter case, the schizophrenic disaster is more likely to follow a course characterized primarily by its close relationship to the nightmares experienced by adolescents and some chronological adults. The conflict between the need for satisfaction and the need for security is said to lower the threshold of consciousness to a level at which the earlier, more primitive, referential processes escape the excluding devices of the self and erupt into consciousness. Sullivan claims that this waking conflict is also a problem-solving effort similar to that operating in troubled dreams and nightmares: a considerable effort at solution of a problem at the level of high orders of reverie processes and subverbal or autistic verbal operations. "As long as this sort of process continues, the patient can be called catatonic."[52] If the person despairs the hebephrenic change may ensue, or a change into paranoid schizophrenia or the paranoid state may occur.

It may be helpful for the understanding of paranoid schizophrenia if one realizes that the schizophrenic (when his condition is not complicated by elements of paranoia) is *not* concerned with problems of blame. According to Sullivan, schizophrenics are especially vulnerable to having blame transferred to *them*. Usually they have not understood people, or how to deal with them, well enough to make others scapegoats.

It happens, however, that in the course of schizophrenic stupor, a patient's nonvalidated thinking processes—the primitive type of referential processes—may randomly hit on the notion of his being Jesus Christ and, perhaps, the world's being made up of people (such as Jews) bent on crucifying him. If this is sufficient to contain the schizophrenic disturbances at the level of awareness, the patient rapidly goes into a bitter, highly systematized paranoid state. However, this is not the usual outcome; if the paranoid development had sufficed, it would have occurred sooner. If the patient had succeeded in the past at making someone else the scapegoat, he would not stay schizophrenic very long.

A certain group of patients, according to Sullivan, do show Christ identifications, yet remain catatonic. They are not paranoid. Often paranoid attitudes do not suffice. Even the catatonic Christ identification may progress to a paranoid phase, but under skillful therapeutic pressure, the Christ identification collapses, and the patient "is again lost in the whole welter of universal patterns and is again definitely stuporous."[53] Sullivan points out that the paranoid schizophrenic can sometimes relapse into stupor, revert to simple schizophrenia, and from that emerge as a social, if not real, recovery. Sullivan believes this shows that the transfer of blame does not really solve the problems of schizophrenics, as is also indicated by the "shocking character" of the persecutions many of them complain of. Paranoid schizophrenics still have a very hard time. When the paranoid state becomes a durable maladjustment, perhaps of years' duration, it remains very unpleasant even though it brings a relative security.

In short, the more paranoid a person is the less schizophrenic are his interpersonal relations. However, ever patient who had undergone the paranoid state whom Sullivan encountered had in his personal history a period of "schizophrenic content," though the latter condition was sometimes hard to discover. Only the patient who has encountered blaming stratagems in his parents or teachers and other such significant people in the culture, and from them learned successfully how to scapegoat others, may elaborate a paranoid distortion of the past, present, and future. But the cost of such a paranoid systematization of experience is "an adoption of hate in the place of a never-quite-realized love. The result of this substitution of hate in place of love as the goal of interpersonal relations is the gradual disintegration of the patient."[54]

The other outcome of the schizophrenic state is hebephrenic dilapidation. While the essentially schizophrenic person is pretty well demoralized, with slight expectation of a brighter, more pleasant future, he is not utterly hopeless, as indicated by many of his utterances and some of his behavior. But a certain proportion of schizophrenics do become hopeless: they despair of becoming human beings acceptable to others. And then, with few exceptions, they leave the field of human relations for good. The hebephrenic "has had such disastrous experiences in his initial, rather frantic, schizophrenic attempt at doing something that he has given it all up as a bad job. That is conspicuously shown by the avoidance of interpersonal contacts and the very disturbing effect of interpersonal pressure on the person with the hebephrenic change."[55] An attitude of resigned separation or alienation from life and an utter hopelessness seems to be the essence of the hebephrenic state. The patient has abandoned the effort at living, and exists on a sort of autobiological level. At the same time he has relinquished, or escaped from, the stress and turmoil and the painfully deep pessimistic expectations of the true schizophrenic state. Condemned to despair, he suffers a feeling of total, utter isolation, and of utter incapacity to do anything that might remedy his situation. Any tie, or even a lifeline, with the real interpersonal world is finally and usually irretrievably broken.

Sullivan claimed that the person who suffers a schizophrenic episode, without having had an genuinely meaningful experience of the preadolescent era, will be characterized by a much prompter appearance of the hebephrenic development. Normally, during preadolescence one first learns to become intimate with another human being, which entails a considerable expansion and deepening of one's values, and thereby a relatively firm attachment to the real interpersonal world—the world of real people.[56] On the other hand, this very tie is conspicuously troublesome to schizophrenics who have experienced some preadolescent intimacy, and who can not dilapidate immediately because, despite their anguish, they still retain a modicum of hope regarding the world.

Not only does the hebephrenic divest himself of, or abandon, the interpersonal abilities developed during the early stages of personality development (truncated and warped though they may be), he is driven to occupying himself with "amusing" zones of interaction to keep himself from being trapped into very disturbing relations with others. However gravely deteriorated he may be, he still retains the various impulses or drives that make up a part of living and cannot be eradicated. Normally they are satisfied in and through interpersonal situations. But the hebephrenic wants no more of the latter and must fall back upon unsocial modes of satisfaction. The satisfaction of needs can be gained without great difficulty in a mental institution (if it is tolerably rational and humane) with minimal contact with people, and in relative contentment. The hebrephrenic can eat, drink, rest, sleep in this fashion. He can more or less continuously manipulate his penis and thus avoid being disturbed by lust, which could be troublesome since it might involve him with another person. And he may possibly "have a wonderful time with the feces."

To further clarify the situation of the hebephrenic, impulses that were once a part of the prepsychotic self, that played a part in the conflict and chaos of the catatonic state, and that were *then* opposed to the impulses whose eruption into consciousness horrified or terrified him, are now *themselves* in much the same relationship to the patient's awareness as were the originally dissociated impulses. The impulses of the prepsychotic self are no longer "on the side of the angels" because they tend to involve him with others. "If they tend strongly to integrate an interpersonal situation, the patient becomes acutely anxious, often becomes seriously disturbed, perhaps acutely hallucinated, excited, assaultive, and more or less randomly destructive."[57]

However, two kinds of experience remain that cannot be handled in the unsocial fashion of the satisfaction of bodily drives. One is loneliness, which the hebephrenic has little or no resources left to deal with. The other is the need for security. Sullivan thought that the hebephrenic deteriorates as the self and its security operations are progressively and rapidly abandoned. The individual is left with a rather constant, unchanging feeling that people regard him with indifference, contempt, scorn, or other negative attitudes. But he gets more or less used to this twilight existence because it is uniform, more or less unchanging without threat of novelty; it has the relative reassurance of the habitual. This is the end state of the hebephrenic change.

This change may appear very early in the course of a schizophrenic episode or it may occur as the termination of a prolonged catatonic state. In any long-continued schizophrenic condition that has not tended markedly to recovery, hebephrenia appears. According to Sullivan, the condition of most patients who have suffered "paranoid schizophrenic" states eventually becomes indistinguishable from the condition of those in whom the hebephrenic change appeared early.

The outstanding characteristics of the hebephrenic state, that is, the signs ordinarily enumerated as its description, are said to be a marked seclusiveness and avoidance of any companionship; a disintegration of language processes (manifested in speech that is "scattered," incoherent, vague, unconnected, or expressing poverty of ideas); and a marked diminution of emotional rapport, so that the patient impresses one as having undergone a dilapidation or impoverishment of the emotional aspects of interpersonal behavior. Sullivan's explanation of the causes of seclusiveness and the reduction of emotional rapport has been described previously. The disintegration of language processes can be explained as concomitants of the disintegration of the self, a very important dimension of which is communicative speech. Psychologically two of the most important functions of language are the communication of ideas and attitudes and the expression of feeling and emotion. And the hebephrenic, for reasons mentioned previously, wants no part of either: they are too threatening to his (relative) "peace of mind," to whatever security he can manage to retain.

While Sullivan discusses a few other signs of the hebephrenic state, I omit them since they are not vital to an understanding of his theory of schizophrenia.

According to Sullivan, the "paranoid maladjustment" and the hebephrenic change are *not* part of schizophrenia but are very unfortunate outcomes of schizophrenic episodes; the essential schizophrenic condition is catatonic schizophrenia.[58] By and large Sullivan's therapy of schizophrenia is oriented toward the treatment of the latter.

Sullivan's ideas on dissociation are relevant to a fuller understanding of schizophrenia. In his Foreword to *Conceptions of Modern Psychiatry* Sullivan wrote that in this lecture series he had ascribed undue importance to dissociation to the neglect of selective inattention, which he had not yet formulated in 1939 when the lectures were delivered. But I think this qualification does not materially alter his conception of dissociation as a functionally separate part of the personality. Selective inattention is an instrumentality of the self by which dissociated dynamisms are kept unconscious, though selective inattention is not the only instrumentality employed for this purpose.

Selective inattention does *not* pertain to the inhibition of motives and hence is quite different from the *suppression* or *repression* of classical psychoanalysis. Its function is the control of consciousness in situations in which anxiety might be aroused. Its clearest formulation is in *Clinical Studies in Psychiatry*. One might call it a misuse of concentration or attention in the traditional sense of those ideas. When one concentrates or attends, he focuses on the relevant aspects of a situation or problem and ignores or inattends everything else, including any distracting elements that might intrude. When one selectively inattends something, he may notice it but does not focus on it or concentrate on it; he therefore fails to perceive or to understand relevant and significant aspects of a situation or problem in order to avoid or minimize anxiety. Of course, very often this operation occurs at the cost of learning highly illuminating aspects of situations that would otherwise be educative. Selective inattention, as I previously mentioned, is an instrumentality of the self; it is part of the restrictive "machinery" of the self. And since the self may also stand in the way of *unfavorable* change, selective inattention must be regarded as at times serving a constructive function when it acts as a barrier against dissociated processes, the emergence of which into consciousness may precipitate panic.

Dissociation is used by Sullivan in two major senses. In one sense, it refers to the inhibition of motives or impulses, with a concomitant exclusion from consciousness of any recognition of their existence. In this sense it is somewhat similar to Freud's concept of repression, though Sullivan said he had never "encountered anything as simple and as comprehensive as the repression of orthodox psychoanalysis." To dissociate is actually to keep some deeply unconscious tendency —or motivational system—functionally split off from the self or, if it has become conscious, to put it out of consciousness in such a fashion that it is isolated from the self-system.

In the second, and related meaning of dissociation, it refers to an aspect of the personality that is functionally separate from and often intensely antipathetic to the self and its values. Some degree of dissociation is ubiquitous. Some impulses are "choked off" in large measure very early in anyone's education. Western culture "does not use part of our impulse equipment . . . part of our adjustive potentialities. . . . But they are not choked off utterly—it is probably impossible to do so. Like the trees growing at the edge of the Grand Canyon, something happens, however terribly distorted."[59] If the impulses constitute a major integrative tendency, a major motivational system, they are not completely divorced from the development that occurs during any stage of growth. "But if a major integrative tendency gets very little place in socialized life, so that it has no material satisfaction in the operations of the self-conscious person, then all that happens is that it is never, in any way, represented in the self-system."[60] Since such a tendency system was never part of the self, it does not require "any great machinery" (such as selective inattention or obsessive substitutive processes) to keep it out. It operates as a separate organization of processes, running on and on, in and out of season, whenever the self-system is not making its presence felt; that is, whenever the self is not alerted, in some interpersonal situation, to any behavior of the self, however obscure, which might arouse the disapproval of significant others, or of one's self.

But other impulse systems that have been a part of the self may, because of some unfortunate experience or series of experiences, cease to be known to the person and vanish into the region in which he does things that he never notices or attends. When they vanish (become dissociated) in this fashion the person no longer accepts them as his. In the course of personality development, a "massive dissociation of impulse systems" before adulthood may occur. The classic psychoanalytic example of such a massive dissociation pertains to sexuality, but almost any impulse system save hunger, thirst, and the like can be ejected from consciousness and functionally isolated from the self. The peculiarities of anyone's development combined with the restrictions of his sociocultural environment determine what drives and motives are acceptable and what must be dissociated.

Since dissociated processes have a significant relation to sleep, I shall briefly discuss it. According to Sullivan the functional importance of sleep, from a psychiatric viewpoint, is the marked relaxation of security operations that occurs in sleep. Sleep is the one phase of life in which one is more or less relieved of the necessity of maintaining security. Many unsatisfied needs and unsatisfied components of needs that cannot be discharged in waking life are, to a degree, satisfied in the "symbolic devices" of sleep. People who are denied sleep for a period of time manifest signs of mental disturbance and their ability to deal with troublesome motivations deteriorates rapidly.

Even in sleep the self-system is not completely in abeyance. Sometimes a person who is severaly anxious while awake may have a frightful nightmare one night that he cannot shake off even when he wakes up; not long after that he becomes overtly schizophrenic. Normally, one maintains dissociation during sleep by a continued vigilance of the dissociative apparatus in the self-system. And the more of the personality that exists in dissociation, the less restful and more troubled by unpleasant dreams and nightmares will one's sleep be. A person in this plight will often not be able to obtain adequate returns from sleep even if he sleeps long hours. In other words, when certain powerful motivational systems are dissociated, the person is unable to relax the self sufficiently to have deep, restful sleep. In general, the tensions of needs and of anxiety are "oppositional" to the tensions of sleeping.

On occasion Sullivan was able to save an incipient schizophrenic from grave disorganization by administering a liberal dose of alcohol, which temporarily enfeebles the "higher centers," making deep sleep possible and thus ensuring a relatively intact personality more amenable to therapy, if it is quickly available.

On the other hand, once the dissociative power of the self has failed and the contents of consciousness have escaped from its control, the sleep of schizophrenics tends to be profound. But the sleep of those patients is said to be very different from relatively normal sleep because it is a "regressive phenomenon." By this Sullivan seems to mean a state reminiscent of early childhood or infancy.

While the self is said to be relatively dormant in sleep it does not disappear.[61] It is what Sullivan calls a perduring aspect of personality. So these dissociated aspects, he says, tend, by fantastic means, to follow a principle that is very markedly manifested in the waking life of those who suffer one of the mental disorders. He claims that the character of the interpersonal phenomena manifested in their sleep is often regressive to archaic modes of awareness. The awareness of the infant is diffuse and nonspecific, for it exists in either the prototaxic or parataxic mode of experience. "We may, therefore, say that the maximum regression of prehending processes is to a sort of an amorphous universe in which one has one's being—doubtless, a fairly early infantile mental state. If there were necessity, one could revert in dreams to that sort of attack upon one's problems."[62] In those who do not suffer from major interpersonal difficulties, regression is not usually "anything like so deep."

I shall close with a brief account of Sullivan's accomplishments in the treatment of schizophrenia at Sheppard and Enoch Pratt Hospital.

First, one must bear in mind that mature people do not suffer schizophrenic illness (with the possible exception of times of catastrophic social change). Sullivan believed that schizophrenia occurs in people who are "fixed" at the preadolescent or early adolescent level of personality development when sex and problems of intimacy with others are pressing problems. During these stages problems of intimacy and problems connected with the sexual drive often take on an almost "preternatural importance," particularly in American society. Failure to handle them successfully constitutes a great social liability, which may in turn have grave consequences for the individual's conviction of personal worth. Other, but probably related, factors such as approaching marriage may help to precipitate a schizophrenic episode. However, they are not the causes of schizophrenia. The variables in the etiology of schizophrenia are apparently multiple. In Sullivan's theory, these variables pertain chiefly to interpersonal relations.

Sullivan believed that the prognosis of a sudden onset of schizophrenia—the "acute dramatic divorcement from more or less commonplace living"—is much better than the insidious onset in which a sudden dramatic break is not seen. The insidious onset implies that personality development has been arrested long before the hospital admission, so that the available human ability and emotional resources useful for a reintegration or resynthesis of anything like an average life situation and normal interpersonal relations are more limited.

Sullivan's success with the patients in the special ward was spectacular and unprecedented. His successor, Dr. William V. Silverberg, of New York City, spent a year at Sheppard, making no essential changes in the organization that Sullivan created there. Silverberg in 1931 summarized his own work as follows: During the year he was at Sheppard he dealt with sixteen schizophrenics in the special 6-bed ward.

"Of these 16 patients, 12 either recovered or improved. Of the 12 cases that had been cured or improved, nine were discharged and three remained under care at the end of the period. Of the 4 unimproved cases, three were discharged and one remained under care. Of the three unimproved, discharged cases, two turned out to be patients who had been ill for some time, without its being known by their families. They had been paranoid for at least two years before coming to the hospital.

"On the basis of these statistics, one sees that 75 percent of the cases going through this organization has been either recovered or improved. If one omits the two chronic cases for whom, as Dr. Sullivan has already said, such a method of treatment, or any method of treatment, seems to be of no great value, it will be seen that about 85 percent of these 14 cases have been either recovered or improved."[63]

Notes

1. HARRY STACK SULLIVAN, *Schizophrenia as a Human Process* with Introduction and Commentaries by HELEN SWICK PERRY (New York: W. W. Norton and Company, 1962).

2. Cf. ROBERT G. MEYER and BERTRAM P. KARON, "The Schizophrenogenic Mother Concept," *Psychiatry*, **30**:173-178, 1967.

3. HARRY STACK SULLIVAN, *The Interpersonal Theory of Psychiatry*, ed. HELEN SWICK PERRY and M ARY LADD GAWEL, with an Introduction by MABEL BLAKE COHEN (New York: W. W. Norton and Company, 1953), p. 326.

4. Cf. HAROLD F. SEARLES, "The Schizophrenic Individual's Experience of his World," *Psychiatry*, **31**:119-131, 1967.

5. HARRY STACK SULLIVAN, *Conceptions of Modern Psychiatry*, with a Foreword by the author and a Critical Appraisal of the Theory by PATRICK MULLAHY (New York: W. W. Norton and Company, 1953), p. 134.

6. SULLIVAN, *The Interpersonal Theory of Psychiatry*, p. 193.

7. SULLIVAN, *Conceptions of Modern Psychiatry*, p. 132.

8. Sullivan points out that the illustration is defective because a person who found the young man so attractive and suitable for genital integration could not be so "healthy." Analogously, the young man would not be motivated by simple, uncomplicated lust.

9. *Ibid.*, p. 133; cf. HARRY STACK SULLIVAN, *The Psychiatric Interview*, ed. HELEN SWICK PERRY and MARY LADD GAWEL, with an Introduction by OTTO ALLEN WILL, JR. (New York: W. W. Norton and Company, 1956), p. 186.

10. Cf. ELLIOT G. MISCHLER and NANCY E. WAXLER (eds.), *Family Processes and Schizophrenia* (New York: Science House, 1968).

11. Cf. MAURICE R. GREEN, "Common problems in the Treatment of Schizophrenia in Adolescents," *Psychiatric Quarterly*, April, 1966.

12. SULLIVAN, *Conceptions of Modern Psychiatry*, p. 133.

13. *Ibid.*, p. 134.

14. *Ibid.*, p. 137.

15. *Ibid.*, p. 138.

16. Sullivan claims that autochthonous ideas precede the occurrence of hallucinations: "Thus while the self-system excludes from awareness clear evidences of a dissociated motivational system, that which is dissociated is represented in awareness by some group of ideas or thoughts which are marked uncannily with utter foreignness—they have nothing to do with one-self." SULLIVAN, *The Interpersonal Theory of Psychiatry*, pp. 360-361.

17. For a discussion of automatisms, see SULLIVAN, *Conceptions of Modern Psychiatry*, and *Clinical Studies in Psychiatry*.

18. SULLIVAN, *Conceptions of Modern Psychiatry*, p. 142.

19. HARRY STACK SULLIVAN, *Clinical Studies in Psychiatry*, ed. HELEN SWICK PERRY, MARY LADD GAWEL, and MARTHA GIBBON, with a Foreword by DEXTER M. BULLARD (New York: W. W. Norton and Company, 1956), p. 318.

20. Cf. HARRY STACK SULLIVAN, "The Relation of Onset to Outcome in Schizophrenia," in SULLIVAN, *Schizophrenia as a Human Process*, pp. 236-244; "The Onset of Schizophrenia," *American Journal of of Psychiatry*, **84**:105-134, 1927-1928, reprinted in SULLIVAN, *Schizophrenia as a Human Process*.

21. SULLIVAN, *Conceptions of Modern Psychiatry*, p. 154.

22. *Ibid.*

23. *Ibid.*, p. 149.

24. Cf. SILVANO ARIETI, *Interpretation of Schizophrenia* (New York: Robert Brunner, 1955).

25. WILLIAM S. SADLER, *Theory and Practice of Psychiatry* (St. Louis, Missouri: The C. V. Mosby Company, 1936), p. 818.

26. SULLIVAN, *Conceptions of Modern Psychiatry*, pp. 151-152.

27. SULLIVAN, *Clinical Studies in Psychiatry*, p. 321.

28. *Ibid.*, p. 323; cf. JAMES C. COLEMAN, *Abnormal Psychology and Modern Life* (3rd ed.; Glenview, Illinois: Scott, Foresman and Company, 1964), pp. 279-281.

29. SULLIVAN, *Conceptions of Modern Psychiatry*, p. 155; cf. SULLIVAN, *Clinical Studies in Psychiatry*, pp. 328-330.

30. GORDON ALLPORT, *Pattern and Growth in Personality* (New York: Holt, Rinehart, and Winston, 1961), p. 112.

31. Cf. MAURICE R. GREEN, "Prelogical Experience in the Thinking Process," *Journal of Issues in Art Education*, **3**:66-78, 1961.

32. SULLIVAN, *Clinical Studies in Psychiatry*, p. 316.

33. *Ibid.*, p. 330

34. *Ibid.*, p. 149.

35. *Ibid.*, p. 311.

36. *Ibid.*, p. 145.

37. *Ibid.*, p. 148.

38. SULLIVAN, *Conceptions of Modern Psychiatry*, p. 159.

39. SULLIVAN, *The Interpersonal Theory of Psychiatry*, pp. 361-362.

40. SULLIVAN, *Clinical Studies in Psychiatry*, p. 335.

41. One wonders if children can be as objective and clear-sighted as this.

42. SULLIVAN, *Clinical Studies in Psychiatry*, p. 147.

43. Cf. HAROLD F. SEARLES, "Sexual Processes in Schizophrenia," *Psychiatry*, **24**:87-95, 1961 (suppl. to No. 2); OTTO ALLEN WILL, JR., "Paranoid Development and the Concept of Self: Psychotherapeutic Intervention," *Psychiatry*, **24**:74-86, 1961.

44. SULLIVAN, *Clinical Studies in Psychiatry*, p. 152.

45. *Ibid.*, pp. 163-164.

46. SULLIVAN, *Clinical Studies in Psychiatry*, p. 155.

47. Cf. PAUL H. WENDER, "Vicious and Virtuous Circles: The Role of Deviation Amplifying Feedback in the Origin and Perpetuation of Behavior," *Psychiatry*, **31**:309-324, 1968.

48. SULLIVAN, *Clinical Studies in Psychiatry*, p. 158.

49. *Ibid.*, p. 307.

50. *Ibid.*, pp. 304-305.

51. *Ibid.*, p. 313.

52. *Ibid.*

53. *Ibid.*, p. 338.

54. SULLIVAN, *Conceptions of Modern Psychiatry*, p. 156; cf. SULLIVAN, *Clinical Studies in Psychiatry*, pp. 160-163.

55. SULLIVAN, *Clinical Studies in Psychiatry*, p. 353.

56. Cf. KURT HAAS, *Understanding Ourselves and Others* (Englewood Cliffs, New Jersey: Prentice-Hall, 1965), pp. 36-84.

57. SULLIVAN, *Conceptions of Modern Psychiatry*, p. 164.

58. SULLIVAN, *The Interpersonal Theory of Psychiatry*, p. 328.

59. SULLIVAN, *Clinical Studies in Psychiatry*, p. 66.

60. *Ibid.*,

61. Cf. *ibid.*, pp. 175-177.

62. SULLIVAN, *Conceptions of Modern Psychiatry*, p. 71.

63. HARRY STACK SULLIVAN, "The Modified Psychoanalytic Treatment of Schizophrenia," discussion in *American Journal of Psychiatry*, **88**:519-540; reprinted in SULLIVAN, *Schizophrenia as a Human Process*, pp. 290-291. Cf. ALFRED H. STANTON, "Milieu Therapy and the Development of Insight," *Psychiatry*, **24**:19-29, 1961 (suppl. to No. 2), and LAWRENCE S. LINN, "The Mental Hospital from the Patient-Perspective," *Psychiatry*, **31**:213-223, 1968.

11 / *The Psychiatric Interview*

As I approach the end of a rather long and taxing effort to provide a comprehensive introduction to Sullivanian psychiatry, I wish to remind the reader that this book is not meant to be—and could not be —a substitute for the published writings and lectures of Sullivan. So I assume that those whose interest in interpersonal psychiatry I may have stimulated and who have not already studied his work intensively will want to study the original sources, especially those who are about to begin a career in psychiatry or clinical psychology. Hence I shall try to provide only a review of Sullivan's formulations of the psychiatric interview and the procedures he employed. As one might expect, he greatly modified, refined, and elaborated the "views" presented in Chapter 5. Perhaps I should call it to the attention of those readers who are young psychiatrists that a good deal has been borrowed over the past twenty or twenty-five years by various psychiatrists and clinical psychologists who have chosen to recast it into their own language.

In *Conceptions of Modern Psychiatry* Sullivan stated that some ten years he had spent in studying schizophrenic conditions convinced him of the interpersonal nature of the psychiatric field. Roughly another ten years (1931–1940) spent in office practice with the "closely related substitutive states, obsessional and other," enabled him to refine and consolidate his earlier insights. The last eight years of Sullivan's life were spent largely in teaching, supervising candidates-in-training, and in consultations with colleagues who sought him out when they got stymied by a patient. At the time of his death he was still actively elaborating and refining the "system" of psychiatry that I have attempted to organize and clarify in this book.

In *Conceptions of Modern Psychiatry* he wrote that the purpose of psychiatry is the understanding of living so that it may be facilitated. Even when this goal is conceived from the standpoint of treating mentally disordered patients one is forced to realize that the social order itself is an important factor that one must take into account in formulating therapeutic goals and the relevant procedures. It "sets the limits" or boundaries within which the patient's interpersonal relations may succeed. There is no way by which he can transcend institutional arrangements, no matter how regrettable or even tragic this may sometimes be. But sooner or later the psychiatrist who adheres to such a perspective sees that the social order not merely sets the limits within which the purpose of psychiatry can be achieved. He realizes that it is the "mediate source" from which the patient's problems spring, and these difficulties in living are themselves signs of difficulties and inadequacies in the social order itself. This is true of *all societies*.

There has never been—and perhaps never will be—a thoroughly rational social order, for that would require that the various institutions of society are truly rationally organized and operated by men who are governed by reason and devoted to the common good (which they somehow learn) and that the members of society also possess enough reason and maturity to run their lives according to the dictates of reason and the common, in contrast to the merely selfish, good. Otherwise, when the members of a society are ignorant of, or reject, rational social norms, even the wisest governors would be ineffectual, whether chosen by popular vote or otherwise. For it is a generally accepted fact that if the members of a society do not respect and support its customs and laws, then the rulers or chosen representatives are helpless to enforce their observance. (I ignore the Marxist fantasy of "the withering away" of the state.) Further considerations of these matters would lead us into a study of the world's great political and social philosophies and of certain current ideas in the political and social sciences. Parenthetically, one suspects that the contemporary upsurge in biochemical and/or neurophysiological researches and "theories" regarding the proximate causes of mental disorders is, *to a degree,* an unconscious recognition of the unpromising social outlook for the foreseeable future.

In 1939, when Sullivan delivered the lectures that were subsequently bound and published, in a limited edition, under the title of *Conceptions of Modern Psychiatry,* he asserted that the level of general insecurity is rising, that the social order is itself gravely disturbed, and that psychiatry as a therapeutic art is confronted with new tasks that require a change of orientation and the perfection of new techniques. But only a small minority of psychiatrists and clinical psychologists took them very seriously. (In fact this was the case with nearly all of Sullivan's ideas in those days.) Liberal-minded psychiatrists and psychologists hastened to refute the notion that the level of general insecurity was rising; it sounded reactionary, somehow a veiled attack on "progress." There was no scientific evidence for this notion, they said, and this was more or less true since in the past psychiatry was far too young and its resources too meagre to have conducted studies like the *Manhattan Project.*[1] According to some, if there was any basis for Sullivan's notion, it was that in previous generations people were not generally aware of psychiatric conceptions: mentally disordered people were not generally recognized as such.

At the present time the social order in the United States of America seems far more gravely "disturbed" and—perhaps something Sullivan could hardly have realized—the human race lives under a constant threat of destruction from thermonuclear war and/or perhaps other lethal forms of warfare. Riots and arson are almost a daily occurrence, erupting in one city after another. The people of the city are afraid to walk in the streets at night. Nor is this all.

It would be strange if the general level of insecurity has not risen since 1939. But this need not seriously detract from the worth of Sullivanian psychiatry when applied in individual and (small) group therapy, wherein it can be efficacious. Man has an extraordinary ability to survive under various kinds of adverse conditions, and, often is able to surmount them. But it must be admitted that never before has he been in such mortal peril.

The reader will have noted that Sullivan conceived psychiatry in two senses. In one sense he adhered to the traditional conception of psychiatry as the study and treatment of mental disorders. But this conception overlaps with a second conception, that psychiatry is a highly specialized branch of social psychology, supplemented by its students' knowledge of human biology. Since psychology is closely interrelated with the major institutions of society and its dominant culture patterns, Sullivan "looked to" the social sciences for help in the development of psychiatry. In recent years there seems to be a gradual rapprochement between psychiatry and the "behavioral sciences," which he had advocated long ago.[2]

In regard to the interview itself, the general cultural and special educational backgrounds of both therapist and patient must also be considered. It is a well-known fact that two (or more) people who have had a similar cultural background can, in general, communicate more easily and precisely than if they have had dissimilar cultural backgrounds. In the latter case, the individuals concerned will have more less different reference frames for interpreting the world, at least some different assumptions about interpersonal relations, and ways of relating to others that may differ sometimes in a subtle way, sometimes in an overt and clear-cut fashion. If at least one of the parties involved is not clearly conscious of these things, then communication may often fail, with possibly serious consequences.

The following is a fairly crude illustration. A college student, a New Yorker, who was spending his summer vacation in Europe, decided to visit Ireland. Unlike so many American tourists, he traveled around the countryside. One day, around noon, when he became hungry, he began to seek out a restaurant. But there were no restaurants for miles around. So he stopped at a farmhouse and explained his predicament to the woman of the house. She invited him in and provided him with a doubtless simple but probably substantial fare. Having eaten, the student, as he was about to leave, in order to show his gratitude, offered to pay her—in rural Ireland, a grossly offensive insult. The ways of life of both parties were so profoundly different that only a superficial type of communication would likely be possible even in everyday intercourse.

As Sullivan wrote, any interview presumes or presupposes the existence of "interlocking" culture patterns, that is, "some approximate identities" in the acculturation of the participants. Language is generally the most notable of these cultural "elements." But in such a situation there is a risk that one or both participants will assume a "full identity" even though there is only a superficial similarity. This sort of occurrence may and perhaps not rarely still does happen in psychoanalytically oriented psychiatry. From the standpoint of psychiatric discussion, psychoanalysts may speak of, or write about, a "mother-fixation" having been the cause of certain conditions. But the conception of a mother-fixation is so wide in range, if not vague and ambiguous in meaning, that it cannot be usefully employed to clarify the varieties and depths of meaning in the pattern of the mother-son relationship. This "master symbol" is, or was, a hindrance to clear thinking, though some patients "love" such a cliché. It "explains" so much that it explains nothing, so a patient who is reluctant to become conscious of, or recognize, anxiety-laden tendencies and attitudes may become an addict of such master symbols, if the therapist himself has not seen through these psychiatric omnibus conceptions.

Sullivan held that "the interview situation," when skillfully conducted by a seasoned therapist, gradually facilitates a gradual evolution of awareness of the people actually concerned. Gradually, as he begins to achieve insight, the patient loses the "parataxic concomitants" with which he has invested, or which he has attributed to, the physician. The latter, meanwhile, refines and clarifies his impressions of what sort of person the patient is. At the same time the therapist must be diligent in preventing the impression a patient sometimes develops as the growth of his awareness progresses, that the purpose of the interview is to humiliate him. If such an impression grows unchecked, therapeutic possibilities become destroyed. But when all goes well, the patient gradually becomes conscious of his parataxic distortions that not only manifest themselves in the therapeutic situation but in his everyday living. Then he can learn to do something about them or, as Sullivan, in the *Psychiatric Interview* (p. 239) stated: therapist and patient work toward uncovering those factors which are concerned in the person's recurrent mistakes, and which lead to his taking ineffective and inappropriate action.

The processes that occur in the interview situation are determined by the whole organization of integrating tendencies that the interview arouses. The perceptions and cognitions of both therapist and patient, as well as the actual verbal exchange, are mediated by their respective self-dynamisms. Everything else that occurs in the interview goes on outside clear consciousness, that is, in the main, selectively inattended or dissociated. Unless the psychiatrist has had wide experience in living and is relatively very secure in the interview situation, he is apt to fail to notice or be unaware of a good deal that goes on. Should the latter eventuality take place, the psychiatrist's formulation of his patient's developmental history as well as his present state is likely to be inconsequential if not "quite irrelevant." What the patient says or "exteriorizes" in an interview is his more or less "cogent streams of reverie process," those not "suppressed" by his self system at least until he has learned to "free associate."

In order to understand that the patient cannot know enough about himself and his interpersonal relations to explain his present difficulties, one must bear the following in mind. The self-dynamism, regardless of its limitations, is the "growing integration" by means of which one, in the main, relates to others for the sake of gaining satisfactions, maintaining as much security as one can, and securing whatever else one may want in dealing with others, either in work, play, or other leisure-time activities. In other words, the self represents the person's meaningful orientation to the world, which is composed chiefly of other people, real or imaginary, or a "blend" of both. Sullivan thought that there was a built-in tendency of the self to maintain its current organization and functional activity. New experience usually has to be "soluble" in the old. Whatever is unprecedented, if it does not make sense in terms of one's ways of experiencing the world, tends to arouse anxiety and, sometimes, fear. For Sullivan the great restrictive, limiting force is anxiety, since it "excludes from [conscious] awareness all the data which would expand the self at the cost of [interpersonal] insecurity." Future investigations may reveal that fear or something else should be given more weight—but that remains to be seen. The loneliness that can be more terrible than anxiety is due to a lack of relatedness to others and not to abstract philosophic reflection on the finiteness of man or his alleged insignificance in some cosmic scheme. In a rapidly changing social order, or in a social order threatened with destruction as was the case with France and some other European countries during World War II, the traditions that bind men together in the solidarity born from the possession of a common culture, the web of interpersonal relations, may be loosened and torn, to be followed by loneliness, a conviction of life's meaninglessness or despair. [3] Even in 1932 Sullivan had an astonishing psychological insight into these things.

Furthermore, in addition to the "resistances" and hindrances to the growth or expansion of consciousness mentioned above, there is, for various causes, a "witting suppression" by the patient of much that *does* come to mind, that *does* appear in his conscious awareness. Therefore, in order to obtain relevant and highly significant information about the sources of difficulties in the patient's interpersonal relations, much more than an interrogation is needed, a point that was brought out in Chapter 5.

"The principal problem of the therapeutic interview," Sullivan wrote, "is that of facilitating the accession to awareness [consciousness] of information which will clarify for the patient the more troublesome aspects of his life."[4] In attempting to accomplish this, the therapist must circumvent the inhibiting processes that would, if one were to try a "direct attack," become manifested in severe anxiety, or anger and resentment. There would probably follow "a disintegration of the therapeutic situation." In circumventing the patient's inhibiting processes, the therapist has also to take into account the fact that one has information about one's experience only to the degree that one has tended to communicate it to another or reflected about it in the manner of communicative speech, that is, in covert vocal or subvocal thought processes. (An instructor's first year as a college teacher is notoriously difficult. For example, he may begin to discuss a topic that he believed he knew well—and is abruptly brought up short. To his discomfiture, he is suddenly made to realize he had not ever thought the topic through.) Sullivan claimed that much of what is ordinarily said to be "repressed" is merely unformulated. The reverie processes connected with the unformulated experiences are either nonverbal or of a highly autistic character. They do not constitute an "image" or effect recall of the unformulated experiences: their form and function are chiefly determined by a need to avoid recall. Often they occur in states of inattentive preoccupation or of abstraction. In other cases they are said to be actively preoccupying, constituting the relatively meaningless recurrent ideation of a substitutive state, such as the obsessional. But in such instances, the "experiential subject-matter," the genuine referent of the reverie processes, is so well disguised that nothing of it can be recalled. This point was described in Chapter 9. Since such reverie processes lack consensual validation, it follows that they "proceed" in the parataxic mode, or, in certain instances, the prototaxic mode.

At this point some of the preconceptions formulated in *Conceptions of Modern Psychiatry* that govern the psychiatric interview need to be mentioned. The first preconception is that the patient is (usually) a stranger and is to be treated as a stranger. There is no reason for the psychiatrist's presuming to adopt either a friendly or an unfriendly attitude. The patient has come for help in his difficulties in living to one who is presumably an expert. The latter's expertness becomes manifested in his "uncovering" the factors or processes at work in the patient's relations with others—"not in omnipotence, omniscience, magical reassurance, persuasion or exhortation."

Secondly, insofar as possible, the "interrogation" proceeds from a given point in a direction that is easy for the patient to follow. Otherwise the psychiatrist's questions do not enable the latter to foresee the current or immediate direction of the inquiry. They do not make much, if any sense, to him, so he may become uncertain or confused —especially if he is suffering a grave mental disorder, such as schizophrenia—and he may thus lose the drift of the psychiatric interrogation. Should that happen, his answers become seemingly pointless, for he has lost any intelligible orientation regarding the inquiry and so his responses become relatively uninterpretable. Sullivan claimed that at the first interview it is often useful to inquire as to what brought him to the therapist; who advised it; and for what purpose. Suppose the patient answered that his father (who thought that there was something wrong with him) took him to see Dr. A., who referred him to Sullivan. The latter then asks, "And what made your father think that?" The patient answers that he does not know but his father said he was acting funny: he didn't want to go out of the house. The therapist then inquires if there has been any marked change in this connection. Did his now wanting to leave the house appear suddenly? "He guesses so, he hated to have people stare at him, so he stayed at home. Why did people stare at him [*not* "What made you think that people were staring at you?"—which would be thoroughly disorganizing to the direction of the inquiry]? He does not know—and is obviously keenly uncomfortable. Were they acquaintances or strangers? He rather morosely says he does not know. I comment, looking at him, that I see no reason why people should stare at him. In most cases, at this point, he will either show relief from tension or show suspicion of my good faith."[5]

The third preconception pertains to the form and manner of asking questions. A direct question in a psychiatric interrogation is not likely to provoke an informative answer. Leaving aside questions of good manners, it is a little like asking a business or professional associate directly, "Do you love your wife?" He may answer, "Yes," "No," "What?" or "Go to hell." One has learned nothing. In any case, people's abstract notions of "love," and of many other things, frequently have little practical relevance in their dealings with people. So when a psychiatrist interrogates a stranger, who happens to be a patient, trying to discover what sort of person he is, or at least to get "some idea" as to the characteristics of the patient, he will be sparing and cautious of direct interrogation. Unless, as in the illustration given above, it has a specific calculated purpose, he will avoid direct interrogation. Instead, he will tend to adopt a more indirect approach, which will be clarified later in this chapter. In essence he will, if he is skillful and lucky, elicit the information he wants by putting together and organizing the indicative statements that have been made to him by the patient in highly personal references, that is, references to his own experiences, not in abstract discussion. However, many of the statements volunteered by the patient require "testing by an inquiry into his supporting ideation." Suppose an informant says, "People stare at me because I am so ugly." Since, he is not, in fact, unattractive in appearance, the therapist (without denial or affirmation) must "uncover" the patient's views about his personal apperance. He may say something like, "Can you tell more about it?" or "I should like to hear more about it." So he learns that the patient's "significant ugliness" is due to a change that has recently taken place in his mouth, such that his lips have become Negroid. And therefore by such an indirect approach the therapist has learned something that is significant. His own conceptions of pulchritude are irrelevant.

The fourth preconception pertains to the general dynamic orientation in the interpretation of interpersonal relations. Whatever else they may—or may not—involve they assume the existence of various kinds of processes, qualities, and relations in human transactions. There is nothing static about personal experience and behavior. There are changes in "velocity" or changes in organization of the individual's relationships, that is, in his interpersonal relations. Some things change rapidly; others slowly. In the psychiatric interview the therapist must be alert to the possibilities of any of these changes occurring. If possible, he must quickly perceive them when they occur. For example, to some degree the organization of the interpersonal relationship changed when Sullivan said to the patient mentioned above that he saw no reason for people's staring at him. Some of the "parataxic elements" changed, which implies a degree of change in the interpersonal situation. The patient may have grown less tense because the therapist enfeebled a shadowy conviction that Sullivan was perceiving the alleged factor making for staring. Alternatively, he might have grown more tense—even less secure—if he suspected that the therapist was trying to deceive him. As Sullivan would say, if the therapist does not remain keenly alert, ready to observe subtle as well as gross changes, God pity the therapy.

The fifth preconception is that every person is much more simply human than unique, from which it follows that no matter "what ails the patient," he is mostly a person like the psychiatrist though he manifests certain significant differences. This assumption is said to imply that a great many of the techniques of interpersonal performances continue to be just as applicable in therapy as elsewhere. For example, if the patient who believed people were staring at him became suspicious of Sullivan's attitude, he would "discourage" the suspiciousness by "showing" irritation, communicated by a change of voice: the sort of response that might occur in a situation between acquaintances or professional colleagues except that a skilled therapist *does not feel* irritated or angry. The therapist does *not* say, "Aha! so you now distrust me"—which incidentally might carry overtones of condescension. In a less neutral and somewhat unfriendly manner, Sullivan might ask, "Perhaps you can say something about the staring?" Should this fail and an impasse is reached, the therapist adopts a new line of inquiry or a new approach. He does not fold his "psychic hands" and sit back.

A sixth preconception is this: In an indefinite, unstructured situation or field one accommodates to the patient's apparent prevailing tendencies. Thus, when the line of inquiry mentioned in the fifth preconception failed, the therapist accepted the fact that it was for the present ended. But though he has been defeated in this particular line of inquiry, at least for the time being, he must avoid any irrational reaction to the rebuff. He does not adopt an Olympian attitude of detachment, as if the whole incident were of no moment. Nor does he punish the patient by in effect telling him, "All right. Go stew in your own juice until I see you again." Instead, the therapist takes up a new line of inquiry, though he maintains the expression of irritation until he and the patient start "moving along" the new line of inquiry, that is, until the therapist has a "simple human reason for changing." An Olympian attitude of pseudodetachment might have been sensed as an imposture by the patient—and he will already have had perhaps a surfeit of innumerable impostures.

The seventh and last preconception mentioned in *Conceptions of Modern Psychiatry* pertains directly to the development of information about the self or self-system. *In general,* according to Sullivan, one cannot accomplish anything constructive in the interview by increasing a patient's anxiety. One must usually avoid questions and interpretations that arouse anxiety because, among other things, it provokes security operations that interfere with the growth of the patient's information and insight. Nevertheless, the psychiatrist must secure information that will lead to formulations that are of rather high probability of correctness. This statement implies that the patient must gain new insight into his interpersonal relations—which is a way of saying that he must gain insight into himself—because otherwise the therapist has no way of checking his hypotheses and interpretations. Unconfirmed interpretations are therapeutically useless. Thus the therapist facilitates the patient's seeking and acquiring new experience that will correct the deficiencies that occurred during the course of his acculturation. This seeking after corrective, educational experience both in and outside of therapy is a way of saying that the person strives to achieve the state of mental health despite previously acquired warps and handicaps.

In *Conceptions of Modern Psychiatry* Sullivan tends to give one the impression that one must carefully avoid therapeutic maneuvers that will arouse anxiety, or more anxiety, in the patient. Yet he clearly acknowledged in *Clinical Studies in Psychiatry* and elsewhere that at times the therapist deliberately offers anxiety-provoking interpretations, as we saw in Chapter 9. But these seem to be exceptions rather than the rule, and the therapist must be very clear about what he is doing and any possible risks involved. There is another and related point (which Maurice R. Green pointed out in a discussion with the writer). Sullivan knew that at times anxiety could serve a constructive function when it helped to "mobilize the patient," that is, prodded him into marshaling his resources for an attack on his problems, instead of, say, "acting out" or otherwise evading any constructive action. Even so, Sullivan seems to have thought that, in general, in therapy anxiety is a formidable enemy.

There are certain factors contributing to the success or failure of the interview that need to be emphasized. For example, the successful conversation between interviewer and interviewee establishes various "consensi." Sullivan claimed that the physician is able to arrive with the patient at an agreement as to the time order of events, as to sequent and consequent, as to cause and effect. There is a progressive enfeeblement of restraint on the patient's ability to make clear statements in consciousness of his unpleasant, embarrassing, or otherwise anxiety-laden statements. He gradually develops the freedom to communicate without the initial inhibiting restraints. From this interchange he gradually learns, among many other things, to substitute socially sanctioned or permissible behavior patterns for those that were enforced by anxiety and for those that were compelled by society's supervisions of his behavior. He may learn to "sublimate" impulses that "society" will not sanction. Thus, the patient who, in the course of the interview, becomes clearly conscious of an impulse whose direct manifestation would probably be disastrous may discover the possibility of finding partial or symbolic satisfactions. Still again, Sullivan says that it occurs to a patient who discovers that he has impulses that would be acceptable to only a few other people that he may "segregate his integrations" or confine his interpersonal relationships to suitable occasions and objects, while discharging the complicating resentments aroused by his individuation, perhaps in games.

In contrast, the goal of occasional treatment is generally alleviation rather than "radical cure," wherein the therapist must sometimes interfere with the growth of consciousness. A radical, prolonged treatment may not be feasible for a number of reasons—not least of which may be financial. For example, a forty-nine-year-old patient, in the face of a chronic disability, was sent to Sullivan for treatment because he was entertaining well-formulated suicidal intentions. This man suffered periods of insomnia that were connected with horrible dreams. His social life was markedly deteriorating. Though he had never engaged in sexual intimacies with women, he had until recently enjoyed their company but they were now becoming repugnant to him. Sullivan relates that on the night before the fourth conference the patient dreamt of "something like a wrestling match" during which the two men engaged in some mutual sexual performance. Moreover, this patient had recounted a somewhat related boyhood experience. But Sullivan carefully provided him with no opportunity to concern himself with thoughts of homosexuality as a part of the motivational structure of the horrible dreams, which were involved in the change in tenor of his life. The indications were said to be chiefly for the remedy of his increasing loneliness, which was undermining the value of his life. For this purpose Sullivan and his patient made a somewhat detailed study of the women who had once been appreciated, a few of whom, it "emerged," were still attractive. These were rather markedly "differentiated women." So a plan was formulated for *specific avoidances* rather than a blanket avoidance and aversion to all women. Presumably the tenor of the patient's life was considerably improved and the horrible and disgusting dreams were alleviated or ceased to occur.

Sullivan also claimed that an optimum performance with patients is not always desirable. In certain psychiatric or psychotherapeutic situations, the life situation of the patient forbids a frank communication of certain conclusions regarding his mental disorder. If the therapist has nothing that will be constructive to offer a patient in such circumstances, he realizes that it is futile, risky, or actually viciously irresponsible to undermine whatever security he has. "Not psychoanalysis alone but modern psychiatry as a whole provides destructively motivated people with peculiarly effective tools for doing harm."[6] However, Sullivan added that there is no valid question of danger in psychoanalytic treatment by a practitioner competent to handle the patient concerned.

The "results" or accomplishments of the interview are said to ensue partly from the interpretation of clearly documented facts, from the building of inferential bridges that carry one from particular concrete instances to a generalized formulation, and partly from considering alternative hypotheses regarding situations in which the patient has proferred misleading formulations. Sullivan discovered that there are a great many misunderstandings about interpretation of the data provided by the patient and about the role of inference. He claimed that psychiatrists, particularly some psychoanalysts, are, or used to be, prone to much interpretation of the material expressed by their patients. The abundance of interpretations was greatly in excess of the need for them. Moreover, an interpretation must never be forced on the patient. (This reminds one of a certain young psychology instructor whose enthusiam for Freudian psychology seems to have exceeded his intelligence, who used to inform his young female undergraduate students that they all suffered from penis envy; and when they protested in bafflement or outrage that they had always been quite content to be females, he explained to them that they had repressed their desires for a man's "most precious possession.")

Sullivan relates his experience with one of several patients with whom he worked and who had previously been treated by classical psychoanalysts. This particular patient had been complimented on the classical character of her "free associating" by her analyst, who "expounded to the patient the meaning of the uninterpretable content —often to the patient's astonishment, sometimes to her perturbation; but by and large, to her final conviction."[7] This analyst, with "charming naïveté," had thought that what was going on in his mind must have some validity for the patient. In contrast, Sullivan said he objected to her uncommunicative verbalizations during the interviews, insisting that while they doubtless had purpose and meaning, they in no way informed the patient or her therapist of anything concerned either in the patient's general difficulty in living, or on the current interpersonal situation. Thus, it was no wonder that the patient had previously failed to resolve some of her difficulties.

As previously noted in Chapter 1, Sullivan very early in his career learned that interpretation should be used sparingly and only under certain conditions. Nevertheless, he held that some interpretations are indispensable if one hopes to achieve therapeutic results in a reasonable length of time. "The first test for any interpretation should be as to its adequacy; does it cover the data to which it is applied? The second test should be as to its exclusiveness: are there other equally plausible hypotheses that cover the data?"[8] If there are, then there is no logical justification of the validity of the proposed interpretation and, in general, it should not be offered.[9] It is vital that the psychiatrist resist precocious conclusions, since almost any inference he may make regarding the patient's preferred communications is often acceptable, if it *does not* clarify the problem being dealt with. The psychiatrist's mistaken inference is not likely to stir up anxiety.

In order to emphasize the importance of interpretation that is as rigorous as the particular inquiry will permit and the necessity for controlled inferences, insofar as possible, Sullivan claimed that a great deal of many people's reverie processes are constituted of what he called "not-processes." Thus a patient may dwell a great deal "about what is not the case." The "not-process" is greatly tributary to a relative security when one realizes that anything *"is* but *one* thing, but is *not* an infinity of other things."[10] Therefore the patient has plenty of leeway to circumvent the *one* formula or statement that would be illuminating—and anxiety-provoking—by employing not-processes to contemplate or mull over innumerable formulations that have no bearing on his difficulty, and that do not arouse discomfort. Hence it is wise for the therapist to ensure, whenever possible, that all statements are offered in a positive, declarative form. "Not the one of a possible infinity of statements as to what the patient does not think, did not do, or does not feel; but the single statement of what he thinks, did, or feels."[11]

But even the positive statements by the patient are said to be usually misleading unless they pertain to a concrete course of relatively impersonal events. His most straightforward account of a conversation he has had with someone or some other interpersonal occurrence is likely to contain a number of parataxic distortions projected on the other persons who were involved. Many patients recite at length statements about the other person's thoughts, motives, and intentions in their accounts. The motives ascribed to others are said to be usually motives into which the patient has rudimentary insight in his own case. This makes his interpretations wholly unreliable. There is no way of knowing what degree of truth, if any, his interpretations have. It is their unquestioned acceptance by the patient that is significant. For his interpretations of other people's motives, without any question or doubt, constitute a significant feature of his own difficulties in interpersonal relations.

There are many other hindrances that arise in the interview. For example, a patient may discuss at great length, allegedly for the purpose of making something clear, while at the same time qualifying, his various statements to an extent that makes the lengthy talk utterly uncommunicative. A patient suffering substitutive disorders such as obsessional neurosis may take refuge in ostensible agreement with his therapist's statement of the actual facts of a situation, once he has grasped them, and then ignore it. "Yes; that is quite true," he may say, while he immediately dismisses the interpretation from his attention, thus asserting an omniscient control over the facts so as to render them unimportant. Sometimes, when patient and therapist reach a consensus, it is short-lived. As soon as the patient has left the psychiatrist's office, something "fatally contradictory" to the consensus may occur to him. In some instances, a patient will manifest a disintegrative process as he is about to leave. "Have we accomplished anything today, Doctor?" In this fashion the significance of the interview is minimized so that only the therapist's opinion seems to matter. Sullivan held that if such a stratagem is not countered, the patient "re-presses" anything significant derived from the interview into a sort of dreamlike vagueness, such that it is none of his business. A patient may also get bogged down with a preoccupation regarding what he *ought* to do. He may engage in a prolonged and wasteful discussion of willpower, choice, decision, free will. Such "productions," of course, get nowhere. Another possibility for wasteful, time-consuming verbalization occurs when a psychoanalyst instructs a certain type of patient "to say instantly every littlest thing that comes into his mind." This may provoke the patient to "charge off in autistic reverie" that serves no therapeutic purpose. Then the analyst may inform the patient that he interprets his behavior as narcissistic self-gratification—to which the latter may reply that he was told to say what comes to his mind and that is all he can do.

One of the perennial problems of psychoanalysis and related psychotherapies is the *"acting out* of troublesome motivations," which can temporarily or even permanently bring the work of therapy to a halt. This familiar occurrence may take place in therapy—as Freud observed long ago when some of his female patients became absorbed indefinitely with their tender feelings, ostensibly toward the therapist —or outside the therapy situation when the patient develops a passionate "love" for someone (usually) of the opposite sex. However, he is not conscious of the significance of his performances. Acting out may pertain to either positive or negative tendencies. When the therapist recognizes such activities, or "dramatizations," he offers his interpretation to the patient of what is going on, with the usual result, though it may take time, that the latter suppresses the activity and verbalizes his motivations. However, there are times when acting out can become a very complicated, even destructive affair. One should not confuse *acting out* with the *transference* of classical psychoanalysis. (Fromm-Reichmann interprets *acting out* as a special form of transference.)[12] In transference, the patient reenacts or relives his "repressed" motivations and experiences originally connected with his parents and/or other significant people in his relationship with his analyst. The patient "displaces" his buried and forgotten "infantile" wishes, drives, and the like to the analyst. This is accomplished chiefly through more or less appropriate vocalization and verbalization and it is not in essence an outright attempt to circumvent anxiety-provoking motivations aroused by the therapeutic situation. However, Sullivan thought that the "acting out" of classical psychoanalysis is an extension of typical, everyday behavior patterns. "Most patients have for years been acting out conflicts, substitutions, and compromises; the benefits of treatment come in large part from their learning to notice what they are doing, and this is greatly expedited by carefully validated verbal statements as to what seems to be going on."[13]

A general reader may begin to wonder what the therapist can reasonably expect the patient to do since he creates all sorts of "resistances." Sullivan asserted that there were three groups of performances that are within human ability, although most people have to learn to do them well. The first is said to be the *noticing of changes in one's body*: voice changes, molar movements, and increases or decreases of tension. The patient must learn to be alert to these matters if he is to discover the unrecognized components of behavior, including the wholly unnoticed actions, such as automatisms, operating in the service of dissociated tendencies. (It is by no means sufficient that the therapist can perceive these things.) Patients who are not specifically interested in noticing changes in somatic tension and in molar movements, Sullivan claims, will be very slow in gaining insight.

The second "collaborative effort" one may reasonably ask for is the *noticing of marginal thoughts*. This is more or less analogous to what an instructor does when he lectures to a class: his "auditor" remains alert to what he is saying and how well he is saying it, whether the lecture seems to be "getting across" to the students or whether he is apparently engaging in a long soliloquy. However, the analogy is imperfect because it is the patient's marginal thoughts occurring during his recital of something or other that are the more useful for the growth of insight. In other words, he may often become intent on telling something to the therapist. His narrative may proceed with difficulty, owing to disturbing marginal thoughts that are threatening to the self, or it may proceed more and more smoothly because of their complex exclusion from consciousness by the self. In either case, it is the marginal processes, whether immediately accessible or not, that matter most because they often provide important data about the patient when they are "exteriorized."

The third possibility of colllaboration is said to be the *prompt statement of all that comes to mind*. As we saw in the discussion in Chapter 5, this is, in general, no easy task. The patient has to learn to trust the therapist and have enough confidence in the therapeutic situation to be able to express the thoughts and feelings that it provokes. Until the patient gains insight into at least one of the parataxic processes, or illusory me-you patterns, that the interpersonal situation provokes, prompt expression of the inner experiences is often an extraordinarily difficult achievement. Until this first great milestone is reached the patient may be bedeviled by all sorts of embarrassing, troublesome, or seemingly irrelevant thoughts and fantasies. He may experience waves of obscenities, distressing recollections of most regrettable past performances, and obsessively offensive thoughts and fantasies about the therapist. False reports may well up in his mind and press for utterance. One may find, or expect to find, almost any thing that is difficult to say, or any idea that seems impossible to verbalize. Sometimes the patient's mind may become "a blank" and he may lapse into a lengthy silence when the therapist does not intervene. Because of such occurrences patients seek relief from the turmoil of thoughts, fantasies, feelings, impulses, that may bedevil them, in a flow of autistic reverie or a circumstantial account of some insignificant current event, or an extravagant report of the marvelous benefits they have already—in some mysterious fashion—obtained by exposure to the psychiatrist or psychotherapist.

An illustration of how a tentative integration may evolve into a firm and reliable collaboration, despite the occasional or sometimes prolonged turmoil of "free association" (once the patient gains some initial insights) is the following. A patient consulted Sullivan because, according to her story, she had to divorce her husband. Naturally Sullivan asked why she was consulting him instead of an attorney. What did she expect from him? As it turned out, this lady was well acquainted with psychiatry. For some time, "when she had been in the throes of indecision" about marrying her husband, she had already been under treatment with another therapist. Sullivan then inquired as to the necessity for getting a divorce; and to his "growing astonishment" learned more and more about the husband's virtues and perfections. But, according to the patient, she had a feeling that her husband interfered with her self-realization. Since she was unable to provide any clues as to the alleged interference Sullivan concluded there was a psychiatric problem involved, and he undertook to discover the facts underlying the patient's situation.

After some three hundred interviews, though he had learned a great deal, he had achieved no certainty about its reliability. Though a great deal of the information obtained was consistent and possibly true, it could also have been a tissue of complex misinterpretation and falsification. For example, very soon after the inquiry began, the patient told Sullivan that she was puzzled because, though she had always heard that mental disorders arose from an unhappy childhood, she enjoyed a childhood that was extraordinarily free from unpleasant incidents. Moreover, she provided considerable "documentation" of her happiness as a child. But when the truth was finally discovered, it turned out that the patient's childhood "had been swamped in amnesia." And its ultimate revelation showed that it had been appalling. The "childhood" that the patient could easily recall was a "serial story" with which she had compensated herself in order to alleviate the pain she suffered in a desolatingly unsatisfactory home.

One day, around the three-hundreth hour of treatment, the patient arrived and came into Sullivan's office in "a peculiar state of agitation." She informed him that she was overwhelmed to discover that he looked quite different from the way she had previously "perceived" him: as a fat old man with white hair (Sullivan was of slender build, with reddish hair, and at the time of this incident was probably in his early or middle forties). This is, of course, an extreme illustration of a parataxic distortion in a treatment situation. Usually such distortions are more subtle and deceptive. In any case, the fat, white-haired old man was "derived" from a personage in her past life. Moreover, the "significant attributes" she perceived in or attributed to her physician were also derived from, or peculiar to, the old man whom she had once known. These things occurred despite the therapist's diligent efforts to avoid misinterpretations and to detect parataxic concomitants. It was only when the patient became conscious of these illusory me-you patterns that the "grandfatherly figure" could be located in his appropriate place in her career. Only then could she become conscious of "something" of his role in her development as the now-accessible discrepancies between her therapist's actual performances and her misconceptions about them became clear and "indicative." With the birth of such insights the therapeutic situation then "lost its tentative quality and became productive of durable results."

Thus Sullivan claimed that until a patient has seen clearly and unmistakably a concrete example of the way in which unresolved situations from the distant past color the perception of present situations and overcomplicate action in them, there can be no material reorganization of personality, no therapeutically satisfactory expansion of the self, no significant insight into the complexities of one's performances or into the unexpected and often disconcerting behavior of others concerned. Until a patient has achieved such an initial insight, there is nothing significantly unique in the treatment situation. Subsequent to that point, the treatment situation becomes one of unprecedented freedom from restraints on the manifestation of constructive impulses. However, this is a gradual affair. There will be recurrences of difficulties, especially when the patient is seriously disordered. Still, a demonstration of what the treatment situation, such as the one illustrated above, can accomplish may provide the confidence and resolution necessary to carry through a long and often harrowing therapeutic endeavor. The accumulating, growing insights bring about a gradual modification of the self-dynamism. Meanwhile the patient is learning that more security may come from *abandoning* a complex security-seeking process than could ever be achieved by it—which in itself adds to one's security and provides further warrant for confronting other anxiety-provoking situations in order to discover what it is that is so threatening about them. In this fashion Sullivan's formula—*that one "achieves mental health to the extent that one becomes aware of one's interpersonal relations"*—becomes really significant to the patient, perhaps especially when he gets discouraged, seemingly forever groping through endless dark alleys of the mind.

Sullivan's formula of the nature of curative change remains a source of insecurity for the patient for a long time, since he "prehends" it as an attack on the core of his personality. It forever denies the ultimate usefulness of the suppressive, the selectively inattending, and the dissociating functions of the self-dynamism. Not for a long time will the patient be able to understand it in recognizable form. "If the patient could seize even the most superficial of its implications, he would take it to mean that one could not make any progress without abandoning the hope of feeling secure in dealing with others."[14] Even if he could, he would never contemplate such a prospect.

Since patients ask questions, as they do for a variety of causes, the physician or therapist in providing an answer has to bear two considerations in mind: (1) the long-range probabilities about the outcome of the treatment, and (2) the immediate situation or phase of treatment and its characteristics. The goal of the treatment, which of course entails the ultimate complete resolution of the patient-therapist relationship, dictates the gradual development of valid insights by the patient into the nature of his personality make-up, the kinds of interpersonal relations that will foster satisfactions, maintain or enhance self-esteem, and support a forward-looking, confident outlook on life. There is a "maturation" of personality to the level at which the person has developed an ability for adult interpersonal relations. In regard to the end or final goal of treatment, the formula mentioned above is offered in succinct form whenever there are no insuperable barriers to that end. Since the momentary present state may be part of an extremely complex parataxic situation, it may demand a great variety of actions or therapeutic maneuvers, a few of which were illustrated in Chapter 9. But in every instance the long-term goal must not be ignored. It is the guiding, controlling orientation from the beginning to the end of therapy, and if it is relinquished, neither physician nor patient can make sense of what they are doing, for no human activity is intelligible if it has no end, however dimly forseen.

At this point in the exposition, a brief summary of the steps which are taken, by means of which the goals of therapy are sought, may be helpful for the general reader. The first effective step that the patient accomplishes in the solution of any problem occurs when he is able to grasp the relevant factors in a "problem-situation" in which he is involved. Usually a *release of alertness* from the inhibiting functions of the self-dynamism is necessary. For example, the release of one's alertness may enable one to become conscious of dissociated impulses that are significant explanatory factors in the clarification of some problem situation in which one is involved. "Repressed," vaguely remembered factors operative in a situation also may be revealed as significant determinants, or suppressive efforts amounting to a "deletion" or clouding of consciousness at some crucial phase of the development of the problem situation may be uncovered. The therapist facilitates the patient's learning how to become conscious of previously unnoticed influences that "cause" interpersonal difficulties by "training" the latter to understand the particular pattern of maladjustive activities he manifests. The understanding is provided in terms of the explanatory conceptions Sullivan had worked out, many of which have been outlined in previous chapters of this book. This learning usually starts from trifling instances rather than from insight into profoundly disturbing, anxiety-provoking occurrences. The intrusion of apparently insnginficant, "accidental" events in the fabric of the patient's daily life or his remembered dreams of rather simple context may provide the psychiatrist with the opportunity to assist in the learning by relatively simple forms of interpretation. For example, he "says something calculated to center attention on the momentary situation, recites in essential outline the course of the significant event as he has heard it, and perhaps asks if there can be something important that was omitted from the account, or if the action could have been meant to have such and such an effect, or if some detail can be recalled that would indicate that such and such an unrecognized end was being pursued."[15] Sullivan adds that in another sort of this apparently insignificant event, he may intervene only to ask, while stressing the importance of the matter by preferably non-verbal, perhaps intonational means, as to how the patient could have been conscious of the motivation of the other person concerned, or what the evidence may be that justifies the assumption that such and such is a durable characteristic of the other person.

As the alertness of the patient becomes less and less circumscribed by the weakening of inhibitory operations of the self, as consciousness of one's experience-and-behavior-patterns expands in range and depth, a time is reached when the patient can *identify* at least one of the parataxic distortions that have for many years "complicated" and confused his perceptions and cognitions of significant other people. (One should bear in mind that this is not a purely intellectualistic affair. The patient's emotions, motivations, attitudes, are, so to speak, tied in with his perceptions and cognitions.) Again, at this stage, it will usually be a quite seemingly insignificant, mildly irrelevant remark, at least at first hearing, that communicates *to the patient* his distorted formulation of the psychiatrist. The patient hears himself say something to and/or about the therapist that sounds off key. Here again the latter's "interpretation" usually facilitates the dawning consciousness of the patient, often by merely an interrupting, seriously expressed question as to what the patient has just expressed. The therapist may recite a repetition of the patient's statement in essential outline. He may inquire about its implication in relation to the psychiatrist or he may ask about the foundation or evidence for the expressed belief. This is perhaps not different in essence from what happens when one rereads a letter he has received to a friend and discovers (perhaps with the aid of a question or two from the latter) that he originally misread the letter by misinterpreting its substance or intent.

The first conscious awareness of "a parataxically illusory personal characterization," that is, of an illusory or distorted me-you pattern, is said to begin the therapeutic process connected with it, as in the instance of the patient who perceived her therapist as a fat, white-haired old man. To be sure, parataxic distortions are usually not that gross, as we have seen in previous chapters. The discovery of a parataxic distortion at first brings a sharp fall in one's level of security; indeed, one may become intensely anxious. One seems to have made a disturbing "mistake"; or a strange and very disquieting "misapprehension" on the therapist's part has somehow occurred. The patient becomes apprehensive, believing that the psychiatrist is annoyed or disappointed, or that his appraisal of him must be unfavorable. If one bears in mind that the patient's self-esteem—his interpersonal security—is often fragile or at least infirm, then the disturbing consciousness of the "mistake" tends to arouse essentially disintegrative, distance-producing security operations. In fact, his efforts at explaining away ("rationalizing") the occurrence as a "mistake" or "misapprehension" in the intercommunicative process is itself a disintegrative security operation. And from Sullivan's point of view, the therapist must step in and counter the disintegrative operation. Naturally one takes into account the type of patient one is dealing with, the severity of his disorder, the stage of therapy reached, and the like. At an early phase of therapy (or at any phase, really), the psychiatrist must not sit back and allow his patient to flounder in embarrassment and misery. So what does he do? One of the things he does *not* do is to try to offer reassurance in terms of his real characteristics. He does *not* say something like: "I can prove that I am not the sadistic son of a bitch you seem to believe I am." Such a maneuevre would *increase* the insecurity of the patient for it implies there was a "mistake" or "misapprehension," which the physician accepts at face value. After having proceeded to clarify the gross outlines of the expressed parataxic distortion, he then makes some such statement as the following: "This impression that you have had about me must have a history, must be the recollection of some such person who was once really important to you—perhaps you can recall someone. Let us listen to whatever comes to mind." Frequently, in the first instance of this kind, though the patient silently, as it were, searches his memory, he can recall no one. Nevertheless, the interpretation, at the very least, will have enabled him to regain security as well as useful information about the sources or conditions of parataxic distortions.

But suppose that the patient does recall the "historic, personal source," the significant other (or others), who possessed, to some approximate degree, the characteristics ascribed to the physician as revealed by the parataxic distortion. Will the "parataxis" then disappear? The answer is no. It would be very psychologically naïve to expect a motivational pattern or a characteristic behavior pattern to dissolve like a soap bubble in one blinding flash of insight. Or, to put this matter another way, it would be dangerously foolish to expect that some fairly sudden insight can immediately alter the structure and functional activity of the self-system. Before a significant change of the self can occur there is probably always a good deal of prepreparation extending over a period of time, with much tentative testing in the real, interpersonal world, or in fantasy or in both. Nevertheless —unless as sometimes happens an even more complex parataxic distortion develops—a truly remarkable and promising thing in the course of the interview does occur. What occurs is insight, as previously described, into the "actual fact of illusory, parataxic distortions" that complicate or undermine the patient's interpersonal relations: the first therapeutic milestone.

Each recurrent recognition of a particular parataxic distortion of the physician is said to bring with it more data as to its historic personal source. There comes a time during the course of therapy at which the patient can vividly recall a series of highly significant occurrences that took place in his interpersonal relations with this person. Gradually this recall expands or generalizes into a more comprehensive, inclusive insight. This comprehensive insight embraces, first, the consequences to the patient of the earlier relationship—that with mother and/or father is a classical instance—on the subsequent course of his dealings with others, including the formulation of ideals of conduct he learned and the relatively fixed valuational judgments of behavior he acquired.

In addition, insights gradually gained into the less obviously interpersonal consequences of the former relationship, which may range from, say, one's failure to finish high school or college, to one's persistent refusal to accept responsibility of any sort, to one's inability to choose an attractive suit or dress when one ventures into a famous department store, to one's overindulgence in alcohol, may also ensue from one's expanded conscious awareness. Such less obviously inter-personal consequences of the former relationship may ramify enor-mously and often enter subtly into the life pattern to which one has adhered for many years.

Insight into direct symbolic "associations" made at the time when the former significant relationship existed also follow from the com-prehensive and growing knowledge of self. Such "associations," if they occurred in connection with a parent during the early years, may also be wide in range and quality. Some of these associations may be conscious, whether "consensually validated" or not; some may have been previously unformulated. Here again the difference between the associations of a normal person and those of some one who suffers a mental disorder differ only in degree—though this difference is usually enormously important for the subsequent fate of the individ-ual concerned. Those readers of this book who are psychiatrists or clinical psychologists will need no illustrations. Perhaps the general reader, unless he wishes to read psychiatric works, may grasp the essential point if he will compare the associations of Dedalus and Bloom in Joyce's *Ulysses* or the marvelous imaginative landscape of associations in Proust's *Remembrance of Things Past.* Of course, the "associations" formed in early and late childhood with significant others are to a large degree governed by one's particular family back-ground. The "associations" of a youngster learned in interaction with his parents, who grows up in Scarsdale, will be vastly different from those of someone who has lived all his early years on a farm or in a small town in, say, the rural South of yesteryear. (Consider the as-sociations of Thomas Wolf's characters in *Look Homeward Angel* and other of his novels, or those of Richard Wright's in *Black Boy,* with those of Harper Lee's *To Kill A Mockingbird.* Younger readers may prefer such novelists as James Baldwin or Saul Bellows.) Equally im-portant in this connection, perhaps, are social class differences of patients.

Finally, as a result of more or less cumulative and comprehensive insights there comes a clarification of "more obscure resymboliza-tions, substitutions, and symptomatic and related actions" that origi-nated in, or occurred in subsequent relation to, the significant relationship. These matters were explicated in the previous discus-sion in Chapters 9 and 10 of obsessionalism, schizophrenia, and the like.

As these "complex remainders" of previous unresolved motivational predispositions, attitudes, and interests "expand into easily understood meaning" the patient generally undergoes much unpleasant emotion. He may bitterly regret the frequently more or less wasted years that he now realizes "stemmed" from the early experiences.

Sullivan held that in the course of identifying all the more parataxically "surviving," unresolved situations of the patient's past, and their consequent dissolutions, there progressively occurs an expanding of the self to the extent that the patient as known to himself is much the same person as the patient behaving with others. Sullivan called this psychiatric cure. It is not clear who would determine this—presumably, though not necessarily, his psychiatrist. Janis, Mahl, Kagan, and Holt provide an excellent summary of personality assessment, which may help to answer the questions of more critical readers.[16] *As a practical matter,* this need not be a grave problem since probably almost every competent, experienced psychiatrist, as a rule, has a pretty good idea when his patients' major personal problems have been resolved. Beyond that, regardless of his personal philosophy, he has no justification for dictating his patient's future course. Of course there have been psychotherapists who like to play God or at least His minister. Obviously these people have missed their calling.

Given a psychiatric cure, there may remain, according to Sullivan, a need for a great deal of experience and education before one progresses to a *social cure.* A social cure "implies" a more abundant life in a community. But it may not be possible to achieve a collaboration with others in the particular community in which one has lived. It may be rich in material goods but squalid in human relations. Sometimes a community is neither rich nor very poor; its members may live out their lives on a deadening level of mediocrity. (Consider the type of community described in *Madame Bovary.*) Or if one lives in a huge metropolis, such as that of New York City, with its ever shifting populations, its celebrated social mobility, its raucous, nervous excitement, its impersonality, one may be forced to live as a stranger in the "English basement" of a small brownstone house. Even so, even if a change of social setting is impractical, Sullivan thought that "adequate mediate relationships" (as in games, sports, hobbies, such as amateur astronomy and radio communications, etc.) and clearly understood reformulations of some of one's interpersonal goals (as in some instances where a dearly wanted marriage and family life cannot be secured and one aims at a career in business or the professions) must "fill the gaps." Whether one achieves social cure or not, Sullivan held that the person who knows himself has mental health. The latter is said to be content with his utilization of the opportunities that come to him, valuing himself as his conduct merits, knowing and mostly obtaining the satisfactions he needs. And "he is greatly secure."[17]

It is hoped that the previous discussion in this chapter will serve as a firm background for a review of *The Psychiatric Interview.* This enormously influential book is based, in part, on two lecture series delivered in 1944 and 1945; in part, on three lectures of a lecture series delivered in 1946–1947. But before I begin a review of the main ideas in *The Psychiatric Interview,* I wish to restate Sullivan's characterizations of thereapeutic conferences. He asserted that all therapeutic conferences are made up of various patterns that can be classified as five types of process. There are, first, occurrences that clarify the immediate interpersonal relationship, such as those that bring about the revelation of parataxic distortions or illusory personifications. Second, there are processes that clarify the patient's actions in some recent interpersonal situation. Such actions may pertain to someone with whom the patient sustains a relatively lasting relationship often discussed in the interviews such as a friend, relative, or boss. Third, in the interview, there are processes, such as thoughts and fantasies, that revert from immediately present and current situations to "relevant" situations im the patient's more remote past. These processes may arise in "free association" or they may occur from more deliberate, directed effort due to the questioning or other prompting of the therapist (for example, "That seems to remind me of something or other you mentioned when you talked about the summers you spent with your Aunt Jane as a child"). Fourth, there are processes in which the patient attempts by means of constructive fantasy to gauge the future consequences of certain aspects of current situations. In other words, one explores in imagination what certain contemporary happenings may lead to in the future. Although Sullivan is not explicit, he seems to mean that the fantasy or "reverie" process is expressed verbally so that the therapist may be able to grasp what is "going on." (A great deal of constructive reverie often occurs *outside* the formal therapeutic situation. Otherwise, if the patient suffers a serious mental disorder, the work of formal therapy is likely to be very limited. Intensive psychotherapy often entails a reconstruction of a very great deal of experience that the person has had perhaps often over a period of twenty or thirty years or longer. With the reconstruction come modification, exploration, discovery, resynthesis, re-creation, and, as a result, perhaps a gradually and radically altered way of life. The time, energy, and effort required for such a task is enormous and superbly difficult. Obviously not every patient has the resources for such an undertaking even if he has what old-fashioned people call the will to attempt it.) Finally there are processes demanded or evoked by some one of numerous possible crisis situations, which occur in or outside of the therapeutic situation.

In the Introduction to *The Psychiatric Interview,* Otto A. Will, Jr., has pointed out that "interview" does not merely designate a certain fixed period of time, but rather a course of interpersonal processes that may be encompassed to some degree in a single conference of sixty or ninety minutes' duration, or developed to a greater extent during the course of several meetings, or elaborated in the many sessions of intensive psychotherapy. However, the essential characteristics and "movements" or activities of the more prolonged or protracted therapy, he thinks, are contained in a single psychiatric interview. Sullivan himself has said or implied this very same thing, leaving the distinction between a particular interview and a protracted series of interviews extending over a period of months or years blurred. Yet it seems doubtful that a single interview could contain all the essential characteristics and occurrences of prolonged intensive psychotherapy as outlined in *The Psychiatric Interview.* The lectures contained in that book chiefly pertain to intensive psychotherapy. To say that the latter has a beginning, a middle, and an end would be an oversimplification. But it very clearly has a beginning, not merely in the temporal sense, but also in the sense that in the early or starting phases, one employs typical procedures that are gradually modified or replaced as the work proceeds. It also clearly has an end, again not in the merely temporal sense (which would be a mere terminus), but also in the sense that, under more or less optimum conditions, the patient has reached a point at which he knows himself well, whether he has been able to resolve all his major difficulties or not. (He may have learned that because of circumstances beyond his control he will never be able to attain optimum security and optimum mental health.) There is a gradual development through various phases, often hindered by "re-sistances" (security operations) or other hindrances within the formal therapeutic situation, or by circumstances external to it. Sullivan, as we have seen, has stated that every particular interview is controlled by the long-range goal of intensive psychotherapy. Hence the particular interview gradually becomes modified, in varying degrees, as the work progresses. That is why Sullivan in his "A Study of Personality" in *Personal Psychopathology* and in *The Psychiatric Interview* distinguishes various stages in the interview process. The division into various phases is no mere pedagogical device. Such an interpretation does not rule out the "open-endedness" of a given interview. As Dr. Will puts it, questions and answers about the interpersonal "field" or interview situation cannot be conclusive, final, and in all ways precise. "They *can* be suggestive, provocative, and useful," he says, "in guiding further inquiry as one participates in and moves along with the process under study." Or, to reiterate a point previously discussed, as Sullivan says in *Conceptions of Modern Psychiatry,* the physician is guided in his response [to questions from the patient] by two considerations: the long-range probabilities about the situation, and the immediate phase of the treatment.[18] So the interview has a beginning, a course of inquiry, and a termination. Many of the basic concepts and assumptions that Sullivan employed in the psychiatric interview have been stated or implied in this and in previous chapters. The field or subject matter of psychiatry is the study of interpersonal relations. This study is carried out primarily by means of the interview situation whether the latter be confined to one or two conferences or extend over a period of years, during most of which time conferences may be held one or twice or five times per week. The role of the therapist is that of a participant observer in a situation created between the observer and his subject, that is, the patient, client, interviewee, or whatever. Sullivan conceived of the interview as a situation con-stituted chiefly of vocal communication in a two-group, more or less voluntarily integrated. That is, some patients actively, deliberately seek treatment, others consent to go into therapy because of pressure put upon them, perhaps by relatives, and still others, particularly patients in mental hospitals, may be more or less compelled to enter into an at least incipient psychiatric interview, though they cannot be compelled to cooperate. It often takes considerable skill, patience, and compassion for a psychiatrist to convince a schizophrenic patient that he might benefit from participation in an interview.

The rationale of the interview is based on a progressively unfolding expert-client (therapist-patient) relationship for the purpose of discovering the client's characteristic patterns of living. The psychiatrist, or expert student of interpersonal relations, seeks to discover those (frequently obscure) patterns of living of the patient that he experiences as particularly troublesome as well as those he experiences as particularly valuable. At some time, perhaps at the beginning, perhaps not for many months, the patient expects to derive benefit, to resolve some or all of his major difficulties in living, from the revelation of his typical ways of life, especially his characteristic interpersonal relationships, which have been molded by his past experiences. Personality is said to demonstrate very strikingly in every situation the perduring effects of the past. The consequences of a particular past occurrence, whether fortunate or unfortunate, may also be extensively intertwined with the consequences of a great many other past events. An indefinitely great deal of what we were and what we experienced though modified and usually elaborated in the course of time, enters into our present behavior and future outlook. For example, childhood is normally vastly different from infancy, but the former does not literally replace the latter. Childhood is the outcome of a continuous modification (due to maturation and experience) of infancy. The continuum is not merely temporal; it is "organic." Every step in personality development normally entails a modification of what one previously experienced and an "elaboration" of new experience such that the next stop contains both elements of the old and of the new in an emergent functional unity. Thus the modification is never so total, so "absolute," that the continuities (intelligence, temperament, emotional and motivational patterns, overt behavior patterns, etc.) in personality become utterly transformed, though often modifications become so great that they ordinarily cease to be recognizable in the ceaseless stream of activity from birth to death. (However, many things do disappear from what Watson called the Life Chart over a period of time.) Change in personality is more or less cumulative, but the form, pattern, organization, of the self-conscious personality, or self-system, as it is manifested in interpersonal relations, tends to endure, and can be radically altered only by great and prolonged effort or by catastrophic experiences.

On the other hand, even fixations or "arrests of development," whether they are manifested in the self-system or partly buried in the dissociated system, do not remain entirely "static." They change, however, slowly.

So when the therapist seeks to discover "what *ails* a person's living," he must, as best he can, learn what sort of person it is who is doing the living, what his personal history is, with whom he is doing the living, and, ideally, what the latters' personal histories are also. Needless to say, as Sullivan might put it, there are often limitations in the way of such an enterprise, especially in regard to those other people who were significant in the patient's life. In general, as we have seen, Sullivan taught that if the therapist is to understand his patient's problems, he must understand him in his dealings with people. Moreover, the patient also has to learn in the course of therapy that his difficulties have to do with his dealings and experiences with others. Still again one must keep in mind that any person's relations and dealings with others have a temporal dimension. All these things have been stated and examined from various angles throughout this book. In essence these are the themes of Sullivanian psychiatry, though their ramifications are profound and often subtle.

The reader will have noted that the interview situation is constituted primarily by vocal, not merely *verbal*, communication. Many people, including some patients, are expert at *concealing* their thoughts, emotions, the character of their interactions, by means of verbal performances. Therefore the psychiatrist or therapist will be wise to pay close attention to "the telltale aspects" of intonation, pronunciation, rate of speech, difficulty in enunciation. In his study of schizophrenics, Sullivan also learned to pay close attention to nonvocal gestures, physical postures of various kinds, the general demeanor of the patient, his characteristic style of walking. He taught that it is by alertness to the importance of all these things as signs or indicators of meaning rather than by exclusive attention only with words spoken that the psychiatric interview becomes efficacious and practical.

However, at certain times, as we have already seen, the psychiatrist, according to Sullivan, should play a very active role in introducing interrogations in order to make sure that he understands what he is being told. And so, during a given interview or early in a particular interview, he would ask "stupid questions." Even though the patient was telling him "the obvious," he could not, or did not, understand, and proceeded to ask further questions. At first, the patient would be annoyed, but after half an hour or so, he would begin to catch on to the fact that there was a reasonable uncertainty about what he meant. He would begin to realize that assertions he made, which seemed "obvious" in meaning, were remarkably uncommunicative. There are said to be few things that do the patient more good in the way of getting toward his more or less clearly formulated desire to benefit from the inquiry than this very care by the interviewer to discover exactly what the client means. Sullivan claimed that almost every time one asks, "Well, do you mean so and so?" the patient becomes a little clearer on what he does mean. "And what a relief it is to him to discover that his true meaning is anything but what he at first says, and that he is at long last uncovering some conventional self-deception that he has been pulling on himself for years."[19]

Furthermore this "dumb" questioning may save the inexperienced interviewer from assuming that he knows something that is not so. If he does make such an assumption, he will discover only belatedly that he has been meandering on a path of private fantasy that could not pertain to what the patient was talking about since the latter, meanwhile, has begun to talk about something that has no connection with what the psychiatrist believed he had been talking about. A part of the interviewer's skill comes from a sort of quiet and constant self-questioning about what he hears: "Does this sentence, this statement, have an unquestionable meaning? Is there any certainty as to what this person means?" Thus success in psychotherapy results, *in part,* from an ever-increasing clarity and precision of intercommunication. The interview situation is a special instance of an interpersonal situation as characterized in previous chapters. It is said to be brought into being by, held together by, and in the course of events, to a certain extent, determined by, *something* in the two people which is *reciprocal,* the manifestations of which coincide approximately in time. The series of interview situations are *"integrated by coincident reciprocal motivation"* of therapist and client. Hence the interviewer, in the very nature of the case, cannot be a detached observer. There is no interview, in the psychiatric sense, *until* he becomes a participant observer. At the same time, he must be eternally alert to the manner in which he is participating. Otherwise he will not understand what he is doing.

It is the interpersonal (reciprocal) processes and the pattern of their course that "generate the data of the interview." The participant observer or interviewer is said to experience the ways in which the interpersonal processes follow one another, what seeming relationships they have to one another, what striking inconsistencies occur, the apparent gaps in the patient's account of something or other, the pauses, short or long, the changes in vocal expression, and the like. "Thus the data of the interview may come, not so much from the answers to questions, but from timing and stress of what was said, the slight misunderstandings here and there, the occasions when the interviewee got off the subject, perhaps volunteering very important facts which had not been asked for, and so on."[20] The interviewer must "watch the course of events," noting how they, as a pattern of ongoing processes, reveal a very wide field of data about the patient. The data have to be interpreted and validated in the progressive course of the interview, inferences have to be drawn from various "facts" or factual statements that have been elicited, and perhaps new lines of inquiry opened up. But the interviewer has nothing with which to begin until he has, by means of participant observation, acquired the information he needs to pursue the inquiry, which is at the same time a continuing therapeutic process or pattern of processes.

As we noted in Chapter 5, Sullivan asserted that the all but inevitable extreme obscurity of the processes early in the interview and the continuing complexity of so many of those processes constituting its course make it extremely useful to be unobtrusively methodical, as well as constantly alert. "In other words, the interviewer is quite clearly aware of the type of significant data that he may reasonably expect in different phases of the interview; he takes steps to secure these data; he validates, or marks for subsequent validation, anything which seems needlessly indefinite or improbable; and he notes most carefully any occasion when material reasonably to be expected *has not* come forth."[21]

For such reasons Sullivan discovered that he could very usefully distinguish four stages in the interview process: (1) *the formal inception;* (2) *the reconnaissance;* (3) *the detailed inquiry;* and (4) *the termination of treatment,* at which point the patient will, if all has in the long run gone well, have achieved psychiatric cure. While each of these stages will be summarized at some length later on in this chapter, they may already suggest to the reader that Sullivan has made still more profound changes in the classical "method" of psychoanalysis he first learned and briefly adopted. He taught that because of the sometimes "impossible complexity" of relations with a comparatively unknown other person it is wise for the interviewer to ingrain in himself an outline of the ways in which the four steps can be taken, while developing patterns of action that will work so effectively and so unnoticed that he will not have to take time out to consider what the next step is to be.

But no outline of therapeutic stages can anticipate the variations—the combinations and permutations of personality factors—that may occur in a personal relationship with a stranger. So he must also be alert for any clues that something unexpected has happened. For it is the *novelties* that appear in an inconspicuously methodical investigation that are said to be the things that distinguish its results. What Sullivan is in effect saying is that every patient is unique and his pattern of difficulties will never be identical with anyone else's. Therefore one must not attempt a mechanical application of his techniques. This is a recognition of what he once called the infinite individuality of nature, including human nature, however conceived. In other words, the psychiatrist is always dealing with patterns of probabilities that appear among the infinite diversities of human life. Thus among the most significant characteristics in the course of processes constituting an interview are the absences of these very processes that all or most of the therapist's previous experience had led him to anticipate. Or the patient may have provided him with information regarding the course of his development, or some phase of his development, whether normal or otherwise, that would lead the interviewer, as a result of all that he has learned, to anticipate that certain other things will have happened. But the patient's account on certain occasions, does not reveal that the expected sequence did occur. Its absence however may be highly revealing. In any event, it may be far too promising to overlook or forget.

Sullivan maintained that the psychiatrist should notice any points at which the patient seems to have no grasp on things that the psychiatrist regards as necessary or important in life, (such as preadolescent intimacy) or in the patient's work (say, cooperation with others). At such points the psychiatrist should offer some hints as to what the information concerning what he wants to discover may be in order to determine whether or not it is lacking. A simple clear comment about what he wants to know may enable the patient to catch on to long streams of implications because there are many people who require only a hint in order to get the point: (For example, "come to think of it, I have been wondering if your wife was your first love").

Throughout, the importance of alertness of the psychiatrist as a participant observer has been stressed. But he must be at all times conscious of the fact that the therapeutic situation is a performance of two people, a transaction, in which the patient's behavior and what he says and does are adjusted, in accordance with the best of his information and ability, to what he guesses or surmises about the therapist. Correspondingly the therapist's comments, questions, remarks, innuendoes, and the like are said to be effective to the degree that he is conscious of the patient's attitude toward him, and also of all that he has learned, at a particular phase in therapy, of the patient's background, his experience, and what sort of person he is. At the same time, as the interview proceeds, the psychiatric interviewer is considering, studying, what the patient could or might mean by what he is saying, how he himself can best formulate what he wishes to communicate to the interviewee while still "observing" and bearing in mind the general pattern of the processes being communicated or discussed.

At the start of the interview situation, or as soon as possible, the therapist must "structure" the situation. In essence this means that both therapist and patient must arrive at an agreement on the overall goal, the end or inclusive "purpose" of the therapy. According to Sullivan, the role of the psychiatrist as an expert in the intricacies of interpersonal relations is due to cultural definition. In other words, society teaches the would-be client that the interviewer is an expert in the field of interpersonal relations, not in surgery, not in how to make enough money to live comfortably while sitting at home with a telephone to communicate with a clever stock broker, nor in any of the thousands of ingenious ways that an "affluent society" enables people to acquire income, prestige, and deference. Therefore Sullivan held that what the patient is taught to expect is the thing he should get. Or if the psychiatrist should effect any variation from it or any departure from it, he should do so in a carefully arranged way. In a humorous fashion, Sullivan gave the illustration of a patient who comes to a psychiatrist in order to learn how to satisfy his thirst for contentment. But the therapist may believe it would be a great thing for the patient to learn how to make a living. According to the cultural role of the psychiatrist, it is permissible for the latter to "wean him from his interest in contentment" and induce him to develop an interest in making a living. But one must take into account the fact that the patient wants—or believes he wants—to know how to gain contentment. (Obviously, Sullivan lived and labored before the age of the Guru.) What he is really saying is that his job is to help the patient achieve a reasonable measure of mental health insofar as circumstances will allow regardless of whatever irrational motives or goals the patient may have acquired. But he must be able to persuade him that he is not acting arbitrarily, and that he is trying to help the patient as best he can. Otherwise the latter will not return.

There are many more details about structuring the interview situation discussed in The *Psychiatric Interview* that I omit, since they seem readily understandable.

A few "general technical considerations" regarding the interview need to be summarized. One of these is "the use of transitions" in interviewing: how to "move about" in the interview situation from one topic to another in such a fashion that the patient can at least "dimly" follow along the path the therapist is going without getting completely lost and confused regarding what the latter is getting at. There is a more or less analagous problem on the formal education level. Instructors who may, or may not, know their subject thoroughly are sometimes very inept when trying to communicate the subject matter of the course to their students. A fairly typical shortcoming of some is suddenly switching from one topic to another without demonstrating any connection between them. Since many students these days are so taken up with "living" (as some of them put it) they will not have studied their assignment for that day or for that week, they cannot see any continuity in the various topics that are presented. (They are among the legions of students who hope to get by with "cramming" for exams.) So a conscientious and competent instructor will carefully explain that a new topic is related to previous topics in certain respects whenever possible.

The therapist's task is, of course, much more difficult. If he does not accomplish a transition from one idea to the next, from one sort of material to another, not only does the patient get lost but very often the interviewer does also, and one or the other may not know it. "The law of diminishing returns then begins to operate with great vigor without the patient's quite realizing it—and often without the psychiatrist's quite realizing it."[22] Ideally, the latter would always proceed, step by step, "with sufficient waving of signal flags," so that there would always be an approximate consensus about what is being discussed. But that is not universally feasible.

Furthermore, Sullivan claimed that it is very easy for an interviewer (or, one might add, for a teacher) to move from one subject or topic to something else that has popped into his mind. If the therapist does this without being clearly conscious of what he has done, he may obtain "the most fantastic ideas" of the interviewee. So one must always know when he changes the subject. The changing of the subject can be effectively accomplished in one of at least three different ways. In one, the *"smooth transition,"* the interviewer makes the transition by a more or less adequate and at least superficially truthful statement to the effect, "Well, now that brings up the topic of so-and-so. Eh?" Or, on many occasions, "Oh, yes, well, sometimes that's due to so-and-so. I wonder if by any chance you've had experience of that kind?" In the second, the *"accented transition,"* the therapist manages to convey a signal that he is going to change the subject. Sullivan would usually "begin to growl, rather like a ball bearing with some sand in it," so as to indicate that something is about to happen. He would do this when he wanted to change the subject emphatically but in such a way that the previous topic is not dismissed and forgotten. The accented change causes a pause, "a sort of empty pause," which is different from the socially conventional, polite sort of pause that often occurs in everyday conversation when one waits for the other fellow to speak. In the accented transition there is a disturbance, a slight jarring, of the patient's attentive set. Then without startling the patient Sullivan would introduce the new topic. The third sort of change is the *"abrupt transition,"* which many interviewers are said to have often employed needlessly or excessively. But Sullivan maintained it has very definite uses at times. The abrupt transition is the rather sudden introduction, without prior warning, of a new topic that has relevance to the ongoing therapeutic process, but the change is made at what could be described as a socially awkward moment. This sort of transition is effected sometimes to avoid dangerous anxiety (threatening to the therapeutic situation, as in the case of the man mentioned previously who had horrible dreams, had lost much interest in life, etc.). The therapist may shift the focus of the particular interview from the informative to the nebulous because the patient has become acutely anxious about something. On the other hand, some interviews "would never get to be psychiatric interviews if the patient were not made anxious."[23] But it has to be properly done. The therapist has to know how to take the patient through an upsetting period to a point at which definitely reassuring material is brought out; or from something that was occurring with greatly increasing risk to the therapeutic situation to something "which is remarkably reassuring." But the therapist must know a great deal about what is, or is not, reassuring. (Reassuring techniques are discussed in Chapter X of *The Psychiatric Interview.*)

The formal inception is the first phase of mapping the interview, which begins usually with the actual, formal reception of the prospective patient or client who comes to a psychiatrist for psychotherapy and an inquiry about, or a reference to, the circumstances of his coming. The manner in which the patient is received can greatly accelerate the achievement of the therapeutic goal or it can make such an achievement virtually impossible. Sullivan held that from the moment the interviewer and interviewee first see each other very important aspects of the psychiatric interview are in progress. And from this very moment, Sullivan goes on to say, the therapist must realize that his own convenience, his own personal background, are not nearly as important as the "assumption" that here is someone to be treated with respectful seriousness because he wants to be benefited, or at least can be benefited. But there is to be no "social hokum." It was pointed out earlier in the chapter that the patient (as a rule, not always) is a stranger and is to be treated accordingly. The therapist acts as if he were expected, greets him by name and *suggests* that he come in. (Never, such hokum as "Oh, *hello,* come in!" That sort of greeting is all right when a man is receiving a young lady in his apartment for other than therapeutic purposes.) While the patient was still at the door, Sullivan would take a good look at him but after that he would not stare at him. Once the patient was in the office Sullivan would indicate a place where he should sit, thus relieving him of the possible uncertainty about it, a seemingly trivial matter that can really be very awkward in a difficult tension-laden situation.

Next Sullivan would tell the prospective patient what he had learned thus far about him. If the patient telephoned to make the appointment, Sullivan might say, "I gathered from our conversation over the telephone that you have a problem of such-and-such a nature" in a slightly questioning tone. In this fashion he would convey to the patient the fact that he had paid attention to whatever data had been presented to him, that he had taken the trouble to notice and to remember what was said to him over the telephone. Insofar as it was feasible, he would try to convey to the client "something" of his impression of why he came. But these initial data—the alleged reason for seeing a psychiatrist—are probably irrelevant. What the patient said over the telephone, for example, may have merely been an excuse for seeing the psychiatrist. Nevertheless by offering an impression of what he heard over the telephone, Sullivan was laying his cards on the table, insofar as such a stratagem was feasible (it might not always be practicable when, for example, he was conducting an initial interview with a certain type of psychotic patient who was referred by another psychiatrist). The purpose of this stratagem was to give the patient at the very beginning an excellent opportunity to "correct the situation," that is, to revise the information the therapist already had got so far. And the patient might say, "Yes, that's right, Doctor," or a great number of other things, such as, "What? Why I never dreamed of it. How is it possible for you to have such a misunderstanding?" In the latter instance, Sullivan would reply somewhat as follows, "Well, now, tell me what really *is* the case?" And he starts to tell his therapist what is (or what he thinks is) the problem. In this fashion, as simply and briefly as possible, the interviewer functions so that no complicating situation arises on first encountering the stranger. The patient begins to think, "Well, we've begun." And he is right. The end of this first phase of the formal inception is said to arrive when the patient has made some statement that the therapist can assume has given the interviewee the feeling that he has transmitted some idea of his problem and of himself. But at this point Sullivan would not try to *discover* what "ails" the patient because no one can understand a client's problems or mental disorder without knowing at least a good deal about that person. The therapist would, however, try to let him believe that he knows something about the reason he has for being there. On accomplishing this, the interviewer has made ready for the second phase, the reconnaissance.

Sullivan taught that throughout the inception of the interview, the psychiatrist should be clearly conscious of how he acts, that is, he should have learned from experience the *usual* impression obtained *of him* in the particular circumstances of encountering the sort of stranger that the client at first glance seems to be. The therapist, in other words, should have "some idea" of how he is affecting the stranger and how he is facilitating or hindering certain things that the client may have thought of doing. Sullivan claimed that the psychiatrist should also have learned what sorts of immediate impressions he himself obtains from the appearance and initial "movements" and vocal behavior of the other person, noting that in such a relationship what one hears first from the other person, no matter "how free and easy" or conventional, represents that person's repertoire of operations or actions to be addressed to a complete stranger. In this situation the psychiatrist is also the stranger to the client, and he must acquire some idea of how the client's behavior affects him. In other words, the therapist should try to be as clearly conscious as possible of his own first impressions of the client.

Because the interview situation is a transaction, the psychiatrist must not only learn to sort out his own impressions of the stranger, he must learn what effect his own immediate impressions have on his own behavior, which in turn affect the client's impression of him. For example, many people are not ordinarily clearly conscious of a great deal they show on their faces and how powerful an effect it may have on others, whether favorable or unfavorable. The psychiatrist must cultivate his alertness in this area also. He must be clearly conscious of his own gestures and what effect they are likely to have in a given situation. Not only must he learn how to act appropriately in the interview situation, he must acquire *"an aptitude to do nothing exterior to his awareness"* that might greatly hinder the development of the interview-transaction, or that will direct its course in an unnecessarily obscure fashion. The vital importance of this is suggested by the fact that many inexperienced interviewers, without knowing it, communicate to their clients a distaste for certain types of data. So they fail to get information which they need to have in order to develop the interview fuller.

Of course, the interviewer has no superhuman ability to know *directly and immediately* what sort of immediate impression of himself he has created in the stranger. But he can and must have useful surmises of *alternative probabilities,* which are partly based on previous experience with clients and partly on the information he has already gathered from his initial observation of the particular client's behavior from the outset. But the best that a psychiatrist can have in the very early phases of the interview is said to be a surmise of perhaps two possible impressions he may have created with the stranger. The alternative probabilities, or the two possible impressions, enable the psychiatrist to explore further, to test his surmises, so that the probability of one increases while that of the other decreases. In this fashion, he approaches reasonable accuracy of impression. One has to be very careful not to close the mind, not to choke off alternative probabilities, once he gets a hunch as to what may be the case. That sort of thing is analogous to precocious interpretation and will make it all too easy for one to make incorrect inferences.

Sullivan taught that the interviewer should be alert to, in order that he can accurately recall, all that he has said and done in the formal inception of each interview he conducts with patients, *so that he can learn to do better*. It is necessary for him to be able to recall a course of processes correctly in regard to "movement and pattern of movement"—that is, in other words, the *timing* or sequence of the occurrences in the interview, what preceded what, what followed what—in order to have the material (the "data") from which he can make a useful analysis of the processes that were involved in and during the transaction. It is from this sort of analysis of the course of a particular interview situation, or of any interview situation, that he can synthesize an improving grasp of the particular aspect of the client's living with which the therapist is concerned at a given time.

Consider the following description of how Sullivan during the stage of the detailed inquiry would attempt to discover what really happened when his obsessional patient became entangled in one of his frequent quarrels with his wife; situations in which things between the two go from bad to worse, and harsh or accusatory statements, accompanied by various defensive stratagems, fly back and forth until both parties are quite disturbed by them.

> As I say, I try to get this [mélange of parataxic me-you patterns] revealed to me by the somewhat guarded communication of the patient. The way that I ask for it is really very simple but does have a somewhat defective effect as well as the appropriate one. I say to the patient that I want to know what happened, who said what next, and so on and so forth. As the patient is reporting, he is apt to get the idea that I am trying to discover just what kind of a polite she-devil he is living with; but the brute fact is that I am trying to get data that are somewhere near what actually happened. I know I may often hear what the other fellow said. I also will hear a great deal of what my patient said, except that it will usually leave out some quite important data—not in any sense deliberately; it will

just happen that a number of the things that show how the melée became more and more inextricably unprofitable will appear in his account of the other person's contribution but not in that of his own. I never expect to get an accurate account of one of these unpleasant flypaper operations early in my relation with a patient; but when I have some notion of what went on, I may depict it in rough outline for the patient to hear it. ....[24]

Sullivan understandably does not make any hard and fast rule about the length of time taken up by the formal inception. It may require more than one conference. The type of person and the sort of disorder he suffers must to some extent dictate the necessary length of time. Furthermore, there is no formal, literal ending of the inception and the beginning of the reconnaissance. Sullivan claims that the series of stages that distinguish the interview are "artificial," "abstract"; that is, one phase is not sharply cut off from the next, and some of the characteristics of one phase to some degree govern all. Thus the excerpt quoted above applies much more to the detailed inquiry than to the beginning phases but they are more or less continuous with it; and several of the therapeutic maneuvers are similar though more tentative and abbreviated during the beginning stages.

In the reconnaissance, the psychiatrist sets out to secure a rough and superficial sketch of the patient's personal-social history. Later on, during the detailed inquiry, he will try to learn the developmental history. Sullivan usually began by saying, "Now, tell me, how old are you? Where were you born? Are your mother and father living?" Should one or both of them have died, he would ask, "When did they die and of what?" These questions may lead to some interesting data. The question about the father's death, for example, may lead to the discovery that the father had not lived in the home for the past twenty years and that the patient does not know whether he is dead or not. Following upon the previously mentioned questions comes a question about the number of siblings, including any who died. It may be significant if a sibling died within the memory span of the client. But it may also be important to learn if any siblings died before he can remember. The reason is that, in such a case, they might have been very significant to his parents, and, therefore, indirectly have a considerable effect on him.

Sullivan would ask about the client's position in the time-order of siblings, trying to make sure he got this information correctly. There was some probability, Sullivan thought, that the fifth and last child in a family (many of his patients must have been born when the United States was still primarily rural, and large families were common), who is the only male child, and who is born ten years after his nearest sibling, will be very spoiled. If the patient occupies that position, Sullivan would, he said, immediately think, "Hah! The probability is that this fellow has gotten away with murder since his early years." But he would also be careful to note any very striking exceptions to that "probability."

Next, he would ask who, besides the parents, was chronically or frequently in the home during the patient's first seven years of life. Thus a maiden aunt or a grandmother who was very frequently in the home might have had a very permanent effect on the client. Sometimes under this sort of questioning the patient will recall that grandma was the only bright spot, or the only decent human being, in his home during the first seven years. And, as Sullivan might say, that is something well worth knowing.

Then he would ask what the father or the mother, or whoever earned the money that supported the family, did for a living. What were the family economic circumstances? Was there at any time a sharp alteration of those circumstances? Marked economic disturbances usually have very marked consequences on the course of personality development. Large adverse economic changes may lead to a tragic revision of the parental ambitions for their offspring with corresponding consequences on the latter's life-goals. The timing of such economic changes is very important. If they occurred, for example, before the patient was eight, they will probably have not only affected the parents but their "utterances and efforts to direct the life of the child." Or if they occurred when he was in his late teens they may have ruined his chances (especially a generation ago) for a university education or a prospective career in one of the professions.

Only those readers who are old enough to have lived through the great Depression can perhaps fully realize the often grave consequences of an abrupt adverse change in economic circumstances on the lives of people. Younger readers may get some idea of the psychological devastation visited upon coutless numbers of people from reading Robert and Helen Lynd's books on *Middletown*. There is no way of knowing the number of victims who suffered permanent scars, or whose lives were ruined, demoralized in varying degrees, up to a point at which, in extreme cases, they became psychotic.

The next step in the reconnaissance is to ask the client—sometimes to his amasement—what sort of person his father was. In the face of such a question a patient may be helpless, and, as it were, dumb. Other clients will not be so helpless. And some will be very vocal. If the client who is helpless is one who lacks verbal formulation, which probably means he has never tried to put into words what he thinks about the male parent, Sullivan would give him a helping hand. "Well, how was he regarded in the community?" If the patient still has no answer, his therapist might say, "What did his pastor think of him?" Or the family doctor, local druggist, grocer, or someone else who was acquainted with the father. "What would they have said about him, offhand?"

After having obtained, if possible, a fair notion of what the father was like, the therapist inquires as to whether the patient's family was a happy one. "Were the parents happily married?" One can see that in this seemingly casual fashion, the therapist has already begun to probe into the probably early beginnings of the patient's difficulties.

And what about the mother? While Sullivan would ask what sort of person the father was, he would ask the client to *describe* his mother. (Sullivan said he could not put into words the reasons he had for asking what sort of person the father was while asking the patient to describe his mother. It is plausible to assume that an important reason was that the mother would normally be by far the more important figure during the early years. The influence of the mother has been emphasized throughout this book while the role of the father has perhaps been underestimated.) Usually the patient will have only a very vague notion of what his mother was like, but his therapist will extract whatever information he can get about her, though he will not spend hours trying to get at the whole truth—which the patient does not have anyway. Eventually the therapist will probably learn a lot more about her, indirectly, if not directly.

Next, any people who were mentioned earlier (aunts, grandparents, and others) come in for some inquiry. The therapist may learn that every summer the client's maternal grandmother took him to the seashore, which he may describe as an ecstatically happy experience, never-to-be-forgotten interludes in a frequently difficult childhood. Or of a vividly remembered older female cousin who visited his home frequently, played with him, told him stories, brought him toys. There may have also been other relatives, such as a male cousin, who taught one the rudiments of certain games, baseball or football, and the like, to whom one may have been deeply attached. One wonders why Sullivan did not pay more attention in his lectures to those "stray people" who were around the house a great deal.

Then Sullivan would inquire about his client's formal educational background, but seemingly in a hurried fashion. This is curious in view of the emphasis he put on experience during the school years both in and outside the classroom in *Conceptions of Modern Psychiatry* and in various unpublished lectures. He seems to deemphasize the role of formal education.[25]

The Sullivanian therapist will want to know his client's occupational history. The latter is said to be much more illuminating than is the educational history in regard to the patient's ability to get on with people and to get somewhere in life. Hence the interviewer wants to learn about everything he has done since leaving school. Sullivan claimed that the "sicker" people are the more they omit from their occupational history. So, after listening to the patient's account, he would say in effect: "Well, aside from these two jobs, you have had no other occupation?" In many instances the answer would be that the client had had many other jobs, but had not held them long. So one should make sure there is more to the occupational history than the interviewee first reports. Sullivan asserted that what he wanted to know pertained to the sorts of jobs, how long he held them, and where, in order to get an idea of whether the person was advancing in his work; whether he was driven by a need for money so that he held a job only long enough to get one that paid more; whether he held each job long enough to know what the work was about and then took another one in a curiously thorough but superficially morbid pattern of learning something about life; whether he quarreled with everyone that he ever tried to work with, and so forth.

Next come questions about the patient's marital status—*not* at this stage about the patient's sex life *per se*. Only inexperienced, inadequately "trained" young therapists will start an inquiry of that sort in the beginning stages of the interview. For one thing, to a highly intelligent patient who is not seriously disordered it may sound fraudulent—and perhaps it is. Or it may be intensely disturbing; so much so that the patient (perhaps wisely) may not return. The Sullivanian psychiatrist will simply ask the patient if he is married. If he is, the next question is, How long? After that comes the question, somewhat casually, "Quite happily?" If the marriage is not a happy one, the patient, hesitating a moment, says, "Yes." Are there any children? If the therapist asks whether it is his first marriage, quite often the client replies with "No, no. I was married before," perhaps sounding as though the interviewer should have known this all along even though no mention had been made of the matter. Then the therapist would want to learn about the early marriage. Was the patient's first wife also his first love? If he hesitates, then the question is followed by the inquiry, "Why did you marry?" Of all the possible answers he might give, a patient sometimes forthrightly replies that it was because the family thought it was a great idea.

According to Sullivan, the reconnaissance may take about twenty minutes in a situation in which he never expected to see the patient again or it might take from seven and a half to fifteen hours, as a rule, when time was not a vital consideration, or even longer. The skill that an interviewer possesses in obtaining and interpreting this outline history is said to have a great deal to do with the ease or difficulty of the subsequent detailed inquiry, that is, the long stretch of intensive psychotherapy. It has previously been pointed out that it would be a mistake to think that all of the reconnaissance is always rather sharply separated from all of the detailed inquiry. Some matters may come up that should be pursued immediately. Moreover, unless the psychiatrist can defer some topic smoothly and in a manner that seems natural to the patient, it is not likely to be the same when it is brought up again later. Suppose the client has said during the social history taking, or reconnaissance, that his mother was a wonderful woman except that she had had a violent temper and at times seemed slightly out of her mind from anger. If the psychiatrist then, without further ado, shifts to an inquiry about someone else the patient is likely to suffer about the baldness of his original statement. Next time the interviewer inquired about the mother he will receive a stream of apologies about what he first said. By this time the psychiatrist cannot be nearly so sure of what he hears about the mother because the patient now believes that it is necessary to be much less frank in his statements. On the other hand, if the interviewer asks for a few examples, of what sort of thing was likely to stir up the mother's violent anger, before proceeding to other matters, he will leave the topic wide open for later inquiry.

The purpose of the social history is, in part, to discover what the grossest landmarks have been in the patient's life up to the present. Nevertheless, by the end of the reconnaissance the psychiatrist will have probably obtained valuable information about many characteristics of his client. Sullivan held that because of the great number of topics covered in the social outline, and because of their real importance and yet apparent lack of relationship, the patient is much more likely to manifest meaningful signs, without perhaps quite knowing it, than he would if he were conversing freely about something in which he more or less had control of the topics. Subsequently, in the detailed inquiry, the Sullivanian therapist will leave the patient more or less in control of the topics, unless for some reason the interviewer must resort to cross-examination. According to Sullivan, "things have to flow." Otherwise, the thoughts and fantasies of the patient are apt to be so disconnected that the therapist does not quite know what he has learned. A discontinuous sequence may amount to little more than a succession of discrete, unrelated entities, or topics, which may be impossible to interpret.

In the reconnaissance, during which the client is "more or less" answering—not a list—but an "organized stream" of questions, in which one question seems to follow "naturally" after the previous one has been answered and end with another question that seems to follow plausibly, the interviewer, by means of alert listening and some "seeing" (of the patient's gestures and movements), is able to pick up a great many clues for further study. While he is obtaining the social history, the interviewer carefully takes note of the relative ease or difficulty of the relationship, which reflects the extent and intensity of the client's concentration on the procedure and his sensitivity to the interviewer. The interpersonal relationship also reflects various attitudes and traits of the interviewee: whether he is reserved, guarded, suspicious, hostile or contemptuous. Also his manner toward the therapist may be defensive, conciliatory, ingratiating, apologetically inferior, superior, supercilious, or respecting. Among other things the interviewer may "pick up" at this stage are included the client's trust or lack of it towards his memory; his attitude toward the social history-taking, that is, whether he feels it puts him at a disadvantage or not; the apparent degree of his need for reassurance, and the like.

According to Sullivan it is useful to conclude the preliminary reconnaissance, especially when it comprises a series of interviews, with a summary statement. He recommended that the psychiatrist tell the patient what he has heard and seen as a problem that seems well within the field of psychiatric competence. In a long psychotherapeutic relationship, especially, it is important to establish the justification for the continued, laborious, often painful, almost always expensive joint endeavor. In general, if treatment situations are not to be self-defeating, the therapist must formulate adequately and present to the patient a problem in living, though not necessarily the most important difficulty he suffers. The latter may be discovered much later during the detailed inquiry. The psychiatric situation is said to be formally established when there is a consensus that the patient and psychiatrist might well talk further about the problem that has emerged from the reconnaissance. The resolution of the problem and perhaps other problems that will emerge subsequently may take two to five or more years. However, in a precisely defined, recurrent problem that a person has in his dealings with others, it is possible, Sullivan held, that a good deal can be done in a rather short time.

The summary should be as brief as possible. In offering it, the therapist should inform the client that he wishes to inform him, without interruption, what has impressed him in the reconnaissance. At the same time the psychiatrist should make it clear that at the end of the summary the patient will be requested to amend and correct those matters that the therapist has misunderstood, and to call his attention to any important matters that he missed. Sullivan asserted that when the psychiatrist at the end of the reconnaissance attempts to summarize what has happened, the patient will have an experience that in some ways is quite startling. The summary reflects back to him in a newly meaningful fashion things that he has known for most or nearly all his life and that he has told the psychiatrist in the interviews. If the latter is competent, and has done his job well, the summary will be "a very uplifting experience," quite often a very enlightening experience and quite often a reassuring experience as well, partly because of the matter-of-fact, historical approach to his problems by the therapist, who has begun to suggest he acquired them in the course of his living with people, not that they were somehow lodged in his genes. Frequently the summary also enlightens the client about some of his conventional evasions and distortions.

Yet there is a very serious question about what to include in the summary, in regard to the patient's problem as the psychiatrist sees it. In psychiatry, for the therapist to be simply and directly frank is often out of the question because it would be as cruel and destructive as possible. Since a great many people are easily exposed, or vulnerable, to extremely severe anxiety, the psychiatrist who bluntly shatters such people's security operations leaves the individual's self-dynamism more or less helpless, if not gravely undermined. So he always has the responsibility, when he presents a problem, especially in the early stages of therapy before a patient can learn how to withstand a good deal of anxiety on occasion, to protect the latter's self-esteem, or, in other words, to make sure his presentation does something more than precipitate anxiety. But the psychiatrist, *at the end of the reconnaissance,* can present problems in such a manner that the patient will not become too anxious to continue the therapy, even if they sometimes constitute a grim picture. By this time the patient will often have developed enough confidence and trust in the psychiatrist that he can really from the grim summary and, so to speak, gird up his loins. For example, in commenting on a patient's recurrent pattern of disparaging others, Sullivan might say, "Well, it seems to me that this pattern of giving lip service and then undermining the other person, which you were forced to develop with Aunt Agatha, has stayed with you ever since."

However, Sullivan taught that sometimes the problems in living that the psychiatrist encounters in the reconnaissance are so grave, so close to the structure of the most serious mental disorders, that it would be disastrous "to toss them in the patient's face." A patient who is deeply disturbed must not be expected to abandon whatever remnants of security he has held on to by agreeing with the psychiatrist that he is psychotic. Yet he should be presented with something helpful. Therefore even though the therapist must omit a direct reference to his psychosis, he can sometimes refer to what are essentially psychotic difficulties with others. Under these circumstances, it is said to be by no means uncommon for the patient to be quite clear on the fact that in a rather objective and undisturbing way the psychiatrist has said, in essence, that he is psychotic. Yet this can frequently be established without provoking serious anxiety in the patient, while he acquires a belief that it might be possible to do something about his disorder with the help of the psychiatrist.

(Somewhat tangentially, it may be well to mention that Sullivan thought that in a series of interviews it can be quite helpful to have the patient prepare a chronology of his life. It may save time especially if the psychiatrist has trouble in keeping track of names, which patients mention, and attaching them to the right people, especially when they mention and name everyone with whom they have had any dealings. "I suggest that the patient prepare a record, showing in one column the date or the year and his age, beginning with his birth and coming up to the present, and in another column, opposite this time scale, brief statements of where he lived, who was living in the household at the given time, and any very significant events, including those that he has been telling me about."[26] Sullivan explained to the client that such a record might help him to recall certain things that had not come up in the early reconnaissance and that it would be very valuable to his therapist in keeping track of the various people and when their influence was felt. The record would save a good deal of time for both, the therapist assured him, while it would aid him in avoiding misunderstandings. Quite often the patient adopted these suggestions and both profited.)

So far in this chapter nothing has been said about what Sullivan used to call the collateral interview. In *The Psychiatric Interview,* its significance seems to be somewhat minimized—except in cases of severe or potentially severe mental disorder—because Sullivan gradually came to the conclusion that it is extremely important to conduct the interview "on the basis of that which is given *in the interview* " itself. Why, he does not directly say. It may be worth noting that psychotherapists generally and literally work from morning until night, very often six days a week, ten or eleven months of the year. An extensive use of the collateral interview would certainly be a very expensive and time-consuming affair.) However, he did maintain that if the patient is seriously disordered or fairly obviously in danger of serious mental disorder, while confronted with making decisions that are far beyond his abilities, he would avail himself of any information bearing on the relevant problem that he could get. However it is often a very delicate problem of technique to decide on what one does with the information. For example, sometimes Sullivan would use the collateral information in (unobtrusively) directing the course of the interview.

In general, there is said to be no reason in the world for not telling the patient about the information he has acquired from other sources *unless* some of the facts he has learned may be very disturbing. It often saves a good deal of time by telling the patient the gross facts as they have been given to him. When he had been misinformed, he would want to hear the correction immediately. On occasion the psychiatrist is told so many disturbing things about a person that they seem to prove that he has a serious mental disorder. But one does not accept these things on faith. The psychiatrist must learn in the interview what the true picture is, what the real state of affairs is; and this may carry implications of possibilities of treatment that had not been implied by the collateral information transmitted.

Before turning to the detailed inquiry, I must take up the topic of free association. In Chapter 5, it was pointed out that Sullivan employed free association extensively after he had passed the stages of the formal inception and reconnaissance. Apparently his subsequent experience with obsessionals and other "types" of neurotics convinced him that however valuable an instrument free association may be it has very serious limitations. From the beginning he knew that it was inapplicable to schizophrenics, at least during their more disturbed periods. Later on he learned that an obsessional patient, if allowed to continue unchecked, can go on "free associating" until he grows old or bankrupt. But he did *not* abandon free association wholesale; nor did several of the students whom he had "trained" or supervised when I knew them. The misunderstanding over this issue probably arose from the fact that, unlike many classical psychoanalysts of his day, he did not try to employ it indiscriminately and uncritically. Just as he learned from his mistakes in the treatment of schizophrenics while he was a young psychiatrist to become a master in the field ("when I think of the mistakes I made with schizophrenics in the early days," he once said to this writer, "my hair stands on end"), so did he learn the uses and abuses of free association.

One never tries, he taught in some of his lectures, to tell a patient what is meant by free association. (Nor did he tell the patient to lie down on the couch and *relax completely* as the first prescription of psychoanalysis as some analysts maintained who flourished when Sullivan was a young psychiatrist. In fact, lying on a couch at any stage in order to engage in the process of free association is not essential but it very often facilitaties the free flow of fantasy and thought when introduced at the proper time. The advantages of this stratagem need not be elaborated.)[27] Sullivan thought that the only way to get a patient to do free association that will do him or the therapist any good is to impress upon him the faculty of his personality to present unknown data by more or less free flow of thought and fantasy.[28] But it had to be, so to speak, "demonstrated" to him. The ideal circumstance for a demonstration occurs when a patient has no answer to a particular inquiry. Thus when the interviewer took up some problem that had emerged in the reconnaissance, and the patient, as it were, ran into blind areas concerning it—when, in other words, the self system inhibited any recall of relevant information—Sullivan would attempt to get the patient to talk more or less at random as things came to mind. And lo! as often as not, things started coming to mind. He would begin to talk; his thoughts would start to circle, "in the most curious fashion," toward the answering of the question. However, there might be, sometimes, many starts and stops before a patient was able to answer a very significant question. In other words, the therapist might attack one of the client's blind spots in the following fashion: "Well, I really wonder what might have been the case; tell me, what comes to your mind." After the patient has experienced a few demonstrations of the fact that free association makes sense, the therapist can lay down useful injunctions as to the unwisdom of his selecting what to report. Thus when the client "has actually accomplished something by a more or less free report of his covert processes, he will begin to understand that the leaving out of ideas because they seem irrelevant or immaterial may cause the therapeutic process to miscarry."[29] However, if a patient should try to "free associate" at length regarding the possible winner of the fifth race at Aqueduct and from there go on to fantasize about the winner of last year's Kentucky Derby, Sullivan would call a halt, saying quite "sardonically," "This seems to be *really* free association, but I wonder what on earth it pertains to." So, in conclusion, he would induct the patient into the reporting of relatively free-flowing thought without prior warning or discourse.

The reasons for the detailed inquiry are multiple. Though the impressions gained from the two initial stages should stand the interviewer in good stead by quickly establishing the procedures that are to be used over the "long haul" of intensive, prolonged psychotherapy, these impressions will have to be revised again and again during the prolonged inquiry. For the impressions are only hypotheses of varying degrees of probability of correctness. So they have to be "tested" carefully, and as exhaustively as time and circumstance will permit. Therefore the therapist must constantly test alternatives, endeavoring to keep an open mind as to the essential correctness of his early impressions. Summarily, the latter have only "purely experimental importance."

The stage of the detailed inquiry is said to be a matter of improving on earlier approximations of understanding what happened to, and what now "ails the patient." But during the detailed exploration, a revolutionary change in one's earlier impressions may occur, as we saw in the instance of the lady who supposedly had such a perfect childhood. One reason is that patients may tell the therapist things they believe will suit him or impress him. Of course such statements do not reveal their "durable characteristics." But they are not trying to deceive the psychiatrist; at least they are not conscious of any effort to deceive or defeat him. One must bear in mind that all their lives they have been trying to say and do things in such a manner that they hope will protect their self-esteem, often without conscious awareness. Since the psychiatrist is not a magician—although he may keep a magic cloak in his clothes closet to wear when he makes a television appearance—he usually cannot, even if he would, suddenly dispel the patient's stratagems and security operations. Hence, in order to protect his self-esteem the latter may for a long time say things that are grossly misleading or subtly color the way he presents things. (There are occasional exceptions or partial exceptions when a very courageous patient is willing and determined to employ the last ounce of energy he possesses and every resource at his command in order to learn the truth about himself as quickly as possible. Then the skillful therapist may have to slow him down because even such a patient can assimilate only a certain amount during a given period of time.)

In addition to the more or less uniquely colored traits of the patient, a general cultural factor has to be considered. In a particular cultural situation, everyone, or almost everyone, knows how he ought to act (as defined by the cultural norms). But very often many people's behavior diverges, in varying degrees from the generally accepted standard. One of the most overtly respected norms of Western peoples is: Thou shalt not steal. Yet there is perhaps no other cultural standard so frequently and pervasively violated as this one. Relatively few people will openly admit to theft, even when they have not "forgotten" about it, which can range from the petty cheating of a supermarket clerk to the most gigantic frauds of an industrial combine. (I leave aside the famous anarchist doctrine that all property is theft; or the Marxist doctrine that all ruling classes are inherently exploitative.)

So if a psychiatrist asks a patient, "How do you believe that you *should* act about so-and-so?" the answer will, in general, tend to be very near or identical with the culturally defined standard regarding one's conduct in the particular situation under discussion. However, if the therapist asks, *"How* did you act in this particular situation, or under such-and-such circumstances?" the answer may be truly amazing. A person "can't tell you accurately how he acted in an important situation unless by almost sheer chance the way he *did* act happened to coincide with his idea of how he *should* have acted—a rather uncommon coincidence in which the answer is just as good as a geographical direction."[30]

Sullivan believed that it seems to be almost impossible for anyone, at least in his dealings with strangers, to say anything that will perfectly and concisely demonstrate that he is inferior to the "demands on his own behavior," the ideals according to which he appraises his own conduct. As a rule, these ideal norms are learned in childhood (and subsequently) from the authority figures. And when the average person violates those norms—an apparently rather common occurrence—he feels guilty, ashamed, anxious. (Sullivan in this context ignores the fact that no society can exist without generalized, shared standards of conduct.) So when a patient starts to report something that does not measure up to his standards, he becomes quickly alerted to the fact that he acted in a manner that he considers wrong, bad, shameful, or whatever. This realization takes place in his covert processes; and it occurs very swiftly, and silently, perhaps in focal awareness, perhaps on the fringes of consciousness.

When the person has done something—or sometimes only thought about something—that he believes to be wrong or shameful or that might evoke a derogatory appraisal by the other fellow, someone who is significant to him, such as the therapist, he aims "a stream of words" at him, trusting that the listening ear is unskeptical. And so the interviewer's work will be taken up with evaluating the stream of words: studious minimization of errors, apologies for failure, extravagant exaggeration of successes, and perhaps a vast array of other security operations. For the patient, like everyone else, wants to protect whatever self-respect he has at all costs even though his efforts, because of the structure of the self system, may often be extremely ineffectual, self-defeating, or self-destructive. Hence it does not seem enough for the therapist to be skillful and as experienced as possible in the details of human living, normal and otherwise. He needs to have human compassion—which, alas! is often in short supply.

In order to be efficacious, the detailed inquiry, the long stretch of intensive psychotherapy must be "exceedingly far" from a conversation composed of simple, correct answers to clear questions. One of the things that often makes it so difficult and uncertain for both participants is the frequent conviction of the patient that what occurs to him, what comes to mind, is not "good enough"—a typical function of the self dynamism. In essence, he may believe, "If I tell the therapist the truth, he won't think well of me." Because of his insecurity, he is convinced that he must put "a good face" on whatever he is saying, else he may make a bad impression or a terrible impression. In effect he is trying to read the interviewer's mind. Since he is not a psychologist or a psychiatrist he does not know that no one can read another's mind, a notion that is best confined to the gypsy tea room. Nor can he realize for quite a while that the expert he is consulting is neither a moral nor a social censor for he has been dealing with people all his life, perhaps, who are quick to disapprove or condemn. (In the last analysis that is one of the most effective ways "society" possesses to maintain continuity of custom and tradition. But these matters are more directly in the domain of the sociologist.) A great many of the covert operations of the patient bring about defects of communication since they stand in the way of direct, unadulterated, unfalsified statements of fact, opinion, prejudice, fear, and the like. The client is too concerned with his private ruminations and fantasies about what the "therapist will think." More generally, Sullivan believed that there is not the remotest chance that any person in this social order, and probably in any social order extant in the world today, will not try to put his best foot forward. As a result, anyone in talking to significant others about his past performances will try to guess what he can say that will minimize any unfavorable aspects of any such given performances. Hence the interviewer has to accept this as a fact of life and not be annoyed by all the complex answers that he will get from his patient when he poses relevant and significant questions. In fact, much of the work of the therapist has to do with evaluating such complex answers.

These matters can—and indeed must—be viewed from another perspective, one that is closely related to what has just been summarized. The interviewee's complex answers, and all other defensive stratagems, are usually designed to ward off anxiety by creating a favorable impression. Along with loneliness, anxiety is something that no one wants. And as we have seen, again and again, people go to great lengths, and often at considerable cost, to evade or minimize it. That is one of the things that the interviewer has to be "eternally" conscious of. He must be alert to evidences of it not only in his patient but in himself. An understanding of its role in therapeutic situations provides the psychiatrist with "the most general grasp possible" of those "movements" of the patient that mislead him. The "movements" (the overt and covert activities) designed to alleviate anxiety may be revealed either in the statements of the informant or in his reaction to the psychiatrist's interpretation of, or insight into, what he hears. Frequently, "if the patient suffered more anxiety, the returns might be highly desirable. He might not need to experience further anxiety about that particular problem. But that fact makes little difference to the patient. Anxiety rules."[31] That is chiefly why the therapist has to employ the procedures that are summarized in this chapter and Chapter 5. That is also why everyone who consults a therapist is very busy interpreting him while he is interpreting the patient or interviewee. Hence a very great part of the work of the participant observer or therapist is said to entail the use of his skill to avoid or circumvent the arousal of unnecessary anxiety in his patient while obtaining dependable indices of what the latter considers to be his significant misfortunes, unfortunate occurrences in his past life, handicaps he has in dealing with people, and the like. But the interviewer must not be "unduly impressed" by his knowledge that anxiety can be an absolute barrier to interpersonal relations, including vocal intercommunication. He must not become too "considerate" of the patient's feelings, for then the latter will spend his time trying to make a good impression, and the therapist will get little or no valuable information. But the interviewer, provided he has had adequate "training," is much less likely to be uncritical and careless with his interpretations, and much too psychologically sophisticated to try to read the other fellow's mind, which can easily result in "projection." Sullivan did not think a therapist should become seriously "ego-involved" with a patient—would in fact consider any personal involvement with his patient therapeutically dangerous. The therapist is an expert in the problems that "ail" patients, but he does not become overtly intimate with any of them. It may be chiefly for this reason that Sullivan neglects "countertransference" in *The Psychiatric Interview*. For Sullivan, countertransference (in the classical Freudian sense) is the result of inadequate skill or of some personal inadequacy. (Yet as a young psychiatrist, he occasionally took enormous personal risks when treating schizophrenics. According to a personal communication from Sullivan, offered many years ago, he would enter the room alone of a violently disturbed patient and talk to him, try to persuade him to eat his meals, and so on. On a quite different occasion, when a hostile professional adversary discovered that he was in grave psychological difficulty he called upon Sullivan for help. So Sullivan left his bed in the middle of the night and went to this man's home and assisted him through a grave personal crisis. One of Sullivan's former students, to whom the writer related this matter, interpreted Sullivan's behavior as motivated by malice. He could not, or would not, entertain any alternative "probability.")

Since psychotherapy is a "system of processes," numerous changes, a great many of them significant changes, occur. Among the significant changes are a *change in the interviewee's attitude*. In one sense a change in another's attitude is fairly easy to observe. But in reference to the interview transactions, changes of a more recondite character have to be observed. The latter are said to be changes in the *interviewer's* attitude as reflected by the interview. In other words, the therapist must ask himself, "What attitude of mine is being reflected by the interviewee?" "What does the patient seem to be experiencing about my attitude toward him?" "What does he believe my feelings toward him are?" Part of the therapist's skill lies in appraising what the patient's probable impression of the former's attitude toward him is or has become. Of course, the patients's impression may or may not be correct. But the interviewee's "operations" are said to provide clues as to what he is experiencing, which in many instances suggest the type of difficulty that he will have with any one who impresses him as superior in capability or in social position. Thus Sullivan claimed that it is quite important to distinguish between the *direct, manifest attitude* of the patient and his *covert attitude* as revealed by his performances, which reflect his impression of the *supposed* attitude of the interviewer.

From the very beginning, the therapist acquires gross rudimentary impressions about his patient, but they have to be refined, analyzed from several points of view. These gross impressions obtained during the first two stages of the interview form the background for the observation of change. First, the interviewer considers how keen the patient is, and in how many areas. Along with this, or in connection with it, he considers the implications the patient draws from the other person's remarks and questions that reveal his general alertness or keeness. Are these implications closely related to what might reasonably be expected or not? The therapist also forms an impression of the intelligence of the patient. The first such impression can be quite misleading, but there are ways of correcting and refining it. For example, inquiry may reveal that the interviewee has made extremely rapid progress in handling complex machinery in an industrial job, a task requiring very high general intelligence. Verbal dexterity or the lack of it may or may not be revealing; it depends on whether the interviewee has had the opportunity for the development of verbal skills. Still another general characteristic the interviewer may observe is the responsiveness of the patient. Responsiveness is said to include a group of complex elements in the personality that ordinarily make for ease or difficulty in living. This responsiveness may vary in range from understanding cooperation to an utter obtuseness such that the patient gets completely lost trying to guess what the interviewer is driving at. Some other general characteristics previously mentioned, pertaining to the "elaboration of observation rather than to observation itself," that is, to the development of skillful observations, are the patient's habitual attitude toward his memory, and his habitual confidence or lack of it about answering questions.

In addition, the following sets of "attitudes," also previously mentioned, suggest patterns of interpersonal relations that the interviewer will employ as starting points in observing change in his relation with the patient. These "attitudes" are suggested by the terms, *reserved, guarded, suspicious, hostile,* or *contemptuous.* The interviewee's manner toward the therapist may also be characterized as *supercilious, superior, conciliatory, deferential,* or *apologetically inferior.* The former set suggests a category of personality *traits,* though Sullivan does not explicitly say so, while the latter seem to pertain chiefly to *ways of relating to authority figures,* that is, attitudes toward people in positions of authority that may be largely outcomes of the set of traits mentioned.

The purpose of observing the changes that appear in such sets of "attitudes" is, in part, that it assists the interviewer in determining whether the situation is improving or deteriorating. In addition, he more or less automatically tries to "pick up" impressions of what there may be in his own performances that have had some bearing, some influence, on the change or changes that have occurred. If the interview is "hard going," the therapist needs to have some idea as to what he did (or did not do) that is responsible for the failure to produce any change. Sullivan taught that if the interviewer knows what he was tying to do, and if he is able to study how well he did it, how flatly it failed or how dramatically it succeeded, then he will have important data related to the motivational system that characterizes the interviewee. This was brought out in Chapter 9.

There are other factors, other areas of major importance, to be considered in regard to the interviewer's gross impression, usually acquired during the first two stages of the interview, of the interviewee's changing impression of the interviewer. The latter may ask himself whether the patient is being impressed by his *expertness* in interpersonal relations. Again the therapist may ask himself whether the patient is becoming more appreciative of the interviewer as an outstanding person. Or, in effect, does the interviewer manifest as much respect as possible for the interviewee's need to feel self-esteem. Thus some, perhaps young and relatively inexperienced, psychiatrists are given to asking blunt questions. Suppose such a therapist is interviewing a teenager about the details of his (or her) sex life. Usually this technique will produce so much anxiety that the adolescent "would not even be able to stutter," so he accomplishes nothing useful. Occasionally, from such a technique, the adolescent will pick up some new ideas about possible sexual ventures that he had not previously thought of. It may also happen that a young male psychiatrist, *at the very first interview,* will start asking blunt questions of an interviewee who is not only a young and very attractive female but brilliant and very articulate. In this case the interviewer may not only infuriate the interviewee but be subjected to an eloquent outburst of scornful replies. "You seem remarkably interested in my sex life, Doctor," she may tell him. "I've read some Freud, so just keep on asking the questions, Doctor, and I'll make up any answers you may want to hear. . . . Shall I tell you a story about masturbation?" Needless to say, the Doctor will never see, or hear from, such an interviewee again.

Sullivan was openly and intensely antagonistic to any notions a therapist might have of engaging in sexual relations with a patient—presumably for the good of the patient. Female patients will often entertain romantic notions about their male psychiatrist. In some cases romantic feelings and fantasies will stimulate reciprocal feelings in him.[32] But a reputable therapist never encourages "acting out" in this area. Aside from all questions of ethics, the patient, according to Sullivan, never seeks out a psychiatrist to help him "fix" his sexual problems (if any) even when he sometimes presents them as his major problem in living. There is no telling how much damage has been done to patients by a certain small minority of so-called therapists who encourage such acting out.

On the other hand, there are interviewers who are so careful not to hurt the patient's feelings when it comes to an inquiry about the details of his sex life that they also do not get any useful information. So, the really understanding interviewer will not be so tender to the interviewee that he prevents the patient from full participation, from doing what he is there for, though the therapist will not make the inquiry more distressing than he can help, however cold and remote he may seem.

There is another area, another major question, about the interviewee's impression of the therapist. "Does he seem to feel a *simplicity of motivation* in the therapist—that the therapist is solely interested in doing a competent job?"[33] That is to say, the interviewer will want to know to what extent the patient seems to believe that his therapist is primarily concerned with getting valid and useful information from which valid conclusions can be inferred about him and his problems. Also, to what extent does the patient seem to believe the interviewer has ulterior motives.

All three areas discussed above—the patient's impressions about his therapist's expertness, his ability as a person to understand interpersonal problems, the character of his motivation—are probed for a definite purpose. The assessment of changes in these areas pertaining to skill, understanding, and motivation of the therapist by the patient will enable the interviewer to determine whether the work of the interview is being vastly expedited or not. If the patient, for example, is not impressed favorably, the data he will present will be more difficult to interpret since his ability to express himself freely and accurately is more, perhaps greatly more, restricted.

Assessing changes is not a separate part or step in the interview process. From the beginning to the end of therapy, the skilled therapist more or less continuously and often almost automatically performs this assessment in the "interstices," as it were, of his interviewing. In other words it is intrinsic to the entire psychotherapeutic activity of the interviewer. Gross impressions of what is going on in the therapeutic "field" are rough hypotheses, which are subjected to continuous or recurrent test and correction. Almost as automatically as a calculating machine the interviewer is sometimes able to appraise negative and positive evidence "of this and that." His appraisal, occurring with little conscious thought, perhaps, enables him to know that, at a given time, the patient is, or is not, improving. "In such a case, the interviewer has so continuously and automatically tested his hypotheses that he knows the answer without bothering to do anything about it very consciously or deliberately."[34]

More often the therapist gains impressions that may or may not be justified when he scrutinizes them. He should then apply more or less specific testing operations in order to refine and increasingly correct his impressions. This may be done by more or less unnoted inference. But one cannot safely and wholly leave the testing of impressions (hypotheses) to relatively unformulated thinking. It is a good idea for the interviewer now and then to reflect on the impressions he has obtained. The very act of beginning to formulate them is said to sort them out into two rough groups, namely, *those about which the therapist has no reasonable doubt,* and, second, *those which, when noted, are open to question.* The latter have to be tested further. The more reliable way to do this is by *"clearly formulated purposed activity":* the therapist asks pertinent critical questions. The answers or responses will indicate whether the hypothesis in question (the impression) is correct' or definitely inadequate.

Throughout the interview, there will be definitely improving communication, or at least periodically there *will,* when everything is going well. On the other hand, there will occasionally be times when, instead, things seem to be going from bad to worse, and the patient is becoming less communicative. But in the case of the inexperienced interviewer, even when communication is improving, he may fail to analyze as carefully and completely as possible "all of the context," that is, "the operations, the remarks, and their patterns" that led to distinct improvements in the interview transaction. When the interviewer does know how the situation got to be going well, if, in other words, he can discover, in the context of what has been occurring, at which points of his "operations," of his interview techniques, the patient's communicability increased, he has very valuable information (based on inference) about the patient's covert processes, especially his covert security operations. Thus the interviewer will have good grounds for inferring what sort of things led the patient to suffer anxiety, what led to improvement in the patient's communication at a particular time so that he experienced relief from the feeling that he might or would make a bad impression, and the like. As the therapist reviews his performances, and the patient's performances, as well, in the continuing transaction, he can begin to apprehend the general pattern of the interviewee's precautions, security operations pertaining to some particular area that were made unnecessary by the timely operations of the interviewer. When the latter does not pay close attention to the more or less episodic improvements at a given phase of therapy, and the improvements that occur from period or phase to the next period or phase, he may miss a great deal of the data that might reveal what the interviewee would be like in a particular more difficult therapeutic situation. So, as pointed out previously, the therapist has to be alert to change, and the conditions for its occurrence.

When things seem to be going from bad to worse, and communication is deteriorating, the therapist, instead of getting upset, should, if he can control his own anxiety, try to study the course of deterioration in the relationship with the patient by means of a retrospective survey. He should try to sort out the time and occasion when things started going badly. It may happen that an interview goes badly from the inception. More frequently a deterioration of communication starts during the reconnaissance. The interviewer may have "fallen over" some security apparatus of the interviewee. Things may have gone well during the first two stages of the inquiry and then, at some point during the detailed inquiry, the interviewer asked a question, to which the patient replied, and thereafter the transaction seemed to go sour.

The interviewer should also try to discover whether the deterioration of communication occurred abruptly or insidiously. In the case of abrupt deterioration, a careful review will provide the therapist with a "hunch" as to what went wrong, which can be tested in various ways. But in the case where things have been insidiously getting worse from the beginning the interviewer has a much more difficult task to perform. First, it may be wise for him to review the factual basis for his previous more favorable appraisal of the situation. Sometimes, he may discover that it was only his own enthusiasm that led him to believe things had been going better in the beginning. Second, in the case in which the interpersonal situation has really been deteriorating, the therapist should review what has happened in order to discover whether anything discouraging pertaining to the ultimate outcome of the interview has occurred. If directly or indirectly the therapist has unwittingly said or done something to discourage the patient's reasonable hopes and expectations about therapy, the patient may lose heart and may want to extricate himself politely from this particular interpersonal situation. Third, it is wise, when things have been going badly, for the therapist to study what relation the current situation has, or might have, to his own attitude toward his patient. The patient may have said something that displeased or offended the psychiatrist. Or the psychiatrist may be suddenly concentrating on something of interest to him such as masturbation or the patient's "forepleasure" activities. Thus the therapist should review his attitudes and/or behavior when the interpersonal situation is insidiously deteriorating. Did he take a dislike to this patient when he first encountered him? Did the patient offend him in some way? Did the therapist manifest undue interest in some communications that the intelligent patient could interpret as a manifestation of a lack of interest in him as a person?

There are numerous other attitudes of the interviewer and/or interviewee that Sullivan mentions as tending to cause deterioration of the interview transaction. For example, anger on the part of the therapist is destructive of psychotherapy. At the very least it will make his patient unnecessarily anxious or more anxious, which entails a deterioration of communication. Frivolity, flippancy, irony, and the like, when employed by the therapist, have a similar destructive effect. Masked or unconscious sadism is a sign that the interviewer needs some psychotherapeutic help himself. The same applies to anger, though a therapist may deliberately appear to be irritated or bored when, say, he wishes to discourage uncommunicative or unproductive "movements" by the patient. Often such attitudes are a "response" to various behaviors of the patient, but this does not relieve the therapist of his responsibility to his patient or lessen the impact of those attitudes.

Patients manifest an extremely broad spectrum of attitudes: blatant hostility, arrogance, insolence, irony, frivolity, boredom, amusement at times, active obstructiveness. But *at no time* must the therapist react *automatically,* perhaps unwittingly, to the patient's expressed attitudes, either by tones of voice, gesture, or words. To various affective "movements" and changes of the patient, he may appear spontaneous, though he never should automatically respond in this fashion. For in the very act of responding automatically, he will eliminate, or fail to grasp, by means of selective inattention probably about half of the useful "data."

Sullivan employed his "theorem of reciprocal emotion" in his outline of the psychiatric interview. Suppose the interviewer, by means of tonal gestures, or by the pattern of his remarks, or both, communicates a need *he* has for reassurance. The most common way interviewers manifest this need is said to be by some form of activity that will "score off," disparage, belittle, or humiliate the patient in the course of the interview. But, by virtue of the situation, wherein the patient is in certain respects in an inferior position, the need of the interviewer cannot, usually, if ever, be met by a complimentary need to reassure. What happens is that the patient's need for security is *aggravated.* If perchance he does develop a pattern of activity that is reciprocal to the interviewer's, it must be an interviewer-reassuring activity, such as a submissive behavior pattern. Otherwise communication between expert and client is disintegrated. The development of a reciprocal pattern of submissiveness is very unfortunate since the interviewee tends to get the impression that he must have certain views in order to please the therapist. Should he submit to such a demand, then the data he proffers the interviewer, unless the latter is remarkably clever at interpretation, will be practically beyond interpretation. The latter will probably not be able to make sense of the information he believes he is getting—except what he reads into it. So an interviewer should never permit a patient to fall into one of those submissive relationships. In such a submissive relationship, also, the patient will develop an "alert foresight" of the rebuff of his own need for reassurance, making it certain that he will protect his self-esteem. The longer such an interpersonal relationship continues, the more is the patient governed or confined by the foresight of any sign that his anxiety will become aggravated—instead of increasing his ability to engage in the free flow of fantasy or provide clear and unfalsified answers to questions.

Sullivan again and again emphasized the fact that the patient's self-system is at all times, but in varying degrees, in opposition to achieving the purpose of the interview. Hence, the expert interviewer must try to circumvent the security operations of the self without increasing the scope or the subtlety of such operations. In this connection, it may be well to repeat that the expert interviewer avoids unnecessary provocation of anxiety while he attempts to obtain missing information that is needed for a reasonably correct assessment of the other person. In order to get to know the patient, the circumstances under which he will experience anxiety, and the general pattern of his security operations designed to ward off or assuage anxiety, the therapist must learn a great deal about the history of the self-system. The social history-taking of the reconnaissance may have provided some important clues, but however important, the reconnaissance constitutes only preliminary spadework as a rule. No one, whether "sick" or healthy, is likely to have enough confidence in a stranger after, say, fifteen interview hours to reveal what he knows about the intimate, and often anxiety-provoking details, of his personal life as it has unfolded through the years. Moreover, he knows more than he thinks he knows but only a skillful therapist will be able to bring to light this fact. That is, only an expert interviewer can prod him or induce him or teach him how to take full advantage of most of the relevant material that is "in" the self-system. Some of this material is manifested in the form of precautionary measures against clear recall and unmistakable manifestations of the consequences of various formative experiences. Some of it exists only in a form that provides an adequate basis for inference about his experiences, and *deficiencies* in his experiences, "of universal developmental significance."

Before I proceed further I think it may be well to recall and reiterate Sullivan's statement that there are three fields of occurrences in the treatment of personality that are "of very great relevance," of very great significance. One field has to do with current events outside the treatment situation. The second pertains to the patient's current relations in the treatment situation. And the third field pertains to the events of the patient's past life. In regard to the last topic Sullivan claimed and emphasized again and again that it is important—often necessary—to discover how difficulties in living, the patient's "problems," started because a study of the developmental history often provides a great deal of information as to what many of the current difficulties "represent." In other words, "their more sophisticated mature manifestations" may be extremely obscure so that a study of how things started, how the difficulties in living originated and developed, stage by stage, may enormously clarify their current manifestations and ramifications. Concomitantly, this study will uncover a great deal of information about what necessary experiences—necessary for mature interpersonal relations—that the patient did not have. In this connection one should pay close attention to "the serial maturation of ability" that characterizes the first twenty-six or twenty-seven years of the patient's life, along with the probable opportunities for experience that he has had. It is well to remember that one cannot have a particular kind of experience until a certain level of maturation of innate capacities has been reached, and perhaps a certain amount of necessary previous experience has been acquired. It is also well to remember that there is often a very subtle interplay of maturation and experience such that some innate potential or actualized capacities may be suppressed, their development delayed, altered, or distorted. Recent investigations reveal that there often is a very complex relationship between innate potential capacity and environmental stimulation.

In the study of personality, signs of personality warp are also uncovered. Such signs are said to be evidence of deficiencies in needed experience, "needed" in the sense that everyone must have it in order to grow up. These signs also are indications of security operations pertaining to these deficiencies. These security operations limit or distort the recognition of subsequent opportunities for remedial experiences and their utilization for further growth. In other words, as the self develops it manifests a very powerful tendency "to influence, if not to control," the direction of its immediate future development. In general, the security operations of the self-dynamism stand in the way of the person's remedying deficiencies in experience, deficiencies that originally brought those security operations into being. That is how the limiting, controlling power of the self is often manifested.

During the detailed inquiry, when the patient has achieved some measure of security in his dealings with the therapist, the interviewer starts the detailed inquiry of the interviewee's development. Sullivan emphasized that his schematization should be employed with flexibility. It is not to be followed in the manner in which a new bride follows the directions of a cookbook—sometimes with unfortunate results for her spouse. To a degree, also, there is an "interaction" of past and current events, that is, a swing, or more or less abrupt transition, from a discussion or study of some past experience to some current one, and conversely. Essentially, that is the major purpose of the detailed history-taking: to clarify for both participants some current difficulty or pattern of difficulties by reference to its origin, development, and ramifications. Otherwise an inquiry into the past would be a mere antiquarian exercise. Finally, one must bear in mind that the self-system, throughout the detailed study of the developmental history, will function in such a fashion that it will hinder the interviewer's inquiry because of the patient's need to maintain precautions against anxiety.

Sullivan claimed that one of the first things that the interviewer might obtain information about is the patient's history of learning toilet habits. Though the patient does not consciously know much about his own toilet training, he often will have picked up some clues about it from his parents. Some of the "really unfortunate people" of the world are said to have been exposed to strict bowel training well before early childhood. Because of their parents' "preternatural" interest in toilet habits, the patient may have suffered rather grave disturbances in living forever after. But the psychiatrist must not ask direct questions about toilet training, for the patient may become intensely annoyed. There are certain signs that may be obscurely reflected in personal cleanliness and other things. For example, how much attention does the patient give to dust that may have accumulated on chairs on which he at one time or another is about to sit? Is he very scrupulous about keeping his clothing from any casual contact with dirt? How often does he send his clothes to be washed or dry cleaned? Is he very careful about preserving the creases in his trousers? Similar questions arise about the care of the hair, finger nails, and the like. In order not to give offense—for the patient may be very proud of his cleanliness and neatness—the interviewer emphasizes the *"estimable qualities of the abnormality"* in the case of a patient who has extraordinary interest in personal cleanliness, good grooming, and similar activities.

Another sign about disorders in learning toilet habits may be reflected, though more subtly, in the patient's attitude toward "dirty words." The interviewer may note that the patient is a little "inhibited," restricted in his freedom to use such words as he knows.

Prolonged enuresis, habitual constipation, recurrent diarrhea, and even an occasional soiling of one's bed are also at least often related to the period of toilet training. Blunt questioning about such matters would, or may, bring communication to a halt. But the interviewer should keep in mind the possible meaning "of little hesitancies," about them. Bearing such possible meanings in mind, he may, for clearly professional reasons, quite simply and frankly, at times, ask rather pointed and ordinarily prohibited questions—provided he has discerned the clues that make such questions relevant. Then the patient will probably not be offended and will be able to provide relevant information.

Next, the interviewer may turn his attention to possible disorders in learning speech habits. They are said to appear as faint suggestions of earlier trouble, such as hesitancy in speech, in oral overactivity, or in manneristic accompaniments of speech at times of stress. The second time a patient shows hesitancy in speech when, for example, he seems to be a little embarrassed, the interviewer, after a pause, making a somewhat abrupt transition, may, say, "Tell me, did you stutter as a child?" And the therapist learns that he did stutter. While it is not very difficult to observe signs of speech disorders in a great many of those who manifest some "suggestion" of an impediment in speech during times of stress for many years after they have conquered the more gross disorders, it is not at first easy to discern signs of such disorders in some others. Some people, while talking, manifest a good many unnecessary movements of the face around the mouth (oral overactivity). Still others display various mannerisms when they are talking, such as pausing for a moment, and then doing something, such as making a gesture of the hand before they can speak freely. Sullivan claimed that all these things suggest that there may be great value in developing an interest in the distortions of personality that occurred as far back as the period of learning speech. He added that the signs that come to the interviewer's attention may all have some relationship to a history of disorders or deficiencies in speech habits, which the interviewer can discover by careful questioning. The patient's history may reveal any of the following: (1) delay in learning to speak, which reflects a morbid situation in which there was no sufficient need for learning speech and "a positive premium" on not learning; (2) stuttering or lisping, either of which may be partly organic in origin, and which have great social disadvantages; (3)

peculiarities of vocabulary, which reflect a defect in the learning of consensual validation; and (4) the continued use of autistic or neologistic terms, reflecting a very serious impairment of an extremely important aspect of socialization, verbal thinking.

Sullivan would then "move" into the juvenile era, leaving a great deal of the exceedingly rich phase of childhood untouched. The reader will recall that in the reconnaissance the interviewer will probably have learned a good deal about the patient's attitudes toward his parents. He would want to learn about the patient's attitude toward games and toward the people who were participants or partners in those games. For many games entail a certain degree of cooperation and competition and often a large element of compromise with one's peers. Such an inquiry may be the easiest approach by the interviewer toward understanding the development of eccentricities and idiosyncracies in the juvenile era. People who have suffered a very stressful juvenile stage of development are said to be very probably not members of New York bridge circles or suburban clubs. Their interest in games is likely to be quite restricted and in people with whom to play them.

However, although some topics have to be approached somewhat indirectly in order to avoid arousing great anxiety, one can ask the patient directly about how he regards competition, since it is an acceptable social pattern in the United States and in various other places. Some people who are arrested in the juvenile era develop an intense ambition owing to their competitiveness. It is worthwhile for the interviewer to study not only how intensely ambitious a person may be but also the character of his goals, and the means he adopts toward achieving them. Once one obtains a communicative answer about competition he then asks the interviewee what he thinks of people who compromise, whether he would compromise, to what degree (easily, sometimes, rarely, never), and what he would compromise on, and similar questions.

"As all this goes on," Sullivan taught, "the interviewer observes whether the interviewee is manifestly competitive in the interview situation—has to know more about things than you do, has to beat you to what you are driving at—or, on the other hand, whether he is unduly conciliatory in an effort to give you the feeling that he agrees with even your lightest utterance. Such things are quite significant; they may be overlooked or misinterpreted unless the interviewer follows some sort of scheme for organizing his thoughts and his procedure."[35]

It is said to be particularly important to distinguish in one's thoughts and perhaps in one's questions the patient's experiences connected with the initial schooling. The reason is that the juvenile era is the first period of correcting warps acquired by nearly everyone in his home during the first two stages. In grammar school one starts to learn social techniques rapidly, to conceal one's "real feelings"; and what occurs subsequently is not very revealing. The psychiatrist will want to learn anything in general he can that will provide a notion of what the interviewee felt toward grammar school. This may be obtained by such questions as, "Did you have a good time? Did you learn a lot? Did you like to learn the sort of things that were offered? Did you have an impression that any teacher was wonderful to you? ..." In some ways, the patient's experiences in school are a reflection of the happiness or lack of it he may have first acquired in the home.

Rather abruptly the interviewer can "leap over" high school to college after he has asked about something that was highly significant for the earlier years of the juvenile era. One reason is that he wants to discourage a too easy appreciation of what he is driving at, which would be a way of unwittingly "telling" the interviewee what security operations he can employ to defeat the purpose of the interview. Sudden transitions interfere with a patient's attempts to adjust "nicely" to the therapist's more or less systematic inquiry by disturbing the mental sets that are already beginning to develop in the patient. Hence the probability that the latter can actually recall what happened to him from the last months of the juvenile era to chronological maturity is increased. If the interviewer learned during the reconnaissance that the patient went to college, he will want to know what his experience there was like. Sullivan thought a generation ago that most college students could be classified in one of two groups: the very studious and the "socialites," for whom college is mostly fun and games. Ordinarily, it was better to be one or the other, rather than to be the exception, in relation to one's future life. In those now seemingly distant days, "the American pattern of normality," according to Sullivan, was "to go to college and spend your parents' money, and to avoid any information that you can elude; that is the more 'normal' pattern of development." Sullivan claimed that in the United States, unless one has a career "spreading before one," it is (or was) better to be a social success than a "stude." In 1969 the "exception" has multiplied though he is still probably in a small minority. But the Sullivanian interviewer will still want to know where his patient stood among the various groups of college students. Was he among the "unduly studious" or the "unduly frivolous," or the "unidentified?" (Soon, in the coming years, the interviewer will hope to broaden his scope. Did the patient attend college in order to evade the draft? Was he a genuine conscientious objector? Or did he belong to a politically activist group? Of course the therapist will employ tact when inquiring into such matters. He is not likely to use a phrase like "evade the draft" or "leftist students' organization," though one cannot be too sure of what the future will bring.)

One of the many things the interviewer inquires about is the patient's interest in boys' or girls' clubs. He will inquire whether the patient before he (or she) became a parent manifested much interest in leading boys' or girls' clubs, that is, in being a "big brother" or a "big sister" for a period of years. If the patient had been such a leader, or had such an interest, it is probably a fairly important clue to inadequacies in his preadolescent experience.

At this point in the interview Sullivan would usually inquire whether the interviewee had a chum, a close friend, during the preadolescent era. Preadolescence, as we know, was regarded as a very crucial step in the person's advance toward maturity. Since the patient would not see any connection between questions about boys' or girls' clubs and the question regarding a chum, Sullivan would make it appear as though there had been a breakdown in communication, requiring a start along a new line of investigation. Then he would ask: "Does anyone stand out in your recollection as having been especially your chum in your early school years?" If the answer is yes, the interviewer will want to learn what became of the friendship and of the friend. He will want to know if the patient and his preadolescent chum are still friends. Sullivan, one must add, emphasized that the interviewer must not be sloppy or careless as he leads up to the crucial questions about chumship; otherwise he is likely to get conventional, misleading, obscuring replies. The reason is that many people believe that they ought to have had preadolescent close friends even if they did not.

Then comes an inquiry about puberty. First, the interviewer must make sure that the patient understands what he is talking about. Merely to introduce the topic, Sullivan would ask, "When did you undergo the puberty change?" Most people have not got the "foggiest idea" because so much else was going on at the same time. It is somewhat like the first day in school. For a great many people, the memory of the first day in school is forever lost, though some can remember it vividly, especially when it introduced them to a strange but enchanting world. (The same qualification may apply to early adolescence, though it is always risky to write about it in a book like this. A great many people seem to experience what they have learned from the "culture" they should or are expected to feel. When such people are very articulate they can drown one in an ocean of words about "love." One or two of James Joyce's short stories contain the essence of adolescent enchantment. Freudian psychiatrists might call it overidealization of the sexual object. Sullivan ignores it.) In any event, Sullivan would search for reliable indices of puberty. When did the patient's voice change? When did he first begin to shave? When did he have orgasm? If the patient is a woman, the interviewer will want to know when she first menstruated, when she first noticed changes in the breasts, and the like. On all of these matters, most people are said to be extremely vague. Yet, as the therapist matter-of-factly inquires about them, the patient may recall something very important about one of them. For example, if the patient's puberty was very late, he is apt to be able to recall something about more than one. Sullivan taught that, if the puberty change occurred two or three years after most of the people in the patient's group had undergone it, this delay could be interpreted as a sign of serious personality warp. Under those circumstances, a great deal of the misery in life is said to be dated from the actual delay in the puberty change, concerning which the patient will have a remarkable amount of information. The delay in the puberty change entails a great deal of misery in the patient's life ever since that time, which becomes illuminated by the patient's information about the beginning of early adolescence and any unfortunate ideas connected with it. This fact was brought out in previous chapters.

Then, having gone thoroughly over all the patient's amnesias, the interviewer "rather categorically" asks: "Is anyone recalled as having been a particularly bad influence in early adolescence?" If the patient hesitates briefly and then says, "Yes," the interviewer must appraise the degree of anxiety that the patient manifests before he decides to proceed, or not to proceed, further on that topic. Generally, when the answer was affiirmative, Sullivan would leave the topic for the time being, while making careful note of it for future reference when it could be more safely explored. The important thing is said to be that there does seem to have been an unfortunate relationship, and, that, in many, many instances it is well for the interviewer to restrain his curiosity and to confine himself to the significant question concerning what became of the relationship. When the patient has treasured it ever since it occurred, that in itself is "interesting," suggestive. If he "exterminated" the relationship as soon as possible, that "sounds pretty healthy."

Without at first ever mentioning them, the interviewer may get "some hints" concerning the freedom with which the patient can contemplate the fact that he has genitals by inquiring what he thinks of risqué or frankly sexual talk. Sullivan claimed that when a person feels that all risqué stories are positively obscene he has probably been subjected to pretty warping influences in bygone years and has not escaped or overcome them. This attitude suggests that he regards sexual behavior as disgraceful, dusgusting, and damned. Then, taking up a somewhat related topic, the interviewer-therapist sets out to discover whether the attitude toward the genitals applies also to the rest of his body. One may approach the topic gently by asking the patient if he is a member of an athletic club, the YMCA or some other organization or group where one may, if willing, expose his body at times, say, in a shower room, and at least a part of it, at other times, in other places, such as the swimming pool. Should the patient be a member of a swimming team, for instance, the interviewer does not have to ask superfluous questions about revealing a part of his body in public. As long as the interviewer avoids giving the impression he has an unjustifiable curiosity of some kind, he may ask his patient if he has any remaining objection to being seen nude by people of the same sex, and similar questions.

By this time, the therapist has led the patient toward thinking a little about later adolescence. One can ask him if he prefers men or women for companionship. Should the patient become a little reserved in the face of such an inquiry, the therapist can always modify his question "amiably" by saying, "Well, it may vary with the moods that you're in. Of course you would prefer the company of women when you are retiring with a view to sexual satisfaction." If the patient looks suspiciously at the therapist, then the latter's assumption is wrong, but he has gained valuable information. But he continues his inquiry with such questions as with whom he likes to dine, and the like. Yet one cannot be too precise without startling the patient. The rule is to ask general questions fairly often as a "method" of transition in order to bring a topic out in the open. After that has been accomplished, one becomes specific.

Sullivan advised that the therapist should find out what the patient's attitude toward solitude is. Some people blissfully enjoy solitude. Others fear it like the plague. Many people are said to be in an "in between" position regarding solitude. (One wonders if increasing urbanization has not caused the majority of people in the United States to dislike solitude or even fear it.) It is when the patient either likes solitude, or does not know what solitude is all about, which probably means he does not often need it, the therapist can ask the following question directly, "Are you ever so lonely that you become restless?" An affirmative answer is highly significant (probably because it suggests that there is a serious barrier to meaningful interpersonal relations.)

With the exception of one or two topics, I believe I have reviewed enough of the developmental history-taking in the detailed inquiry to provide the reader with an overall picture of Sullivan's suggested outline for obtaining data about how the patient has got to be what he is. It is not a definitive outline. Sullivan expected his students to utilize their own knowledge and experience to "fill in many of the details." So there seems to be no need to summarize every detail of his outline.

He recommended that the interviewer inquire into the patient's use of alcohol and of his possible use of narcotics. This is to be followed by an investigation of the patient's eating habits, his sleep habits and sleep functions or, roughly, dreamings. Then comes the topic of sex which, though it has been amply discussed in previous chapters, is such a hallowed subject in psychiatry that one cannot pass over it. Sullivan rejected the Freudian idea that sexuality is a "mirror of personality."

When the topic of genital sexual behavior, and related matters, has been introduced, the interviewer may say, "Well, and what of the sex life? Are you very restrained in such things, or are you quite free? Are you promiscuous?" The last question may provoke some kind of sputtering response, but it may also provoke the patient to talk about his sex life if only to defend himself. In any event, having got some sort of information, the interviewer may continue with, "Well, how long has it been true? I don't suppose you've always been like that. Give me a notion of the history of your sexual experience. For example, when did it begin?" For reasons previously explained, it is necessary to learn the beginning of things. Sullivan would be satisfied at this point if the patient can tell him "a little bit of something" about the first sexual encounter since he would already have gathered almost all the data he needed to guess about the latter's major problems and his probable adjustment to the life circumstances that may be before him. The interviewer is "really sparring around" for something he may have missed in the previous interviews. He is not really searching for anything "more intimately sexual" than how the interviewee relates to members of the opposite sex, that is, as friends or enemies. If the informant appears to be "notoriously normal" in his sexual behavior (that is, "protesting" too much), the interviewer will attempt to discover whether his genital performances are really autoerotic, whether in other words, he is using the other person's genitals in lieu of his own hands. The therapist will also try to find out whether the patient's heterosexual performances are really security operations: activities designed primarily to maintain or enhance his prestige. Still again the interviewer will want to know whether the interviewee's heterosexual operations are designed to satisfy him and his partner.

Inquiries about the patient's sex life make possible an easy transition to the subject of marriage and his history of courtship. The reconnaissance will already have provided a good deal of information about these things. Now one may seek an assessment of the interpersonal patterns characterizing the interviewee's married life: his satisfactions and dissatisfactions, his securities and insecurities. Who runs things? Or who is "the person who is run?" Or do husband and wife "happily share in their dominance over each other?" Who are the people, such as in-laws, that are influencing "the mate?" Another and never-to-be-forgotten piece of required information has to do with whether the mate is harassed by a necessity of keeping up with the Joneses. Is the patient (or his spouse) deeply disappointed with the marriage relationship? However, much of this information is inferred from answers to indirect or oblique questions. One often avoids direct and possibly embarrassing questions about many of these details of the interviewee's marriage relationship.

Other inquiries concerning parenthood, vocational history, and avocational interests follow but it does not seem necessary to review them.

In connection with the developmental history, Sullivan suggested a schematization of the personified self (that to which we refer when we say "I" or "Me" and what others call the "self concept"), which is a subsystem of the self or self-dynamism.

First of all one inquires about what the patient esteems and what he disparages about himself. The latter is much harder to find out. Second, the interviewer will want to know to what kinds of experience the patient's self-esteem is unreasonably vulnerable. It may be of interest to note in passing that some people have a knack for *consciously* attacking another's vulnerable spots—especially if they do not think he will or can retaliate swiftly or cruelly. Third, the therapist makes inquiries regarding the interviewee's security operations after he has been discomposed, made upset or anxious—and *knows* it. (When he does not know it, he will tend to employ different security operations: annoyance, irritation, anger, etc.) There are many ways by which individuals react when this happens. Fourth, the interviewer will inquire as to the interviewee's reserves of security. This has to be analyzed into more specific characterizations. For example, can the interviewee relate characteristics of himself, of his life, which are, beyond reasonable doubt, estimable? Does he have exalted purposes in life that he demonstrates *in action* rather than merely speech? A number of people profess exalted purposes while in fact they lead petty or self-centered lives. Still again, the therapist will want to learn if the patient harbors secret sources of shame or enduring regret. A famous illustration from literature comes to mind: Hawthorne's *The Scarlet Letter.* When there are such secret sources of shame or enduring regret, the interviewer inquires about their relation to the person's justification of his life. Without a justification of some sort, sometimes they will generate gnawing doubts about the worth of life itself, like an unhealed ulcer slowly sapping the victim's vitality. Of course, almost anyone who has been "really in touch" with what has happened to him from childhood onward will have some enduring regrets, and he may not escape lasting shame about one thing or another. But that does not necessarily entail the loss or lack of a reserve of security or self-esteem. The sort of justification for living he has or believes he has will tip the balance in either direction: toward a great reserve of security or concealed self-recrimination, shame, and regret.

But how does the interviewer discover these things? He must inquire as to the manner the patient habitually seeks to be regarded. "Does he seek to give the impression to most people that he is amiable, considerate, kind, and thoughtful; or—somewhat the reverse of these—does he seek to convey the impression that he is thoughtless, severe, cruel, inconsiderate or austere?"[36] The impression that a person seems to be trying to convey indicates the way he has found suitable for dealing with life situations, which in turn reveals data about the personified self. But one must also bear in mind that what one consciously tries to convey is not necessarily what he will convey since there are aspects of his self, and of his entire personality, that are not ordinarily accessible to him. For the general reader, the following fairly minor illustration may serve. Once when Sullivan was talking to the writer about a well-known professor of psychology, whom Sullivan believed to be a rather hostile person who ordinarily strove to convey a benevolent attitude, he said, "Watch Professor Jones's face in repose when he thinks he is not being observed." Needless to say, this suggestion was meant to provide only one clue as to what might lie in back of the attitude that the professor apparently had consciously organized in his dealings with others.

In the same inquiry regarding the personified self, the interviewer seeks to discover what is the usual attitude shown by the patient toward servants, "and after some considerable digression", what attitude he sustains toward animals, that is, toward inferior creatures.

Among other things the interviewer will try to discover is the interviewee's attitude toward others in relatively unaccustomed interpersonal situations and contacts as compared with his attitude in familiar situations. How does he relate to socially superior people? Is his attitude disturbed? Does he become anxious? Or does he remain self-confident and assured? Analogously, how does he relate to the less fortunate, socially inferior people? Does he "pull rank"? Or is he gracious and unassuming? In this connection, one would like to mention that it can be enlightening to observe the way some people treat department store clerks or taxi drivers. Sullivan used to say that anyone who has to deal with the public day in and day out is not likely to sustain a sweet disposition. The fact that at least a small minority of people who constantly deal with the public in large cities still seem to preserve a genuine amiable attitude is a minor miracle. (A disturbance of attitude is said to be sometimes marked also when a person visits a country whose language and customs are different.)

Another important trait that the interviewer hopes to find out about pertains to real humor, "with the capacity for maintaining a sense of proportion as to his place in the tapestry of life." In other words, real humor is one of the marks of a more mature person. But it is often confused with a lot of other things: *vide* certain television programs.

"And lastly," Sullivan said, "how dearly does the interviewee actually value his life, and how steadfastly, and for how long, has he so valued it? Here I refer to a sense of proportion which is perhaps even broader than the life-saving real sense of humor. What does the person consider to be worth more than himself? For what would he really sacrifice his life? When did that come to be the case? How unalterable is it? How much of it is a matter of mood? As I have said, all of these data bear on a consideration of the personified self of the interviewee, in contrast with all the other data that the interviewer may pick up in an interview."[37]

The Psychiatric Interview contains a chapter on "Diagnostic Signs and Patterns of Mental Disorder." In order to avoid repetition of a good deal of previous discussions in this and other chapters of this book, I will not review it. However, for the general reader it may be useful to bring up one point. In the interview, the therapist is said to be able to make diagnostic observations on the basis of *signs* as they are verified by symptoms reported by the patient. The signs can be observed more or less objectively. Signs include depression, elation, overdramatic extravagance about matters of fact (when this is patterned it becomes a familiar behavior pattern of the hysteric), psychopathic fluency of speech (wherein the patient can give a fluent and superficially plausible account of a most estimable past and anticipated very good future), fatigue phenomena, disturbance of verbal communication, disturbance in the gestural components of communication, among others. But symptoms are *reported* by the patient because only the patient experiences the symptoms. The psychiatrist must not always take signs at face value. He must inquire into the meaning of the signs; that is, he must determine whether there are corresponding symptoms that are experienced by the patient. Otherwise he runs the risk of making gross errors of interpretation.

Every interview situation, even though it may have continued for years, as in prolonged psychotherapy, finally, of course, reaches a termination (or interruption, owing to a variety of causes). In terminating the interview or in interrupting it for any length of time the important thing is said to be to consolidate whatever progress has been achieved. Progress is measured by the degree to which the purpose of the therapy has been realized. This progress is objective, not a mere change of the patient's state of mind. In other words, his maladjustment or his difficulties in living have been alleviated or resolved. This does not mean that he will forever after enjoy abounding bliss. For anyone, life presents very real problems that cannot be dealt with by psychotherapy because they are part of the nature of things. For example, a severe economic depression can—because it has—cause untold misery to millions of normal people. A limited war, that is, a nonthermonuclear war (I assume there would be no problems following upon the latter) can bring devastation and death to hundreds of thousands of people. An invasion of a country by a foreign power, such as that which in recent years occurred in Hungary and Czechoslovakia, can bring demoralization or death to countless hapless individuals. Exploitation, in varying degrees, seems to be endemic. So do intergroup hatreds. Turning from the national and international scene, one can observe the widespread misfortunes visited upon a myriad of individuals: the death of a spouse, physical illnesses whose number can scarcely be counted, cultural deprivation, personal misfortunes due to local circumstances beyond one's control, and the like. The list is endless. So it needs to be emphasized that the psychiatrist can no more solve all of life's problems than can a surgeon or a politician. *There is no lasting solution, and perhaps no solution at all, to all of life's problems*—except death. A blind optimism is almost as bad as hopeless pessimism. The kinds of problems with which psychiatrists and clinical psychologists deal are widespread but so are those of the internist or surgeon. The field of mental disorders is primarily the area that encompasses Sullivan's "difficulties in living," though not entirely so. His techniques of therapy are also primarily aimed at the alleviation or cure of mental disorders, but again not exclusively. Sullivan's work embraces a spectrum of personal problems that at one end are more or less exclusively those of the clinician, and at the other, those that imperceptibly merge with the problems studied by social psychologists.

The consolidating of the interview's purpose is said to be done, grossly, by the following four steps: (1) The interviewer makes a *final statement* to the interviewee summarizing what he has learned during the course of the interview; (2) the interviewer gives the interviewee a *prescription of action* in which the interviewee is now to engage; (3) the interviewer makes a *final assessment* of the probable effects on the life course of the interviewee that may reasonably be expected from the statement and prescription; and (4) there is a *formal leave-taking* between the interviewer and the interviewee.[38]

The formulation of the first step seems self-explanatory. In it, the therapist offers his gross conclusions of which he is by this time quite sure. If the patient believes the formulation is inadequate, then the interviewer should take more time and make his summation adequate. If the patient is a person who must engage in all kinds of doubting, the therapist merely ignores it and continues with his summation.

The final summation in a good many interviews leaves things out. If the prognosis is unfavorable, the therapist almost never mentions it in this last summary. He most emphatically carefully avoids destroying whatever chance in life the person has left. One must never "close all doors to a person." He should be encouraged to depart with hope and with an improved grasp on what has been troubling him.

The prescription of action has to be carefully carried out. Sullivan claimed that there were few things so harrowing (to him) as the occasional psychiatrist who knows a great deal about right and wrong, how things should be done, what is good taste, and the like. Such a psychiatrist is said to often feel a missionary spirit so that he wants to pass on his own values to his patient, which is in effect a general prescription for action, not mere advice. This is not only hard on the patient, but it creates difficulty for any other psychiatrist who may try to help the patient at some later date, if things are not going well in the latter's life.

Sullivan taught that the interviewer should offer a particular prescription for action, in certain circumstances, whether he plans to see the patient again or is presumably carrying out his final interview with him. When the interview was interrupted, even if briefly, Sullivan would offer a prescription "in the nature of homework" as a setting for the next session. In regard to some point that puzzled him he might say, "The business of how so-and-so came about is obscure. Well, maybe it will come back to you by next time." Thus he has given the patient something to do meanwhile. Anyway, regardless of such a suggestion, the latter will do some homework before the next meeting, though the psychiatrist may have better judgment about what might be useful, and also necessary or valuable in some anticipated course of action.

Sullivan asserted that if the interviewer does not plan to see the patient again he may prescribe that he find someone with whom to do intensive psychotherapy, or, in the case of an employment interview, that the interviewee look for a kind of job that is different from the one he is seeking. "In other words, the interviewer indicates a course of events in which the interviewee might engage and which, in the interviewer's opinion, in view of the data accumulated, would improve his chances of success and satisfaction in life."[39]

On certain occasions Sullivan undertook to give advice most vigorously, including a recommendation that a psychotic patient sign himself or herself into a mental hospital if an when he or she felt called upon to act violently or destructively toward the "troublesome" people with whom the person worked. Sometimes he "disadvised" a course of action "with force." Suppose a patient asserted that he was going to do something that would almost certainly be disastrous, and it was clear that he meant it, Sullivan would say "No!" emphatically, following this up with, "Merciful God! Let us consider what will follow that." Then he would depict the probable course of events as he expected them to unfold. After that he would ask the patient if he had done more than anticipate the obvious. Unless the interviewee could show that he was excessively pessimistic or wrong, then the latter had to face up to a situation with clear foresight of disaster. Under such circumstances very few people will go ahead with plans that, if carried out, will bring disastrous consequences.

In the final assessment, the interviewer gives thought as to how the interviewee is going to receive what has been offered to him, the final survey and prescription of action, in this last interview. The skillful therapist knows how to direct his final statement and prescription of action in such a way that they depict a reasonably constructive picture from the point of view of the patient. The interviewer will be wise to assess what this picture is, trying to make sure that it is a constructive one.

Much good work in psychotherapy can be "horribly garbled or completely destroyed" in the last few minutes of the final interview. So it is said to be very important that the interviewer, as soon as he can, find a way of detaching himself from the interview situation without awkwardness and without prejudice. Certain patients frantically reach for more of something or for some "great formula." The therapist must know how to "exclude a patient" once the interview situation has come to an end. He must know how to make "a clean-cut, respectful finish" that does not confuse what has been accomplished. Thus, in the final minutes, the psychiatrist must not go over things, and he must not explain what is now clearer than it ever will be if he repeats himself.

I have left to the very end a discussion of Sullivan's ideas on the treatment of schizophrenics.[40] All I want to do is elaborate certain points that were briefly summarized in Chapter 1. Much of what has been said in this chapter applies to schizophrenics as well, but only after they have recovered from their more disturbed states and are willing to take a chance on the therapist. In this connection, I wish to refer the reader to Mary Julian White's superb paper "Sullivan and Treatment" in *The Contributions of Harry Stack Sullivan.* It will supplement not only this final review, but the entire chapter, even though she errs on at least one point: that Sullivan "gave up the use of free association after having carefully used the method for a number of years." As long as he carried on intensive psychotherapy, he never did; but he learned that it has serious limitations. So he used it when he thought it was appropriate, but he was too brilliant and original a therapist to rely on any one "method." In the course of his career he used several techniques, including the utilization of hypnosis and chemotherapy, which is discussed in *Personal Psychopathology.* Parenthetically, his outstanding failure was perhaps with manic-depressives because, I suspect, he could not stand their "mania." Anyone who knew Sullivan can conjure up a comical picture of him getting his hair mussed up by one of them. (Can anyone imagine Freud in a similar situation?) As Redlich and Freedman have said: "To spend an hour a day with a manic patient, letting him associate freely (which he does all too readily) can be more a filibuster than treatment." Nevertheless, some of Sullivan's former students and colleagues (Mabel Cohen, Robert Cohen, Frieda Fromm-Reichmann, *et al.)* made spectacular progress in the treatment and understanding of manic-depressives.

Schizophrenics are people who are bedeviled by feelings of inferiority, loneliness, and failure in living. They are said to be remarkably shy, low in their self-esteem, and rather convinced that they are not highly appreciated by others long before they suffer the grave psychosis. Driven by certain insoluble problems in interpersonal relations, some of which have been discussed, they are forced to abandon, at least temporarily, the more adult patterns of living, including the cognitive and other features of socialized living. In *waking life* they revert to the types of thought processes that characterize late infancy and childhood. But this does not mean they abandon the struggle to live, as their symptoms and experiences so eloquently testify. For Sullivan the essential schizophrenic condition or state is the catatonic.

Sullivan taught that the catatonic schizophrenic, who is often mute and engages in practically none of the communication by gesture on which we ordinarily depend, seems to many very strange and very inaccessible. Nevertheless, even though he cannot communicate, he is "in touch with events." In treating such a person Sullivan would proceed, owing to the restrictions imposed on him, by operating with an almost purely hypothetical other person. "Because of the extreme handicaps on any real interchange with this person," he said, "there is a very great possibility of the most serious error in his understanding me, and there is also a strong possibility that a great deal of what I might be inclined to guess or to say to him will be profoundly irrelevant."[41] Therefore, Sullivan said he reduced his attempts at communication to certain things that seemed to him so very highly probable that the chances of their being irrelevant were small. He related how he would talk slowly and carefully, perhaps saying the same thing several ways, not necessarily in succession, but still trying to cover the ground from various angles. Should the patient be or remain "in touch," his therapist will have achieved the objective of the interview, provided he has correctly guessed what was profoundly important to the patient at the time, and provided, also, that he has expressed it in language that was meaningful at the time so that it connects in the patient's mind with the correct implications rather than with some very highly autistic content. In other words, if the patient was willing to trust his therapist enough to listen to what he was trying to say, and if the therapist hit upon matters that are meaningful and relevant to what is going on in the patient's mind, or on significant matters that he can correctly understand, the therapist will have achieved the purpose of the interview. The objective is primarily the patient's receiving "some durable benefit." At this stage of therapy with a catatonic schizophrenic, the durable benefit is said to be simply that the patient get the idea that his therapist is really interested in him, that he is taking a lot of trouble over him, that he knows something about what has probably happened in the patient's past, and that he (the therapist) is dealing with urgent matters of real importance. In this way, the patient might—and often did—get the impression that the therapist knew something "about what ailed" him and was interested in him as a person—never as a "case." Sullivan spent months at a time with some of these catatonic schizophrenics, engaging in this kind of therapy. Eventually a significant number of patients emerged from the catatonic stupor and were able to participate in the interview as described above.

Needless to say, any psychiatrist who conducts this kind of therapy with mute patients will suffer stress. After a time he may abandon it for less stressful and perhaps more lucrative work. "It is very sad indeed," Sullivan related, "to be confronted with fifty minutes of an utterly uncommunicative patient, when you have only one or two ideas that seem to meet the criterion of being highly probable."[42] Eventually he realized that it was not the length of time he spent that counted but the seriousness of his effort to avoid any possible misunderstanding in communicating what he had to say, and the keenness of his interest in what had happened to the patient. After the psychiatrist has done his best in these respects, he must call it quits and depart before he becomes discouraged. To continue beyond that point would serve no useful therapeutic purpose. Furthermore, the catatonic, despite the psychiatrist's most skillful work, and profound interest, may decide that he does not "want to come to America."

Sullivan's technique of interrogation and reassurance of an ambulatory schizophrenic was as follows. He claimed that the therapist must have a lively plan of action before he attacks the problem of discovering what really worries the patient. Since it is easier for him to talk about past problems than to talk about what makes him extremely anxious, terrified, or "panicky" about the present, the therapist can get good hunches in hearing him tell of his past history. So he steers the interview accordingly. Finally, one may ask, "What really is haunting you all the time?" Suppose the patient says "I am a homosexual." The psychiatrist must *not* assume that this statement means the same thing to the patient as it might to him, but he should observe that it is extremely important to the patient. The therapist may say something to the effect that he does not think it is as awful as the patient does. Nevertheless, Sullivan claimed it is risky for the patient to think he is a homosexual, or to know he is. So the therapist then proceeds smoothly and more or less automatically to ask, "Now what in the world makes you think so?" Most frequently the answer will be, "Well, you damn well know I am, Doctor." To which the therapist will reply, "Well, I don't know what you mean by being homosexual—it hadn't occurred to me. What makes you think you are? Do you know anything that points that way?" Always, the patient does know. Following upon the latter's account of a homosexual experience, Sullivan would proceed to ask about the circumstances. He would inquire as to whether the patient sought it or whether it was forced upon him. Sullivan would proceed thus in a matter-of-fact, commonplace fashion, regardless of the answers, which in itself tends to be reassuring. If the Doctor talks as though he were inquiring about a weather forecast, he can scarcely be horrified over what he has heard. Then Sullivan would make the "final movement." This final movement occurs when the patient does not seem to be so tense as he was at the terrible admission. Gazing into the future, so to speak, he would say, "Oh, yes, I can see how it looks that way to you now." At that, he was through with the particular interview, having done everything he could to protect his relationship with the patient and prevent him from going into a panic over his admissions. He has *suggested* that the patient may be wrong, which carries an implication that both will talk some more, continue the inquiry. It is not the end of the world.

Sullivan taught the importance "of carefully putting almost a scaffolding under the patient's self-system."[43] The therapist must build a "me-you pattern" between him and the patient that is of an utterly previously unexperienced solidity and dependability. "Only then can you get to the point where you can deal with disturbing material without causing this sudden disturbance of the self-function of suppressing more primitive types of mental process, with, as a result, the abolition of communication and God knows what results in the patient, in the sense of what finally comes out as a result of your efforts."[44] In this connection the psychiatrist must not play the role of the Great Physician who holds out the balm of cure. The schizophrenic has enough inferiority feelings without having to deal with a Great Man. Nor must the therapist toss out a great statement of where the patient's difficulties lie and where wisdom might be found. The latter's self-system could not tolerate them—even if he could understand what the Great Man is talking about. (It seems to be a general rule that a therapist who treats any sort of patient must carefully avoid conveying such an imposture.) If the psychiatrist fails to adhere to these injunctions his schizophrenic patient will relapse into primitive referential processes. Thus Sullivan asserted that the therapist must neither attempt direct communication of security nor be so superior that it is impossible for an extremely insecure person to imagine himself being on the same level.

So the psychiatrist has to structure the relationship with his patient by, first, circumventing any avoidable, foreseeable disturbance of the schizophrenic's security. He must exercise exquisite care in circumventing unnecessary bad jolts to the patient. This will give him a good chance to preserve communication—and if there is no communication there is no therapy.[45] One must bear in mind that the precise meaning of words in the therapist's mind are probably by no means identical with the patient's meaning of words, in which a "residual" of autistic meaning is considerable. Therefore, Sullivan taught that the psychiatrist's statements must always be as near the commonplace, as near as possible to the everyday use of words, as he can make them. But when the insecurity of the patient is aroused by all sorts of things over which the therapist has no control the latter can still maintain a "feeling of familiarity" with what is being said without the conceit of believing that he is intimately following what is happening. Nor should the psychiatrist become upset, ready to start climbing the walls. As long as he regards the schizophrenic's behavior "as part of the universe," the patient knows that there is someone who, though he may not understand, regards the patient's behavior as not terribly and horribly strange. During his more lucid moments and by a great deal of fairly lucid reflection, the patient realizes that the psychiatrist does not look upon him as terribly strange and barely human. "That immediately reduces the gravity of being schizophrenic." The patient is said to note that someone else seems to consider his communications as not desirable, something to get rid of, if possible, though by no means fantastic. Also, by his attitude the psychiatrist has made the positive contribution to the patient's realization that at last he has encountered someone who will be a real help, instead of a delusional help, which may have been the case in the past, to be followed by a sharp rebuff and disappointment. Such an achievement seems to be effected very largely by the psychiatrist's great care in assuming or accepting the probabilities (of improvement and greater understanding) from the point of view of the patient as he reflects upon the therapist's operations. But this idea needs clarification.

Sullivan said that since the schizophrenic has a whole pattern of inadequate security dynamisms, whose inadequacy has been a terribly impressive aspect of all his previous life, it is a pretty good bet that the instances in which he has succeeded have left very little easily accessible evidence. In such circumstances, Sullivan adds, an occasional success can either precipitate him into an excitement or is immediately followed by a firm conviction that, "Well, it's probably a mistake on my part—at least it won't last and the next thing that happens will be bad."[46] It seems that in many of people's very insecure operations during the course of living, if the other fellow obviously expects one *not* to do what he wants, one is apt to get so puzzled about it that he does not do it. Thus the schizophrenic person is said to practically guarantee a great deal of woe for himself. Hence the psychiatrist cannot resort to neat reassuring questions that he might use with an obsessional patient, such as "I presume you don't think a great deal about drinking your morning coffee. And for God's sake, don't begin, otherwise you'll drown yourself." This may be roughly interpreted as "It isn't necessary to plague oneself with thinking about, or doubting the meaning of, every incident in life." One cannot employ such a stratagem of reassurance with a schizophrenic because he probably has "sputtered in his coffee" or dropped a cup of coffee on someone's lap—a reminder of very painful past experiences connected with eating.

Sullivan claimed that a good many of the therapeutic operations calculated to increase the schizophrenic's feeling of security must be done *indirectly.* But one must never be *obscure* if only because that would increase the difficulties of communication. Suppose a patient has decided that he never was married to a woman who claims she is his wife—even though most of the time he is more or less conscious of the fact that he did participate in a marriage ceremony. At such a denial the psychiatrist may say, "I can understand your having doubts, or even a tendency to deny the marriage." The significant term in this statement is "doubts," which is placed in this particular context. The psychiatrist then would or should go on to other things for the patient will *at the time* give no attention to the context of doubt. The latter is not likely to repond to something he does not follow. That seems to be a characteristic of schizophrenics. Subsequently, when there is no pressure from the therapist's presence and the patient feels calm, he will tend to think, "Why, I *did* marry that woman. Now why do I say she isn't my wife? Oh yeah, that doctor! He said *doubting* or denying!

Christ, yes! I suppose that's the fact. I got so used to saying 'How in hell *could* I have married this woman' that finally I decided I hadn't."[47] Thus the patient tends to catch on to the fact the therapist seems to understand that in a dilemma he has long periods of unhappy doubting. And so in successful therapy with schizophrenics Sullivan was able, step by step, or stage by stage, to help bring them back to a state in which the interview techniques reviewed in this chapter could be employed, though not necessarily in every detail. I think he would have scoffed at the idea that the therapist must first bring a psychotic patient back to a neurotic state. In all likelihood he would have denounced it as an instance of the misuse of categorial thinking.

I have written enough, I believe, to provide the reader with a fairly comprehensive exposition of Sullivan's therapeutic techniques. Much more could be written, including a review of his techniques of treating obsessional people, which is described chiefly in *Clinical Studies in Psychiatry*. But I think I can safely leave the rest to the interested reader for perusal at his leisure. As another supplement to this chapter, young psychiatrists and clinical psychologists may find Wolberg's *The Technique of Psychotherapy* very helpful.[48] Even though his summary of Sullivanian therapy (pp. 235-241) is very feeble, he seems to share a great many ideas on therapy with Sullivan.

The influence of interpersonal psychiatry is now very great and seems likely to increase. Sullivan set forth many concepts that he did not live to develop, providing a rich harvest for others to reap.

Notes

1. Leo Srole, Thomas S. Langer, Stanley T. Michael, Marvin K. Opler, and Thomas A. C. Rennie, *Mental Health in the Metropolis* (New York: McGraw-Hill Book Company, 1962).

2. See, for example, Otto Klineberg and Richard Christie (eds.), *Perspectives in Social Psychology* (New York: Holt, Rinehart and Winston, 1965).

3. Cf. Harry Stack Sullivan, *Conceptions of Modern Psychiatry,* with a Foreword by the author and a Critical Appraisal of the Theory by Patrick Mullahy (New York: W. W. Norton and Company, 1953)., pp. 193-195, and George Lichtheim, "Alienation," *International Encyclopedia of the Social Sciences,* Vol. I.

4. Sullivan, *Conceptions of Modern Psychiatry,* p. 185.

5. *Ibid.,* pp. 93-94.

6. *Ibid.,* 214-215.

7. *Ibid.,* pp. 186-187.

8. *Ibid.,* p. 187.

9. Cf. John Dewey, *Logic: The Theory of Inquiry* (New York: Henry Holt and Company, 1938), pp. 104-180 and chap. 24, "Social Inquiry."

10. Sullivan, *Conceptions of Modern Psychiatry,* pp. 187-188.

11. *Ibid.,* p. 188.

12. Frieda Fromm-Reichmann, *Principles of Intensive Psychotherapy* (Chicago, Illinois: University of Chicago Press, 1950), p. 103.

13. Sullivan, *Conceptions of Modern Psychiatry,* p. 223.

14. *Ibid.,* p. 207.

15. *Ibid.,* p. 234.

16. Irving L. Janis, George F. Mahl, Jerome Kagan, and Robert R. Holt, *Personality: Dynamics, Development, and Assessment* (New York: Harcourt, Brace,

and World, 1969), Part IV, "Assessing Personality."

17. Cf. ERWIN SINGER, *Key Concepts in Psychotherapy* (New York: Random House, 1965).

18. SULLIVAN, *Conceptions in Modern Psychiatry,* p. 208.

19. HARRY STACK SULLIVAN, *The Psychiatric Interview,* ed. HELEN SWICK PERRY and MARY LADD GAWEL, with an Introduction by OTTO ALLEN WILL, JR. (New York: W. W. Norton and Company, 1954), p. 21.

20. *Ibid.,* p. 54.

21. *Ibid.,* p. 55.

22. *Ibid.,* p. 46.

23. *Ibid.,* p. 49.

24. HARRY STACK SULLIVAN, *Clinical Studies in Psychiatry,* ed. HELEN SWICK PERRY, MARY LADD GAWEL, and MARTHA GIBBON, with a Foreword by DEXTER M. BULLARD (New York: W. W. Norton and Company, 1956), pp. 275-276.

25. SULLIVAN, *The Psychiatric Interview,* p. 75.

26. *Ibid.,* p. 89.

27. See, for example, JANIS, MAHL, KAGAN, and HOLT, *op. cit.,* pp. 210-213, 618-620, 718-720.

28. SULLIVAN, *The Psychiatric Interview,* p. 83.

29. *Ibid.,* p. 84.

30. *Ibid.,* p. 97.

31. *Ibid.,* p. 101.

32. See, for example, EDWIN KASIN, "Interpretation as Active Nurture: An Interpersonal Perspective," in EMMANUEL F. HAMMER (ed.), *Use of Interpretation in Treatment* (New York: Grune and Stratton, 1968).

33. SULLIVAN, *The Psychiatric Interview,* p. 121.

34. *Ibid.,* pp. 111-112.

35. *Ibid.,* pp. 154-155.

36. *Ibid.,* p. 180.

37. *Ibid.,* p. 182.

38. *Ibid.,* pp. 209-210.

39. *Ibid.,* p. 212.

40. Cf. SILVANO ARIETI, *Interpretation of Schizophrenia* (New York: Basic Books, 1955).

41. SULLIVAN, *The Psychiatric Interview,* pp. 206-207.

42. *Ibid.,* pp. 207-208.

43. SULLIVAN, *Clinical Studies in Psychiatry,* p. 363.

44. *Ibid.*

45. Cf. SULLIVAN, *The Psychiatric Interview,* chap. 10.

46. SULLIVAN, *Clinical Studies in Psychiatry,* p. 368.

47. *Ibid.,* p. 370.

48. LEWIS R. WOLBERG, *The Technique of Psychotherapy* (2nd ed.; New York: Grune and Stratton, 1967).

12/Some Recent Developments

I begin this chapter with an apology to all those distinguished psychiatrists and psychologists who have made substantial contributions to interpersonal psychiatry—sometimes called "transactional" psychoanalysis or "transactional" psychiatry—during the past fifteen years. In order to do justice to this ever-growing field, one would have to write another large volume. In any event, Judd Marmor and some of his associates have done a good deal in providing a compendium of recent developments.[1] Ironically, he does not mention Sullivan at all, though that is now of no great importance. In an introductory essay, "New Directions in Psychoanalytic Theory and Therapy," Marmor raises the old and hackneyed issue, whether the "new directions" covered in *Modern Psychoanalysis* can rightly be called *psychoanalysis*. And he suggests that, from a scientific point of view, the question is irrelevant. The essential, logical relevant question would run something like this: How valid are these new ideas? Another relevant question might be: Are the techniques of psychotherapy that are employed in connection with these ideas efficacious, and if so, to what extent? Still again, one might ask: In what ways, or to what degree, are they superior to Freudian classical psychoanalysis? Fifty years from now, the question: Is it psychoanalysis? is going to sound rather silly. Freud will have his rightful place—whatever it may be—in the history of psychiatry (or more generally, in the history of thought) and that will be that.

But, as I mentioned earlier, there are extrapsychiatric considerations, usually unavowed, involved: considerations of "economics," prestige, power, and the like. So Marmor feels called upon to answer the traditional question—Yes, he says, the new directions are psycho-analytic if, as he believes, the essence of Freud's great contribution has to do with the recognition of the fact that human behavior is motivated (a view Freud shared with many others); that this motivation is often largely unconscious (a view Freud also shared with many others, though it was chiefly he who saw the implications of this view); that the human personality is shaped by experiential as well as biological determinants (one of the least original of Freud's ideas, and one that he did not see very profoundly); that functional personality disorders are the result of contradictory and conflictful "inputs or feedbacks"; and that early developmental experiences are significant determinants in shaping subsequent perceptions and reactions in adolescence and adulthood. (There is one thing in particular that classical psychoanalysts would insist upon, now increasingly called into question—the allegedly pervasive function of sexuality *from infancy* onward, which Marmor, like Sullivan, does not accept.) Let it be granted, then, that Freud was a giant, the loftiest figure in modern psychiatry, but he must not be allowed to stand in the way of those who can have progressed far beyond him. During the 1930's and 1940's, if not longer, a whole generation of psychoanalysts worshipped blindly at his feet with the result that the entire period in classical psychoanalysis from Brill to Zilboorg was largely sterile.

Marmor has pointed out that traditionally psychoanalysis has been considered to be (1) a method of investigation of thoughts and feelings of which the subject is unconscious; (2) a theory of human personality; and (3) a technique of therapy. He says that the psychoanalytic method of investigating unconscious processes remains unquestioned. Perhaps it should remain unquestioned, but its value is not universally recognized, especially among many psychologists who have their own methods. Although I think Marmor is right in thinking that psychoanalysis is by far the best method for uncovering unconscious psychological processes, I suggest that Sullivan's adaptation of the classical Freudian approach is a vast improvement, partly because he abandoned the "mirror model," making psychoanalysis more flexible, more of a transactional affair, less of an esoteric discipline that has to remain pure and undefiled, unencumbered by needless and dogmatic interpretations and assumptions. Marmor also notes that Freudian *theory* of human behavior has not equally well stood the test of time, though certain ideas ("constructs") regarding conflict, repression, transference (though this point is questionable if Freud's formulation be literally adopted), and unconscious psychological processes are still extremely efficacious. Marmor *should* have said they are "effective" because they are, within varying limits, true. But he says the data on which they were based can be dealt with just as effectively within other frames of reference, such as those of communication theory or learning theory—but he does not attempt to validate his assertion. No doubt they have important things to offer psychoanalysis, just as sociology and cultural anthropology do. Marmor all too easily accepts the idea that different frames of reference are equally useful or valid.[2] That would have to be demonstrated, and I do not think it has. Equally questionable is his notion that psychoanalysis *as a technique of therapy* has failed to fulfill its original high promise. I suggest that what I wrote about psychoanalysis as a method of inquiry applies here too. In other words, it is Freud's theory of human nature allied with his "mirror model" that have gravely hindered a more effective use of psychoanalytic technique. Although Freud was a giant, he was blind in one eye (instinctivism). Hence the house that Freud built rested on flimsy foundations. It had to be restructured, set on more firm foundations, and greatly expanded. More than anyone else Sullivan was the man who effectively began this work and to a very significant extent succeeded. Meanwhile, others have been busy working along similar lines, or extending his work, often with impressive results.

There seems to be no need to be pessimistic about psychoanalytic technique, provided one accepts Sullivan's "variant" of it, as in fact Marmor does. To be sure it is not universally applicable. It makes demands that a great many people cannot meet. So what? A great many people are unable to learn calculus—even if their lives depend on it. But no one—so far—has suggested that it is too "limited."

The time has arrived when psychoanalysts, whether Freudian or "neo-freudian," should surrender the dream that their techniques are potentially capable of "curing" functional illness no matter what the native endowment or life circumstances of the patient. Since psychoanalysis is a transactional affair, it cannot control or even modify all the circumstances governing the life of any and every patient. For example, psychoanalysis is not suited or applicable to a person with an IQ of, say, ninety. Psychiatrists and clinical psychologists have created techniques of therapy that can be of considerable help to those who are less endowed or less fortunate. Although psychoanalysis is not *essentially* a therapy designed only for those in the upper-income brackets, it is of necessity limited to those whose intelligence, drive, and life situation are not inferior to an, as yet, indefinitely specifiable range of human powers and life situations.

Actually Marmor is not nearly as pessimistic about psychoanalysis as he appears. The following passage makes that clear:

> At the level of individual therapy, the emphasis is changing from one in which the therapist does something to the patient by "analyzing" him, to an examination of the nature of the reciprocal interaction between therapist and patient. The nature and quality of this transactional system is now seen as the crucial factor in achieving therapeutic progress rather than the former assumption that that which was crucial was the nature of the repetitive insights that the analyst gave to the patient. As a consequence, the therapist is no longer viewed as a neutral, impersonal conveyor of interpretations, but rather as an active human participant in a verbal and nonverbal, affective as well as cognitive, reciprocal interaction in which *both* participants "change" over the course of time. In this view, the personality of the therapist is seen as an important factor which needs to be evaluated and understood just as fully as that of the patient. . . . Moreover, in recognition of the fact that both patient and therapist, as open systems, are products of their surrounding media, an understanding of class differences, value systems, group-linked verbal and behavioral patterns, and the like becomes highly relevant and indeed essential for optimal therapeutic effectiveness. . . .[3]

Apparently as a result of his work with hysterics, Freud thought at least during the major part of his career that the etiology of mental disorder always entailed a significant sexual factor. Also as a result of his work with hysterics, he created his famous "theory" of infantile sexuality. There is no need to attempt another recital of these matters. At present this theory is being rapidly discredited, though not in every detail. Leon Salzman's paper "Sexuality in Psychoanalytic Theory" seems to contain an excellent overview of this highly controversial subject.[4] Salzman claims that psychoanalytic investigations took their initial impetus from the libido theory, which presumed that the sexual instinct was the major directing force in human development. Sex was regarded primarily as an instinct. But it was studied "in terms of the aim or object of the drive rather than as an activity between two people in which a multitude of reactions, responses, and interactions occur."[5] Since sex in man generally is said to occur in an atmosphere of tenderness and mutual regard, it resembles animal activity only to the extent that it is an act of procreation. Hence, in man the biological significance of sex is only a small part of its total significance. Salzman points out that in recent years there has been a much greater emphasis on the interpersonal aspects of sex behavior, by a number of investigators, a development that takes into account the extraordinary capacity of sex to fulfill many of man's needs aside from the biological function of procreation. Sexual disorders, as well as other mental disorders, are said to be seen as complications of personality development as a whole rather than of sexual development in particular. The reader will recall that Sullivan published very similar ideas forty years ago.

Not only are the physiological mechanisms involved in coitus among primates in general functional before the individual is capable of reproduction, but social experience, it has been discovered, clearly influences the capacity to perform the act. Patterns of sexual behavior and performance seem to depend rather considerably on learned experience through contact with parents, siblings, and other members of society. As a biological model for the comprehension of personality development and its deviations, instinct theory is largely outmoded.

Granted that sexual activity is a source of intense pleasure and enjoyment, one need not assume that the latter occurs for the sake of procreation. "Adaptive behavior does not require a reward to encourage its performance, since it is beyond the choice of the animal and therefore is obligatory and compulsive."[6] But in the case of man, he *can* choose, and abandon sexual behavior if he is sufficiently motivated, that is, if other goals seem far superior, as in the case of the religious, namely, monks, nuns, and others. Salzman asserts that the impetus for sex activity under ordinary circumstances rarely arises out of species-preservation needs, but comes from its enormous potentialities for satisfaction of various kinds.

Long ago C. G. Jung pointed out that Freud's ideas about infantile sexuality were an outgrowth of his work with adults. Salzman calls attention to the fact that since it is almost impossible to get direct data from adults regarding experiences prior to age four and similarly difficult to get statements of the meaning of the four-year-old's behavior, the information is all extrapolated from later years with data derived from free association or dream analysis. It is also true that some of the interpretations made in child analysis of three-or-four-year-old behavior are heavily influenced by the preconceptions of the observer and confirm the sexual nature of the oedipal attachment if one believes it to be present in the first place. Evidence from direct observational studies is said to be scanty and does not always confirm Freud's views. Though intensive studies of children are badly needed, the reader should exercise caution in crediting interpretations of infantile behavior derived from information that assumes a preexisting theory of the ubiquity of sexual behavior in children. In other words, if one believes, *a priori,* in the existence and ubiquity of infantile sexuality, then he will probably have no great difficulty "discovering" it in his work since *all* human behavior has to be interpreted and does not carry its meaning on its face, unrelated to past experiences, though conventional modes of interpretation may seem to "prove" otherwise. That is one of the things every young psychiatrist should be taught. He should never be forced or indoctrinated to accept *any* theory or interpretation that he cannot in fact or in principle learn to verify by investigation. That is why Sullivan "harped upon" the necessity of having alternative hypotheses.

Salzman goes on to say that recent research by D. E. Berlyne and others suggests that much activity of higher animals, and probably man, is concerned with obtaining stimuli with no manifest goal except to maintain levels of sensory experience and that traditional explanations of such behavior in terms of biological drives such as sex and survival are probably irrelevant. Much of such "exploratory" behavior is said to involve seeking out, novelty, change, complexity, and variety, having no specific adaptive motivation, either sexual, aggressive, or defensive. Such studies cast doubt on the traditional Freudian interpretation of certain preverbal patterns of behavior as being sexual in nature.

Preverbal behavior must be appraised without resort to fixed preconceptions about infantile sexuality. "The activity of the infant who passes his hand over his entire anatomy and particularly his mouth may simply be exploratory. Similarly, the handling of the genitals along with the earlobes, blanket, and so forth *may* have no special significance aside from the infant's need to explore his environment and his own body, receiving sensory input from his skin as well as from his lips, ears, penis, or genital area. At this time, and for a long time to come, the genital area is almost exclusively identified with urination. A great deal of the child's play, whether with the same or opposite sex, often involves mutual exploration or manipulation."[7] Because some children's games resemble adult sexual play, adults often interpret such games as sexual in nature. But an adult observer has no justification for interpreting such behavior as other than exploratory unless the participants are at some level aware that such play is sexual in the adult sense. Salzman affirms Sullivan's interpretation that because of an abundance of special nerve endings, the glans of the penis may become a favorite organ for manipulation. Similarly it is asserted that a focus on the penis or the female genital area by anxious, prudish, or puritanical parents can give these areas undue significance and cause associations with shame, loathing, or disgust even prior to gonadal maturation.

An interested reader will want to peruse other important topics in Salzman's essay regarding the role of sex in human development, sex differences, orgasm in the female, homosexuality, and sexual deviations. The essay makes clear that most of Freud's ideas on sexuality and its role in human life are either erroneous or extremely dubious.[8]

Interpersonal psychiatry ("interpersonal psychoanalysis") originated in Sullivan's work with schizophrenics just as classical psychoanalysis originated in Freud's work with hysterical neurotics. Of the many recent studies of schizophrenia a discussion of one or two of the papers published by Otto Allen Will, Jr., who has done a good deal of distinguished work in this field, seems most appropriate. In "Schizophrenia and Psychotherapy," Will has written that through the years in which he has had any formal contact with schizophrenic behavior there has extended one unifying thread, namely, that patient and therapist come together, are together, or as Sullivan would say, "integrate a situation" often unhappily and with distrust.[9] Patient and therapist are together in a difficult situation, in which each is curious, fearful, and driven to discover something of himself and the other. Will not only interprets change in terms of growth and learning but he also sees it as accompanied by trepidation, uncertainty, pain, and the lingering apprehension that the way one has chosen to go is the wrong way, permitting no return or no alternative.

In regard to schizophrenia and the psychotherapeutic encounter, he believes that schizophrenic behavior has its social origins in infancy. Will wrote that during this period, before the acquisition of speech skills and well-defined object identity, in the experience of the person who becomes schizophrenic human relatedness, interpersonal relations, are marked by anxiety and excessive ambiguity, doubt, and uncertainty regarding self-identity and "object relations." It is during infancy, he added, that there *begins* dissociation of systems of sentiments reflecting painful, inadequately perceived and differentiated, poorly formulated experience. The dissociation of such sentiments is extremely unfortunate, since they must be available to the person's consciousness in later life for the purpose of integrating complex, intimate attachments to other people if he is going to live a reasonably normal, healthy existence. In the case of the schizophrenic, the difficulties and failures that *originate* in the early years of his life interfere with the acquisition of (social) skills in the succeeding developmental stages, and at the same time have not been adequately corrected by later experience. Will claims that the appearance of gross behavioral distortions in the adolescence of some people who have previously made outwardly "good adjustments" may reflect social pressures to find suitable expression of the needs for intimacy and sexuality and to meet cultural demands for a public demonstration of, and a personal acceptance of, self-identity and of independence from earlier ties. So he emphasizes the interplay between the sequential unfolding of biologic potential and living experience but he does not attempt to characterize possible inadequacies in terms of a chemical-neurological-structural background. Summarily, the person who manifests psychotic behavior is said to be an individual who has not developed a clear-cut, satisfying, dependable concept of himself or of the motivations and expected behavior of others. The human relationships that he requires make him anxious. The schizophrenic's judgment, perception, and foresight, in his dealings with others, are seriously impaired by learning defects, by the dissociation of important motivational systems, "and by the recurrent, uncontrollable intrusion into awareness of poorly comprehended and frightening fragments of these latter, adding to familiar and seemingly 'normal' processes of thought a quality of the strange, the uncanny and the mad."[10]

Like Sullivan, Will regards hebephrenic and paranoid modes of conduct as behavioral "solutions" of the more acute, confusional schizophrenic episode. Will also believes that, although hebephrenic and paranoid behaviors serve to reduce anxiety, they constitute grave oversimplifications of experience and do not readily yield to a psychotherapeutic intervention, which requires further interpersonal development, though he does not think people who manifest such behaviors are "hopeless."

In a brief review, I cannot do justice to Will's various formulations of schizophrenia and related matters. However, I wish to let him speak for himself regarding his treatment procedures. The following excerpt is taken from another paper.

When I first met Miss X she looked younger than her twenty-nine years. She was slender, blonde, and her unlined face was often vacuous, seemingly unmarked by the violence of her emotions. She had been obviously "mentally" ill since the age of seventeen, and had been continuously hospitalized for the past five years. We worked together for seven years, at the end of which time she was discharged as "recovered." Obviously she did not return to some long-past state of alleged good health, she did not recover her youth, she did not make up for lost experience, and her personality was not entirely remade. However, certain useful changes were noted as follows: (1) major systems of concepts required for the integration of durable interpersonal relationships were no longer dissociated; (2) personal identity had been clarified, comprehended in terms of previous experience, and was verifiable with others; (3) attitudes toward family members had been altered, and she was not dependent on them or estranged from them; (4) autistic thinking and communicative defects were no longer prominent; and (5) she displayed insight, in that she could discuss her difficulties and their possible relationship to various events in her life. She also recovered the ability to grow, to learn, to engage in new experience, to welcome human contact, to endure separation and uncertainty, and to find intimacy while accepting a degree of loneliness. After the termination of therapy some ten years ago, Miss X graduated from college, found a career, and entered into satisfying intimate relationships with both men and women.

At the beginning of therapy with me, Miss X lived on the closed ward of a psychiatric hospital with twelve other psychotic female patients, several of whom were chronically ill and markedly regressed. She denied sickness or being a patient, said that she was illegally held in a prison, and fought to leave whenever the ward door was opened. Her days were marked by frequent outbursts of rage and panic, in which she screamed, attacked personnel, ripped her clothing, broke furnishings, bit and cut herself, tried to escape, and was controlled by being placed in a pack or locked alone in her room, where she was isolated over ninety per cent of the time.

Because of Miss X's destructiveness, she usually wore a hospital gown, and her room was furnished only with a rubber-covered mattress on the floor. She often voided and defecated on the floor. Usually she refused to eat, saying she was not hungry or that the food was poisoned, and was tube-fed daily, as she had been with rare exception for the past five years.

Miss X's behavior drove others away; her cold aloofness, her assaultiveness, her paranoid accusations, her long periods of muteness, her incontinence, and the daily struggles about food were found to be intolerable. In the years of hospitalization her identity became increasingly unclear; she was a "chronic schizophrenic" rather than a person. To her the role of patient was unacceptable, being equated with defeat, disgrace, and hopelessness; she rejected it, claiming to be a prisoner, or no one, or dead, no available living identity seeming meaningful. She was involved in a dangerous oversimplification of action and thought by stereotype.

When our work began, Miss X was not schizophrenic in the same sense that she had been some twelve years before. Through the years the schizophrenic process had been complicated by the failure of thereapeutic efforts, by growing social isolation, by despair, and by a chronic state of low morale shared by patient and staff. At this time she showed no interest in seeing me, ran from me or attacked me, was often mute, and would stay in the room with me only when I locked the door. She became intensely anxious at any attempt to discuss her past, present, or future, insisting that I was not a physician and that my only design was to harm her.

The Background of the Disorder

What follows is a brief and superficial account of Miss X's life before we met on the hospital ward.

Miss X was the youngest of two children in a family of comfortable financial circumstances and good social position. What seemed to be a mutually destructive realtionship between the contemptuously dominating mother and the artistically talented and resentfully subservient father was concealed from the community by the family's façade of conventionality. The older sister had a "nervous breakdown" while in college, received psychiatric treatment, and later died in an automobile accident.

No one thought of Miss X as being ill until her late adolescence. She made an excellent record as student, athlete, and group leader, and was socially popular. At the age of seventeen she became obsessionally meticulous, withdrawn, and depressed, and shortly after high-school graduation attempted suicide. Briefly hospitalized, she refused psychiatric care and was soon discharged.

During the next seven years she made increasingly failing efforts to lead a conventional life, moving restlessly from one transient interest to another. She developed a fear of being constipated, refused food, and became emaciated; her menses ceased, she was bedridden because of weakness, and the diagnosis of anorexia nervosa was made. Throughout these years, Miss X denied that she had any difficulties. At the age of twenty-four she was said to "have" dementia praecox, and spent the next five years in various psychiatric institutions, where she was frequently murderously assaultive, at times catatonic and posturing, required tube-feeding, and refused to talk with therapists. She received several series of insulin coma and electroshock without improvement, and was said to show evidence of "deterioration." She was transferred to Chestnut Lodge under sedation, and on arrival was comatose; her lips were cyanotic, respiration 12 per minute, pulse rate 44, systolic blood pressure 80, rectal temperature 97°F., height 5 feet 6 inches, and weight 68 pounds.

From this report we cannot speak with assurance of heredity, metabolic disturbance, cultural influence, or social experience as determinants of disorders. We can say that whatever combination of factors led to the disturbance was not of sufficient influence to maintain it indefinitely or to produce effects that would permanently prevent the patient from living closer to her potentialities. Much of the behavior could be seen to be useful in dealing with anxiety, a failing self-esteem, an uncertain identity, and increasing isolation; it often could be identified as expressing motivation (in awareness or not), as having been learned, and as "making sense." Of particular importance, such behavior, found to be inadequate or no longer required, could be modified by further processes of learning.

Miss X's unclear sense of identity, her defects in communicative ability, and her long concealment of internal disorganization by social conformity seemed to be a reflection in her personality structure of the social structure of the family. The diagnosis of schizophrenia came after seven years of what was at best a marginal adjustment. The evidences of disorder before the more obvious adolescent crisis did not attract serious attention in the troubled family. The "onset" of schizophrenia is often found on close inspection to be prolonged, the final disaster a culminating event in a long series of adjustive efforts to continue social contacts, to communicate, and to preserve a minimum of self-esteem. The totality of the organism is eventually involved in this process, as evidenced in the case of Miss X by anorexia, constipation, weight loss, amenorrhea, sleep disturbances, anxiety, depression, fatigue, catatonic posturing, delusional elaboration, hallucination, panic, and a lack of clarity about her own identity and needs.

The Concept of Organization

As my work with Miss X continued, I tacitly assumed that what went on in her living outside of the sessions with me would somehow be managed for her benefit, be supportive of therapy, and need not be a direct concern of mine. This was not a realistic view, as Miss X told me very little about herself, she was forcibly controlled by others, and she often roused more hatred than tenderness in others. Her fate was in the hands of many people whose activities were not well coordinated, not directed by clearly formulated concepts of disorder, therapeutic approach, or anticipated goals, and not clearly communicated one to the other. If the disorder of the patient's personality reflected the social structure of the family, it thus might be perpetuated in the structure of the hospital. It was too easy to ascribe the patient's behavior entirely to her "disease," minimizing or overlooking the destructive aspects of the institutional culture.

The following dimensions seemed to me to be of particular significance in the patient's hospital existence: (1) the physical environment; (2) the culture of the ward and the hospital in general; (3) the social field of the family; and (4) the relationship with the therapist.

These dimensions, or operational areas, are not functionally separate but are merged in a continuum in which the patient must find meaning. Useful work in one area may be disadvantaged by defects in another. The efforts in all areas should be coordinated, information from one should be available to others, and destructive competitiveness between areas recognized and eliminated.

We should remind ourselves that all of the above takes place in the dimension of time. The perception of time is determined in part by the culture and past experience; it also varies with the "level" of anxiety and one's role in a situation. The measure of time is not the same for patient, family member, nurse, and doctor, but for each it has significance not to be denied. For Miss X the time of her youth was in hospitals.

There follow brief accounts of certain experiences in the treatment of Miss X, relevant to the above-mentioned areas of interest and representative of efforts—often awkward and poorly timed— to coordinate various aspects of a psychotherapeutic approach.

The Physical Surroundings.

The ward on which Miss X lived was dismal. The walls were dark and without decoration, lighting was dim, the windows were heavily screened, furniture was durable but uncomfortable and unattractive, there were no movable lamps and no pictures, and the floors were bare. Several of the rooms were closed by heavy doors containing small windows or peepholes. There were no private bathrooms. Patients were moved from one room to another in response to administrative necessity, and single rooms were usually reserved for those who were "upset" and required "isolation." The "day room" was small and occasionally used as an emergency bedroom, and the screened porch opening off the ward was frequently shut off because of inclement weather or patients' attempts to escape. As the ward was on the fourth floor, access to the out-of-doors was difficult and, for many patients, infrequent. The restlessness and sudden explosive outbursts of some patients intensified the feeling of being crowded. Privacy was an unavailable luxury.

The physical surroundings conveyed to both staff and patients a message of unchanging hopelessness. For the patients the timeless quality was emphasized by the absence of clocks, calendars, current literature, and by their isolation from the daily routines of the outside world. Miss X had no personal possessions on the ward to remind her of a happier past to suggest a more promising future. There was nothing to confirm her identity as a woman and as a person of sensitivity. Her own low self-esteem was reflected in her environment.

Although we could not at this time modify the entire ward, we did redecorate Miss X's room. The walls were repainted and the worn flooring replaced. More attractive clothing was provided, and she was given her violin and typewriter to keep in her room, and a calendar and watch despite her protestations that time did not exist. However, Miss X's disturbed behavior continued, and at the end of the third year it was evident that she had become involved in a seemingly unyielding hospital routine that perpetuated her difficulties. She was then moved to another section of the hospital where she had a private room and bath, and special nursing. Furniture, radio, pictures, books, potted plants, and so on, were provided, and although there were days when she moved everything out of her room, insisting that she wanted no thing or person near her, she did not destroy these possessions.

In the fifth and sixth year Miss X lived in a single room in a small cottage with about six other patients. The room was provided with furnishings from her home—her bed, rugs, pictures, lamps, chairs, and books. In the last year of our work she lived in a small apartment near the hospital. At first this was sparsely furnished, but slowly she was able to admit more color and life, until the surroundings reflected no longer despair but her increasing hope and confidence.

Comment: Miss X's perception of space and time and her concept of identity were distorted in periods of panic, her despair further complicated her evaluation of events, and the duration of her incarceration had led her to feel stuck in the time-binding repetitiveness of existence in a series of mental hospitals. The hospital building had not been designed for the care of psychiatric patients, and it was our opinion that the housing was itself destructive to the patients' interests. We wanted to modify this environment or get Miss X out of it, but found, as is often the case, that institutional tradition resisted change. Some staff members were offended by the suggestion that all was not being done for the patients' good, and some insisted that the patients' destructiveness required a "stripped" and barren ward. Others feared that the patient was being "babied" and might be "spoiled" by being given "special" attention. Our aim was simply to provide a more conventional, attractive living situation, reasonably suitable to anyone. We had come to think that no one "in his right mind" would want to live on the ward.

In carrying out the above moves we were not operating with a clearly formulated concept of human spatial needs. However, we are becoming aware that space has communicative significance varying from one culture to another, and that the human requirement for a certain amount of space is biologically fundamental. The anthropologist Edward T. Hall writes on this subject as follows: "Man has many needs, drives, or tropisms. Of these, food, sex, and affirmation are perhaps those most commonly considered. The need to lay claim to and organize territory, as well as to maintain a pattern of discrete distances from our fellows, may prove to be just as basic."

Hall and others have studied the cultural and personal variations in spatial requirements and usage. Of particular interest to the psychiatrist are the size and forms of space best suited to the needs of various patients—the regressed catatonic, the hostile and restless paranoid, those in states of panic, and so on. Although I do not have the answers to such matters, I consider the physical environment to be of great significance in the care of psychiatric patients. I favor the following environmental features in a therapeutic program:

1. Space in which patients can move about without unavoidably violating the territories of others

2. A place in which one can be alone and find quiet

3. A distribution of space permitting a patient to move, as he feels the need, from privacy, to contact with a small group (of two or three), and to a larger group (of eight to ten), having some freedom to choose his associates

4. Privacy in toilet and bathing facilities

5. Ready availability of personal possessions and items from home to reinforce a sense of identity apart from the institution

6. Clocks, calendars, and current publications to help correct distortions of time

7. Furnishings of varied colors and textures—attention being given to auditory, tactile, and visual input.

The Social Environment

When I first met Miss X, she lived in a situation of disturbance. Most of the patients on the ward had been hospitalized for several years in various institutions, had received a multiplicity of therapies without lasting benefit, and had little confidence in anything psychiatric. Several were incontinent of urine and feces, some were assaultive, some confused, and others huddled in corners in near-isolation. More communicative and effective patients grouped together and, on improvement, left. The general attitude of the patient group was one of despair and hostility, despite the fact that all were seen regularly by psychotherapists. The more permanent group of patients had its own organization—a hierarchical system of control by force and fear—that was not openly revealed to staff. Patients had to adjust to their therapists, to the ward administrative physician, to staff members of each shift, to the patient in-group, and to whatever requirements filtered in to them from the world "outside."

Members of the nursing staff felt harassed by the demands and expectations of administrator, therapist, and patients, and were discouraged by the chronicity of the situation. Despite their talk of patients improving, it was evident that they often had little confidence in such improvement occurring, and felt required to conceal their own feelings of anger, frustration, and despair. In reviewing this situation we were particularly impressed by the following:

1. The social system was complicated, a patient having to develop some form of relationship and communication with many and various people, who came and went (often unpredictably), and who communicated in different modes and with diverse degrees of effectiveness.

2. Patients were exposed to obscure, mixed messages. For example, words might be of faith in improvement, whereas the physical surroundings and the nonverbal structure conveyed a different meaning. This conflict of messages might resemble a patient's home situation, furthering disorder by seeming to require a unification of incompatible messages, a distortion of them, or an ignoring of some.

3. Certain of Miss X's basic needs were met no matter what she did—that is, she was bathed, fed, dressed, housed, and protected from serious physical injury. She no longer bore responsibility for her living, being treated as if she were helpless and hopeless, and thus had little opportunity to learn to recognize or adequately express her own needs.

4. Staff members, often feeling denied and ineffective in their professional roles and in their worth as humans, experienced a diffusion of identity. Both patients and personnel dealt with the anxiety accompanying such diffusion by denial, withdrawal, or the use of oversimplified stereotyped views of the other.

In an effort to reduce the frequency of conflicting and obscure messages and the isolation of one communication system from another, I talked with some of the nurses on the ward after each session with Miss X. I told them something of what had gone on with the patient, and shared with them my own doubts, uncertainties, anger, and hope—hearing, as I did so, more of their own feelings. In regular biweekly ward staff meetings, open expression of thought and emotion was encouraged, and there was gradually revealed not only discouragement, hostility, frustration, and contempt, but also affection and hope. At times the patient's mother joned these sessions. The discussion[s] were frequently awkward and painful, and the anxiety was so intense that at times the integrity and continuance of the organization seemed threatened.

Despite our work, Miss X was not greatly improved, and by the end of the third year I thought that she had become involved in a chronic state in which feelings of anger and despair, while often denied, were being reinforced by all participants. She was then moved to her own room in another section of the hospital and for the next year was not a part of a formal ward organization. During the day she was in the care of two people—a female nurse from 8 A.M. to 4 P.M. and a male aide from 4 P.M. to midnight. During the early morning hours she was restricted to her room, rarely making any demands on the regular staff. The aide and the nurse became intensely involved with Miss X—as did I; that is, our relationship was marked by emotion, perplexity, and obscure motivations. Each day I met with the aide and nurse for brief conferences in which we spoke as freely as we could about our experiencing of the patient and each other. As Miss X was at times grossly disturbed, and our own feelings were frequently tempestuous, we recurrently found ourselves at odds with each other and the patient. At the end of a year the nurse and aide left for other duties, and Miss X, who at first denied their being of any importance to her, was now able to grieve at the separation.

For the next two years Miss X lived in the open cottage, in a single room with her own furnishings. Although she could be alone when she wished—by remaining in her room or going for a walk—she had become more tolerant of others and by choice spent time with patients and staff members. Sometimes her anxiety was so great that she would have none of us close to her, and then would insist that she could never live in the world and that we were cruel not to leave her entirely alone. During this period there were increasing contacts with the world outside the hospital; she took a university correspondence course, studied typing with

an instructor who came to the hospital to teach, made her first
visits home, and shopped and spent time in town.

During the last year she lived in an apartment near the hospital.
She saw me for her "hours" and frequently had long talks with a
nurse of whom she had grown very fond; but her interests turned
increasingly from us to new acquaintances in the community and
at college.[11]

Following upon this excerpt, Will provides some enlightening comments and information. He writes that through the years of hospitalization Miss X had become less a person and more a "case." There was
a tendency among hospital staff members to think of her as a "schizophrenic" or as a "disturbed patient" rather than as a person. One
reason for moving her from the ward to a private room in another
section of the hospital was to circumvent the restrictive rigidity of
such "stereotypes" harbored by both staff and patient. Will informs
us that he favored her living in a social situation of greater simplicity
in which a durable, comprehensible relationship with a few people
could be developed, the source of authority more clearly determined,
cause-and-effect relationships clarified, identity simplified, "feedback" localized, and the input of conflicting messages (roughly, conflicting communications) reduced or eliminated. The therapist and
his assistants acquainted the patient with their comings and goings,
in order to foster her living in a simpler, more comprehensible environment. They were not secretive with her, trying to encourage the
development of foresight by reducing the fear and uncertainty of the
present while at the same time attempting to make the future more
easily predictable and demonstrably less threatening than Miss X's
previous life experience had been. Her removal to more sequestered
quarters also made it possible for the therapist and his assistants to
increase useful communication in their conferences. In contrast to the
time when the patient was in contact with relatively large numbers of
personnel, they could focus more accurately on occurrences actually
relevant to Miss X's behavior and on their own experiences in connection with her treatment. In the patient's previous situation, while she
lived on the dark, undecorated, dimly lit ward, they could not do so.
After she had been put in a room of her own, Will and his assistants
also increasingly required of Miss X that she be responsible for her
own behavior. Within the widening limits of her tolerance, she was
also exposed to an increasing number and variety of social contacts.

Throughout this period, Will and his assistants worked with Miss X on the problem of needs. Her therapist writes that it seemed she was unclear concerning her own needs and how to communicate them to others. Staff members would often say, "I don't know what she wants. Nothing satisfies her. I don't think *she* knows." The patient claimed that she did not need food or companionship, giving her therapist the impression that if left unattended she would die. Her apparent lack of certain fundamental needs is said to have further estranged her from those who believed such needs to be vital in their own living. They thought she was incomprehensible or a hypocrite or lazy. Miss X manifested no recognition of certain tension patterns. Though she might feel ill at ease, fearful, or "sick," she did not understand what the particular feeling meant, trying to explain it with a rationalization. Her tension states might involve an unrecognized need for food, for rest, for physical contact, for tenderness, and the like.

So her psychiatrist, with the help of his assistants, tried to identify a particular need of Miss X, while realizing that behavior may serve both need-satisfying and anxiety-reducing functions. At the same time, they realized that the original, undeveloped need may have been poorly elaborated, though altered by intervening time (perhaps covering a number of years), experience, and the growth of the organism. As Sullivan used to say, nothing in the human personality is static. The therapist, in order to help Miss X, began with simple needs (for food, rest, etc.), preferably needs not associated with great anxiety, and attempted to provide satisfactions in ways that were acceptable to the patient. (Sullivan had taught that satisfactions may serve to help identify the related needs.) With as little arousal of anxiety as possible, a need is said to have been "identified to the patient," although Will does not inform us as to how this process was carried out. (Sometimes a parent may identify a need for a child by telling him, "you are restless" or "you are bored" on several suitable occasions and then show the child how to do something that will relieve the restlessness or boredom. In this fashion the need for, say, a meaningful activity may be "identified" to the child.)

Following upon this identification process, or perhaps, concurrently, the therapist encouraged Miss X to recognize, formulate, and express the (hitherto unformulated) tension as need in communicable language, "opening the way for the renewal of object relationship[s] and the recognition and acceptance of desire."[12] In this fashion Will and his assistants enabled the patient to learn that she (or he, in other analogous circumstances) could express and gratify a need overtly, openly, without fear of being rejected, or being made to feel anxious or being controlled by another person, or becoming unduly obligated to him, or abandoning her identity. In a way, this technique illustrates, in a poignant fashion, how much has to be learned during the entire process of acculturation. It also illustrates Sullivan's "theorem" of reciprocal emotional and motivational patterns. For example, with the help of her therapist Miss X gradually learned that the need to receive affection may be accompanied by the need to give affection. She was also helped to recognize other people's needs: those of the nurse, therapist, other patients, relatives. At the same time, this patient was encouraged to accept responsibility for expressing and securing satisfaction for her needs just as she was encouraged to endure frustration without recourse to denial and failure to recognize want. Will also claims that through all of this a patient, such as Miss X, as her self-assurance grew, may be able to accept the often frightening idea that one needs others, is bound to other human beings, accepting the fact that separation and loss are inevitable aspects of living.

The overriding conception that Will employs, one might add, is that the therapeutic experience is a learning experience. The therapist is said to be a model, a controlling force, a person with values, and a teacher, as well as being more traditionally one who tries to comprehend and help his patient gain understanding from what the two are able to "observe" together.

Will gives a brief account of Miss X's family background. He writes that when Miss X first came to the hospital, her parents were turning to what they considered a "last resort." She had spent five years in various mental hospitals before she was transferred to Chestnut Lodge, which at one time was a famous institution, chiefly owing to Sullivan's and Frieda Fromm-Reichmann's connection with it. Though Miss X's parents had become discouraged and pessimistic about further psychiatric care, they did not know what else to do. They brought her to one more mental hospital because they wanted to be able to say that they had done everything possible for their daughter. But Will claims that behind their conventional expressions of hope for recovery and their conscious wishes for Miss X to get better and be happy, as they put it, were hidden or inadequately recognized feelings of shame, guilt, despair, resentment, hatred, and the wish that she would die, which they unwittingly revealed in a statement that "she might be better off dead than suffering so."

Will met Miss X's mother shortly after he began work with her; then he met her father and, later, her sister. The father is said to have been polite, vague, and remarkably uninformative about the patient, while the mother was composed and distant, giving a history of her ill daughter that revealed little. The sister, who was openly hostile toward Miss X, wanted nothing to do with her. Though Will saw little more of the father and sister after the first meetings, he talked with the mother every month or two when she visited the hospital. In the fifth year of Miss X's treatment at Chestnut Lodge the mother occasionally took part in staff discussions about her daughter's care.

Though the patient was obviously improved in the fifth year, her parents decided at that time to transfer her elsewhere. Will relates that it became evident that although they wanted Miss X to "get well," they had no clear conception of what they meant, having for so long known her only as a child or "sick." He adds that they resisted change in the patient and clung to the *status quo* just as the hospital staff at times had done. Only after Will discussed their fears of change, and their resentment of her destructive behavior with the parents was he able to continue work with the patient.

This "all too brief account of Miss X's family" introduces some reflections of the therapist on family organization.[13] The family group is said to be a reflection of the larger culture in which it exists and is itself a social field whose equilibrium reflects and influences the behavior of its constituents. Will claims that the family organization may resist change in itself, restrict the growth of its members, resenting the intrusion of ideas that seem threatening to its integrity. Thus, a patient's family may oppose his increasing independence while consciously desiring his improvement, and withdraw him from treatment when he shows signs of improvement. Such an action is said to be an indication that the patient *and his illness* are an integral part of the family, suggesting that a change in the patient requires adjustive changes in those intimately related to him. Will writes that if the family does not reinclude the patient and his "sickness" (whether in actuality or in fantasy) and if its members cannot alter, in keeping with the patient's growth, the equilibrium may be readjusted by pathological developments in someone other than the patient. This may be manifested by the person's withdrawal, a development of "physical illness," mental disturbance, or even by death. In this connection he quotes Strindberg: ". . . for me the family has become an organism, such as in plants, a whole of which I am a part. Alone I could not exist, and I could not exist with the children, without their mother. The family is a network of veins which are knit together; if one is severed my life runs out with the blood that drenches the sand."

In discussing the doctor-patient relationship, Will relates that for the first three years she was at Chestnut Lodge, Miss X did not want to have anything to do with him. Since she would not come to his office he went to her room on the ward and often locked the door when she did not want to remain with him. She was mute for long stretches of time, periodically assaultive and always rejecting. Not surprisingly, during those years her therapist felt ineffective, discouraged, and angry. Miss X is said to have insisted that Will was not a physician, that he had no rightful concern with her, that she did not know his name, and so forth. The past, present, or future could not be discussed. Any approach, or topic, at some time or other, precipitated panic, assault, or withdrawal. The patient did not "confirm" Will as a therapist, or as a human being, behaving toward him as a "stereotyped," malevolent inhuman creature. In later years, Miss X is said to have spoken of this denial as follows: "I didn't want you to mean anything—not even to know your name. Everything had gone away. If we were nothing, there was nothing to lose." (One could hardly find a more vivid formulation of "quintessential loneliness" and despair.) Will states that little occurred during those first three years to encourage the patient or those interested in her. Like a frightened and hungry robin in the winter snow, hovering near an open farmhouse door, her small advances were obliterated by retreats. Her therapist asserts that it was as if she dared not consider hope. It seemed that for Miss X hope was too fragile—too easily and too quickly crushed—even to be spoken of or permitted in her thoughts. Hence, the time was marked by a sort of rhythm of approach and withdrawal, promise and disappointment.

It was after she had been moved to her own room, with special nursing care, at the end of the third year, that Miss X began to speak more openly of her isolation and despair. Will relates that she talked to the nurse, and to the aide, and to him, though she would accept only one, distantly and briefly, while the others were pushed aside. It took her a long time to be able to deal comfortably and overtly with several relationships at the same time. Each day she wrote long notes. Each day she tore them up, knowing that her therapist would retrieve them from the wastebasket in order to piece them together and read them. One fragment of her notes, written one day, contained the following: "I can face death easier than life. . . . It means warmth, coolness, and freedom. . . . It means no people . . . [and] the end of separation. . . . I want separation to be over. . . . No one understands what I say. . . . I think that I am dead now; I died and didn't know it. I have been dead for ten years [the period of hospitalization]."

Miss X continued to experience periods of disturbance. Will narrates that sometimes he sat on the floor nearby if she crawled under her bed, and how, when she attacked, he held her arms. He sat, or read to himself and frequently to her, during her periods of silence. When circumstances allowed, the two often walked on the grounds or in the town. They went driving and shopping together.

Miss X became more overtly interested in others, in the fifth year, and less hostile and distant. Then an "upsurge of hopefulness" appeared in the staff and a "turning to her." By the end of the fifth year, the ten years of tube-feeding were at an end and the patient began to eat regularly. The therapist lifted the restrictions under which she lived in the hospital. He and his aides "no longer pursued her," depending on her to come to them with her needs; and with increasing confidence she did. Will asserts that for a time Miss X became insistently dependent on him, a state of affairs that he accepted. The last two years of their work, he writes, was more conventionally psychotherapeutic. As the patient spoke more freely, her therapist had less to say, occasionally venturing an interpretive suggestion when the evidence seemed to warrant such a maneuver. At length the time came for her to go, though her therapist, feeling some reluctance at her leaving, suggested some aspects of her earlier life might merit further analysis. But she pointed out to him that this was unnecessary, which was true, and she was free to depart.

In a brief conclusion, Will asserts that in long therapeutic endeavors, the therapist may be the major—and necessary—element of consistency in a plethora of medical and administrative procedures and routines. A patient is said to be often exposed to a series of nurses, administrative physicians, and others, and to many variations in administrative policy. A troubled and discouraged chronically ill patient needs some one person to persist in the doctor-patient relationship, who will help coordinate the multiple aspects of the therapeutic program. (To perhaps any patient, who has spent time in any kind of hospital and who is unfamiliar with hospital routines, the physicians, nurses, aides, technicians, seem to come suddenly out of the walls.) This person must be deeply concerned with the welfare of the patient and able to withstand anxiety and disturbance. He must also be able to enjoy the pleasure he may derive from self-growth and enhancement of self-knowledge as well as from the self-development and increasing self-knowledge in another.

As a therapist, Will seems to have contributed mightily to all those changes.[14]

Manic and depressive behavior disorders are said to make up a large group of disorders characterized by profound disturbances of affect (feeling and emotion) without deterioration. According to Redlich and Freedman, it is a heterogeneous grouping, in which disorders ranging from presumably endogenous psychoses to abnormal grief are included. Manic-depressive behavior disorders designate two important characteristics, namely the extremes of pathological affect and the repetitive, alternating, or cyclic attacks.[15] Thus, cyclothymic people are given to profound mood swings, as Sullivan described their behavior in *The Psychiatric Interview*. When they are "up," he says, nothing can get them "down" (at least this seems to have been true a generation ago), and when they are "down" nothing can get them "up" (again, such was the state of affairs a generation ago). "When elation ... reaches the frankly hypomanic state, the person, even though he may look frightened, acts as if he were feeling fine; he is very gay, and he wants to cheer you up—and now and then he probably pulls some most inopportune wisecracks to do so. It is hard to keep him on the topic long enough to find anything that carries conviction; and in fact he must get up quite often, and fumble with and admire some of the objects on your desk—and I always feel that next he will have to muss my hair to show how good he feels. It is very much like having the office full of jumping beans."[16] Sullivan thought that the behavior of cyclothymic people may be looked upon as an obscure expression of movements away from the experience of anxiety—depression or an unhappy manic state being more tolerable than anxiety itself. Rarely is the anxiety felt as such apparently. It is extraordinarily difficult, Sullivan claimed, to isolate the occurrence that threatens to expose the anxiety and that in turn triggers the patterns known as manic and depressive. Depression in the manic-depressive psychosis is said to be a preoccupation of consciousness with a very restricted progression of grief-provoking ideas, along with a more or less striking reduction of activity of the person. Sometimes he acts in a clearly punitive fashion.

Sullivan related his experiences with the disturbed daughter of a "society woman." When he interviewed the patient, she had quieted down, he says, to what might be described as a hypomanic state. Although she was "well above normal key" in the sense that it would be extremely difficult to find anyone who could talk as fast as she could, she did not otherwise exhibit "terribly impressive" manic behavior. She was not elated. In fact, when she was "galloping across" obviously very painful data, she at times looked extremely unhappy. Sullivan asserted that she was not highly distractible; and in one sense, he added, it might even be said that she was not distractible at all, since she would keep to material that was relevant to her life situation, which is not characteristic of distractibility. Nevertheless, she manifested a "residual feature" of the hypomanic state: she "moved with great speed over the surface" of relevant material and never "dipped down." She did not develop any topic in depth. Thus she is said to have unhesitatingly expressed hatred for her mother, based on fear of her mother's evil effects on her. In the interviews with Sullivan she revealed a great deal of historic data regarding this hatred, including a vast documentation of the reasonableness of her hatred. But the striking thing was, he said, not the slightest trace of any benefit seemed to result from the "wonderfully adequate insight into the type of deviltry she had grown up with."[17] But so far as her therapist could tell, not the slightest benefit resulted. "She never slowed down, and she never gave anything a chance to sneak by the self," as it were. She provided glimpses of an extremely unhappy life, accompanied by an appropriate emotional facial expression. The more painful her recital of her past became, the more she was apt to look sad and harassed. Sometimes on such occasions, she shed tears.

Though this girl provided "the strangest kind of hypomanic picture," in subsequent years she had some ups and downs, supporting the notion that her disorder was a "curious fragment" of something that can occur in a manic-depressive personality.

Another problem that interested Sullivan a good deal was the "element of duration" in relation to onset in states of excitement, but he was unable to fathom it. It is true that people can go into a lurid manic state quite swiftly but this does not seem to be a really quite sudden onset. In the manic, the state of excitement "grows by accretion" so that the change occurs from a hardly observable beginning to a very perceptible state. Thus the appearance of the excitement is said to be not *sudden,* or abrupt, even though the excitement may increase very rapidly in the course of, say, twenty-four hours: the person may pass from an irritable, uncomfortable type of active existence to a psychotic excitement. Since Sullivan—quite uncharacteristically—had the "feeling" that the manic-depressive psychosis cannot be explained without a good deal of attention to obscure, intricate "complexes of factors" in bodily organization, the growth by accretion in excitement is part of the "argument" in favor of somatological factors being involved in the manic-depressive. He also thought that depression deepens in much the same way, though it is not nearly as easy to observe because quite often the person's depression impresses people as being related to a particular event, and deepens, perhaps, from there on.

Although Sullivan's attempt to formulate the manic state in "personality terms"—in terms of interpersonal relations—was not very successful, he thought that there is a great deal of obvious hostility in quite a number of these excitements. For example, he recalled a patient he had seen, who, at the height of his excitement, could not resist the impulse to strike the night supervisor, a man twice his age, and in general a pretty kindly person. This is said to have been a clear instance of the ungovernable necessity for destructiveness and injury to others that appears in some patients at the height of their excitement, and that appears to be part "of the picture," even if masked. In some other patients, one does not observe direct hostility, but when one studies what they did as part of the manic hyperactivity he will discover that it represents "a long string of violations and so on." Sullivan mentions the "most amiable manic" he had ever known, a woman who happened to be wealthy. "Her family would know that she had had an attack when she would drive down the main street at 60 miles an hour and wave to the traffic cop, who was so flabbergasted that he didn't even whistle at her."[18] To her family that meant "she was well up" and the time for the mental hospital had arrived. She is said to have been an amazingly genial and amiable woman and her therapist never saw her in any other condition. But Sullivan asserted when one looked at *what* she did when she got excited, one could see that she violated all sorts of standards, *"although she did it gayly."*

The discharge of other motivational systems was much less strikingly consistent to him. Thus there are said to be people who, as they become excited, have a great expansion of lust and engage in really manic sexual relations, while there are others who become excited only after they have become simply impotent, and though lust may color their thoughts it does not express itself in any access of genital behavior. In the life of the patient, motivational sets sometimes appear in excitement with rather startling clarity that have hitherto only obscurely manifested themselves during the ordinary waking state. For example, when the "overloading" of sublimated lust is followed by excitement, then it will often reveal the thing that has been sublimated. Imagine a person who has not given any striking suggestion of sexual deviation. Imagine further, that fairly early in life he has had slight warnings that he had a barrier to any real attachment to a woman, which had manifested itself as an undue interest in members of his own sex, though all these things had been "gathered into a sublimatory way of life." Sullivan tended to think that as long as lust is the motivational system that is being sublimated, such a person will "blow up into an excitement." This may be manifested by his engaging in his first homosexual affair during the excitement. For people who have overloaded a sublimatory way of dealing with people, this kind of occurrence might be considered almost pathognomonic.

At one time, this excitement, following upon the collapse of the sublimatory organization of a motivational system such as lust, was thought to be the beginning of a manic-depressive history. Gradually Sullivan arrived at the conclusion that this is improbable, though the excitement is at first apt to be rather typically manic, it becomes less typically so in the course of time, winding up as a definite schizophrenic illness. He surmised that excitement in adolescents may be special instances of the same sort of thing. In his long experience, he said he had discovered that excitements *never* initiated a manic-depressive history, always, instead, initiating schizophrenia. Sullivan mentions the course of several youngsters whom he had seen brought into the hospital in a state of manic excitement. He discovered, however, that when they began to quiet down that he heard them express very "foggy concepts," which he interpreted as more or less *unusual* implicit operations. Yet they were soon discharged from the hospital and would return home, or go back to where they came from, "or something of that sort" after having been labeled social recoveries or regarded as much improved. Perhaps a year later they were back in the hospital in an excited state, which no physician could interpret as that of a manic-depressive. Now they definitely manifested *catatonic excitements.* Sullivan surmised that these younger people had developed a pretty extensive sublimatory organization as part of their make-up, though *it did not involve any patterned type of sexual interest* since they had not yet progressed to this stage of personality growth. The sublimatory organization that is said to have collapsed involved such things as hatred and fear of a parent. If the psychiatrist will study these youngsters from this viewpoint, he may discover that they have been more and more frantically driven by attempts to maintain social approval for unacceptable motivation. "And the thing finally gets to be physical overactivity; the person starts a lot of new things before he finishes the other things and so on, and you can almost see the excitement develop before your eyes." This excitement is the forerunner of schizophrenia. In contrast, Sullivan thought that manic excitement is clearly related to rage, for manics, even the amiable ones, traverse all sorts of conventions and commit plenty of offenses against others.

Sullivan provides a brief discussion of the transition from a manic-depressive type of illness to a settled paranoid state, and involutional illness in relation to manic-depressive psychosis, which is largely a descriptive, marginal comment. He has reservations about the Kraepelinian characterization of manic-depressive psychosis, wherein there are recurrent depressions and excitements, or recurrent depressions or recurrent excitements: both phases may occur in cycles, or only one phase may recur at more or less regular intervals. But observation reveals that regularity is not an essential part of these occurrences.

Sullivan was unable to explain the psychogenesis of the manic-depressive psychosis. But a generation later Redlich and Freedman declared that "pathogenesis" of manic-depressive psychosis and related disorders "is still obscure."[19] They declare it is desirable to reserve "depression," a term first used by Adolf Meyer, for a *syndrome.* Depression should not be confused with sadness. "Mania" also is a term that names a syndrome, not to be confused with euphoria and elation. Since the following pages will be devoted to depression and depressive states, one must call attention to the distinction between

reactive depressions and *endogenous depressions.* Reactive depressions are
said to be severe and long lasting reactions to stimuli that ordinarily
produce grief, "a complex and characteristic response to a loss."[20]
Since other writers disagree on this characterization, it may be regarded as tentative. Endogenous depressions are said to refer to
inner processes that produce the disorder; but since no one seems to
know what these processes are, "endogenous depression" merely
calls attention to the fact that the etiological variables of depression
are not well understood.

"In all too many cases," Redlich and Freedman write, "the boundary between psychotic and neurotic depression is blurred. It seems
almost that the more we learn about these syndromes the less we are
able to maintain our old diagnostic scheme. To many clinicians neurotic depression designates a relatively mild psychogenic depression.
Such states can be enduring or can show marked fluctuations. The
symptoms are similar though less pronounced than in a severe
depression, but obviously, it is difficult to delineate clearly the severe
and the mild."[21]

Since it appears that "depressives" manifest a syndrome that Sullivan did not understand, or not very well, I propose to give a brief
summary of some recent contributions regarding the more or less
clearly delineated disorder of depression. Bonime has stated that
depressive living has a basic dynamic consistency prevading all its
variations in intensity and setting, from neurotic sulking to psychotic
mania or functionally paralytic retardation.[22] He claims that the outstanding elements of this disorder are *manipulativeness, aversion to influence* by others, which is the constant corollary to manipulativeness, an
unwillingness to give gratification, hostility, and *anxiety.* Manipulativeness
is said to cover much of the so-called dependency, which is the indirect demand for service comprising all the techniques of helplessness, seduction, and moral blackmail. At the same time, the highly
manipulative person interprets the actions of other people as designed to manipulate and exploit him. In order to counter this threat
he will do everything he possibly can. He experiences the providing
of gratification to others as a way of becoming the victim of exploitation. Unless he anticipates the outcome as an investment, he fights
against being the means or source of pleasure for someone else.
Failure of such security operations produces anger. The anger may
result in direct punitive action or may serve to deprive others of

pleasure or may succeed in compelling the immunities and indulgences originally sought. In order to keep the peace, as it were, a spouse, for example, will often give in and placate a sulking partner rather than suffer his sulken withdrawal. The failure or anticipation of failure of manipulative activities may cause not only anger but also anxiety since the depressive experiences it as a threat to his effectiveness as a person, which is a way of saying he suffers a sense of inferiority and inadequacy as an individual. All these security operations of the depressive inevitably deprive him of ordinary, available gratification. This loss, in turn, makes him still more determined to compel others to provide the gratifications he wants and to insure that they do not secure gratifications from him. Such aspects of the depressive's behavior are said to constitute the primary obstacles to therapeutic progress.

Bonime asserts that there is a necessity for constant examination of depression in all its more simple forms, for a constant effort on learning to recognize and deal with, and also on engaging the patient in recognizing and dealing with, all his *minor* depressions. Every depressive is said to have a history of these minor depressions. In fact, all neurotics suffer them, though they very often are not thought of, or dealt with, as depressions because they take on various guises. The latter usually are "sulks and mopes." Several illustrations are given: Someone who does not get his own way, perhaps even "galantly" acquiescing in the gratification of someone else's needs instead of his own, who then sulks; someone who loses in a game or in an argument who turns out to be a "bad loser." It can be someone who, perhaps, because he cannot have his own way in an interpersonal relationship, or fails to impress the other one favorably, or cannot elicit a desired response, is given to feel rejected. Feeling rejected is said to be usually sullen, punitive, covert anger. The sullen response may arouse anxiety, especially if the person then anticipates rejection. (One has the impression that such behavior patterns are not rare among many people considered to be normal, though such patterns in these cases may be less frequent and intense.) As a final illustration, there is the "pathos maneuver" ("No matter how hard I try, I always seem to say or do the wrong thing") which is designed to blackmail or "melt" the other person, who then may feel compelled to relent and reverse his attitude or position. In the therapeutic relationship, minor depressions, manifested in tears, silences, sadnesses, may be sought, discovered, and found to be identical with everyday behavior, past and present, as it occurs in relation to elders, juniors, and peers. These minor depressions occur in the individual's interpersonal relations with the same and opposite sex.

Bonime emphatically asserts (in the "Discussion") that, in his view, depression is "a sick way of relating to other human beings." It is a functional interpersonal disorder. Of course the physician has to ask himself when treating a person who appears to be a depressive, "Is this something of a characterological disorder or is this state brought about by some endogenous physiological cause?" It is granted that the physician must be alert to the possibility of underlying disease. A person who appears to be unwilling to exert himself, for example, may possibly have emphysema, or a cardiac condition, or any allergy. However, such a state of affairs would *not* be a *depression.* Bonime claims that in the case of a depression, the therapist tries to deal with interpersonal disorders, with the practices, the interpersonal relations of the individual.

The essence of his therapeutic technique when dealing with depressives is to examine with the patient his depression as something that is his "practice": "a sick way of relating to others." The therapist aims to discover the nature of his way of relating to others. How does this way of relating to others produce a painful existence for him? Though the depressive comes to the therapist with what he considers an affliction, the latter examines how he lives. Bonime asserts that outstanding psychoanalysts such as Edith Jacobson and Frieda Fromm-Reichmann have recognized the necessity, when dealing with a depressive, for engaging more actively, affectively with him than with other sorts of patients. Both are said to have emphasized the necessity for being responsive in a personal way to demands of depressives, and both employed the stratagem of first, giving a clear indication of limits, and, second, of showing open resentment toward the efforts of the patient to go beyond these limits. Bonime claims that the focus of the therapeutic endeavor must be the engagement of the patient in exploring and recognizing the contexts and the patterns of sulks, of poor losing, of feeling rejected, of begrudging pleasure to others, of wet blanketing. In the case of minor depressions, this kind of focus can lead to an alteration of the patient's personality, and, "in a meaningful way," prevent the progressive development of the profoundly depression-prone character. But in the already evolved seriously depressive pattern of interpersonal relations, the acute episodes may be usefully clarified by the examination of "the biographic longitudinal panorama of these minor depressions," that is, roughly, by what Sullivan called the detailed interview. Bonime asserts that, above all else, the intense collaboration required in the intensive therapeutic interview, extending over a long period, constitutes in itself a new, profoundly therapeutic kind of interpersonal experience. The patient is said to engage in a cooperative experience in which he is influenced by another, and simultaneously affords this other a genuine gratification. In the course of the intensive collaboration, he begins to mobilize and draw upon his most valuable personal resources. He develops increasing confidence and security in relation to continuing interpersonal functional success, achieving more personal satisfaction cooperatively than he could ever possibly achieve in the unremitting anxiety-and-anger-ridden pursuit of unreciprocated services from others. Thus the psychotherapy of the depressive entails assisting the person toward a reorientation in living such that he may be able to achieve a more rewarding use of his own resources instead of a dogged insistence upon mobilizing and exploiting the resources of others.

From a somewhat different vantage point and orientation, Spiegel concentrates on problems of communication in the interpretation of depression and the technique of treatment.[23] She thinks that though every kind of personality and every psychopathologic syndrome has its characteristic communication pattern, difficulties in communication play a particular role in the depressive patient, forming part of the depressive syndrome and contributing to the barrier between him and others generally, and between him and his therapist in particular. Disorders in communication have baffled many therapists who have attempted to treat depressive patients. Thus, the enterprise of psychotherapy is said to depend on the establishment of communication with the patient for its feasibility while it also entails repair of the communication process as one of its therapeutic goals.

As Bonime in effect alleged, Spiegel also claims that though depression is generally considered in terms of massive psychiatric illness, it wears many guises and does not respect time, place, or person. As a transient experience, she says, it is familiar to everyone by reason of the human condition, the nature of man living in the world. It follows that the therapist, whether he is conscious of it or not, has within himself a latent kinship with the patient. Such a link is threatening and the therapist may deny it. But he must be able to confront it in himself if he is to work effectively with depressives. "It is interesting," she adds, "that in the clinical context depression is generally thought of first as the retardation variety," [that], in the form of agitation, it is thought of only as a distant second; and that it is regarded least frequently in its manifestations of open rage and even violence toward others. This may be due, in part, to the fact that, at least fairly generally, therapists find retardation depression as the most depleting to witness and the most threatening with which to identify. From the clinical and objective side, it is said to be the most overt and clearly demarcated variety and thereby lends itself to being used as the basic model of depression, whose variants are attributable to additional dynamisms.

Spiegel characterizes retardation depression as follows: low energy; mood of sadness, dejection, boredom, emptiness; low self-esteem, which is openly experienced with very little defense against it; diminution of communication, particularly intraphysically and interpersonally, with restriction of cognitive processes.

In treating a depressive Spiegel often would ask herself, "What's going on in me?" As we saw in the previous chapter, it is necessary for the interviewer to be eternally alert to his own mental processes, directly, and also as they are reflected back to him from the patient. Thus Spiegel would also ask herself, "Was I really so tired that a particular patient's heaviness was sufficient to sedate me? Was there something she was doing that I missed?" The therapist would also ask the patient for a description of her side of the experience. This "double question" is said to be based on the premise that something goes on within the patient, or in some nonverbal interchange between patient and therapist, that is susceptible of the patient's recognition as experience in itself and then of verbal communication. Spiegel also claims that a therapist experiences a patient through the "primal mode of communication of body language." By this she means that the patient, by means of bodily expression, communicates attitudes, moods, emotions, states of well being. The therapist's consciousness of this mode of communication may enable him to be more therapeutically effective, for it tells him of things that are going on in the patient and facilitates his helping the patient to become conscious of what has happened to him in the past or is happening in the present.

The paucity and constriction of the depressive patient's verbal communication is said to be only one step above the baseline of silence, one of the things that tends to baffle the psychotherapist who works with him. "The impoverishment of verbal communication involves not only his utterances, but the play in the variety of language, a reduction below the person's competence and performance when not depressed. Sentences may be repetitious in form, language, and ideas; the range of ideas is limited, and verbal imagery may shrink to the vanishing point."[24] The reduction of the dream-imagery and in the patient's impression that dreaming itself has diminished bears out the statement about the profundity of the shrinkage of imagery in the mental life as a whole. To the silence of despair or mute unfocused resentment, of tension and "staticness," to which the person in a retarded depression is prone, are added the character of the patient's verbal communication, coupled with the diminished range of "affect-expression" in the voice, to make any cognitive interplay—any exchange of thought—difficult, boring, wearying, baffling, discouraging, unless the therapist is highly skillful and emotionally secure. Under such circumstances, combined with his "ambience of fatality," it is said to be quite a test of the therapist's own resistance and even his sense of identity to work with a depressed patient, remaining "sensitive to him" and not "caught up" in the depletion of the self that afflicts him.

Spiegel asserts that though interpersonal communication may be viewed as a brief encounter between persons involved in a specific transaction, from the long-range perspective, communication is a longitudinal process, one extending through "overarching" time covering a large portion of the patient's life. It is subject to development, "maturation," and shaping by personal experience in the life history of the individual. Communication is not only a means in interpersonal relations, as in the exchange of ideas; it is a process whose fulfillment brings its own gratification, its own enjoyment. Thus, the psychotherapist who deals with the depressive may appropriately concern himself with both the establishment of communication in the running transactions, the interpersonal relations between him and the patient, and also in the more inclusive sense of helping the latter to enrich his life experience.

Spiegel gives a vivid account of some of the difficulties in communication with a depressive. In a particular therapeutic interview she had become dubious about the progress of the work and weary from the stress of trying to communicate with a tensely silent patient. As she attempted to "unwind," she relates that she became conscious of the fact that her jaws were clenched, her neck arched back rigidly with her head thrust forward. "I became aware that I sat tensely poised in sessions with this patient, in strained and sustained alert attention for the crumb of verbal or open emotional communication that did not come."[25] She writes that she was unmoving, sitting with elbows ridigly digging into the arms of the chair, her posture one of dogged entrenchment. Thus both therapist and patient had become entrenched. An inquiry into both aspects of this experience enabled the patient to become conscious of what her attitude was: refusal to let the therapist "reach" her, or to talk or to experience emotion freely. On becoming conscious of what her attitude was, the patient was then able to recapture the "mood of adolescence" with its long dreary quarrels with mother, which culminated in dogged silence after the quarrels with mother had reached a stalemate. In short, it is necessary for the therapist to be able to recognize the nonverbal aspects of the therapist-patient transaction. Otherwise he will be less likely to understand what is going on and less likely to be able to help the patient to understand the various transactions in which he is participating as well as his therapist.

Perhaps one other thing needs to be emphasized. To a patient in the depth of depression, free association in the classical sense is not usually within his power. In order to activate the patient's latent powers of communication on various levels, the therapist must reach "toward the patient through various modes of communication," drawing upon various kinds of communicational content, including his own immediate experience of the patient.

In a very thought-provoking paper Green has taken up the problem of depression in adolescents. He quotes an arresting passage from G. Stanley Hall (1904), one of the great pioneers in psychology:

> The same youth with all his brazen effrontery may feel a distrust of self and a sinking of heart, which all his bravado is needed to hide. He doubts his own powers, is perilously anxious about his future, his self-love is wounded and humiliated in innumerable ways keenly felt, perhaps at heart resented, with a feeling of impotence to resist. The collapsing moods bring a sense of abasement and a complacency to all that comes, suggesting spiritlessness.

Youth often fears itself lacking in some essential trait of manhood or womanhood, or wanting the qualities of success. He is often vanquished in innumerable rivalries and competitions that now make so much of life, and loses heart and faith. The world seems all the more hopeless because of the great demands which the opposite mood (more arrogant and demanding) has imposed. Sometimes a sense of shame from purely imaginary causes is so poignant as to plunge the soul for a time into the deepest and most doleful dumps; fancied slights suggest despair, and in place of wanted self-confidence there is a retiring bashfulness; which no coaxing or encouragement of friends can overcome or fathom, and which may express itself only in some secret diary or perhaps in prayer.[26]

Of course many, perhaps most, boys from twelve to eighteen do not appear to have had these experiences, at least to a significant degree. Green claims that there are among them "our organization men," adolescents who seem to know what they want: youths who look calm, capable, confident, secure; who are neither too deviant nor too conforming, neither too happy nor too sad. They are youths who appear to do all the right things and apparently cause no trouble for themselves, their family, or their society. Green believes, however, if such a youngster goes through all the adolescent years without at some time feeling disturbed, he misses out on a very important experience (which may cause him to take a more profound look at himself and his world). Not that all disturbances are valuable and worthwhile. *Morbid* depression is said to be invariably destructive and incapacitating, not only to those suffering it but also often to others who are near and dear.

Green asserts that depression in this age group, as in any other, can be manifest, latent, or masked; that it can be reactive or endogenous; neurotic, borderline, or psychotic. It may be associated with any other physical or mental illness or occur "in almost pure culture" as an entity in itself, incomprehensible at times to the sufferer himself, his family or even his therapist. Depression may appear to be a seemingly realistic outcome of the actually unfortunate circumstances that one experiences as a member of one's race, or religion or social class; it may appear to be a seemingly equally realistic response to one's hereditary make-up or to one's immediate environment (as in the case of a soldier during wartime when his "Buddy" gets killed). Green asserts that depression may be expressed in the form of shallow or even very profound criticism of one's parents, society, or even humanity itself. A variety of aggressive, defiant, and disobedient behaviors may serve as an analogous outlet. Still again, it may be expressed through numerous physical symptoms or various psychological reactions, including neurotic or regressive symptoms.

The adolescent phase of personality development is said to comprise four main areas of challenge, stress, task, and concern for the individual who has reached that phase: the drive for independence and competence; control of impulsive tendencies with the development of a guiding sense of values; sexual role clarification and fulfillment; and the selection of educational and vocational career operations. "All these areas have their beginnings in early childhood and may or may not ever be fully realized and evolved throughout the course of one's life."[27] Green claims that the combination of vulnerability and promise that is so characteristic of these adolescent years makes the adolescent especially attractive to adults for exploitation, identification, or simply love and admiration. He quotes Hinsie and Campbell (1960) to the effect that depressions are so frequently seen in youth of both sexes that the term "adolescent depression" would not be out of place. Green also quotes Grinker, Miller, Sabshin, Nunn, and Nunnally (1961), who said that the essence of depression is comprised by a factor describing characteristics of hopelessness, helplessness, failure, sadness, unworthiness, guilt, and internal suffering. Grinker *et al.* also assert that the depressive makes no appeal to the outside world; no conviction that receiving anything from the environment would change how the patients feel. "There is," they say, "a self-concept of 'badness.'"[28]

Gould, Chief of Adolescent Services at the Bellevue Psychiatric Division has written:

"On our Service, we see a fair number of children and adolescents who show many of the classic symptoms of depression, such as (1) loss of interest in social environment and loss of drive; (2) feelings of sadness and emptiness; (3) eating disturbances (anorexia mostly, bulimia occasionally); (4) sleeping disturbances (insomnia mostly, "oversleeping" occasionally); (5) hypomotility; and (6) feelings of loneliness."[29]

Gould also wrote in the same paper:

"Depression, with its accompanying feeling of loneliness, is an excruciating state which is generally avoided or masked in the young-ster. Impulsivity, which is more in evidence in children and adoles-cents than in adults, combines with the depressive state, resulting in behavior which cloaks the depression."

In 1935, Leo Kanner in *Child Psychiatry* wrote:

"It is in an atmosphere of gloom and fear that the soil is prepared for thoughts of self-destruction; especially the dread of failure in school with ensuing ridicule and punishment on the part of strict and unrelenting parents, the fear of the brutalities of an alcoholic and tyrannical father, and the misconceptions about the prophecied ill results of masturbation have been known to make children desper-ately wish to end their lives. . . . Some of the highly intelligent, solitary and educationally misguided children living in an eccentric environ-ment with artificial 'aesthetic standards,' undigested belletristic senti-mentalism and false romanticism are apt to breed unwholesome notions of *Weltschmerz.* "[30]

Green adds that today (1965) Kanner's *Weltschmerz* might be con-tained in popular teenage misconceptions of Zen "nothingness," ex-istentialist "despair," and LSD "superreality."

William James in his *Principles of Psychology* (1890) called attention to the rapid expansion of the self in adolescence, which sharply increases its vulnerability to a crippling of personality. James wrote: ". . . but the worst alterations of the self come from present perversions of sensi-bility and impulse which leave the past undisturbed, but induce the patient to think that the present 'me' is an altogether new personality. Something of this sort happens normally in the rapid expansion of the whole character, intellectual as well as volitional, which takes place after the time of puberty."[31] As Green points out, this rapid expansion of the self during adolescence has been characterized in recent litera-ture by the clichéd expression of "identity crisis."

In regard to treatment, Green claims that because the adolescent is so unsure of his developing adult identity, which is just coming into being, and is so defensive and touchy about his narrow, limited juve-nile identity that he wants to put behind him, he poses a special problem for the therapist's style and technique of psychotherapy. First of all, he is said to have good reason to distrust much of what the adult world is trying to sell him, both literally and figuratively. Secondly, because of the speed of the changes he is experiencing, he has to make more stressful effort in order to maintain values, [self-] directions and orientations. His rapid shifts in mood, role and sense of self may cause the "empathic instrument" of the therapist's skill to be sorely tried. It is often necessary for the therapist to exercise spontaneous initiative in sharing experiences. He must undertake a very flexible and very active technique. Use of food and soda pop is said to be sometimes helpful. Green writes that contact with parents and other family members is often necessary and should be shared with the patient. The therapist must help the adolescent to affirm the ties and continuities he chooses from the past of his juvenile and childhood life with his family, while at the same time supporting him in his efforts to sever those aspects of his past from which he chooses to free himself. "He must also be strengthened in the understanding and incorporation of a future dimension into his present-day thinking, for it is only in the insightful prospect of a future that he is solidly based, however sketchy or incomplete. In this prospect he can feel his powers and he can feel the meaningful purpose and goal of his existence, as well as his therapeutic endeavor. This future may comprise tomorrow, next week, next month, next year or even ten years ahead, depending upon the particular adolescent and his situation."[32] By confronting him with the fact that his existence has a future dimension (which he can ignore only at the risk of suffering permanent misery or worse), he may sometimes be prevented from evading the complexities of his confusion, rebellion, love, and pride, which often cripple the adolescent in his everyday decisions. Green suggests that effective help at this time may accomplish in a shorter period what is so difficult and sometimes impossible to accomplish in later life: the prevention of the recurrence of paralyzing despair and constricting self-depreciatory rumination.[33]

Anthony Storr, an English psychiatrist, has made an attempt at a character study of Winston Churchill.[34] Since he did not know Churchill, he has had to rely upon available written evidence. This, Storr realizes, is a project full of risk, since he is deprived of "those special insights which can only be attained in the consulting room." Storr points out that in the analytical treatment of a patient, the psychiatrist is able to check the validity of the hypotheses that he proffers by the patient's response, and by the changes that occur in the patient as a result of his increased comprehension of himself. As the long process of analysis continues, he writes, errors will gradually be eliminated and the truth recognized by both parties in the analytical transaction. When deprived of the constant appraisal and reappraisal that occurs in prolonged, intensive psychotherapy, psychiatrists who attempt biographical studies of great men are apt to allow theory to outrun discretion. The Freud-Bullitt disastrous study of Woodrow Wilson is a famous example.

In his essay, Storr, nevertheless, advances a hypothesis that he thinks is warranted by the facts. But he is careful to say that his own study is tentative. Storr's essay is not, of course, meant to belittle Churchill. Indeed he believes it was due to the latter's courage that Britain owes its escape from Nazi tyranny. But Storr adds it is no disservice to a great man to draw attention to his humanity, nor to point out, that, like other men, he has had imperfections and flaws. In fact, he claims that had Churchill been a stable and equable man he could never have inspired Britain. While many a political leader might have tried to rally his country with brave words, in 1940, although his heart was full of despair, only a man "who had known and faced despair in himself could carry conviction at such a moment."[35] Storr asserts that only a man who knew what it was to discern a gleam of hope in a hopeless situation, whose courage was beyond reason, and whose aggressive spirit burned at its fiercest when he was hemmed in and surrounded by enemies, could have given emotional reality to the words of defiance that rallied and sustained Britain in the menacing summer of 1940. It was because all his life Churchill had battled against his own despair that he could communicate to others the conviction that despair can be overcome.

Like his ancestor, the first Duke of Marlborough, Churchill suffered from prolonged and recurrent fits of depression. Though this may surprise some general readers, it is a fact that many great men—as well as countless ordinary people—have suffered from recurrent depressions. Among those great men, according to Storr, were Goethe, Schumann, Luther, and Tolstoy. Churchill himself named his depression Black Dog, which he was able to control and largely master until advanced old age combined with the narrowing of his cerebral arteries undermined his resistance during the last five years of his life. Storr admits that the relation between great achievement and the depressive character ("temperament") has yet to be determined in detail, but he thinks that, in some natures, depression acts as a spur. "When depression is overwhelming, the sufferer relapses into gloom and an inactivity which may be so profound as to render him immobile. To avoid this state of misery is of prime importance; and so the depressive, before his despair becomes too severe, may recurrently force himself into activity, deny himself rest and relaxation, and accomplish more than most men are capable of, just because he cannot afford to stop."[36]

Storr is one of those psychiatrists who believe that a hereditary factor enters into the etiology of depression, though he admits it is uncertain how much weight should be attached to it. He also believes it probable that physique and character are intimately connected, and that the structure and shape of the body reflect genetic rather than environmental influences. Though a man's "cast of mind" is largely influenced by the way he is brought up and educated, his physical endowment is more apt to be a product of heredity, though modifiable to some extent by external circumstances. Churchill began life with considerable handicaps. Storr quotes Lord Moran, Churchill's personal physician, as follows: "I could see this sensitive boy, bullied and beaten at his school, grow up into a man, small in stature, with thin, unmuscular limbs, and the white delicate hands of a woman; there was no hair on his chest, and he spoke with a lisp and a slight stutter."[37] While at Sandhurst, he wrote (1893): I am cursed with so feeble a body, that I can scarcely support the fatigues of the day." The physical courage that, in youth and adult life, he so consistently and rashly displayed, according to Storr, was not based on any natural superiority of physique, but rather on his determination to be tough despite his physical disadvantages. His courage was not something he took for granted but sprang, it seems, from a determination to prove himself, a compensation for inner doubts of his own bravery. At his second preparatory school he is said to have been frightened by other boys throwing cricket balls at him, and to have had taken refuge behind some trees. This became a shameful memory, which rankled, causing him very early in life to resolve that he would be as tough as anyone could be.

Storr draws upon W. H. Sheldon's formulations of physique and temperament. According to Sheldon there are three main components in a man's physical make-up characterized as endomorphy, mesomorphy, and ectomorphy. Closely allied to the subject's physique, Sheldon thinks, is a scale of temperament comprising three sets of twenty basic traits. (I pass over the question as to whether Sheldon has not confused temperamental characteristics with character traits.) The three chief varieties of temperament connected with the three kinds of physique are viscerotonia, somatotonia, and cerebrotonia.

Churchill's physique was predominantly endomophic. "His massive head, the small size of his chest compared with his abdomen, the rounded contours of his body, and the small size of his extremities were all characteristic. So was his smooth, soft skin, which was so delicate that he always wore specially obtained silk underwear."[38] Following Sheldon's formulations, one would anticipate such a physique to be predominantly viscerotonic in temperament: "earthy, unhurried, deliberate and predictable." Storr writes that Churchill does actually rate high on eleven out of the twenty viscerotonic traits, but he also scores almost equally high on somatotonia, the temperament that is allied to the powerful and athletic frame of the mesomorph. So Storr calls attention to Sheldon's idea that men whose "temperament" differs widely from that which accords with their physique are particularly subject to psychological conflict, since they are at odds "with their own emotional constitution." Churchill is said to have been a very much more aggressive and dominant individual than one would expect from his basic physique. He "loved" risk and physical adventure, possessed enormous energy, and manifested a pugnacious assertiveness. These are characteristics and traits that are normally associated with a heavily muscled mesomorph, not an endomorph. Hence Storr concludes that Churchill was a man who, to a marked extent, forced himself to go against his own inner nature. His aggressiveness, his courage, and his domineering ("dominant") behavior were the product of deliberate decision and iron will.

In order to penetrate the complex make-up of his subject, Storr also resorts to another typology, that of C. G. Jung, claiming that Churchill was undoubtedly highly extroverted. The reader who is not familiar with Jung's book *Psychological Types* will recall from the discussion in a previous chapter of this book that the extrovert is a person who is oriented toward the events and features of the external world, not toward his own inner life and "the recesses of his own soul." The extrovert is primarily interested in action, not in abstract ideas or the subleties of philosophy, and when troubled he seeks to do things that will distract him rather than explore his inner life in order to discover the causes of his disturbance. Philosophy had little interest for Churchill, and religion, none at all. One cannot imagine him reading

Greek drama and poetry in the trenches, had he been a soldier, as did Harold Macmillan during World War I.

Storr also believes that of Jung's subdivision of types into thinking, feeling, sensation, and intuition, the last-mentioned fits Churchill almost perfectly. In *Psychological Types* Jung wrote: "Whenever intuition predominates, a particular and unmistakable psychology presents itself. . . . The intuitive is never to be found among the generally recognized reality values, but is always present where possibilities exist. He has a keen nose for things in the bud pregnant with future promise. . . . Thinking and feeling, the indispensable components of conviction, are, with him inferior functions, possessing no decisive weight: hence they lack the power to offer any lasting resistance to the force of intuition." According to Jung, from these things come the intuitive's lack of judgment and also his "weak consideration for the welfare of his neighbors." The intuitive is "not infrequently put down as a ruthless and immoral adventurer," a characterization often applied to Churchill in his youth, according to Storr, "and yet his capacity to inspire his fellow-men with courage, or to kindle enthusiasm for something new, is unrivalled."[39]

C. P. Snow in an essay on Churchill commented on his lack of judgment, which was "seriously defective." But Snow also wrote: "Judgment is a fine thing: but it is not all that uncommon. Deep insight is much rarer. Churchill had flashes of that kind of insight, dug up from his own nature, independent of influences, owing nothing to anyone outside himself. Sometimes it was a better guide than judgment: in the ultimate crisis when he came to power, there were times when judgment itself could, though it did not need to, become a source of weakness. . . ."[40] When Hitler came to power, Churchill is said to have employed one of his deep insights.

Storr believes this kind of insight can also be called intuition. However, he is careful to point out that in many respects intuition is an unreliable guide, and some of Churchill's were "badly wrong." Undoubtedly. But he incautiously accepts the popular notion that Churchill's "major strategic conception," the invasion of Gallipoli, in World War I was a failure. Actually, according to the eminent military strategist, Captain Basil Liddell Hart, it was *the execution* of this apparently sound conception that went wrong—and this was not Churchill's fault.[41] On the other hand Storr gives him far too much credit for his ideas on the development of the tank.[42] It was, I think, during World

War II that many of Churchill's "intuitions" proved to be disastrously wrong but I shall content myself with referring the reader to the various specialists who have appraised Churchill's career in *Churchill Revised* for a more comprehensive and balanced picture of his achievements and failures.

Storr thinks that Jung's description of the extroverted intuitive, who is lacking in judgment, has much to offer that applies to Churchill. The latter "could never think for long at a time. Although he had brilliant ideas, he was hardly susceptible to reason and could not follow a consecutive argument when presented to him by others. His famous demand that all ideas should be presented to him on a half sheet of paper is an illustration of this point."[43] Alanbrooke wrote in his wartime diary of him that planned strategy was not his "strong card," that he preferred to work by intuition and by impulse. Not only was he not good at examining all the implications of any course he favored; in fact, he often refused to look at them.[44] Moreover, he was, in many respects, deficient in feeling, possessing little appreciation of the feelings of others.

Throughout the years, Churchill struggled with his Black Dog. Moran, in his book, relates the following interchange held on August 14, 1944.

"When I was young," Churchill ruminated in the conversation with Moran, "for two or three years the light faded out of the picture. I did my work. I sat in the House of Commons, but black depression settled on me. It helped me to talk to Clemmie about it. I don't like standing near the edge of a platform when an express train is passing through. I like to stand right back and if possible to get a pillar between me and the train. . . ."[45]

Then Moran told him that the "Black Dog business" was inherited from his ancestors. "You have fought against it all your life. That is why you dislike visiting hospitals. You always avoid anything that is depressing." At this, Churchill stared at Moran as if he knew too much.

Later in his book, Moran quotes a communication with the dying Brendan Bracken to the effect that when Churchill was a mere boy he deliberately set out to change his nature, to be tough and full of rude spirits.

"It has not been easy for him," Bracken asserted. "You see, Charles, Winston has always been a 'despairer.' Orpen, who painted him after the Dardanelles, used to speak of the misery in his face. He called him the man of misery. Winston was so sure then that he would take no further part in public life. There seemed nothing left to live for. It made him very sad. Then, in his years in the wilderness, before the Second War, he kept saying: 'I'm finished.' He said that about twice a day. He was quite certain that he would never get back to office, for everyone seemed to regard him as a wild man. And he missed the red boxes awfully. Winston has always been wretched unless he was occupied. You know what he has been like since he resigned. Why, he told me that he prays every day for death."[46]

Many depressives are said to deny themselves rest or relaxation because they cannot afford to stop, and if they are compelled to do so by circumstances, the black cloud comes down upon them. Several times this happened to Churchill: when he left the Admiralty in May, 1915; when he did not hold office during the thirties; when he lost the election of 1945; and when old age forced his final retirement. Though he employed various inventions to cope with the depression he suffered when he was no longer fully occupied by affairs of state, including painting, writing, and bricklaying, he did not wholly succeed. Storr attempts to explain why. He claims that a man's genetic inheritance may predispose him to depression but whether he actually suffers from it or not is likely to depend upon his early experiences within the family. Storr claims that psychoanalysis, from which he borrows many of his ideas, assumes that the psychological disturbances from which people suffer are related to the whole emotional climate in which they were reared, and that neurosis and psychosis in adult life are explicable in terms of a failure of the environment to meet the needs of the particular individual under scrutiny at a time when those needs are paramount.

One salient characteristic of adults who suffer from depression is said to be their inordinate dependence on external sources to maintain self-esteem. While normal people may mourn or experience disappointment, they do not become or remain severely depressed for long in the face of misadventure, being fairly easily consoled by what is left to them because they have an inner source of self-esteem. In contrast, depressives are much more vulnerable. "If one thing in the world goes wrong, they are apt to be thrown into despair." Attempts to comfort them are useless. In a depressive, disappointment, bereavement, rejection, may trigger a reaction of total hopelessness, since such a person does not possess an inner resource of self-esteem to which he can fall back upon to sustain him when visited by trouble or misfortune. The ministrations of others are equally ineffective. Storr adds that if, at a deep inner level, a person feels himself to be predominantly bad or unlovable, an actual rejection in the external world will bring this depressive belief to the surface, and no amount of reassurance from well-wishers will, for a time, persuade him of his real worth.

According to Storr, psychoanalysts have assumed that this vulnerability is the result of a rather early failure in the relationship between the child and his parents. "In the ordinary course of events, a child takes in love with his mother's milk. A child who is wanted, loved, played with, cuddled will incorporate within himself a lively sense of his own value; and will therefore surmount the inevitable setbacks and disappointments of childhood with no more than temporary sorrow, secure in the belief that the world is predominantly a happy place, and that he has a favored place in it. And this pattern [if very unfortunate circumstances do not intervene] will generally persist throughout life."[47]

On the other hand, when a child is unwanted, rejected, or disapproved of by his parents, he will gain no such conviction. Even when in subsequent years he experiences periods of success and happiness, they will not convince him that he is lovable. Nor will they convince him that life is worth living. In the course of life, he may dedicate a whole career to the pursuit of power, the conquest of women, or the acquisition of wealth, only to be faced, in the end, with despair or futility for he cannot shake off the underlying conviction of worthlessness first acquired from his experiences with his parents. Nor can any amount of wordly success compensate him for his lack of a sense of value as a person. Sarah Churchill in her book *A Thread in the Tapestry* relates that on one of his birthdays, when the family had been listening to the radio and reading "the always generous newspaper euologies," and she had exclaimed in wonderment at all the things her father had done in his life, he replied, "I have achieved a great deal to achieve nothing in the end."[48] As Storr so well expresses it, despite everything Churchill had done, there was still a void at the heart of his being.

"What," Storr asks, "were the childhood origins of Churchill's depressive disposition?" To some extent, the answer has to be speculative. But certain data are available for consideration foremost of which is parental neglect. When Churchill was a baby, in accordance with the custom of those days, he was not fed by his mother, a celebrated and beautiful lady. Instead he was handed over to the care of a wet nurse, about whom nothing is known. When he was born, his mother, Lady Randolph, was only twenty and much too immersed in the fashionable life of the aristocracy to be much concerned about her infant son. The brilliant Lord Randolph, who was deeply involved in politics, showed only a remote interest in his son and heir. Thus in the vital years of early childhood, Winston received extremely little affection or support from his parents. Storr writes that the person who saved him from emotional starvation was Mrs. Everest, the nanny who was engaged early in 1875 within a few months of his birth, and who remained his chief support and confidante until she died when Churchill was twenty. Until the end of his own life her photograph hung in his room. In his novel *Savrola,* she is immortalized as the nanny (and housekeeper) whose devotion, according to Churchill, is perhaps "the only disinterested affection in the world."

Storr points out that happy children do not ask *why* their mothers or anyone else love them, merely accepting it as a fact of their existence. Only those who are not loved, or are not loved enough, as children, are surprised that anyone should be fond of them, and who seek for an explanation of the love that more fortunate children accept as a matter of course. Churchill was one of these. People who suffer from depression are said to be always asking themselves why anyone should love them. They may often believe they are entitled to respect or to admiration or awe; but to love—never. There is no doubt that Winston Churchill's parents were neglectful. His son, Randolph Churchill wrote: "The neglect and lack of interest in him shown by his parents were remarkable, even judged by the standards of late Victorian and Edwardian days. His letters to his mother from his various schools abound in pathetic requests for letters and for visits, if not from her, from Mrs. Everest and his brother Jack. Lord Randolph was a busy politician with his whole interest absorbed in politics. Lady Randolph was caught up in the whirl of fashionable society and seems to have taken very little interest in her son until he began to make his name resound through the world. It will later be seen how neglectful she was in writing to him when he was for three years a subaltern in India and when his father and Mrs. Everest were dead. His brother

Jack, more than five years younger, could not be a satisfactory corre-spondent and Winston was to feel exceptionally lonely and aban-doned."[49]

It seems that one is justified in assuming that Winston Churchill was deprived of that inner source of self-esteem upon which, most predominantly, happy persons rely, and which serves to carry them through the inevitable disappointments and reverses of human exist-ence, by the cold neglect of his parents. And he tried to make up for this early deprivation and to sustain his self-esteem in various ways. Storr claims that the first and most obvious trait of character that he developed as a response to his deprivation was ambition. But it was not the normal ambition of a young man reared in the competitive climate of Western civilization. It was an inordinate compensatory and compulsive drive that made him unpopular when he was a young man. When it becomes a compulsive drive, ambition is the direct outcome of early deprivation. But why? A child who has little convic-tion of his own worth tends to seek recognition and acclaim from external achievement, especially if he has the social and ancestral background of a Churchill. Success, or even the hope of success, whether financial, political, or artistic in youth, especially, can be effec-tive in warding off depression in those who are liable to this disorder. But as a man gets older, the inevitable decay of hope during middle age accounts for the fact that severe attacks of depression usually become more common.

Moreover, extreme, compulsive ambition is not based upon a so-ber, objective appraisal of one's gifts and deficiencies. There is always said to be an element of fantasy, unrelated to actual achievement. In Churchill's case, it took the form of a conviction that one is being reserved for a special purpose, whether by the Deity or by Fate. But it is remarkable that this conviction persisted throughout the greater part of his life until, at the age of sixty-five, through a remarkable convergence of fortuitous circumstances, his fantasy found expres-sion in reality. He even told Moran, "This cannot be accident, it must be design. I was kept for this job." Throughout his life, despite nu-merous setbacks and bitter disappointments, Churchill's schoolboy dreams of future greatness, of a heroic mission, persisted. In 1945, his conviction became a reality.

Storr, following Freudian theory, believes the conviction of being special is a reflection of "infantile omnipotence." Despite the infant's utter helplessness, he creates the illusion that he is powerful. In the normal course of events, "a number of willing slaves hasten to fulfill the needs of the infant." The constant care and attention of these willing slaves creates in the infant who has no appreciation of his realistic situation in the world a feeling of omnipotence. For he has only to utter a few sounds, perhaps, or to raise his arms in ineffable appeal, and the slaves appear, as if by magic, to minister to him. Because of maturation and increasing experience, the youngster gradually learns that his desires are not always paramount, and that he must sometimes subordinate his demands to the needs of others who take precedence. Storr asserts that this is especially true in a family where there are other children. In the rough and tumble of competition with brothers and sisters, one learns the hard lesson that he is not the center of the universe. An only child may not outgrow this early phase of development, and this was more or less the case with Churchill. Even though he was not an only child, his brother Jack was sufficiently younger for Winston to have held his "solitary position" during the first five years of his life. "Paradoxically, it is children who are deprived as well as solitary who retain the sense of omnipotence." A failure to satisfy a child's need for total care and total acceptance during the earliest part of his life is said to leave him with a sense of something missing and something yearned for. In later life he may try to so contrive or create conditions in which his lightest whim is immediately attended to (much after the fashion of a very spoiled child whose parents foolishly try to cater to his every whim) and resent the fact that this is not always possible.

This characteristic was markedly evident in Churchill. During one of his illnesses there were two nurses to minister to his needs and demands. His wife said to Moran: "Winston is a pasha. If he cannot clap his hands for a servant he calls for Walter as he enters the house. If it were left to him he'd have the nurses for the rest of his life. He would like two in his room, two in the passage. He is never so happy, Charles, as he is when one of the nurses is doing something for him while Walter puts on his socks."[50] Storr comments that Churchill's arrogance, impatience, and lack of consideration for others must have been extremely difficult to live with. However, Storr adds that these traits were "softened by his magnanimity." One wonders how so egocentric an individual could inspire devotion in those who served under him, whose immediate needs he seldom considered. Storr suggests that men who demand and need a great deal of attention from others are manifesting a childlike helplessness that evokes an appropriate response, however difficult these people may be. His wife related that the one time Churchill had been on the Underground was during the general strike. "He went round and round," she said, "not knowing where to get out and had to be rescued eventually."

His having been an aristocrat must have been of considerable help to him. Even though his parents grossly neglected him, there always was Mrs. Everest to wait upon him and minister to his needs and whims until she died. Subsequently, his wife, valet, doctor, and "innumerable attendants and servants" took over the job. Storr writes that those ("of us") who are old enough to remember the days in which the aristocracy and the upper middle class took it for granted that the ordinary details of living, food, clothes, travel, and so on would be taken care of by some minion or other, and who have since learned to take care of themselves, can recall that the existence of servants did minister to their self-esteem. The sense of belonging to a privileged class is said to be some mitigation for the feeling of rejection. Within that privileged class, the Churchill family enjoyed particular distinction, which Winston must have learned early in life to appreciate.

A child whose emotional needs are not gratified or only partially gratified will generally react to this frustration by hostility. Badly behaved, difficult children are (at least often) those who are unloved. For them all authority is hostile. Churchill is said to have been no exception. But there is another, and poignant, side to even the most rebellious and intransigent children. In imagination they create a picture of parents they would like to have. Thus the negative image of authority as rejecting, cruel, and neglectful is said to be balanced by a positive image of idealized parents who are invariably loving, tender, and understanding. The more removed and isolated from his real parents, the more will he persist in his fantasies of imaginary, idealized parents. Real parents are not godlike figures: they share all the human limitations and imperfections, sometimes loving, sometimes hating, sometimes acutely conscious of a child's needs, sometimes ignorant, unimaginative, uncomprehending, imperceptive, oblivious of the child's strange, new world. Reared in the intimacy of an ordinary family, the child soon amalgamates his images of good and bad parents, of good and bad people, learning to realize in the course of time that, in other human beings as in himself, good and bad qualities are inextricably intertwined. Storr also points out that delinquent and emotionally disturbed children, whose parents are neglectful or actually cruel, still maintain that they are really "good," blaming themselves for the parents' inadequacies. Idealization of parents, in such cases, acts as a defensive and protective function. Weak and defenseless, a small child cannot bear to believe that there are no adults who love, support, and guide him. He could not survive the Arctic winter of utter indifference. So if there are no adults or elder siblings who care for him, he invents imaginary, idealized parents.

Winston Churchill idealized his mother. Of her he wrote: "She shone for me like the Evening Star. I loved her dearly—but at a distance." For many years, he retained a romantic view of women, based on his idealization of his beautiful mother. His friend Violet Bonham Carter has related that he had a lively susceptibility to beauty, glamor, radiance, and those who possessed those qualities were not subjected to analysis. He assumed as a matter of course that they possessed all the cardinal virtues. If one openly questioned the accuracy of such a romantic picture of women, he was affronted. But here again, like the Evening Star, they shone from afar. Although in his youth, he was "emotionally involved" with at least three girls before he married, in his latter years he took little notice of women. But the romantic vision is said to have persisted, attaching itself to the figure of Queen Elizabeth II.

Storr thinks that Churchill's idealization of his father was even more remarkable, since the latter was so consistently disapproving of, or uninterested in, his small son. Yet the small boy hero-worshiped him, a phenomenon that apparently can be explained only with the help of the same psychological mechanism outlined in relation to his idealization of his mother. "The image remained upon its pedestal," according to Violet Bonham Carter, "intact and glorious. Until the end he worshiped at the altar of his Unknown Father." His flesh-and-blood father is said to have remained entirely unknown to him, to have never talked intimately with him, and to have seldom written to him except to reprove him. Even though Winston Churchill published a two-volume biography of Lord Randolph in 1906, he was memorializing an image, not a real father whose life he shared.

There is another side, as it were, to idealization. When children suffer their parents' neglect or lack of affection, they react with hostility as well as idealization. Storr tells us that Churchill's obstinacy, resentment of authority, and willfulness were manifest very early in his life. The school authorities at the boarding school to which he was sent before his eighth birthday became the recipients of the hostility that he must have (unconsciously) felt toward his parents, though he never manifested it because of his idealization of them. The reports from the school authorities describe him as repeatedly late for class. From being "a regular pickle" in his earliest report, he progressed to "troublesome," "very bad," "constant trouble to everybody," and "very naughty." Though he did not remain long at this school—less than two years—he himself has told how much he hated it. Storr believes it is likely that he was removed from this school because of the severe beatings he received from the headmaster, a sadistic clergyman who enjoyed inflicting as many as twenty strokes of the birch upon the bare buttocks of the helpless little boys under his care. But Churchill was not cowed. The stupid, cruel behavior of the headmaster probably served to reinforce his intolerance toward authority. Yet he did not complain in his early letters from school, reporting himself to be happy, though he subsequently admitted this was the opposite of the truth. Very frequently small boys conceal the misery they suffer at boarding school from their parents. "Ignorance of what the world is really like may lead them to suppose that ill-treatment and lack of sympathetic understanding is the expected lot of boys; and that if they are unhappy, it is a sign of weakness and their own fault."[51] Storr asserts that this is especially true of those with a depressive tendency, for the hostility they feel toward parents and other authorities easily becomes turned inward against themselves. Since they believe they ought to be happy, they report themselves as happy, easily deceiving imperceptive parents who are not concerned to discover the truth about the real feelings and attitudes of their offspring.

Freud discovered an intimate connection between depression and hostility. The emotionally deprived child who later becomes prey to depression is said to have enormous difficulty in the discharge of his hostility. Though he resents those who have neglected or deprived him, he cannot risk expressing this hostility against the very people on whom he depends for the gratification of his needs. If he should express his hostility toward them, he will be still further deprived of the approval and affection he requires so profoundly. During periods of depression this hostility becomes diverted from expression against others and redirected inward against the self, bringing about a devaluation, or increasing devaluation, of himself, sometimes to the point where he feels worthless, as in the case of Churchill at times: "I have achieved a great deal to achieve nothing in the end." This dilemma, so to speak, drives some depressives to seek for opponents in the external world. When they find them, they experience great relief, since the opponents are justifiable objects on whom they can lavishly vent their justifiable wrath. Fighting enemies held a strong emotional appeal for Churchill, and when he was faced with an enemy whom he believed to be wholly evil, it nourished and strengthened his enormous vitality. Hitler provided him with the opportunity to employ, with happiness and great gusto, the full force of his enormous aggressiveness. Against such an archdemon he could employ all his aggressive powers without pangs of conscience.

Storr alleges that Churchill was never happy unless he was fully occupied, asleep, or holding the floor. Violet Bonham Carter has told that he had to be perpetually active or else he relapsed into "dark moments of impatience and frustration." As early as 1895 he wrote to his mother from Aldershot that he was getting into a state of mental stagnation when even letter writing became an effort and when any reading but that of monthly magazines—and rereading "Papa's speeches"—were impossible. Apparently he suffered apprehensions galore (fears of sleeping near a balcony for example, or traveling by airplane or of traveling by ship). In early youth he believed he would die young. He showed an early tendency to hypochondriasis. In 1910, Lucy Masterman reported of him: "He thought he had got every mortal disease under heaven, and was very much inclined to dine off slops and think about the latter end."[52] Though Storr does not think that Churchill was suicidal, he thinks it likely that death had a kind of fascination for him against which he had to defend himself. A secret longing for peace generally possesses men who have to be hyperactive in order to protect themselves against depression. For them, "the garden of Prosperpina" has a special appeal.

Although Churchill performed inadequately in most school subjects, he discovered that he had a gift for words. Storr relates that when he first met Violet Bonham Carter, he asked her whether she thought that words had a magic and a music quite independent of their meaning. Churchill thought they did. The magic of words is said to have become a part of his inner world of make-believe, in which he lived a large part of his life. "His imagination was really creative; and it expressed itself in rhetoric, in an ornate phraseology which soon soared above the sober and often intransigent facts of reality. This was why he was always having to be restrained by his advisers; by his civil servants when he was Home Secretary; by his chiefs of staff, especially Alanbrooke, when he was Prime Minister."[53] Since he could clothe his ideas in magnificent language, he could inspire himself as well as others by the magic of words. Storr thinks it likely that Churchill used his writing as a fence against the depression that invariably descended upon him when he was forced to be inactive. Painting served a similar function. After his resignation from the Admiralty in 1915 following upon the failure of the Dardanelles expedition, for which he was unjustly blamed, he was despairing. Of this period he himself wrote: "And then it was that the Muse of Painting came to my rescue—out of charity and out of chivalry, because after all she had nothing to do with me—and said, 'Are these toys any good to you? They amuse some people.' "[54]

Storr pushes his analysis of Churchill's character as cooly and relentlessly as if he were a client who had sought psychiatric help from him. He reminds us that people of Churchill's type of psychological structure find it hard to learn that they are not the center of the universe. Owing to the lack of intimate affectional relations, first with parents, and later with other persons, "they remain egocentrically oriented." In a rather quaint phraseology, Storr writes that every baby starts life in a predominantly solipsistic state (while Sullivan would say that every infant first experiences life in the prototaxic mode). Most babies, as they grow, he writes, "progress to a more mature emotional condition in which it is realized not only that other people have desires and needs, but also that one's own desires and needs interact with them in such a way that one can both satisfy and be satisfied simultaneously." When a child is deprived of approval and affection, he can form no such conceptions (because he has no models from whom he can learn them). So he is unable to put away childish emotions and attitudes, making inordinate demands on other people while he is barely conscious, if at all, of the possibility that he might give them much. Churchill was like that. Although he could be generous to defeated enemies, he remained all his life extremely demanding, insensitive to the needs and requirements of others, including men like Alanbrooke, who, time and again by wise counsel, saved him from disastrous military blunders. Churchill's "principle love-object," according to Storr, "remained himself, because that self had never, in childhood, been satisfied."[55]

In Churchill, oral character traits persisted, both literally and metaphorically. One of his earliest school reports described him as greedy. All through his life he is said to have needed feeding at frequent intervals. He was dependent on alcohol. As perhaps everyone who remembers the newspaper pictures published during the period of World War II knows, he was a heavy smoker of cigars. Storr tells us that he was also "greedy for approval." If he showed his intimates a manuscript of what he was writing, he wanted unadulterated praise. Any friend who dared an adverse comment on any of his ideas or creations met with the reproach, "You are not on my side." From his failure to receive total and uncritical acceptance as a child, he inherited this either/or attitude: a division of the world into black and white, with no greys, no shadings, no mixtures. John Dewey's statement that all character is "speckled" would have been incomprehensible to him. Because of his naïve, childish appraisals of people he was uncritical in his relationships with friends, to whom he was intensely loyal. And from them he expected the same attitudes. Storr writes of him: "He remained hungry—hungry for fame, for adulation, for success, and for power; and although he gained all these in full measure, the end of his life showed that he never assimilated them into himself, but remained unsatisfied."[56]

This is, to be sure, a psychiatric commonplace: the child who is unloved, unapproved, neglected, consciously or otherwise, develops an insatiable need for love and approval—provided, of course, that he has not been so terribly damaged that he abandons all hope and effort, perhaps seeking total solace in alcohol or drugs.

Storr informs us that the end of Churchill's life makes melancholy reading. After his retirement in 1955, according to Moran, "Winston made little effort to hide his distaste for what was left to him of life." The Black Dog finally overcame him. Although Moran ends his story five years before Churchill's death, he has revealed that he sank into a state of indifference and apathy. He gave up reading, spoke seldom and for hours sat before the fire in what Storr thinks must have amounted to a depressive stupor. Such was the end of the "heroic visionary" who rallied Britain in 1940. Old age had finally conquered his dogged determination, his resilience in the aftermath of many defects and failures, and the courage to stand firm when all seemed lost.

While it seems likely that no future biographer can ignore Storr's brilliant analysis of Churchill's character, on the basis of the presently available data about his life, I think a psychiatrist's view is of necessity narrow in scope. What did Churchill's achievements add up to in the end? We are all of us the heirs to Churchill's—and Roosevelt's—successes and failures. Hence I want to end this chapter on a different note, and one that bears some relation to my essay in the Appendix, and, what is infinitely more important, to the "mess" we are all in, and which promises to endure for a long, long time. Consider the estimate of Hart. He regards Churchill as having been "a wonderful man," who shone out of the gloom of an era of mediocrities in the democracies. Not only did he compel admiration by his virtuosity, he also inspired affection, supreme egocentric though he was. Though he revealed at times a long view, he was inclined to act on a short view, "prompted by his tactical sense as well as blinded by the force of his feelings." When he went into action his fighting instinct is said to have governed his course, his emotions to have swamped his calculations so that when his reason reasserted itself it was too late. "Thus when he got his hand on the helm in 1939, too late to avert the danger he had foreseen, events continued to move with the same inevitability of tragedy as in the preceding period, toward further danger that he did not foresee."[57]

It would be more accurate, perhaps, to say that he did not foresee it in time. Possibly in the end it would not have greatly mattered, since he lost the power of ultimate decision—to Roosevelt and his advisers. Hart—whose authority can scarcely be successfully challenged—writes that once the cross-channel landing was achieved, not only Alanbrooke, who headed the British Chiefs of Staff, but Churchill himself ceased "to have any important influence on the course of the war—or on its sequel."[58] In fact, Churchill had earlier proclaimed himself to be merely Roosevelt's "lieutenant."[59] Nevertheless, for a long time he shared the American President's blindness to the further danger.

The danger was—and is—Russia. (Communist China, to be sure, is now an added danger, thanks to the conduct of the war and its aftermath.) According to Hart, a very great blindness prevailed in London and Washington regarding the grand strategy of the war. "Through it," he writes, "the Western democracies have been in fresh and greater peril ever since the war ended."[60] This is said to be due to a too intense concentration on the short-term object, and a failure to take a long view. This failure was epitomized by Churchill himself, with his implacable insistence on "the defeat, ruin, and slaughter of Hitler, *to the exclusion of all other purposes.*" (Italics added.) "Churchill, as well as Roosevelt," Hart proclaims, "seems to have been blind to the obvious fact that the complete destruction of Germany's and Japan's power of *defense* was bound to give Soviet Russia the chance to dominate Eastern Europe and Asia."[61]

Perhaps when Churchill retired in 1955 to sit and brood by the fire, his despondency was nourished by more than his defective character and advanced age.

Now that I have virtually completed the somewhat difficult task of writing this book, I wish to add a few thoughts concerning Sullivan's cultural background, which may be contrasted with Freud's German-Austrian background, with its famous idealistic and quasi-idealistic concepts regarding the interpretation of sense experience. That is, according to the latter view, there supposedly are principles of interpretation more or less native to the human mind, without which one could not understand the world. Sullivan inherited a tradition that was more pragmatic, less given to interpreting experience by means of *a priori* concepts. There is a tendency in Freudian psychoanalysis to interpret human experience and behavior according to fixed principles of interpretation. *"Das Ich"* of German philosophy, for example, is very different from the empirical self of William James, which Sullivan inherited with the great enrichment given to it by Cooley and the refinement of formulation contributed by Mead. In interpersonal psychiatry, the empirical self became the self-dynamism. Thus, the self-conscious personality is not a fixed entity: Though it usually has a relatively stabile organization, it is never literally twice the same. It begins to develop in infancy, "grows" for an indefinitely great number of years, and somewhere along the individual's career begins to decline. Moreover, at any given time, the self-dynamism has a greater or lesser scope, depending partly on the nature and quality of the interpersonal situations in which one is "integrated." This scope is often manifested in me-you patterns. Sullivan believed that the psychiatrist who has a ready-made inflexible set of principles and categories with which to "analyze" his patient may be doing his patient a serious disservice.

Chapter 12 provides evidence that Sullivan's ideas and techniques are being widely employed, with very promising results. These ideas and techniques are no longer the property of any one school. Hence, they are now largely immune to the ideological commitments, prejudices, and misunderstandings of individual psychiatrists. They "belong" to the entire psychiatric (and psychological) enterprise. So, I believe, that in the history of modern psychiatry, Sullivan will be ranked second only to Freud.

Notes

1. JUDD MARMOR (ed.), *Modern Psychoanalysis: New Directions and Perspectives* (New York: Basic Books, 1968).

2. Cf. JURGEN RUESCH, "Psychoanalysis Between Two Cultures" in Marmor, *op. cit.*, chap. 3.

3. MARMOR, *op. cit.*, pp. 8-9.

4. *Ibid.*, pp. 123-145.

5. *Ibid.*, p. 124.

6. *Ibid.*, p. 125.

7. *Ibid.*, p. 127.

8. Cf. LOUIS BREGER, "Motivation, Energy and Cognitive Structure in Psychoanalytic Theory," in MARMOR, *op. cit.*, chap. 2.

9. OTTO A. WILL, JR., "Schizophrenia and Psychotherapy," in MARMOR, *op. cit.*, p. 568.

10. *Ibid.*, p. 569.

11. OTTO A. WILL, JR., "Schizophrenia and the Phychotherapeutic Field," *Contemporary Psychoanalysis*, 1:11-20, 1964.

12. *Ibid.*, p. 21.

13. Cf. THEODORE LIDZ, "The Influence of Family Studies on the Treatment of Schizophrenia," *Psychiatry*, 32:237-251, 1969.

14. Cf. OTTO A. WILL, JR., "Paranoid Development and the Concept of Self: Psychotherapeutic Intervention," *Psychiatry*, 24:74-86, 1961 (suppl. to No. 2); "The Reluctant Patient, the Unwanted Psychotherapist—and Coercion," *Contemporary Psychoanalysis*, 5:1-31, 1968; HAROLD F. SEARLES, "The Schizophrenic Individual's Experience of His World," *Psychiatry*, 31:119-131, 1967.

15. FREDERIC C. REDLICH and DANIEL X. FREEDMAN, *The Theory and Practice of Psychiatry* (New York: Basic Books, 1966), p. 534.

16. HARRY STACK SULLIVAN, *The Psychiatric Interview,* ed. HELEN SWICK PERRY and MARY LADD GAWEL, with an Introduction by OTTO ALLEN WILL, JR. (New York: W. W. Norton and Company, 1954), p. 200.

17. HARRY STACK SULLIVAN, *Clinical Studies in Psychiatry,* ed. HELEN SWICK PERRY, MARY LADD GAWEL, and MARTHA GIBBON, with a Foreword by DEXTER M. BULLARD (New York: W. W. Norton and Company, 1956), pp. 284-285.

18. *Ibid.,* p. 289.

19. REDLICH AND FREEDMAN, *op. cit.,* p. 533.

20. *ibid.,* p. 534.

21. *Ibid.,* pp. 546-547.

22. WALTER BONIME, "A Psychotherapeutic Approach to Depression," *Contemporary Psychoanalysis,* **2**:48-53, 1965.

23. ROSE SPIEGEL, "Communication with Depressive Patients," *Contemporary Psychoanalysis,* **2**:30-35, 1965.

24. *Ibid.*

25. *Ibid.*

26. MAURICE R. GREEN, "Depression in Adolescence," *Contemporary Psychoanalysis,* **2**:42-47, 1965.

27. *Ibid.*

28. *Ibid.*

29. *Ibid.* Quoted from R. E. GOULD, "Suicide Problems in Children and Adolescents," *American Journal of Psychiatry,* April, 1964.

30. GREEN, *op. cit.* Quoted from LEO KANNER, *Child Psychiatry* (Springfield, Illinois: Charles C Thomas, 1935), p. 509.

31. GREEN, *op. cit.* Quoted from WILLIAM JAMES, *Principles of Psychology* (New York: Dover Press, 1890), Vol. I, p. 345.

32. GREEN, *op. cit.*

33. Cf. ELIZABETH KLEINBERGER, "Depression in Infancy and Childhood," *Contemporary Psychoanalysis,* **2**:36-40, 1965.

34. ANTHONY STORR, "The Man," in A. J. P. TAYLOR, ROBERT RHODES JONES, J. H. PLUMB, BASIL LIDDELL HART, and ANTHONY STORR, *Churchill Revised: A Critical Assessment* (New York: Dial Press, 1969), pp. 229-274.

35. *Ibid.,* pp. 230-231.

36. *Ibid.,* pp. 231-232.

37. *Ibid.,* pp. 234-235. Quoted from LORD MORAN, *The Later Churchills* (London: The Macmillan Company, 1958), pp. 287-288.

38. STORR, *op. cit.,* p. 236.

39. *Ibid.,* p. 238.

40. *Ibid.* Quoted from C. P. SNOW, *Varieties of Men* (London: The Macmillan Company, 1967), p. 125.

41. BASIL LIDDELL HART, "The Military Srategist," in TAYLOR, JONES, PLUMB, HART, AND STORR, *op. cit.*

42. *Ibid.*

43. STORR, *op. cit.*, p. 239.

44. *Ibid.*

45. *Ibid.* Quoted from LORD MORAN, *op. cit.*, p. 167.

46. STORR, *op. cit.*, p. 241. Quoted from LORD MORAN, *op. cit.*, p. 754.

47. STORR, *op. cit.*, pp. 243-244.

48. *Ibid.*, p. 244.

49. *Ibid.*, pp. 249-250. Quoted from RANDOLPH CHURCHILL, *Winston S. Churchill*, Vol. I, *Youth: 1877-1900* (London: Heinemann, 1966), p. 45.

50. STORR, *op. cit.* Quoted from LORD MORAN, *op. cit.*, p. 433.

51. STORR, *op. cit.*, p. 258.

52. *Ibid.*, p. 263.

53. *Ibid.*, p. 264.

54. *Ibid.*, p. 267.

55. *Ibid.*, p. 269.

56. *Ibid.*, p. 270.

57. HART, *op. cit.*, p. 225.

58. *Ibid.*, pp. 218-219.

59. *Ibid.*, p. 219.

60. *Ibid.*, p. 221.

61. *Ibid.* Cf. CORNELIAS RYAN, *The Last Battle* (New York: Simon and Schuster, 1966).

Bibliography

ABRAHAM, KARL. *Selected Papers on Psychoanalysis.* London: Hogarth Press, 1927.

ALLPORT, FLOYD H. *Theories of Perception and the Concept of Structure.* New York: John Wiley and Sons, 1955.

ALLPORT GORDON W. *Personality.* New York: McGraw-Hill Book Company, 1937.

————. *Pattern and Growth in Personality.* New York: Holt, Rinehart, and Winston, 1961.

ARIETI, SILVANO. *Interpretation of Schizophrenia.* New York: Robert Brunner, 1955.

————. *The Intrapsychic Self.* New York: Basic Books, 1967.

BARRETT, WILLIAM. *Irrational Man.* New York: Doubleday and Company, 1958.

BEARD, CHARLES, and MARY BEARD. *The Rise of American Civilization.* New York: The Macmillan Company, 1930.

BENEDICT, RUTH. "Continuities and Discontinuities in Cultural Patterning," in Patrick Mullahy (ed.) *A Study of Personal Relations,* 1967.

BENNIS, WARREN G., EDGAR H. SCHEIN, DAVID E. BERLEW, and FRED I. STEELE (eds.). *Interpersonal Dynamics: Essays and Readings on Human Interaction.* Homewood, Illinois: The Dorsey Press, 1964.

BERELSON, BERNARD, and GARY A. STEINER. *Human Behavior.* New York: Harcourt, Brace, and World, 1964.

BERMAN, LEO. "Countertransference and Attitudes of the Analyst in the Therapeutic Process," in Mabel Blake Cohen (ed.), *Advances in Psychiatry,* 1959.

BERNARD, HAROLD W., and WESLEY C. HUCKINS (eds.). *Readings in Human Development.* Boston, Massachusetts: Allyn and Bacon, 1967.

BONIME, WALTER. "A Psychotherapeutic Approach to Depression," *Contemporary Psychoanalysis,* **2**:48-53, 1965.

BRACKBILL, YVONNE (ed.). *Infancy and Early Childhood.* New York: The Free Press of Glencoe, 1967.

BRAND, HOWARD (ed.). *The Study of Personality.* New York: John Wiley and Sons, 1954.

BREGER, LOUIS. "Motivation, Energy and Cognitive Structure in Psychoanalytic Theory," in Judd Marmor (ed.), *Modern Psychoanalysis: New Directions and Perspectives,* 1968.

BRENNER, CHARLES. *An Elementary Textbook of Psychoanalysis.* New York: International Universities Press, 1955.

BRILL, A. A. (trans. and ed.). *The Basic Writings of Sigmund Freud.* New York: Random House, 1938.

BROWNELL, BAKER. *The Human Community: Its Philosophy and Practice for a Time of Crisis.* New York: Harper and Brothers, 1950.

CHRZANOWSKI, GERARD. "Interpersonal View of Phobias," *Voices,* Fall, 1967.

CHURCH, JOSEPH. *Language and the Discovery of Reality.* New York: Random House, 1966.

CHURCHILL, RANDOLPH. *Winston S. Churchill.* London: Heinemann, 1966.

COHEN, JOHN. *Humanistic Psychology.* London: Allen and Unwin, 1958; New York: Crowell-Collier Publishing Company, 1962.

COHEN, MABEL BLAKE (ed.). *Advances in Psychiatry.* New York: W. W. Norton and Company, 1959.

COLEMAN, JAMES C. *Abnormal Psychology and Modern Life.* Glenview, Illinois: Scott, Foresman and Company, 1964.

COOLEY, CHARLES HORTON. *Social Organization.* New York: Charles Scribner's Sons, 1909.

CORWIN, RONALD G. *A Sociology of Education: Emerging Patterns of Class, Status, and Power in the Public Schools.* New York: Appleton-Century-Crofts, 1965.

Current Biography. New York: H. W. Wilson Company, 1942.

DEWEY, JOHN. *Human Nature and Conduct.* New York: Henry Holt and Company, 1922.

———. *Experience and Nature.* New York: The Open Court Publishing Company, 1929.

————. *The Quest for Certainty.* New York: Minton, Balch and Company, 1929.

————. *Individualism, Old and New.* New York: Minton, Balch and Company, 1930.

————. *Philosophy and Civilization.* New York: Minton, Balch and Company, 1931.

————. *Philosophy and Civilization.* New York: Minton Balch and Company, 1931.

————. *Art as Experience.* New York: Minton, Balch and Company, 1934.

————. *Logic: The Theory of Inquiry.* New York: henry Holt and Company, 1938.

————. "The Unity of the Human Being," in Joseph Ratner (ed.), *Intelligence in the Modern World: John Dewey's Philosophy,* 1939.

DRAPER, GEORGE. *Beaumont Foundation Lectures.* Baltimore, Maryland: Williams and Wilkins, 1928.

————. *Diseases and the Man.* New York: The Macmillan Company, 1930.

DUMONT, MATTHEW. *The Absurd Healer: Perspectives of a Community Psychiatrist.* New York: Science House, 1968.

DUNHAM, ALBERT MILLER, JR. "The Concept of Tension in Philosophy," *Psychiatry,* **1**:79-120, 1938.

FORD, DONALD H., and HUGH B. URBAN. *Systems of Psychotherapy.* New York: John Wiley and Sons, 1963.

FOREST, TESS. "The Family Dynamics of the Oedipus Drama," *Contemporary Psychoanalysis,* **4**:138-160, 1968.

FRANK, L. K. "The Management of Tensions," *American Journal of Sociology,* **33**:705-736, 1928.

FREUD, SIGMUND. *An Outline of Psychoanalysis.* New York: W. W. Norton and Company, 1949.

————. *On Dreams,* trans. James Strachey. New York: W. W. Norton and Company, 1952.

————. *Civilization and Its Discontents,* trans., ed., James Strachey. New York: W. W. Norton and Company, 1962.

————. *Therapy and Technique,* ed. with and introduction by Philip Rieff. New York: Crowell-Collier Publishing Company, 1965.

FROMM-REICHMANN, FRIEDA. *Principles of Intensive Psychotherapy.* Chicago, Illinois: University of Chicago Press, 1950.

GIBSON, JAMES J. *The Senses Considered as Perceptual Systems.* Boston, Massachusetts: Houghton Mifflin Company, 1966.

GORDON, JESSE E. *Personality and Behavior.* New York: The Macmillan Company, 1963.

GOULD, R. E. "Suicide Problems in Children and Adolescents," *American Journal of Psychiatry,* April, 1964.

GREEN, ARNOLD W. *Sociology.* New York: McGraw-Hill Book Company, 1952.

GREEN, MAURICE R. "Prelogical Experience in the Thinking Process," *Journal of Issues in Art Education,* 3:66-78, 1961.

———. "Prelogical Processes and Participant Communication," *Psychiatric Quarterly,* October, 1961.

———. "Depression in Adolescence," *Contemporary Psychoanalysis,* 2:42-47, 1965.

———. "Common Problems in the Treatment of Schizophrenia in Adolescents," *Psychiatric Quarterly,* April, 1966.

———. "The Problem of Identity Crisis," in Jules Masserman (ed.), *Science and Psychoanalysis,* 1966.

GUTHRIE, ROBERT V. *Psychology in the World Today.* Reading, Massachusetts: Addison-Wesley Publishing Company, 1968.

HAAS, KURT. *Understanding Ourselves and Others.* Engelwood Cliffs, New Jersey: Prentice-Hall, 1965.

HACKER, ANDREW. "A Country Called Corporate America," *New York Times Magazine,* July 3, 1966.

HAIRE, NORMAN (ed.). *Sexual Reform Congress.* London: Kegan Paul, Trench, Trubner and Company, 1930.

HALL, CALVIN S. "A Cognitive Theory of Dream Symbols," in David C. McClelland (ed.), *Studies in Motivation,* 1955.

———, and GARDNER LINDZEY. *Theories of Personality.* New York: John Wiley and Sons, 1957.

HAMMER, EMMANUEL F. (ed.). *Use of Interpretation in Treatment.* New York: Grune and Stratton, 1968.

HANSEN, MARCUS LEE. *The Immigrant in American History,* ed., with a Foreword, by Arthur M. Schlesinger. New York: Harper and Row, 1964.

HART, HORNELL. "Family Life and the Fulfillment of Personality," *American Journal of Psychiatry,* 10:7-17, 1930.

HAVENS, LESTON. "Main Currents of Psychiatric Development," *In-*

ternational Journal of Psychiatry, 5:288-310, 1968.

HEIDER, FRITZ. *The Psychology of Interpersonal Relations.* New York: John Wiley and Sons, 1958.

HEILBRONER, ROBERT L. *The Future as History.* New York: Harper and Row, 1968.

HILGARD, ERNEST R., and RICHARD C. ATKINSON. *Introduction to Psychology.* New Yrork: Harcourt, Brace, and World, 1967.

HOLT, ROBERT R. "Experimental Methods in Clinical Psychology," in Benjamin B. Wolman (ed.), *Handbook of Clinical Psychology,* 1965.

HOOK, SIDNEY. *American Philosophers at Work.* New York: Criterion Books, 1956.

———. "Naturalism and First Principles," in Sidney Hook, *American Philosophers at Work,* 1956.

———. *The Quest for Being.* New York: Dell Publishing Company, 1961.

HORNEY, KAREN. *New Ways in Psychoanalysis.* New York: W. W. Norton and Company, 1939.

HURLOCK, ELIZABETH B. *Developmental Psychology.* New York: McGraw-Hill Book Company, 1959.

HUTT, MAX L., ROBERT L. ISAACSON, and MILTON L. BLUM, *The Science of Behavioral Psychology/The Science of Interpersonal Behavior.* New York: Harper and Row, 1967.

JAENSCH, ERICH R. *Eidetic Imagery,* trans. Oscar Oeser. London: Kegan Paul, Trench, Trubner, 1930.

JAMES, WILLIAM. *Principles of Psychology.* New York: Dover Press, 1890.

JANIS, IRVINGL., GEORGE F. MAHL, JEROME KAGAN, and ROBERT R. HOLT. *Personality: Dynamics, Development, and Assessment.* New York: Harcourt, Brace, and World, 1969.

JERSILD, ARTHUR T. *Child Psychology.* Englewood Cliffs, New Jersey: Prentice-Hall, 1960.

———. *The Psychology of Adolescence.* New York: The Macmillan Company, 1963.

JONES, W. T. *A History of Western Philosophy.* New York: Harcourt, Brace and Company, 1952.

KANNER, LEO. *Child Psychiatry.* Springfield, Illinois: Charles C Thomas, 1935.

KAPLAN, BERT (ed.). *Studying Personality Cross-Culturally.* New York: Harper and Row, 1961.

KARDINER, ABRAM, AARON KARUSH, and LIONEL OVESEY. "A Methodological Study of Freudian Theory," *International Journal of Psychiatry*, **2**:489-541, 1966.

KARLEN, ARNO. "The Unmarried Marrieds on Campus," *New York Times Magazine*, January 26, 1969.

KASANIN, J. S. (ed.). *Language and Thought in Schizophrenia: Collected Papers.* Berkeley and Los Angeles: University of California Press, 1944.

KASIN, EDWIN. "Interpretation as Active Nurture: An Interpersonal Perspective," in Emmanuel F. Hammer (ed.), *Use of Interpretation in Treatment*, 1968.

KENDLER, HOWARD H. *Basic Psychology.* New York: Appleton-Century-Crofts, 1968.

KENNAN, GEORGE F. *Memoirs.* Boston, Massachusetts: Little, Brown and Company, 1967.

KERR, WALTER. "What Can They Do Next?" *New York Times Magazine*, February 2, 1969.

KLEINBERGER, Elizabeth. "Depression in Infancy and Childhood," *Contemporary Psychoanalysis*, **2**:36-40, 1965.

KLINEBERG, OTTO. "Discussion," in Patrick Mullahy (ed.), *The Contributions of Harry Stack Sullivan*, 1967.

————, and RICHARD CHRISTIE (eds.). *Perspectives in Social Psychology.* New York: Holt, Rinehart, and Winston, 1965.

KRECH, DAVID, RICHARD S. CRUTCHFIELD, and EGERTON L. BALLACHEY. *Individual in Society.* New York: McGraw-Hill Book Company, 1962.

KRISTOL, IRVING. "The Old Politics, the New Politics, and the New, New Politics," *New York Times Magazine*, November 24, 1968.

KROCK, ARTHUR. *Memoirs.* New York: Funk and Wagnalls, 1968.

LASSWELL, HAROLD. *Psychopathology and Politics.* Chicago, Illinois: University of Chicago Press, 1930.

LICHTHEIM, GEORGE. "Alienation," *International Encyclopedia of the Social Sciences*, Vol. I.

LIDDELL HART, BASIL. "The Military Strategist," in A. J. P. Taylor, Robert Rhodes Jones, J. H. Plumb, Basil Liddell Hart, and Anthony Storr, *Churchill Revised: A Critical Assessment*, 1969.

LIDZ, THEODORE. "The Influence of Family Studies on the Treatment of Schizophrenia," *Psychiatry*, **32**:237-251, 1969.

LIEF, ALFRED (ed.). *The Commonsense Psychiatry of Dr. Adolph Meyer.* New York: McGraw-Hill Book Company, 1948.

LINDZEY, GARDNER (ed.). *Handbook of Social Psychology.* Cambridge, Massachusetts: Addison-Wesley Publishing Company, 1954.

————, and CALVIN S. HALL. *Theories of Personality: Primary Sources and Research.* New York: The Macmillan Company, 1949.

LINN, LAWRENCE S. "The Mental Hospital from the Patient-Perspective," *Psychiatry,* **31**:213-223, 1968.

MAAS, HENRY S. "Preadolescent Peer Relations and Adult Intimacy," *Psychiatry,* **31**:161-172, 1968.

McCLELLAND, DAVID C. (ed.). *Studies in Motivation.* New York: Appleton-Century-Crofts, 1955.

MACCOBY, ELEANOR E., and NATHAN MACCOBY. "The Interview: A Tool of Social Science," in Gardner Lindzey (ed.), *Handbook of Social Psychology,* 1954.

McCURDY, HAROLD GRIER. *The Personal World.* New York: Harcourt, Brace, and World, 1961.

McDOUGALL, WILLIAM. *Outline of Psychology.* New York: Charles Scribner's Sons, 1924.

MacIVER, ROBERT M. *Society.* New York: Farrar and Rinehart, 1937.

McKEACHIE, WILBERT JAMES, and CHARLOTTE LACKNER DOYLE. *Psychology.* Reading, Massachusetts: Addison-Wesley Publishing Company, 1966.

MALINOWSKI, BRONISLAW. *The Father in Primitive Psychology.* New York: W. W. Norton and Company, 1927.

————. *The Sexual Life of Savages in Northwestern Melanesia.* New York: Liveright, 1929.

MARMOR, JUDD (ed.). *Modern Psychoanalysis: New Directions and Perspectives.* New York: Basic Books, 1968.

————. "New Directions in Psychoanalytic Theory and Therapy," in Judd Marmor (ed.), *Modern Psychoanalysis: New Directions and Perspectives,* 1968.

MASSERMAN, JULES (ed.). *Science and Psychoanalysis.* New York: Grune and Stratton, 1966.

MATARAZZO, JOSEPH D. "The Interview," in Benjamin B. Wolman (ed.), *Handbook of Clinical Psychology,* 1965.

MEYER, ADOLPH. "An Attempt at Analysis of the Neurotic Constitution," *American Journal of Psychology,* **14**:90-103, 1903.

MEYER, ROBERT G., BERTRAM P. KARON "The Schizophrenic Mother Concept," *Psychiatry,* **30**:173-178, 1967.

MILL, JOHN STUART. *Utilitarianism.* New York: Library of Liberal Arts, 1957.

MISCHLER, ELLIOT G., and NANCY E. WAXLER (eds.). *Family Process and*

Schizophrenia. New York: Science House, 1968.

MISIAK, HENRYK, and VIRGINIA STROUDT SEXTON. *History of Psychology.* New York: Grune and Stratton, 1966.

MORAN, LORD. *The Later Churchills.* London: The Macmillan Company, 1958.

MORGAN, CLIFFORD T., and RICHARD A. KING. *Introduction to Psychology.* New York: McGraw-Hill Book Company, 1966.

MULLAHY, PATRICK. *Oedipus Myth and Complex.* New York: Hermitage Press, 1948.

———. "Will, Choice and Ends," *Psychiatry,* **12**:379-386, 1949.

———. "A Philosophy of Personality," *Psychiatry,* **13**:417-437, 1950. Reprinted in Howard Brand (ed.), *The Study of Personality,* 1954.

———. *The Contributions of Harry Stack Sullivan.* New York: Science House, 1967.

———(ed.). *A Study of Interpersonal Relations.* New York: Science House, 1967.

———. "The Interpersonal Current in Psychiatric Development," *International Journal of Psychiatry,* **2**:131-143, 1968.

———. "Interpersonal Theory," *International Encyclopedia of the Social Sciences,* Vol. XV, pp. 398-405.

MUNN, NORMAN L. *Psychology.* Boston, Massachusetts: Houghton Mifflin Company, 1966.

MURPHY, GARDNER. *Personality.* New York: Harper and Brothers, 1947.

PERRY, HELEN SWICK. "Commentary," in Harry Stack Sullivan, *Schizophrenia as a Human Process,* 1962.

———. "Introduction," to Harry Stack Sullivan, *Schizophrenia as a Human Process,* 1962.

Psychiatry, 1949.

RANDALL, JOHN HERMAN, JR. *Nature and Historical Experience.* New York: Columbia University Press, 1958.

———, and JUSTUS BUCHLOR. *Philosophy: An Introduction.* New York: Barnes and Noble, 1942.

RATNER, JOSEPH (ed.). *Intelligence in the Modern World: John Dewey's Philosophy.* New York: Random House, 1939.

REDL, FRITZ, and DAVID WINEMAN. *Children Who Hate.* New York: Collier Books, 1962.

REDLICH, FREDERIC C., and DANIEL X. FREEDMAN. *The Theory and Practice of Psychiatry.* New York: Basic Books, 1966.

RUESCH, JURGEN. *Psychoanalysis Between Two Cultures.*

SADLER, WILLIAM S. *Theory and Practice of Psychiatry.* St. Louis, Missouri: The C. V. Mosby Company, 1936.

SALZMAN, LEON. *Developments in Psychoanalysis.* New York: Grune and Stratton, 1962.

————. "Obsessions and Phobias," *Contemporary Psychoanalysis,* Fall, 1965.

————. *The Obsessive Personality.* New York: Science House, 1968.

SCHACHTEL, ERNEST. *Metamorphosis.* New York: Basic Books, 1959.

SCHECHTER, DAVID E. "The Oedipus Complex: Considerations of Ego Development and Parental Interaction," *Contemporary Psychoanalysis,* 4:111-137, 1968.

SEARLES, HAROLD F. "Sexual Processes in Schizophrenia," *Psychiatry,* 24:87-95, 1961 (suppl. to No. 2).

————. "The Schizophrenic Individual's Experience of His World," *Psychiatry,* 31:119-131, 1967.

SHAND, ALEXANDER F. *The Foundations of Character.* London: Macmillan and Company, 1914.

SHIBOTANI, TAMOTSO. *Society and Personality.* Englewood Cliffs, New Jersey: Prentice-Hall, 1961.

SINGER, ERWIN. *Key Concepts in Psychotherapy.* New York: Random House, 1965.

SNOW, C. P. *Variety of Men.* London: The Macmillan Company, 1967.

SPEARMAN, CHARLES. *The Nature of "Intelligence" and the Principles of Cognition.* London: Macmillan and Company, 1923.

SPIEGEL, ROSE. "Communication with Depressive Patients," *Contemporary Psychoanalysis,* 2:30-35, 1965.

SPRANGER, EDUARD. *Types of Man,* trans. Paul J. W. Pigors. Halle, Germany: Max Niemer Verlag, 1928.

SRB, ADRIAN M., RAY D. OWEN, and ROBERT S. EDGER. *General Genetics.* San Francisco, California: W. H. Freeman and Company, 1965.

SROLE, LEO, THOMAS S. LANGER, STANLEY T. MICHAEL, MARVIN K. OPLER, and THOMAS A. C. RENNIE. *Mental Health in the Metropolis.* New York: McGraw-Hill Book Company, 1962.

STANTON, ALFRED H. "Milieu Therapy and the Development of Insight," *Psychiatry,* 24:19-29, 1961 (suppl. to No. 2).

STONE, L. JOSEPH, and JOSEPH CHURCH. *Childhood and Adolescence.* New York: Random House, 1957.

STORR, ANTHONY. "The Man," in A. J. P. Taylor, Robert Rhodes

684 : *Bibliography*

Jones, J. H. Plumb, Basil Liddell Hart, and Anthony Storr, *Churchill Revised: A Critical Assessment,* 1969.

STRAUSS, ANSELM (ed.). *George Herbert Mead on Social Psychology.* Chicago, Illinois: University of Chicago Press, 1964.

SULLIVAN, HARRY STACK. "Schizophrenia: Its Conservative and Malignant Features," *American Journal of Psychiatry,* **81**:77-91, 1924-1925. Reprinted in Harry Stack Sullivan, *Schizophrenia as a Human Process,* 1962.

———. "The Oral Complex," *Psychoanalytic Review,* **12**:31-38, 1925.

———. "Peculiarity of Thought in Schizophrenia," *American Journal of Psychiatry,* **82**:21-86, 1925-1926. Reprinted in Harry Stack Sullivan, *Schizophrenia as a Human Process,* 1962.

———. "Erogenous Maturation," *Psychoanalytic Review,* **13**:1-15, 1926.

———. "The Importance of a Study of Symbols in Psychiatry," *Psyche* (London), **1**:81-93, 1926.

———. "Regression: A Consideration of Reversive Mental Processes," *State Hospital Quarterly,* **11**:208-217, 387-394, 651-668, 1926.

———. "Affective Experience in Early Schizophrenia," *American Journal of Psychiatry,* **83**:467-483, 1926-1927.

———. "The Common Field of Research and Clinical Psychiatry," *Psychiatric Quarterly,* **1**:276-291, 1927. Reprinted in Harry Stack Sullivan, *Schizophrenia as a Human Process,* 1962.

———. "The Onset of Schizophrenia," *American Journal of Psychiatry,* **84**:105-134, 1927-1928. Reprinted in Harry Stack Sullivan, *Schizophrenia as a Human Process,* 1962.

———. "Tentative Criteria of Malignancy in Schizophrenia," *American Journal of Psychiatry,* **84**:759-782, 1927-1928. Reprinted in Harry Stack Sullivan, *Schizophrenia as a Human Process,* 1962.

———. "Research in Schizophrenia," *American Journal of Psychiatry,* **86**:553-567, 1929. Reprinted in Harry Stack Sullivan, *Schizophrenia as a Human Process,* 1962.

———. "Archaic Sexual Culture and Schizophrenia," in Norman Haire (ed.), *Sexual Reform Congress.* London: Kegan Paul, Trench, Trubner and Company, 1930.

———. "Schizophrenic Individuals as a Source of Data for Comparative Investigation of Personality," in *Proceedings, Second Colloquium on Personality Investigation.* Baltimore, Maryland: The Johns Hopkins

Press, 1930. Reprinted inHarry Stack Sullivan, *Schizophrenia as a Human Process,* 1962.

———. "Environmental Factors in Etiology and Course Under Treatment of Schizophrenia," *Medical Journal and Record,* 1931.

———. "The Modified Psychoanalytic Treatment of Schizophrenia," *American Journal of Psychiatry,* 11:519-536, 1931. Reprinted in Harry Stack Sullivan, *Schizophrenia as a Human Process,* 1962.

———. "Socio-Psychiatric Research," *American Journal of Psychiatry,* 10:977-991, 1931. Reprinted in Harry Stack Sullivan, *Schizophrenia as a Human Process,* 1962.

———. "Training of the General Medical Student in Psychiatry," *American Journal of Orthopsychiatry,* 1:371-379, 1931.

———. "Mental Disorders," *Encyclopedia of the Social Sciences,* 10:313-319. New York: The Macmillan Company, 1933. Reprinted in Harry Stack Sullivan, *Schizophrenia as a Human Process,* 1962.

———. "Psychiatry," *Encyclopedia of the Social Sciences,* 12:578-580. New York: The Macmillan Company, 1934. Reprinted in Harry Stack Sullivan, *The Fusion of Psychiatry and Social Science,* 1964.

———. "Psychiatric Training as a Prerequisite to Psychoanalytic Practice," *American Journal of Psychiatry,* 91:1117-1126, 1934-1935. Reprinted in Harry Stack Sullivan, *Schizophrenia as a Human Process,* 1962.

———. "A Note on the Implications of Psychiatry, the Study of Interpersonal Relations, for Investigations in the Social Sciences," *American Journal of Sociology,* 42:846-861, 1936-1937. Reprinted in Harry Stack Sullivan, *The Fusion of Psychiatry and Social Science,* 1964.

———. "A Note on Formulating the Relationship of the Individual and the Group," *American Journal of Sociology,* 44:932-937, 1938-1939. Reprinted in Harry Stack Sullivan, *The Fusion of Psychiatry and Social Science,* 1964.

———. "Psychiatry: Introduction to the Study of Interpersonal Relations," *Psychiatry,* 1:121-134, 1939.

———. "The Language of Schizophrenia," in J. S. Kasanin (ed.), *Language and Thought in Schizophrenia: Collected Papers,* 1944.

———. "The Meaning of Anxiety in Psychiatry and in Life," *Psychiatry,* 11:1-13, 1948. Reprinted in Harry Stack Sullivan, *The Fusion of Psychiatry and Social Science,* 1964.

———. "The Illusion of Personal Individuality," *Psychiatry,* 13:317-

332, 1950. Reprinted in Harry Stack Sullivan, *The Fusion of Psychiatry and Social Science,* 1964.

———. *Conceptions of Modern Psychiatry,* with a Foreword by the author and a Critical Appraisal of the Theory by Patrick Mullahy. New York: W. W. Norton and Company, 1953.

———. *The Interpersonal Theory of Psychiatry,* ed. Helen Swick Perry and Mary Ladd Gawel, with an Introduction by Mabel Blake Cohen. New York: W. W. Norton and Company, 1953.

———. *The Psychiatric Interview,* ed. Helen Swick Perry and Mary Ladd Gawel, with an Introduction by Otto Allen Will, Jr. New York: W. W. Norton and Company, 1954.

———. *Clinical Studies in Psychiatry,* ed. with a Foreword by Dexter M. Bullard. New York: W. W. Norton and Company, 1956.

———. "Dissociative Processes," in Harry Stack Sullivan, *Clinical Studies in Psychiatry,* 1956.

———. "The Paranoid Dynamism," in Harry Stack Sullivan, *Clinical Studies in Psychiatry,* 1956.

———. *Schizophrenia as a Human Process,* with Introduction and Commentaries by Helen Swick Perry. New York: W. W. Norton and Company, 1962.

———. "The Relations of Onset to Outcome in Schizophrenia," in Harry Stack Sullivan, *Schizophrenia as a Human Process,* 1962.

———. *The Fusion of Psychiatry and Social Science,* with an Introduction and Commentaries by Helen Swick Perry. New York: W. W. Norton and Company, 1964.

———. "The Data of Psychiatry," in Harry Stack Sullivan, *The Fusion of Psychiatry and Social Science,* 1964.

———. *Farewell Lectures*, unpublished.

———. *Personal Psychopathology.* Copyright 1965 by William Alanson White Psychiatric Foundation, Washington, D.C. Unpublished.

Szasz, Thomas S. "Mental Illness Is a Myth," *New York Times Magazine,* June 12, 1966. Reprinted in Robert V. Guthrie, *Psychology in the World Today,* 1968.

Taylor, A. J. P., Robert Rhodes Jones, J. H. Plumb, Basil Liddell Hart, and Anthony Storr. *Churchill Revised: A Critical Assessment.* New York: Dial Press, 1969.

Thompson, Clara, and Patrick Mullahy. *Psychoanalysis: Evolution and Development.* New York: Hermitage Press, 1950.

TITIEV, MISCHA. *The Science of Man.* New York: Holt, Rinehart, and Winston, 1963.

VOLKART, EDMUND H. (ed.). *Social Behavior and Personality: Contributions of W. I. Thomas to Theory and Social Research.* New York: Social Science Research Council, 1951.

WANN, T. W. (ed.). *Behaviorism and Phenomenology.* Chicago, Illinois: University of Chicago Press, 1964.

WENDER, PAUL H. "Vicious and Virtuous Circles: The Role of Deviation Amplifying Feedback in the Origin and Perpetuation of Behavior," *Psychiatry,* **31**:309-324, 1968.

WHITE, MARY JULIAN. "Sullivan and Treatment," in Patrick Mullahy (ed.), *The Contributions of Harry Stack Sullivan,* 1967.

WHITE, ROBERT W. *Lives in Progress.* New York: The Dryden Press, 1952.

WILL, OTTO A., JR. "Paranoid Development and the Concept of Self: Psychotherapeutic Intervention," *Psychiatry,* **24**:74-86, 1961.

———. "Schizophrenia and the Psychotherapeutic Field," *Contemporary Psychoanalysis,* **1**:11-20, 1964.

———. "The Reluctant Patient, the Unwanted Psychotherapist—and Coercion," *Contemporary Psychoanalysis,* **5**:1-31, 1968.

———. "Schizophrenia and Psychotherapy," in Judd Marmor (ed.), *Modern Psychoanalysis: New Directions and Perspectives,* 1968.

WOLBERG, LEWIS R. *The Technique of Psychotherapy.* New York: Grune and Stratton, 1967.

WOLMAN, BENJAMIN B. *Contemporary Theories and Systems in Psychology.* New York: Harper and Brothers, 1960.

——— (ed.). *Handbook of Clinical Psychology.* New York: McGraw-Hill Book Company, 1965.

Index

A

Abnormal fears, 304

Abraham, Karl, 228

Abstracts of experience, 38

Accommodation, 390, 391

Accommodative associations, 233

Actions, 82-83

Activity-types, 80

Adler, A., ii

Adjustive mental processes, 82, 84

Adjustive potentialities, 250

Adjustment, 240, 243, 245, 246

Adolescence, 92, 126, 167, 175, 407, 508, 595, 650
   depression in, 647-651
   late, 167, 417-420
   and religion, 413-414

Adolescent dating, 410

Adolescent sexual behavior, 167, 170

Adolescent sexuality, 176
   and schizophrenia, 87-88

Adolescents, homosexual phase of, 99

Agee, James, 312, 407

Aggressive tendencies, 371

Alanbrooke, Lord, 666, 668

Alcoholism, 8

Algonagnic state, 437-439, 445

Alienation, Negro, 416

Allport, Gordon, 227, 229, 288, 396, 499

American Psychiatric Association, 5

Amnesia, 477-478, 594

Anal eroticism, 68

Anal zone of interaction, 350

Analytic situation, 206

Anger, 305-306, 378

Antianxiety, 368

Anxiety, 245, 252, 295, 303-306, 351, 352, 367-369, 370, 372, 374, 378, 394, 412, 483-484
   infant, 345
   rationalization of, 316

Anxiety equivalents, 276

Anxiety gradient, 356

Anxiety neurosis, 9

Anxiety states, 275, 276

Apathy, 352

Aristotle, 347, 402
Artistic orientation, 228
Asthenic type, 228
Athletic type, 228
Auchinchloss, Louis, 200
Auditory hallucinations, 11
Auditory imagery, 228
Autistic symbol activity, 340
Autistic thinking, 372
Autoerotic activity, 350, 364
Autoerotic interests, 231
Autoerotism, 134
Automatic writing, 273, 491
Automatisms, 244, 465, 491
Autosexual activity, 177
Aversion vector, 63
Avoidance, 258
Awkwardness, varieties of, 411-412

B

Bad Father, the, 495
Bad Mother, the, 490, 495
Baldwin, James, 547
Barnard, Harold W., 186
Behavior, 76
Bellows, Saul, 547
Bergson, Henri, 41
Berlyne, D. E., 618
Biological adaptation, 245
Biological equipment, 305
Biotypes, 228
Biting oral type, 228
Blame dynamism, transference of, 165,
    166, 244, 262, 439, 440
Blocking, 500
Blum, Milton L., 285
Board of Examiners, U.S. Army Medi-
    cal Corps, 2
Bohemian type, 229
Bonime, Walter, 641-644
Borderline intellect, 228

Bracken, Brendan, 656
Brain, the, 42
Brain disorders, 8
Brenner, Charles, 213
Brill, H., i, 614
Brownell, Baker, 400

C

Carter, Violet Bonham, 663, 665
Castration fear, 141
Catatonia, 495, 499
Catatonic schizophrenia, 20, 25, 32,
    95, 498
Catatonic stupor, 496-498
Central unpleasantness, 259
Chapman, Ross McClure, 3
Change, 128, 129
Character, 160, 161
Character disorders, 8
Child psychology, 122
Childhood, 124
Chromosomes, 77
Church, Joseph, 54, 372, 410, 414
Churchill, Randolph, 659
Churchill, Sarah, 658
Churchill, Winston, 651-669
Classificatory schemes, 425, 427
Cognitions, 396
Cohen, Mabel, 604
Cohen, Robert, 604
Coleman, James C., 9, 10
Collaborative intimacy, 412
Collective unconscious, 17
Communal existence, 76, 77, 335
Communication, 110
    and language, 120
Compensation, 243, 253-254
Competitiveness, 326, 591
Complex, 54, 55
Complex image, 336
Compulsive neurosis, 467

Conative situations, 46
Conceit, 320
Conflict, 256-257
Conscience, 161, 162
Consciously chosen actions, 82-83
Consensual validation, 52, 84, 85, 342, 366
Continuity of structure, 362
Conversion, 277
Conversion hysteria, 476
Cooley, Charles Horton, 7, 52, 138, 257
Corporal punishment, 358
Countertransference, 114, 218
Covert processes, 458
Crazy guilt, 316, 317
Creative mental processes, 82, 85
Creative type, 229
Crystal gazing, 273
Cultural distortions, and schizophrenia, 18, 89
Cultural controls, and schozophrenia, 25

D

Dawson, Christopher, 120
Death wish, 210
Defense mechanisms, 491
Defense reactions, 243, 256-257
Delusions, 10-11
Dementia praecox, 17, 18, 29
Deoxyribonucleic acid (DNA), 77
Depression, 22, 23, 245, 279, 640-649
Destructive instinct, 210
Deutsch, Martin, 354
Developmental arrest, 382
Dewey, John, vi, vii, 51, 75, 121, 268, 347, 400, 401, 402, 667
Diagnosis, 433
Difficulty, dynamisms of, 240-281, 427, 429, 430
Disease, 425

Disgust reactions, 63
Disintegration, 372, 373
Dissociated dynamism, 446
Dissociated processes, 270
Dissociation, 136, 137, 154, 155, 158, 244, 258, 272-273, 296, 297, 299, 466, 484, 515, 516
  in catatonic schizophrenia, 32, 87, 96, 97
Domhoff, G. Williams, 326
Dominant ordination, 231
Dooley, Lucille, 6
Dos Passos, John, 200
Dostoevsky, Feodor, 191
Dramatizations, 377, 382
Draper, George, 228
Dream interpretation, 207, 208, 209, 210, 211, 213, 214, 215, 220
Dream-work, 212
Dreams, 218, 441, 442
Dreiser, Theodore, 200
Drug addiction, 8
Dunlop, Knight, 108
Dynamisms, 18, 270
  of difficulty, 240-281, 427, 429, 430

E

Economic orientation, 229
Ecstatic absorption, 487
Ego, the, 59, 62, 69, 201, 202, 212, 213
Ego-alien character, 445
Ekstein, Rudolf, iv-v
Electra complex, 67, 142, 387
Emotional attachments, 387
Empathy, 134, 143, 196, 344
Endogenous depressions, 641
Energy path, 63
Energy transformations, 343
Envy, 321-326
Equilibration, 343
Erogeny, 177, 178
Eros, 210

Erroneous attitudes, and schizophrenia, 19
Essential sequence, 9-10
Ethics, 700-724
Euphoria, 344, 346, 351, 352
Everest, Mrs., 659, 662
Excitement, 245, 278
Expressive mechanism, 259
Expulsive anal type, 228
Externally controlled mental processes, 83
Extroversion, 229, 230, 231

F

Falling in love, 409-410
Fantasy processes, 82, 83, 85
Farrell, James, 200
Fear, 304-305, 367, 369, 370, 374
  of ostracism, 358
Fear states, in schizophrenia, 23
Federal Board for Vocational Education, 2
Ferenczi, Sandor, 56, 61
Forgetting, 244, 258
Free association, 7, 112, 540, 573, 574
Freedman, Daniel X., 2, 445, 604, 636, 640, 641
Free-fantasy exploration 221, 223, 225
Freud, Sigmund, i, ii, iii, iv, 7, 9, 33, 53-54, 59, 61, 62, 66, 67, 69, 71, 109, 113-114, 127, 128, 134, 136, 141, 150, 176, 177, 193, 197, 201, 202, 204, 209, 210, 211, 215, 218, 221, 227, 232, 252, 255-256, 260, 267, 268, 270, 284, 294, 296, 315, 317, 327, 344, 350, 377, 386, 387, 392, 395, 397, 414, 538, 604, 614, 615, 616, 617, 664
Friendship, 233
Fromm-Reichmann, Frieda, 538, 604, 632, 643

Functional activity, 78, 335
Functional psychoses, 8, 10

G

Gang sociality, 170
Genetic hypothesis of mental structure and functions, 54
Genetic organization, 77
Genetic structure, 134
Genital lust dynamism, 178, 413, 487
  see also Lust dynamism
Genital phobia, 95, 100, 134, 410-411
Genital zone of interaction, 407
Global responses, 338
Globus hystericus, 276
Goal-seeking behavior, 76
Good Father, the, 495
Good Mother, the, 495
Gould, R. E., 649-650
Grandeur, delusion of, 10
Grave psychosis, the, 8, 19, 483
Green, Maurice R., 215, 533, 647-651
Grief, 277-278, 311-315
Guilt, 315-317
  delusion of, 10
Gustatory hallucinations, 11
Gutmann, James, vi

H

Hadley, Ernest E., 6
Hall, Calvin S., 232
Hall, G. Stanley, 647-648
Hallucinated utterances, 490
Hallucinations, 11, 491
Hallucinosis, 273, 491, 492
Handler, Oscar, 324-325
Hansen, Marcus Lee, 325
Hatred, 307-308
Havens, Leston, 424, 425
Hawthorne, Nathaniel, 598
Hebephrenia, 25, 467, 513, 514

Hebephrenic dilapidation, 95, 512
Heredity, 128, 129
Heteroerotic interest, 231
Heteroerotism, 134
Heterosexual behavior, 178
Heterosexual intimacy, 408-409
Hoch, August, 26
Holt, Robert R., 548
Homoerotic interest, 231
Homoerotism, 134
Homosexual behavior, 178, 405
Homosexuality, 100, 171, 327
    and schizophrenia, 97-99, 441
Huckins, Wesley C., 186
Human dynamics, 243-245
Human organism, explained, 343
Hutt, Max L., 285, 334
Hypnosis, 224, 225
Hypochondria, 9, 433-435, 438
Hypochondriacal delusions, 10
Hypomania, 278-279
Hysteria, 8, 9, 471-477, 479

I

Id, the, 59, 201, 202
Idealization, 181, 182, 183, 184
Ideas, 268
Identification, 377
Idiot intellect, 228
Illusory me-you patterns, 292-294
Imbecile intellect, 228
Implicit processes, 458
Impulsive actions, 82, 85
Inattention, selective, 201, 299, 339,
    514-515
Incapacitation, 244
    defenses by, 266
Incipient schizophrenia, 95
Indifference, teaching by, 365-366
Individual, the, 76
Infancy, 124
Infant anxiety, 345

Infant personifications, 353, 360-364,
    376
Infantile experiences, 44, 54-55, 130-
    134, 139
Infantile sexuality, 134, 140, 616
Influence, delusion of, 11
Information, kinds of, 84
Initial warp, 432
Innate actions, 82
Innate determiners, 76
Instincts, 296
Integrating tendencies, 300
Integration, of personality, 373
Interaction, 246
Interpersonal intimacy, 401
Interpersonal psychiatry, 335, 619
Interpersonal relations, vi-vii, 5, 152
    and personality, 284-330
Interpersonal situations, 240
Interpersonally valid information, 84
Interpretation, in interview, 536, 537
Interpsychic processes, 284
Interview, 198, 200, 205, 226, 523-610
Intimacy:
    collaborative, 412
    heterosexual, 408-409
    and lust, 412
    need for, 508
Intimacy impulse, 129
Intimate association, 170
Intrapsychic processes, 245, 284, 285
Introversion, 229, 230, 231
Isaacson, Robert L., 285, 334

J

Jackson, Donald, 483
Jacobson, Edith, 643
Jaensch, Eric R., 228
Jaensch, Walter, 228
James, William, 81, 151, 320, 361, 414,
    650, 669
Janis, Irving L., 548

Jealousy, 326-330

Jelliffe, Smith Ely, 39

Jersild, Arthur J., 186, 339, 340, 372, 392, 409, 410, 414

Johnson, Charles, 416

Joyce, James, 191, 547, 594

Jung, C. G., ii, 7, 17, 39, 108, 229, 232, 363, 397, 491, 617, 654, 655, 656

Juvenile delinquency, 8

Juvenile era, 91, 125, 145, 147, 152, 162, 164, 165, 318-319, 358, 367, 390-391, 393, 395, 397, 398, 399, 591, 592

K

Kagan, Jerome, 548

Kendler, Howard H., 45

King, Richard A., 369

Kinship, 232

Kraepelin, Emil, 425

Kretschmer, Ernst, 228

L

Language, 51-53
  and communication, 120

Late adolescence, 167

Learned actions, 82

Lee, Harper, 547

Leptosomatic type, 228

Levy, David, 350

Levy-Bruhl, L., 62

Lewin, Kurt, 110

Libido, 33

Libido theory, 252

Liddell Hart, Basil, 655, 668-669

Life history, of schizophrenics, 90

Life instinct, 210

Lindzey, Gardner, 232

Local actions, 78

Loneliness, 358, 406-407, 411

Love, 401, 402

Love affairs, 329, 401-402

Lust dynamism, 299, 348, 349, 407, 410, 412-413, 435
  see also Genital lust dynamism

M

Maas, Henry S., 401

McDougall, William, 70, 71, 75, 138

Macmillan, Harold, 655

Magic, 449, 496

Mahl, George F., 548

Maladjustive processes, 247-248, 252, 258, 280

Malevolence, 381-382

Malinowski, Bronislaw, 142

Mania, 640

Manic-depressive psychosis, 8, 280, 638-640

Manic excitement, 279

Marmor, Judd, 613-616

Marriage, 127, 408

Masterman, Lucy, 665

Masturbation conflict, 95

Matarazzo, Joseph D., 226

Mead, George Herbert, 7, 81, 101, 363

Medical Corps, U.S. Army, 2

Medical education, 4, 198

Medical School, University of Maryland, 5

Mediumistic speech, 273

Mental disorders, 8, 105, 106, 110, 377

Mental health, 76, 106, 240, 241, 247, 251 264, 346, 415

Mental illness, 241, 247, 264, 304, 385, 413

Mental life, 296
  of schizophrenics, 86

Mental processes, 82, 83-86

Mental situations, 41

Mental typography, 268

Mentation, 37, 39
  see also Mind

Metapsychology, 284
Meyer, Adolf, ii, iii, 7, 29, 39, 75, 232, 640
Me-You patterns, 292-294, 498
Midadolescence, 126, 167, 178, 180, 507
Migraine headaches, 8
Mind, 37, 40-41, 42, 75, 76, 78
    see also Mentation
Misiak, Henryk, 228
Modes of experience, 336
Moral behavior, 99
Moran, Lord, 653, 656, 667
Morbid ambition, 326
Morbid grieving, 245, 314
Morgan, Clifford T., 369
Mother, the, and the self, 102
Mothering, 132-133, 484
Motivation, and schizophrenia, 88
Multiple personality, 271
Murphy, Gardner, 110

N

Negativism, 244, 265-266
Nerve impulses, 42
Negro, alienation of, 416
Neuroses, 8, 9
    anxiety, 9
    compulsive, 467
    obsessive-compulsive, 8, 9, 337, 460, 462, 464, 466, 467, 468, 471
    and psychoses, 9, 31
Neurasthenia, 9, 19
Newton, Isaac, 287
Nihilistic delusions, 10
Nonadjustive processes, 244, 247, 248, 252, 280
Normal intellect, 228
"Not-me" processes, 296

O

Obsessional behavior, 445-466
Obsessional personality, 144

Obsessive-compulsive neurosis, 8, 9, 337, 460, 462, 464, 466, 467, 468, 471
Obsessive preoccupations, 245
O'Connor, Edwin, 200, 325
Oedipus complex, 14, 66, 142, 295, 296, 386-387, 475
O'Hara, John, 200
Olfactory hallucinations, 11
Olfactory imagery, 228
Ontogenesis of personality, 45
Oral activity, of infants, 138
Oral behavior, 124
Oral complex, 59
Oral dynamism, 59
Ordinate associations, 233
Organism-environmental complex, 240, 330
Organization, 269
Organization man, 399
Organism, defined, 135
Orgasm, 179, 185
Orpen, Sir William N. M., 656-657
Orthodox psychoanalytic theory, 75
Ostracism, fear of, 358
Overvaluation, 320

P

Panic, 244-245, 274, 484-486, 489, 495
    in schizophrenia, 93-94
Paranoia, 438, 439, 442, 443, 444, 445, 501, 503, 504, 505, 506, 508, 509, 640
Paranoid attitudes, 262, 264
Paranoid dynamism, 261
Paranoid schizophrenia, 490
Paranoid state, 95
Parataxic complexity, 498
Parataxic concomitance, 300-301
Parataxic distortion, 295, 431
Parataxic mode, 48, 337, 338, 339, 341, 372

Parataxic patterns, 291, 292
Parataxis, 546
Parents, dealing with, 204-205
Partial adjustment, 243
Pathological liar, 146
Pederasty, and schizophrenia, 24
Perception, 42
Perplexity, in schizophrenia, 22
Perry, Helen S., 3, 4, 6
Persecution, delusion of, 10
Persecutory trends, in schizophrenia, 21, 493
Persona, 397
Personal equation, 192
Personal interview, 191, 195, 198, 200
Personal-environmental complex, 80
Personality, 101, 135, 193, 223, 241-242, 271, 287, 289, 297, 486, 587, 588
    intercommunication of, 195
    in interpersonal relations, 119, 284-330
    and social sciences, 192
Personality development, 129, 334-420
Personality typologies, 227-234
Personally valid information, 84
Personifications, infant, 353, 360-364, 376
Phasic variation, 346
Phenomenological consciousness, 41
Philistine type, 229
Phipps Clinic, Johns Hopkins University, Baltimore, Maryland, iii
Phobias, 275
Physician, role of, 215
Piaget, Jean, 347
Pleasure principle, 344
Podhoretz, Norman, 399
Preadolescence, 91, 126, 167, 168, 170, 173, 174, 401-407, 512, 593
Preconcept, 54, 55, 58
Preconscious system, 268

Preoccupations, 378
Preverbal behavior, 618
Previous experience, 110
Pride, 317-319
Primary emotions, 77
Primary genital phobia, 410-411, 470
Primitive mental processes, 82, 83, 85, 86
Primordial fear, 275
Prodromal schizophrenia, 21
Prognosis, 433
Projection, 262
Prototaxic mode, 83, 337, 344, 352, 499
Proust, Marcel, 191
Pseudosublimation, 443
Psyche, 284, 285, 289, 330
Psychiatric interview, 215, 523-610
Psychiatric research, 108
Psychiatry, 5, 6
Psychic region, 267
Psychical system, 268
Psychoanalysis, 613-616
Psychobiology, 192
Psychology, 192
Psychoneuroses, 8, 30-31
Psychopathic personality, 8, 144
Psychopathology, 119
Psychophysiologic disorders, 8
Psychoses:
    functional, 8, 10
    manic-depressive, 8, 638-640
    and neuroses, 9, 31
Psychosomatic disorders, 303, 379
Psychotic symptoms, 10
Puberty, 593-594
Punishment, corporal, 358
Purposive behavior, 76

R

Rage, 306-307
Rage behavior, 308-311

Randolph, Lady, 659, 663
Randolph, Lord, 659, 663
Rational insight, 197, 198
Rationalization, 244, 260-261, 377
    of anxiety, 316
Reactive depressions, 641
Reality-controlled mental processes,
    82, 83
Re-cognition, 352
Redlich, Frederick C., 2, 445, 604, 636,
    640, 641
Reevaluation, 223
Reference, delusion of, 11
Referential processes, 371-372
Reflected appraisals, 363
Reflex actions, 82
Regression, 56-58, 86, 244, 274, 315,
    434, 436, 437, 488
Rehabilitation Division, Federal Board
    of Vocational Education, 2
Religion, and adolescence, 413-414
Religious orientation, 229
Repetition compulsion, 128, 294
Repression, 137, 158, 244, 259-260,
    267, 297, 515
Resentment, 378, 379
Retardation depression, 645
Retentive anal type, 228
Retinal zone of interaction, 349
Retrograde falsification, 244
Revery processes, 83, 84, 86, 436, 488
Romantic attachments, 340
Romantic love, 401, 402, 403
Roosevelt, Franklin D., 668
Russell, Bertrand, 41, 478

S

Sadism, 156, 157
Salzman, Leon, 471, 616-619
Saint Elizabeth's Hospital, Washing-
    ton, D.C., ii-iii, 3
Santayana, George, 414

Schizophrenia, 7, 8, 14-33, 40, 86-104,
    270, 280, 362-370, 429, 604-610
    catatonic, 20, 25, 32, 95, 498
    child, 363
    and homosexuality, 441
    language behavior in, 51-53
    and obsessional neurosis, 467
    paranoid, 490
    and sleep deprivation, 80-81
    Sullivan's theory of, 483-519
Schizophrenic stupor, 511
Schizophrenics, 206
Schooling, 592-593
Secondary elaboration, 310
Selective inattention, 201, 299, 339,
    514-515
Selective Service System, 5
Self, the, 81, 201, 202, 241, 298, 308,
    485-486, 517
    and the mother, 102
    somatic schematization of, 140
Self-consciousness, 81
Self concept, 598
Self-deception, 290
Self dynamism, 69, 71, 101, 159, 201,
    290, 297, 300, 350, 359, 360, 361,
    367, 390, 397, 456, 472, 484, 542,
    543, 669
Self-esteem, 56, 92, 99, 100, 119, 155,
    241, 250, 252, 253, 255, 259, 329,
    350, 361, 369, 370, 411, 545
Self-fulfillment, 415
Self-idealization, 166, 167
Self-regard, 62, 69
Self-respect, 104, 119, 173, 241, 249,
    262
Self system, 201, 362, 396, 517
Self-understanding, 197
Sense organs, 42
Sentiment, 59, 70
Sex factor, in schizophrenia, 18
Sex reform, 100

Sexton, Virginia S., 228
Sexual behavior, 231, 596-597
    adolescent, 167-170
Sexual experimentation, 408
Sexual satisfaction, need for, 265
Sexual situations, 172
Sexuality:
    adolescent, 176
    infantile, 134, 140, 616
    and schizophrenia, 87-88, 103
Shand, Alexander F., 69, 71
Sheldon, W. H., 653, 654
Sheppard and Enoch Pratt Hospital,
Baltimore, Maryland, iii, 3, 4, 7, 26,
    89, 109, 111, 483, 503, 518
Shibotani, Tamotso, 42-43
Significant people, 101
Silverberg, William V., 109, 483, 518
Sin, delusion of, 10
Sleep, 80, 214, 317, 346, 434, 441, 443,
    444, 516, 517
Sloane, R. Bruce, iv
Snow, C. P., 655
Social accommodation, 390, 391
Social experience, 88
Social sciences, and personality, 192
Social subordination, 390
Socialization, 145
    handicap to, 147
Socializing impulse, 129
Socrates, 395, 677
Solipsism, 17
Solitude, 596
Somnambulism, 273
Spearman, Charles, 46
Speech habits, 590
Spiegel, Rose, 644-647
Split personality, 273
Spranger, Edouard, 228
Status, 104
Status quo, 247
Stendahl, 191

Stereotypes, 181, 182, 183
Stomach ulcers, 8
Stone, L. Joseph, 372, 410, 414
Storr, Anthony, 651-668
Structure, continuity of, 362
Sublimation, 243, 255, 356, 371, 372,
    395, 443, 486, 487, 489
Subordinate ordination, 231, 390
Subrogative relationships, 232
Substitutive processes, 466
Subverbal processes, 296
Successful living, 240
Sucking oral type, 228
Suckling, 60, 62, 131
Suicide, 280
Sullivan, Harry Stack:
    early life of, 1-2
    cultural background of, 669-670
    and Freud, 7
    and Johns Hopkins University, iii
    in New York, 5
    and psychiatry, 105, 108
    and *Psychiatry*, 6
    and psychology, 75
    at Saint Elizabeth's Hospital, Wash-
        ington, D.C., ii-iii, 3
    at Sheppard and Enoch Pratt Hos-
        pital, Baltimore, Maryland, iii, 3,
        4, 7, 26, 89, 109, 111, 483, 503, 518
    and UNESCO, 6
    and U.S. Veterans Bureau, 2-3
    at University of Maryland, 5
    and White, iii, 3
    and World Federation for Mental
        Health, 6
Sullivan, Timothy, 2
Superego, 161, 162, 201, 202, 212, 315-
    316
Superior intellect, 228
Suppression, 244, 258-259, 515
Symbol activities, 340-341
Symbol systems, 37-71

Symbolic segregation, 350
Symptoms, 425
Syndromes, 425, 433
Syntaxic mode, 337, 340, 342, 366, 385

T

Tactile hallucinations, 11
Tactile imagery, 228
Teleological vitalism, 54
Temperament, 227-228
Temperamental differences, 134
Tension, 336, 343, 346
Terror, 305, 489
Thanatos, 210
Theorem of escape, 367
Theoretical orientation, 229
Therapy techniques, 191
Thomas, Dorothy Swaine, 149
Thomas, W. I., 229
Thompson, Clara, 1, 2, 184
Thompson, Elizabeth B., 186
Thumb sucking, 134
Tics, 491
Timely interpretation, 113
Toilet training, 63, 589-590
Tolstoy, Leo, 191
Total actions, 78
Total activity, 83
Total situation, 79
Totalitarianism, 107
Trance phenomena, 273
Transcendental ego, 330
Transference, 113, 194, 294
    of blame dynamism, 165, 166, 244, 262, 439, 440

U

Unconscious, the, 53-54
Unconscious self, 267
UNESCO, 6

V

Verbal behavior, 120
Verbal magic, 455, 456, 458
Veterans Bureau, U.S., 3
Violence, in schizophrenia, 27-28
Visual hallucinations, 11
Visual imagery, 228

W

Washington School of Psychiatry, 6
Watson, John B., 267, 358, 552
White, Mary Julian, 604
White, William Alanson, ii, iii, 3, 7, 17, 39
Will, Otto A., Jr., 194, 550, 619-636
William Alanson White Institute of Psychiatry, Psychoanalysis and Psychology, New York City, 6
William Alanson White Psychiatric Foundation, Washington, D.C., v, 5-6
Wolberg, Lewis R., 610
Wolfe, Thomas, 547
World Federation for Mental Health, 6
Wright, Richard, 547

Z

Zilboorg, Gregory, 614
Zones of interaction, 348-350

SENTRY EDITIONS

1. A Week on the Concord and Merrimack Rivers
   by Henry David Thoreau
2. A Diary from Dixie *by Mary Boykin Chesnut,*
   edited by Ben Ames Williams
3. The Education of Henry Adams: An Autobiography
4. J.B. *by Archibald MacLeish*
5. John C. Calhoun *by Margaret L. Coit*
6. The Maritime History of Massachusetts: 1783–1860
   by Samuel Eliot Morison
7. My Antonia *by Willa Cather*
8. Patterns of Culture *by Ruth Benedict*
9. Sam Clemens of Hannibal *by Dixon Wecter*
10. The Great Crash, 1929 *by John Kenneth Galbraith*
11. The Year of Decision: 1846 *by Bernard DeVoto*
12. Young Man with a Horn *by Dorothy Baker*
13. Mein Kampf *by Adolf Hitler*
14. The Vital Center *by Arthur M. Schlesinger, Jr.*
15. The Course of Empire *by Bernard DeVoto*
16. O Pioneers! *by Willa Cather*
17. The Armada *by Garrett Mattingly*
18. American Capitalism *by John Kenneth Galbraith*
19. The Emancipation of Massachusetts *by Brooks Adams*
20. Beyond the Hundredth Meridian *by Wallace Stegner*
21. Paul Revere and the World He Lived In *by Esther Forbes*
22. Chosen Country *by John Dos Passos*
23. The Tragic Era *by Claude G. Bowers*
24. Parkinson's Law *by C. Northcote Parkinson*
25. Across the Wide Missouri *by Bernard DeVoto*
26. Manhattan Transfer *by John Dos Passos*
27. A Cartoon History of Architecture *by Osbert Lancaster*
28. The Song of the Lark *by Willa Cather*
29. A Mirror for Witches *by Esther Forbes*
30. The Collected Poems of Archibald MacLeish
31. The Journals of Lewis and Clark
   edited by Bernard DeVoto
32. Builders of the Bay Colony *by Samuel Eliot Morison*
33. Mont-Saint-Michel and Chartres *by Henry Adams*
34. Laughing Boy *by Oliver La Farge*
35. Wild America *by Roger Tory Peterson and James Fisher*
36. Paths to the Present *by Arthur M. Schlesinger*
37. U.S.A. *by John Dos Passos*
38. Economic Development *by John Kenneth Galbraith*
39. The Crisis of the Old Order *by Arthur M. Schlesinger, Jr.*
40. Three Soldiers *by John Dos Passos*
41. The Road to Xanadu *by John Livingston Lowes*

(continued on next page)

42. More in Sorrow *by Wolcott Gibbs*
43. The Coming of the New Deal
   by Arthur M. Schlesinger, Jr.
44. The Big Sky *by A. B. Guthrie, Jr.*
45. The Dartmouth Bible *edited by Roy B. Chamberlin and Herman Feldman*
46. The Far Side of Paradise *by Arthur Mizener*
47. The Politics of Upheaval *by Arthur M. Schlesinger, Jr.*
48. Jefferson and Hamilton *by Claude G. Bowers*
49. The Price of Union *by Herbert Agar*
50. Mark Twain's America *and* Mark Twain at Work
   by Bernard DeVoto
51. Jefferson in Power *by Claude G. Bowers*
52. Fifty Best American Short Stories 1915–1965
   edited by Martha Foley
53. Names on the Land *by George R. Stewart*
54. Two Kinds of Time *by Graham Peck*
55. The Young Jefferson 1743–1789 *by Claude G. Bowers*
56. The Promised Land *by Mary Antin*
57. Personal History *by Vincent Sheean*
58. The New Industrial State *by John Kenneth Galbraith*
59. The Battle of Gettysburg *by Frank A. Haskell,*
   edited by Bruce Catton
60. On Becoming a Person *by Carl R. Rogers*
61. A History of Mexico *by Henry Bamford Parkes*
62. Flaubert and Madame Bovary *by Francis Steegmuller*
63. Paths of American Thought
   edited by Arthur M. Schlesinger, Jr., and Morton White
64. The South Since the War *by Sidney Andrews*
65. The Elizabethan World *by Lacey Baldwin Smith*
66. Literature and the Sixth Sense *by Philip Rahv*
67. Turbulent Years *by Irving Bernstein*
68. Renaissance Diplomacy *by Garrett Mattingly*
69. The Death of the Past *by J. H. Plumb*
70. The Affluent Society *by John Kenneth Galbraith*
71. The Way We Go to War *by Merlo J. Pusey*
72. Roosevelt and Morgenthau *by John Morton Blum*
73. The Lean Years *by Irving Bernstein*
74. Henry VIII *by Lacey Baldwin Smith*
75. Presidential Government *by James MacGregor Burns*
76. Silent Spring *by Rachel Carson*
77. The Book of Family Therapy *by Andrew Ferber,*
   Marilyn Mendelsohn, and Augustus Napier
78. The Beginnings of Modern American Psychiatry
   by Patrick Mullahy
79. A World Restored *by Henry A. Kissinger*